American Prisoners of War

Held at
Quebec
during the War of 1812

8 June 1813–11 December 1814

Transcribed by
Eric Eugene Johnson

Society of the War of 1812
in the
State of Ohio

HERITAGE BOOKS
2011

HERITAGE BOOKS
AN IMPRINT OF HERITAGE BOOKS, INC.

Books, CDs, and more—Worldwide

For our listing of thousands of titles see our website
at
www.HeritageBooks.com

Published 2011 by
HERITAGE BOOKS, INC.
Publishing Division
100 Railroad Ave. #104
Westminster, Maryland 21157

Copyright © 2011 Eric Eugene Johnson

All rights reserved. No part of this book may be reproduced or transmitted in any form or by any means, electronic or mechanical, including photocopying, recording or by any information storage and retrieval system without written permission from the author, except for the inclusion of brief quotations in a review.

International Standard Book Numbers
Paperbound: 978-0-7884-5274-1
Clothbound: 978-0-7884-8709-5

Introduction

This is a transcription of prisoner of war records of American soldiers, sailors, marines, privateers and civilians held by the British Empire at the internment facility at Quebec, Lower Canada, during the War of 1812. All of the men were captured during the various land battles or naval actions on or around the Great Lakes or Lake Champlain.

This volume was compiled from a copy of the *General Entry Book of American Prisoners of War* ledger of the British Admiralty made by the Public Record Office in London, Great Britain (ADM 103 / 362). This ledger contains the information on the American prisoners of war who were interned between 8 June 1813 – 11 December 1814 at Quebec. Some of the men were captured before this June date and were later transferred to Quebec.

The *General Entry Book* records are composed of lines for the recording of names of those incarcerated. The record of each prisoner is found on two facing pages. The clerk making the entries wrote the page number on the upper right side page of the book.

The columns across the top of the left side:
Current Number
By What Ship, or how taken
Time When – Day, Month, Year
Place Where
Of What Ship or Corps
Whether Man of War, Privateer or Merchant Vessel
Prisoners' Names

The columns across the top of the right side:
Quality
Time when received into Custody – Day, Month, Year
From what Ship or whence received
Exchanged, Discharged, Died, or Escaped
Time When – Day, Month, Year
Whither, and by what order, or Number of Re-entry

The *General Entry Book* contains the names of 1,987 prisoners of war, numbered from one through 1,990 with one name inserted between the lines and three numbers which were not used. There are seventy-seven pages in this ledger. The names of some of the prisoners of war are missing. The copy of this ledger which was obtained from the Public Record Office is missing from one to three names at the bottom of each page. Only 1,834 prisoners of war are contained in this volume.

The penmanship in this ledger is very good but the spelling of non-familiar names was done phonetically. By the hand writing, it appears that two clerks entered the information. The second clerk used the first initial of the given name for enlisted personnel. He did spell out the given names of officers.

For historic accuracy, the names of many of the ships and battles from which the men were captured were corrected. The U.S. Schooner *Somers* was listed as "*Summers*" while the U.S. Schooner *Julia* was listed as "*Juliet.*" The names of two famous battles, Lundy's Lane and Chippewa, had a number of various spellings. There were many other corrections.

Two American ships by the name of "*Growler*" were captured by the British during the War of 1812. The U.S. Schooner *Growler* was captured on Lake Ontario while the U.S. Sloop *Growler* was captured on Lake Champlain.

There are 1,503 soldiers listed in this volume compared to 297 sailors. For the most part, the soldiers were exchanged for British soldiers during prisoner of war exchanges and they were sent back to the United States. The sailors were sent to other prisoner of war camps in eastern Canada or they were transported to the United Kingdom. Only four U.S. Marines were identified in this ledger as were twenty-nine civilian men.

The biggest surprise was finding Eliza Romley listed as a prisoner of war in a men's facility. She was not a civilian but a sailor who was captured on Lake Champlain on the U.S. Sloop *Growler*. She was captured on 3 June 1813 and released twenty-two days later when her true identity was discovered. Her rank is listed as "woman" so it is not known what duty she performed while serving aboard this ship.

The ledger shows that sixty-seven men died while interned at Quebec. A few of the men died from wounds received in battle. Eleven men had the opportunity of escaping. A total of seventy-one men volunteered to serve with the New Brunswick Fencibles rather than staying in a POW facility. The New Brunswick Fencibles was a regiment of the British Army.

Three American generals are listed in this ledger. Brigadier General William Henry Winder is listed twice. He was captured at the Battle of Stoney Creek and later during the Battle of Fort Niagara. He was in command of Washington, DC, when the British captured the city and burnt the government buildings.

The other two generals were Brigadier General James Winchester who was captured at the Battle of the River Raisin and Brigadier General John Chandler who was captured at the Battle of Stoney Creek.

Any errors or omissions are regretted and are the fault of the transcriber.

Eric Eugene Johnson

President (2008-2011)
Society of the War of 1812 in the State of Ohio

In memory of

Harrison Scott Baker II
1950 – 2008

- In memory of those who did not return -

The Dead

Ayers, John	Kimball, Benjamin W.
Bacon, Jabbec	Knight, Andrew
Bartley, William	Lackey, Amasa
Bascomb, Samuel	Lain, Benjamin
Carver, William	Lamb, Josiah P.
Churchill, Oliver	Lander, Charles
Clement, Daniel	Lanton, Peory
Coaswell, Allanson	Lewis, John
Coombe, Isaac	Libby, Thadedus
Cory, Asa	Martin, Silvanus
Cotton, Seth	McIntyre, James
Davis, Stephen	McMillen, Archibald
Dearborn, Soloman	Merrill, Eli
Dearing, John	Mitchell, William
Defriend, John	Moody, John
Dyer, Isaac	Moore, Jonas
Easter, Stephen	Parker, Edward
Eaton, William	Patterson, John
Fenning, Charles	Paul, Simeon
Finney, Elihu	Plainloir, John
Foster, Nathaniel	Pratt, Nathaniel
Frost, Phineas	Pratt, Walter
Goodnow, Elisha	Reed, Isaac
Green, Eli	Robinson, Nathan
Guton, Thomas	Root, John
Hallz or Hall, Orin or Horace	Sanborn, John L.
Halted, John	Shaver, George
Harrodon, Elisha	Sinclair, Jacob
Hooker, Oris	Smith, Jonathan
Hooper, Simon	Smith, Stephen
Howard, Joseph	Smith, William
Hunt, Soloman	Till, James
Ingalls, Jonathan	Tuffs, William
Judd, William	

- Those who die in service to the United States should not be forgotten –

- Table of Contents -

Introduction	iii
The Dead	vii
Alphabetical listing of names	1
Numeric listings by prison number	205
Crew listing by U.S. ship	225
Soldiers listing by battle	229
United States Marines and civilians	246

American Prisoners of War held at Quebec during the War of 1812

Abbett, John   Prisoner 1832. Rank: Private - By what ship or how taken: Troops - Time when: 17 Sep 1814 - Place where: Fort Erie - Of what ship or corps: Land forces - Whether man of war, privateer or merchant vessel: Taken on shore - Time when received into custody: 1 Nov 1814 - From what ship or whence received: Montreal - Exchanged, discharged, died, or escape: Discharged - Time when: 8 Nov 1814 - Whither, and by what order, or number or re-entry: S. George No. 575 for Halifax by order of Sir George Provost

Abby, Horace B.   Prisoner 1895. Rank: Corporal - By what ship or how taken: Troops - Time when: 17 Sep 1814 - Place where: Fort Erie - Of what ship or corps: Land forces - Whether man of war, privateer or merchant vessel: Taken on shore - Time when received into custody: 1 Nov 1814 - From what ship or whence received: Montreal - Exchanged, discharged, died, or escape: Discharged - Time when: 8 Nov 1814 - Whither, and by what order, or number or re-entry: S. George No. 575 for Halifax by order of Sir George Provost

Aberts, Michael   Prisoner 862. Rank: Private - By what ship or how taken: Troops - Time when: 26 Jun 1813 - Place where: Beaver Dam - Of what ship or corps: Land forces - Whether man of war, privateer or merchant vessel: Taken on shore - Time when received into custody: 7 Jul 1813 - From what ship or whence received: Steamboat - Exchanged, discharged, died, or escape: Discharged - Time when: 10 Aug 1813 - Whither, and by what order, or number or re-entry: HM Ship Malpomena

Ackley, William   Prisoner 452. Rank: Private - By what ship or how taken: Troops - Time when: 24 Jun 1813 - Place where: Beaver Dam - Of what ship or corps: Malabar & Hydia - Whether man of war, privateer or merchant vessel: Taken on shore - Time when received into custody: 7 Jul 1813 - From what ship or whence received: Steamboat - Exchanged, discharged, died, or escape: Discharged - Time when: 10 Aug 1813 - Whither, and by what order, or number or re-entry: HM Ship Regulius by order of Sir George Provost

Adams, George   Prisoner 1956. Rank: Musician - By what ship or how taken: Troops - Time when: 23 Oct 1814 - Place where: Fort Erie - Of what ship or corps: Land forces - Whether man of war, privateer or merchant vessel: Taken on shore - Time when received into custody: 11 Dec 1814 - From what ship or whence received: Montreal - Exchanged, discharged, died, or escape: Discharged - Time when: 13 Mar 1815 - Whither, and by what order, or number or re-entry: United States

Adney, William D.   Prisoner 1764. Rank: Sergeant - By what ship or how taken: Troops - Time when: 7 Sep 1814 - Place where: Fort Erie - Of what ship or corps: Land forces - Whether man of war, privateer or merchant vessel: Taken on shore - Time when received into custody: 1 Nov 1814 - From what ship or whence received: Montreal - Exchanged, discharged, died, or escape: Discharged - Time when: 8 Nov 1814 - Whither, and by what order, or number or re-entry: S. George No. 575 for Halifax by order of Sir George Provost

Agen, John   Prisoner 638. Rank: Private - By what ship or how taken: Troops - Time when: 24 Jun 1813 - Place where: Stoney Point - Of what ship or corps: Land forces - Whether man of war, privateer or merchant vessel: Taken on shore - Time when received into custody: 7 Jul 1813 - From what ship or whence received: Steamboat - Exchanged, discharged, died, or escape: Discharged - Time when: 10 Aug 1813 - Whither, and by what order, or number or re-entry: HM Ship Regulius by order of Sir George Provost

Alfen, John   Prisoner 108. Rank: Private - By what ship or how taken: Boats & Troops - Time when: 28 May 1813 - Place where: Stoney Point, Henderson Harbor - Of what ship or corps: Land forces - Whether man of war, privateer or merchant vessel: Taken on shore - Time when received into custody: 8 Jun 1813 - From what ship or whence received: Batteaux - Exchanged, discharged, died, or escape: Discharged - Time when: 31 Oct 1813 - Whither, and by what order, or number or re-entry: Malabar Transport

Allen, Ira   Prisoner 1526. Rank: Citizen - By what ship or how taken: Troops - Time when: 25 Jul 1814 - Place where: Lundy's Lane - Of what ship or corps: Land forces - Whether man of war, privateer or merchant vessel: Taken on shore - Time when received into custody: 30 Aug 1814 - From what ship or whence received: Lady Delaval Schooner 578 - Exchanged, discharged, died, or escape: Discharged - Time when: 8 Oct 1814 - Whither, and by what order, or number or re-entry: Queen No. 415

Allen, Isaac   Prisoner 213. Rank: Private - By what ship or how taken: Boats & Troops - Time when: 3 Jun 1813 - Place where: Lake Champlain - Of what ship or corps: Growler - Whether man of war, privateer or merchant vessel: Man of War - Time when received into custody: 9 Jun 1813 - From what ship or whence received: Batteaux - Exchanged, discharged, died, or escape: Discharged - Time when: 31 Oct 1813 - Whither, and by what order, or number or re-entry: Malabar Transport

Allen, J.   Prisoner 1474. Rank: Private - By what ship or how taken: Troops - Time when: 16 Jul 1814 - Place where: Queenstown - Of what ship or corps: Land forces - Whether man of war, privateer or merchant vessel: Taken on shore - Time when received into custody: 12 Aug 1814 - From what ship or whence received: Royal Seaman No. 289

American Prisoners of War held at Quebec during the War of 1812

Transport - Exchanged, discharged, died, or escape: Discharged - Time when: 8 Oct 1814 - Whither, and by what order, or number or re-entry: Queen No. 415

Allen, John   Prisoner 282. Rank: Private - By what ship or how taken: Troops - Time when: 6 Jun 1813 - Place where: Stoney Point - Of what ship or corps: Land forces - Whether man of war, privateer or merchant vessel: Taken on shore - Time when received into custody: 28 Jun 1813 - From what ship or whence received: Batteaux - Exchanged, discharged, died, or escape: Discharged - Time when: 31 Oct 1813 - Whither, and by what order, or number or re-entry: Malabar Transport

Allen, Samuel   Prisoner 1554. Rank: Private - By what ship or how taken: Troops - Time when: 25 Jul 1814 - Place where: Lundy's Lane - Of what ship or corps: Land forces - Whether man of war, privateer or merchant vessel: Taken on shore - Time when received into custody: 30 Aug 1814 - From what ship or whence received: Lady Delaval Schooner 578 - Exchanged, discharged, died, or escape: Discharged - Time when: 8 Oct 1814 - Whither, and by what order, or number or re-entry: Queen No. 415

Ames, Oliver   Prisoner 49. Rank: Private - By what ship or how taken: Boats & Troops - Time when: 28 May 1813 - Place where: Stoney Point, Henderson Harbor - Of what ship or corps: Land forces - Whether man of war, privateer or merchant vessel: Taken on shore - Time when received into custody: 8 Jun 1813 - From what ship or whence received: Batteaux - Exchanged, discharged, died, or escape: Discharged - Time when: - Whither, and by what order, or number or re-entry: HM Ship Success

Ames, Thomas   Prisoner 978. Rank: Private - By what ship or how taken: Troops - Time when: 5 Jul 1813 - Place where: Fort Schisher - Of what ship or corps: Land forces - Whether man of war, privateer or merchant vessel: Taken on shore - Time when received into custody: 5 Sep 1813 - From what ship or whence received: Steamboat - Exchanged, discharged, died, or escape: Discharged - Time when: 31 Oct 1813 - Whither, and by what order, or number or re-entry: Malabar Transport

Amyets, John   Prisoner 1348. Rank: Private - By what ship or how taken: Troops - Time when: 19 Dec 1813 - Place where: Fort Niagara - Of what ship or corps: Land forces - Whether man of war, privateer or merchant vessel: Taken on shore - Time when received into custody: 29 Jan 1814 - From what ship or whence received: Montreal by land carriage - Exchanged, discharged, died, or escape: Discharged - Time when: 4 May 1814 - Whither, and by what order, or number or re-entry: United States

Anderson, Henry   Prisoner 579. Rank: Private - By what ship or how taken: Troops - Time when: 26 Jun 1813 - Place where: Beaver Dam - Of what ship or corps: Land forces - Whether man of war, privateer or merchant vessel: Taken on shore - Time when received into custody: 13 Jul 1813 - From what ship or whence received: Steamboat - Exchanged, discharged, died, or escape: Discharged - Time when: 9 Aug 1813 - Whither, and by what order, or number or re-entry: HM Ship Wasp

Anderson, Peter   Prisoner 1278. Rank: Private - By what ship or how taken: Troops - Time when: 19 Dec 1813 - Place where: Fort Niagara - Of what ship or corps: Land forces - Whether man of war, privateer or merchant vessel: Taken on shore - Time when received into custody: 29 Jan 1814 - From what ship or whence received: Montreal by land carriage - Exchanged, discharged, died, or escape: Discharged - Time when: 4 May 1814 - Whither, and by what order, or number or re-entry: United States

Andrews, David   Prisoner 458. Rank: Private - By what ship or how taken: Troops - Time when: 24 Jun 1813 - Place where: Beaver Dam - Of what ship or corps: Malabar & Hydia - Whether man of war, privateer or merchant vessel: Taken on shore - Time when received into custody: 7 Jul 1813 - From what ship or whence received: Steamboat - Exchanged, discharged, died, or escape: Discharged - Time when: 10 Aug 1813 - Whither, and by what order, or number or re-entry: HM Ship Regulius by order of Sir George Provost

Andrews, Edward   Prisoner 727. Rank: Private - By what ship or how taken: Troops - Time when: 26 Jun 1813 - Place where: Beaver Dam - Of what ship or corps: Land forces - Whether man of war, privateer or merchant vessel: Taken on shore - Time when received into custody: 7 Jul 1813 - From what ship or whence received: Steamboat - Exchanged, discharged, died, or escape: Discharged - Time when: 10 Aug 1813 - Whither, and by what order, or number or re-entry: HM Ship Regulius by order of Sir George Provost

Andrews, Stephen   Prisoner 647. Rank: Private - By what ship or how taken: Troops - Time when: 24 Jun 1813 - Place where: Stoney Point - Of what ship or corps: Land forces - Whether man of war, privateer or merchant vessel: Taken on shore - Time when received into custody: 7 Jul 1813 - From what ship or whence received: Steamboat - Exchanged, discharged, died, or escape: Discharged - Time when: 10 Aug 1813 - Whither, and by what order, or number or re-entry: HM Ship Regulius by order of Sir George Provost

American Prisoners of War held at Quebec during the War of 1812

Ansol, Philip   Prisoner 743. Rank: Private - By what ship or how taken: Troops - Time when: 26 Jun 1813 - Place where: Beaver Dam - Of what ship or corps: Land forces - Whether man of war, privateer or merchant vessel: Taken on shore - Time when received into custody: 7 Jul 1813 - From what ship or whence received: Steamboat - Exchanged, discharged, died, or escape: Discharged - Time when: 10 Aug 1813 - Whither, and by what order, or number or re-entry: HM Ship Regulius by order of Sir George Provost

Archer, Robert   Prisoner 1396. Rank: Private - By what ship or how taken: Troops - Time when: 19 Dec 1813 - Place where: Fort Niagara - Of what ship or corps: Land forces - Whether man of war, privateer or merchant vessel: Taken on shore - Time when received into custody: 29 Jan 1814 - From what ship or whence received: Montreal by land carriage - Exchanged, discharged, died, or escape: Discharged - Time when: 4 May 1814 - Whither, and by what order, or number or re-entry: United States

Arell, Richard   Prisoner 527. Rank: Lieutenant - By what ship or how taken: Troops - Time when: 24 Jun 1813 - Place where: Beaver Dam - Of what ship or corps: Land forces - Whether man of war, privateer or merchant vessel: Taken on shore - Time when received into custody: 13 Jul 1813 - From what ship or whence received: Steamboat - Exchanged, discharged, died, or escape: Discharged - Time when: 10 Aug 1813 - Whither, and by what order, or number or re-entry: HM Ship Regulius by order of Sir George Provost

Armstrong, Earl   Prisoner 1703. Rank: Private - By what ship or how taken: Troops - Time when: 25 Jul 1814 - Place where: Lundy's Lane - Of what ship or corps: Land forces - Whether man of war, privateer or merchant vessel: Taken on shore - Time when received into custody: 23 Oct 1814 - From what ship or whence received: Montreal - Exchanged, discharged, died, or escape: Discharged - Time when: 8 Nov 1814 - Whither, and by what order, or number or re-entry: S. George No. 575 for Halifax

Armstrong, George   Prisoner 1916. Rank: Private - By what ship or how taken: Troops - Time when: 17 Sep 1814 - Place where: Fort Erie - Of what ship or corps: Land forces - Whether man of war, privateer or merchant vessel: Taken on shore - Time when received into custody: 1 Nov 1814 - From what ship or whence received: Montreal - Exchanged, discharged, died, or escape: Discharged - Time when: 8 Nov 1814 - Whither, and by what order, or number or re-entry: S. George No. 575 for Halifax by order of Sir George Provost

Armstrong, Isaac   Prisoner 1915. Rank: Private - By what ship or how taken: Troops - Time when: 17 Sep 1814 - Place where: Fort Erie - Of what ship or corps: Land forces - Whether man of war, privateer or merchant vessel: Taken on shore - Time when received into custody: 1 Nov 1814 - From what ship or whence received: Montreal - Exchanged, discharged, died, or escape: Discharged - Time when: 8 Nov 1814 - Whither, and by what order, or number or re-entry: S. George No. 575 for Halifax by order of Sir George Provost

Armstrong, Thomas   Prisoner 1140. Rank: Private - By what ship or how taken: Troops - Time when: 22 Jan 1812 - Place where: Rapids Prince Reason - Of what ship or corps: Land forces - Whether man of war, privateer or merchant vessel: Taken on shore - Time when received into custody: 25 Nov 1813 - From what ship or whence received: Town Goal - Exchanged, discharged, died, or escape: Discharged - Time when: 21 Apr 1814 - Whither, and by what order, or number or re-entry: United States

Armstrong, William   Prisoner 466. Rank: Private - By what ship or how taken: Troops - Time when: 24 Jun 1813 - Place where: Beaver Dam - Of what ship or corps: Malabar & Hydia - Whether man of war, privateer or merchant vessel: Taken on shore - Time when received into custody: 7 Jul 1813 - From what ship or whence received: Steamboat - Exchanged, discharged, died, or escape: Discharged - Time when: 10 Aug 1813 - Whither, and by what order, or number or re-entry: HM Ship Regulius by order of Sir George Provost

Arnold, James   Prisoner 1356. Rank: Private - By what ship or how taken: Troops - Time when: 19 Dec 1813 - Place where: Fort Niagara - Of what ship or corps: Land forces - Whether man of war, privateer or merchant vessel: Taken on shore - Time when received into custody: 29 Jan 1814 - From what ship or whence received: Montreal by land carriage - Exchanged, discharged, died, or escape: Discharged - Time when: 4 May 1814 - Whither, and by what order, or number or re-entry: United States

Arthur, James   Prisoner 584. Rank: Private - By what ship or how taken: Troops - Time when: 26 Jun 1813 - Place where: Beaver Dam - Of what ship or corps: Land forces - Whether man of war, privateer or merchant vessel: Taken on shore - Time when received into custody: 13 Jul 1813 - From what ship or whence received: Steamboat - Exchanged, discharged, died, or escape: Discharged - Time when: 10 Aug 1813 - Whither, and by what order, or number or re-entry: HM Ship Regulius by order of Sir George Provost

Artis, John   Prisoner 491. Rank: Private - By what ship or how taken: Troops - Time when: 24 Jun 1813 - Place where: Beaver Dam - Of what ship or corps: Land forces - Whether man of war, privateer or merchant vessel: Taken on shore - Time when received into custody: 7 Jul 1813 - From what ship or whence received: Steamboat - Exchanged, discharged,

American Prisoners of War held at Quebec during the War of 1812

died, or escape: Discharged - Time when: 10 Aug 1813 - Whither, and by what order, or number or re-entry: HM Ship Regulius by order of Sir George Provost

Asher, Frederick   Prisoner 927.   Rank: Private - By what ship or how taken: Troops - Time when: 26 Jun 1813 - Place where: Beaver Dam - Of what ship or corps: Land forces - Whether man of war, privateer or merchant vessel: Taken on shore - Time when received into custody: 21 Jul 1813 - From what ship or whence received: Steamboat - Exchanged, discharged, died, or escape: Discharged - Time when: 10 Aug 1813 - Whither, and by what order, or number or re-entry: HM Ship Malpomena

Atchley, Daniel   Prisoner 1406.   Rank: Private - By what ship or how taken: Troops - Time when: 19 Dec 1813 - Place where: Fort Niagara - Of what ship or corps: Land forces - Whether man of war, privateer or merchant vessel: Taken on shore - Time when received into custody: 29 Jan 1814 - From what ship or whence received: Montreal by land carriage - Exchanged, discharged, died, or escape: Discharged - Time when: 4 May 1814 - Whither, and by what order, or number or re-entry: United States

Atchley, Joseph   Prisoner 1350.   Rank: Private - By what ship or how taken: Troops - Time when: 19 Dec 1813 - Place where: Fort Niagara - Of what ship or corps: Land forces - Whether man of war, privateer or merchant vessel: Taken on shore - Time when received into custody: 29 Jan 1814 - From what ship or whence received: Montreal by land carriage - Exchanged, discharged, died, or escape: Discharged - Time when: 4 May 1814 - Whither, and by what order, or number or re-entry: United States

Atherton, William   Prisoner 1157.   Rank: Private - By what ship or how taken: Troops - Time when: 5 May 1813 - Place where: Rapids Prince Reason - Of what ship or corps: Land forces - Whether man of war, privateer or merchant vessel: Taken on shore - Time when received into custody: 25 Nov 1813 - From what ship or whence received: Town Goal - Exchanged, discharged, died, or escape: Discharged - Time when: 12 Mar 1814 - Whither, and by what order, or number or re-entry: New Brunswick Fencibles

Atkins, Henry   Prisoner 1670.   Rank: Seaman - By what ship or how taken: Gun Boats - Time when: 25 Aug 1814 - Place where: Lake Ontario - Of what ship or corps: Taken on a gigg - Whether man of war, privateer or merchant vessel: Man of War - Time when received into custody: 23 Oct 1814 - From what ship or whence received: Montreal - Exchanged, discharged, died, or escape: Discharged - Time when: 7 Nov 1814 - Whither, and by what order, or number or re-entry: Transport Freedom No. 582 by orders of his Excellency Sir George Provost

Atwood, E.   Prisoner 1587.   Rank: Seaman - By what ship or how taken: Gun Boats - Time when: 12 Aug 1814 - Place where: Fort Erie - Of what ship or corps: Ohio - Whether man of war, privateer or merchant vessel: Man of War - Time when received into custody: 5 Oct 1814 - From what ship or whence received: Montreal - Exchanged, discharged, died, or escape: Discharged - Time when: 10 Nov 1814 - Whither, and by what order, or number or re-entry: Freedom No. 582

Austin, William   Prisoner 1782.   Rank: Private - By what ship or how taken: Troops - Time when: 7 Sep 1814 - Place where: Fort Erie - Of what ship or corps: Land forces - Whether man of war, privateer or merchant vessel: Taken on shore - Time when received into custody: 1 Nov 1814 - From what ship or whence received: Montreal - Exchanged, discharged, died, or escape: Discharged - Time when: 8 Nov 1814 - Whither, and by what order, or number or re-entry: S. George No. 575 for Halifax by order of Sir George Provost

Avery, A.   Prisoner 1627.   Rank: Private - By what ship or how taken: Troops - Time when: 6 Sep 1814 - Place where: Plattsburg - Of what ship or corps: Land forces - Whether man of war, privateer or merchant vessel: Taken on shore - Time when received into custody: 5 Oct 1814 - From what ship or whence received: Montreal - Exchanged, discharged, died, or escape: Discharged - Time when: 8 Oct 1814 - Whither, and by what order, or number or re-entry: H.M. Ship Ceylon

Avery, Matlass   Prisoner 964.   Rank: Private - By what ship or how taken: Troops - Time when: 5 Jul 1813 - Place where: Fort Schisher - Of what ship or corps: Land forces - Whether man of war, privateer or merchant vessel: Taken on shore - Time when received into custody: 5 Sep 1813 - From what ship or whence received: Steamboat - Exchanged, discharged, died, or escape: Discharged - Time when: 2 Nov 1813 - Whither, and by what order, or number or re-entry: Malabar Transport

Avery, Richard   Prisoner 963.   Rank: Private - By what ship or how taken: Troops - Time when: 5 Jul 1813 - Place where: Fort Schisher - Of what ship or corps: Land forces - Whether man of war, privateer or merchant vessel: Taken on shore - Time when received into custody: 5 Sep 1813 - From what ship or whence received: Steamboat - Exchanged, discharged, died, or escape: Discharged - Time when: 31 Oct 1813 - Whither, and by what order, or number or re-entry: Malabar Transport

American Prisoners of War held at Quebec during the War of 1812

Ayers, John   Prisoner 138. Rank: Private - By what ship or how taken: Boats & Troops - Time when: 28 May 1813 - Place where: Stoney Point, Henderson Harbor - Of what ship or corps: Land forces - Whether man of war, privateer or merchant vessel: Taken on shore - Time when received into custody: 8 Jul 1813 - From what ship or whence received: Batteaux - Exchanged, discharged, died, or escape: Died - Time when: 15 Aug 1813 - Whither, and by what order, or number or re-entry:

Ayrus, Samuel   Prisoner 1907. Rank: Corporal - By what ship or how taken: Troops - Time when: 17 Sep 1814 - Place where: Fort Erie - Of what ship or corps: Land forces - Whether man of war, privateer or merchant vessel: Taken on shore - Time when received into custody: 1 Nov 1814 - From what ship or whence received: Montreal - Exchanged, discharged, died, or escape: Discharged - Time when: 8 Nov 1814 - Whither, and by what order, or number or re-entry: S. George No. 575 for Halifax by order of Sir George Provost

Bacon, Jabbec   Prisoner 40. Rank: Private - By what ship or how taken: Boats & Troops - Time when: 28 May 1813 - Place where: Stoney Point, Henderson Harbor - Of what ship or corps: Land forces - Whether man of war, privateer or merchant vessel: Taken on shore - Time when received into custody: 8 Jun 1813 - From what ship or whence received: Batteaux - Exchanged, discharged, died, or escape: Died - Time when: 6 Aug 1813 - Whither, and by what order, or number or re-entry:

Bacon, Moses   Prisoner 1831. Rank: Private - By what ship or how taken: Troops - Time when: 17 Sep 1814 - Place where: Fort Erie - Of what ship or corps: Land forces - Whether man of war, privateer or merchant vessel: Taken on shore - Time when received into custody: 1 Nov 1814 - From what ship or whence received: Montreal - Exchanged, discharged, died, or escape: Discharged - Time when: 8 Nov 1814 - Whither, and by what order, or number or re-entry: S. George No. 575 for Halifax by order of Sir George Provost

Bacon, Nathan   Prisoner 632. Rank: Private - By what ship or how taken: Troops - Time when: 24 Jun 1813 - Place where: Stoney Point - Of what ship or corps: Land forces - Whether man of war, privateer or merchant vessel: Taken on shore - Time when received into custody: 7 Jul 1813 - From what ship or whence received: Steamboat - Exchanged, discharged, died, or escape: Discharged - Time when: 10 Aug 1813 - Whither, and by what order, or number or re-entry: HM Ship Regulius by order of Sir George Provost

Badger, Ephraim T.   Prisoner 934. Rank: Private - By what ship or how taken: Troops - Time when: 26 Jun 1813 - Place where: Beaver Dam - Of what ship or corps: Land forces - Whether man of war, privateer or merchant vessel: Taken on shore - Time when received into custody: 21 Jul 1813 - From what ship or whence received: Steamboat - Exchanged, discharged, died, or escape: Discharged - Time when: 10 Aug 1813 - Whither, and by what order, or number or re-entry: HM Ship Malpomena

Baker, Daniel B.   Prisoner 334. Rank: Private - By what ship or how taken: Boats & Troops - Time when: 6 Jun 1813 - Place where: Stoney Point - Of what ship or corps: Land forces - Whether man of war, privateer or merchant vessel: Taken on shore - Time when received into custody: 28 Jun 1813 - From what ship or whence received: Quebec of Quebec - Exchanged, discharged, died, or escape: Discharged - Time when: 31 Oct 1813 - Whither, and by what order, or number or re-entry: Malabar Transport

Baker, George   Prisoner 952. Rank: Private - By what ship or how taken: Troops - Time when: 5 Jul 1813 - Place where: Fort Schisher - Of what ship or corps: Land forces - Whether man of war, privateer or merchant vessel: Taken on shore - Time when received into custody: 5 Sep 1813 - From what ship or whence received: Steamboat - Exchanged, discharged, died, or escape: Discharged - Time when: 31 Oct 1813 - Whither, and by what order, or number or re-entry: Malabar Transport

Baker, John   Prisoner 678. Rank: Private - By what ship or how taken: Troops - Time when: 26 Jun 1813 - Place where: Beaver Dam - Of what ship or corps: Land forces - Whether man of war, privateer or merchant vessel: Taken on shore - Time when received into custody: 7 Jul 1813 - From what ship or whence received: Steamboat - Exchanged, discharged, died, or escape: Discharged - Time when: 10 Aug 1813 - Whither, and by what order, or number or re-entry: HM Ship Regulius by order of Sir George Provost

Baker, Lloyd   Prisoner 1791. Rank: Private - By what ship or how taken: Troops - Time when: 7 Sep 1814 - Place where: Fort Erie - Of what ship or corps: Land forces - Whether man of war, privateer or merchant vessel: Taken on shore - Time when received into custody: 1 Nov 1814 - From what ship or whence received: Montreal - Exchanged, discharged, died, or escape: Discharged - Time when: 8 Nov 1814 - Whither, and by what order, or number or re-entry: S. George No. 575 for Halifax by order of Sir George Provost

Baker, Philip   Prisoner 1034. Rank: Seaman - By what ship or how taken: Lord Melvin - Time when: 10 Aug 1813 - Place where: Lake Ontario - Of what ship or corps: Growler - Whether man of war, privateer or merchant vessel: Man of War - Time when received into custody: 5 Sep 1813 - From what ship or whence received: Steamboat - Exchanged,

American Prisoners of War held at Quebec during the War of 1812

discharged, died, or escape: Discharged - Time when: 21 Sep 1813 - Whither, and by what order, or number or re-entry: Mersey Transport

Baker, Samuel   Prisoner 1030. Rank: Seaman - By what ship or how taken: Lord Melvin - Time when: 10 Aug 1813 - Place where: Lake Ontario - Of what ship or corps: Growler - Whether man of war, privateer or merchant vessel: Man of War - Time when received into custody: 5 Sep 1813 - From what ship or whence received: Steamboat - Exchanged, discharged, died, or escape: Discharged - Time when: 31 Oct 1813 - Whither, and by what order, or number or re-entry: Malabar Transport

Baker, Samuel   Prisoner 1778. Rank: Corporal - By what ship or how taken: Troops - Time when: 7 Sep 1814 - Place where: Fort Erie - Of what ship or corps: Land forces - Whether man of war, privateer or merchant vessel: Taken on shore - Time when received into custody: 1 Nov 1814 - From what ship or whence received: Montreal - Exchanged, discharged, died, or escape: Discharged - Time when: 8 Nov 1814 - Whither, and by what order, or number or re-entry: S. George No. 575 for Halifax by order of Sir George Provost

Baldwyn, John   Prisoner 1752. Rank: Private - By what ship or how taken: Gun Boats - Time when: 3 Sep 1814 - Place where: Lake Huron - Of what ship or corps: Tigress - Whether man of war, privateer or merchant vessel: Man of War - Time when received into custody: 1 Nov 1814 - From what ship or whence received: Montreal - Exchanged, discharged, died, or escape: Discharged - Time when: 8 Nov 1814 - Whither, and by what order, or number or re-entry: S. George No. 575 for Halifax by order of Sir George Provost

Ballard, James H.   Prisoner 1667. Rank: Lieutenant - By what ship or how taken: Troops - Time when: 17 Sep 1814 - Place where: Fort Erie - Of what ship or corps: Land forces - Whether man of war, privateer or merchant vessel: Taken on shore - Time when received into custody: 23 Oct 1814 - From what ship or whence received: Montreal - Exchanged, discharged, died, or escape: Discharged - Time when: 10 Nov 1814 - Whither, and by what order, or number or re-entry: Transport Stately No. 408 for Halifax

Ballard, John   Prisoner 188. Rank: Private - By what ship or how taken: Boats & Troops - Time when: 3 Jun 1813 - Place where: Lake Champlain - Of what ship or corps: Growler - Whether man of war, privateer or merchant vessel: Man of War - Time when received into custody: 9 Jun 1813 - From what ship or whence received: Batteaux - Exchanged, discharged, died, or escape: Discharged - Time when: 31 Oct 1813 - Whither, and by what order, or number or re-entry: Malabar Transport

Banger, Thomas   Prisoner 1093. Rank: Private - By what ship or how taken: Troops - Time when: 24 Aug 1813 - Place where: Fort George - Of what ship or corps: Land forces - Whether man of war, privateer or merchant vessel: Taken on shore - Time when received into custody: 10 Oct 1813 - From what ship or whence received: Steamboat - Exchanged, discharged, died, or escape: Discharged - Time when: 31 Oct 1813 - Whither, and by what order, or number or re-entry: Malabar Transport

Bangs, Seth   Prisoner 41. Rank: Private - By what ship or how taken: Boats & Troops - Time when: 28 May 1813 - Place where: Stoney Point, Henderson Harbor - Of what ship or corps: Land forces - Whether man of war, privateer or merchant vessel: Taken on shore - Time when received into custody: 8 Jun 1813 - From what ship or whence received: Batteaux - Exchanged, discharged, died, or escape: Discharged - Time when: 31 Oct 1813 - Whither, and by what order, or number or re-entry: Malabar Transport

Baninstine, John   Prisoner 875. Rank: Private - By what ship or how taken: Troops - Time when: 26 Jun 1813 - Place where: Beaver Dam - Of what ship or corps: Land forces - Whether man of war, privateer or merchant vessel: Taken on shore - Time when received into custody: 7 Jul 1813 - From what ship or whence received: Steamboat - Exchanged, discharged, died, or escape: Discharged - Time when: 10 Aug 1813 - Whither, and by what order, or number or re-entry: HM Ship Malpomena

Banker, Christian   Prisoner 1236. Rank: Sergeant - By what ship or how taken: Troops - Time when: 19 Dec 1813 - Place where: Fort Niagara - Of what ship or corps: Land forces - Whether man of war, privateer or merchant vessel: Taken on shore - Time when received into custody: 29 Jan 1814 - From what ship or whence received: Montreal by land carriage - Exchanged, discharged, died, or escape: Discharged - Time when: 4 May 1814 - Whither, and by what order, or number or re-entry: United States

Baptise, John   Prisoner 1786. Rank: Private - By what ship or how taken: Troops - Time when: 7 Sep 1814 - Place where: Fort Erie - Of what ship or corps: Land forces - Whether man of war, privateer or merchant vessel: Taken on shore - Time when received into custody: 1 Nov 1814 - From what ship or whence received: Montreal - Exchanged, discharged, died, or escape: Discharged - Time when: 8 Nov 1814 - Whither, and by what order, or number or re-entry: S. George No. 575 for Halifax by order of Sir George Provost

American Prisoners of War held at Quebec during the War of 1812

Barber, John   Prisoner 842. Rank: Private - By what ship or how taken: Troops - Time when: 26 Jun 1813 - Place where: Beaver Dam - Of what ship or corps: Land forces - Whether man of war, privateer or merchant vessel: Taken on shore - Time when received into custody: 7 Jul 1813 - From what ship or whence received: Steamboat - Exchanged, discharged, died, or escape: Discharged - Time when: 31 Oct 1813 - Whither, and by what order, or number or re-entry: Malabar Transport

Barber, William   Prisoner 171. Rank: Boy - By what ship or how taken: Boats & Troops - Time when: 3 Jun 1813 - Place where: Lake Champlain - Of what ship or corps: Growler - Whether man of war, privateer or merchant vessel: Man of War - Time when received into custody: 9 Jun 1813 - From what ship or whence received: Batteaux - Exchanged, discharged, died, or escape: Discharged - Time when: 6 Oct 1813 - Whither, and by what order, or number or re-entry:

Barker, John   Prisoner 841. Rank: Private - By what ship or how taken: Troops - Time when: 26 Jun 1813 - Place where: Beaver Dam - Of what ship or corps: Land forces - Whether man of war, privateer or merchant vessel: Taken on shore - Time when received into custody: 7 Jul 1813 - From what ship or whence received: Steamboat - Exchanged, discharged, died, or escape: Discharged - Time when: 10 Aug 1813 - Whither, and by what order, or number or re-entry: HM Ship Malpomena

Barker, Robert   Prisoner 1065. Rank: Private - By what ship or how taken: Troops - Time when: 24 Jun 1813 - Place where: Beaver Dam - Of what ship or corps: Land forces - Whether man of war, privateer or merchant vessel: Taken on shore - Time when received into custody: 5 Sep 1813 - From what ship or whence received: Steamboat - Exchanged, discharged, died, or escape: Discharged - Time when: 10 Sep 1813 - Whither, and by what order, or number or re-entry: Volunteered for the army

Barlow, John   Prisoner 907. Rank: Private - By what ship or how taken: Troops - Time when: 26 Jun 1813 - Place where: Beaver Dam - Of what ship or corps: Land forces - Whether man of war, privateer or merchant vessel: Taken on shore - Time when received into custody: 21 Jul 1813 - From what ship or whence received: Steamboat - Exchanged, discharged, died, or escape: Discharged - Time when: 10 Aug 1813 - Whither, and by what order, or number or re-entry: HM Ship Malpomena

Barnes, E.   Prisoner 1479. Rank: Private - By what ship or how taken: Troops - Time when: 15 Jul 1814 - Place where: St. Davids - Of what ship or corps: Land forces - Whether man of war, privateer or merchant vessel: Taken on shore - Time when received into custody: 12 Aug 1814 - From what ship or whence received: Royal Seaman No. 289 Transport - Exchanged, discharged, died, or escape: Discharged - Time when: 8 Oct 1814 - Whither, and by what order, or number or re-entry: Queen No. 415

Barnes, Jacob   Prisoner 1361. Rank: Private - By what ship or how taken: Troops - Time when: 19 Dec 1813 - Place where: Fort Niagara - Of what ship or corps: Land forces - Whether man of war, privateer or merchant vessel: Taken on shore - Time when received into custody: 29 Jan 1814 - From what ship or whence received: Montreal by land carriage - Exchanged, discharged, died, or escape: Discharged - Time when: 4 May 1814 - Whither, and by what order, or number or re-entry: United States

Barnes, Samuel   Prisoner 896. Rank: Private - By what ship or how taken: Troops - Time when: 26 Jun 1813 - Place where: Beaver Dam - Of what ship or corps: Land forces - Whether man of war, privateer or merchant vessel: Taken on shore - Time when received into custody: 7 Jul 1813 - From what ship or whence received: Steamboat - Exchanged, discharged, died, or escape: Discharged - Time when: 10 Aug 1813 - Whither, and by what order, or number or re-entry: HM Ship Malpomena

Barnes, Seth   Prisoner 339. Rank: Private - By what ship or how taken: Boats & Troops - Time when: 22 Feb 1813 - Place where: Hedgesburgh - Of what ship or corps: Land forces - Whether man of war, privateer or merchant vessel: Taken on shore - Time when received into custody: 28 Jun 1813 - From what ship or whence received: Mary of Quebec - Exchanged, discharged, died, or escape: Discharged - Time when: 8 Oct 1813 - Whither, and by what order, or number or re-entry: H.M. Ship Ceylon

Barnes, Thomas   Prisoner 734. Rank: Private - By what ship or how taken: Troops - Time when: 26 Jun 1813 - Place where: Beaver Dam - Of what ship or corps: Land forces - Whether man of war, privateer or merchant vessel: Taken on shore - Time when received into custody: 7 Jul 1813 - From what ship or whence received: Steamboat - Exchanged, discharged, died, or escape: Discharged - Time when: 10 Aug 1813 - Whither, and by what order, or number or re-entry: HM Ship Regulius by order of Sir George Provost

Barnes, William   Prisoner 1512. Rank: Private - By what ship or how taken: Troops - Time when: 25 Jul 1814 - Place where: Lundy's Lane - Of what ship or corps: Land forces - Whether man of war, privateer or merchant vessel: Taken on shore - Time when received into custody: 30 Aug 1814 - From what ship or whence received: Lady Delaval Schooner 578 - Exchanged, discharged, died, or escape: Discharged - Time when: 8 Oct 1814 - Whither, and by what order, or number

American Prisoners of War held at Quebec during the War of 1812

or re-entry: Queen No. 415

Barrett, Dyer   Prisoner 1792. Rank: Sergeant - By what ship or how taken: Troops - Time when: 7 Sep 1814 - Place where: Fort Erie - Of what ship or corps: Land forces - Whether man of war, privateer or merchant vessel: Taken on shore - Time when received into custody: 1 Nov 1814 - From what ship or whence received: Montreal - Exchanged, discharged, died, or escape: Discharged - Time when: 8 Nov 1814 - Whither, and by what order, or number or re-entry: S. George No. 575 for Halifax by order of Sir George Provost

Barron, John   Prisoner 366. Rank: Private - By what ship or how taken: Troops - Time when: 6 Jun 1813 - Place where: Stoney Point - Of what ship or corps: Land forces - Whether man of war, privateer or merchant vessel: Taken on shore - Time when received into custody: 28 Jun 1813 - From what ship or whence received: Mary of Quebec - Exchanged, discharged, died, or escape: Discharged - Time when: 31 Oct 1813 - Whither, and by what order, or number or re-entry: Malabar Transport

Bartlett, James   Prisoner 758. Rank: Private - By what ship or how taken: Troops - Time when: 26 Jun 1813 - Place where: Beaver Dam - Of what ship or corps: Land forces - Whether man of war, privateer or merchant vessel: Taken on shore - Time when received into custody: 7 Jul 1813 - From what ship or whence received: Steamboat - Exchanged, discharged, died, or escape: Discharged - Time when: 10 Aug 1813 - Whither, and by what order, or number or re-entry: HM Ship Malpomena

Barto, Selis   Prisoner 786. Rank: Private - By what ship or how taken: Troops - Time when: 26 Jun 1813 - Place where: Beaver Dam - Of what ship or corps: Land forces - Whether man of war, privateer or merchant vessel: Taken on shore - Time when received into custody: 7 Jul 1813 - From what ship or whence received: Steamboat - Exchanged, discharged, died, or escape: Discharged - Time when: 10 Aug 1813 - Whither, and by what order, or number or re-entry: HM Ship Malpomena

Barttey, William   Prisoner 363. Rank: Private - By what ship or how taken: Troops - Time when: 6 Jun 1813 - Place where: Stoney Point - Of what ship or corps: Land forces - Whether man of war, privateer or merchant vessel: Taken on shore - Time when received into custody: 28 Jun 1813 - From what ship or whence received: Mary of Quebec - Exchanged, discharged, died, or escape: Died - Time when: 13 Aug 1813 - Whither, and by what order, or number or re-entry:

Bascomb, Samuel   Prisoner 1222. Rank: Private - By what ship or how taken: Troops - Time when: 19 Dec 1813 - Place where: Fort Niagara - Of what ship or corps: Land forces - Whether man of war, privateer or merchant vessel: Taken on shore - Time when received into custody: 29 Jan 1814 - From what ship or whence received: Montreal by land carriage - Exchanged, discharged, died, or escape: Died - Time when: 21 Apr 1814 - Whither, and by what order, or number or re-entry: Gun shot wound

Batch, George   Prisoner 464. Rank: Private - By what ship or how taken: Troops - Time when: 24 Jun 1813 - Place where: Beaver Dam - Of what ship or corps: Malabar & Hydia - Whether man of war, privateer or merchant vessel: Taken on shore - Time when received into custody: 7 Jul 1813 - From what ship or whence received: Steamboat - Exchanged, discharged, died, or escape: Discharged - Time when: 31 Oct 1813 - Whither, and by what order, or number or re-entry: Malabar Transport

Batehelor, Orsen   Prisoner 50. Rank: Private - By what ship or how taken: Boats & Troops - Time when: 28 May 1813 - Place where: Stoney Point, Henderson Harbor - Of what ship or corps: Land forces - Whether man of war, privateer or merchant vessel: Taken on shore - Time when received into custody: 8 Jun 1813 - From what ship or whence received: Batteaux - Exchanged, discharged, died, or escape: Discharged - Time when: 31 Oct 1813 - Whither, and by what order, or number or re-entry: Malabar Transport

Batts, James   Prisoner 687. Rank: Private - By what ship or how taken: Troops - Time when: 26 Jun 1813 - Place where: Beaver Dam - Of what ship or corps: Land forces - Whether man of war, privateer or merchant vessel: Taken on shore - Time when received into custody: 7 Jul 1813 - From what ship or whence received: Steamboat - Exchanged, discharged, died, or escape: Discharged - Time when: 10 Aug 1813 - Whither, and by what order, or number or re-entry: HM Ship Regulius by order of Sir George Provost

Batty, Joseph   Prisoner 153. Rank: Ensign - By what ship or how taken: Boats & Troops - Time when: 3 Jun 1813 - Place where: Lake Champlain - Of what ship or corps: Growler - Whether man of war, privateer or merchant vessel: Man of War - Time when received into custody: 8 Jul 1813 - From what ship or whence received: Batteaux - Exchanged, discharged, died, or escape: Discharged - Time when: 31 Oct 1813 - Whither, and by what order, or number or re-entry: Malabar Transport

American Prisoners of War held at Quebec during the War of 1812

Bay, John   Prisoner 879. Rank: Private - By what ship or how taken: Troops - Time when: 26 Jun 1813 - Place where: Beaver Dam - Of what ship or corps: Land forces - Whether man of war, privateer or merchant vessel: Taken on shore - Time when received into custody: 7 Jul 1813 - From what ship or whence received: Steamboat - Exchanged, discharged, died, or escape: Discharged - Time when: 10 Aug 1813 - Whither, and by what order, or number or re-entry: HM Ship Malpomena

Bays, Jacob   Prisoner 290. Rank: Private - By what ship or how taken: Boats & Troops - Time when: 6 Jun 1813 - Place where: Stoney Point - Of what ship or corps: Land forces - Whether man of war, privateer or merchant vessel: Taken on shore - Time when received into custody: 28 Jun 1813 - From what ship or whence received: Quebec of Quebec - Exchanged, discharged, died, or escape: Discharged - Time when: 31 Oct 1813 - Whither, and by what order, or number or re-entry: Malabar Transport

Beals, John   Prisoner 471. Rank: Private - By what ship or how taken: Troops - Time when: 24 Jun 1813 - Place where: Beaver Dam - Of what ship or corps: Malabar & Hydia - Whether man of war, privateer or merchant vessel: Taken on shore - Time when received into custody: 7 Jul 1813 - From what ship or whence received: Steamboat - Exchanged, discharged, died, or escape: Discharged - Time when: 10 Aug 1813 - Whither, and by what order, or number or re-entry: HM Ship Regulius by order of Sir George Provost

Beals, William   Prisoner 1192. Rank: Citizen - By what ship or how taken: - Time when: - Place where: - Of what ship or corps: - Whether man of war, privateer or merchant vessel: - Time when received into custody: 12 Dec 1813 - From what ship or whence received: Town Goal - Exchanged, discharged, died, or escape: Discharged - Time when: 4 May 1814 - Whither, and by what order, or number or re-entry: United States

Bear , Henry   Prisoner 293. Rank: Private - By what ship or how taken: Boats & Troops - Time when: 6 Jun 1813 - Place where: Stoney Point - Of what ship or corps: Land forces - Whether man of war, privateer or merchant vessel: Taken on shore - Time when received into custody: 28 Jun 1813 - From what ship or whence received: Quebec of Quebec - Exchanged, discharged, died, or escape: Discharged - Time when: 31 Oct 1813 - Whither, and by what order, or number or re-entry: Malabar Transport

Beard, John   Prisoner 511. Rank: Private - By what ship or how taken: Troops - Time when: 24 Jun 1813 - Place where: Beaver Dam - Of what ship or corps: Land forces - Whether man of war, privateer or merchant vessel: Taken on shore - Time when received into custody: 7 Jul 1813 - From what ship or whence received: Steamboat - Exchanged, discharged, died, or escape: Discharged - Time when: 10 Aug 1813 - Whither, and by what order, or number or re-entry: HM Ship Regulius by order of Sir George Provost

Beard, Richard   Prisoner 436. Rank: Private - By what ship or how taken: Troops - Time when: 24 Jun 1813 - Place where: Beaver Dam - Of what ship or corps: Land forces - Whether man of war, privateer or merchant vessel: Taken on shore - Time when received into custody: 7 Jul 1813 - From what ship or whence received: Steamboat - Exchanged, discharged, died, or escape: Discharged - Time when: 10 Aug 1813 - Whither, and by what order, or number or re-entry: HM Ship Regulius by order of Sir George Provost

Beard, William C.   Prisoner 251. Rank: Lieutenant - By what ship or how taken: Boats & Troops - Time when: 24 Jun 1813 - Place where: Rec in charge of Beauport - Of what ship or corps: Land forces - Whether man of war, privateer or merchant vessel: Taken on shore - Time when received into custody: 24 Jun 1813 - From what ship or whence received: At Beauport - Exchanged, discharged, died, or escape: Discharged - Time when: 10 Aug 1813 - Whither, and by what order, or number or re-entry: Per order His Exellency Sir George Prevost

Beck, Andrew   Prisoner 278. Rank: Musician - By what ship or how taken: Troops - Time when: 6 Jun 1813 - Place where: Stoney Point - Of what ship or corps: Land forces - Whether man of war, privateer or merchant vessel: Taken on shore - Time when received into custody: 28 Jun 1813 - From what ship or whence received: Batteaux - Exchanged, discharged, died, or escape: Discharged - Time when: 31 Oct 1813 - Whither, and by what order, or number or re-entry: Malabar Transport

Beckford, John   Prisoner 1080. Rank: Private - By what ship or how taken: Troops - Time when: 24 Aug 1813 - Place where: Fort George - Of what ship or corps: Land forces - Whether man of war, privateer or merchant vessel: Taken on shore - Time when received into custody: 10 Oct 1813 - From what ship or whence received: Steamboat - Exchanged, discharged, died, or escape: Discharged - Time when: 31 Oct 1813 - Whither, and by what order, or number or re-entry: Malabar Transport

Beech, James   Prisoner 1116. Rank: Private - By what ship or how taken: Troops - Time when: 17 Oct 1813 - Place where: Red Mills - Of what ship or corps: Land forces - Whether man of war, privateer or merchant vessel: Taken on shore - Time when received into custody: 12 Oct 1813 - From what ship or whence received: Steamboat - Exchanged, discharged, died, or escape: Discharged - Time when: 31 Oct 1813 - Whither, and by what order, or number or re-entry: Malabar

American Prisoners of War held at Quebec during the War of 1812

Transport

Beers, James   Prisoner 1602. Rank: Private - By what ship or how taken: Troops - Time when: 12 Aug 1814 - Place where: Fort Erie - Of what ship or corps: Land forces - Whether man of war, privateer or merchant vessel: Taken on shore - Time when received into custody: 5 Oct 1814 - From what ship or whence received: Montreal - Exchanged, discharged, died, or escape: Discharged - Time when: 8 Oct 1814 - Whither, and by what order, or number or re-entry: H.M. Ship Ceylon

Befarr, Leonard   Prisoner 819. Rank: Private - By what ship or how taken: Troops - Time when: 26 Jun 1813 - Place where: Beaver Dam - Of what ship or corps: Land forces - Whether man of war, privateer or merchant vessel: Taken on shore - Time when received into custody: 7 Jul 1813 - From what ship or whence received: Steamboat - Exchanged, discharged, died, or escape: Discharged - Time when: 10 Aug 1813 - Whither, and by what order, or number or re-entry: HM Ship Malpomena

Belcher, Joseph   Prisoner 16. Rank: Corporal - By what ship or how taken: Boats & Troops - Time when: 28 May 1813 - Place where: Stoney Point, Henderson Harbor - Of what ship or corps: Land forces - Whether man of war, privateer or merchant vessel: Taken on shore - Time when received into custody: 8 Jun 1813 - From what ship or whence received: Batteaux - Exchanged, discharged, died, or escape: Discharged - Time when: 18 Sep 1813 - Whither, and by what order, or number or re-entry: Dick Transport

Bell, J. H.   Prisoner 1658. Rank: Sergeant - By what ship or how taken: Troops - Time when: 22 Jul 1812 - Place where: River Raisin - Of what ship or corps: Land forces - Whether man of war, privateer or merchant vessel: Taken on shore - Time when received into custody: 5 Oct 1814 - From what ship or whence received: Montreal - Exchanged, discharged, died, or escape: Discharged - Time when: 8 Oct 1814 - Whither, and by what order, or number or re-entry: H.M. Ship Ceylon

Bell, Orling   Prisoner 1906. Rank: Private - By what ship or how taken: Troops - Time when: 17 Sep 1814 - Place where: Fort Erie - Of what ship or corps: Land forces - Whether man of war, privateer or merchant vessel: Taken on shore - Time when received into custody: 1 Nov 1814 - From what ship or whence received: Montreal - Exchanged, discharged, died, or escape: Discharged - Time when: 8 Nov 1814 - Whither, and by what order, or number or re-entry: S. George No. 575 for Halifax by order of Sir George Provost

Belluite, Leve   Prisoner 817. Rank: Private - By what ship or how taken: Troops - Time when: 26 Jun 1813 - Place where: Beaver Dam - Of what ship or corps: Land forces - Whether man of war, privateer or merchant vessel: Taken on shore - Time when received into custody: 7 Jul 1813 - From what ship or whence received: Steamboat - Exchanged, discharged, died, or escape: Discharged - Time when: 31 Oct 1813 - Whither, and by what order, or number or re-entry: Malabar Transport

Benedick, Henry   Prisoner 1797. Rank: Corporal - By what ship or how taken: Troops - Time when: 7 Sep 1814 - Place where: Fort Erie - Of what ship or corps: Land forces - Whether man of war, privateer or merchant vessel: Taken on shore - Time when received into custody: 1 Nov 1814 - From what ship or whence received: Montreal - Exchanged, discharged, died, or escape: Discharged - Time when: 8 Nov 1814 - Whither, and by what order, or number or re-entry: S. George No. 575 for Halifax by order of Sir George Provost

Bennett, James W.   Prisoner 1235. Rank: Private - By what ship or how taken: Troops - Time when: 19 Dec 1813 - Place where: Fort Niagara - Of what ship or corps: Land forces - Whether man of war, privateer or merchant vessel: Taken on shore - Time when received into custody: 29 Jan 1814 - From what ship or whence received: Montreal by land carriage - Exchanged, discharged, died, or escape: Discharged - Time when: 28 Feb 1814 - Whither, and by what order, or number or re-entry: John D. Thomas Transport No. 23

Bennett, John   Prisoner 1972. Rank: Citizen - By what ship or how taken: Troops - Time when: 2 Nov 1814 - Place where: Saint Lawrence - Of what ship or corps: Land forces - Whether man of war, privateer or merchant vessel: Taken on shore - Time when received into custody: 11 Dec 1814 - From what ship or whence received: Montreal - Exchanged, discharged, died, or escape: Discharged - Time when: 13 Mar 1815 - Whither, and by what order, or number or re-entry: United States

Benton, John   Prisoner 1838. Rank: Private - By what ship or how taken: Troops - Time when: 17 Sep 1814 - Place where: Fort Erie - Of what ship or corps: Land forces - Whether man of war, privateer or merchant vessel: Taken on shore - Time when received into custody: 1 Nov 1814 - From what ship or whence received: Montreal - Exchanged, discharged, died, or escape: Discharged - Time when: 8 Nov 1814 - Whither, and by what order, or number or re-entry: S. George No. 575 for Halifax by order of Sir George Provost

Berg, Lawrence   Prisoner 348. Rank: Able seaman - By what ship or how taken: Gun Boats - Time when: 3 Jun 1813 - Place

American Prisoners of War held at Quebec during the War of 1812

where: Lake Champlain - Of what ship or corps: Growler - Whether man of war, privateer or merchant vessel: Man of War - Time when received into custody: 28 Jun 1813 - From what ship or whence received: Mary of Quebec - Exchanged, discharged, died, or escape: Discharged - Time when: 22 Aug 1813 - Whither, and by what order, or number or re-entry: Hydra No. 434

Bertel, Edward   Prisoner 967. Rank: Private - By what ship or how taken: Troops - Time when: 5 Jul 1813 - Place where: Fort Schisher - Of what ship or corps: Land forces - Whether man of war, privateer or merchant vessel: Taken on shore - Time when received into custody: 5 Sep 1813 - From what ship or whence received: Steamboat - Exchanged, discharged, died, or escape: Discharged - Time when: 31 Oct 1813 - Whither, and by what order, or number or re-entry: Malabar Transport

Berwick, George W.   Prisoner 1355. Rank: Private - By what ship or how taken: Troops - Time when: 19 Dec 1813 - Place where: Fort Niagara - Of what ship or corps: Land forces - Whether man of war, privateer or merchant vessel: Taken on shore - Time when received into custody: 29 Jan 1814 - From what ship or whence received: Montreal by land carriage - Exchanged, discharged, died, or escape: Discharged - Time when: 4 May 1814 - Whither, and by what order, or number or re-entry: United States

Bevins, John H.   Prisoner 1822. Rank: Private - By what ship or how taken: Troops - Time when: 17 Sep 1814 - Place where: Fort Erie - Of what ship or corps: Land forces - Whether man of war, privateer or merchant vessel: Taken on shore - Time when received into custody: 1 Nov 1814 - From what ship or whence received: Montreal - Exchanged, discharged, died, or escape: Discharged - Time when: 8 Nov 1814 - Whither, and by what order, or number or re-entry: S. George No. 575 for Halifax by order of Sir George Provost

Bilby, Henry   Prisoner 1106. Rank: Private - By what ship or how taken: Troops - Time when: 17 Oct 1813 - Place where: Red Mills - Of what ship or corps: Land forces - Whether man of war, privateer or merchant vessel: Taken on shore - Time when received into custody: 12 Oct 1813 - From what ship or whence received: Steamboat - Exchanged, discharged, died, or escape: Discharged - Time when: 31 Oct 1813 - Whither, and by what order, or number or re-entry: Malabar Transport

Bingham, Isaac   Prisoner 1126. Rank: Private - By what ship or how taken: Troops - Time when: 5 May 1813 - Place where: Rapids Prince Reason - Of what ship or corps: Land forces - Whether man of war, privateer or merchant vessel: Taken on shore - Time when received into custody: 25 Nov 1813 - From what ship or whence received: Town Goal - Exchanged, discharged, died, or escape: Discharged - Time when: 4 May 1814 - Whither, and by what order, or number or re-entry: United States

Bird, John D.   Prisoner 1570. Rank: Midshipman - By what ship or how taken: Gun Boats - Time when: 12 Aug 1814 - Place where: Fort Erie - Of what ship or corps: Somers - Whether man of war, privateer or merchant vessel: Man of War - Time when received into custody: 16 Sep 1814 - From what ship or whence received: Steamboat - Exchanged, discharged, died, or escape: Discharged - Time when: 10 Nov 1814 - Whither, and by what order, or number or re-entry: Lord Cartheart No. 161 for Halifax

Birk, John   Prisoner 541. Rank: Private By what ship or how taken: Troops Time when: 24 Jun 1813 - Place where: Beaver Dam - Of what ship or corps: Land forces - Whether man of war, privateer or merchant vessel: Taken on shore - Time when received into custody: 13 Jul 1813 - From what ship or whence received: Steamboat - Exchanged, discharged, died, or escape: Discharged - Time when: 31 Oct 1813 - Whither, and by what order, or number or re-entry: Malabar Transport

Bishop, James   Prisoner 1296. Rank: Private - By what ship or how taken: Troops - Time when: 19 Dec 1813 - Place where: Fort Niagara - Of what ship or corps: Land forces - Whether man of war, privateer or merchant vessel: Taken on shore - Time when received into custody: 29 Jan 1814 - From what ship or whence received: Montreal by land carriage - Exchanged, discharged, died, or escape: Discharged - Time when: 27 Feb 1814 - Whither, and by what order, or number or re-entry: Volunteered for New Brunswick Fencibles

Bishop, Jesse   Prisoner 610. Rank: Private - By what ship or how taken: Troops - Time when: 26 Jun 1813 - Place where: Stoney Point - Of what ship or corps: Land forces - Whether man of war, privateer or merchant vessel: Taken on shore - Time when received into custody: 7 Jul 1813 - From what ship or whence received: Steamboat - Exchanged, discharged, died, or escape: Discharged - Time when: 10 Aug 1813 - Whither, and by what order, or number or re-entry: HM Ship Regulius by order of Sir George Provost

Bishop, Job   Prisoner 1771. Rank: Corporal - By what ship or how taken: Troops - Time when: 7 Sep 1814 - Place where: Fort Erie - Of what ship or corps: Land forces - Whether man of war, privateer or merchant vessel: Taken on shore - Time when received into custody: 1 Nov 1814 - From what ship or whence received: Montreal - Exchanged, discharged, died, or escape: Discharged - Time when: 8 Nov 1814 - Whither, and by what order, or number or re-entry: S. George

American Prisoners of War held at Quebec during the War of 1812

No. 575 for Halifax by order of Sir George Provost

Bishop, Josiah   Prisoner 1327. Rank: Sergeant - By what ship or how taken: Troops - Time when: 19 Dec 1813 - Place where: Fort Niagara - Of what ship or corps: Land forces - Whether man of war, privateer or merchant vessel: Taken on shore - Time when received into custody: 29 Jan 1814 - From what ship or whence received: Montreal by land carriage - Exchanged, discharged, died, or escape: Discharged - Time when: 4 May 1814 - Whither, and by what order, or number or re-entry: United States

Bissure, Theodore   Prisoner 923. Rank: Private - By what ship or how taken: Troops - Time when: 26 Jun 1813 - Place where: Beaver Dam - Of what ship or corps: Land forces - Whether man of war, privateer or merchant vessel: Taken on shore - Time when received into custody: 21 Jul 1813 - From what ship or whence received: Steamboat - Exchanged, discharged, died, or escape: Discharged - Time when: 10 Aug 1813 - Whither, and by what order, or number or re-entry: HM Ship Malpomena

Black, C.   Prisoner 1592. Rank: Seaman - By what ship or how taken: Gun Boats - Time when: 12 Aug 1814 - Place where: Fort Erie - Of what ship or corps: Somers - Whether man of war, privateer or merchant vessel: Man of War - Time when received into custody: 5 Oct 1814 - From what ship or whence received: Montreal - Exchanged, discharged, died, or escape: Discharged - Time when: 10 Nov 1814 - Whither, and by what order, or number or re-entry: Freedom No. 582

Black, John   Prisoner 508. Rank: Private - By what ship or how taken: Troops - Time when: 24 Jun 1813 - Place where: Beaver Dam - Of what ship or corps: Land forces - Whether man of war, privateer or merchant vessel: Taken on shore - Time when received into custody: 7 Jul 1813 - From what ship or whence received: Steamboat - Exchanged, discharged, died, or escape: Discharged - Time when: 10 Aug 1813 - Whither, and by what order, or number or re-entry: HM Ship Regulius by order of Sir George Provost

Blairdie, Phillip   Prisoner 1923. Rank: Private - By what ship or how taken: Troops - Time when: 17 Sep 1814 - Place where: Fort Erie - Of what ship or corps: Land forces - Whether man of war, privateer or merchant vessel: Taken on shore - Time when received into custody: 1 Nov 1814 - From what ship or whence received: Montreal - Exchanged, discharged, died, or escape: Discharged - Time when: 14 Nov 1814 - Whither, and by what order, or number or re-entry: Soverign No. 628 for Halifax

Blake, Jonathan   Prisoner 1950. Rank: Sergeant - By what ship or how taken: Troops - Time when: 17 Sep 1814 - Place where: Fort Erie - Of what ship or corps: Land forces - Whether man of war, privateer or merchant vessel: Taken on shore - Time when received into custody: 11 Dec 1814 - From what ship or whence received: Montreal - Exchanged, discharged, died, or escape: Discharged - Time when: 13 Mar 1815 - Whither, and by what order, or number or re-entry: United States

Blake, William   Prisoner 1955. Rank: Private - By what ship or how taken: Troops - Time when: 23 Oct 1814 - Place where: Fort Erie - Of what ship or corps: Land forces - Whether man of war, privateer or merchant vessel: Taken on shore - Time when received into custody: 11 Dec 1814 - From what ship or whence received: Montreal - Exchanged, discharged, died, or escape: Discharged - Time when: 13 Mar 1815 - Whither, and by what order, or number or re-entry: United States

Blancet, Levi   Prisoner 1769. Rank: Corporal - By what ship or how taken: Troops - Time when: 7 Sep 1814 - Place where: Fort Erie - Of what ship or corps: Land forces - Whether man of war, privateer or merchant vessel: Taken on shore - Time when received into custody: 1 Nov 1814 - From what ship or whence received: Montreal - Exchanged, discharged, died, or escape: Discharged - Time when: 8 Nov 1814 - Whither, and by what order, or number or re-entry: S. George No. 575 for Halifax by order of Sir George Provost

Blancet, Levy   Prisoner 111. Rank: Corporal - By what ship or how taken: Boats & Troops - Time when: 28 May 1813 - Place where: Stoney Point, Henderson Harbor - Of what ship or corps: Land forces - Whether man of war, privateer or merchant vessel: Taken on shore - Time when received into custody: 8 Jun 1813 - From what ship or whence received: Batteaux - Exchanged, discharged, died, or escape: Discharged - Time when: 31 Oct 1813 - Whither, and by what order, or number or re-entry: Malabar Transport

Blanch, James   Prisoner 544. Rank: Sergeant - By what ship or how taken: Troops - Time when: 24 Jun 1813 - Place where: Beaver Dam - Of what ship or corps: Land forces - Whether man of war, privateer or merchant vessel: Taken on shore - Time when received into custody: 13 Jul 1813 - From what ship or whence received: Steamboat - Exchanged, discharged, died, or escape: Discharged - Time when: 13 Dec 1813 - Whither, and by what order, or number or re-entry: United States

American Prisoners of War held at Quebec during the War of 1812

Blank, Samuel   Prisoner 1000. Rank: Seaman - By what ship or how taken: Earl Moria - Time when: 10 Aug 1813 - Place where: Lake Ontario - Of what ship or corps: Julia - Whether man of war, privateer or merchant vessel: Man of War - Time when received into custody: 5 Sep 1813 - From what ship or whence received: Steamboat - Exchanged, discharged, died, or escape: Discharged - Time when: 31 Oct 1813 - Whither, and by what order, or number or re-entry: Malabar Transport

Blogs, Mordericke   Prisoner 487. Rank: Private - By what ship or how taken: Troops - Time when: 24 Jun 1813 - Place where: Beaver Dam - Of what ship or corps: Land forces - Whether man of war, privateer or merchant vessel: Taken on shore - Time when received into custody: 7 Jul 1813 - From what ship or whence received: Steamboat - Exchanged, discharged, died, or escape: Discharged - Time when: 10 Aug 1813 - Whither, and by what order, or number or re-entry: HM Ship Regulius by order of Sir George Provost

Blosea, Nathaniel   Prisoner 993. Rank: Seaman - By what ship or how taken: Earl Moria - Time when: 10 Aug 1813 - Place where: Lake Ontario - Of what ship or corps: Julia - Whether man of war, privateer or merchant vessel: Man of War - Time when received into custody: 5 Sep 1813 - From what ship or whence received: Steamboat - Exchanged, discharged, died, or escape: Discharged - Time when: 4 May 1814 - Whither, and by what order, or number or re-entry: United States

Blue, Henry   Prisoner 894. Rank: Private - By what ship or how taken: Troops - Time when: 26 Jun 1813 - Place where: Beaver Dam - Of what ship or corps: Land forces - Whether man of war, privateer or merchant vessel: Taken on shore - Time when received into custody: 7 Jul 1813 - From what ship or whence received: Steamboat - Exchanged, discharged, died, or escape: Discharged - Time when: 10 Aug 1813 - Whither, and by what order, or number or re-entry: HM Ship Malpomena

Blyth, John   Prisoner 1413. Rank: Private - By what ship or how taken: Troops - Time when: 19 Dec 1813 - Place where: Fort Niagara - Of what ship or corps: Land forces - Whether man of war, privateer or merchant vessel: Taken on shore - Time when received into custody: 29 Jan 1814 - From what ship or whence received: Montreal by land carriage - Exchanged, discharged, died, or escape: Discharged - Time when: 4 May 1814 - Whither, and by what order, or number or re-entry: United States

Boarmaster, Henry   Prisoner 352. Rank: Private - By what ship or how taken: Troops - Time when: 6 Jun 1813 - Place where: Stoney Point - Of what ship or corps: Land forces - Whether man of war, privateer or merchant vessel: Taken on shore - Time when received into custody: 28 Jun 1813 - From what ship or whence received: Mary of Quebec - Exchanged, discharged, died, or escape: Discharged - Time when: 22 Aug 1813 - Whither, and by what order, or number or re-entry: Hydra No. 434

Boersther, Charles G.   Prisoner 929. Rank: Lieutenant Colonel - By what ship or how taken: Troops - Time when: 26 Jun 1813 - Place where: Beaver Dam - Of what ship or corps: Land forces - Whether man of war, privateer or merchant vessel: Taken on shore - Time when received into custody: 21 Jul 1813 - From what ship or whence received: Steamboat - Exchanged, discharged, died, or escape: Discharged - Time when: 10 Aug 1813 - Whither, and by what order, or number or re-entry: HM Ship Malpomena

Bogea, John   Prisoner 835. Rank: Private - By what ship or how taken: Troops - Time when: 26 Jun 1813 - Place where: Beaver Dam - Of what ship or corps: Land forces - Whether man of war, privateer or merchant vessel: Taken on shore - Time when received into custody: 7 Jul 1813 - From what ship or whence received: Steamboat - Exchanged, discharged, died, or escape: Discharged - Time when: 10 Aug 1813 - Whither, and by what order, or number or re-entry: HM Ship Malpomena

Boggs, Lyman   Prisoner 414. Rank: Sergeant - By what ship or how taken: Troops - Time when: 24 Jun 1813 - Place where: Beaver Dam - Of what ship or corps: Land forces - Whether man of war, privateer or merchant vessel: Taken on shore - Time when received into custody: 7 Jul 1813 - From what ship or whence received: Steamboat - Exchanged, discharged, died, or escape: Discharged - Time when: 8 Oct 1813 - Whither, and by what order, or number or re-entry: H.M. Ship Ceylon

Bonney, William   Prisoner 39. Rank: Private - By what ship or how taken: Boats & Troops - Time when: 28 May 1813 - Place where: Stoney Point, Henderson Harbor - Of what ship or corps: Land forces - Whether man of war, privateer or merchant vessel: Taken on shore - Time when received into custody: 8 Jun 1813 - From what ship or whence received: Batteaux - Exchanged, discharged, died, or escape: Discharged - Time when: 31 Oct 1813 - Whither, and by what order, or number or re-entry: Malabar Transport

Boohm, Joseph   Prisoner 478. Rank: Private - By what ship or how taken: Troops - Time when: 24 Jun 1813 - Place where: Beaver Dam - Of what ship or corps: Land forces - Whether man of war, privateer or merchant vessel: Taken on shore - Time when received into custody: 7 Jul 1813 - From what ship or whence received: Steamboat - Exchanged,

American Prisoners of War held at Quebec during the War of 1812

discharged, died, or escape: Discharged - Time when: 10 Aug 1813 - Whither, and by what order, or number or re-entry: HM Ship Regulius by order of Sir George Provost

Booth, George   Prisoner 496. Rank: Private - By what ship or how taken: Troops - Time when: 24 Jun 1813 - Place where: Beaver Dam - Of what ship or corps: Land forces - Whether man of war, privateer or merchant vessel: Taken on shore - Time when received into custody: 7 Jul 1813 - From what ship or whence received: Steamboat - Exchanged, discharged, died, or escape: Discharged - Time when: 10 Aug 1813 - Whither, and by what order, or number or re-entry: HM Ship Regulius by order of Sir George Provost

Booth, John   Prisoner 761. Rank: Private - By what ship or how taken: Troops - Time when: 26 Jun 1813 - Place where: Beaver Dam - Of what ship or corps: Land forces - Whether man of war, privateer or merchant vessel: Taken on shore - Time when received into custody: 7 Jul 1813 - From what ship or whence received: Steamboat - Exchanged, discharged, died, or escape: Discharged - Time when: 10 Aug 1813 - Whither, and by what order, or number or re-entry: HM Ship Malpomena

Booth, Richard   Prisoner 44. Rank: Private - By what ship or how taken: Boats & Troops - Time when: 28 May 1813 - Place where: Stoney Point, Henderson Harbor - Of what ship or corps: Land forces - Whether man of war, privateer or merchant vessel: Taken on shore - Time when received into custody: 8 Jun 1813 - From what ship or whence received: Batteaux - Exchanged, discharged, died, or escape: Discharged - Time when: 4 May 1814 - Whither, and by what order, or number or re-entry: United States

Bossell, John   Prisoner 1276. Rank: Corporal - By what ship or how taken: Troops - Time when: 19 Dec 1813 - Place where: Fort Niagara - Of what ship or corps: Land forces - Whether man of war, privateer or merchant vessel: Taken on shore - Time when received into custody: 29 Jan 1814 - From what ship or whence received: Montreal by land carriage - Exchanged, discharged, died, or escape: Discharged - Time when: 24 Feb 1814 - Whither, and by what order, or number or re-entry: Volunteered for New Brunswick Fencibles

Bosson, Thaddius   Prisoner 116. Rank: Private - By what ship or how taken: Boats & Troops - Time when: 28 May 1813 - Place where: Stoney Point, Henderson Harbor - Of what ship or corps: Land forces - Whether man of war, privateer or merchant vessel: Taken on shore - Time when received into custody: 8 Jun 1813 - From what ship or whence received: Batteaux - Exchanged, discharged, died, or escape: Discharged - Time when: 31 Oct 1813 - Whither, and by what order, or number or re-entry: Malabar Transport

Boston, Daniel   Prisoner 158. Rank: Able seaman - By what ship or how taken: Boats & Troops - Time when: 3 Jun 1813 - Place where: Lake Champlain - Of what ship or corps: Eagle - Whether man of war, privateer or merchant vessel: Man of War - Time when received into custody: 9 Jun 1813 - From what ship or whence received: Batteaux - Exchanged, discharged, died, or escape: Discharged - Time when: 10 Dec 1813 - Whither, and by what order, or number or re-entry: United States

Bourdineou, Elijhua   Prisoner 1731. Rank: Seaman - By what ship or how taken: Gun Boats - Time when: 6 Sep 1814 - Place where: Lake Huron - Of what ship or corps: Scorpion - Whether man of war, privateer or merchant vessel: Man of War - Time when received into custody: 1 Nov 1814 - From what ship or whence received: Montreal - Exchanged, discharged, died, or escape: Discharged - Time when: 7 Nov 1814 - Whither, and by what order, or number or re-entry: Transport Freedom No. 582 by orders of his Excellency Sir George Provost

Bowe, Artemus   Prisoner 946. Rank: Sergeant - By what ship or how taken: Troops - Time when: 26 Jun 1813 - Place where: Beaver Dam - Of what ship or corps: Land forces - Whether man of war, privateer or merchant vessel: Taken on shore - Time when received into custody: 21 Jul 1813 - From what ship or whence received: Steamboat - Exchanged, discharged, died, or escape: Discharged - Time when: 10 Aug 1813 - Whither, and by what order, or number or re-entry: HM Ship Malpomena

Bowen, Joseph   Prisoner 1155. Rank: Corporal - By what ship or how taken: Troops - Time when: 5 May 1813 - Place where: Rapids Prince Reason - Of what ship or corps: Land forces - Whether man of war, privateer or merchant vessel: Taken on shore - Time when received into custody: 25 Nov 1813 - From what ship or whence received: Town Goal - Exchanged, discharged, died, or escape: Discharged - Time when: 4 May 1814 - Whither, and by what order, or number or re-entry: United States

Bowen, Pearce   Prisoner 1790. Rank: Corporal - By what ship or how taken: Troops - Time when: 7 Sep 1814 - Place where: Fort Erie - Of what ship or corps: Land forces - Whether man of war, privateer or merchant vessel: Taken on shore - Time when received into custody: 1 Nov 1814 - From what ship or whence received: Montreal - Exchanged, discharged, died, or escape: Discharged - Time when: 8 Nov 1814 - Whither, and by what order, or number or re-entry: S. George No. 575 for Halifax by order of Sir George Provost

American Prisoners of War held at Quebec during the War of 1812

Bowen, Thomas   Prisoner 283. Rank: Private - By what ship or how taken: Troops - Time when: 6 Jun 1813 - Place where: Stoney Point - Of what ship or corps: Land forces - Whether man of war, privateer or merchant vessel: Taken on shore - Time when received into custody: 28 Jun 1813 - From what ship or whence received: Batteaux - Exchanged, discharged, died, or escape: Discharged - Time when: 31 Oct 1813 - Whither, and by what order, or number or re-entry: HM Ship Success

Bowen, William   Prisoner 432. Rank: Private - By what ship or how taken: Troops - Time when: 24 Jun 1813 - Place where: Beaver Dam - Of what ship or corps: Land forces - Whether man of war, privateer or merchant vessel: Taken on shore - Time when received into custody: 7 Jul 1813 - From what ship or whence received: Steamboat - Exchanged, discharged, died, or escape: Discharged - Time when: 10 Aug 1813 - Whither, and by what order, or number or re-entry: HM Ship Regulius by order of Sir George Provost

Bowers, George   Prisoner 1634. Rank: Private - By what ship or how taken: Troops - Time when: 25 Jul 1814 - Place where: Lundy's Lane - Of what ship or corps: Land forces - Whether man of war, privateer or merchant vessel: Taken on shore - Time when received into custody: 5 Oct 1814 - From what ship or whence received: Montreal - Exchanged, discharged, died, or escape: Discharged - Time when: 8 Nov 1814 - Whither, and by what order, or number or re-entry: George No. 575 for Halifax by orders of Sir George Provost

Bowers, Jesse   Prisoner 895. Rank: Private - By what ship or how taken: Troops - Time when: 26 Jun 1813 - Place where: Beaver Dam - Of what ship or corps: Land forces - Whether man of war, privateer or merchant vessel: Taken on shore - Time when received into custody: 7 Jul 1813 - From what ship or whence received: Steamboat - Exchanged, discharged, died, or escape: Discharged - Time when: 10 Aug 1813 - Whither, and by what order, or number or re-entry: H.M. Ship Malpomena

Bowers, Joseph   Prisoner 1459. Rank: Private - By what ship or how taken: Troops - Time when: 6 May 1814 - Place where: Oswago - Of what ship or corps: Land forces - Whether man of war, privateer or merchant vessel: Taken on shore - Time when received into custody: 12 Aug 1814 - From what ship or whence received: Royal Seaman No. 289 Transport - Exchanged, discharged, died, or escape: Discharged - Time when: 8 Oct 1814 - Whither, and by what order, or number or re-entry: Queen No. 415

Bowice, Joseph   Prisoner 904. Rank: Drummer - By what ship or how taken: Troops - Time when: 26 Jun 1813 - Place where: Beaver Dam - Of what ship or corps: Land forces - Whether man of war, privateer or merchant vessel: Taken on shore - Time when received into custody: 21 Jul 1813 - From what ship or whence received: Steamboat - Exchanged, discharged, died, or escape: Discharged - Time when: 10 Aug 1813 - Whither, and by what order, or number or re-entry: HM Ship Malpomena

Bowlett, Nathaniel   Prisoner 1238. Rank: Private - By what ship or how taken: Troops - Time when: 19 Dec 1813 - Place where: Fort Niagara - Of what ship or corps: Land forces - Whether man of war, privateer or merchant vessel: Taken on shore - Time when received into custody: 29 Jan 1814 - From what ship or whence received: Montreal by land carriage - Exchanged, discharged, died, or escape: Discharged - Time when: 27 Feb 1814 - Whither, and by what order, or number or re-entry: Volunteered for New Brunswick Fencibles

Bowtell, H.   Prisoner 1593. Rank: Corporal - By what ship or how taken: Troops - Time when: 12 Aug 1814 - Place where: Fort Erie - Of what ship or corps: Land forces - Whether man of war, privateer or merchant vessel: Taken on shore - Time when received into custody: 5 Oct 1814 - From what ship or whence received: Montreal - Exchanged, discharged, died, or escape: Discharged - Time when: 8 Oct 1814 - Whither, and by what order, or number or re-entry: H.M. Ship Ceylon

Bowyer, George   Prisoner 304. Rank: Private - By what ship or how taken: Boats & Troops - Time when: 6 Jun 1813 - Place where: Stoney Point - Of what ship or corps: Land forces - Whether man of war, privateer or merchant vessel: Taken on shore - Time when received into custody: 28 Jun 1813 - From what ship or whence received: Quebec of Quebec - Exchanged, discharged, died, or escape: Discharged - Time when: 31 Oct 1813 - Whither, and by what order, or number or re-entry: Malabar Transport

Boyce, John   Prisoner 22. Rank: Private - By what ship or how taken: Boats & Troops - Time when: 28 May 1813 - Place where: Stoney Point, Henderson Harbor - Of what ship or corps: Land forces - Whether man of war, privateer or merchant vessel: Taken on shore - Time when received into custody: 8 Jun 1813 - From what ship or whence received: Batteaux - Exchanged, discharged, died, or escape: Discharged - Time when: 31 Oct 1813 - Whither, and by what order, or number or re-entry: Malabar Transport

Boyd, Samuel   Prisoner 385. Rank: Private - By what ship or how taken: Troops - Time when: 6 Jun 1813 - Place where: Stoney Point - Of what ship or corps: Land forces - Whether man of war, privateer or merchant vessel: Taken on shore - Time when received into custody: 28 Jun 1813 - From what ship or whence received: Mary of Quebec - Exchanged, discharged, died, or escape: Discharged - Time when: 31 Oct 1813 - Whither, and by what order, or number or re-entry: Malabar Transport

Boyd, William   Prisoner 1346. Rank: Private - By what ship or how taken: Troops - Time when: 19 Dec 1813 - Place where: Fort Niagara - Of what ship or corps: Land forces - Whether man of war, privateer or merchant vessel: Taken on shore - Time when received into custody: 29 Jan 1814 - From what ship or whence received: Montreal by land carriage - Exchanged, discharged, died, or escape: Discharged - Time when: 4 May 1814 - Whither, and by what order, or number or re-entry: United States

Boyer, Nelson   Prisoner 585. Rank: Private - By what ship or how taken: Troops - Time when: 26 Jun 1813 - Place where: Beaver Dam - Of what ship or corps: Land forces - Whether man of war, privateer or merchant vessel: Taken on shore - Time when received into custody: 13 Jul 1813 - From what ship or whence received: Steamboat - Exchanged, discharged, died, or escape: Discharged - Time when: 10 Aug 1813 - Whither, and by what order, or number or re-entry: HM Ship Regulius by order of Sir George Provost

Boyley, Moses   Prisoner 1733. Rank: Seaman - By what ship or how taken: Gun Boats - Time when: 6 Sep 1814 - Place where: Lake Huron - Of what ship or corps: Scorpion - Whether man of war, privateer or merchant vessel: Man of War - Time when received into custody: 1 Nov 1814 - From what ship or whence received: Montreal - Exchanged, discharged, died, or escape: Discharged - Time when: 7 Nov 1814 - Whither, and by what order, or number or re-entry: Transport Freedom No. 582 by orders of his Excellency Sir George Provost

Brace, Stephen   Prisoner 1152. Rank: Private - By what ship or how taken: Troops - Time when: 5 May 1813 - Place where: Rapids Prince Reason - Of what ship or corps: Land forces - Whether man of war, privateer or merchant vessel: Taken on shore - Time when received into custody: 25 Nov 1813 - From what ship or whence received: Town Goal - Exchanged, discharged, died, or escape: Discharged - Time when: 4 May 1814 - Whither, and by what order, or number or re-entry: United States

Bradford, John   Prisoner 362. Rank: Private - By what ship or how taken: Troops - Time when: 6 Jun 1813 - Place where: Stoney Point - Of what ship or corps: Land forces - Whether man of war, privateer or merchant vessel: Taken on shore - Time when received into custody: 28 Jun 1813 - From what ship or whence received: Mary of Quebec - Exchanged, discharged, died, or escape: Discharged - Time when: 31 Oct 1813 - Whither, and by what order, or number or re-entry: Malabar Transport

Bradford, Samuel   Prisoner 242. Rank: Captain - By what ship or how taken: Boats & Troops - Time when: 24 Jun 1813 - Place where: Rec in charge of Beauport - Of what ship or corps: Land forces - Whether man of war, privateer or merchant vessel: Taken on shore - Time when received into custody: 9 Jun 1813 - From what ship or whence received: Steamboat - Exchanged, discharged, died, or escape: Discharged - Time when: 10 Aug 1813 - Whither, and by what order, or number or re-entry: Per order His Exellency Sir George Prevost

Bradley, S.   Prisoner 1475. Rank: Private - By what ship or how taken: Troops - Time when: 14 Jul 1814 - Place where: St. Davids - Of what ship or corps: Land forces - Whether man of war, privateer or merchant vessel: Taken on shore - Time when received into custody: 12 Aug 1814 - From what ship or whence received: Royal Seaman No. 289 Transport - Exchanged, discharged, died, or escape: Discharged - Time when: 8 Oct 1814 - Whither, and by what order, or number or re-entry: Queen No. 415

Bradshaw, Edward   Prisoner 426. Rank: Private - By what ship or how taken: Troops - Time when: 24 Jun 1813 - Place where: Beaver Dam - Of what ship or corps: Land forces - Whether man of war, privateer or merchant vessel: Taken on shore - Time when received into custody: 7 Jul 1813 - From what ship or whence received: Steamboat - Exchanged, discharged, died, or escape: Discharged - Time when: 31 Oct 1813 - Whither, and by what order, or number or re-entry: Malabar Transport

Brakeman, Lodowick   Prisoner 937. Rank: Private - By what ship or how taken: Troops - Time when: 26 Jun 1813 - Place where: Beaver Dam - Of what ship or corps: Land forces - Whether man of war, privateer or merchant vessel: Taken on shore - Time when received into custody: 21 Jul 1813 - From what ship or whence received: Steamboat - Exchanged, discharged, died, or escape: Discharged - Time when: 10 Aug 1813 - Whither, and by what order, or number or re-entry: HM Ship Malpomena

Brandon, Samuel   Prisoner 1250. Rank: Sergeant - By what ship or how taken: Troops - Time when: 19 Dec 1813 - Place where: Fort Niagara - Of what ship or corps: Land forces - Whether man of war, privateer or merchant vessel: Taken on shore - Time when received into custody: 29 Jan 1814 - From what ship or whence received: Montreal by land carriage - Exchanged, discharged, died, or escape: Discharged - Time when: 27 Feb 1814 - Whither, and by what order, or number or re-entry: Volunteered for New Brunswick Fencibles

American Prisoners of War held at Quebec during the War of 1812

Brauntsman, Daniel   Prisoner 1256. Rank: Private - By what ship or how taken: Troops - Time when: 19 Dec 1813 - Place where: Fort Niagara - Of what ship or corps: Land forces - Whether man of war, privateer or merchant vessel: Taken on shore - Time when received into custody: 29 Jan 1814 - From what ship or whence received: Montreal by land carriage - Exchanged, discharged, died, or escape: Discharged - Time when: 27 Feb 1814 - Whither, and by what order, or number or re-entry: Volunteered for New Brunswick Fencibles

Brenhard, Arnold   Prisoner 1819. Rank: Private - By what ship or how taken: Troops - Time when: 17 Sep 1814 - Place where: Fort Erie - Of what ship or corps: Land forces - Whether man of war, privateer or merchant vessel: Taken on shore - Time when received into custody: 1 Nov 1814 - From what ship or whence received: Montreal - Exchanged, discharged, died, or escape: Discharged - Time when: 8 Nov 1814 - Whither, and by what order, or number or re-entry: S. George No. 575 for Halifax by order of Sir George Provost

Brett, Francis   Prisoner 1430. Rank: Cassenzer - By what ship or how taken: - Time when: Jul 1813 - Place where: St. Johns - Of what ship or corps: Posheu - Whether man of war, privateer or merchant vessel: Man of War - Time when received into custody: 24 May 1814 - From what ship or whence received: Mary Transport No. 360 Halifax - Exchanged, discharged, died, or escape: Discharged - Time when: 4 May 1814 - Whither, and by what order, or number or re-entry: United States

Bridge, Franklin   Prisoner 199. Rank: Sergeant - By what ship or how taken: Boats & Troops - Time when: 3 Jun 1813 - Place where: Lake Champlain - Of what ship or corps: Eagle - Whether man of war, privateer or merchant vessel: Man of War - Time when received into custody: 9 Jun 1813 - From what ship or whence received: Batteaux - Exchanged, discharged, died, or escape: Discharged - Time when: 8 Oct 1813 - Whither, and by what order, or number or re-entry: H.M. Ship Ceylon

Bridgeman, W.   Prisoner 1487. Rank: Private - By what ship or how taken: Troops - Time when: 25 Jul 1814 - Place where: Lundy's Lane - Of what ship or corps: Land forces - Whether man of war, privateer or merchant vessel: Taken on shore - Time when received into custody: 12 Aug 1814 - From what ship or whence received: Royal Seaman No. 289 Transport - Exchanged, discharged, died, or escape: Discharged - Time when: 8 Oct 1814 - Whither, and by what order, or number or re-entry: Queen No. 415

Briggs, William   Prisoner 1232. Rank: Private - By what ship or how taken: Troops - Time when: 19 Dec 1813 - Place where: Fort Niagara - Of what ship or corps: Land forces - Whether man of war, privateer or merchant vessel: Taken on shore - Time when received into custody: 29 Jan 1814 - From what ship or whence received: Montreal by land carriage - Exchanged, discharged, died, or escape: Discharged - Time when: 4 May 1814 - Whither, and by what order, or number or re-entry: United States

Brine, Thomas   Prisoner 981. Rank: Private - By what ship or how taken: Troops - Time when: 5 Jul 1813 - Place where: Fort Schisher - Of what ship or corps: Land forces - Whether man of war, privateer or merchant vessel: Taken on shore - Time when received into custody: 5 Sep 1813 - From what ship or whence received: Steamboat - Exchanged, discharged, died, or escape: Discharged - Time when: 4 May 1814 - Whither, and by what order, or number or re-entry: United States

Brink, Orson   Prisoner 180. Rank: Private - By what ship or how taken: Boats & Troops - Time when: 3 Jun 1813 - Place where: Lake Champlain - Of what ship or corps: Growler - Whether man of war, privateer or merchant vessel: Man of War - Time when received into custody: 9 Jun 1813 - From what ship or whence received: Batteaux - Exchanged, discharged, died, or escape: Discharged - Time when: 31 Oct 1813 - Whither, and by what order, or number or re-entry: Malabar Transport

Brison, James   Prisoner 435. Rank: Private - By what ship or how taken: Troops - Time when: 24 Jun 1813 - Place where: Beaver Dam - Of what ship or corps: Land forces - Whether man of war, privateer or merchant vessel: Taken on shore - Time when received into custody: 7 Jul 1813 - From what ship or whence received: Steamboat - Exchanged, discharged, died, or escape: Discharged - Time when: 10 Aug 1813 - Whither, and by what order, or number or re-entry: HM Ship Regulius by order of Sir George Provost

Broadist, Moses   Prisoner 444. Rank: Private - By what ship or how taken: Troops - Time when: 24 Jun 1813 - Place where: Beaver Dam - Of what ship or corps: Land forces - Whether man of war, privateer or merchant vessel: Taken on shore - Time when received into custody: 7 Jul 1813 - From what ship or whence received: Steamboat - Exchanged, discharged, died, or escape: Discharged - Time when: 10 Aug 1813 - Whither, and by what order, or number or re-entry: HM Ship Regulius by order of Sir George Provost

Bromley, Salmon   Prisoner 1302. Rank: Private - By what ship or how taken: Troops - Time when: 19 Dec 1813 - Place where: Fort Niagara - Of what ship or corps: Land forces - Whether man of war, privateer or merchant vessel: Taken on shore - Time when received into custody: 29 Jan 1814 - From what ship or whence received: Montreal by land carriage -

American Prisoners of War held at Quebec during the War of 1812

Exchanged, discharged, died, or escape: Discharged - Time when: 27 Feb 1814 - Whither, and by what order, or number or re-entry: Volunteered for New Brunswick Fencibles

Bronaugh, Thomas   Prisoner 1133. Rank: Private - By what ship or how taken: Troops - Time when: 5 May 1813 - Place where: Rapids Prince Reason - Of what ship or corps: Land forces - Whether man of war, privateer or merchant vessel: Taken on shore - Time when received into custody: 25 Nov 1813 - From what ship or whence received: Town Goal - Exchanged, discharged, died, or escape: Discharged - Time when: 4 May 1814 - Whither, and by what order, or number or re-entry: United States

Brookes, Joseph   Prisoner 1914. Rank: Private - By what ship or how taken: Troops - Time when: 17 Sep 1814 - Place where: Fort Erie - Of what ship or corps: Land forces - Whether man of war, privateer or merchant vessel: Taken on shore - Time when received into custody: 1 Nov 1814 - From what ship or whence received: Montreal - Exchanged, discharged, died, or escape: Discharged - Time when: 8 Nov 1814 - Whither, and by what order, or number or re-entry: S. George No. 575 for Halifax by order of Sir George Provost

Brown, Francis   Prisoner 789. Rank: Private - By what ship or how taken: Troops - Time when: 26 Jun 1813 - Place where: Beaver Dam - Of what ship or corps: Land forces - Whether man of war, privateer or merchant vessel: Taken on shore - Time when received into custody: 7 Jul 1813 - From what ship or whence received: Steamboat - Exchanged, discharged, died, or escape: Discharged - Time when: 10 Aug 1813 - Whither, and by what order, or number or re-entry: HM Ship Malpomena

Brown, Henry   Prisoner 1071. Rank: Corporal - By what ship or how taken: Troops - Time when: 24 Aug 1813 - Place where: Fort George - Of what ship or corps: Land forces - Whether man of war, privateer or merchant vessel: Taken on shore - Time when received into custody: 10 Oct 1813 - From what ship or whence received: Steamboat - Exchanged, discharged, died, or escape: Discharged - Time when: 31 Oct 1813 - Whither, and by what order, or number or re-entry: Malabar Transport

Brown, Henry   Prisoner 1735. Rank: Seaman - By what ship or how taken: Gun Boats - Time when: 6 Sep 1814 - Place where: Lake Huron - Of what ship or corps: Scorpion - Whether man of war, privateer or merchant vessel: Man of War - Time when received into custody: 1 Nov 1814 - From what ship or whence received: Montreal - Exchanged, discharged, died, or escape: Discharged - Time when: 7 Nov 1814 - Whither, and by what order, or number or re-entry: Transport Freedom No. 582 by orders of his Excellency Sir George Provost

Brown, James   Prisoner 948. Rank: Boy - By what ship or how taken: Troops - Time when: 26 Jun 1813 - Place where: Beaver Dam - Of what ship or corps: Land forces - Whether man of war, privateer or merchant vessel: Taken on shore - Time when received into custody: 21 Jul 1813 - From what ship or whence received: Steamboat - Exchanged, discharged, died, or escape: Discharged - Time when: 10 Aug 1813 - Whither, and by what order, or number or re-entry: HM Ship Malpomena

Brown, James   Prisoner 350. Rank: Private - By what ship or how taken: Troops - Time when: 6 Jun 1813 - Place where: Stoney Point - Of what ship or corps: Land forces - Whether man of war, privateer or merchant vessel: Taken on shore - Time when received into custody: 28 Jun 1813 - From what ship or whence received: Mary of Quebec - Exchanged, discharged, died, or escape: Discharged - Time when: 4 May 1814 - Whither, and by what order, or number or re-entry: United States

Brown, John   Prisoner 1445. Rank: Corporal - By what ship or how taken: Troops - Time when: 6 May 1814 - Place where: Oswago - Of what ship or corps: Land forces - Whether man of war, privateer or merchant vessel: Taken on shore - Time when received into custody: 12 Aug 1814 - From what ship or whence received: Royal Seaman No. 289 Transport - Exchanged, discharged, died, or escape: Discharged - Time when: 8 Oct 1814 - Whither, and by what order, or number or re-entry: Queen No. 415

Brown, John   Prisoner 506. Rank: Private - By what ship or how taken: Troops - Time when: 24 Jun 1813 - Place where: Beaver Dam - Of what ship or corps: Land forces - Whether man of war, privateer or merchant vessel: Taken on shore - Time when received into custody: 7 Jul 1813 - From what ship or whence received: Steamboat - Exchanged, discharged, died, or escape: Discharged - Time when: 9 Aug 1813 - Whither, and by what order, or number or re-entry: HM Ship Wasp

Brown, John   Prisoner 1704. Rank: Private - By what ship or how taken: Troops - Time when: 10 Sep 1814 - Place where: Plattsburg - Of what ship or corps: Land forces - Whether man of war, privateer or merchant vessel: Taken on shore - Time when received into custody: 23 Oct 1814 - From what ship or whence received: Montreal - Exchanged, discharged, died, or escape: Discharged - Time when: 8 Nov 1814 - Whither, and by what order, or number or re-entry: S. George No. 575 for Halifax

American Prisoners of War held at Quebec during the War of 1812

Brown, Joseph   Prisoner 1347. Rank: Private - By what ship or how taken: Troops - Time when: 19 Dec 1813 - Place where: Fort Niagara - Of what ship or corps: Land forces - Whether man of war, privateer or merchant vessel: Taken on shore - Time when received into custody: 29 Jan 1814 - From what ship or whence received: Montreal by land carriage - Exchanged, discharged, died, or escape: Discharged - Time when: 4 May 1814 - Whither, and by what order, or number or re-entry: United States

Brown, Michael   Prisoner 757. Rank: Private - By what ship or how taken: Troops - Time when: 26 Jun 1813 - Place where: Beaver Dam - Of what ship or corps: Land forces - Whether man of war, privateer or merchant vessel: Taken on shore - Time when received into custody: 7 Jul 1813 - From what ship or whence received: Steamboat - Exchanged, discharged, died, or escape: Discharged - Time when: 10 Aug 1813 - Whither, and by what order, or number or re-entry: HM Ship Malpomena

Brown, Perry W.   Prisoner 747. Rank: Private - By what ship or how taken: Troops - Time when: 26 Jun 1813 - Place where: Beaver Dam - Of what ship or corps: Land forces - Whether man of war, privateer or merchant vessel: Taken on shore - Time when received into custody: 7 Jul 1813 - From what ship or whence received: Steamboat - Exchanged, discharged, died, or escape: Discharged - Time when: 10 Aug 1813 - Whither, and by what order, or number or re-entry: HM Ship Regulius by order of Sir George Provost

Brown, R.   Prisoner 1621. Rank: Private - By what ship or how taken: Gun Boats - Time when: 15 Aug 1814 - Place where: Fort Erie - Of what ship or corps: Land forces - Whether man of war, privateer or merchant vessel: Taken on shore - Time when received into custody: 5 Oct 1814 - From what ship or whence received: Montreal - Exchanged, discharged, died, or escape: Discharged - Time when: 8 Oct 1814 - Whither, and by what order, or number or re-entry: H.M. Ship Ceylon

Brown, Rufus   Prisoner 1811. Rank: Private - By what ship or how taken: Troops - Time when: 17 Sep 1814 - Place where: Fort Erie - Of what ship or corps: Land forces - Whether man of war, privateer or merchant vessel: Taken on shore - Time when received into custody: 1 Nov 1814 - From what ship or whence received: Montreal - Exchanged, discharged, died, or escape: Discharged - Time when: 8 Nov 1814 - Whither, and by what order, or number or re-entry: S. George No. 575 for Halifax by order of Sir George Provost

Brown, Thomas   Prisoner 1503. Rank: Private - By what ship or how taken: Troops - Time when: 19 Jul 1814 - Place where: 4 Mile Creek - Of what ship or corps: Land forces - Whether man of war, privateer or merchant vessel: Taken on shore - Time when received into custody: 19 Aug 1814 - From what ship or whence received: Triton No. 438 Transport - Exchanged, discharged, died, or escape: Discharged - Time when: 8 Oct 1814 - Whither, and by what order, or number or re-entry: Queen No. 415

Brown, Thomas   Prisoner 1028. Rank: Seaman - By what ship or how taken: Lord Melvin - Time when: 10 Aug 1813 - Place where: Lake Ontario - Of what ship or corps: Growler - Whether man of war, privateer or merchant vessel: Man of War - Time when received into custody: 5 Sep 1813 - From what ship or whence received: Steamboat - Exchanged, discharged, died, or escape: Discharged - Time when: 4 May 1814 - Whither, and by what order, or number or re-entry: United States

Brown, William   Prisoner 1692. Rank: Musician - By what ship or how taken: Troops - Time when: 29 Dec 1813 - Place where: Buffalo - Of what ship or corps: Land forces - Whether man of war, privateer or merchant vessel: Taken on shore - Time when received into custody: 23 Oct 1814 - From what ship or whence received: Montreal - Exchanged, discharged, died, or escape: Discharged - Time when: 8 Nov 1814 - Whither, and by what order, or number or re-entry: S. George No. 575 for Halifax

Brown, William   Prisoner 1253. Rank: Private - By what ship or how taken: Troops - Time when: 19 Dec 1813 - Place where: Fort Niagara - Of what ship or corps: Land forces - Whether man of war, privateer or merchant vessel: Taken on shore - Time when received into custody: 29 Jan 1814 - From what ship or whence received: Montreal by land carriage - Exchanged, discharged, died, or escape: Discharged - Time when: 27 Feb 1814 - Whither, and by what order, or number or re-entry: Volunteered for New Brunswick Fencibles

Brownhill, John   Prisoner 791. Rank: Private - By what ship or how taken: Troops - Time when: 26 Jun 1813 - Place where: Beaver Dam - Of what ship or corps: Land forces - Whether man of war, privateer or merchant vessel: Taken on shore - Time when received into custody: 7 Jul 1813 - From what ship or whence received: Steamboat - Exchanged, discharged, died, or escape: Discharged - Time when: 10 Aug 1813 - Whither, and by what order, or number or re-entry: HM Ship Malpomena

Brownwell, D.   Prisoner 1633. Rank: Private - By what ship or how taken: Troops - Time when: 25 Jul 1814 - Place where: Lundy's Lane - Of what ship or corps: Land forces - Whether man of war, privateer or merchant vessel: Taken on shore - Time when received into custody: 5 Oct 1814 - From what ship or whence received: Montreal - Exchanged,

American Prisoners of War held at Quebec during the War of 1812

discharged, died, or escape: Discharged - Time when: 8 Oct 1814 - Whither, and by what order, or number or re-entry: H.M. Ship Ceylon

Bruce, William   Prisoner 1501. Rank: Private - By what ship or how taken: Troops - Time when: 26 Jul 1814 - Place where: Lundy's Lane - Of what ship or corps: Land forces - Whether man of war, privateer or merchant vessel: Taken on shore - Time when received into custody: 19 Aug 1814 - From what ship or whence received: Triton No. 438 Transport - Exchanged, discharged, died, or escape: Discharged - Time when: 8 Oct 1814 - Whither, and by what order, or number or re-entry: Queen No. 415

Bryan, J.   Prisoner 1582. Rank: Seaman - By what ship or how taken: Gun Boats - Time when: 12 Aug 1814 - Place where: Fort Erie - Of what ship or corps: Somers - Whether man of war, privateer or merchant vessel: Man of War - Time when received into custody: 5 Oct 1814 - From what ship or whence received: Montreal - Exchanged, discharged, died, or escape: Discharged - Time when: 10 Nov 1814 - Whither, and by what order, or number or re-entry: Freedom No. 582

Bryce, James   Prisoner 659. Rank: Private - By what ship or how taken: Troops - Time when: 24 Jun 1813 - Place where: Stoney Point - Of what ship or corps: Land forces - Whether man of war, privateer or merchant vessel: Taken on shore - Time when received into custody: 7 Jul 1813 - From what ship or whence received: Steamboat - Exchanged, discharged, died, or escape: Discharged - Time when: 10 Aug 1813 - Whither, and by what order, or number or re-entry: HM Ship Regulius by order of Sir George Provost

Buchanan, John   Prisoner 1380. Rank: Private - By what ship or how taken: Troops - Time when: 19 Dec 1813 - Place where: Fort Niagara - Of what ship or corps: Land forces - Whether man of war, privateer or merchant vessel: Taken on shore - Time when received into custody: 29 Jan 1814 - From what ship or whence received: Montreal by land carriage - Exchanged, discharged, died, or escape: Discharged - Time when: 4 May 1814 - Whither, and by what order, or number or re-entry: United States

Buckley, Elis   Prisoner 1883. Rank: Private - By what ship or how taken: Troops - Time when: 17 Sep 1814 - Place where: Fort Erie - Of what ship or corps: Land forces - Whether man of war, privateer or merchant vessel: Taken on shore - Time when received into custody: 1 Nov 1814 - From what ship or whence received: Montreal - Exchanged, discharged, died, or escape: Discharged - Time when: 8 Nov 1814 - Whither, and by what order, or number or re-entry: S. George No. 575 for Halifax by order of Sir George Provost

Buel, Jeremiah   Prisoner 987. Rank: Purser Steward - By what ship or how taken: Lord McMillien - Time when: 10 Aug 1813 - Place where: Lake Ontario - Of what ship or corps: Growler - Whether man of war, privateer or merchant vessel: Man of War - Time when received into custody: 5 Sep 1813 - From what ship or whence received: Steamboat - Exchanged, discharged, died, or escape: Discharged - Time when: 31 Oct 1813 - Whither, and by what order, or number or re-entry: Malabar Transport

Bull, Benjamin S.   Prisoner 812. Rank: Sergeant - By what ship or how taken: Troops - Time when: 26 Jun 1813 - Place where: Beaver Dam - Of what ship or corps: Land forces - Whether man of war, privateer or merchant vessel: Taken on shore - Time when received into custody: 7 Jul 1813 - From what ship or whence received: Steamboat - Exchanged, discharged, died, or escape: Discharged - Time when: 10 Aug 1813 - Whither, and by what order, or number or re-entry: HM Ship Malpomena

Bull, William   Prisoner 646. Rank: Private - By what ship or how taken: Troops - Time when: 24 Jun 1813 - Place where: Stoney Point - Of what ship or corps: Land forces - Whether man of war, privateer or merchant vessel: Taken on shore - Time when received into custody: 7 Jul 1813 - From what ship or whence received: Steamboat - Exchanged, discharged, died, or escape: Discharged - Time when: 10 Aug 1813 - Whither, and by what order, or number or re-entry: HM Ship Regulius by order of Sir George Provost

Bunnell, David C.   Prisoner 1723. Rank: Purser Steward - By what ship or how taken: Gun Boats - Time when: 6 Sep 1814 - Place where: Lake Huron - Of what ship or corps: Scorpion - Whether man of war, privateer or merchant vessel: Man of War - Time when received into custody: 28 Oct 1814 - From what ship or whence received: Montreal - Exchanged, discharged, died, or escape: Discharged - Time when: 7 Nov 1814 - Whither, and by what order, or number or re-entry: Transport Freedom No. 582 by orders of his Excellency Sir George Provost

Burch, Levi   Prisoner 1968. Rank: Private - By what ship or how taken: Troops - Time when: 17 Oct 1814 - Place where: Chippawa - Of what ship or corps: Land forces - Whether man of war, privateer or merchant vessel: Taken on shore - Time when received into custody: 11 Dec 1814 - From what ship or whence received: Montreal - Exchanged, discharged, died, or escape: Discharged - Time when: 13 Mar 1815 - Whither, and by what order, or number or re-entry: United States

American Prisoners of War held at Quebec during the War of 1812

Burd, Benjamin E.   Prisoner 535. Rank: Lieutenant - By what ship or how taken: Troops - Time when: 24 Jun 1813 - Place where: Beaver Dam - Of what ship or corps: Land forces - Whether man of war, privateer or merchant vessel: Taken on shore - Time when received into custody: 13 Jul 1813 - From what ship or whence received: Steamboat - Exchanged, discharged, died, or escape: Discharged - Time when: 10 Aug 1813 - Whither, and by what order, or number or re-entry: HM Ship Regulius by order of Sir George Provost

Burees, Viris   Prisoner 1226. Rank: Private - By what ship or how taken: Troops - Time when: 19 Dec 1813 - Place where: Fort Niagara - Of what ship or corps: Land forces - Whether man of war, privateer or merchant vessel: Taken on shore - Time when received into custody: 29 Jan 1814 - From what ship or whence received: Montreal by land carriage - Exchanged, discharged, died, or escape: Discharged - Time when: 4 May 1814 - Whither, and by what order, or number or re-entry: United States

Burk, Edward   Prisoner 1913. Rank: Private - By what ship or how taken: Troops - Time when: 17 Sep 1814 - Place where: Fort Erie - Of what ship or corps: Land forces - Whether man of war, privateer or merchant vessel: Taken on shore - Time when received into custody: 1 Nov 1814 - From what ship or whence received: Montreal - Exchanged, discharged, died, or escape: Discharged - Time when: 8 Nov 1814 - Whither, and by what order, or number or re-entry: S. George No. 575 for Halifax by order of Sir George Provost

Burlue, Gilbert   Prisoner 754. Rank: Private - By what ship or how taken: Troops - Time when: 26 Jun 1813 - Place where: Beaver Dam - Of what ship or corps: Land forces - Whether man of war, privateer or merchant vessel: Taken on shore - Time when received into custody: 7 Jul 1813 - From what ship or whence received: Steamboat - Exchanged, discharged, died, or escape: Discharged - Time when: 10 Aug 1813 - Whither, and by what order, or number or re-entry: HM Ship Malpomena

Burns, Andrew   Prisoner 633. Rank: Private - By what ship or how taken: Troops - Time when: 24 Jun 1813 - Place where: Stoney Point - Of what ship or corps: Land forces - Whether man of war, privateer or merchant vessel: Taken on shore - Time when received into custody: 7 Jul 1813 - From what ship or whence received: Steamboat - Exchanged, discharged, died, or escape: Discharged - Time when: 10 Aug 1813 - Whither, and by what order, or number or re-entry: HM Ship Regulius by order of Sir George Provost

Burns, John E.   Prisoner 1835. Rank: Private - By what ship or how taken: Troops - Time when: 17 Sep 1814 - Place where: Fort Erie - Of what ship or corps: Land forces - Whether man of war, privateer or merchant vessel: Taken on shore - Time when received into custody: 1 Nov 1814 - From what ship or whence received: Montreal - Exchanged, discharged, died, or escape: Discharged - Time when: 8 Nov 1814 - Whither, and by what order, or number or re-entry: S. George No. 575 for Halifax by order of Sir George Provost

Burrell, John   Prisoner 454. Rank: Private - By what ship or how taken: Troops - Time when: 24 Jun 1813 - Place where: Beaver Dam - Of what ship or corps: Malabar & Hydia - Whether man of war, privateer or merchant vessel: Taken on shore - Time when received into custody: 7 Jul 1813 - From what ship or whence received: Steamboat - Exchanged, discharged, died, or escape: Discharged - Time when: 10 Aug 1813 - Whither, and by what order, or number or re-entry: HM Ship Regulius by order of Sir George Provost

Burtle, Dovis   Prisoner 1720. Rank: Private - By what ship or how taken: Gun Boats - Time when: 6 Sep 1814 - Place where: Lake Huron - Of what ship or corps: Scorpion - Whether man of war, privateer or merchant vessel: Man of War - Time when received into custody: 28 Oct 1814 - From what ship or whence received: Montreal - Exchanged, discharged, died, or escape: Discharged - Time when: 10 Nov 1814 - Whither, and by what order, or number or re-entry: Transport Stately No. 408 for Halifax

Burtsell, David   Prisoner 1318. Rank: Private - By what ship or how taken: Troops - Time when: 19 Dec 1813 - Place where: Fort Niagara - Of what ship or corps: Land forces - Whether man of war, privateer or merchant vessel: Taken on shore - Time when received into custody: 29 Jan 1814 - From what ship or whence received: Montreal by land carriage - Exchanged, discharged, died, or escape: Discharged - Time when: 27 Feb 1814 - Whither, and by what order, or number or re-entry: Volunteered for New Brunswick Fencibles

Bush, Hollower   Prisoner 1438. Rank: Private - By what ship or how taken: Gun Boats - Time when: 29 May 1814 - Place where: Sacketts Harbor - Of what ship or corps: Land forces - Whether man of war, privateer or merchant vessel: Taken on shore - Time when received into custody: 12 Aug 1814 - From what ship or whence received: Royal Seaman No. 289 Transport - Exchanged, discharged, died, or escape: Discharged - Time when: 8 Nov 1814 - Whither, and by what order, or number or re-entry: S. George No. 575

Buskerk, Garrett   Prisoner 1400. Rank: Private - By what ship or how taken: Troops - Time when: 19 Dec 1813 - Place where: Fort Niagara - Of what ship or corps: Land forces - Whether man of war, privateer or merchant vessel: Taken on shore - Time when received into custody: 29 Jan 1814 - From what ship or whence received: Montreal by land carriage -

American Prisoners of War held at Quebec during the War of 1812

Exchanged, discharged, died, or escape: Discharged - Time when: 4 May 1814 - Whither, and by what order, or number or re-entry: United States

Bussell, D.   Prisoner 1600. Rank: Private - By what ship or how taken: Troops - Time when: 12 Aug 1814 - Place where: Fort Erie - Of what ship or corps: Land forces - Whether man of war, privateer or merchant vessel: Taken on shore - Time when received into custody: 5 Oct 1814 - From what ship or whence received: Montreal - Exchanged, discharged, died, or escape: Discharged - Time when: 8 Oct 1814 - Whither, and by what order, or number or re-entry: H.M. Ship Ceylon

Butman, Benjamin   Prisoner 184. Rank: Sergeant - By what ship or how taken: Boats & Troops - Time when: 3 Jun 1813 - Place where: Lake Champlain - Of what ship or corps: Eagle - Whether man of war, privateer or merchant vessel: Man of War - Time when received into custody: 9 Jun 1813 - From what ship or whence received: Batteaux - Exchanged, discharged, died, or escape: Discharged - Time when: 8 Oct 1813 - Whither, and by what order, or number or re-entry: H.M. Ship Ceylon

Butsman, D.   Prisoner 1615. Rank: Private - By what ship or how taken: Gun Boats - Time when: 12 Aug 1814 - Place where: Fort Erie - Of what ship or corps: Land forces - Whether man of war, privateer or merchant vessel: Taken on shore - Time when received into custody: 5 Oct 1814 - From what ship or whence received: Montreal - Exchanged, discharged, died, or escape: Discharged - Time when: 8 Oct 1814 - Whither, and by what order, or number or re-entry: H.M. Ship Ceylon

Butterfield, Abraham   Prisoner 1818. Rank: Private - By what ship or how taken: Troops - Time when: 17 Sep 1814 - Place where: Fort Erie - Of what ship or corps: Land forces - Whether man of war, privateer or merchant vessel: Taken on shore - Time when received into custody: 1 Nov 1814 - From what ship or whence received: Montreal - Exchanged, discharged, died, or escape: Discharged - Time when: 8 Nov 1814 - Whither, and by what order, or number or re-entry: S. George No. 575 for Halifax by order of Sir George Provost

Byrn, Phillip   Prisoner 1129. Rank: Sergeant - By what ship or how taken: Troops - Time when: 5 May 1813 - Place where: Rapids Prince Reason - Of what ship or corps: Land forces - Whether man of war, privateer or merchant vessel: Taken on shore - Time when received into custody: 25 Nov 1813 - From what ship or whence received: Town Goal - Exchanged, discharged, died, or escape: Discharged - Time when: 4 May 1814 - Whither, and by what order, or number or re-entry: United States

Cady, Daniel G.   Prisoner 977. Rank: Private - By what ship or how taken: Troops - Time when: 5 Jul 1813 - Place where: Fort Schisher - Of what ship or corps: Land forces - Whether man of war, privateer or merchant vessel: Taken on shore - Time when received into custody: 5 Sep 1813 - From what ship or whence received: Steamboat - Exchanged, discharged, died, or escape: Discharged - Time when: 31 Oct 1813 - Whither, and by what order, or number or re-entry: Malabar Transport

Cahall, E.   Prisoner 1645. Rank: Private - By what ship or how taken: Troops - Time when: 19 Dec 1813 - Place where: Niagara - Of what ship or corps: Land forces - Whether man of war, privateer or merchant vessel: Taken on shore - Time when received into custody: 5 Oct 1814 - From what ship or whence received: Montreal - Exchanged, discharged, died, or escape: Discharged - Time when: 8 Oct 1814 - Whither, and by what order, or number or re-entry: H.M. Ship Ceylon

Caknary, James   Prisoner 571. Rank: Private - By what ship or how taken: Troops - Time when: 26 Jun 1813 - Place where: Beaver Dam - Of what ship or corps: Land forces - Whether man of war, privateer or merchant vessel: Taken on shore - Time when received into custody: 13 Jul 1813 - From what ship or whence received: Steamboat - Exchanged, discharged, died, or escape: Discharged - Time when: 10 Aug 1813 - Whither, and by what order, or number or re-entry: HM Ship Regulius by order of Sir George Provost

Caldwell, Nathaniel   Prisoner 1823. Rank: Private - By what ship or how taken: Troops - Time when: 17 Sep 1814 - Place where: Fort Erie - Of what ship or corps: Land forces - Whether man of war, privateer or merchant vessel: Taken on shore - Time when received into custody: 1 Nov 1814 - From what ship or whence received: Montreal - Exchanged, discharged, died, or escape: Discharged - Time when: 8 Nov 1814 - Whither, and by what order, or number or re-entry: S. George No. 575 for Halifax by order of Sir George Provost

Calkins, Eliphel   Prisoner 784. Rank: Private - By what ship or how taken: Troops - Time when: 26 Jun 1813 - Place where: Beaver Dam - Of what ship or corps: Land forces - Whether man of war, privateer or merchant vessel: Taken on shore - Time when received into custody: 7 Jul 1813 - From what ship or whence received: Steamboat - Exchanged, discharged, died, or escape: Discharged - Time when: 10 Aug 1813 - Whither, and by what order, or number or re-entry: HM Ship Malpomena

American Prisoners of War held at Quebec during the War of 1812

Calliham, Francis   Prisoner 1211. Rank: Boy - By what ship or how taken: Troops - Time when: 19 Dec 1813 - Place where: Fort Niagara - Of what ship or corps: Land forces - Whether man of war, privateer or merchant vessel: Taken on shore - Time when received into custody: 18 Jan 1814 - From what ship or whence received: Montreal by land carriage - Exchanged, discharged, died, or escape: Discharged - Time when: 4 May 1814 - Whither, and by what order, or number or re-entry: United States

Campbell, Frederick   Prisoner 1653. Rank: Private - By what ship or how taken: Troops - Time when: 11 Nov 1813 - Place where: Williamsburg - Of what ship or corps: Land forces - Whether man of war, privateer or merchant vessel: Taken on shore - Time when received into custody: 5 Oct 1814 - From what ship or whence received: Montreal - Exchanged, discharged, died, or escape: Discharged - Time when: 8 Oct 1814 - Whither, and by what order, or number or re-entry: H.M. Ship Ceylon

Campbell, James   Prisoner 198. Rank: Private - By what ship or how taken: Boats & Troops - Time when: 3 Jun 1813 - Place where: Lake Champlain - Of what ship or corps: Growler - Whether man of war, privateer or merchant vessel: Man of War - Time when received into custody: 9 Jun 1813 - From what ship or whence received: Batteaux - Exchanged, discharged, died, or escape: Discharged - Time when: 31 Oct 1813 - Whither, and by what order, or number or re-entry: Malabar Transport

Campbell, Jesse   Prisoner 1464. Rank: Private - By what ship or how taken: Gun Boats - Time when: 29 May 1814 - Place where: Sandy Creek - Of what ship or corps: Land forces - Whether man of war, privateer or merchant vessel: Taken on shore - Time when received into custody: 12 Aug 1814 - From what ship or whence received: Royal Seaman No. 289 Transport - Exchanged, discharged, died, or escape: Discharged - Time when: 8 Oct 1814 - Whither, and by what order, or number or re-entry: Queen No. 415

Campbell, Joseph   Prisoner 1081. Rank: Private - By what ship or how taken: Troops - Time when: 24 Aug 1813 - Place where: Fort George - Of what ship or corps: Land forces - Whether man of war, privateer or merchant vessel: Taken on shore - Time when received into custody: 10 Oct 1813 - From what ship or whence received: Steamboat - Exchanged, discharged, died, or escape: Discharged - Time when: 31 Oct 1813 - Whither, and by what order, or number or re-entry: Malabar Transport

Campbell, Mathew   Prisoner 358. Rank: Private - By what ship or how taken: Troops - Time when: 6 Jun 1813 - Place where: Stoney Point - Of what ship or corps: Land forces - Whether man of war, privateer or merchant vessel: Taken on shore - Time when received into custody: 28 Jun 1813 - From what ship or whence received: Mary of Quebec - Exchanged, discharged, died, or escape: Discharged - Time when: 7 Aug 1813 - Whither, and by what order, or number or re-entry: H.M. Ship Cievare

Campbell, Oliver   Prisoner 1821. Rank: Private - By what ship or how taken: Troops - Time when: 17 Sep 1814 - Place where: Fort Erie - Of what ship or corps: Land forces - Whether man of war, privateer or merchant vessel: Taken on shore - Time when received into custody: 1 Nov 1814 - From what ship or whence received: Montreal - Exchanged, discharged, died, or escape: Discharged - Time when: 8 Nov 1814 - Whither, and by what order, or number or re-entry: S. George No. 575 for Halifax by order of Sir George Provost

Campbell, William   Prisoner 217. Rank: Private - By what ship or how taken: Boats & Troops - Time when: 3 Jun 1813 - Place where: Lake Champlain - Of what ship or corps: Growler - Whether man of war, privateer or merchant vessel: Man of War - Time when received into custody: 9 Jun 1813 - From what ship or whence received: Batteaux - Exchanged, discharged, died, or escape: Discharged - Time when: 31 Oct 1813 - Whither, and by what order, or number or re-entry: Malabar Transport

Cann, John   Prisoner 706. Rank: Private - By what ship or how taken: Troops - Time when: 26 Jun 1813 - Place where: Beaver Dam - Of what ship or corps: Land forces - Whether man of war, privateer or merchant vessel: Taken on shore - Time when received into custody: 7 Jul 1813 - From what ship or whence received: Steamboat - Exchanged, discharged, died, or escape: Discharged - Time when: 10 Aug 1813 - Whither, and by what order, or number or re-entry: HM Ship Regulius by order of Sir George Provost

Cannon, Dominick   Prisoner 867. Rank: Private - By what ship or how taken: Troops - Time when: 26 Jun 1813 - Place where: Beaver Dam - Of what ship or corps: Land forces - Whether man of war, privateer or merchant vessel: Taken on shore - Time when received into custody: 7 Jul 1813 - From what ship or whence received: Steamboat - Exchanged, discharged, died, or escape: Discharged - Time when: 10 Aug 1813 - Whither, and by what order, or number or re-entry: HM Ship Malpomena

Capatity, William   Prisoner 519. Rank: Private - By what ship or how taken: Troops - Time when: 24 Jun 1813 - Place where: Beaver Dam - Of what ship or corps: Land forces - Whether man of war, privateer or merchant vessel: Taken on shore - Time when received into custody: 7 Jul 1813 - From what ship or whence received: Steamboat - Exchanged,

American Prisoners of War held at Quebec during the War of 1812

discharged, died, or escape: Discharged - Time when: 9 Aug 1813 - Whither, and by what order, or number or re-entry: HM Ship Wasp

Carmody, Dalby   Prisoner 512. Rank: Private - By what ship or how taken: Troops - Time when: 24 Jun 1813 - Place where: Beaver Dam - Of what ship or corps: Land forces - Whether man of war, privateer or merchant vessel: Taken on shore - Time when received into custody: 7 Jul 1813 - From what ship or whence received: Steamboat - Exchanged, discharged, died, or escape: Discharged - Time when: 9 Aug 1813 - Whither, and by what order, or number or re-entry: HM Ship Wasp

Carnes, Joseph   Prisoner 159. Rank: Able seaman - By what ship or how taken: Boats & Troops - Time when: 3 Jun 1813 - Place where: Lake Champlain - Of what ship or corps: Eagle - Whether man of war, privateer or merchant vessel: Man of War - Time when received into custody: 9 Jun 1813 - From what ship or whence received: Batteaux - Exchanged, discharged, died, or escape: Discharged - Time when: - Whither, and by what order, or number or re-entry: Harbingar Transport

Carpenter, John   Prisoner 450. Rank: Private - By what ship or how taken: Troops - Time when: 24 Jun 1813 - Place where: Beaver Dam - Of what ship or corps: Malabar & Hydia - Whether man of war, privateer or merchant vessel: Taken on shore - Time when received into custody: 7 Jul 1813 - From what ship or whence received: Steamboat - Exchanged, discharged, died, or escape: Discharged - Time when: 10 Aug 1813 - Whither, and by what order, or number or re-entry: HM Ship Regulius by order of Sir George Provost

Carr, James   Prisoner 882. Rank: Private - By what ship or how taken: Troops - Time when: 26 Jun 1813 - Place where: Beaver Dam - Of what ship or corps: Land forces - Whether man of war, privateer or merchant vessel: Taken on shore - Time when received into custody: 7 Jul 1813 - From what ship or whence received: Steamboat - Exchanged, discharged, died, or escape: Discharged - Time when: 10 Aug 1813 - Whither, and by what order, or number or re-entry: HM Ship Malpomena

Carr, John   Prisoner 1751. Rank: Private - By what ship or how taken: Gun Boats - Time when: 6 Sep 1814 - Place where: Lake Huron - Of what ship or corps: Scorpion - Whether man of war, privateer or merchant vessel: Man of War - Time when received into custody: 1 Nov 1814 - From what ship or whence received: Montreal - Exchanged, discharged, died, or escape: Discharged - Time when: 8 Nov 1814 - Whither, and by what order, or number or re-entry: S. George No. 575 for Halifax by order of Sir George Provost

Carr, William   Prisoner 621. Rank: Private - By what ship or how taken: Troops - Time when: 24 Jun 1813 - Place where: Stoney Point - Of what ship or corps: Land forces - Whether man of war, privateer or merchant vessel: Taken on shore - Time when received into custody: 7 Jul 1813 - From what ship or whence received: Steamboat - Exchanged, discharged, died, or escape: Discharged - Time when: 10 Aug 1813 - Whither, and by what order, or number or re-entry: HM Ship Regulius by order of Sir George Provost

Carrall, T.   Prisoner 1642. Rank: Private - By what ship or how taken: Troops - Time when: 10 Sep 1814 - Place where: Plattsburg - Of what ship or corps: Land forces - Whether man of war, privateer or merchant vessel: Taken on shore - Time when received into custody: 5 Oct 1814 - From what ship or whence received: Montreal - Exchanged, discharged, died, or escape: Discharged - Time when: 8 Oct 1814 - Whither, and by what order, or number or re-entry: H.M. Ship Ceylon

Carroll, Isaac   Prisoner 683. Rank: Private - By what ship or how taken: Troops - Time when: 26 Jun 1813 - Place where: Beaver Dam - Of what ship or corps: Land forces - Whether man of war, privateer or merchant vessel: Taken on shore - Time when received into custody: 7 Jul 1813 - From what ship or whence received: Steamboat - Exchanged, discharged, died, or escape: Discharged - Time when: 10 Aug 1813 - Whither, and by what order, or number or re-entry: HM Ship Regulius by order of Sir George Provost

Carroll, Martin   Prisoner 1840. Rank: Private - By what ship or how taken: Troops - Time when: 17 Sep 1814 - Place where: Fort Erie - Of what ship or corps: Land forces - Whether man of war, privateer or merchant vessel: Taken on shore - Time when received into custody: 1 Nov 1814 - From what ship or whence received: Montreal - Exchanged, discharged, died, or escape: Discharged - Time when: 8 Nov 1814 - Whither, and by what order, or number or re-entry: S. George No. 575 for Halifax by order of Sir George Provost

Carry, Daniel   Prisoner 349. Rank: Private - By what ship or how taken: Gun Boats - Time when: 3 Jun 1813 - Place where: Lake Champlain - Of what ship or corps: Growler - Whether man of war, privateer or merchant vessel: Man of War - Time when received into custody: 28 Jun 1813 - From what ship or whence received: Mary of Quebec - Exchanged, discharged, died, or escape: Discharged - Time when: 31 Oct 1813 - Whither, and by what order, or number or re-entry: Malabar Transport

American Prisoners of War held at Quebec during the War of 1812

Carter, Marthil   Prisoner 790. Rank: Private - By what ship or how taken: Troops - Time when: 26 Jun 1813 - Place where: Beaver Dam - Of what ship or corps: Land forces - Whether man of war, privateer or merchant vessel: Taken on shore - Time when received into custody: 7 Jul 1813 - From what ship or whence received: Steamboat - Exchanged, discharged, died, or escape: Discharged - Time when: 10 Aug 1813 - Whither, and by what order, or number or re-entry: HM Ship Malpomena

Carthwright, George   Prisoner 1760. Rank: Private - By what ship or how taken: Gun Boats - Time when: 3 Sep 1814 - Place where: Lake Huron - Of what ship or corps: Tigress - Whether man of war, privateer or merchant vessel: Man of War - Time when received into custody: 1 Nov 1814 - From what ship or whence received: Montreal - Exchanged, discharged, died, or escape: Discharged - Time when: 8 Nov 1814 - Whither, and by what order, or number or re-entry: S. George No. 575 for Halifax by order of Sir George Provost

Carver, William   Prisoner 32. Rank: Private - By what ship or how taken: Boats & Troops - Time when: 28 May 1813 - Place where: Stoney Point, Henderson Harbor - Of what ship or corps: Land forces - Whether man of war, privateer or merchant vessel: Taken on shore - Time when received into custody: 8 Jun 1813 - From what ship or whence received: Batteaux - Exchanged, discharged, died, or escape: Died - Time when: 12 Sep 1813 - Whither, and by what order, or number or re-entry: Dysentery

Case, John   Prisoner 1714. Rank: Lieutenant - By what ship or how taken: Troops - Time when: 17 Sep 1814 - Place where: Fort Erie - Of what ship or corps: Land forces - Whether man of war, privateer or merchant vessel: Taken on shore - Time when received into custody: 28 Oct 1814 - From what ship or whence received: Montreal - Exchanged, discharged, died, or escape: Discharged - Time when: 10 Nov 1814 - Whither, and by what order, or number or re-entry: Transport Stately No. 408 for Halifax

Cashman, William   Prisoner 795. Rank: Private - By what ship or how taken: Troops - Time when: 26 Jun 1813 - Place where: Beaver Dam - Of what ship or corps: Land forces - Whether man of war, privateer or merchant vessel: Taken on shore - Time when received into custody: 7 Jul 1813 - From what ship or whence received: Steamboat - Exchanged, discharged, died, or escape: Discharged - Time when: 10 Aug 1813 - Whither, and by what order, or number or re-entry: HM Ship Malpomena

Cavry, James   Prisoner 520. Rank: Private - By what ship or how taken: Troops - Time when: 24 Jun 1813 - Place where: Beaver Dam - Of what ship or corps: Land forces - Whether man of war, privateer or merchant vessel: Taken on shore - Time when received into custody: 7 Jul 1813 - From what ship or whence received: Steamboat - Exchanged, discharged, died, or escape: Discharged - Time when: 9 Aug 1813 - Whither, and by what order, or number or re-entry: HM Ship Wasp

Cawthorn, Eleazer   Prisoner 1134. Rank: Private - By what ship or how taken: Troops - Time when: 5 May 1813 - Place where: Rapids Prince Reason - Of what ship or corps: Land forces - Whether man of war, privateer or merchant vessel: Taken on shore - Time when received into custody: 25 Nov 1813 - From what ship or whence received: Town Goal - Exchanged, discharged, died, or escape: Discharged - Time when: 4 May 1814 - Whither, and by what order, or number or re-entry: United States

Cedus, Francis   Prisoner 1746. Rank: Seaman - By what ship or how taken: Gun Boats - Time when: 3 Sep 1814 - Place where: Lake Huron - Of what ship or corps: Tigress - Whether man of war, privateer or merchant vessel: Man of War - Time when received into custody: 1 Nov 1814 - From what ship or whence received: Montreal - Exchanged, discharged, died, or escape: Discharged - Time when: 7 Nov 1814 - Whither, and by what order, or number or re-entry: Transport Freedom No. 582 by orders of his Excellency Sir George Provost

Celley, Paul   Prisoner 310. Rank: Private - By what ship or how taken: Boats & Troops - Time when: 6 Jun 1813 - Place where: Stoney Point - Of what ship or corps: Land forces - Whether man of war, privateer or merchant vessel: Taken on shore - Time when received into custody: 28 Jun 1813 - From what ship or whence received: Quebec of Quebec - Exchanged, discharged, died, or escape: Discharged - Time when: 31 Oct 1813 - Whither, and by what order, or number or re-entry: HM Ship Success

Cerkhill, James W.   Prisoner 542. Rank: Private - By what ship or how taken: Troops - Time when: 24 Jun 1813 - Place where: Beaver Dam - Of what ship or corps: Land forces - Whether man of war, privateer or merchant vessel: Taken on shore - Time when received into custody: 13 Jul 1813 - From what ship or whence received: Steamboat - Exchanged, discharged, died, or escape: Discharged - Time when: 10 Aug 1813 - Whither, and by what order, or number or re-entry: HM Ship Regulius by order of Sir George Provost

Cermour, Robert   Prisoner 1322. Rank: Private - By what ship or how taken: Troops - Time when: 19 Dec 1813 - Place where: Fort Niagara - Of what ship or corps: Land forces - Whether man of war, privateer or merchant vessel: Taken on shore - Time when received into custody: 29 Jan 1814 - From what ship or whence received: Montreal by land carriage -

American Prisoners of War held at Quebec during the War of 1812

Exchanged, discharged, died, or escape: Discharged - Time when: 4 May 1814 - Whither, and by what order, or number or re-entry: United States

Chambers, Henry   Prisoner 821. Rank: Private - By what ship or how taken: Troops - Time when: 26 Jun 1813 - Place where: Beaver Dam - Of what ship or corps: Land forces - Whether man of war, privateer or merchant vessel: Taken on shore - Time when received into custody: 7 Jul 1813 - From what ship or whence received: Steamboat - Exchanged, discharged, died, or escape: Discharged - Time when: 10 Aug 1813 - Whither, and by what order, or number or re-entry: HM Ship Malpomena

Chambers, James   Prisoner 1717. Rank: Ensign - By what ship or how taken: Gun Boats - Time when: 6 Sep 1814 - Place where: Lake Huron - Of what ship or corps: Scorpion - Whether man of war, privateer or merchant vessel: Man of War - Time when received into custody: 28 Oct 1814 - From what ship or whence received: Montreal - Exchanged, discharged, died, or escape: Discharged - Time when: 10 Nov 1814 - Whither, and by what order, or number or re-entry: Transport Stately No. 408 for Halifax

Chambers, Samuel   Prisoner 1051. Rank: Private - By what ship or how taken: Lord Melvin - Time when: 10 Aug 1813 - Place where: Lake Ontario - Of what ship or corps: Growler - Whether man of war, privateer or merchant vessel: Man of War - Time when received into custody: 5 Sep 1813 - From what ship or whence received: Steamboat - Exchanged, discharged, died, or escape: Discharged - Time when: 31 Oct 1813 - Whither, and by what order, or number or re-entry: Malabar Transport

Chandler, John   Prisoner 254. Rank: Brigadier General - By what ship or how taken: Boats & Troops - Time when: 24 Jun 1813 - Place where: Stoney Point - Of what ship or corps: Land forces - Whether man of war, privateer or merchant vessel: Taken on shore - Time when received into custody: 24 Jun 1813 - From what ship or whence received: Steamboat - Exchanged, discharged, died, or escape: Discharged - Time when: 21 Apr 1814 - Whither, and by what order, or number or re-entry: United States

Chapin, Cyrenius   Prisoner 1213. Rank: Lieutenant Colonel - By what ship or how taken: Troops - Time when: 19 Dec 1813 - Place where: Fort Niagara - Of what ship or corps: Land forces - Whether man of war, privateer or merchant vessel: Taken on shore - Time when received into custody: 28 Jan 1814 - From what ship or whence received: Montreal by land carriage - Exchanged, discharged, died, or escape: Discharged - Time when: 4 May 1814 - Whither, and by what order, or number or re-entry: United States

Chapman, Eliphea   Prisoner 586. Rank: Private - By what ship or how taken: Troops - Time when: 26 Jun 1813 - Place where: Beaver Dam - Of what ship or corps: Land forces - Whether man of war, privateer or merchant vessel: Taken on shore - Time when received into custody: 13 Jul 1813 - From what ship or whence received: Steamboat - Exchanged, discharged, died, or escape: Discharged - Time when: 10 Aug 1813 - Whither, and by what order, or number or re-entry: HM Ship Regulius by order of Sir George Provost

Chase, John   Prisoner 1221. Rank: Private - By what ship or how taken: Troops - Time when: 19 Dec 1813 - Place where: Fort Niagara - Of what ship or corps: Land forces - Whether man of war, privateer or merchant vessel: Taken on shore - Time when received into custody: 29 Jan 1814 - From what ship or whence received: Montreal by land carriage - Exchanged, discharged, died, or escape: Discharged - Time when: 4 May 1814 - Whither, and by what order, or number or re-entry: United States

Chase, Joshua   Prisoner 263. Rank: Servant - By what ship or how taken: Boats & Troops - Time when: 24 Jun 1813 - Place where: Stoney Point - Of what ship or corps: Land forces - Whether man of war, privateer or merchant vessel: Taken on shore - Time when received into custody: 24 Jun 1813 - From what ship or whence received: Steamboat - Exchanged, discharged, died, or escape: Discharged - Time when: - Whither, and by what order, or number or re-entry: Harbingar Transport

Cheek, William   Prisoner 1401. Rank: Private - By what ship or how taken: Troops - Time when: 19 Dec 1813 - Place where: Fort Niagara - Of what ship or corps: Land forces - Whether man of war, privateer or merchant vessel: Taken on shore - Time when received into custody: 29 Jan 1814 - From what ship or whence received: Montreal by land carriage - Exchanged, discharged, died, or escape: Discharged - Time when: 4 May 1814 - Whither, and by what order, or number or re-entry: United States

Cheney, Elijhua   Prisoner 1802. Rank: Private - By what ship or how taken: Troops - Time when: 17 Sep 1814 - Place where: Fort Erie - Of what ship or corps: Land forces - Whether man of war, privateer or merchant vessel: Taken on shore - Time when received into custody: 1 Nov 1814 - From what ship or whence received: Montreal - Exchanged, discharged, died, or escape: Discharged - Time when: 8 Nov 1814 - Whither, and by what order, or number or re-entry: S. George No. 575 for Halifax by order of Sir George Provost

American Prisoners of War held at Quebec during the War of 1812

Chick, Nathaniel   Prisoner 1393. Rank: Wheelwright - By what ship or how taken: Troops - Time when: 19 Dec 1813 - Place where: Fort Niagara - Of what ship or corps: Land forces - Whether man of war, privateer or merchant vessel: Taken on shore - Time when received into custody: 29 Jan 1814 - From what ship or whence received: Montreal by land carriage - Exchanged, discharged, died, or escape: Discharged - Time when: 4 May 1814 - Whither, and by what order, or number or re-entry: United States

Childers, Joseph   Prisoner 801. Rank: Private - By what ship or how taken: Troops - Time when: 26 Jun 1813 - Place where: Beaver Dam - Of what ship or corps: Land forces - Whether man of war, privateer or merchant vessel: Taken on shore - Time when received into custody: 7 Jul 1813 - From what ship or whence received: Steamboat - Exchanged, discharged, died, or escape: Discharged - Time when: 10 Aug 1813 - Whither, and by what order, or number or re-entry: HM Ship Malpomena

Chrise, John   Prisoner 884. Rank: Private - By what ship or how taken: Troops - Time when: 26 Jun 1813 - Place where: Beaver Dam - Of what ship or corps: Land forces - Whether man of war, privateer or merchant vessel: Taken on shore - Time when received into custody: 7 Jul 1813 - From what ship or whence received: Steamboat - Exchanged, discharged, died, or escape: Discharged - Time when: 10 Aug 1813 - Whither, and by what order, or number or re-entry: HM Ship Malpomena

Christian, Charles P.   Prisoner 1680. Rank: Sergeant - By what ship or how taken: Troops - Time when: 30 Jul 1814 - Place where: Fort Erie - Of what ship or corps: Land forces - Whether man of war, privateer or merchant vessel: Taken on shore - Time when received into custody: 23 Oct 1814 - From what ship or whence received: Montreal - Exchanged, discharged, died, or escape: Discharged - Time when: 8 Nov 1814 - Whither, and by what order, or number or re-entry: S. George No. 575 for Halifax

Christian, Humphrey   Prisoner 918. Rank: Private - By what ship or how taken: Troops - Time when: 26 Jun 1813 - Place where: Beaver Dam - Of what ship or corps: Land forces - Whether man of war, privateer or merchant vessel: Taken on shore - Time when received into custody: 21 Jul 1813 - From what ship or whence received: Steamboat - Exchanged, discharged, died, or escape: Discharged - Time when: 4 May 1814 - Whither, and by what order, or number or re-entry: United States

Christie, John   Prisoner 1053. Rank: Private - By what ship or how taken: Lord Melvin - Time when: 10 Aug 1813 - Place where: Lake Ontario - Of what ship or corps: Growler - Whether man of war, privateer or merchant vessel: Man of War - Time when received into custody: 5 Sep 1813 - From what ship or whence received: Steamboat - Exchanged, discharged, died, or escape: Discharged - Time when: - Whither, and by what order, or number or re-entry: HM Ship Success

Christopher, Samuel   Prisoner 440. Rank: Private - By what ship or how taken: Troops - Time when: 24 Jun 1813 - Place where: Beaver Dam - Of what ship or corps: Land forces - Whether man of war, privateer or merchant vessel: Taken on shore - Time when received into custody: 7 Jul 1813 - From what ship or whence received: Steamboat - Exchanged, discharged, died, or escape: Discharged - Time when: 10 Aug 1813 - Whither, and by what order, or number or re-entry: HM Ship Regulius by order of Sir George Provost

Church , Jesse   Prisoner 1713. Rank: Lieutenant - By what ship or how taken: Troops - Time when: 17 Sep 1814 - Place where: Fort Erie - Of what ship or corps: Land forces - Whether man of war, privateer or merchant vessel: Taken on shore - Time when received into custody: 28 Oct 1814 - From what ship or whence received: Montreal - Exchanged, discharged, died, or escape: Discharged - Time when: 10 Nov 1814 - Whither, and by what order, or number or re-entry: Transport Stately No. 408 for Halifax

Churchill, Oliver   Prisoner 79. Rank: Private - By what ship or how taken: Boats & Troops - Time when: 28 May 1813 - Place where: Stoney Point, Henderson Harbor - Of what ship or corps: Land forces - Whether man of war, privateer or merchant vessel: Taken on shore - Time when received into custody: 8 Jun 1813 - From what ship or whence received: Batteaux - Exchanged, discharged, died, or escape: Died - Time when: 28 Jul 1813 - Whither, and by what order, or number or re-entry: Dysentery

Churchill, Worthy L.   Prisoner 1705. Rank: Lieutenant Colonel - By what ship or how taken: Troops - Time when: 17 Sep 1814 - Place where: Fort Erie - Of what ship or corps: Land forces - Whether man of war, privateer or merchant vessel: Taken on shore - Time when received into custody: 28 Oct 1814 - From what ship or whence received: Montreal - Exchanged, discharged, died, or escape: Discharged - Time when: 10 Nov 1814 - Whither, and by what order, or number or re-entry: Transport Stately No. 408 for Halifax

Claffin, George   Prisoner 1794. Rank: Corporal - By what ship or how taken: Troops - Time when: 7 Sep 1814 - Place where: Fort Erie - Of what ship or corps: Land forces - Whether man of war, privateer or merchant vessel: Taken on shore - Time when received into custody: 1 Nov 1814 - From what ship or whence received: Montreal - Exchanged,

American Prisoners of War held at Quebec during the War of 1812

discharged, died, or escape: Discharged - Time when: 8 Nov 1814 - Whither, and by what order, or number or re-entry: S. George No. 575 for Halifax by order of Sir George Provost

Clarey, Timothy   Prisoner 1970. Rank: Corporal - By what ship or how taken: Troops - Time when: 17 Oct 1814 - Place where: Chippawa - Of what ship or corps: Land forces - Whether man of war, privateer or merchant vessel: Taken on shore - Time when received into custody: 11 Dec 1814 - From what ship or whence received: Montreal - Exchanged, discharged, died, or escape: Discharged - Time when: 13 Mar 1815 - Whither, and by what order, or number or re-entry: United States

Clark, Abraham   Prisoner 538. Rank: Lieutenant - By what ship or how taken: Troops - Time when: 24 Jun 1813 - Place where: Beaver Dam - Of what ship or corps: Land forces - Whether man of war, privateer or merchant vessel: Taken on shore - Time when received into custody: 13 Jul 1813 - From what ship or whence received: Steamboat - Exchanged, discharged, died, or escape: Discharged - Time when: 10 Aug 1813 - Whither, and by what order, or number or re-entry: HM Ship Regulius by order of Sir George Provost

Clark, Benjamin   Prisoner 76. Rank: Private - By what ship or how taken: Boats & Troops - Time when: 28 May 1813 - Place where: Stoney Point, Henderson Harbor - Of what ship or corps: Land forces - Whether man of war, privateer or merchant vessel: Taken on shore - Time when received into custody: 8 Jun 1813 - From what ship or whence received: Batteaux - Exchanged, discharged, died, or escape: Discharged - Time when: 31 Oct 1813 - Whither, and by what order, or number or re-entry: Malabar Transport

Clark, Charles   Prisoner 1412. Rank: Drummer - By what ship or how taken: Troops - Time when: 19 Dec 1813 - Place where: Fort Niagara - Of what ship or corps: Land forces - Whether man of war, privateer or merchant vessel: Taken on shore - Time when received into custody: 29 Jan 1814 - From what ship or whence received: Montreal by land carriage - Exchanged, discharged, died, or escape: Discharged - Time when: 4 May 1814 - Whither, and by what order, or number or re-entry: United States

Clark, Henry   Prisoner 1372. Rank: Private - By what ship or how taken: Troops - Time when: 19 Dec 1813 - Place where: Fort Niagara - Of what ship or corps: Land forces - Whether man of war, privateer or merchant vessel: Taken on shore - Time when received into custody: 29 Jan 1814 - From what ship or whence received: Montreal by land carriage - Exchanged, discharged, died, or escape: Discharged - Time when: 4 May 1814 - Whither, and by what order, or number or re-entry: United States

Clark, James   Prisoner 462. Rank: Private - By what ship or how taken: Troops - Time when: 24 Jun 1813 - Place where: Beaver Dam - Of what ship or corps: Malabar & Hydia - Whether man of war, privateer or merchant vessel: Taken on shore - Time when received into custody: 7 Jul 1813 - From what ship or whence received: Steamboat - Exchanged, discharged, died, or escape: Discharged - Time when: 10 Aug 1813 - Whither, and by what order, or number or re-entry: HM Ship Regulius by order of Sir George Provost

Clark, Joseph   Prisoner 1715. Rank: Ensign - By what ship or how taken: Troops - Time when: 17 Sep 1814 - Place where: Fort Erie - Of what ship or corps: Land forces - Whether man of war, privateer or merchant vessel: Taken on shore - Time when received into custody: 28 Oct 1814 - From what ship or whence received: Montreal - Exchanged, discharged, died, or escape: Discharged - Time when: 15 Oct 1814 - Whither, and by what order, or number or re-entry: Wolga No. 377

Clark, Sheldren   Prisoner 854. Rank: Private - By what ship or how taken: Troops - Time when: 26 Jun 1813 - Place where: Beaver Dam - Of what ship or corps: Land forces - Whether man of war, privateer or merchant vessel: Taken on shore - Time when received into custody: 7 Jul 1813 - From what ship or whence received: Steamboat - Exchanged, discharged, died, or escape: Discharged - Time when: 10 Aug 1813 - Whither, and by what order, or number or re-entry: HM Ship Malpomena

Clark, Stephen   Prisoner 461. Rank: Private - By what ship or how taken: Troops - Time when: 24 Jun 1813 - Place where: Beaver Dam - Of what ship or corps: Malabar & Hydia - Whether man of war, privateer or merchant vessel: Taken on shore - Time when received into custody: 7 Jul 1813 - From what ship or whence received: Steamboat - Exchanged, discharged, died, or escape: Discharged - Time when: 10 Aug 1813 - Whither, and by what order, or number or re-entry: HM Ship Regulius by order of Sir George Provost

Clarke, John   Prisoner 827. Rank: Corporal - By what ship or how taken: Troops - Time when: 26 Jun 1813 - Place where: Beaver Dam - Of what ship or corps: Land forces - Whether man of war, privateer or merchant vessel: Taken on shore - Time when received into custody: 7 Jul 1813 - From what ship or whence received: Steamboat - Exchanged, discharged, died, or escape: Discharged - Time when: 10 Aug 1813 - Whither, and by what order, or number or re-entry: HM Ship Malpomena

American Prisoners of War held at Quebec during the War of 1812

Clarke, Norman   Prisoner 1262. Rank: Private - By what ship or how taken: Troops - Time when: 19 Dec 1813 - Place where: Fort Niagara - Of what ship or corps: Land forces - Whether man of war, privateer or merchant vessel: Taken on shore - Time when received into custody: 29 Jan 1814 - From what ship or whence received: Montreal by land carriage - Exchanged, discharged, died, or escape: Discharged - Time when: 4 May 1814 - Whither, and by what order, or number or re-entry: United States

Clauts, William   Prisoner 787. Rank: Private - By what ship or how taken: Troops - Time when: 26 Jun 1813 - Place where: Beaver Dam - Of what ship or corps: Land forces - Whether man of war, privateer or merchant vessel: Taken on shore - Time when received into custody: 7 Jul 1813 - From what ship or whence received: Steamboat - Exchanged, discharged, died, or escape: Discharged - Time when: 10 Aug 1813 - Whither, and by what order, or number or re-entry: HM Ship Malpomena

Clawson, Henry   Prisoner 986. Rank: D. Gun. - By what ship or how taken: Earl Moria - Time when: 10 Aug 1813 - Place where: Lake Ontario - Of what ship or corps: Julia - Whether man of war, privateer or merchant vessel: Man of War - Time when received into custody: 5 Sep 1813 - From what ship or whence received: Steamboat - Exchanged, discharged, died, or escape: Discharged - Time when: 1 Nov 1813 - Whither, and by what order, or number or re-entry: Cartheart Transport

Clay, Elijah   Prisoner 307. Rank: Private - By what ship or how taken: Boats & Troops - Time when: 6 Jun 1813 - Place where: Stoney Point - Of what ship or corps: Land forces - Whether man of war, privateer or merchant vessel: Taken on shore - Time when received into custody: 28 Jun 1813 - From what ship or whence received: Quebec of Quebec - Exchanged, discharged, died, or escape: Discharged - Time when: 31 Oct 1813 - Whither, and by what order, or number or re-entry: Malabar Transport

Clayton, Fariner   Prisoner 1816. Rank: Private - By what ship or how taken: Troops - Time when: 17 Sep 1814 - Place where: Fort Erie - Of what ship or corps: Land forces - Whether man of war, privateer or merchant vessel: Taken on shore - Time when received into custody: 1 Nov 1814 - From what ship or whence received: Montreal - Exchanged, discharged, died, or escape: Discharged - Time when: 8 Nov 1814 - Whither, and by what order, or number or re-entry: S. George No. 575 for Halifax by order of Sir George Provost

Clayton, Thomas   Prisoner 305. Rank: Private - By what ship or how taken: Boats & Troops - Time when: 6 Jun 1813 - Place where: Stoney Point - Of what ship or corps: Land forces - Whether man of war, privateer or merchant vessel: Taken on shore - Time when received into custody: 28 Jun 1813 - From what ship or whence received: Quebec of Quebec - Exchanged, discharged, died, or escape: Discharged - Time when: 7 Aug 1813 - Whither, and by what order, or number or re-entry: H.M. Ship Cievare

Clement, Daniel   Prisoner 693. Rank: Sergeant - By what ship or how taken: Troops - Time when: 26 Jun 1813 - Place where: Beaver Dam - Of what ship or corps: Land forces - Whether man of war, privateer or merchant vessel: Taken on shore - Time when received into custody: 7 Jul 1813 - From what ship or whence received: Steamboat - Exchanged, discharged, died, or escape: Died - Time when: 3 Aug 1813 - Whither, and by what order, or number or re-entry:

Clews, Thomas   Prisoner 1676. Rank: Seaman - By what ship or how taken: Gun Boats - Time when: 10 Aug 1814 - Place where: Lake Ontario - Of what ship or corps: Forsyth - Whether man of war, privateer or merchant vessel: Man of War - Time when received into custody: 23 Oct 1814 - From what ship or whence received: Montreal - Exchanged, discharged, died, or escape: Discharged - Time when: 7 Nov 1814 - Whither, and by what order, or number or re-entry: Transport Freedom No. 582 by orders of his Excellency Sir George Provost

Clyne, Isaac   Prisoner 960. Rank: Private - By what ship or how taken: Troops - Time when: 5 Jul 1813 - Place where: Fort Schisher - Of what ship or corps: Land forces - Whether man of war, privateer or merchant vessel: Taken on shore - Time when received into custody: 5 Sep 1813 - From what ship or whence received: Steamboat - Exchanged, discharged, died, or escape: Discharged - Time when: 31 Oct 1813 - Whither, and by what order, or number or re-entry: Malabar Transport

Coalbath, John F.   Prisoner 1770. Rank: Sergeant - By what ship or how taken: Troops - Time when: 7 Sep 1814 - Place where: Fort Erie - Of what ship or corps: Land forces - Whether man of war, privateer or merchant vessel: Taken on shore - Time when received into custody: 1 Nov 1814 - From what ship or whence received: Montreal - Exchanged, discharged, died, or escape: Discharged - Time when: 8 Nov 1814 - Whither, and by what order, or number or re-entry: S. George No. 575 for Halifax by order of Sir George Provost

Coalbough, Michael   Prisoner 1263. Rank: Private - By what ship or how taken: Troops - Time when: 19 Dec 1813 - Place where: Fort Niagara - Of what ship or corps: Land forces - Whether man of war, privateer or merchant vessel: Taken on shore - Time when received into custody: 29 Jan 1814 - From what ship or whence received: Montreal by land carriage - Exchanged, discharged, died, or escape: Discharged - Time when: 4 May 1814 - Whither, and by what order, or

American Prisoners of War held at Quebec during the War of 1812

number or re-entry: United States

Coaswell, Allanson   Prisoner 1229. Rank: Private - By what ship or how taken: Troops - Time when: 19 Dec 1813 - Place where: Fort Niagara - Of what ship or corps: Land forces - Whether man of war, privateer or merchant vessel: Taken on shore - Time when received into custody: 29 Jan 1814 - From what ship or whence received: Montreal by land carriage - Exchanged, discharged, died, or escape: Died - Time when: 5 Mar 1814 - Whither, and by what order, or number or re-entry: Phrenitis

Coates, Elizha   Prisoner 1261. Rank: Private - By what ship or how taken: Troops - Time when: 19 Dec 1813 - Place where: Fort Niagara - Of what ship or corps: Land forces - Whether man of war, privateer or merchant vessel: Taken on shore - Time when received into custody: 29 Jan 1814 - From what ship or whence received: Montreal by land carriage - Exchanged, discharged, died, or escape: Discharged - Time when: 4 May 1814 - Whither, and by what order, or number or re-entry: United States

Cobb, John   Prisoner 235. Rank: Private - By what ship or how taken: Boats & Troops - Time when: 3 Jun 1813 - Place where: Lake Champlain - Of what ship or corps: Growler - Whether man of war, privateer or merchant vessel: Man of War - Time when received into custody: 9 Jun 1813 - From what ship or whence received: Batteaux - Exchanged, discharged, died, or escape: Discharged - Time when: 31 Oct 1813 - Whither, and by what order, or number or re-entry: Malabar Transport

Cole, Andrew   Prisoner 566. Rank: Private - By what ship or how taken: Troops - Time when: 26 Jun 1813 - Place where: Beaver Dam - Of what ship or corps: Land forces - Whether man of war, privateer or merchant vessel: Taken on shore - Time when received into custody: 13 Jul 1813 - From what ship or whence received: Steamboat - Exchanged, discharged, died, or escape: Discharged - Time when: 10 Aug 1813 - Whither, and by what order, or number or re-entry: HM Ship Regulius by order of Sir George Provost

Cole, Benjamin   Prisoner 1973. Rank: Citizen - By what ship or how taken: Troops - Time when: 2 Nov 1814 - Place where: Saint Lawrence - Of what ship or corps: Land forces - Whether man of war, privateer or merchant vessel: Taken on shore - Time when received into custody: 11 Dec 1814 - From what ship or whence received: Montreal - Exchanged, discharged, died, or escape: Discharged - Time when: 13 Mar 1815 - Whither, and by what order, or number or re-entry: United States

Cole, Henry   Prisoner 1827. Rank: Private - By what ship or how taken: Troops - Time when: 17 Sep 1814 - Place where: Fort Erie - Of what ship or corps: Land forces - Whether man of war, privateer or merchant vessel: Taken on shore - Time when received into custody: 1 Nov 1814 - From what ship or whence received: Montreal - Exchanged, discharged, died, or escape: Discharged - Time when: 8 Nov 1814 - Whither, and by what order, or number or re-entry: S. George No. 575 for Halifax by order of Sir George Provost

Collins, Robert   Prisoner 710. Rank: Private - By what ship or how taken: Troops - Time when: 26 Jun 1813 - Place where: Beaver Dam - Of what ship or corps: Land forces - Whether man of war, privateer or merchant vessel: Taken on shore - Time when received into custody: 7 Jul 1813 - From what ship or whence received: Steamboat - Exchanged, discharged, died, or escape: Discharged - Time when: 10 Aug 1813 - Whither, and by what order, or number or re-entry: HM Ship Regulius by order of Sir George Provost

Colman, Charles   Prisoner 244. Rank: Private - By what ship or how taken: Boats & Troops - Time when: 24 Jun 1813 - Place where: Rec in charge of Beauport - Of what ship or corps: Land forces - Whether man of war, privateer or merchant vessel: Taken on shore - Time when received into custody: 9 Jun 1813 - From what ship or whence received: Steamboat - Exchanged, discharged, died, or escape: Discharged - Time when: 8 Oct 1813 - Whither, and by what order, or number or re-entry: H.M. Ship Ceylon

Comfort, R.   Prisoner 1480. Rank: Private - By what ship or how taken: Troops - Time when: 15 Jul 1814 - Place where: St. Davids - Of what ship or corps: Land forces - Whether man of war, privateer or merchant vessel: Taken on shore - Time when received into custody: 12 Aug 1814 - From what ship or whence received: Royal Seaman No. 289 Transport - Exchanged, discharged, died, or escape: Discharged - Time when: 8 Oct 1814 - Whither, and by what order, or number or re-entry: Queen No. 415

Conkey, Joshua   Prisoner 249. Rank: Captain - By what ship or how taken: Boats & Troops - Time when: 24 Jun 1813 - Place where: Rec in charge of Beauport - Of what ship or corps: Land forces - Whether man of war, privateer or merchant vessel: Taken on shore - Time when received into custody: 24 Jun 1813 - From what ship or whence received: At Beauport - Exchanged, discharged, died, or escape: Discharged - Time when: 10 Aug 1813 - Whither, and by what order, or number or re-entry: Per order His Exellency Sir George Prevost

Conkey, Tebena   Prisoner 340. Rank: Sergeant - By what ship or how taken: Boats & Troops - Time when: 22 Feb 1813 - Place

American Prisoners of War held at Quebec during the War of 1812

where: Hedgesburgh - Of what ship or corps: Land forces - Whether man of war, privateer or merchant vessel: Taken on shore - Time when received into custody: 28 Jun 1813 - From what ship or whence received: Mary of Quebec - Exchanged, discharged, died, or escape: Discharged - Time when: 10 Aug 1813 - Whither, and by what order, or number or re-entry: Per order His Exellency Sir George Prevost

Conklin, John F. Prisoner 1919. Rank: Corporal - By what ship or how taken: Troops - Time when: 17 Sep 1814 - Place where: Fort Erie - Of what ship or corps: Land forces - Whether man of war, privateer or merchant vessel: Taken on shore - Time when received into custody: 1 Nov 1814 - From what ship or whence received: Montreal - Exchanged, discharged, died, or escape: Discharged - Time when: 8 Nov 1814 - Whither, and by what order, or number or re-entry: S. George No. 575 for Halifax by order of Sir George Provost

Connor, John Prisoner 1049. Rank: Private - By what ship or how taken: Lord Melvin - Time when: 10 Aug 1813 - Place where: Lake Ontario - Of what ship or corps: Growler - Whether man of war, privateer or merchant vessel: Man of War - Time when received into custody: 5 Sep 1813 - From what ship or whence received: Steamboat - Exchanged, discharged, died, or escape: Discharged - Time when: 31 Oct 1813 - Whither, and by what order, or number or re-entry: Malabar Transport

Connor, William Prisoner 1888. Rank: Private - By what ship or how taken: Troops - Time when: 17 Sep 1814 - Place where: Fort Erie - Of what ship or corps: Land forces - Whether man of war, privateer or merchant vessel: Taken on shore - Time when received into custody: 1 Nov 1814 - From what ship or whence received: Montreal - Exchanged, discharged, died, or escape: Discharged - Time when: 8 Nov 1814 - Whither, and by what order, or number or re-entry: S. George No. 575 for Halifax by order of Sir George Provost

Conway, Michael Prisoner 408. Rank: Private - By what ship or how taken: Troops - Time when: 24 Jun 1813 - Place where: Beaver Dam - Of what ship or corps: Land forces - Whether man of war, privateer or merchant vessel: Taken on shore - Time when received into custody: 7 Jul 1813 - From what ship or whence received: Steamboat - Exchanged, discharged, died, or escape: Discharged - Time when: 31 Oct 1813 - Whither, and by what order, or number or re-entry: Malabar Transport

Conwell, John Prisoner 603. Rank: Private - By what ship or how taken: Troops - Time when: 26 Jun 1813 - Place where: Stoney Point - Of what ship or corps: Land forces - Whether man of war, privateer or merchant vessel: Taken on shore - Time when received into custody: 7 Jul 1813 - From what ship or whence received: Steamboat - Exchanged, discharged, died, or escape: Discharged - Time when: 10 Aug 1813 - Whither, and by what order, or number or re-entry: HM Ship Regulius by order of Sir George Provost

Cook, Haz. Prisoner 629. Rank: Private - By what ship or how taken: Troops - Time when: 24 Jun 1813 - Place where: Stoney Point - Of what ship or corps: Land forces - Whether man of war, privateer or merchant vessel: Taken on shore - Time when received into custody: 7 Jul 1813 - From what ship or whence received: Steamboat - Exchanged, discharged, died, or escape: Discharged - Time when: 10 Aug 1813 - Whither, and by what order, or number or re-entry: HM Ship Regulius by order of Sir George Provost

Cook, John H. Prisoner 844. Rank: Sergeant - By what ship or how taken: Troops - Time when: 26 Jun 1813 - Place where: Beaver Dam - Of what ship or corps: Land forces - Whether man of war, privateer or merchant vessel: Taken on shore - Time when received into custody: 7 Jul 1813 - From what ship or whence received: Steamboat - Exchanged, discharged, died, or escape: Discharged - Time when: 10 Aug 1813 - Whither, and by what order, or number or re-entry: HM Ship Malpomena

Cook, Joseph Prisoner 135. Rank: Private - By what ship or how taken: Boats & Troops - Time when: 28 May 1813 - Place where: Stoney Point, Henderson Harbor - Of what ship or corps: Land forces - Whether man of war, privateer or merchant vessel: Taken on shore - Time when received into custody: 8 Jul 1813 - From what ship or whence received: Batteaux - Exchanged, discharged, died, or escape: Discharged - Time when: 31 Oct 1813 - Whither, and by what order, or number or re-entry: Malabar Transport

Cook, Robert Prisoner 72. Rank: Private - By what ship or how taken: Boats & Troops - Time when: 28 May 1813 - Place where: Stoney Point, Henderson Harbor - Of what ship or corps: Land forces - Whether man of war, privateer or merchant vessel: Taken on shore - Time when received into custody: 8 Jun 1813 - From what ship or whence received: Batteaux - Exchanged, discharged, died, or escape: Discharged - Time when: 31 Oct 1813 - Whither, and by what order, or number or re-entry: Malabar Transport

Cook, William Prisoner 591. Rank: Private - By what ship or how taken: Troops - Time when: 26 Jun 1813 - Place where: Stoney Point - Of what ship or corps: Land forces - Whether man of war, privateer or merchant vessel: Taken on shore - Time when received into custody: 7 Jul 1813 - From what ship or whence received: Steamboat - Exchanged, discharged, died, or escape: Discharged - Time when: 10 Aug 1813 - Whither, and by what order, or number or re-

American Prisoners of War held at Quebec during the War of 1812

entry: HM Ship Regulius by order of Sir George Provost

Coombe, Isaac   Prisoner 1975. Rank: Private - By what ship or how taken: Troops - Time when: 2 Nov 1814 - Place where: Fort Erie - Of what ship or corps: Land forces - Whether man of war, privateer or merchant vessel: Taken on shore - Time when received into custody: - From what ship or whence received: - Exchanged, discharged, died, or escape: Died - Time when: 22 Dec 1814 - Whither, and by what order, or number or re-entry: Typhus Fever

Copner, J.   Prisoner 1499. Rank: Private - By what ship or how taken: Troops - Time when: 25 Jul 1814 - Place where: Lundy's Lane - Of what ship or corps: Land forces - Whether man of war, privateer or merchant vessel: Taken on shore - Time when received into custody: 19 Aug 1814 - From what ship or whence received: Triton No. 438 Transport - Exchanged, discharged, died, or escape: Discharged - Time when: 8 Oct 1814 - Whither, and by what order, or number or re-entry: Queen No. 415

Corbin, James   Prisoner 1164. Rank: Corporal - By what ship or how taken: Troops - Time when: 5 May 1813 - Place where: Fort Dearborn - Of what ship or corps: Land forces - Whether man of war, privateer or merchant vessel: Taken on shore - Time when received into custody: 25 Nov 1813 - From what ship or whence received: Town Goal - Exchanged, discharged, died, or escape: Discharged - Time when: 12 Mar 1814 - Whither, and by what order, or number or re-entry: New Brunswick Fencibles

Cord, Jacob   Prisoner 690. Rank: Private - By what ship or how taken: Troops - Time when: 26 Jun 1813 - Place where: Beaver Dam - Of what ship or corps: Land forces - Whether man of war, privateer or merchant vessel: Taken on shore - Time when received into custody: 7 Jul 1813 - From what ship or whence received: Steamboat - Exchanged, discharged, died, or escape: Discharged - Time when: 10 Aug 1813 - Whither, and by what order, or number or re-entry: HM Ship Regulius by order of Sir George Provost

Corkins, Joel   Prisoner 392. Rank: Private - By what ship or how taken: Troops - Time when: 6 Jun 1813 - Place where: Stoney Point - Of what ship or corps: Land forces - Whether man of war, privateer or merchant vessel: Taken on shore - Time when received into custody: 28 Jun 1813 - From what ship or whence received: Mary of Quebec - Exchanged, discharged, died, or escape: Discharged - Time when: 4 May 1814 - Whither, and by what order, or number or re-entry: United States

Cornell, G.   Prisoner 1574. Rank: Carpenter - By what ship or how taken: Gun Boats - Time when: 12 Aug 1814 - Place where: Fort Erie - Of what ship or corps: Ohio - Whether man of war, privateer or merchant vessel: Man of War - Time when received into custody: 5 Oct 1814 - From what ship or whence received: Montreal - Exchanged, discharged, died, or escape: Discharged - Time when: 10 Nov 1814 - Whither, and by what order, or number or re-entry: Freedom No. 582

Corsey, John   Prisoner 991. Rank: Seaman - By what ship or how taken: Earl Moria - Time when: 10 Aug 1813 - Place where: Lake Ontario - Of what ship or corps: Julia - Whether man of war, privateer or merchant vessel: Man of War - Time when received into custody: 5 Sep 1813 - From what ship or whence received: Steamboat - Exchanged, discharged, died, or escape: Discharged - Time when: 31 Oct 1813 - Whither, and by what order, or number or re-entry: Malabar Transport

Cory, Asa   Prisoner 121. Rank: Private - By what ship or how taken: Boats & Troops - Time when: 28 May 1813 - Place where: Stoney Point, Henderson Harbor - Of what ship or corps: Land forces - Whether man of war, privateer or merchant vessel: Taken on shore - Time when received into custody: 8 Jun 1813 - From what ship or whence received: Batteaux - Exchanged, discharged, died, or escape: Died - Time when: 20 Oct 1813 - Whither, and by what order, or number or re-entry:

Cottes, Edward   Prisoner 134. Rank: Private - By what ship or how taken: Boats & Troops - Time when: 28 May 1813 - Place where: Stoney Point, Henderson Harbor - Of what ship or corps: Land forces - Whether man of war, privateer or merchant vessel: Taken on shore - Time when received into custody: 8 Jul 1813 - From what ship or whence received: Batteaux - Exchanged, discharged, died, or escape: Discharged - Time when: 31 Oct 1813 - Whither, and by what order, or number or re-entry: Malabar Transport

Cotton, Seth   Prisoner 1481. Rank: Private - By what ship or how taken: Troops - Time when: 15 Jul 1814 - Place where: St. Davids - Of what ship or corps: Land forces - Whether man of war, privateer or merchant vessel: Taken on shore - Time when received into custody: 12 Aug 1814 - From what ship or whence received: Royal Seaman No. 289 Transport - Exchanged, discharged, died, or escape: Died - Time when: 2 Sep 1814 - Whither, and by what order, or number or re-entry: Dysentery

American Prisoners of War held at Quebec during the War of 1812

Count , Levin   Prisoner 443. Rank: Private - By what ship or how taken: Troops - Time when: 24 Jun 1813 - Place where: Beaver Dam - Of what ship or corps: Land forces - Whether man of war, privateer or merchant vessel: Taken on shore - Time when received into custody: 7 Jul 1813 - From what ship or whence received: Steamboat - Exchanged, discharged, died, or escape: Discharged - Time when: 10 Aug 1813 - Whither, and by what order, or number or re-entry: HM Ship Regulius by order of Sir George Provost

Countryman, Elias   Prisoner 335. Rank: Private - By what ship or how taken: Boats & Troops - Time when: 6 Jun 1813 - Place where: Stoney Point - Of what ship or corps: Land forces - Whether man of war, privateer or merchant vessel: Taken on shore - Time when received into custody: 28 Jun 1813 - From what ship or whence received: Quebec of Quebec - Exchanged, discharged, died, or escape: Discharged - Time when: 31 Oct 1813 - Whither, and by what order, or number or re-entry: HM Ship Success

Courtney, George   Prisoner 465. Rank: Private - By what ship or how taken: Troops - Time when: 24 Jun 1813 - Place where: Beaver Dam - Of what ship or corps: Malabar & Hydia - Whether man of war, privateer or merchant vessel: Taken on shore - Time when received into custody: 7 Jul 1813 - From what ship or whence received: Steamboat - Exchanged, discharged, died, or escape: Discharged - Time when: 7 Aug 1813 - Whither, and by what order, or number or re-entry: H.M. Ship Cievare

Cox, John   Prisoner 337. Rank: Private - By what ship or how taken: Boats & Troops - Time when: 6 Jun 1813 - Place where: Stoney Point - Of what ship or corps: Land forces - Whether man of war, privateer or merchant vessel: Taken on shore - Time when received into custody: 28 Jun 1813 - From what ship or whence received: Quebec of Quebec - Exchanged, discharged, died, or escape: Discharged - Time when: 31 Oct 1813 - Whither, and by what order, or number or re-entry: Malabar Transport

Crabtree, John   Prisoner 738. Rank: Private - By what ship or how taken: Troops - Time when: 26 Jun 1813 - Place where: Beaver Dam - Of what ship or corps: Land forces - Whether man of war, privateer or merchant vessel: Taken on shore - Time when received into custody: 7 Jul 1813 - From what ship or whence received: Steamboat - Exchanged, discharged, died, or escape: Discharged - Time when: 10 Aug 1813 - Whither, and by what order, or number or re-entry: HM Ship Regulius by order of Sir George Provost

Craft, George B.   Prisoner 1324. Rank: Private - By what ship or how taken: Troops - Time when: 19 Dec 1813 - Place where: Fort Niagara - Of what ship or corps: Land forces - Whether man of war, privateer or merchant vessel: Taken on shore - Time when received into custody: 29 Jan 1814 - From what ship or whence received: Montreal by land carriage - Exchanged, discharged, died, or escape: Discharged - Time when: 4 May 1814 - Whither, and by what order, or number or re-entry: United States

Cranson, John H.   Prisoner 141. Rank: Lieutenant - By what ship or how taken: Boats & Troops - Time when: 28 May 1813 - Place where: Stoney Point, Henderson Harbor - Of what ship or corps: Land forces - Whether man of war, privateer or merchant vessel: Taken on shore - Time when received into custody: 8 Jul 1813 - From what ship or whence received: Batteaux - Exchanged, discharged, died, or escape: Discharged - Time when: 13 Dec 1813 - Whither, and by what order, or number or re-entry: United States

Cranstone, John   Prisoner 961. Rank: Private - By what ship or how taken: Troops - Time when: 5 Jul 1813 - Place where: Fort Schisher - Of what ship or corps: Land forces - Whether man of war, privateer or merchant vessel: Taken on shore - Time when received into custody: 5 Sep 1813 - From what ship or whence received: Steamboat - Exchanged, discharged, died, or escape: Discharged - Time when: 31 Oct 1813 - Whither, and by what order, or number or re-entry: Malabar Transport

Crarmey, Edward   Prisoner 564. Rank: Private - By what ship or how taken: Troops - Time when: 26 Jun 1813 - Place where: Beaver Dam - Of what ship or corps: Land forces - Whether man of war, privateer or merchant vessel: Taken on shore - Time when received into custody: 13 Jul 1813 - From what ship or whence received: Steamboat - Exchanged, discharged, died, or escape: - Time when: - Whither, and by what order, or number or re-entry:

Cravertson, George   Prisoner 792. Rank: Private - By what ship or how taken: Troops - Time when: 26 Jun 1813 - Place where: Beaver Dam - Of what ship or corps: Land forces - Whether man of war, privateer or merchant vessel: Taken on shore - Time when received into custody: 7 Jul 1813 - From what ship or whence received: Steamboat - Exchanged, discharged, died, or escape: Discharged - Time when: 10 Aug 1813 - Whither, and by what order, or number or re-entry: HM Ship Malpomena

Crawford, William   Prisoner 1495. Rank: Private - By what ship or how taken: Troops - Time when: 25 Jul 1814 - Place where: Lundy's Lane - Of what ship or corps: Land forces - Whether man of war, privateer or merchant vessel: Taken on shore - Time when received into custody: 19 Aug 1814 - From what ship or whence received: Triton No. 438 Transport - Exchanged, discharged, died, or escape: Discharged - Time when: 8 Oct 1814 - Whither, and by what order, or number

American Prisoners of War held at Quebec during the War of 1812

or re-entry: Queen No. 415

Crayton, William   Prisoner 382.   Rank: Private - By what ship or how taken: Troops - Time when: 6 Jun 1813 - Place where: Stoney Point - Of what ship or corps: Land forces - Whether man of war, privateer or merchant vessel: Taken on shore - Time when received into custody: 28 Jun 1813 - From what ship or whence received: Mary of Quebec - Exchanged, discharged, died, or escape: Discharged - Time when: 31 Oct 1813 - Whither, and by what order, or number or re-entry: Malabar Transport

Creighton, Hugh   Prisoner 1427.   Rank: Private - By what ship or how taken: Troops - Time when: 19 Dec 1813 - Place where: Fort Niagara - Of what ship or corps: Land forces - Whether man of war, privateer or merchant vessel: Taken on shore - Time when received into custody: 29 Jan 1814 - From what ship or whence received: Montreal by land carriage - Exchanged, discharged, died, or escape: Discharged - Time when: 4 May 1814 - Whither, and by what order, or number or re-entry: United States

Crocker, Benjamin   Prisoner 662.   Rank: Private - By what ship or how taken: Troops - Time when: 24 Jun 1813 - Place where: Stoney Point - Of what ship or corps: Land forces - Whether man of war, privateer or merchant vessel: Taken on shore - Time when received into custody: 7 Jul 1813 - From what ship or whence received: Steamboat - Exchanged, discharged, died, or escape: Discharged - Time when: 10 Aug 1813 - Whither, and by what order, or number or re-entry: HM Ship Regulius by order of Sir George Provost

Crocker, John   Prisoner 1167.   Rank: Private - By what ship or how taken: Troops - Time when: 5 May 1813 - Place where: Rapids Prince Reason - Of what ship or corps: Land forces - Whether man of war, privateer or merchant vessel: Taken on shore - Time when received into custody: 25 Nov 1813 - From what ship or whence received: Town Goal - Exchanged, discharged, died, or escape: Discharged - Time when: 12 Mar 1814 - Whither, and by what order, or number or re-entry: New Brunswick Fencibles

Cronkling, Henry M.   Prisoner 1565.   Rank: Lieutenant - By what ship or how taken: Gun Boats - Time when: 12 Aug 1814 - Place where: Fort Erie - Of what ship or corps: Ohio - Whether man of war, privateer or merchant vessel: Man of War - Time when received into custody: 16 Sep 1814 - From what ship or whence received: Steamboat - Exchanged, discharged, died, or escape: Discharged - Time when: 10 Nov 1814 - Whither, and by what order, or number or re-entry: Lord Cartheart No. 161 for Halifax

Crosby, James   Prisoner 1079.   Rank: Private - By what ship or how taken: Troops - Time when: 24 Aug 1813 - Place where: Fort George - Of what ship or corps: Land forces - Whether man of war, privateer or merchant vessel: Taken on shore - Time when received into custody: 10 Oct 1813 - From what ship or whence received: Steamboat - Exchanged, discharged, died, or escape: Discharged - Time when: 31 Oct 1813 - Whither, and by what order, or number or re-entry: Malabar Transport

Cross, Barnebus   Prisoner 1378.   Rank: Private - By what ship or how taken: Troops - Time when: 19 Dec 1813 - Place where: Fort Niagara - Of what ship or corps: Land forces - Whether man of war, privateer or merchant vessel: Taken on shore - Time when received into custody: 29 Jan 1814 - From what ship or whence received: Montreal by land carriage - Exchanged, discharged, died, or escape: Discharged - Time when: 22 Feb 1814 - Whither, and by what order, or number or re-entry: Volunteered for New Brunswick Fencibles

Crossby, William   Prisoner 1898.   Rank: Sergeant - By what ship or how taken: Troops - Time when: 17 Sep 1814 - Place where: Fort Erie - Of what ship or corps: Land forces - Whether man of war, privateer or merchant vessel: Taken on shore - Time when received into custody: 1 Nov 1814 - From what ship or whence received: Montreal - Exchanged, discharged, died, or escape: Discharged - Time when: 8 Nov 1814 - Whither, and by what order, or number or re-entry: S. George No. 575 for Halifax by order of Sir George Provost

Crouch, Henry   Prisoner 1712.   Rank: Captain - By what ship or how taken: Troops - Time when: 17 Sep 1814 - Place where: Fort Erie - Of what ship or corps: Land forces - Whether man of war, privateer or merchant vessel: Taken on shore - Time when received into custody: 28 Oct 1814 - From what ship or whence received: Montreal - Exchanged, discharged, died, or escape: Discharged - Time when: 10 Nov 1814 - Whither, and by what order, or number or re-entry: Transport Stately No. 408 for Halifax

Crundle, Joshua   Prisoner 1684.   Rank: Sergeant Major - By what ship or how taken: Troops - Time when: 16 Aug 1814 - Place where: Detroit - Of what ship or corps: Land forces - Whether man of war, privateer or merchant vessel: Taken on shore - Time when received into custody: 23 Oct 1814 - From what ship or whence received: Montreal - Exchanged, discharged, died, or escape: Discharged - Time when: 8 Nov 1814 - Whither, and by what order, or number or re-entry: S. George No. 575 for Halifax

Cummings, David   Prisoner 930.   Rank: Captain - By what ship or how taken: Troops - Time when: 26 Jun 1813 - Place where:

American Prisoners of War held at Quebec during the War of 1812

Beaver Dam - Of what ship or corps: Land forces - Whether man of war, privateer or merchant vessel: Taken on shore - Time when received into custody: 21 Jul 1813 - From what ship or whence received: Steamboat - Exchanged, discharged, died, or escape: Discharged - Time when: 4 May 1814 - Whither, and by what order, or number or re-entry: United States

Cummings, John L.   Prisoner 1566. Rank: Midshipman - By what ship or how taken: Gun Boats - Time when: 12 Aug 1814 - Place where: Fort Erie - Of what ship or corps: Ohio - Whether man of war, privateer or merchant vessel: Man of War - Time when received into custody: 16 Sep 1814 - From what ship or whence received: Steamboat - Exchanged, discharged, died, or escape: Discharged - Time when: 10 Nov 1814 - Whither, and by what order, or number or re-entry: Lord Cartheart No. 161 for Halifax

Cune, Thomas   Prisoner 503. Rank: Private - By what ship or how taken: Troops - Time when: 24 Jun 1813 - Place where: Beaver Dam - Of what ship or corps: Land forces - Whether man of war, privateer or merchant vessel: Taken on shore - Time when received into custody: 7 Jul 1813 - From what ship or whence received: Steamboat - Exchanged, discharged, died, or escape: Discharged - Time when: 10 Aug 1813 - Whither, and by what order, or number or re-entry: HM Ship Regulius by order of Sir George Provost

Cunningham, Kellup   Prisoner 604. Rank: Private - By what ship or how taken: Troops - Time when: 26 Jun 1813 - Place where: Stoney Point - Of what ship or corps: Land forces - Whether man of war, privateer or merchant vessel: Taken on shore - Time when received into custody: 7 Jul 1813 - From what ship or whence received: Steamboat - Exchanged, discharged, died, or escape: Discharged - Time when: 10 Aug 1813 - Whither, and by what order, or number or re-entry: HM Ship Regulius by order of Sir George Provost

Curtis, Morgan   Prisoner 1376. Rank: Private - By what ship or how taken: Troops - Time when: 19 Dec 1813 - Place where: Fort Niagara - Of what ship or corps: Land forces - Whether man of war, privateer or merchant vessel: Taken on shore - Time when received into custody: 29 Jan 1814 - From what ship or whence received: Montreal by land carriage - Exchanged, discharged, died, or escape: Discharged - Time when: 9 Mar 1814 - Whither, and by what order, or number or re-entry: Volunteered for New Brunswick Fencibles

Curtis, Uria   Prisoner 829. Rank: Private - By what ship or how taken: Troops - Time when: 26 Jun 1813 - Place where: Beaver Dam - Of what ship or corps: Land forces - Whether man of war, privateer or merchant vessel: Taken on shore - Time when received into custody: 7 Jul 1813 - From what ship or whence received: Steamboat - Exchanged, discharged, died, or escape: Discharged - Time when: 10 Aug 1813 - Whither, and by what order, or number or re-entry: HM Ship Malpomena

Curtis, Zeba   Prisoner 1608. Rank: Private - By what ship or how taken: Troops - Time when: 6 Sep 1814 - Place where: Plattsburg - Of what ship or corps: Land forces - Whether man of war, privateer or merchant vessel: Taken on shore - Time when received into custody: 5 Oct 1814 - From what ship or whence received: Montreal - Exchanged, discharged, died, or escape: Discharged - Time when: 8 Oct 1814 - Whither, and by what order, or number or re-entry: H.M. Ship Ceylon

Cushing, William   Prisoner 1525. Rank: Private - By what ship or how taken: Troops - Time when: 25 Jul 1814 - Place where: Lundy's Lane - Of what ship or corps: Land forces - Whether man of war, privateer or merchant vessel: Taken on shore - Time when received into custody: 30 Aug 1814 - From what ship or whence received: Lady Delaval Schooner 578 - Exchanged, discharged, died, or escape: Discharged - Time when: 8 Oct 1814 - Whither, and by what order, or number or re-entry: Queen No. 415

Cutler, Leonard   Prisoner 1440. Rank: Private - By what ship or how taken: Troops - Time when: 6 May 1814 - Place where: Oswago - Of what ship or corps: Land forces - Whether man of war, privateer or merchant vessel: Taken on shore - Time when received into custody: 12 Aug 1814 - From what ship or whence received: Royal Seaman No. 289 Transport - Exchanged, discharged, died, or escape: Discharged - Time when: 8 Oct 1814 - Whither, and by what order, or number or re-entry: Queen No. 415

Dabine, J.   Prisoner 1577. Rank: Seaman - By what ship or how taken: Gun Boats - Time when: 12 Aug 1814 - Place where: Fort Erie - Of what ship or corps: Somers - Whether man of war, privateer or merchant vessel: Man of War - Time when received into custody: 5 Oct 1814 - From what ship or whence received: Montreal - Exchanged, discharged, died, or escape: Discharged - Time when: 10 Nov 1814 - Whither, and by what order, or number or re-entry: Freedom No. 582

Daggert, Thomas   Prisoner 484. Rank: Private - By what ship or how taken: Troops - Time when: 24 Jun 1813 - Place where: Beaver Dam - Of what ship or corps: Land forces - Whether man of war, privateer or merchant vessel: Taken on shore - Time when received into custody: 7 Jul 1813 - From what ship or whence received: Steamboat - Exchanged, discharged, died, or escape: Discharged - Time when: 10 Aug 1813 - Whither, and by what order, or number or re-

American Prisoners of War held at Quebec during the War of 1812

entry: HM Ship Regulius by order of Sir George Provost

Daggett, Josiah   Prisoner 38. Rank: Private - By what ship or how taken: Boats & Troops - Time when: 28 May 1813 - Place where: Stoney Point, Henderson Harbor - Of what ship or corps: Land forces - Whether man of war, privateer or merchant vessel: Taken on shore - Time when received into custody: 8 Jun 1813 - From what ship or whence received: Batteaux - Exchanged, discharged, died, or escape: Discharged - Time when: 31 Oct 1813 - Whither, and by what order, or number or re-entry: Malabar Transport

Daggett, Lewis   Prisoner 31. Rank: Corporal - By what ship or how taken: Boats & Troops - Time when: 28 May 1813 - Place where: Stoney Point, Henderson Harbor - Of what ship or corps: Land forces - Whether man of war, privateer or merchant vessel: Taken on shore - Time when received into custody: 8 Jun 1813 - From what ship or whence received: Batteaux - Exchanged, discharged, died, or escape: Discharged - Time when: 31 Oct 1813 - Whither, and by what order, or number or re-entry: Malabar Transport

Dallas, D.   Prisoner 1543. Rank: Private - By what ship or how taken: Troops - Time when: 25 Jul 1814 - Place where: Lundy's Lane - Of what ship or corps: Land forces - Whether man of war, privateer or merchant vessel: Taken on shore - Time when received into custody: 30 Aug 1814 - From what ship or whence received: Lady Delaval Schooner 578 - Exchanged, discharged, died, or escape: Discharged - Time when: 8 Oct 1814 - Whither, and by what order, or number or re-entry: Queen No. 415

Dalyrumple, John   Prisoner 1891. Rank: Private - By what ship or how taken: Troops - Time when: 17 Sep 1814 - Place where: Fort Erie - Of what ship or corps: Land forces - Whether man of war, privateer or merchant vessel: Taken on shore - Time when received into custody: 1 Nov 1814 - From what ship or whence received: Montreal - Exchanged, discharged, died, or escape: Discharged - Time when: 8 Nov 1814 - Whither, and by what order, or number or re-entry: S. George No. 575 for Halifax by order of Sir George Provost

Dandridge, Richard   Prisoner 676. Rank: Corporal - By what ship or how taken: Troops - Time when: 26 Jun 1813 - Place where: Beaver Dam - Of what ship or corps: Land forces - Whether man of war, privateer or merchant vessel: Taken on shore - Time when received into custody: 7 Jul 1813 - From what ship or whence received: Steamboat - Exchanged, discharged, died, or escape: Discharged - Time when: 10 Aug 1813 - Whither, and by what order, or number or re-entry: HM Ship Regulius by order of Sir George Provost

Danforth, Joseph F.   Prisoner 193. Rank: Private - By what ship or how taken: Boats & Troops - Time when: 3 Jun 1813 - Place where: Lake Champlain - Of what ship or corps: Eagle - Whether man of war, privateer or merchant vessel: Man of War - Time when received into custody: 9 Jun 1813 - From what ship or whence received: Batteaux - Exchanged, discharged, died, or escape: Discharged - Time when: 31 Oct 1813 - Whither, and by what order, or number or re-entry: Malabar Transport

Darling, Gamaliel   Prisoner 1568. Rank: Sailing Master - By what ship or how taken: Gun Boats - Time when: 12 Aug 1814 - Place where: Fort Erie - Of what ship or corps: Somers - Whether man of war, privateer or merchant vessel: Man of War - Time when received into custody: 16 Sep 1814 - From what ship or whence received: Steamboat - Exchanged, discharged, died, or escape: Discharged - Time when: 10 Nov 1814 - Whither, and by what order, or number or re-entry: Lord Cartheart No. 161 for Halifax

Darling, Thomas   Prisoner 1310. Rank: Private - By what ship or how taken: Troops - Time when: 19 Dec 1813 - Place where: Fort Niagara - Of what ship or corps: Land forces - Whether man of war, privateer or merchant vessel: Taken on shore - Time when received into custody: 29 Jan 1814 - From what ship or whence received: Montreal by land carriage - Exchanged, discharged, died, or escape: Discharged - Time when: 4 May 1814 - Whither, and by what order, or number or re-entry: United States

Davidson, John   Prisoner 606. Rank: Private - By what ship or how taken: Troops - Time when: 26 Jun 1813 - Place where: Stoney Point - Of what ship or corps: Land forces - Whether man of war, privateer or merchant vessel: Taken on shore - Time when received into custody: 7 Jul 1813 - From what ship or whence received: Steamboat - Exchanged, discharged, died, or escape: Discharged - Time when: 31 Oct 1813 - Whither, and by what order, or number or re-entry: Malabar Transport

Davis, Benjamin   Prisoner 574. Rank: Private - By what ship or how taken: Troops - Time when: 26 Jun 1813 - Place where: Beaver Dam - Of what ship or corps: Land forces - Whether man of war, privateer or merchant vessel: Taken on shore - Time when received into custody: 13 Jul 1813 - From what ship or whence received: Steamboat - Exchanged, discharged, died, or escape: Discharged - Time when: 10 Aug 1813 - Whither, and by what order, or number or re-entry: HM Ship Regulius by order of Sir George Provost

American Prisoners of War held at Quebec during the War of 1812

Davis, Elnathan   Prisoner 326. Rank: Private - By what ship or how taken: Boats & Troops - Time when: 6 Jun 1813 - Place where: Stoney Point - Of what ship or corps: Land forces - Whether man of war, privateer or merchant vessel: Taken on shore - Time when received into custody: 28 Jun 1813 - From what ship or whence received: Quebec of Quebec - Exchanged, discharged, died, or escape: Discharged - Time when: 31 Oct 1813 - Whither, and by what order, or number or re-entry: Malabar Transport

Davis, Ezra   Prisoner 598. Rank: Private - By what ship or how taken: Troops - Time when: 26 Jun 1813 - Place where: Stoney Point - Of what ship or corps: Land forces - Whether man of war, privateer or merchant vessel: Taken on shore - Time when received into custody: 7 Jul 1813 - From what ship or whence received: Steamboat - Exchanged, discharged, died, or escape: Discharged - Time when: 10 Aug 1813 - Whither, and by what order, or number or re-entry: HM Ship Regulius by order of Sir George Provost

Davis, Hugh   Prisoner 807. Rank: Private - By what ship or how taken: Troops - Time when: 26 Jun 1813 - Place where: Beaver Dam - Of what ship or corps: Land forces - Whether man of war, privateer or merchant vessel: Taken on shore - Time when received into custody: 7 Jul 1813 - From what ship or whence received: Steamboat - Exchanged, discharged, died, or escape: Discharged - Time when: 10 Aug 1813 - Whither, and by what order, or number or re-entry: HM Ship Malpomena

Davis, John   Prisoner 677. Rank: Private - By what ship or how taken: Troops - Time when: 26 Jun 1813 - Place where: Beaver Dam - Of what ship or corps: Land forces - Whether man of war, privateer or merchant vessel: Taken on shore - Time when received into custody: 7 Jul 1813 - From what ship or whence received: Steamboat - Exchanged, discharged, died, or escape: Discharged - Time when: 10 Aug 1813 - Whither, and by what order, or number or re-entry: HM Ship Regulius by order of Sir George Provost

Davis, John   Prisoner 1096. Rank: Private - By what ship or how taken: Troops - Time when: 24 Aug 1813 - Place where: Fort George - Of what ship or corps: Land forces - Whether man of war, privateer or merchant vessel: Taken on shore - Time when received into custody: 10 Oct 1813 - From what ship or whence received: Steamboat - Exchanged, discharged, died, or escape: Discharged - Time when: 31 Oct 1813 - Whither, and by what order, or number or re-entry: Malabar Transport

Davis, Moses   Prisoner 23. Rank: Private - By what ship or how taken: Boats & Troops - Time when: 28 May 1813 - Place where: Stoney Point, Henderson Harbor - Of what ship or corps: Land forces - Whether man of war, privateer or merchant vessel: Taken on shore - Time when received into custody: 8 Jun 1813 - From what ship or whence received: Batteaux - Exchanged, discharged, died, or escape: Discharged - Time when: 31 Oct 1813 - Whither, and by what order, or number or re-entry: Malabar Transport

Davis, Peter   Prisoner 1214. Rank: Ensign - By what ship or how taken: Troops - Time when: 19 Dec 1813 - Place where: Fort Niagara - Of what ship or corps: Land forces - Whether man of war, privateer or merchant vessel: Taken on shore - Time when received into custody: 28 Jan 1814 - From what ship or whence received: Montreal by land carriage - Exchanged, discharged, died, or escape: Discharged - Time when: 4 May 1814 - Whither, and by what order, or number or re-entry: United States

Davis, Richard   Prisoner 935. Rank: Private - By what ship or how taken: Troops - Time when: 26 Jun 1813 - Place where: Beaver Dam - Of what ship or corps: Land forces - Whether man of war, privateer or merchant vessel: Taken on shore - Time when received into custody: 21 Jul 1813 - From what ship or whence received: Steamboat - Exchanged, discharged, died, or escape: Discharged - Time when: 10 Aug 1813 - Whither, and by what order, or number or re-entry: HM Ship Malpomena

Davis, Stephen   Prisoner 81. Rank: Private - By what ship or how taken: Boats & Troops - Time when: 28 May 1813 - Place where: Stoney Point, Henderson Harbor - Of what ship or corps: Land forces - Whether man of war, privateer or merchant vessel: Taken on shore - Time when received into custody: 8 Jun 1813 - From what ship or whence received: Batteaux - Exchanged, discharged, died, or escape: Died - Time when: 10 Aug 1813 - Whither, and by what order, or number or re-entry:

Davis, Theddeck   Prisoner 602. Rank: Private - By what ship or how taken: Troops - Time when: 26 Jun 1813 - Place where: Stoney Point - Of what ship or corps: Land forces - Whether man of war, privateer or merchant vessel: Taken on shore - Time when received into custody: 7 Jul 1813 - From what ship or whence received: Steamboat - Exchanged, discharged, died, or escape: Discharged - Time when: 10 Aug 1813 - Whither, and by what order, or number or re-entry: HM Ship Regulius by order of Sir George Provost

Davis, Thomas   Prisoner 477. Rank: Private - By what ship or how taken: Troops - Time when: 24 Jun 1813 - Place where: Beaver Dam - Of what ship or corps: Land forces - Whether man of war, privateer or merchant vessel: Taken on shore - Time when received into custody: 7 Jul 1813 - From what ship or whence received: Steamboat - Exchanged,

American Prisoners of War held at Quebec during the War of 1812

discharged, died, or escape: Discharged - Time when: 10 Aug 1813 - Whither, and by what order, or number or re-entry: HM Ship Regulius by order of Sir George Provost

Davis, Thomas   Prisoner 1900.   Rank: Private - By what ship or how taken: Troops - Time when: 17 Sep 1814 - Place where: Fort Erie - Of what ship or corps: Land forces - Whether man of war, privateer or merchant vessel: Taken on shore - Time when received into custody: 1 Nov 1814 - From what ship or whence received: Montreal - Exchanged, discharged, died, or escape: Discharged - Time when: 8 Nov 1814 - Whither, and by what order, or number or re-entry: S. George No. 575 for Halifax by order of Sir George Provost

Davis, Thomas   Prisoner 1048.   Rank: Private - By what ship or how taken: Lord Melvin - Time when: 10 Aug 1813 - Place where: Lake Ontario - Of what ship or corps: Growler - Whether man of war, privateer or merchant vessel: Man of War - Time when received into custody: 5 Sep 1813 - From what ship or whence received: Steamboat - Exchanged, discharged, died, or escape: Discharged - Time when: 31 Oct 1813 - Whither, and by what order, or number or re-entry: Malabar Transport

Davis, William   Prisoner 1484.   Rank: Private - By what ship or how taken: Troops - Time when: 25 Jul 1814 - Place where: Lundy's Lane - Of what ship or corps: Land forces - Whether man of war, privateer or merchant vessel: Taken on shore - Time when received into custody: 12 Aug 1814 - From what ship or whence received: Royal Seaman No. 289 Transport - Exchanged, discharged, died, or escape: Discharged - Time when: 8 Oct 1814 - Whither, and by what order, or number or re-entry: Queen No. 415

Davisson, John   Prisoner 483.   Rank: Private - By what ship or how taken: Troops - Time when: 24 Jun 1813 - Place where: Beaver Dam - Of what ship or corps: Land forces - Whether man of war, privateer or merchant vessel: Taken on shore - Time when received into custody: 7 Jul 1813 - From what ship or whence received: Steamboat - Exchanged, discharged, died, or escape: Discharged - Time when: 10 Aug 1813 - Whither, and by what order, or number or re-entry: HM Ship Regulius by order of Sir George Provost

Day, Andrew D.   Prisoner 1798.   Rank: Private - By what ship or how taken: Troops - Time when: 7 Sep 1814 - Place where: Fort Erie - Of what ship or corps: Land forces - Whether man of war, privateer or merchant vessel: Taken on shore - Time when received into custody: 1 Nov 1814 - From what ship or whence received: Montreal - Exchanged, discharged, died, or escape: Discharged - Time when: 8 Nov 1814 - Whither, and by what order, or number or re-entry: S. George No. 575 for Halifax by order of Sir George Provost

Day, John   Prisoner 1251.   Rank: Blacksmith - By what ship or how taken: Troops - Time when: 19 Dec 1813 - Place where: Fort Niagara - Of what ship or corps: Land forces - Whether man of war, privateer or merchant vessel: Taken on shore - Time when received into custody: 29 Jan 1814 - From what ship or whence received: Montreal by land carriage - Exchanged, discharged, died, or escape: Discharged - Time when: 27 Feb 1814 - Whither, and by what order, or number or re-entry: Volunteered for New Brunswick Fencibles

de Fredrick, Peter   Prisoner 1872.   Rank: Private - By what ship or how taken: Troops - Time when: 17 Sep 1814 - Place where: Fort Erie - Of what ship or corps: Land forces - Whether man of war, privateer or merchant vessel: Taken on shore - Time when received into custody: 1 Nov 1814 - From what ship or whence received: Montreal - Exchanged, discharged, died, or escape: Discharged - Time when: 8 Nov 1814 - Whither, and by what order, or number or re-entry: S. George No. 575 for Halifax

de Masters, Foster   Prisoner 1436.   Rank: Sergeant - By what ship or how taken: Gun Boats - Time when: 29 May 1814 - Place where: Sacketts Harbor - Of what ship or corps: Land forces - Whether man of war, privateer or merchant vessel: Taken on shore - Time when received into custody: 12 Aug 1814 - From what ship or whence received: Royal Seaman No. 289 Transport - Exchanged, discharged, died, or escape: Discharged - Time when: 8 Oct 1814 - Whither, and by what order, or number or re-entry: Queen No. 415

Dearborn, D.   Prisoner 1473.   Rank: Private - By what ship or how taken: Troops - Time when: 15 Jul 1814 - Place where: Chippewa - Of what ship or corps: Land forces - Whether man of war, privateer or merchant vessel: Taken on shore - Time when received into custody: 12 Aug 1814 - From what ship or whence received: Royal Seaman No. 289 Transport - Exchanged, discharged, died, or escape: Discharged - Time when: 8 Oct 1814 - Whither, and by what order, or number or re-entry: Queen No. 415

Dearborn, Soloman   Prisoner 80.   Rank: Private - By what ship or how taken: Boats & Troops - Time when: 28 May 1813 - Place where: Stoney Point, Henderson Harbor - Of what ship or corps: Land forces - Whether man of war, privateer or merchant vessel: Taken on shore - Time when received into custody: 8 Jun 1813 - From what ship or whence received: Batteaux - Exchanged, discharged, died, or escape: Died - Time when: 23 Jul 1813 - Whither, and by what order, or number or re-entry: Dysentery

American Prisoners of War held at Quebec during the War of 1812

Dearing, John   Prisoner 82. Rank: Private - By what ship or how taken: Boats & Troops - Time when: 28 May 1813 - Place where: Stoney Point, Henderson Harbor - Of what ship or corps: Land forces - Whether man of war, privateer or merchant vessel: Taken on shore - Time when received into custody: 8 Jun 1813 - From what ship or whence received: Batteaux - Exchanged, discharged, died, or escape: Died - Time when: 28 Sep 1813 - Whither, and by what order, or number or re-entry: Typhus Fever

Deason, David   Prisoner 1067. Rank: Lieutenant - By what ship or how taken: Lord Melvin - Time when: 10 Aug 1813 - Place where: Lake Ontario - Of what ship or corps: Growler - Whether man of war, privateer or merchant vessel: Man of War - Time when received into custody: 5 Sep 1813 - From what ship or whence received: Steamboat - Exchanged, discharged, died, or escape: Discharged - Time when: 16 Nov 1813 - Whither, and by what order, or number or re-entry: To United States

Decker, Joseph   Prisoner 919. Rank: Private - By what ship or how taken: Troops - Time when: 26 Jun 1813 - Place where: Beaver Dam - Of what ship or corps: Land forces - Whether man of war, privateer or merchant vessel: Taken on shore - Time when received into custody: 21 Jul 1813 - From what ship or whence received: Steamboat - Exchanged, discharged, died, or escape: Discharged - Time when: 10 Aug 1813 - Whither, and by what order, or number or re-entry: HM Ship Malpomena

Decker, Zeli   Prisoner 1105. Rank: Private - By what ship or how taken: Troops - Time when: 24 Aug 1813 - Place where: Fort George - Of what ship or corps: Land forces - Whether man of war, privateer or merchant vessel: Taken on shore - Time when received into custody: 12 Oct 1813 - From what ship or whence received: Steamboat - Exchanged, discharged, died, or escape: Discharged - Time when: 31 Oct 1813 - Whither, and by what order, or number or re-entry: Malabar Transport

Defriend, John   Prisoner 324. Rank: Private - By what ship or how taken: Boats & Troops - Time when: 6 Jun 1813 - Place where: Stoney Point - Of what ship or corps: Land forces - Whether man of war, privateer or merchant vessel: Taken on shore - Time when received into custody: 28 Jun 1813 - From what ship or whence received: Quebec of Quebec - Exchanged, discharged, died, or escape: Died - Time when: 17 Jul 1813 - Whither, and by what order, or number or re-entry: Dysentery

Dellaghon, George   Prisoner 711. Rank: Private - By what ship or how taken: Troops - Time when: 26 Jun 1813 - Place where: Beaver Dam - Of what ship or corps: Land forces - Whether man of war, privateer or merchant vessel: Taken on shore - Time when received into custody: 7 Jul 1813 - From what ship or whence received: Steamboat - Exchanged, discharged, died, or escape: Discharged - Time when: 10 Aug 1813 - Whither, and by what order, or number or re-entry: HM Ship Regulius by order of Sir George Provost

Delshaven, Michael   Prisoner 852. Rank: Private - By what ship or how taken: Troops - Time when: 26 Jun 1813 - Place where: Beaver Dam - Of what ship or corps: Land forces - Whether man of war, privateer or merchant vessel: Taken on shore - Time when received into custody: 7 Jul 1813 - From what ship or whence received: Steamboat - Exchanged, discharged, died, or escape: Discharged - Time when: 10 Aug 1813 - Whither, and by what order, or number or re-entry: HM Ship Malpomena

Dempsey, George   Prisoner 890. Rank: Private - By what ship or how taken: Troops - Time when: 26 Jun 1813 - Place where: Beaver Dam - Of what ship or corps: Land forces - Whether man of war, privateer or merchant vessel: Taken on shore - Time when received into custody: 7 Jul 1813 - From what ship or whence received: Steamboat - Exchanged, discharged, died, or escape: Discharged - Time when: 10 Aug 1813 - Whither, and by what order, or number or re-entry: HM Ship Malpomena

Denenberg, William   Prisoner 1755. Rank: Private - By what ship or how taken: Gun Boats - Time when: 3 Sep 1814 - Place where: Lake Huron - Of what ship or corps: Tigress - Whether man of war, privateer or merchant vessel: Man of War - Time when received into custody: 1 Nov 1814 - From what ship or whence received: Montreal - Exchanged, discharged, died, or escape: Discharged - Time when: 8 Nov 1814 - Whither, and by what order, or number or re-entry: S. George No. 575 for Halifax by order of Sir George Provost

Denison, John   Prisoner 1845. Rank: Corporal - By what ship or how taken: Troops - Time when: 17 Sep 1814 - Place where: Fort Erie - Of what ship or corps: Land forces - Whether man of war, privateer or merchant vessel: Taken on shore - Time when received into custody: 1 Nov 1814 - From what ship or whence received: Montreal - Exchanged, discharged, died, or escape: Discharged - Time when: 8 Nov 1814 - Whither, and by what order, or number or re-entry: S. George No. 575 for Halifax by order of Sir George Provost

Denison, Luther   Prisoner 1789. Rank: Private - By what ship or how taken: Troops - Time when: 7 Sep 1814 - Place where: Fort Erie - Of what ship or corps: Land forces - Whether man of war, privateer or merchant vessel: Taken on shore - Time when received into custody: 1 Nov 1814 - From what ship or whence received: Montreal - Exchanged,

American Prisoners of War held at Quebec during the War of 1812

discharged, died, or escape: Discharged - Time when: 8 Nov 1814 - Whither, and by what order, or number or re-entry: S. George No. 575 for Halifax by order of Sir George Provost

Denmade, Edward Prisoner 448. Rank: Private - By what ship or how taken: Troops - Time when: 24 Jun 1813 - Place where: Beaver Dam - Of what ship or corps: Land forces - Whether man of war, privateer or merchant vessel: Taken on shore - Time when received into custody: 7 Jul 1813 - From what ship or whence received: Steamboat - Exchanged, discharged, died, or escape: Discharged - Time when: 7 Aug 1813 - Whither, and by what order, or number or re-entry: H.M. Ship Cievare

Denning, J. Prisoner 1584. Rank: Seaman - By what ship or how taken: Gun Boats - Time when: 12 Aug 1814 - Place where: Fort Erie - Of what ship or corps: Ohio - Whether man of war, privateer or merchant vessel: Man of War - Time when received into custody: 5 Oct 1814 - From what ship or whence received: Montreal - Exchanged, discharged, died, or escape: Discharged - Time when: 10 Nov 1814 - Whither, and by what order, or number or re-entry: Freedom No. 582

Dennis, Patrick M. Prisoner 666. Rank: Private - By what ship or how taken: Troops - Time when: 24 Jun 1813 - Place where: Stoney Point - Of what ship or corps: Land forces - Whether man of war, privateer or merchant vessel: Taken on shore - Time when received into custody: 7 Jul 1813 - From what ship or whence received: Steamboat - Exchanged, discharged, died, or escape: Discharged - Time when: 9 Aug 1813 - Whither, and by what order, or number or re-entry: HM Ship Wasp

Dennison, J. Prisoner 1607. Rank: Private - By what ship or how taken: Troops - Time when: 6 Sep 1814 - Place where: Plattsburg - Of what ship or corps: Land forces - Whether man of war, privateer or merchant vessel: Taken on shore - Time when received into custody: 5 Oct 1814 - From what ship or whence received: Montreal - Exchanged, discharged, died, or escape: Discharged - Time when: 8 Oct 1814 - Whither, and by what order, or number or re-entry: H.M. Ship Ceylon

Dennison, Washington Prisoner 150. Rank: Ensign - By what ship or how taken: Boats & Troops - Time when: 3 Jun 1813 - Place where: Lake Champlain - Of what ship or corps: Growler - Whether man of war, privateer or merchant vessel: Man of War - Time when received into custody: 8 Jul 1813 - From what ship or whence received: Batteaux - Exchanged, discharged, died, or escape: Discharged - Time when: 13 Dec 1813 - Whither, and by what order, or number or re-entry: United States

Denton, Charles Prisoner 421. Rank: Corporal - By what ship or how taken: Troops - Time when: 24 Jun 1813 - Place where: Beaver Dam - Of what ship or corps: Land forces - Whether man of war, privateer or merchant vessel: Taken on shore - Time when received into custody: 7 Jul 1813 - From what ship or whence received: Steamboat - Exchanged, discharged, died, or escape: Discharged - Time when: 7 Aug 1813 - Whither, and by what order, or number or re-entry: H.M. Ship Cievare

Dervalt, Alvin Prisoner 755. Rank: Corporal - By what ship or how taken: Troops - Time when: 26 Jun 1813 - Place where: Beaver Dam - Of what ship or corps: Land forces - Whether man of war, privateer or merchant vessel: Taken on shore - Time when received into custody: 7 Jul 1813 - From what ship or whence received: Steamboat - Exchanged, discharged, died, or escape: - Time when: - Whither, and by what order, or number or re-entry:

Desheates, Peter Prisoner 809. Rank: Private - By what ship or how taken: Troops - Time when: 26 Jun 1813 - Place where: Beaver Dam - Of what ship or corps: Land forces - Whether man of war, privateer or merchant vessel: Taken on shore - Time when received into custody: 7 Jul 1813 - From what ship or whence received: Steamboat - Exchanged, discharged, died, or escape: - Time when: - Whither, and by what order, or number or re-entry:

Devenus, J. Prisoner 1575. Rank: Seaman - By what ship or how taken: Gun Boats - Time when: 12 Aug 1814 - Place where: Fort Erie - Of what ship or corps: Ohio - Whether man of war, privateer or merchant vessel: Man of War - Time when received into custody: 5 Oct 1814 - From what ship or whence received: Montreal - Exchanged, discharged, died, or escape: Discharged - Time when: 10 Nov 1814 - Whither, and by what order, or number or re-entry: Freedom No. 582

Dickenson, J. Prisoner 1644. Rank: Private - By what ship or how taken: Troops - Time when: 19 Dec 1813 - Place where: Niagara - Of what ship or corps: Land forces - Whether man of war, privateer or merchant vessel: Taken on shore - Time when received into custody: 5 Oct 1814 - From what ship or whence received: Montreal - Exchanged, discharged, died, or escape: Discharged - Time when: 8 Oct 1814 - Whither, and by what order, or number or re-entry: H.M. Ship Ceylon

Diffenderffer, Henry Prisoner 1391. Rank: Private - By what ship or how taken: Troops - Time when: 19 Dec 1813 - Place where: Fort Niagara - Of what ship or corps: Land forces - Whether man of war, privateer or merchant vessel: Taken on shore - Time when received into custody: 29 Jan 1814 - From what ship or whence received: Montreal by land carriage - Exchanged, discharged, died, or escape: Discharged - Time when: 4 May 1814 - Whither, and by what order, or

American Prisoners of War held at Quebec during the War of 1812

number or re-entry: United States

Dill, Peter   Prisoner 543. Rank: Private - By what ship or how taken: Troops - Time when: 24 Jun 1813 - Place where: Beaver Dam - Of what ship or corps: Land forces - Whether man of war, privateer or merchant vessel: Taken on shore - Time when received into custody: 13 Jul 1813 - From what ship or whence received: Steamboat - Exchanged, discharged, died, or escape: Discharged - Time when: 31 Oct 1813 - Whither, and by what order, or number or re-entry: Malabar Transport

Diver, David   Prisoner 1063. Rank: Private - By what ship or how taken: Troops - Time when: 24 Jun 1813 - Place where: Beaver Dam - Of what ship or corps: Land forces - Whether man of war, privateer or merchant vessel: Taken on shore - Time when received into custody: 5 Sep 1813 - From what ship or whence received: Steamboat - Exchanged, discharged, died, or escape: Discharged - Time when: 24 Nov 1813 - Whither, and by what order, or number or re-entry: H.M. Ship Aeolus

Dixon, James   Prisoner 425. Rank: Private - By what ship or how taken: Troops - Time when: 24 Jun 1813 - Place where: Beaver Dam - Of what ship or corps: Land forces - Whether man of war, privateer or merchant vessel: Taken on shore - Time when received into custody: 7 Jul 1813 - From what ship or whence received: Steamboat - Exchanged, discharged, died, or escape: Discharged - Time when: 31 Oct 1813 - Whither, and by what order, or number or re-entry: Malabar Transport

Dodd, Moses   Prisoner 1911. Rank: Private - By what ship or how taken: Troops - Time when: 17 Sep 1814 - Place where: Fort Erie - Of what ship or corps: Land forces - Whether man of war, privateer or merchant vessel: Taken on shore - Time when received into custody: 1 Nov 1814 - From what ship or whence received: Montreal - Exchanged, discharged, died, or escape: Discharged - Time when: 8 Nov 1814 - Whither, and by what order, or number or re-entry: S. George No. 575 for Halifax by order of Sir George Provost

Doddson, Thomas S.   Prisoner 913. Rank: Private - By what ship or how taken: Troops - Time when: 26 Jun 1813 - Place where: Beaver Dam - Of what ship or corps: Land forces - Whether man of war, privateer or merchant vessel: Taken on shore - Time when received into custody: 21 Jul 1813 - From what ship or whence received: Steamboat - Exchanged, discharged, died, or escape: Discharged - Time when: 31 Oct 1813 - Whither, and by what order, or number or re-entry: Malabar Transport

Dodge, John   Prisoner 1626. Rank: Private - By what ship or how taken: Troops - Time when: 11 Sep 1814 - Place where: Plattsburg - Of what ship or corps: Land forces - Whether man of war, privateer or merchant vessel: Taken on shore - Time when received into custody: 5 Oct 1814 - From what ship or whence received: Montreal - Exchanged, discharged, died, or escape: Discharged - Time when: 8 Oct 1814 - Whither, and by what order, or number or re-entry: H.M. Ship Ceylon

Dogherty, James   Prisoner 1417. Rank: Private - By what ship or how taken: Troops - Time when: 19 Dec 1813 - Place where: Fort Niagara - Of what ship or corps: Land forces - Whether man of war, privateer or merchant vessel: Taken on shore - Time when received into custody: 29 Jan 1814 - From what ship or whence received: Montreal by land carriage - Exchanged, discharged, died, or escape: Discharged - Time when: 4 May 1814 - Whither, and by what order, or number or re-entry: United States

Dogherty, Jared   Prisoner 1264. Rank: Private - By what ship or how taken: Troops - Time when: 19 Dec 1813 - Place where: Fort Niagara - Of what ship or corps: Land forces - Whether man of war, privateer or merchant vessel: Taken on shore - Time when received into custody: 29 Jan 1814 - From what ship or whence received: Montreal by land carriage - Exchanged, discharged, died, or escape: Discharged - Time when: 4 May 1814 - Whither, and by what order, or number or re-entry: United States

Dolf, Joseph   Prisoner 1453. Rank: Private - By what ship or how taken: Troops - Time when: 6 May 1814 - Place where: Oswago - Of what ship or corps: Land forces - Whether man of war, privateer or merchant vessel: Taken on shore - Time when received into custody: 12 Aug 1814 - From what ship or whence received: Royal Seaman No. 289 Transport - Exchanged, discharged, died, or escape: Discharged - Time when: 8 Oct 1814 - Whither, and by what order, or number or re-entry: Queen No. 415

Donaldson, Thomas   Prisoner 716. Rank: Private - By what ship or how taken: Troops - Time when: 26 Jun 1813 - Place where: Beaver Dam - Of what ship or corps: Land forces - Whether man of war, privateer or merchant vessel: Taken on shore - Time when received into custody: 7 Jul 1813 - From what ship or whence received: Steamboat - Exchanged, discharged, died, or escape: Discharged - Time when: 31 Oct 1813 - Whither, and by what order, or number or re-entry: Malabar Transport

Doolittle, William   Prisoner 1918. Rank: Private - By what ship or how taken: Troops - Time when: 17 Sep 1814 - Place where:

American Prisoners of War held at Quebec during the War of 1812

Fort Erie - Of what ship or corps: Land forces - Whether man of war, privateer or merchant vessel: Taken on shore - Time when received into custody: 1 Nov 1814 - From what ship or whence received: Montreal - Exchanged, discharged, died, or escape: Discharged - Time when: 8 Nov 1814 - Whither, and by what order, or number or re-entry: S. George No. 575 for Halifax by order of Sir George Provost

Doti, Ambrose   Prisoner 1847. Rank: Citizen - By what ship or how taken: Troops - Time when: 17 Sep 1814 - Place where: Fort Erie - Of what ship or corps: Land forces - Whether man of war, privateer or merchant vessel: Taken on shore - Time when received into custody: 1 Nov 1814 - From what ship or whence received: Montreal - Exchanged, discharged, died, or escape: Discharged - Time when: 8 Nov 1814 - Whither, and by what order, or number or re-entry: S. George No. 575 for Halifax by order of Sir George Provost

Douay, H.   Prisoner 1606. Rank: Private - By what ship or how taken: Troops - Time when: 6 Sep 1814 - Place where: Plattsburg - Of what ship or corps: Land forces - Whether man of war, privateer or merchant vessel: Taken on shore - Time when received into custody: 5 Oct 1814 - From what ship or whence received: Montreal - Exchanged, discharged, died, or escape: Discharged - Time when: 8 Oct 1814 - Whither, and by what order, or number or re-entry: H.M. Ship Ceylon

Doud, John   Prisoner 501. Rank: Private - By what ship or how taken: Troops - Time when: 24 Jun 1813 - Place where: Beaver Dam - Of what ship or corps: Land forces - Whether man of war, privateer or merchant vessel: Taken on shore - Time when received into custody: 7 Jul 1813 - From what ship or whence received: Steamboat - Exchanged, discharged, died, or escape: Discharged - Time when: 9 Aug 1813 - Whither, and by what order, or number or re-entry: HM Ship Wasp

Dougherty, William   Prisoner 739. Rank: Private - By what ship or how taken: Troops - Time when: 26 Jun 1813 - Place where: Beaver Dam - Of what ship or corps: Land forces - Whether man of war, privateer or merchant vessel: Taken on shore - Time when received into custody: 7 Jul 1813 - From what ship or whence received: Steamboat - Exchanged, discharged, died, or escape: Discharged - Time when: 31 Oct 1813 - Whither, and by what order, or number or re-entry: Malabar Transport

Doughtery, Hamilton   Prisoner 507. Rank: Private - By what ship or how taken: Troops - Time when: 24 Jun 1813 - Place where: Beaver Dam - Of what ship or corps: Land forces - Whether man of war, privateer or merchant vessel: Taken on shore - Time when received into custody: 7 Jul 1813 - From what ship or whence received: Steamboat - Exchanged, discharged, died, or escape: Discharged - Time when: 10 Aug 1813 - Whither, and by what order, or number or re-entry: HM Ship Regulius by order of Sir George Provost

Doughty, Elias   Prisoner 323. Rank: Private - By what ship or how taken: Boats & Troops - Time when: 6 Jun 1813 - Place where: Stoney Point - Of what ship or corps: Land forces - Whether man of war, privateer or merchant vessel: Taken on shore - Time when received into custody: 28 Jun 1813 - From what ship or whence received: Quebec of Quebec - Exchanged, discharged, died, or escape: Discharged - Time when: 31 Oct 1813 - Whither, and by what order, or number or re-entry: Malabar Transport

Douglas, Caleb   Prisoner 1632. Rank: Private - By what ship or how taken: Troops - Time when: 6 Sep 1814 - Place where: Plattsburg - Of what ship or corps: Land forces - Whether man of war, privateer or merchant vessel: Taken on shore - Time when received into custody: 5 Oct 1814 - From what ship or whence received: Montreal - Exchanged, discharged, died, or escape: Discharged - Time when: 8 Oct 1814 - Whither, and by what order, or number or re-entry: H.M. Ship Ceylon

Douglass, Luther   Prisoner 1830. Rank: Private - By what ship or how taken: Troops - Time when: 17 Sep 1814 - Place where: Fort Erie - Of what ship or corps: Land forces - Whether man of war, privateer or merchant vessel: Taken on shore - Time when received into custody: 1 Nov 1814 - From what ship or whence received: Montreal - Exchanged, discharged, died, or escape: Discharged - Time when: 8 Nov 1814 - Whither, and by what order, or number or re-entry: S. George No. 575 for Halifax by order of Sir George Provost

Dours, William   Prisoner 989. Rank: Seaman - By what ship or how taken: Lord Melvin - Time when: 10 Aug 1813 - Place where: Lake Ontario - Of what ship or corps: Growler - Whether man of war, privateer or merchant vessel: Man of War - Time when received into custody: 5 Sep 1813 - From what ship or whence received: Steamboat - Exchanged, discharged, died, or escape: Discharged - Time when: 31 Oct 1813 - Whither, and by what order, or number or re-entry: Malabar Transport

Dover, D.   Prisoner 1466. Rank: Private - By what ship or how taken: Gun Boats - Time when: 29 May 1814 - Place where: Sandy Creek - Of what ship or corps: Land forces - Whether man of war, privateer or merchant vessel: Taken on shore - Time when received into custody: 12 Aug 1814 - From what ship or whence received: Royal Seaman No. 289 Transport - Exchanged, discharged, died, or escape: Discharged - Time when: 8 Oct 1814 - Whither, and by what order,

American Prisoners of War held at Quebec during the War of 1812

or number or re-entry: Queen No. 415

Doyle, James   Prisoner 265. Rank: Private - By what ship or how taken: Boats & Troops - Time when: 24 Jun 1813 - Place where: Stoney Point - Of what ship or corps: Land forces - Whether man of war, privateer or merchant vessel: Taken on shore - Time when received into custody: 24 Jun 1813 - From what ship or whence received: Steamboat - Exchanged, discharged, died, or escape: Escaped - Time when: - Whither, and by what order, or number or re-entry:

Drake, Eliasha   Prisoner 223. Rank: Private - By what ship or how taken: Boats & Troops - Time when: 3 Jun 1813 - Place where: Lake Champlain - Of what ship or corps: Growler - Whether man of war, privateer or merchant vessel: Man of War - Time when received into custody: 9 Jun 1813 - From what ship or whence received: Batteaux - Exchanged, discharged, died, or escape: Discharged - Time when: 31 Oct 1813 - Whither, and by what order, or number or re-entry: Malabar Transport

Drake, George William   Prisoner 1374. Rank: Private - By what ship or how taken: Troops - Time when: 19 Dec 1813 - Place where: Fort Niagara - Of what ship or corps: Land forces - Whether man of war, privateer or merchant vessel: Taken on shore - Time when received into custody: 29 Jan 1814 - From what ship or whence received: Montreal by land carriage - Exchanged, discharged, died, or escape: Discharged - Time when: 4 May 1814 - Whither, and by what order, or number or re-entry: United States

Drake, W.   Prisoner 1482. Rank: Private - By what ship or how taken: Troops - Time when: 14 Jul 1814 - Place where: St. Davids - Of what ship or corps: Land forces - Whether man of war, privateer or merchant vessel: Taken on shore - Time when received into custody: 12 Aug 1814 - From what ship or whence received: Royal Seaman No. 289 Transport - Exchanged, discharged, died, or escape: Discharged - Time when: 8 Oct 1814 - Whither, and by what order, or number or re-entry: Queen No. 415

Draper, Francis   Prisoner 262. Rank: Servant - By what ship or how taken: Boats & Troops - Time when: 24 Jun 1813 - Place where: Stoney Point - Of what ship or corps: Land forces - Whether man of war, privateer or merchant vessel: Taken on shore - Time when received into custody: 24 Jun 1813 - From what ship or whence received: Steamboat - Exchanged, discharged, died, or escape: Discharged - Time when: 21 Apr 1814 - Whither, and by what order, or number or re-entry: United States

Draton, Joseph   Prisoner 1311. Rank: Private - By what ship or how taken: Troops - Time when: 19 Dec 1813 - Place where: Fort Niagara - Of what ship or corps: Land forces - Whether man of war, privateer or merchant vessel: Taken on shore - Time when received into custody: 29 Jan 1814 - From what ship or whence received: Montreal by land carriage - Exchanged, discharged, died, or escape: Discharged - Time when: 4 May 1814 - Whither, and by what order, or number or re-entry: United States

Dresser, Thomas   Prisoner 214. Rank: Private - By what ship or how taken: Boats & Troops - Time when: 3 Jun 1813 - Place where: Lake Champlain - Of what ship or corps: Growler - Whether man of war, privateer or merchant vessel: Man of War - Time when received into custody: 9 Jun 1813 - From what ship or whence received: Batteaux - Exchanged, discharged, died, or escape: Discharged - Time when: 31 Oct 1813 - Whither, and by what order, or number or re-entry: Malabar Transport

Drew, Ira   Prisoner 140. Rank: Lieutenant - By what ship or how taken: Boats & Troops - Time when: 28 May 1813 - Place where: Stoney Point, Henderson Harbor - Of what ship or corps: Land forces - Whether man of war, privateer or merchant vessel: Taken on shore - Time when received into custody: 8 Jul 1813 - From what ship or whence received: Batteaux - Exchanged, discharged, died, or escape: Discharged - Time when: 10 Aug 1813 - Whither, and by what order, or number or re-entry: Per order His Exellency Sir George Prevost

Drummin, John   Prisoner 800. Rank: Private - By what ship or how taken: Troops - Time when: 26 Jun 1813 - Place where: Beaver Dam - Of what ship or corps: Land forces - Whether man of war, privateer or merchant vessel: Taken on shore - Time when received into custody: 7 Jul 1813 - From what ship or whence received: Steamboat - Exchanged, discharged, died, or escape: Discharged - Time when: 10 Aug 1813 - Whither, and by what order, or number or re-entry: HM Ship Malpomena

Dubois, David   Prisoner 699. Rank: Private - By what ship or how taken: Troops - Time when: 26 Jun 1813 - Place where: Beaver Dam - Of what ship or corps: Land forces - Whether man of war, privateer or merchant vessel: Taken on shore - Time when received into custody: 7 Jul 1813 - From what ship or whence received: Steamboat - Exchanged, discharged, died, or escape: Discharged - Time when: 10 Aug 1813 - Whither, and by what order, or number or re-entry: HM Ship Regulius by order of Sir George Provost

Duffy, Ebenezer   Prisoner 1013. Rank: Seaman - By what ship or how taken: Earl Moria - Time when: 10 Aug 1813 - Place where: Lake Ontario - Of what ship or corps: Julia - Whether man of war, privateer or merchant vessel: Man of War -

American Prisoners of War held at Quebec during the War of 1812

Time when received into custody: 5 Sep 1813 - From what ship or whence received: Steamboat - Exchanged, discharged, died, or escape: Discharged - Time when: 31 Oct 1813 - Whither, and by what order, or number or re-entry: Malabar Transport

Duguenom, Charles   Prisoner 459. Rank: Private - By what ship or how taken: Troops - Time when: 24 Jun 1813 - Place where: Beaver Dam - Of what ship or corps: Malabar & Hydia - Whether man of war, privateer or merchant vessel: Taken on shore - Time when received into custody: 7 Jul 1813 - From what ship or whence received: Steamboat - Exchanged, discharged, died, or escape: Discharged - Time when: 10 Aug 1813 - Whither, and by what order, or number or re-entry: HM Ship Regulius by order of Sir George Provost

Dulman, George   Prisoner 874. Rank: Private - By what ship or how taken: Troops - Time when: 26 Jun 1813 - Place where: Beaver Dam - Of what ship or corps: Land forces - Whether man of war, privateer or merchant vessel: Taken on shore - Time when received into custody: 7 Jul 1813 - From what ship or whence received: Steamboat - Exchanged, discharged, died, or escape: Discharged - Time when: 10 Aug 1813 - Whither, and by what order, or number or re-entry: HM Ship Malpomena

Duncan, Mathew   Prisoner 154. Rank: Ensign - By what ship or how taken: Boats & Troops - Time when: 3 Jun 1813 - Place where: Lake Champlain - Of what ship or corps: Growler - Whether man of war, privateer or merchant vessel: Man of War - Time when received into custody: 8 Jul 1813 - From what ship or whence received: Batteaux - Exchanged, discharged, died, or escape: Discharged - Time when: 18 Sep 1813 - Whither, and by what order, or number or re-entry: Dick Transport

Dungan, Benjamin   Prisoner 365. Rank: Private - By what ship or how taken: Troops - Time when: 6 Jun 1813 - Place where: Stoney Point - Of what ship or corps: Land forces - Whether man of war, privateer or merchant vessel: Taken on shore - Time when received into custody: 28 Jun 1813 - From what ship or whence received: Mary of Quebec - Exchanged, discharged, died, or escape: Discharged - Time when: 31 Oct 1813 - Whither, and by what order, or number or re-entry: Malabar Transport

Dunklebury, J.   Prisoner 1544. Rank: Private - By what ship or how taken: Troops - Time when: 25 Jul 1814 - Place where: Lundy's Lane - Of what ship or corps: Land forces - Whether man of war, privateer or merchant vessel: Taken on shore - Time when received into custody: 30 Aug 1814 - From what ship or whence received: Lady Delaval Schooner 578 - Exchanged, discharged, died, or escape: Discharged - Time when: 8 Oct 1814 - Whither, and by what order, or number or re-entry: Queen No. 415

Dunn, Joel   Prisoner 1896. Rank: Sergeant - By what ship or how taken: Troops - Time when: 17 Sep 1814 - Place where: Fort Erie - Of what ship or corps: Land forces - Whether man of war, privateer or merchant vessel: Taken on shore - Time when received into custody: 1 Nov 1814 - From what ship or whence received: Montreal - Exchanged, discharged, died, or escape: Discharged - Time when: 8 Nov 1814 - Whither, and by what order, or number or re-entry: S. George No. 575 for Halifax by order of Sir George Provost

Dunn, William   Prisoner 1029. Rank: Seaman - By what ship or how taken: Lord Melvin - Time when: 10 Aug 1813 - Place where: Lake Ontario - Of what ship or corps: Growler - Whether man of war, privateer or merchant vessel: Man of War - Time when received into custody: 5 Sep 1813 - From what ship or whence received: Steamboat - Exchanged, discharged, died, or escape: Discharged - Time when: 1 Nov 1813 - Whither, and by what order, or number or re-entry: The Hero for England

Dunning, Jesse   Prisoner 417. Rank: Sergeant - By what ship or how taken: Troops - Time when: 24 Jun 1813 - Place where: Beaver Dam - Of what ship or corps: Land forces - Whether man of war, privateer or merchant vessel: Taken on shore - Time when received into custody: 7 Jul 1813 - From what ship or whence received: Steamboat - Exchanged, discharged, died, or escape: Discharged - Time when: 31 Oct 1813 - Whither, and by what order, or number or re-entry: Malabar Transport

Duvall, J.   Prisoner 1604. Rank: Private - By what ship or how taken: Troops - Time when: 12 Aug 1814 - Place where: Fort Erie - Of what ship or corps: Land forces - Whether man of war, privateer or merchant vessel: Taken on shore - Time when received into custody: 5 Oct 1814 - From what ship or whence received: Montreal - Exchanged, discharged, died, or escape: Discharged - Time when: 8 Oct 1814 - Whither, and by what order, or number or re-entry: H.M. Ship Ceylon

American Prisoners of War held at Quebec during the War of 1812

Dyer, Daniel   Prisoner 167. Rank: Boy - By what ship or how taken: Boats & Troops - Time when: 3 Jun 1813 - Place where: Lake Champlain - Of what ship or corps: Eagle - Whether man of war, privateer or merchant vessel: Man of War - Time when received into custody: 9 Jun 1813 - From what ship or whence received: Batteaux - Exchanged, discharged, died, or escape: Discharged - Time when: 31 Oct 1813 - Whither, and by what order, or number or re-entry: Malabar Transport

Dyer, Isaac   Prisoner 165. Rank: Able seaman - By what ship or how taken: Boats & Troops - Time when: 3 Jun 1813 - Place where: Lake Champlain - Of what ship or corps: Eagle - Whether man of war, privateer or merchant vessel: Man of War - Time when received into custody: 9 Jun 1813 - From what ship or whence received: Batteaux - Exchanged, discharged, died, or escape: Died - Time when: 10 Sep 1813 - Whither, and by what order, or number or re-entry: Dysentery

Dyke, Elijhua   Prisoner 1868. Rank: Private - By what ship or how taken: Troops - Time when: 17 Sep 1814 - Place where: Fort Erie - Of what ship or corps: Land forces - Whether man of war, privateer or merchant vessel: Taken on shore - Time when received into custody: 1 Nov 1814 - From what ship or whence received: Montreal - Exchanged, discharged, died, or escape: Discharged - Time when: 8 Nov 1814 - Whither, and by what order, or number or re-entry: S. George No. 575 for Halifax

Eades, Thomas   Prisoner 1375. Rank: Private - By what ship or how taken: Troops - Time when: 19 Dec 1813 - Place where: Fort Niagara - Of what ship or corps: Land forces - Whether man of war, privateer or merchant vessel: Taken on shore - Time when received into custody: 29 Jan 1814 - From what ship or whence received: Montreal by land carriage - Exchanged, discharged, died, or escape: Discharged - Time when: 4 May 1814 - Whither, and by what order, or number or re-entry: United States

Easter, Stephen   Prisoner 45. Rank: Private - By what ship or how taken: Boats & Troops - Time when: 28 May 1813 - Place where: Stoney Point, Henderson Harbor - Of what ship or corps: Land forces - Whether man of war, privateer or merchant vessel: Taken on shore - Time when received into custody: 8 Jun 1813 - From what ship or whence received: Batteaux - Exchanged, discharged, died, or escape: Died - Time when: 28 Jun 1813 - Whither, and by what order, or number or re-entry:

Eastman, Henry   Prisoner 1681. Rank: Sergeant - By what ship or how taken: Troops - Time when: 13 Aug 1814 - Place where: Fort Erie - Of what ship or corps: Land forces - Whether man of war, privateer or merchant vessel: Taken on shore - Time when received into custody: 23 Oct 1814 - From what ship or whence received: Montreal - Exchanged, discharged, died, or escape: Discharged - Time when: 8 Nov 1814 - Whither, and by what order, or number or re-entry: S. George No. 575 for Halifax

Eaton, George   Prisoner 1619. Rank: Private - By what ship or how taken: Gun Boats - Time when: 15 Aug 1814 - Place where: Fort Erie - Of what ship or corps: Land forces - Whether man of war, privateer or merchant vessel: Taken on shore - Time when received into custody: 5 Oct 1814 - From what ship or whence received: Montreal - Exchanged, discharged, died, or escape: Discharged - Time when: 8 Oct 1814 - Whither, and by what order, or number or re-entry: H.M. Ship Ceylon

Eaton, H. P.   Prisoner 1540. Rank: Private - By what ship or how taken: Troops - Time when: 25 Jul 1814 - Place where: Lundy's Lane - Of what ship or corps: Land forces - Whether man of war, privateer or merchant vessel: Taken on shore - Time when received into custody: 30 Aug 1814 - From what ship or whence received: Lady Delaval Schooner 578 - Exchanged, discharged, died, or escape: Discharged - Time when: 8 Oct 1814 - Whither, and by what order, or number or re-entry: Queen No. 415

Eaton, Moses   Prisoner 1168. Rank: Private - By what ship or how taken: Troops - Time when: 5 May 1813 - Place where: Rapids Prince Reason - Of what ship or corps: Land forces - Whether man of war, privateer or merchant vessel: Taken on shore - Time when received into custody: 25 Nov 1813 - From what ship or whence received: Town Goal - Exchanged, discharged, died, or escape: Discharged - Time when: 12 Mar 1814 - Whither, and by what order, or number or re-entry: New Brunswick Fencibles

Eaton, William   Prisoner 578. Rank: Private - By what ship or how taken: Troops - Time when: 26 Jun 1813 - Place where: Beaver Dam - Of what ship or corps: Land forces - Whether man of war, privateer or merchant vessel: Taken on shore - Time when received into custody: 13 Jul 1813 - From what ship or whence received: Steamboat - Exchanged, discharged, died, or escape: Died - Time when: 23 Aug 1813 - Whither, and by what order, or number or re-entry:

Edgets, Horan   Prisoner 1850. Rank: Private - By what ship or how taken: Troops - Time when: 17 Sep 1814 - Place where: Fort Erie - Of what ship or corps: Land forces - Whether man of war, privateer or merchant vessel: Taken on shore - Time when received into custody: 1 Nov 1814 - From what ship or whence received: Montreal - Exchanged, discharged, died, or escape: Discharged - Time when: 8 Nov 1814 - Whither, and by what order, or number or re-entry:

American Prisoners of War held at Quebec during the War of 1812

S. George No. 575 for Halifax by order of Sir George Provost

Edging, M.   Prisoner 1636. Rank: Private - By what ship or how taken: Troops - Time when: 15 Aug 1814 - Place where: Fort Erie - Of what ship or corps: Land forces - Whether man of war, privateer or merchant vessel: Taken on shore - Time when received into custody: 5 Oct 1814 - From what ship or whence received: Montreal - Exchanged, discharged, died, or escape: Discharged - Time when: 8 Oct 1814 - Whither, and by what order, or number or re-entry: H.M. Ship Ceylon

Edson, Nathan   Prisoner 1181. Rank: Private - By what ship or how taken: Troops - Time when: 5 May 1813 - Place where: Rapids - Of what ship or corps: Land forces - Whether man of war, privateer or merchant vessel: Taken on shore - Time when received into custody: 25 Nov 1813 - From what ship or whence received: Town Goal - Exchanged, discharged, died, or escape: Discharged - Time when: 4 May 1814 - Whither, and by what order, or number or re-entry: United States

Edy, Charles   Prisoner 1820. Rank: Private - By what ship or how taken: Troops - Time when: 17 Sep 1814 - Place where: Fort Erie - Of what ship or corps: Land forces - Whether man of war, privateer or merchant vessel: Taken on shore - Time when received into custody: 1 Nov 1814 - From what ship or whence received: Montreal - Exchanged, discharged, died, or escape: Discharged - Time when: 8 Nov 1814 - Whither, and by what order, or number or re-entry: S. George No. 575 for Halifax by order of Sir George Provost

Ella, John   Prisoner 33. Rank: Private - By what ship or how taken: Boats & Troops - Time when: 28 May 1813 - Place where: Stoney Point, Henderson Harbor - Of what ship or corps: Land forces - Whether man of war, privateer or merchant vessel: Taken on shore - Time when received into custody: 8 Jun 1813 - From what ship or whence received: Batteaux - Exchanged, discharged, died, or escape: Discharged - Time when: 31 Oct 1813 - Whither, and by what order, or number or re-entry: Malabar Transport

Elmore, Philip   Prisoner 737. Rank: Private - By what ship or how taken: Troops - Time when: 26 Jun 1813 - Place where: Beaver Dam - Of what ship or corps: Land forces - Whether man of war, privateer or merchant vessel: Taken on shore - Time when received into custody: 7 Jul 1813 - From what ship or whence received: Steamboat - Exchanged, discharged, died, or escape: Discharged - Time when: 10 Aug 1813 - Whither, and by what order, or number or re-entry: HM Ship Regulius by order of Sir George Provost

Elton, Moses   Prisoner 1397. Rank: Private - By what ship or how taken: Troops - Time when: 19 Dec 1813 - Place where: Fort Niagara - Of what ship or corps: Land forces - Whether man of war, privateer or merchant vessel: Taken on shore - Time when received into custody: 29 Jan 1814 - From what ship or whence received: Montreal by land carriage - Exchanged, discharged, died, or escape: Discharged - Time when: 4 May 1814 - Whither, and by what order, or number or re-entry: United States

Ely, Daniel   Prisoner 1742. Rank: Seaman - By what ship or how taken: Gun Boats - Time when: 3 Sep 1814 - Place where: Lake Huron - Of what ship or corps: Tigress - Whether man of war, privateer or merchant vessel: Man of War - Time when received into custody: 1 Nov 1814 - From what ship or whence received: Montreal - Exchanged, discharged, died, or escape: Discharged - Time when: 7 Nov 1814 - Whither, and by what order, or number or re-entry: Transport Freedom No. 582 by orders of his Excellency Sir George Provost

Emery, Stephen   Prisoner 313. Rank: Sergeant - By what ship or how taken: Boats & Troops - Time when: 6 Jun 1813 - Place where: Stoney Point - Of what ship or corps: Land forces - Whether man of war, privateer or merchant vessel: Taken on shore - Time when received into custody: 28 Jun 1813 - From what ship or whence received: Quebec of Quebec - Exchanged, discharged, died, or escape: Discharged - Time when: 31 Oct 1813 - Whither, and by what order, or number or re-entry: Malabar Transport

Emmins, Henry   Prisoner 858. Rank: Private - By what ship or how taken: Troops - Time when: 26 Jun 1813 - Place where: Beaver Dam - Of what ship or corps: Land forces - Whether man of war, privateer or merchant vessel: Taken on shore - Time when received into custody: 7 Jul 1813 - From what ship or whence received: Steamboat - Exchanged, discharged, died, or escape: Discharged - Time when: 10 Aug 1813 - Whither, and by what order, or number or re-entry: HM Ship Malpomena

Emmins, Phillip   Prisoner 168. Rank: Boy - By what ship or how taken: Boats & Troops - Time when: 3 Jun 1813 - Place where: Lake Champlain - Of what ship or corps: Eagle - Whether man of war, privateer or merchant vessel: Man of War - Time when received into custody: 9 Jun 1813 - From what ship or whence received: Batteaux - Exchanged, discharged, died, or escape: Discharged - Time when: 18 Sep 1813 - Whither, and by what order, or number or re-entry: Dick Transport

Enas, Abner   Prisoner 1980. Rank: Master's Mate - By what ship or how taken: Gun Boats - Time when: 3 Sep 1814 - Place where: Lake Huron - Of what ship or corps: Tigress - Whether man of war, privateer or merchant vessel: Man of War - Time when received into custody: 30 Dec 1814 - From what ship or whence received: Montreal - Exchanged, discharged, died, or escape: Discharged - Time when: 13 Mar 1815 - Whither, and by what order, or number or re-entry: United States

English, John   Prisoner 577. Rank: Private - By what ship or how taken: Troops - Time when: 26 Jun 1813 - Place where: Beaver Dam - Of what ship or corps: Land forces - Whether man of war, privateer or merchant vessel: Taken on shore - Time when received into custody: 13 Jul 1813 - From what ship or whence received: Steamboat - Exchanged, discharged, died, or escape: Discharged - Time when: 31 Oct 1813 - Whither, and by what order, or number or re-entry: Malabar Transport

Ervin, James B.   Prisoner 270. Rank: Sergeant - By what ship or how taken: Troops - Time when: 6 Jun 1813 - Place where: Stoney Point - Of what ship or corps: Land forces - Whether man of war, privateer or merchant vessel: Taken on shore - Time when received into custody: 28 Jun 1813 - From what ship or whence received: Batteaux - Exchanged, discharged, died, or escape: Discharged - Time when: 31 Oct 1813 - Whither, and by what order, or number or re-entry: Malabar Transport

Ervin, John   Prisoner 309. Rank: Private - By what ship or how taken: Boats & Troops - Time when: 6 Jun 1813 - Place where: Stoney Point - Of what ship or corps: Land forces - Whether man of war, privateer or merchant vessel: Taken on shore - Time when received into custody: 28 Jun 1813 - From what ship or whence received: Quebec of Quebec - Exchanged, discharged, died, or escape: Discharged - Time when: 31 Oct 1813 - Whither, and by what order, or number or re-entry: Malabar Transport

Ervin, Lewis   Prisoner 627. Rank: Private - By what ship or how taken: Troops - Time when: 24 Jun 1813 - Place where: Stoney Point - Of what ship or corps: Land forces - Whether man of war, privateer or merchant vessel: Taken on shore - Time when received into custody: 7 Jul 1813 - From what ship or whence received: Steamboat - Exchanged, discharged, died, or escape: Discharged - Time when: 31 Oct 1813 - Whither, and by what order, or number or re-entry: Malabar Transport

Erwing, Patrick   Prisoner 1174. Rank: Private - By what ship or how taken: Troops - Time when: 5 May 1813 - Place where: Rapids Prince Reason - Of what ship or corps: Land forces - Whether man of war, privateer or merchant vessel: Taken on shore - Time when received into custody: 25 Nov 1813 - From what ship or whence received: Town Goal - Exchanged, discharged, died, or escape: Discharged - Time when: 12 Mar 1814 - Whither, and by what order, or number or re-entry: New Brunswick Fencibles

Estes, Edward   Prisoner 233. Rank: Private - By what ship or how taken: Boats & Troops - Time when: 3 Jun 1813 - Place where: Lake Champlain - Of what ship or corps: Eagle - Whether man of war, privateer or merchant vessel: Man of War - Time when received into custody: 9 Jun 1813 - From what ship or whence received: Batteaux - Exchanged, discharged, died, or escape: Discharged - Time when: 2 Nov 1813 - Whither, and by what order, or number or re-entry: Malabar Transport

Estty, Israel   Prisoner 1795. Rank: Private - By what ship or how taken: Troops - Time when: 7 Sep 1814 - Place where: Fort Erie - Of what ship or corps: Land forces - Whether man of war, privateer or merchant vessel: Taken on shore - Time when received into custody: 1 Nov 1814 - From what ship or whence received: Montreal - Exchanged, discharged, died, or escape: Discharged - Time when: 8 Nov 1814 - Whither, and by what order, or number or re-entry: S. George No. 575 for Halifax by order of Sir George Provost

Eton, Ambrose   Prisoner 776. Rank: Private - By what ship or how taken: Troops - Time when: 26 Jun 1813 - Place where: Beaver Dam - Of what ship or corps: Land forces - Whether man of war, privateer or merchant vessel: Taken on shore - Time when received into custody: 7 Jul 1813 - From what ship or whence received: Steamboat - Exchanged, discharged, died, or escape: Discharged - Time when: 10 Aug 1813 - Whither, and by what order, or number or re-entry: HM Ship Malpomena

Evans, Edward   Prisoner 398. Rank: Private - By what ship or how taken: Troops - Time when: 6 Jun 1813 - Place where: Stoney Point - Of what ship or corps: Land forces - Whether man of war, privateer or merchant vessel: Taken on shore - Time when received into custody: 28 Jun 1813 - From what ship or whence received: Mary of Quebec - Exchanged, discharged, died, or escape: Discharged - Time when: 7 Aug 1813 - Whither, and by what order, or number or re-entry: H.M. Ship Cievare

Evans, James   Prisoner 317. Rank: Private - By what ship or how taken: Boats & Troops - Time when: 6 Jun 1813 - Place where: Stoney Point - Of what ship or corps: Land forces - Whether man of war, privateer or merchant vessel: Taken on shore - Time when received into custody: 28 Jun 1813 - From what ship or whence received: Quebec of Quebec - Exchanged, discharged, died, or escape: Discharged - Time when: 7 Aug 1813 - Whither, and by what order, or number

American Prisoners of War held at Quebec during the War of 1812

or re-entry: H.M. Ship Cievare

Evans, Thomas   Prisoner 53. Rank: Private - By what ship or how taken: Boats & Troops - Time when: 28 May 1813 - Place where: Stoney Point, Henderson Harbor - Of what ship or corps: Land forces - Whether man of war, privateer or merchant vessel: Taken on shore - Time when received into custody: 8 Jun 1813 - From what ship or whence received: Batteaux - Exchanged, discharged, died, or escape: Discharged - Time when: 31 Oct 1813 - Whither, and by what order, or number or re-entry: Malabar Transport

Evener, Christian   Prisoner 314. Rank: Private - By what ship or how taken: Boats & Troops - Time when: 6 Jun 1813 - Place where: Stoney Point - Of what ship or corps: Land forces - Whether man of war, privateer or merchant vessel: Taken on shore - Time when received into custody: 28 Jun 1813 - From what ship or whence received: Quebec of Quebec - Exchanged, discharged, died, or escape: Discharged - Time when: 31 Oct 1813 - Whither, and by what order, or number or re-entry: Malabar Transport

Everett, John   Prisoner 1040. Rank: Seaman - By what ship or how taken: Lord Melvin - Time when: 10 Aug 1813 - Place where: Lake Ontario - Of what ship or corps: Growler - Whether man of war, privateer or merchant vessel: Man of War - Time when received into custody: 5 Sep 1813 - From what ship or whence received: Steamboat - Exchanged, discharged, died, or escape: Discharged - Time when: 31 Oct 1813 - Whither, and by what order, or number or re-entry: Malabar Transport

Evertson, Benjamin   Prisoner 712. Rank: Private - By what ship or how taken: Troops - Time when: 26 Jun 1813 - Place where: Beaver Dam - Of what ship or corps: Land forces - Whether man of war, privateer or merchant vessel: Taken on shore - Time when received into custody: 7 Jul 1813 - From what ship or whence received: Steamboat - Exchanged, discharged, died, or escape: Discharged - Time when: 31 Oct 1813 - Whither, and by what order, or number or re-entry: Malabar Transport

Ewings, James   Prisoner 1363. Rank: Private - By what ship or how taken: Troops - Time when: 19 Dec 1813 - Place where: Fort Niagara - Of what ship or corps: Land forces - Whether man of war, privateer or merchant vessel: Taken on shore - Time when received into custody: 29 Jan 1814 - From what ship or whence received: Montreal by land carriage - Exchanged, discharged, died, or escape: Discharged - Time when: 4 May 1814 - Whither, and by what order, or number or re-entry: United States

Fagan, Phillip   Prisoner 1952. Rank: Private - By what ship or how taken: Troops - Time when: 23 Oct 1814 - Place where: Fort Erie - Of what ship or corps: Land forces - Whether man of war, privateer or merchant vessel: Taken on shore - Time when received into custody: 11 Dec 1814 - From what ship or whence received: Montreal - Exchanged, discharged, died, or escape: Discharged - Time when: 13 Mar 1815 - Whither, and by what order, or number or re-entry: United States

Fairchild, Cyrus   Prisoner 1112. Rank: Private - By what ship or how taken: Troops - Time when: 17 Oct 1813 - Place where: Red Mills - Of what ship or corps: Land forces - Whether man of war, privateer or merchant vessel: Taken on shore - Time when received into custody: 12 Oct 1813 - From what ship or whence received: Steamboat - Exchanged, discharged, died, or escape: Discharged - Time when: 31 Oct 1813 - Whither, and by what order, or number or re-entry: Malabar Transport

Fairfield, Soloman   Prisoner 834. Rank: Private - By what ship or how taken: Troops - Time when: 26 Jun 1813 - Place where: Beaver Dam - Of what ship or corps: Land forces - Whether man of war, privateer or merchant vessel: Taken on shore - Time when received into custody: 7 Jul 1813 - From what ship or whence received: Steamboat - Exchanged, discharged, died, or escape: Discharged - Time when: 10 Aug 1813 - Whither, and by what order, or number or re-entry: HM Ship Malpomena

Falcon, John   Prisoner 1758. Rank: Private - By what ship or how taken: Gun Boats - Time when: 3 Sep 1814 - Place where: Lake Huron - Of what ship or corps: Tigress - Whether man of war, privateer or merchant vessel: Man of War - Time when received into custody: 1 Nov 1814 - From what ship or whence received: Montreal - Exchanged, discharged, died, or escape: Discharged - Time when: 8 Nov 1814 - Whither, and by what order, or number or re-entry: S. George No. 575 for Halifax by order of Sir George Provost

Farmham, Gauis   Prisoner 1275. Rank: Sergeant - By what ship or how taken: Troops - Time when: 19 Dec 1813 - Place where: Fort Niagara - Of what ship or corps: Land forces - Whether man of war, privateer or merchant vessel: Taken on shore - Time when received into custody: 29 Jan 1814 - From what ship or whence received: Montreal by land carriage - Exchanged, discharged, died, or escape: Discharged - Time when: 28 Feb 1814 - Whither, and by what order, or number or re-entry: Soverign Transport No. 628

American Prisoners of War held at Quebec during the War of 1812

Farr, Chester W.   Prisoner 1853. Rank: Private - By what ship or how taken: Troops - Time when: 17 Sep 1814 - Place where: Fort Erie - Of what ship or corps: Land forces - Whether man of war, privateer or merchant vessel: Taken on shore - Time when received into custody: 1 Nov 1814 - From what ship or whence received: Montreal - Exchanged, discharged, died, or escape: Discharged - Time when: 8 Nov 1814 - Whither, and by what order, or number or re-entry: S. George No. 575 for Halifax

Farrard, Michael   Prisoner 1383. Rank: Private - By what ship or how taken: Troops - Time when: 19 Dec 1813 - Place where: Fort Niagara - Of what ship or corps: Land forces - Whether man of war, privateer or merchant vessel: Taken on shore - Time when received into custody: 29 Jan 1814 - From what ship or whence received: Montreal by land carriage - Exchanged, discharged, died, or escape: Discharged - Time when: 4 May 1814 - Whither, and by what order, or number or re-entry: United States

Farrell, Michael   Prisoner 837. Rank: Private - By what ship or how taken: Troops - Time when: 26 Jun 1813 - Place where: Beaver Dam - Of what ship or corps: Land forces - Whether man of war, privateer or merchant vessel: Taken on shore - Time when received into custody: 7 Jul 1813 - From what ship or whence received: Steamboat - Exchanged, discharged, died, or escape: Discharged - Time when: 31 Oct 1813 - Whither, and by what order, or number or re-entry: Malabar Transport

Farrell, Richard   Prisoner 1736. Rank: Seaman - By what ship or how taken: Gun Boats - Time when: 3 Sep 1814 - Place where: Lake Huron - Of what ship or corps: Tigress - Whether man of war, privateer or merchant vessel: Man of War - Time when received into custody: 1 Nov 1814 - From what ship or whence received: Montreal - Exchanged, discharged, died, or escape: Discharged - Time when: 7 Nov 1814 - Whither, and by what order, or number or re-entry: Transport Freedom No. 582 by orders of his Excellency Sir George Provost

Faunce, Peter   Prisoner 453. Rank: Private - By what ship or how taken: Troops - Time when: 24 Jun 1813 - Place where: Beaver Dam - Of what ship or corps: Malabar & Hydia - Whether man of war, privateer or merchant vessel: Taken on shore - Time when received into custody: 7 Jul 1813 - From what ship or whence received: Steamboat - Exchanged, discharged, died, or escape: Discharged - Time when: 7 Aug 1813 - Whither, and by what order, or number or re-entry: H.M. Ship Cievare

Fay, Hey.   Prisoner 1630. Rank: Militia - By what ship or how taken: Troops - Time when: 6 Sep 1814 - Place where: Plattsburg - Of what ship or corps: Land forces - Whether man of war, privateer or merchant vessel: Taken on shore - Time when received into custody: 5 Oct 1814 - From what ship or whence received: Montreal - Exchanged, discharged, died, or escape: Discharged - Time when: 8 Oct 1814 - Whither, and by what order, or number or re-entry: H.M. Ship Ceylon

Feders, Jacob   Prisoner 1454. Rank: Private - By what ship or how taken: Troops - Time when: 6 May 1814 - Place where: Oswago - Of what ship or corps: Land forces - Whether man of war, privateer or merchant vessel: Taken on shore - Time when received into custody: 12 Aug 1814 - From what ship or whence received: Royal Seaman No. 289 Transport - Exchanged, discharged, died, or escape: Discharged - Time when: 8 Oct 1814 - Whither, and by what order, or number or re-entry: Queen No. 415

Felton, John   Prisoner 1721. Rank: Boat. Mate - By what ship or how taken: Gun Boats - Time when: 6 Sep 1814 - Place where: Lake Huron - Of what ship or corps: Scorpion - Whether man of war, privateer or merchant vessel: Man of War - Time when received into custody: 28 Oct 1814 - From what ship or whence received: Montreal - Exchanged, discharged, died, or escape: Discharged - Time when: 7 Nov 1814 - Whither, and by what order, or number or re-entry: Transport Freedom No. 582 by orders of his Excellency Sir George Provost

Fenning, Charles   Prisoner 1320. Rank: Private - By what ship or how taken: Troops - Time when: 19 Dec 1813 - Place where: Fort Niagara - Of what ship or corps: Land forces - Whether man of war, privateer or merchant vessel: Taken on shore - Time when received into custody: 29 Jan 1814 - From what ship or whence received: Montreal by land carriage - Exchanged, discharged, died, or escape: Died - Time when: 5 Jun 1814 - Whither, and by what order, or number or re-entry: Asceles

Ferrish, Barney   Prisoner 1061. Rank: Private - By what ship or how taken: Troops - Time when: 24 Jun 1813 - Place where: Beaver Dam - Of what ship or corps: Land forces - Whether man of war, privateer or merchant vessel: Taken on shore - Time when received into custody: 5 Sep 1813 - From what ship or whence received: Steamboat - Exchanged, discharged, died, or escape: Discharged - Time when: 31 Oct 1813 - Whither, and by what order, or number or re-entry: Malabar Transport

Field, Eli   Prisoner 10. Rank: Private - By what ship or how taken: Boats & Troops - Time when: 28 May 1813 - Place where: Stoney Point, Henderson Harbor - Of what ship or corps: Land forces - Whether man of war, privateer or merchant vessel: Taken on shore - Time when received into custody: 8 Jun 1813 - From what ship or whence received: Batteaux

American Prisoners of War held at Quebec during the War of 1812

- Exchanged, discharged, died, or escape: Discharged - Time when: 31 Oct 1813 - Whither, and by what order, or number or re-entry: Malabar Transport

Fields, Thomas   Prisoner 876. Rank: Private - By what ship or how taken: Troops - Time when: 26 Jun 1813 - Place where: Beaver Dam - Of what ship or corps: Land forces - Whether man of war, privateer or merchant vessel: Taken on shore - Time when received into custody: 7 Jul 1813 - From what ship or whence received: Steamboat - Exchanged, discharged, died, or escape: Discharged - Time when: 10 Aug 1813 - Whither, and by what order, or number or re-entry: HM Ship Malpomena

Filkins, John F.   Prisoner 600. Rank: Private - By what ship or how taken: Troops - Time when: 26 Jun 1813 - Place where: Stoney Point - Of what ship or corps: Land forces - Whether man of war, privateer or merchant vessel: Taken on shore - Time when received into custody: 7 Jul 1813 - From what ship or whence received: Steamboat - Exchanged, discharged, died, or escape: Discharged - Time when: 10 Aug 1813 - Whither, and by what order, or number or re-entry: HM Ship Regulius by order of Sir George Provost

Fincher, Jesse   Prisoner 1297. Rank: Private - By what ship or how taken: Troops - Time when: 19 Dec 1813 - Place where: Fort Niagara - Of what ship or corps: Land forces - Whether man of war, privateer or merchant vessel: Taken on shore - Time when received into custody: 29 Jan 1814 - From what ship or whence received: Montreal by land carriage - Exchanged, discharged, died, or escape: Discharged - Time when: 4 May 1814 - Whither, and by what order, or number or re-entry: United States

Finney, Elihu   Prisoner 110. Rank: Private - By what ship or how taken: Boats & Troops - Time when: 28 May 1813 - Place where: Stoney Point, Henderson Harbor - Of what ship or corps: Land forces - Whether man of war, privateer or merchant vessel: Taken on shore - Time when received into custody: 8 Jun 1813 - From what ship or whence received: Batteaux - Exchanged, discharged, died, or escape: Died - Time when: 28 Jul 1813 - Whither, and by what order, or number or re-entry: Dysentery

Finney, Samuel   Prisoner 107. Rank: Private - By what ship or how taken: Boats & Troops - Time when: 28 May 1813 - Place where: Stoney Point, Henderson Harbor - Of what ship or corps: Land forces - Whether man of war, privateer or merchant vessel: Taken on shore - Time when received into custody: 8 Jun 1813 - From what ship or whence received: Batteaux - Exchanged, discharged, died, or escape: Discharged - Time when: 31 Oct 1813 - Whither, and by what order, or number or re-entry: Malabar Transport

Fisher, Anthony   Prisoner 351. Rank: Private - By what ship or how taken: Troops - Time when: 6 Jun 1813 - Place where: Stoney Point - Of what ship or corps: Land forces - Whether man of war, privateer or merchant vessel: Taken on shore - Time when received into custody: 28 Jun 1813 - From what ship or whence received: Mary of Quebec - Exchanged, discharged, died, or escape: Discharged - Time when: 31 Oct 1813 - Whither, and by what order, or number or re-entry: Malabar Transport

Fisher, Jacob   Prisoner 626. Rank: Private - By what ship or how taken: Troops - Time when: 24 Jun 1813 - Place where: Stoney Point - Of what ship or corps: Land forces - Whether man of war, privateer or merchant vessel: Taken on shore - Time when received into custody: 7 Jul 1813 - From what ship or whence received: Steamboat - Exchanged, discharged, died, or escape: Discharged - Time when: 10 Aug 1813 - Whither, and by what order, or number or re-entry: HM Ship Regulius by order of Sir George Provost

Fistock, Thomas   Prisoner 998. Rank: Seaman - By what ship or how taken: Earl Moria - Time when: 10 Aug 1813 - Place where: Lake Ontario - Of what ship or corps: Julia - Whether man of war, privateer or merchant vessel: Man of War - Time when received into custody: 5 Sep 1813 - From what ship or whence received: Steamboat - Exchanged, discharged, died, or escape: Discharged - Time when: 31 Oct 1813 - Whither, and by what order, or number or re-entry: Malabar Transport

Fitz, Charles   Prisoner 714. Rank: Private - By what ship or how taken: Troops - Time when: 26 Jun 1813 - Place where: Beaver Dam - Of what ship or corps: Land forces - Whether man of war, privateer or merchant vessel: Taken on shore - Time when received into custody: 7 Jul 1813 - From what ship or whence received: Steamboat - Exchanged, discharged, died, or escape: Discharged - Time when: 10 Aug 1813 - Whither, and by what order, or number or re-entry: HM Ship Regulius by order of Sir George Provost

Fitzgerald, Aaron   Prisoner 109. Rank: Private - By what ship or how taken: Boats & Troops - Time when: 28 May 1813 - Place where: Stoney Point, Henderson Harbor - Of what ship or corps: Land forces - Whether man of war, privateer or merchant vessel: Taken on shore - Time when received into custody: 8 Jun 1813 - From what ship or whence received: Batteaux - Exchanged, discharged, died, or escape: Discharged - Time when: 4 May 1814 - Whither, and by what order, or number or re-entry: United States

American Prisoners of War held at Quebec during the War of 1812

Fitzgerald, John   Prisoner 295.   Rank: Private - By what ship or how taken: Boats & Troops - Time when: 6 Jun 1813 - Place where: Stoney Point - Of what ship or corps: Land forces - Whether man of war, privateer or merchant vessel: Taken on shore - Time when received into custody: 28 Jun 1813 - From what ship or whence received: Quebec of Quebec - Exchanged, discharged, died, or escape: Discharged - Time when: 7 Aug 1813 - Whither, and by what order, or number or re-entry: H.M. Ship Cievare

Fleming, Henry   Prisoner 524.   Rank: Captain - By what ship or how taken: Troops - Time when: 24 Jun 1813 - Place where: Beaver Dam - Of what ship or corps: Land forces - Whether man of war, privateer or merchant vessel: Taken on shore - Time when received into custody: 13 Jul 1813 - From what ship or whence received: Steamboat - Exchanged, discharged, died, or escape: Discharged - Time when: 13 Dec 1813 - Whither, and by what order, or number or re-entry: United States

Fleming, William   Prisoner 1154.   Rank: Private - By what ship or how taken: Troops - Time when: 5 May 1813 - Place where: Rapids Prince Reason - Of what ship or corps: Land forces - Whether man of war, privateer or merchant vessel: Taken on shore - Time when received into custody: 25 Nov 1813 - From what ship or whence received: Town Goal - Exchanged, discharged, died, or escape: Discharged - Time when: 4 May 1814 - Whither, and by what order, or number or re-entry: United States

Flemmings, Joseph   Prisoner 367.   Rank: Private - By what ship or how taken: Troops - Time when: 6 Jun 1813 - Place where: Stoney Point - Of what ship or corps: Land forces - Whether man of war, privateer or merchant vessel: Taken on shore - Time when received into custody: 28 Jun 1813 - From what ship or whence received: Mary of Quebec - Exchanged, discharged, died, or escape: Discharged - Time when: 31 Oct 1813 - Whither, and by what order, or number or re-entry: Malabar Transport

Flury, Francis   Prisoner 1759.   Rank: Private - By what ship or how taken: Gun Boats - Time when: 3 Sep 1814 - Place where: Lake Huron - Of what ship or corps: Tigress - Whether man of war, privateer or merchant vessel: Man of War - Time when received into custody: 1 Nov 1814 - From what ship or whence received: Montreal - Exchanged, discharged, died, or escape: Discharged - Time when: 8 Nov 1814 - Whither, and by what order, or number or re-entry: S. George No. 575 for Halifax by order of Sir George Provost

Fobes, Quen   Prisoner 83.   Rank: Private - By what ship or how taken: Boats & Troops - Time when: 28 May 1813 - Place where: Stoney Point, Henderson Harbor - Of what ship or corps: Land forces - Whether man of war, privateer or merchant vessel: Taken on shore - Time when received into custody: 8 Jun 1813 - From what ship or whence received: Batteaux - Exchanged, discharged, died, or escape: Discharged - Time when: 31 Oct 1813 - Whither, and by what order, or number or re-entry: Malabar Transport

Folks, John   Prisoner 1452.   Rank: Private - By what ship or how taken: Troops - Time when: 6 May 1814 - Place where: Oswago - Of what ship or corps: Land forces - Whether man of war, privateer or merchant vessel: Taken on shore - Time when received into custody: 12 Aug 1814 - From what ship or whence received: Royal Seaman No. 289 Transport - Exchanged, discharged, died, or escape: Discharged - Time when: 8 Oct 1814 - Whither, and by what order, or number or re-entry: Queen No. 415

Folson, John   Prisoner 1953.   Rank: Private - By what ship or how taken: Troops - Time when: 16 Oct 1814 - Place where: Lyons Creek - Of what ship or corps: Land forces - Whether man of war, privateer or merchant vessel: Taken on shore - Time when received into custody: 11 Dec 1814 - From what ship or whence received: Montreal - Exchanged, discharged, died, or escape: Discharged - Time when: 13 Mar 1815 - Whither, and by what order, or number or re-entry: United States

Fontaine, John J.   Prisoner 1564.   Rank: Lieutenant - By what ship or how taken: Troops - Time when: 15 Aug 1814 - Place where: Fort Erie - Of what ship or corps: Land forces - Whether man of war, privateer or merchant vessel: Taken on shore - Time when received into custody: 16 Sep 1814 - From what ship or whence received: Steamboat - Exchanged, discharged, died, or escape: Discharged - Time when: 15 Nov 1814 - Whither, and by what order, or number or re-entry: Wolga No. 377

Foot, Henry   Prisoner 329.   Rank: Private - By what ship or how taken: Boats & Troops - Time when: 6 Jun 1813 - Place where: Stoney Point - Of what ship or corps: Batteaux - Whether man of war, privateer or merchant vessel: Taken on shore - Time when received into custody: 28 Jun 1813 - From what ship or whence received: Quebec of Quebec - Exchanged, discharged, died, or escape: Discharged - Time when: 31 Oct 1813 - Whither, and by what order, or number or re-entry: Malabar Transport

Forrest, Arthur   Prisoner 634.   Rank: Private - By what ship or how taken: Troops - Time when: 24 Jun 1813 - Place where: Stoney Point - Of what ship or corps: Land forces - Whether man of war, privateer or merchant vessel: Taken on shore - Time when received into custody: 7 Jul 1813 - From what ship or whence received: Steamboat - Exchanged,

American Prisoners of War held at Quebec during the War of 1812

discharged, died, or escape: Discharged - Time when: 10 Aug 1813 - Whither, and by what order, or number or re-entry: HM Ship Regulius by order of Sir George Provost

Forrester, Peter   Prisoner 1227. Rank: Private - By what ship or how taken: Troops - Time when: 19 Dec 1813 - Place where: Fort Niagara - Of what ship or corps: Land forces - Whether man of war, privateer or merchant vessel: Taken on shore - Time when received into custody: 29 Jan 1814 - From what ship or whence received: Montreal by land carriage - Exchanged, discharged, died, or escape: Discharged - Time when: 4 May 1814 - Whither, and by what order, or number or re-entry: United States

Foster, John   Prisoner 54. Rank: Private - By what ship or how taken: Boats & Troops - Time when: 28 May 1813 - Place where: Stoney Point, Henderson Harbor - Of what ship or corps: Land forces - Whether man of war, privateer or merchant vessel: Taken on shore - Time when received into custody: 8 Jun 1813 - From what ship or whence received: Batteaux - Exchanged, discharged, died, or escape: Discharged - Time when: 4 May 1814 - Whither, and by what order, or number or re-entry: United States

Foster, Nathaniel   Prisoner 231. Rank: Private - By what ship or how taken: Boats & Troops - Time when: 3 Jun 1813 - Place where: Lake Champlain - Of what ship or corps: Eagle - Whether man of war, privateer or merchant vessel: Man of War - Time when received into custody: 9 Jun 1813 - From what ship or whence received: Batteaux - Exchanged, discharged, died, or escape: Died - Time when: 28 Aug 1813 - Whither, and by what order, or number or re-entry: Typhus Fever

Fowler, James   Prisoner 1595. Rank: Corporal - By what ship or how taken: Troops - Time when: 12 Aug 1814 - Place where: Fort Erie - Of what ship or corps: Land forces - Whether man of war, privateer or merchant vessel: Taken on shore - Time when received into custody: 5 Oct 1814 - From what ship or whence received: Montreal - Exchanged, discharged, died, or escape: Discharged - Time when: 8 Oct 1814 - Whither, and by what order, or number or re-entry: H.M. Ship Ceylon

Francisco, John   Prisoner 708. Rank: Private - By what ship or how taken: Troops - Time when: 26 Jun 1813 - Place where: Beaver Dam - Of what ship or corps: Land forces - Whether man of war, privateer or merchant vessel: Taken on shore - Time when received into custody: 7 Jul 1813 - From what ship or whence received: Steamboat - Exchanged, discharged, died, or escape: Discharged - Time when: 10 Aug 1813 - Whither, and by what order, or number or re-entry: HM Ship Regulius by order of Sir George Provost

Frank, Christian F.   Prisoner 701. Rank: Private - By what ship or how taken: Troops - Time when: 26 Jun 1813 - Place where: Beaver Dam - Of what ship or corps: Land forces - Whether man of war, privateer or merchant vessel: Taken on shore - Time when received into custody: 7 Jul 1813 - From what ship or whence received: Steamboat - Exchanged, discharged, died, or escape: Discharged - Time when: 10 Aug 1813 - Whither, and by what order, or number or re-entry: HM Ship Regulius by order of Sir George Provost

Frankling, G.   Prisoner 1828. Rank: Private - By what ship or how taken: Troops - Time when: 17 Sep 1814 - Place where: Fort Erie - Of what ship or corps: Land forces - Whether man of war, privateer or merchant vessel: Taken on shore - Time when received into custody: 1 Nov 1814 - From what ship or whence received: Montreal - Exchanged, discharged, died, or escape: Discharged - Time when: 8 Nov 1814 - Whither, and by what order, or number or re-entry: S. George No. 575 for Halifax by order of Sir George Provost

Frasel, Hubbard   Prisoner 438. Rank: Private - By what ship or how taken: Troops - Time when: 24 Jun 1813 - Place where: Beaver Dam - Of what ship or corps: Land forces - Whether man of war, privateer or merchant vessel: Taken on shore - Time when received into custody: 7 Jul 1813 - From what ship or whence received: Steamboat - Exchanged, discharged, died, or escape: Discharged - Time when: 10 Aug 1813 - Whither, and by what order, or number or re-entry: HM Ship Regulius by order of Sir George Provost

Frayman, James   Prisoner 277. Rank: Private - By what ship or how taken: Troops - Time when: 6 Jun 1813 - Place where: Stoney Point - Of what ship or corps: Land forces - Whether man of war, privateer or merchant vessel: Taken on shore - Time when received into custody: 28 Jun 1813 - From what ship or whence received: Batteaux - Exchanged, discharged, died, or escape: Discharged - Time when: 31 Oct 1813 - Whither, and by what order, or number or re-entry: Malabar Transport

Frederick, Henry   Prisoner 1203. Rank: Lieutenant - By what ship or how taken: Troops - Time when: 19 Dec 1813 - Place where: Fort Niagara - Of what ship or corps: Land forces - Whether man of war, privateer or merchant vessel: Taken on shore - Time when received into custody: 18 Jan 1814 - From what ship or whence received: Montreal by land carriage - Exchanged, discharged, died, or escape: Discharged - Time when: 4 May 1814 - Whither, and by what order, or number or re-entry: United States

American Prisoners of War held at Quebec during the War of 1812

Free, Almond   Prisoner 1077. Rank: Private - By what ship or how taken: Troops - Time when: 24 Aug 1813 - Place where: Fort George - Of what ship or corps: Land forces - Whether man of war, privateer or merchant vessel: Taken on shore - Time when received into custody: 10 Oct 1813 - From what ship or whence received: Steamboat - Exchanged, discharged, died, or escape: Discharged - Time when: 31 Oct 1813 - Whither, and by what order, or number or re-entry: Malabar Transport

Freeborne, John   Prisoner 144. Rank: Master's Mate - By what ship or how taken: Boats & Troops - Time when: 3 Jun 1813 - Place where: Lake Champlain - Of what ship or corps: Eagle - Whether man of war, privateer or merchant vessel: Man of War - Time when received into custody: 8 Jul 1813 - From what ship or whence received: Batteaux - Exchanged, discharged, died, or escape: Discharged - Time when: 4 May 1814 - Whither, and by what order, or number or re-entry: United States

Freeman, James   Prisoner 315. Rank: Private - By what ship or how taken: Boats & Troops - Time when: 6 Jun 1813 - Place where: Stoney Point - Of what ship or corps: Land forces - Whether man of war, privateer or merchant vessel: Taken on shore - Time when received into custody: 28 Jun 1813 - From what ship or whence received: Quebec of Quebec - Exchanged, discharged, died, or escape: Discharged - Time when: 4 May 1814 - Whither, and by what order, or number or re-entry: United States

Frehen, Edward   Prisoner 1059. Rank: Private - By what ship or how taken: Troops - Time when: 24 Jun 1813 - Place where: Beaver Dam - Of what ship or corps: Land forces - Whether man of war, privateer or merchant vessel: Taken on shore - Time when received into custody: 5 Sep 1813 - From what ship or whence received: Steamboat - Exchanged, discharged, died, or escape: Discharged - Time when: 31 Oct 1813 - Whither, and by what order, or number or re-entry: Malabar Transport

French, Thomas   Prisoner 1889. Rank: Private - By what ship or how taken: Troops - Time when: 17 Sep 1814 - Place where: Fort Erie - Of what ship or corps: Land forces - Whether man of war, privateer or merchant vessel: Taken on shore - Time when received into custody: 1 Nov 1814 - From what ship or whence received: Montreal - Exchanged, discharged, died, or escape: Discharged - Time when: 8 Nov 1814 - Whither, and by what order, or number or re-entry: S. George No. 575 for Halifax by order of Sir George Provost

Frickes, John   Prisoner 174. Rank: Able seaman - By what ship or how taken: Boats & Troops - Time when: 3 Jun 1813 - Place where: Lake Champlain - Of what ship or corps: Growler - Whether man of war, privateer or merchant vessel: Man of War - Time when received into custody: 9 Jun 1813 - From what ship or whence received: Batteaux - Exchanged, discharged, died, or escape: Discharged - Time when: 4 May 1814 - Whither, and by what order, or number or re-entry: United States

Frink, Rupel   Prisoner 924. Rank: Private - By what ship or how taken: Troops - Time when: 26 Jun 1813 - Place where: Beaver Dam - Of what ship or corps: Land forces - Whether man of war, privateer or merchant vessel: Taken on shore - Time when received into custody: 21 Jul 1813 - From what ship or whence received: Steamboat - Exchanged, discharged, died, or escape: Discharged - Time when: 10 Aug 1813 - Whither, and by what order, or number or re-entry: HM Ship Malpomena

Frost, Phineas   Prisoner 222. Rank: Private - By what ship or how taken: Boats & Troops - Time when: 3 Jun 1813 - Place where: Lake Champlain - Of what ship or corps: Growler - Whether man of war, privateer or merchant vessel: Man of War - Time when received into custody: 9 Jun 1813 - From what ship or whence received: Batteaux - Exchanged, discharged, died, or escape: Died - Time when: 22 Oct 1813 - Whither, and by what order, or number or re-entry:

Fry, Jacob   Prisoner 1446. Rank: Sergeant - By what ship or how taken: Troops - Time when: 6 May 1814 - Place where: Oswago - Of what ship or corps: Land forces - Whether man of war, privateer or merchant vessel: Taken on shore - Time when received into custody: 12 Aug 1814 - From what ship or whence received: Royal Seaman No. 289 Transport - Exchanged, discharged, died, or escape: Discharged - Time when: 8 Oct 1814 - Whither, and by what order, or number or re-entry: Queen No. 415

Fuller, Chester   Prisoner 1561. Rank: Private - By what ship or how taken: Troops - Time when: 25 Jul 1814 - Place where: Lundy's Lane - Of what ship or corps: Land forces - Whether man of war, privateer or merchant vessel: Taken on shore - Time when received into custody: 30 Aug 1814 - From what ship or whence received: Lady Delaval Schooner 578 - Exchanged, discharged, died, or escape: Discharged - Time when: - Whither, and by what order, or number or re-entry: H.M. Ship Ceylon

Fuller, James   Prisoner 781. Rank: Private - By what ship or how taken: Troops - Time when: 26 Jun 1813 - Place where: Beaver Dam - Of what ship or corps: Land forces - Whether man of war, privateer or merchant vessel: Taken on shore - Time when received into custody: 7 Jul 1813 - From what ship or whence received: Steamboat - Exchanged, discharged, died, or escape: Discharged - Time when: 10 Aug 1813 - Whither, and by what order, or number or re-

American Prisoners of War held at Quebec during the War of 1812

entry: HM Ship Malpomena

Fuller, John B.   Prisoner 1928. Rank: Private - By what ship or how taken: Troops - Time when: 17 Sep 1814 - Place where: Fort Erie - Of what ship or corps: Land forces - Whether man of war, privateer or merchant vessel: Taken on shore - Time when received into custody: 1 Nov 1814 - From what ship or whence received: Montreal - Exchanged, discharged, died, or escape: Discharged - Time when: 13 Mar 1815 - Whither, and by what order, or number or re-entry: United States

Fullerton, William   Prisoner 595. Rank: Private - By what ship or how taken: Troops - Time when: 26 Jun 1813 - Place where: Stoney Point - Of what ship or corps: Land forces - Whether man of war, privateer or merchant vessel: Taken on shore - Time when received into custody: 7 Jul 1813 - From what ship or whence received: Steamboat - Exchanged, discharged, died, or escape: Discharged - Time when: 10 Aug 1813 - Whither, and by what order, or number or re-entry: HM Ship Regulius by order of Sir George Provost

Furbush, Joshua   Prisoner 162. Rank: Able seaman - By what ship or how taken: Boats & Troops - Time when: 3 Jun 1813 - Place where: Lake Champlain - Of what ship or corps: Eagle - Whether man of war, privateer or merchant vessel: Man of War - Time when received into custody: 9 Jun 1813 - From what ship or whence received: Batteaux - Exchanged, discharged, died, or escape: Discharged - Time when: 4 May 1814 - Whither, and by what order, or number or re-entry: United States

Furguson, John   Prisoner 955. Rank: Corporal - By what ship or how taken: Troops - Time when: 5 Jul 1813 - Place where: Fort Schisher - Of what ship or corps: Land forces - Whether man of war, privateer or merchant vessel: Taken on shore - Time when received into custody: 5 Sep 1813 - From what ship or whence received: Steamboat - Exchanged, discharged, died, or escape: - Time when: - Whither, and by what order, or number or re-entry: In the town goal

Gale, J. G.   Prisoner 1618. Rank: Private - By what ship or how taken: Gun Boats - Time when: 15 Aug 1814 - Place where: Fort Erie - Of what ship or corps: Land forces - Whether man of war, privateer or merchant vessel: Taken on shore - Time when received into custody: 5 Oct 1814 - From what ship or whence received: Montreal - Exchanged, discharged, died, or escape: Discharged - Time when: 8 Oct 1814 - Whither, and by what order, or number or re-entry: H.M. Ship Ceylon

Galispie, Martin   Prisoner 1748. Rank: Private - By what ship or how taken: Gun Boats - Time when: 6 Sep 1814 - Place where: Lake Huron - Of what ship or corps: Scorpion - Whether man of war, privateer or merchant vessel: Man of War - Time when received into custody: 1 Nov 1814 - From what ship or whence received: Montreal - Exchanged, discharged, died, or escape: Discharged - Time when: 8 Nov 1814 - Whither, and by what order, or number or re-entry: S. George No. 575 for Halifax by order of Sir George Provost

Galloway, Samuel   Prisoner 1511. Rank: Major - By what ship or how taken: Troops - Time when: 5 Jul 1814 - Place where: Chippewa - Of what ship or corps: Land forces - Whether man of war, privateer or merchant vessel: Taken on shore - Time when received into custody: 25 Aug 1814 - From what ship or whence received: Steamboat - Exchanged, discharged, died, or escape: Discharged - Time when: 10 Nov 1814 - Whither, and by what order, or number or re-entry: Transport Stately No. 408 for Halifax

Gardner, Hiram   Prisoner 1784. Rank: Private - By what ship or how taken: Troops - Time when: 7 Sep 1814 - Place where: Fort Erie - Of what ship or corps: Land forces - Whether man of war, privateer or merchant vessel: Taken on shore - Time when received into custody: 1 Nov 1814 - From what ship or whence received: Montreal - Exchanged, discharged, died, or escape: Discharged - Time when: 8 Nov 1814 - Whither, and by what order, or number or re-entry: S. George No. 575 for Halifax by order of Sir George Provost

Garland, John   Prisoner 1885. Rank: Private - By what ship or how taken: Troops - Time when: 17 Sep 1814 - Place where: Fort Erie - Of what ship or corps: Land forces - Whether man of war, privateer or merchant vessel: Taken on shore - Time when received into custody: 1 Nov 1814 - From what ship or whence received: Montreal - Exchanged, discharged, died, or escape: Discharged - Time when: 8 Nov 1814 - Whither, and by what order, or number or re-entry: S. George No. 575 for Halifax by order of Sir George Provost

Garland, Levy   Prisoner 442. Rank: Private - By what ship or how taken: Troops - Time when: 24 Jun 1813 - Place where: Beaver Dam - Of what ship or corps: Land forces - Whether man of war, privateer or merchant vessel: Taken on shore - Time when received into custody: 7 Jul 1813 - From what ship or whence received: Steamboat - Exchanged, discharged, died, or escape: Discharged - Time when: 10 Aug 1813 - Whither, and by what order, or number or re-entry: HM Ship Regulius by order of Sir George Provost

Gates, Horatio   Prisoner 1304. Rank: Private - By what ship or how taken: Troops - Time when: 19 Dec 1813 - Place where:

American Prisoners of War held at Quebec during the War of 1812

Fort Niagara - Of what ship or corps: Land forces - Whether man of war, privateer or merchant vessel: Taken on shore - Time when received into custody: 29 Jan 1814 - From what ship or whence received: Montreal by land carriage - Exchanged, discharged, died, or escape: Discharged - Time when: 4 May 1814 - Whither, and by what order, or number or re-entry: United States

Gates, Jacob   Prisoner 793. Rank: Private - By what ship or how taken: Troops - Time when: 26 Jun 1813 - Place where: Beaver Dam - Of what ship or corps: Land forces - Whether man of war, privateer or merchant vessel: Taken on shore - Time when received into custody: 7 Jul 1813 - From what ship or whence received: Steamboat - Exchanged, discharged, died, or escape: Discharged - Time when: 10 Aug 1813 - Whither, and by what order, or number or re-entry: HM Ship Malpomena

Gazlir, John   Prisoner 1200. Rank: Seaman - By what ship or how taken: - Time when: - Place where: - Of what ship or corps: - Whether man of war, privateer or merchant vessel: - Time when received into custody: 18 Jan 1814 - From what ship or whence received: Montreal by land carriage - Exchanged, discharged, died, or escape: Discharged - Time when: 4 May 1814 - Whither, and by what order, or number or re-entry: United States

Gentry, John   Prisoner 1387. Rank: Private - By what ship or how taken: Troops - Time when: 19 Dec 1813 - Place where: Fort Niagara - Of what ship or corps: Land forces - Whether man of war, privateer or merchant vessel: Taken on shore - Time when received into custody: 29 Jan 1814 - From what ship or whence received: Montreal by land carriage - Exchanged, discharged, died, or escape: Discharged - Time when: 4 May 1814 - Whither, and by what order, or number or re-entry: United States

George, John   Prisoner 1266. Rank: Corporal - By what ship or how taken: Troops - Time when: 19 Dec 1813 - Place where: Fort Niagara - Of what ship or corps: Land forces - Whether man of war, privateer or merchant vessel: Taken on shore - Time when received into custody: 29 Jan 1814 - From what ship or whence received: Montreal by land carriage - Exchanged, discharged, died, or escape: Discharged - Time when: 4 May 1814 - Whither, and by what order, or number or re-entry: United States

German, J.   Prisoner 1563. Rank: Private - By what ship or how taken: Troops - Time when: 25 Jul 1814 - Place where: Lundy's Lane - Of what ship or corps: Land forces - Whether man of war, privateer or merchant vessel: Taken on shore - Time when received into custody: 16 Sep 1814 - From what ship or whence received: Steamboat - Exchanged, discharged, died, or escape: Discharged - Time when: - Whither, and by what order, or number or re-entry: H.M. Ship Ceylon

Gibbs, Eusebais   Prisoner 1240. Rank: Civilian - By what ship or how taken: Troops - Time when: 19 Dec 1813 - Place where: Fort Niagara - Of what ship or corps: Land forces - Whether man of war, privateer or merchant vessel: Taken on shore - Time when received into custody: 29 Jan 1814 - From what ship or whence received: Montreal by land carriage - Exchanged, discharged, died, or escape: Discharged - Time when: 27 Feb 1814 - Whither, and by what order, or number or re-entry: Volunteered for New Brunswick Fencibles

Gibbs, John   Prisoner 1023. Rank: Quarter Gunner - By what ship or how taken: Lord Melvin - Time when: 10 Aug 1813 - Place where: Lake Ontario - Of what ship or corps: Growler - Whether man of war, privateer or merchant vessel: Man of War - Time when received into custody: 5 Sep 1813 - From what ship or whence received: Steamboat - Exchanged, discharged, died, or escape: Discharged - Time when: - Whither, and by what order, or number or re-entry: HM Ship Success

Gibson, Ebenezer   Prisoner 232. Rank: Private - By what ship or how taken: Boats & Troops - Time when: 3 Jun 1813 - Place where: Lake Champlain - Of what ship or corps: Growler - Whether man of war, privateer or merchant vessel: Man of War - Time when received into custody: 9 Jun 1813 - From what ship or whence received: Batteaux - Exchanged, discharged, died, or escape: Discharged - Time when: 31 Oct 1813 - Whither, and by what order, or number or re-entry: Malabar Transport

Gibson, Fortune   Prisoner 1062. Rank: Private - By what ship or how taken: Troops - Time when: 24 Jun 1813 - Place where: Beaver Dam - Of what ship or corps: Land forces - Whether man of war, privateer or merchant vessel: Taken on shore - Time when received into custody: 5 Sep 1813 - From what ship or whence received: Steamboat - Exchanged, discharged, died, or escape: Discharged - Time when: 31 Oct 1813 - Whither, and by what order, or number or re-entry: Malabar Transport

Gibson, Samuel   Prisoner 1990. Rank: Seaman - By what ship or how taken: Troops - Time when: - Place where: - Of what ship or corps: George - Whether man of war, privateer or merchant vessel: Man of War - Time when received into custody: - From what ship or whence received: - Exchanged, discharged, died, or escape: Discharged - Time when: 13 Mar 1815 - Whither, and by what order, or number or re-entry: United States

American Prisoners of War held at Quebec during the War of 1812

Gifford, Francis   Prisoner 1277. Rank: Private - By what ship or how taken: Troops - Time when: 19 Dec 1813 - Place where: Fort Niagara - Of what ship or corps: Land forces - Whether man of war, privateer or merchant vessel: Taken on shore - Time when received into custody: 29 Jan 1814 - From what ship or whence received: Montreal by land carriage - Exchanged, discharged, died, or escape: Discharged - Time when: 4 May 1814 - Whither, and by what order, or number or re-entry: United States

Gilbert, Abique   Prisoner 898. Rank: Private - By what ship or how taken: Troops - Time when: 26 Jun 1813 - Place where: Beaver Dam - Of what ship or corps: Land forces - Whether man of war, privateer or merchant vessel: Taken on shore - Time when received into custody: 7 Jul 1813 - From what ship or whence received: Steamboat - Exchanged, discharged, died, or escape: Discharged - Time when: 10 Aug 1813 - Whither, and by what order, or number or re-entry: HM Ship Malpomena

Gilbert, John C.   Prisoner 1194. Rank: Citizen - By what ship or how taken: - Time when: - Place where: - Of what ship or corps: - Whether man of war, privateer or merchant vessel: - Time when received into custody: 12 Dec 1813 - From what ship or whence received: Town Goal - Exchanged, discharged, died, or escape: Discharged - Time when: 29 Mar 1814 - Whither, and by what order, or number or re-entry: United States

Gilbreath, John   Prisoner 1207. Rank: Lieutenant - By what ship or how taken: Troops - Time when: 19 Dec 1813 - Place where: Fort Niagara - Of what ship or corps: Land forces - Whether man of war, privateer or merchant vessel: Taken on shore - Time when received into custody: 18 Jan 1814 - From what ship or whence received: Montreal by land carriage - Exchanged, discharged, died, or escape: Discharged - Time when: 4 May 1814 - Whither, and by what order, or number or re-entry: United States

Gilchrist, James   Prisoner 1176. Rank: Private - By what ship or how taken: Troops - Time when: 5 May 1813 - Place where: Rapids Prince Reason - Of what ship or corps: Land forces - Whether man of war, privateer or merchant vessel: Taken on shore - Time when received into custody: 25 Nov 1813 - From what ship or whence received: Town Goal - Exchanged, discharged, died, or escape: Discharged - Time when: 12 Mar 1814 - Whither, and by what order, or number or re-entry: New Brunswick Fencibles

Giles, John   Prisoner 1599. Rank: Private - By what ship or how taken: Troops - Time when: 12 Aug 1814 - Place where: Fort Erie - Of what ship or corps: Land forces - Whether man of war, privateer or merchant vessel: Taken on shore - Time when received into custody: 5 Oct 1814 - From what ship or whence received: Montreal - Exchanged, discharged, died, or escape: Discharged - Time when: 8 Oct 1814 - Whither, and by what order, or number or re-entry: H.M. Ship Ceylon

Gill, Emauel   Prisoner 1761. Rank: Private - By what ship or how taken: Gun Boats - Time when: 6 Sep 1814 - Place where: Lake Huron - Of what ship or corps: Scorpion - Whether man of war, privateer or merchant vessel: Man of War - Time when received into custody: 1 Nov 1814 - From what ship or whence received: Montreal - Exchanged, discharged, died, or escape: Discharged - Time when: 8 Nov 1814 - Whither, and by what order, or number or re-entry: S. George No. 575 for Halifax by order of Sir George Provost

Gill, William   Prisoner 1468. Rank: Private - By what ship or how taken: Gun Boats - Time when: 29 May 1814 - Place where: Sandy Creek - Of what ship or corps: Land forces - Whether man of war, privateer or merchant vessel: Taken on shore - Time when received into custody: 12 Aug 1814 - From what ship or whence received: Royal Seaman No. 289 Transport - Exchanged, discharged, died, or escape: Discharged - Time when: 8 Oct 1814 - Whither, and by what order, or number or re-entry: Queen No. 415

Gillet, Eleazer   Prisoner 1817. Rank: Private - By what ship or how taken: Troops - Time when: 17 Sep 1814 - Place where: Fort Erie - Of what ship or corps: Land forces - Whether man of war, privateer or merchant vessel: Taken on shore - Time when received into custody: 1 Nov 1814 - From what ship or whence received: Montreal - Exchanged, discharged, died, or escape: Discharged - Time when: 8 Nov 1814 - Whither, and by what order, or number or re-entry: S. George No. 575 for Halifax by order of Sir George Provost

Gillies, James   Prisoner 1662. Rank: Cornet Dragoons - By what ship or how taken: - Time when: - Place where: - Of what ship or corps: - Whether man of war, privateer or merchant vessel: - Time when received into custody: 13 Oct 1814 - From what ship or whence received: Montreal - Exchanged, discharged, died, or escape: Discharged - Time when: 8 Oct 1814 - Whither, and by what order, or number or re-entry: Wolga No. 377

American Prisoners of War held at Quebec during the War of 1812

Gillis, Walter   Prisoner 1679. Rank: Master - By what ship or how taken: Gun Boats - Time when: 4 Aug 1814 - Place where: Lake Ontario - Of what ship or corps: Jack - Whether man of war, privateer or merchant vessel: Man of War - Time when received into custody: 23 Oct 1814 - From what ship or whence received: Montreal - Exchanged, discharged, died, or escape: Discharged - Time when: 10 Nov 1814 - Whither, and by what order, or number or re-entry: Lord Cartheart No. 161 for Halifax

Gilllispie, William   Prisoner 1097. Rank: Private - By what ship or how taken: Troops - Time when: 24 Aug 1813 - Place where: Fort George - Of what ship or corps: Land forces - Whether man of war, privateer or merchant vessel: Taken on shore - Time when received into custody: 10 Oct 1813 - From what ship or whence received: Steamboat - Exchanged, discharged, died, or escape: Discharged - Time when: 31 Oct 1813 - Whither, and by what order, or number or re-entry: Malabar Transport

Gillmore, John   Prisoner 1640. Rank: Private - By what ship or how taken: Troops - Time when: 6 Sep 1814 - Place where: Plattsburg - Of what ship or corps: Land forces - Whether man of war, privateer or merchant vessel: Taken on shore - Time when received into custody: 5 Oct 1814 - From what ship or whence received: Montreal - Exchanged, discharged, died, or escape: Discharged - Time when: 13 Mar 1815 - Whither, and by what order, or number or re-entry: United States

Ginning, Stephen   Prisoner 1813. Rank: Private - By what ship or how taken: Troops - Time when: 17 Sep 1814 - Place where: Fort Erie - Of what ship or corps: Land forces - Whether man of war, privateer or merchant vessel: Taken on shore - Time when received into custody: 1 Nov 1814 - From what ship or whence received: Montreal - Exchanged, discharged, died, or escape: Discharged - Time when: 8 Nov 1814 - Whither, and by what order, or number or re-entry: S. George No. 575 for Halifax by order of Sir George Provost

Gitchell, Josiah   Prisoner 164. Rank: Able seaman - By what ship or how taken: Boats & Troops - Time when: 3 Jun 1813 - Place where: Lake Champlain - Of what ship or corps: Eagle - Whether man of war, privateer or merchant vessel: Man of War - Time when received into custody: 9 Jun 1813 - From what ship or whence received: Batteaux - Exchanged, discharged, died, or escape: Discharged - Time when: 10 Oct 1813 - Whither, and by what order, or number or re-entry: Orlando Transport

Givin, James   Prisoner 521. Rank: Private - By what ship or how taken: Troops - Time when: 24 Jun 1813 - Place where: Beaver Dam - Of what ship or corps: Land forces - Whether man of war, privateer or merchant vessel: Taken on shore - Time when received into custody: 7 Jul 1813 - From what ship or whence received: Steamboat - Exchanged, discharged, died, or escape: Discharged - Time when: 10 Aug 1813 - Whither, and by what order, or number or re-entry: HM Ship Regulius by order of Sir George Provost

Glenn, James   Prisoner 1392. Rank: Private - By what ship or how taken: Troops - Time when: 19 Dec 1813 - Place where: Fort Niagara - Of what ship or corps: Land forces - Whether man of war, privateer or merchant vessel: Taken on shore - Time when received into custody: 29 Jan 1814 - From what ship or whence received: Montreal by land carriage - Exchanged, discharged, died, or escape: Discharged - Time when: 4 May 1814 - Whither, and by what order, or number or re-entry: United States

Goble, Daniel   Prisoner 1829. Rank: Private - By what ship or how taken: Troops - Time when: 17 Sep 1814 - Place where: Fort Erie - Of what ship or corps: Land forces - Whether man of war, privateer or merchant vessel: Taken on shore - Time when received into custody: 1 Nov 1814 - From what ship or whence received: Montreal - Exchanged, discharged, died, or escape: Discharged - Time when: 8 Nov 1814 - Whither, and by what order, or number or re-entry: S. George No. 575 for Halifax by order of Sir George Provost

Godard, Lewis   Prisoner 250. Rank: Lieutenant - By what ship or how taken: Boats & Troops - Time when: 24 Jun 1813 - Place where: Rec in charge of Beauport - Of what ship or corps: Land forces - Whether man of war, privateer or merchant vessel: Taken on shore - Time when received into custody: 24 Jun 1813 - From what ship or whence received: At Beauport - Exchanged, discharged, died, or escape: Discharged - Time when: 10 Aug 1813 - Whither, and by what order, or number or re-entry: Per order His Exellency Sir George Prevost

Godwin, Kimmel   Prisoner 533. Rank: Lieutenant - By what ship or how taken: Troops - Time when: 24 Jun 1813 - Place where: Beaver Dam - Of what ship or corps: Land forces - Whether man of war, privateer or merchant vessel: Taken on shore - Time when received into custody: 13 Jul 1813 - From what ship or whence received: Steamboat - Exchanged, discharged, died, or escape: Discharged - Time when: 10 Aug 1813 - Whither, and by what order, or number or re-entry: HM Ship Regulius by order of Sir George Provost

Gonsolby, Samuel   Prisoner 1848. Rank: Private - By what ship or how taken: Troops - Time when: 17 Sep 1814 - Place where: Fort Erie - Of what ship or corps: Land forces - Whether man of war, privateer or merchant vessel: Taken on shore - Time when received into custody: 1 Nov 1814 - From what ship or whence received: Montreal - Exchanged, discharged, died, or escape: Discharged - Time when: 8 Nov 1814 - Whither, and by what order, or number or re-entry: S. George No. 575 for Halifax by order of Sir George Provost

Goodall, J.   Prisoner 1616. Rank: Private - By what ship or how taken: Gun Boats - Time when: 12 Aug 1814 - Place where: Fort Erie - Of what ship or corps: Land forces - Whether man of war, privateer or merchant vessel: Taken on shore - Time when received into custody: 5 Oct 1814 - From what ship or whence received: Montreal - Exchanged, discharged, died, or escape: Discharged - Time when: 8 Oct 1814 - Whither, and by what order, or number or re-entry: H.M. Ship Ceylon

Goodnow, Elisha   Prisoner 13. Rank: Private - By what ship or how taken: Boats & Troops - Time when: 28 May 1813 - Place where: Stoney Point, Henderson Harbor - Of what ship or corps: Land forces - Whether man of war, privateer or merchant vessel: Taken on shore - Time when received into custody: 8 Jun 1813 - From what ship or whence received: Batteaux - Exchanged, discharged, died, or escape: Died - Time when: 13 May 1814 - Whither, and by what order, or number or re-entry: Debility

Goodrich, Henry C.   Prisoner 811. Rank: Private - By what ship or how taken: Troops - Time when: 26 Jun 1813 - Place where: Beaver Dam - Of what ship or corps: Land forces - Whether man of war, privateer or merchant vessel: Taken on shore - Time when received into custody: 7 Jul 1813 - From what ship or whence received: Steamboat - Exchanged, discharged, died, or escape: Discharged - Time when: 10 Aug 1813 - Whither, and by what order, or number or re-entry: HM Ship Malpomena

Goodwin, James   Prisoner 1056. Rank: Seaman - By what ship or how taken: Boats & Troops - Time when: 3 Jun 1813 - Place where: Lake Champlain - Of what ship or corps: Eagle - Whether man of war, privateer or merchant vessel: Man of War - Time when received into custody: 5 Sep 1813 - From what ship or whence received: Steamboat - Exchanged, discharged, died, or escape: Discharged - Time when: 18 Sep 1813 - Whither, and by what order, or number or re-entry: Dick Transport

Goodwin, Joseph   Prisoner 681. Rank: Private - By what ship or how taken: Troops - Time when: 26 Jun 1813 - Place where: Beaver Dam - Of what ship or corps: Land forces - Whether man of war, privateer or merchant vessel: Taken on shore - Time when received into custody: 7 Jul 1813 - From what ship or whence received: Steamboat - Exchanged, discharged, died, or escape: Discharged - Time when: 10 Aug 1813 - Whither, and by what order, or number or re-entry: HM Ship Regulius by order of Sir George Provost

Goodwin, Richard   Prisoner 331. Rank: Private - By what ship or how taken: Boats & Troops - Time when: 6 Jun 1813 - Place where: Stoney Point - Of what ship or corps: Land forces - Whether man of war, privateer or merchant vessel: Taken on shore - Time when received into custody: 28 Jun 1813 - From what ship or whence received: Quebec of Quebec - Exchanged, discharged, died, or escape: Discharged - Time when: 31 Oct 1813 - Whither, and by what order, or number or re-entry: Malabar Transport

Goodwin, Simeon   Prisoner 1117. Rank: Private - By what ship or how taken: Troops - Time when: 17 Oct 1813 - Place where: Red Mills - Of what ship or corps: Land forces - Whether man of war, privateer or merchant vessel: Taken on shore - Time when received into custody: 12 Oct 1813 - From what ship or whence received: Steamboat - Exchanged, discharged, died, or escape: Discharged - Time when: 31 Oct 1813 - Whither, and by what order, or number or re-entry: Malabar Transport

Gordon, John   Prisoner 1556. Rank: Private - By what ship or how taken: Troops - Time when: 25 Jul 1814 - Place where: Lundy's Lane - Of what ship or corps: Land forces - Whether man of war, privateer or merchant vessel: Taken on shore - Time when received into custody: 30 Aug 1814 - From what ship or whence received: Lady Delaval Schooner 578 - Exchanged, discharged, died, or escape: Discharged - Time when: 8 Oct 1814 - Whither, and by what order, or number or re-entry: Queen No. 415

Gorman, Edward   Prisoner 859. Rank: Private - By what ship or how taken: Troops - Time when: 26 Jun 1813 - Place where: Beaver Dam - Of what ship or corps: Land forces - Whether man of war, privateer or merchant vessel: Taken on shore - Time when received into custody: 7 Jul 1813 - From what ship or whence received: Steamboat - Exchanged, discharged, died, or escape: Discharged - Time when: 10 Aug 1813 - Whither, and by what order, or number or re-entry: HM Ship Malpomena

Gosset, Stephen   Prisoner 373. Rank: Private - By what ship or how taken: Troops - Time when: 6 Jun 1813 - Place where: Stoney Point - Of what ship or corps: Land forces - Whether man of war, privateer or merchant vessel: Taken on shore - Time when received into custody: 28 Jun 1813 - From what ship or whence received: Mary of Quebec - Exchanged, discharged, died, or escape: Discharged - Time when: 31 Oct 1813 - Whither, and by what order, or number or re-entry: Malabar Transport

American Prisoners of War held at Quebec during the War of 1812

Gouldsmith, Thomas   Prisoner 1983. Rank: Private - By what ship or how taken: Troops - Time when: 25 Jul 1814 - Place where: Lake Ontario - Of what ship or corps: Land forces - Whether man of war, privateer or merchant vessel: Taken on shore - Time when received into custody: 30 Dec 1814 - From what ship or whence received: Montreal - Exchanged, discharged, died, or escape: Discharged - Time when: 13 Mar 1815 - Whither, and by what order, or number or re-entry: United States

Gowan, Thomas   Prisoner 1651. Rank: Private - By what ship or how taken: Troops - Time when: 19 Dec 1813 - Place where: Niagara - Of what ship or corps: Land forces - Whether man of war, privateer or merchant vessel: Taken on shore - Time when received into custody: 5 Oct 1814 - From what ship or whence received: Montreal - Exchanged, discharged, died, or escape: Discharged - Time when: 8 Oct 1814 - Whither, and by what order, or number or re-entry: H.M. Ship Ceylon

Grant, A. T.   Prisoner 1562. Rank: Citizen - By what ship or how taken: Troops - Time when: 25 Jul 1814 - Place where: Lundy's Lane - Of what ship or corps: Land forces - Whether man of war, privateer or merchant vessel: Taken on shore - Time when received into custody: 12 Sep 1814 - From what ship or whence received: Lady Delaval Schooner 578 - Exchanged, discharged, died, or escape: Discharged - Time when: - Whither, and by what order, or number or re-entry: H.M. Ship Ceylon

Graves, Abraham   Prisoner 142. Rank: Ensign - By what ship or how taken: Boats & Troops - Time when: 28 May 1813 - Place where: Stoney Point, Henderson Harbor - Of what ship or corps: Land forces - Whether man of war, privateer or merchant vessel: Taken on shore - Time when received into custody: 8 Jul 1813 - From what ship or whence received: Batteaux - Exchanged, discharged, died, or escape: Discharged - Time when: 10 Aug 1813 - Whither, and by what order, or number or re-entry: HM Ship Regulius

Graves, Darius   Prisoner 763. Rank: Private - By what ship or how taken: Troops - Time when: 26 Jun 1813 - Place where: Beaver Dam - Of what ship or corps: Land forces - Whether man of war, privateer or merchant vessel: Taken on shore - Time when received into custody: 7 Jul 1813 - From what ship or whence received: Steamboat - Exchanged, discharged, died, or escape: Discharged - Time when: 10 Aug 1813 - Whither, and by what order, or number or re-entry: HM Ship Malpomena

Gray, John D.   Prisoner 878. Rank: Private - By what ship or how taken: Troops - Time when: 26 Jun 1813 - Place where: Beaver Dam - Of what ship or corps: Land forces - Whether man of war, privateer or merchant vessel: Taken on shore - Time when received into custody: 7 Jul 1813 - From what ship or whence received: Steamboat - Exchanged, discharged, died, or escape: Discharged - Time when: 10 Aug 1813 - Whither, and by what order, or number or re-entry: HM Ship Malpomena

Gray, Samuel   Prisoner 764. Rank: Private - By what ship or how taken: Troops - Time when: 26 Jun 1813 - Place where: Beaver Dam - Of what ship or corps: Land forces - Whether man of war, privateer or merchant vessel: Taken on shore - Time when received into custody: 7 Jul 1813 - From what ship or whence received: Steamboat - Exchanged, discharged, died, or escape: Discharged - Time when: 10 Aug 1813 - Whither, and by what order, or number or re-entry: HM Ship Regulius by order of Sir George Provost

Grayson, John   Prisoner 1319. Rank: Corporal - By what ship or how taken: Troops - Time when: 19 Dec 1813 - Place where: Fort Niagara - Of what ship or corps: Land forces - Whether man of war, privateer or merchant vessel: Taken on shore - Time when received into custody: 29 Jan 1814 - From what ship or whence received: Montreal by land carriage - Exchanged, discharged, died, or escape: Discharged - Time when: 27 Feb 1814 - Whither, and by what order, or number or re-entry: Volunteered for New Brunswick Fencibles

Gready, Martin   Prisoner 1075. Rank: Private - By what ship or how taken: Troops - Time when: 24 Aug 1813 - Place where: Fort George - Of what ship or corps: Land forces - Whether man of war, privateer or merchant vessel: Taken on shore - Time when received into custody: 10 Oct 1813 - From what ship or whence received: Steamboat - Exchanged, discharged, died, or escape: Discharged - Time when: 31 Oct 1813 - Whither, and by what order, or number or re-entry: Malabar Transport

Greaves, Philander   Prisoner 1241. Rank: Civilian - By what ship or how taken: Troops - Time when: 19 Dec 1813 - Place where: Fort Niagara - Of what ship or corps: Land forces - Whether man of war, privateer or merchant vessel: Taken on shore - Time when received into custody: 29 Jan 1814 - From what ship or whence received: Montreal by land carriage - Exchanged, discharged, died, or escape: Discharged - Time when: 27 Feb 1814 - Whither, and by what order, or number or re-entry: Volunteered for New Brunswick Fencibles

Greemo, Paul   Prisoner 1147. Rank: Private - By what ship or how taken: Troops - Time when: 15 Aug 1812 - Place where: Rapids Prince Reason - Of what ship or corps: Land forces - Whether man of war, privateer or merchant vessel: Taken on shore - Time when received into custody: 25 Nov 1813 - From what ship or whence received: Town Goal -

American Prisoners of War held at Quebec during the War of 1812

Exchanged, discharged, died, or escape: Discharged - Time when: 21 Apr 1814 - Whither, and by what order, or number or re-entry: United States

Green, Eli   Prisoner 55. Rank: Private - By what ship or how taken: Boats & Troops - Time when: 28 May 1813 - Place where: Stoney Point, Henderson Harbor - Of what ship or corps: Land forces - Whether man of war, privateer or merchant vessel: Taken on shore - Time when received into custody: 8 Jun 1813 - From what ship or whence received: Batteaux - Exchanged, discharged, died, or escape: Died - Time when: 23 Jul 1813 - Whither, and by what order, or number or re-entry: Dysentery

Green, James   Prisoner 176. Rank: Able seaman - By what ship or how taken: Boats & Troops - Time when: 3 Jun 1813 - Place where: Lake Champlain - Of what ship or corps: Growler - Whether man of war, privateer or merchant vessel: Man of War - Time when received into custody: 9 Jun 1813 - From what ship or whence received: Batteaux - Exchanged, discharged, died, or escape: Discharged - Time when: 7 Oct 1813 - Whither, and by what order, or number or re-entry: General Kempt Transport

Green, Jeremiah N.   Prisoner 1309. Rank: Private - By what ship or how taken: Troops - Time when: 19 Dec 1813 - Place where: Fort Niagara - Of what ship or corps: Land forces - Whether man of war, privateer or merchant vessel: Taken on shore - Time when received into custody: 29 Jan 1814 - From what ship or whence received: Montreal by land carriage - Exchanged, discharged, died, or escape: Discharged - Time when: 4 May 1814 - Whither, and by what order, or number or re-entry: United States

Green , John   Prisoner 516. Rank: Private - By what ship or how taken: Troops - Time when: 24 Jun 1813 - Place where: Beaver Dam - Of what ship or corps: Land forces - Whether man of war, privateer or merchant vessel: Taken on shore - Time when received into custody: 7 Jul 1813 - From what ship or whence received: Steamboat - Exchanged, discharged, died, or escape: Discharged - Time when: 10 Aug 1813 - Whither, and by what order, or number or re-entry: HM Ship Regulius by order of Sir George Provost

Green, Samuel   Prisoner 1754. Rank: Private - By what ship or how taken: Gun Boats - Time when: 3 Sep 1814 - Place where: Lake Huron - Of what ship or corps: Tigress - Whether man of war, privateer or merchant vessel: Man of War - Time when received into custody: 1 Nov 1814 - From what ship or whence received: Montreal - Exchanged, discharged, died, or escape: Discharged - Time when: 8 Nov 1814 - Whither, and by what order, or number or re-entry: S. George No. 575 for Halifax by order of Sir George Provost

Green, Thomas   Prisoner 954. Rank: Private - By what ship or how taken: Troops - Time when: 5 Jul 1813 - Place where: Fort Schisher - Of what ship or corps: Land forces - Whether man of war, privateer or merchant vessel: Taken on shore - Time when received into custody: 5 Sep 1813 - From what ship or whence received: Steamboat - Exchanged, discharged, died, or escape: Discharged - Time when: 31 Oct 1813 - Whither, and by what order, or number or re-entry: Malabar Transport

Green, Thomas   Prisoner 983. Rank: Sergeant - By what ship or how taken: Troops - Time when: 5 Jul 1813 - Place where: Fort Schisher - Of what ship or corps: Land forces - Whether man of war, privateer or merchant vessel: Taken on shore - Time when received into custody: 5 Sep 1813 - From what ship or whence received: Steamboat - Exchanged, discharged, died, or escape: Discharged - Time when: 31 Oct 1813 - Whither, and by what order, or number or re-entry: Malabar Transport

Green, William   Prisoner 160. Rank: Boy - By what ship or how taken: Boats & Troops - Time when: 3 Jun 1813 - Place where: Lake Champlain - Of what ship or corps: Eagle - Whether man of war, privateer or merchant vessel: Man of War - Time when received into custody: 9 Jun 1813 - From what ship or whence received: Batteaux - Exchanged, discharged, died, or escape: Discharged - Time when: 18 Sep 1813 - Whither, and by what order, or number or re-entry: Regulius Transport

Greenley, William   Prisoner 1359. Rank: Private - By what ship or how taken: Troops - Time when: 19 Dec 1813 - Place where: Fort Niagara - Of what ship or corps: Land forces - Whether man of war, privateer or merchant vessel: Taken on shore - Time when received into custody: 29 Jan 1814 - From what ship or whence received: Montreal by land carriage - Exchanged, discharged, died, or escape: Discharged - Time when: 4 May 1814 - Whither, and by what order, or number or re-entry: United States

Gregory, Francis H.   Prisoner 1716. Rank: Lieutenant - By what ship or how taken: Gun Boats - Time when: 6 Sep 1814 - Place where: Lake Huron - Of what ship or corps: Scorpion - Whether man of war, privateer or merchant vessel: Man of War - Time when received into custody: 28 Oct 1814 - From what ship or whence received: Montreal - Exchanged, discharged, died, or escape: Discharged - Time when: 10 Nov 1814 - Whither, and by what order, or number or re-entry: Lord Cartheart No. 161 for Halifax

American Prisoners of War held at Quebec during the War of 1812

Grey, James   Prisoner 704. Rank: Private - By what ship or how taken: Troops - Time when: 26 Jun 1813 - Place where: Beaver Dam - Of what ship or corps: Land forces - Whether man of war, privateer or merchant vessel: Taken on shore - Time when received into custody: 7 Jul 1813 - From what ship or whence received: Steamboat - Exchanged, discharged, died, or escape: Discharged - Time when: 10 Aug 1813 - Whither, and by what order, or number or re-entry: HM Ship Regulius by order of Sir George Provost

Griffin, John   Prisoner 485. Rank: Private - By what ship or how taken: Troops - Time when: 24 Jun 1813 - Place where: Beaver Dam - Of what ship or corps: Land forces - Whether man of war, privateer or merchant vessel: Taken on shore - Time when received into custody: 7 Jul 1813 - From what ship or whence received: Steamboat - Exchanged, discharged, died, or escape: Discharged - Time when: 10 Aug 1813 - Whither, and by what order, or number or re-entry: HM Ship Regulius by order of Sir George Provost

Griffin, William   Prisoner 1745. Rank: Seaman - By what ship or how taken: Gun Boats - Time when: 3 Sep 1814 - Place where: Lake Huron - Of what ship or corps: Tigress - Whether man of war, privateer or merchant vessel: Man of War - Time when received into custody: 1 Nov 1814 - From what ship or whence received: Montreal - Exchanged, discharged, died, or escape: Discharged - Time when: 7 Nov 1814 - Whither, and by what order, or number or re-entry: Transport Freedom No. 582 by orders of his Excellency Sir George Provost

Griffiths, William   Prisoner 1573. Rank: Quarter Gunner - By what ship or how taken: Gun Boats - Time when: 12 Aug 1814 - Place where: Fort Erie - Of what ship or corps: Somers - Whether man of war, privateer or merchant vessel: Man of War - Time when received into custody: 5 Oct 1814 - From what ship or whence received: Montreal - Exchanged, discharged, died, or escape: Discharged - Time when: 10 Nov 1814 - Whither, and by what order, or number or re-entry: Freedom No. 582

Grimes, John   Prisoner 816. Rank: Private - By what ship or how taken: Troops - Time when: 26 Jun 1813 - Place where: Beaver Dam - Of what ship or corps: Land forces - Whether man of war, privateer or merchant vessel: Taken on shore - Time when received into custody: 7 Jul 1813 - From what ship or whence received: Steamboat - Exchanged, discharged, died, or escape: Discharged - Time when: 10 Aug 1813 - Whither, and by what order, or number or re-entry: HM Ship Malpomena

Grinder, John   Prisoner 1787. Rank: Private - By what ship or how taken: Troops - Time when: 7 Sep 1814 - Place where: Fort Erie - Of what ship or corps: Land forces - Whether man of war, privateer or merchant vessel: Taken on shore - Time when received into custody: 1 Nov 1814 - From what ship or whence received: Montreal - Exchanged, discharged, died, or escape: Discharged - Time when: 8 Nov 1814 - Whither, and by what order, or number or re-entry: S. George No. 575 for Halifax by order of Sir George Provost

Griner, George   Prisoner 873. Rank: Private - By what ship or how taken: Troops - Time when: 26 Jun 1813 - Place where: Beaver Dam - Of what ship or corps: Land forces - Whether man of war, privateer or merchant vessel: Taken on shore - Time when received into custody: 7 Jul 1813 - From what ship or whence received: Steamboat - Exchanged, discharged, died, or escape: Discharged - Time when: 10 Aug 1813 - Whither, and by what order, or number or re-entry: HM Ship Malpomena

Grisold, James   Prisoner 1694. Rank: Private - By what ship or how taken: Troops - Time when: 30 Jul 1814 - Place where: Chippewa - Of what ship or corps: Land forces - Whether man of war, privateer or merchant vessel: Taken on shore - Time when received into custody: 23 Oct 1814 - From what ship or whence received: Montreal - Exchanged, discharged, died, or escape: Discharged - Time when: 7 Jan 1814 - Whither, and by what order, or number or re-entry: S. George No. 575 for Halifax

Griswold, Samuel B.   Prisoner 537. Rank: Lieutenant - By what ship or how taken: Troops - Time when: 24 Jun 1813 - Place where: Beaver Dam - Of what ship or corps: Land forces - Whether man of war, privateer or merchant vessel: Taken on shore - Time when received into custody: 13 Jul 1813 - From what ship or whence received: Steamboat - Exchanged, discharged, died, or escape: Discharged - Time when: 13 Dec 1813 - Whither, and by what order, or number or re-entry: United States

Groomes, Richard   Prisoner 1162. Rank: Corporal - By what ship or how taken: Troops - Time when: 5 May 1813 - Place where: Fort Maggie - Of what ship or corps: Land forces - Whether man of war, privateer or merchant vessel: Taken on shore - Time when received into custody: 25 Nov 1813 - From what ship or whence received: Town Goal - Exchanged, discharged, died, or escape: Discharged - Time when: 12 Mar 1814 - Whither, and by what order, or number or re-entry: New Brunswick Fencibles

Grouse, Frederick   Prisoner 441. Rank: Private - By what ship or how taken: Troops - Time when: 24 Jun 1813 - Place where: Beaver Dam - Of what ship or corps: Land forces - Whether man of war, privateer or merchant vessel: Taken on shore - Time when received into custody: 7 Jul 1813 - From what ship or whence received: Steamboat - Exchanged,

discharged, died, or escape: Discharged - Time when: 10 Aug 1813 - Whither, and by what order, or number or re-entry: HM Ship Regulius by order of Sir George Provost

Groves, George   Prisoner 1290. Rank: Private - By what ship or how taken: Troops - Time when: 19 Dec 1813 - Place where: Fort Niagara - Of what ship or corps: Land forces - Whether man of war, privateer or merchant vessel: Taken on shore - Time when received into custody: 29 Jan 1814 - From what ship or whence received: Montreal by land carriage - Exchanged, discharged, died, or escape: Discharged - Time when: 4 May 1814 - Whither, and by what order, or number or re-entry: United States

Gruet, James   Prisoner 863. Rank: Private - By what ship or how taken: Troops - Time when: 26 Jun 1813 - Place where: Beaver Dam - Of what ship or corps: Land forces - Whether man of war, privateer or merchant vessel: Taken on shore - Time when received into custody: 7 Jul 1813 - From what ship or whence received: Steamboat - Exchanged, discharged, died, or escape: Discharged - Time when: 10 Aug 1813 - Whither, and by what order, or number or re-entry: HM Ship Malpomena

Gruet, William   Prisoner 870. Rank: Private - By what ship or how taken: Troops - Time when: 26 Jun 1813 - Place where: Beaver Dam - Of what ship or corps: Land forces - Whether man of war, privateer or merchant vessel: Taken on shore - Time when received into custody: 7 Jul 1813 - From what ship or whence received: Steamboat - Exchanged, discharged, died, or escape: Discharged - Time when: 10 Aug 1813 - Whither, and by what order, or number or re-entry: HM Ship Malpomena

Guest, Charles   Prisoner 1218. Rank: Private - By what ship or how taken: Troops - Time when: 19 Dec 1813 - Place where: Fort Niagara - Of what ship or corps: Land forces - Whether man of war, privateer or merchant vessel: Taken on shore - Time when received into custody: 29 Jan 1814 - From what ship or whence received: Montreal by land carriage - Exchanged, discharged, died, or escape: Discharged - Time when: 4 May 1814 - Whither, and by what order, or number or re-entry: United States

Gulintine, James   Prisoner 1879. Rank: Private - By what ship or how taken: Troops - Time when: 17 Sep 1814 - Place where: Fort Erie - Of what ship or corps: Land forces - Whether man of war, privateer or merchant vessel: Taken on shore - Time when received into custody: 1 Nov 1814 - From what ship or whence received: Montreal - Exchanged, discharged, died, or escape: Discharged - Time when: 8 Nov 1814 - Whither, and by what order, or number or re-entry: S. George No. 575 for Halifax by order of Sir George Provost

Gunies, Michael   Prisoner 551. Rank: Sergeant - By what ship or how taken: Troops - Time when: 26 Jun 1813 - Place where: Beaver Dam - Of what ship or corps: Land forces - Whether man of war, privateer or merchant vessel: Taken on shore - Time when received into custody: 13 Jul 1813 - From what ship or whence received: Steamboat - Exchanged, discharged, died, or escape: Discharged - Time when: 10 Aug 1813 - Whither, and by what order, or number or re-entry: HM Ship Regulius by order of Sir George Provost

Gunison, James   Prisoner 1118. Rank: Private - By what ship or how taken: Troops - Time when: 17 Oct 1813 - Place where: Red Mills - Of what ship or corps: Land forces - Whether man of war, privateer or merchant vessel: Taken on shore - Time when received into custody: 12 Oct 1813 - From what ship or whence received: Steamboat - Exchanged, discharged, died, or escape: Discharged - Time when: 31 Oct 1813 - Whither, and by what order, or number or re-entry: Malabar Transport

Gustavas, John   Prisoner 1677. Rank: Seaman - By what ship or how taken: Gun Boats - Time when: 10 Aug 1814 - Place where: Lake Ontario - Of what ship or corps: Forsyth - Whether man of war, privateer or merchant vessel: Man of War - Time when received into custody: 23 Oct 1814 - From what ship or whence received: Montreal - Exchanged, discharged, died, or escape: Discharged - Time when: 7 Nov 1814 - Whither, and by what order, or number or re-entry: Transport Freedom No. 582 by orders of his Excellency Sir George Provost

Guton, Thomas   Prisoner 320. Rank: Private - By what ship or how taken: Boats & Troops - Time when: 6 Jun 1813 - Place where: Stoney Point - Of what ship or corps: Land forces - Whether man of war, privateer or merchant vessel: Taken on shore - Time when received into custody: 28 Jun 1813 - From what ship or whence received: Quebec of Quebec - Exchanged, discharged, died, or escape: Died - Time when: 23 Aug 1813 - Whither, and by what order, or number or re-entry:

Guynnup, John   Prisoner 1055. Rank: Private - By what ship or how taken: Lord Melvin - Time when: 10 Aug 1813 - Place where: Lake Ontario - Of what ship or corps: Growler - Whether man of war, privateer or merchant vessel: Man of War - Time when received into custody: 5 Sep 1813 - From what ship or whence received: Steamboat - Exchanged, discharged, died, or escape: Discharged - Time when: 31 Oct 1813 - Whither, and by what order, or number or re-entry: Malabar Transport

American Prisoners of War held at Quebec during the War of 1812

Haddard, Whitman   Prisoner 1805. Rank: Private - By what ship or how taken: Troops - Time when: 17 Sep 1814 - Place where: Fort Erie - Of what ship or corps: Land forces - Whether man of war, privateer or merchant vessel: Taken on shore - Time when received into custody: 1 Nov 1814 - From what ship or whence received: Montreal - Exchanged, discharged, died, or escape: Discharged - Time when: 8 Nov 1814 - Whither, and by what order, or number or re-entry: S. George No. 575 for Halifax by order of Sir George Provost

Hagan, Thomas   Prisoner 1349. Rank: Sergeant - By what ship or how taken: Troops - Time when: 19 Dec 1813 - Place where: Fort Niagara - Of what ship or corps: Land forces - Whether man of war, privateer or merchant vessel: Taken on shore - Time when received into custody: 29 Jan 1814 - From what ship or whence received: Montreal by land carriage - Exchanged, discharged, died, or escape: Discharged - Time when: 4 May 1814 - Whither, and by what order, or number or re-entry: United States

Hagar, Henry   Prisoner 7. Rank: Private - By what ship or how taken: Boats & Troops - Time when: 28 May 1813 - Place where: Stoney Point, Henderson Harbor - Of what ship or corps: Land forces - Whether man of war, privateer or merchant vessel: Taken on shore - Time when received into custody: 8 Jun 1813 - From what ship or whence received: Batteaux - Exchanged, discharged, died, or escape: Discharged - Time when: 31 Oct 1813 - Whither, and by what order, or number or re-entry: Malabar Transport

Hagar, John   Prisoner 740. Rank: Private - By what ship or how taken: Troops - Time when: 26 Jun 1813 - Place where: Beaver Dam - Of what ship or corps: Land forces - Whether man of war, privateer or merchant vessel: Taken on shore - Time when received into custody: 7 Jul 1813 - From what ship or whence received: Steamboat - Exchanged, discharged, died, or escape: Discharged - Time when: 10 Aug 1813 - Whither, and by what order, or number or re-entry: HM Ship Regulius by order of Sir George Provost

Hagerty, Thomas   Prisoner 1884. Rank: Private - By what ship or how taken: Troops - Time when: 17 Sep 1814 - Place where: Fort Erie - Of what ship or corps: Land forces - Whether man of war, privateer or merchant vessel: Taken on shore - Time when received into custody: 1 Nov 1814 - From what ship or whence received: Montreal - Exchanged, discharged, died, or escape: Discharged - Time when: 8 Nov 1814 - Whither, and by what order, or number or re-entry: S. George No. 575 for Halifax by order of Sir George Provost

Haggerty, Leve   Prisoner 806. Rank: Private - By what ship or how taken: Troops - Time when: 26 Jun 1813 - Place where: Beaver Dam - Of what ship or corps: Land forces - Whether man of war, privateer or merchant vessel: Taken on shore - Time when received into custody: 7 Jul 1813 - From what ship or whence received: Steamboat - Exchanged, discharged, died, or escape: Discharged - Time when: 10 Aug 1813 - Whither, and by what order, or number or re-entry: HM Ship Malpomena

Hagherty, Mathew   Prisoner 623. Rank: Private - By what ship or how taken: Troops - Time when: 24 Jun 1813 - Place where: Stoney Point - Of what ship or corps: Land forces - Whether man of war, privateer or merchant vessel: Taken on shore - Time when received into custody: 7 Jul 1813 - From what ship or whence received: Steamboat - Exchanged, discharged, died, or escape: Discharged - Time when: 9 Aug 1813 - Whither, and by what order, or number or re-entry: HM Ship Wasp

Haidy, Amos   Prisoner 840. Rank: Private - By what ship or how taken: Troops - Time when: 26 Jun 1813 - Place where: Beaver Dam - Of what ship or corps: Land forces - Whether man of war, privateer or merchant vessel: Taken on shore - Time when received into custody: 7 Jul 1813 - From what ship or whence received: Steamboat - Exchanged, discharged, died, or escape: Discharged - Time when: 10 Aug 1813 - Whither, and by what order, or number or re-entry: HM Ship Malpomena

Haines, Daniel   Prisoner 209. Rank: Private - By what ship or how taken: Boats & Troops - Time when: 3 Jun 1813 - Place where: Lake Champlain - Of what ship or corps: Eagle - Whether man of war, privateer or merchant vessel: Man of War - Time when received into custody: 9 Jun 1813 - From what ship or whence received: Batteaux - Exchanged, discharged, died, or escape: Discharged - Time when: 31 Oct 1813 - Whither, and by what order, or number or re-entry: Malabar Transport

Haines, Joel   Prisoner 1307. Rank: Private - By what ship or how taken: Troops - Time when: 19 Dec 1813 - Place where: Fort Niagara - Of what ship or corps: Land forces - Whether man of war, privateer or merchant vessel: Taken on shore - Time when received into custody: 29 Jan 1814 - From what ship or whence received: Montreal by land carriage - Exchanged, discharged, died, or escape: Discharged - Time when: 4 May 1814 - Whither, and by what order, or number or re-entry: United States

Halbert, Lotha   Prisoner 1444. Rank: Private - By what ship or how taken: Troops - Time when: 6 May 1814 - Place where: Oswago - Of what ship or corps: Land forces - Whether man of war, privateer or merchant vessel: Taken on shore - Time when received into custody: 12 Aug 1814 - From what ship or whence received: Royal Seaman No. 289

American Prisoners of War held at Quebec during the War of 1812

Transport - Exchanged, discharged, died, or escape: Discharged - Time when: 8 Oct 1814 - Whither, and by what order, or number or re-entry: Queen No. 415

Hale, William   Prisoner 639. Rank: Private - By what ship or how taken: Troops - Time when: 24 Jun 1813 - Place where: Stoney Point - Of what ship or corps: Land forces - Whether man of war, privateer or merchant vessel: Taken on shore - Time when received into custody: 7 Jul 1813 - From what ship or whence received: Steamboat - Exchanged, discharged, died, or escape: Discharged - Time when: 10 Aug 1813 - Whither, and by what order, or number or re-entry: HM Ship Regulius by order of Sir George Provost

Halison, Jacob   Prisoner 1252. Rank: Private - By what ship or how taken: Troops - Time when: 19 Dec 1813 - Place where: Fort Niagara - Of what ship or corps: Land forces - Whether man of war, privateer or merchant vessel: Taken on shore - Time when received into custody: 29 Jan 1814 - From what ship or whence received: Montreal by land carriage - Exchanged, discharged, died, or escape: Discharged - Time when: 27 Feb 1814 - Whither, and by what order, or number or re-entry: Volunteered for New Brunswick Fencibles

Hall, Allen   Prisoner 1171. Rank: Private - By what ship or how taken: Troops - Time when: 5 May 1813 - Place where: Rapids Prince Reason - Of what ship or corps: Land forces - Whether man of war, privateer or merchant vessel: Taken on shore - Time when received into custody: 25 Nov 1813 - From what ship or whence received: Town Goal - Exchanged, discharged, died, or escape: Discharged - Time when: 12 Mar 1814 - Whither, and by what order, or number or re-entry: New Brunswick Fencibles

Hall, Aug. C.   Prisoner 936. Rank: Private - By what ship or how taken: Troops - Time when: 26 Jun 1813 - Place where: Beaver Dam - Of what ship or corps: Land forces - Whether man of war, privateer or merchant vessel: Taken on shore - Time when received into custody: 21 Jul 1813 - From what ship or whence received: Steamboat - Exchanged, discharged, died, or escape: Discharged - Time when: 10 Aug 1813 - Whither, and by what order, or number or re-entry: HM Ship Malpomena

Hall, Daniel   Prisoner 1887. Rank: Private - By what ship or how taken: Troops - Time when: 17 Sep 1814 - Place where: Fort Erie - Of what ship or corps: Land forces - Whether man of war, privateer or merchant vessel: Taken on shore - Time when received into custody: 1 Nov 1814 - From what ship or whence received: Montreal - Exchanged, discharged, died, or escape: Discharged - Time when: 8 Nov 1814 - Whither, and by what order, or number or re-entry: S. George No. 575 for Halifax by order of Sir George Provost

Hall, Lot   Prisoner 85. Rank: Private - By what ship or how taken: Boats & Troops - Time when: 28 May 1813 - Place where: Stoney Point, Henderson Harbor - Of what ship or corps: Land forces - Whether man of war, privateer or merchant vessel: Taken on shore - Time when received into custody: 8 Jun 1813 - From what ship or whence received: Batteaux - Exchanged, discharged, died, or escape: Discharged - Time when: 31 Oct 1813 - Whither, and by what order, or number or re-entry: Malabar Transport

Hall, William   Prisoner 1337. Rank: Private - By what ship or how taken: Troops - Time when: 19 Dec 1813 - Place where: Fort Niagara - Of what ship or corps: Land forces - Whether man of war, privateer or merchant vessel: Taken on shore - Time when received into custody: 29 Jan 1814 - From what ship or whence received: Montreal by land carriage - Exchanged, discharged, died, or escape: Discharged - Time when: 4 May 1814 - Whither, and by what order, or number or re-entry: United States

Hallz or Hall, Orin or Horace   Prisoner 1082. Rank: Private - By what ship or how taken: Troops - Time when: 24 Aug 1813 - Place where: Fort George - Of what ship or corps: Land forces - Whether man of war, privateer or merchant vessel: Taken on shore - Time when received into custody: 10 Oct 1813 - From what ship or whence received: Steamboat - Exchanged, discharged, died, or escape: Died - Time when: 28 Mar 1814 - Whither, and by what order, or number or re-entry: Phrenitis

Halted, John   Prisoner 488. Rank: Private - By what ship or how taken: Troops - Time when: 24 Jun 1813 - Place where: Beaver Dam - Of what ship or corps: Land forces - Whether man of war, privateer or merchant vessel: Taken on shore - Time when received into custody: 7 Jul 1813 - From what ship or whence received: Steamboat - Exchanged, discharged, died, or escape: Died - Time when: 5 Jul 1813 - Whither, and by what order, or number or re-entry: Dysentery

Ham, Robert   Prisoner 225. Rank: Private - By what ship or how taken: Boats & Troops - Time when: 3 Jun 1813 - Place where: Lake Champlain - Of what ship or corps: Eagle - Whether man of war, privateer or merchant vessel: Man of War - Time when received into custody: 9 Jun 1813 - From what ship or whence received: Batteaux - Exchanged, discharged, died, or escape: Discharged - Time when: 31 Oct 1813 - Whither, and by what order, or number or re-entry: Malabar Transport

American Prisoners of War held at Quebec during the War of 1812

Ham, Rufus   Prisoner 211. Rank: Private - By what ship or how taken: Boats & Troops - Time when: 3 Jun 1813 - Place where: Lake Champlain - Of what ship or corps: Growler - Whether man of war, privateer or merchant vessel: Man of War - Time when received into custody: 9 Jun 1813 - From what ship or whence received: Batteaux - Exchanged, discharged, died, or escape: Discharged - Time when: 31 Oct 1813 - Whither, and by what order, or number or re-entry: Malabar Transport

Hamilton, James   Prisoner 910. Rank: Private - By what ship or how taken: Troops - Time when: 26 Jun 1813 - Place where: Beaver Dam - Of what ship or corps: Land forces - Whether man of war, privateer or merchant vessel: Taken on shore - Time when received into custody: 21 Jul 1813 - From what ship or whence received: Steamboat - Exchanged, discharged, died, or escape: Discharged - Time when: 10 Aug 1813 - Whither, and by what order, or number or re-entry: HM Ship Malpomena

Hamilton, John   Prisoner 1243. Rank: Private - By what ship or how taken: Troops - Time when: 19 Dec 1813 - Place where: Fort Niagara - Of what ship or corps: Land forces - Whether man of war, privateer or merchant vessel: Taken on shore - Time when received into custody: 29 Jan 1814 - From what ship or whence received: Montreal by land carriage - Exchanged, discharged, died, or escape: Discharged - Time when: 27 Feb 1814 - Whither, and by what order, or number or re-entry: Volunteered for New Brunswick Fencibles

Hammond, Jed.   Prisoner 1451. Rank: Private - By what ship or how taken: Troops - Time when: 6 May 1814 - Place where: Oswago - Of what ship or corps: Land forces - Whether man of war, privateer or merchant vessel: Taken on shore - Time when received into custody: 12 Aug 1814 - From what ship or whence received: Royal Seaman No. 289 Transport - Exchanged, discharged, died, or escape: Discharged - Time when: 8 Oct 1814 - Whither, and by what order, or number or re-entry: Queen No. 415

Hammond, S.   Prisoner 1516. Rank: Private - By what ship or how taken: Troops - Time when: 25 Jul 1814 - Place where: Lundy's Lane - Of what ship or corps: Land forces - Whether man of war, privateer or merchant vessel: Taken on shore - Time when received into custody: 30 Aug 1814 - From what ship or whence received: Lady Delaval Schooner 578 - Exchanged, discharged, died, or escape: Discharged - Time when: 8 Oct 1814 - Whither, and by what order, or number or re-entry: Queen No. 415

Hamwood, George   Prisoner 124. Rank: Private - By what ship or how taken: Boats & Troops - Time when: 28 May 1813 - Place where: Stoney Point, Henderson Harbor - Of what ship or corps: Land forces - Whether man of war, privateer or merchant vessel: Taken on shore - Time when received into custody: 8 Jun 1813 - From what ship or whence received: Batteaux - Exchanged, discharged, died, or escape: Discharged - Time when: 10 Oct 1813 - Whither, and by what order, or number or re-entry: H.M. Ship Diver

Handing, Amasa   Prisoner 1299. Rank: Private - By what ship or how taken: Troops - Time when: 19 Dec 1813 - Place where: Fort Niagara - Of what ship or corps: Land forces - Whether man of war, privateer or merchant vessel: Taken on shore - Time when received into custody: 29 Jan 1814 - From what ship or whence received: Montreal by land carriage - Exchanged, discharged, died, or escape: Discharged - Time when: 4 May 1814 - Whither, and by what order, or number or re-entry: United States

Hankins, Gilbreath   Prisoner 1371. Rank: Sergeant - By what ship or how taken: Troops - Time when: 19 Dec 1813 - Place where: Fort Niagara - Of what ship or corps: Land forces - Whether man of war, privateer or merchant vessel: Taken on shore - Time when received into custody: 29 Jan 1814 - From what ship or whence received: Montreal by land carriage - Exchanged, discharged, died, or escape: Discharged - Time when: 4 May 1814 - Whither, and by what order, or number or re-entry: United States

Hansel, William   Prisoner 1336. Rank: Private - By what ship or how taken: Troops - Time when: 19 Dec 1813 - Place where: Fort Niagara - Of what ship or corps: Land forces - Whether man of war, privateer or merchant vessel: Taken on shore - Time when received into custody: 29 Jan 1814 - From what ship or whence received: Montreal by land carriage - Exchanged, discharged, died, or escape: Discharged - Time when: 4 May 1814 - Whither, and by what order, or number or re-entry: United States

Hanyan, Elihu   Prisoner 855. Rank: Private - By what ship or how taken: Troops - Time when: 26 Jun 1813 - Place where: Beaver Dam - Of what ship or corps: Land forces - Whether man of war, privateer or merchant vessel: Taken on shore - Time when received into custody: 7 Jul 1813 - From what ship or whence received: Steamboat - Exchanged, discharged, died, or escape: Discharged - Time when: 10 Aug 1813 - Whither, and by what order, or number or re-entry: HM Ship Malpomena

Hard, Daniel   Prisoner 1107. Rank: Corporal - By what ship or how taken: Troops - Time when: 17 Oct 1813 - Place where: Red Mills - Of what ship or corps: Land forces - Whether man of war, privateer or merchant vessel: Taken on shore - Time when received into custody: 12 Oct 1813 - From what ship or whence received: Steamboat - Exchanged,

American Prisoners of War held at Quebec during the War of 1812

discharged, died, or escape: Discharged - Time when: 31 Oct 1813 - Whither, and by what order, or number or re-entry: Malabar Transport

Hardy, Andrew H.   Prisoner 1519. Rank: Private - By what ship or how taken: Troops - Time when: 25 Jul 1814 - Place where: Lundy's Lane - Of what ship or corps: Land forces - Whether man of war, privateer or merchant vessel: Taken on shore - Time when received into custody: 30 Aug 1814 - From what ship or whence received: Lady Delaval Schooner 578 - Exchanged, discharged, died, or escape: Discharged - Time when: 10 Nov 1814 - Whither, and by what order, or number or re-entry: Soverign Transport No. 628 to Halifax by orders of Sir George Provost

Hardy, Elisha   Prisoner 399. Rank: Private - By what ship or how taken: Troops - Time when: 6 Jun 1813 - Place where: Stoney Point - Of what ship or corps: Land forces - Whether man of war, privateer or merchant vessel: Taken on shore - Time when received into custody: 28 Jun 1813 - From what ship or whence received: Mary of Quebec - Exchanged, discharged, died, or escape: Discharged - Time when: 24 Nov 1813 - Whither, and by what order, or number or re-entry: H.M. Ship Aeolus

Hargood, George   Prisoner 698. Rank: Private - By what ship or how taken: Troops - Time when: 26 Jun 1813 - Place where: Beaver Dam - Of what ship or corps: Land forces - Whether man of war, privateer or merchant vessel: Taken on shore - Time when received into custody: 7 Jul 1813 - From what ship or whence received: Steamboat - Exchanged, discharged, died, or escape: Discharged - Time when: 10 Aug 1813 - Whither, and by what order, or number or re-entry: HM Ship Regulius by order of Sir George Provost

Harkness, James   Prisoner 657. Rank: Private - By what ship or how taken: Troops - Time when: 24 Jun 1813 - Place where: Stoney Point - Of what ship or corps: Land forces - Whether man of war, privateer or merchant vessel: Taken on shore - Time when received into custody: 7 Jul 1813 - From what ship or whence received: Steamboat - Exchanged, discharged, died, or escape: Discharged - Time when: 10 Aug 1813 - Whither, and by what order, or number or re-entry: HM Ship Regulius by order of Sir George Provost

Harley, George   Prisoner 1308. Rank: Private - By what ship or how taken: Troops - Time when: 19 Dec 1813 - Place where: Fort Niagara - Of what ship or corps: Land forces - Whether man of war, privateer or merchant vessel: Taken on shore - Time when received into custody: 29 Jan 1814 - From what ship or whence received: Montreal by land carriage - Exchanged, discharged, died, or escape: Discharged - Time when: 4 May 1814 - Whither, and by what order, or number or re-entry: United States

Harper, William   Prisoner 1225. Rank: Private - By what ship or how taken: Troops - Time when: 19 Dec 1813 - Place where: Fort Niagara - Of what ship or corps: Land forces - Whether man of war, privateer or merchant vessel: Taken on shore - Time when received into custody: 29 Jan 1814 - From what ship or whence received: Montreal by land carriage - Exchanged, discharged, died, or escape: Discharged - Time when: 27 Feb 1814 - Whither, and by what order, or number or re-entry: Volunteered for New Brunswick Fencibles

Harrington, Estes   Prisoner 951. Rank: Sergeant - By what ship or how taken: Troops - Time when: 5 Jul 1813 - Place where: Fort Schisher - Of what ship or corps: Land forces - Whether man of war, privateer or merchant vessel: Taken on shore - Time when received into custody: 5 Sep 1813 - From what ship or whence received: Steamboat - Exchanged, discharged, died, or escape: Discharged - Time when: 31 Oct 1813 - Whither, and by what order, or number or re-entry: Malabar Transport

Harris, James   Prisoner 1943. Rank: Private - By what ship or how taken: Troops - Time when: 17 Sep 1814 - Place where: Fort Erie - Of what ship or corps: Land forces - Whether man of war, privateer or merchant vessel: Taken on shore - Time when received into custody: 1 Nov 1814 - From what ship or whence received: Montreal - Exchanged, discharged, died, or escape: Discharged - Time when: 13 Mar 1815 - Whither, and by what order, or number or re-entry: United States

Harris, James   Prisoner 175. Rank: Able seaman - By what ship or how taken: Boats & Troops - Time when: 3 Jun 1813 - Place where: Lake Champlain - Of what ship or corps: Growler - Whether man of war, privateer or merchant vessel: Man of War - Time when received into custody: 9 Jun 1813 - From what ship or whence received: Batteaux - Exchanged, discharged, died, or escape: Discharged - Time when: 31 Oct 1813 - Whither, and by what order, or number or re-entry: Malabar Transport

Harris, James   Prisoner 1422. Rank: Private - By what ship or how taken: Troops - Time when: 19 Dec 1813 - Place where: Fort Niagara - Of what ship or corps: Land forces - Whether man of war, privateer or merchant vessel: Taken on shore - Time when received into custody: 29 Jan 1814 - From what ship or whence received: Montreal by land carriage - Exchanged, discharged, died, or escape: Discharged - Time when: 4 May 1814 - Whither, and by what order, or number or re-entry: United States

American Prisoners of War held at Quebec during the War of 1812

Harris, Robert   Prisoner 1032. Rank: Seaman - By what ship or how taken: Lord Melvin - Time when: 10 Aug 1813 - Place where: Lake Ontario - Of what ship or corps: Growler - Whether man of war, privateer or merchant vessel: Man of War - Time when received into custody: 5 Sep 1813 - From what ship or whence received: Steamboat - Exchanged, discharged, died, or escape: Discharged - Time when: 31 Oct 1813 - Whither, and by what order, or number or re-entry: Malabar Transport

Harrodon, Elisha   Prisoner 42. Rank: Private - By what ship or how taken: Boats & Troops - Time when: 28 May 1813 - Place where: Stoney Point, Henderson Harbor - Of what ship or corps: Land forces - Whether man of war, privateer or merchant vessel: Taken on shore - Time when received into custody: 8 Jun 1813 - From what ship or whence received: Batteaux - Exchanged, discharged, died, or escape: Died - Time when: 15 Jul 1813 - Whither, and by what order, or number or re-entry: Dysentery

Hart, John   Prisoner 1650. Rank: Private - By what ship or how taken: Troops - Time when: 19 Dec 1813 - Place where: Niagara - Of what ship or corps: Land forces - Whether man of war, privateer or merchant vessel: Taken on shore - Time when received into custody: 5 Oct 1814 - From what ship or whence received: Montreal - Exchanged, discharged, died, or escape: Discharged - Time when: 8 Oct 1814 - Whither, and by what order, or number or re-entry: H.M. Ship Ceylon

Hartman, Andrew   Prisoner 818. Rank: Corporal - By what ship or how taken: Troops - Time when: 26 Jun 1813 - Place where: Beaver Dam - Of what ship or corps: Land forces - Whether man of war, privateer or merchant vessel: Taken on shore - Time when received into custody: 7 Jul 1813 - From what ship or whence received: Steamboat - Exchanged, discharged, died, or escape: Discharged - Time when: 10 Aug 1813 - Whither, and by what order, or number or re-entry: HM Ship Malpomena

Hartwell, Calvin   Prisoner 1930. Rank: Private - By what ship or how taken: Troops - Time when: 17 Sep 1814 - Place where: Fort Erie - Of what ship or corps: Land forces - Whether man of war, privateer or merchant vessel: Taken on shore - Time when received into custody: 1 Nov 1814 - From what ship or whence received: Montreal - Exchanged, discharged, died, or escape: Discharged - Time when: 13 Mar 1815 - Whither, and by what order, or number or re-entry: United States

Harvey, Charles   Prisoner 1326. Rank: Sergeant - By what ship or how taken: Troops - Time when: 19 Dec 1813 - Place where: Fort Niagara - Of what ship or corps: Land forces - Whether man of war, privateer or merchant vessel: Taken on shore - Time when received into custody: 29 Jan 1814 - From what ship or whence received: Montreal by land carriage - Exchanged, discharged, died, or escape: Discharged - Time when: 4 May 1814 - Whither, and by what order, or number or re-entry: United States

Harvey, Luther   Prisoner 19. Rank: Musician - By what ship or how taken: Boats & Troops - Time when: 28 May 1813 - Place where: Stoney Point, Henderson Harbor - Of what ship or corps: Land forces - Whether man of war, privateer or merchant vessel: Taken on shore - Time when received into custody: 8 Jun 1813 - From what ship or whence received: Batteaux - Exchanged, discharged, died, or escape: Discharged - Time when: 31 Oct 1813 - Whither, and by what order, or number or re-entry: Malabar Transport

Harvey, Peter   Prisoner 1027. Rank: Seaman - By what ship or how taken: Lord Melvin - Time when: 10 Aug 1813 - Place where: Lake Ontario - Of what ship or corps: Growler - Whether man of war, privateer or merchant vessel: Man of War - Time when received into custody: 5 Sep 1813 - From what ship or whence received: Steamboat - Exchanged, discharged, died, or escape: Discharged - Time when: 1 Nov 1813 - Whither, and by what order, or number or re-entry: Lord Cartheart Transport

Harvey, William   Prisoner 195. Rank: Private - By what ship or how taken: Boats & Troops - Time when: 3 Jun 1813 - Place where: Lake Champlain - Of what ship or corps: Eagle - Whether man of war, privateer or merchant vessel: Man of War - Time when received into custody: 9 Jun 1813 - From what ship or whence received: Batteaux - Exchanged, discharged, died, or escape: Discharged - Time when: 31 Oct 1813 - Whither, and by what order, or number or re-entry: HM Ship Success

Hassar, George   Prisoner 416. Rank: Sergeant - By what ship or how taken: Troops - Time when: 24 Jun 1813 - Place where: Beaver Dam - Of what ship or corps: Land forces - Whether man of war, privateer or merchant vessel: Taken on shore - Time when received into custody: 7 Jul 1813 - From what ship or whence received: Steamboat - Exchanged, discharged, died, or escape: Discharged - Time when: 8 Oct 1813 - Whither, and by what order, or number or re-entry: H.M. Ship Ceylon

Hately, John   Prisoner 836. Rank: Private - By what ship or how taken: Troops - Time when: 26 Jun 1813 - Place where: Beaver Dam - Of what ship or corps: Land forces - Whether man of war, privateer or merchant vessel: Taken on shore - Time when received into custody: 7 Jul 1813 - From what ship or whence received: Steamboat - Exchanged, discharged, died, or escape: Discharged - Time when: 10 Aug 1813 - Whither, and by what order, or number or re-entry: HM Ship Malpomena

Havwood, Abijah   Prisoner 139. Rank: Private - By what ship or how taken: Boats & Troops - Time when: 28 May 1813 - Place where: Stoney Point, Henderson Harbor - Of what ship or corps: Land forces - Whether man of war, privateer or merchant vessel: Taken on shore - Time when received into custody: 8 Jul 1813 - From what ship or whence received: Batteaux - Exchanged, discharged, died, or escape: Escaped - Time when: 3 Sep 1813 - Whither, and by what order, or number or re-entry:

Haydon, Daniel   Prisoner 794. Rank: Private - By what ship or how taken: Troops - Time when: 26 Jun 1813 - Place where: Beaver Dam - Of what ship or corps: Land forces - Whether man of war, privateer or merchant vessel: Taken on shore - Time when received into custody: 7 Jul 1813 - From what ship or whence received: Steamboat - Exchanged, discharged, died, or escape: Discharged - Time when: 10 Aug 1813 - Whither, and by what order, or number or re-entry: HM Ship Malpomena

Hayes, Patrick   Prisoner 1321. Rank: Private - By what ship or how taken: Troops - Time when: 19 Dec 1813 - Place where: Fort Niagara - Of what ship or corps: Land forces - Whether man of war, privateer or merchant vessel: Taken on shore - Time when received into custody: 29 Jan 1814 - From what ship or whence received: Montreal by land carriage - Exchanged, discharged, died, or escape: Discharged - Time when: 4 May 1814 - Whither, and by what order, or number or re-entry: United States

Haynes, Clement   Prisoner 650. Rank: Corporal - By what ship or how taken: Troops - Time when: 24 Jun 1813 - Place where: Stoney Point - Of what ship or corps: Land forces - Whether man of war, privateer or merchant vessel: Taken on shore - Time when received into custody: 7 Jul 1813 - From what ship or whence received: Steamboat - Exchanged, discharged, died, or escape: Discharged - Time when: 10 Aug 1813 - Whither, and by what order, or number or re-entry: HM Ship Regulius by order of Sir George Provost

Hayway, Archibald   Prisoner 57. Rank: Private - By what ship or how taken: Boats & Troops - Time when: 28 May 1813 - Place where: Stoney Point, Henderson Harbor - Of what ship or corps: Land forces - Whether man of war, privateer or merchant vessel: Taken on shore - Time when received into custody: 8 Jun 1813 - From what ship or whence received: Batteaux - Exchanged, discharged, died, or escape: Discharged - Time when: 31 Oct 1813 - Whither, and by what order, or number or re-entry: Malabar Transport

Head, William   Prisoner 1364. Rank: Sergeant - By what ship or how taken: Troops - Time when: 19 Dec 1813 - Place where: Fort Niagara - Of what ship or corps: Land forces - Whether man of war, privateer or merchant vessel: Taken on shore - Time when received into custody: 29 Jan 1814 - From what ship or whence received: Montreal by land carriage - Exchanged, discharged, died, or escape: Discharged - Time when: 4 May 1814 - Whither, and by what order, or number or re-entry: United States

Headman, Charles   Prisoner 1009. Rank: Seaman - By what ship or how taken: Earl Moria - Time when: 10 Aug 1813 - Place where: Lake Ontario - Of what ship or corps: Julia - Whether man of war, privateer or merchant vessel: Man of War - Time when received into custody: 5 Sep 1813 - From what ship or whence received: Steamboat - Exchanged, discharged, died, or escape: Discharged - Time when: 31 Oct 1813 - Whither, and by what order, or number or re-entry: Malabar Transport

Heath, John   Prisoner 9. Rank: Private - By what ship or how taken: Boats & Troops - Time when: 28 May 1813 - Place where: Stoney Point, Henderson Harbor - Of what ship or corps: Land forces - Whether man of war, privateer or merchant vessel: Taken on shore - Time when received into custody: 8 Jun 1813 - From what ship or whence received: Batteaux - Exchanged, discharged, died, or escape: Discharged - Time when: 4 May 1814 - Whither, and by what order, or number or re-entry: United States

Hedderick, George   Prisoner 287. Rank: Private - By what ship or how taken: Boats & Troops - Time when: 6 Jun 1813 - Place where: Stoney Point - Of what ship or corps: Land forces - Whether man of war, privateer or merchant vessel: Taken on shore - Time when received into custody: 28 Jun 1813 - From what ship or whence received: Quebec of Quebec - Exchanged, discharged, died, or escape: Discharged - Time when: 31 Oct 1813 - Whither, and by what order, or number or re-entry: Malabar Transport

Heddon, Amas   Prisoner 688. Rank: Private - By what ship or how taken: Troops - Time when: 26 Jun 1813 - Place where: Beaver Dam - Of what ship or corps: Land forces - Whether man of war, privateer or merchant vessel: Taken on shore - Time when received into custody: 7 Jul 1813 - From what ship or whence received: Steamboat - Exchanged, discharged, died, or escape: Discharged - Time when: 10 Aug 1813 - Whither, and by what order, or number or re-entry: HM Ship Regulius by order of Sir George Provost

American Prisoners of War held at Quebec during the War of 1812

Heding, Henry Prisoner 845. Rank: Private - By what ship or how taken: Troops - Time when: 26 Jun 1813 - Place where: Beaver Dam - Of what ship or corps: Land forces - Whether man of war, privateer or merchant vessel: Taken on shore - Time when received into custody: 7 Jul 1813 - From what ship or whence received: Steamboat - Exchanged, discharged, died, or escape: Discharged - Time when: 10 Aug 1813 - Whither, and by what order, or number or re-entry: HM Ship Malpomena

Hemmick, George Prisoner 261. Rank: Private - By what ship or how taken: Boats & Troops - Time when: 24 Jun 1813 - Place where: Stoney Point - Of what ship or corps: Land forces - Whether man of war, privateer or merchant vessel: Taken on shore - Time when received into custody: 24 Jun 1813 - From what ship or whence received: Steamboat - Exchanged, discharged, died, or escape: Discharged - Time when: 13 Dec 1813 - Whither, and by what order, or number or re-entry: United States

Henderson, Amos Prisoner 1954. Rank: Private - By what ship or how taken: Troops - Time when: 23 Oct 1814 - Place where: Fort Erie - Of what ship or corps: Land forces - Whether man of war, privateer or merchant vessel: Taken on shore - Time when received into custody: 11 Dec 1814 - From what ship or whence received: Montreal - Exchanged, discharged, died, or escape: Discharged - Time when: 13 Mar 1815 - Whither, and by what order, or number or re-entry: United States

Henderson, George W. Prisoner 1925. Rank: Private - By what ship or how taken: Troops - Time when: 17 Sep 1814 - Place where: Fort Eric - Of what ship or corps: Land forces - Whether man of war, privateer or merchant vessel: Taken on shore - Time when received into custody: 1 Nov 1814 - From what ship or whence received: Montreal - Exchanged, discharged, died, or escape: Discharged - Time when: 14 Nov 1814 - Whither, and by what order, or number or re-entry: Soverign No. 628 for Halifax

Hendricks, John Prisoner 1100. Rank: Private - By what ship or how taken: Troops - Time when: 24 Aug 1813 - Place where: Fort George - Of what ship or corps: Land forces - Whether man of war, privateer or merchant vessel: Taken on shore - Time when received into custody: 12 Oct 1813 - From what ship or whence received: Steamboat - Exchanged, discharged, died, or escape: Discharged - Time when: 31 Oct 1813 - Whither, and by what order, or number or re-entry: Malabar Transport

Henon, James Prisoner 966. Rank: Private - By what ship or how taken: Troops - Time when: 5 Jul 1813 - Place where: Fort Schisher - Of what ship or corps: Land forces - Whether man of war, privateer or merchant vessel: Taken on shore - Time when received into custody: 5 Sep 1813 - From what ship or whence received: Steamboat - Exchanged, discharged, died, or escape: Discharged - Time when: 31 Oct 1813 - Whither, and by what order, or number or re-entry: Malabar Transport

Henry, George Prisoner 799. Rank: Private - By what ship or how taken: Troops - Time when: 26 Jun 1813 - Place where: Beaver Dam - Of what ship or corps: Land forces - Whether man of war, privateer or merchant vessel: Taken on shore - Time when received into custody: 7 Jul 1813 - From what ship or whence received: Steamboat - Exchanged, discharged, died, or escape: Discharged - Time when: 10 Aug 1813 - Whither, and by what order, or number or re-entry: HM Ship Malpomena

Henry, George Prisoner 599. Rank: Private - By what ship or how taken: Troops - Time when: 26 Jun 1813 - Place where: Stoney Point - Of what ship or corps: Land forces - Whether man of war, privateer or merchant vessel: Taken on shore - Time when received into custody: 7 Jul 1813 - From what ship or whence received: Steamboat - Exchanged, discharged, died, or escape: Discharged - Time when: 9 Aug 1813 - Whither, and by what order, or number or re-entry: HM Ship Wasp

Henry, James Prisoner 510. Rank: Private - By what ship or how taken: Troops - Time when: 24 Jun 1813 - Place where: Beaver Dam - Of what ship or corps: Land forces - Whether man of war, privateer or merchant vessel: Taken on shore - Time when received into custody: 7 Jul 1813 - From what ship or whence received: Steamboat - Exchanged, discharged, died, or escape: Discharged - Time when: 9 Aug 1813 - Whither, and by what order, or number or re-entry: HM Ship Wasp

Henry, John Prisoner 1869. Rank: Private - By what ship or how taken: Troops - Time when: 17 Sep 1814 - Place where: Fort Erie - Of what ship or corps: Land forces - Whether man of war, privateer or merchant vessel: Taken on shore - Time when received into custody: 1 Nov 1814 - From what ship or whence received: Montreal - Exchanged, discharged, died, or escape: Discharged - Time when: 8 Nov 1814 - Whither, and by what order, or number or re-entry: S. George No. 575 for Halifax

Henry, Samuel Prisoner 685. Rank: Private - By what ship or how taken: Troops - Time when: 26 Jun 1813 - Place where: Beaver Dam - Of what ship or corps: Land forces - Whether man of war, privateer or merchant vessel: Taken on shore - Time when received into custody: 7 Jul 1813 - From what ship or whence received: Steamboat - Exchanged,

discharged, died, or escape: Discharged - Time when: 10 Aug 1813 - Whither, and by what order, or number or re-entry: HM Ship Regulius by order of Sir George Provost

Herley, John   Prisoner 1841. Rank: Private - By what ship or how taken: Troops - Time when: 17 Sep 1814 - Place where: Fort Erie - Of what ship or corps: Land forces - Whether man of war, privateer or merchant vessel: Taken on shore - Time when received into custody: 1 Nov 1814 - From what ship or whence received: Montreal - Exchanged, discharged, died, or escape: Discharged - Time when: 8 Nov 1814 - Whither, and by what order, or number or re-entry: S. George No. 575 for Halifax by order of Sir George Provost

Heron, James E.   Prisoner 1210. Rank: Asst. Comsy of Purch - By what ship or how taken: Troops - Time when: 19 Dec 1813 - Place where: Fort Niagara - Of what ship or corps: Land forces - Whether man of war, privateer or merchant vessel: Taken on shore - Time when received into custody: 18 Jan 1814 - From what ship or whence received: Montreal by land carriage - Exchanged, discharged, died, or escape: Discharged - Time when: 31 Jan 1814 - Whither, and by what order, or number or re-entry: To United States

Herrick, Eli   Prisoner 203. Rank: Corporal - By what ship or how taken: Boats & Troops - Time when: 3 Jun 1813 - Place where: Lake Champlain - Of what ship or corps: Growler - Whether man of war, privateer or merchant vessel: Man of War - Time when received into custody: 9 Jun 1813 - From what ship or whence received: Batteaux - Exchanged, discharged, died, or escape: Discharged - Time when: 31 Oct 1813 - Whither, and by what order, or number or re-entry: Malabar Transport

Herrick, Oliver   Prisoner 149. Rank: Captain - By what ship or how taken: Boats & Troops - Time when: 3 Jun 1813 - Place where: Lake Champlain - Of what ship or corps: Growler - Whether man of war, privateer or merchant vessel: Man of War - Time when received into custody: 8 Jul 1813 - From what ship or whence received: Batteaux - Exchanged, discharged, died, or escape: Discharged - Time when: 10 Aug 1813 - Whither, and by what order, or number or re-entry: Per order His Exellency Sir George Prevost

Herring, John   Prisoner 494. Rank: Private - By what ship or how taken: Troops - Time when: 24 Jun 1813 - Place where: Beaver Dam - Of what ship or corps: Land forces - Whether man of war, privateer or merchant vessel: Taken on shore - Time when received into custody: 7 Jul 1813 - From what ship or whence received: Steamboat - Exchanged, discharged, died, or escape: Discharged - Time when: 10 Aug 1813 - Whither, and by what order, or number or re-entry: HM Ship Regulius by order of Sir George Provost

Hervey, John   Prisoner 839. Rank: Private - By what ship or how taken: Troops - Time when: 26 Jun 1813 - Place where: Beaver Dam - Of what ship or corps: Land forces - Whether man of war, privateer or merchant vessel: Taken on shore - Time when received into custody: 7 Jul 1813 - From what ship or whence received: Steamboat - Exchanged, discharged, died, or escape: Discharged - Time when: 10 Aug 1813 - Whither, and by what order, or number or re-entry: HM Ship Malpomena

Hewins, Thomas   Prisoner 1165. Rank: Sergeant - By what ship or how taken: Troops - Time when: 27 Oct 1812 - Place where: Rapids - Of what ship or corps: Land forces - Whether man of war, privateer or merchant vessel: Taken on shore - Time when received into custody: 25 Nov 1813 - From what ship or whence received: Town Goal - Exchanged, discharged, died, or escape: Discharged - Time when: 12 Mar 1814 - Whither, and by what order, or number or re-entry: New Brunswick Fencibles

Hickins, Francis   Prisoner 920. Rank: Private - By what ship or how taken: Troops - Time when: 26 Jun 1813 - Place where: Beaver Dam - Of what ship or corps: Land forces - Whether man of war, privateer or merchant vessel: Taken on shore - Time when received into custody: 21 Jul 1813 - From what ship or whence received: Steamboat - Exchanged, discharged, died, or escape: Discharged - Time when: 10 Aug 1813 - Whither, and by what order, or number or re-entry: HM Ship Malpomena

Hickling, William   Prisoner 1833. Rank: Private - By what ship or how taken: Troops - Time when: 17 Sep 1814 - Place where: Fort Erie - Of what ship or corps: Land forces - Whether man of war, privateer or merchant vessel: Taken on shore - Time when received into custody: 1 Nov 1814 - From what ship or whence received: Montreal - Exchanged, discharged, died, or escape: Discharged - Time when: 8 Nov 1814 - Whither, and by what order, or number or re-entry: S. George No. 575 for Halifax by order of Sir George Provost

Hicks, Isaac   Prisoner 1052. Rank: Private - By what ship or how taken: Lord Melvin - Time when: 10 Aug 1813 - Place where: Lake Ontario - Of what ship or corps: Growler - Whether man of war, privateer or merchant vessel: Man of War - Time when received into custody: 5 Sep 1813 - From what ship or whence received: Steamboat - Exchanged, discharged, died, or escape: Discharged - Time when: 31 Oct 1813 - Whither, and by what order, or number or re-entry: Malabar Transport

American Prisoners of War held at Quebec during the War of 1812

Higgins, Hiram   Prisoner 1864.   Rank: Corporal - By what ship or how taken: Troops - Time when: 17 Sep 1814 - Place where: Fort Erie - Of what ship or corps: Land forces - Whether man of war, privateer or merchant vessel: Taken on shore - Time when received into custody: 1 Nov 1814 - From what ship or whence received: Montreal - Exchanged, discharged, died, or escape: Discharged - Time when: 8 Nov 1814 - Whither, and by what order, or number or re-entry: S. George No. 575 for Halifax

Hiler, Peter   Prisoner 1859.   Rank: Private - By what ship or how taken: Troops - Time when: 17 Sep 1814 - Place where: Fort Erie - Of what ship or corps: Land forces - Whether man of war, privateer or merchant vessel: Taken on shore - Time when received into custody: 1 Nov 1814 - From what ship or whence received: Montreal - Exchanged, discharged, died, or escape: Discharged - Time when: 8 Nov 1814 - Whither, and by what order, or number or re-entry: S. George No. 575 for Halifax

Hill, Allen   Prisoner 1373.   Rank: Private - By what ship or how taken: Troops - Time when: 19 Dec 1813 - Place where: Fort Niagara - Of what ship or corps: Land forces - Whether man of war, privateer or merchant vessel: Taken on shore - Time when received into custody: 29 Jan 1814 - From what ship or whence received: Montreal by land carriage - Exchanged, discharged, died, or escape: Discharged - Time when: 4 May 1814 - Whither, and by what order, or number or re-entry: United States

Hill, Valentine   Prisoner 1796.   Rank: Private - By what ship or how taken: Troops - Time when: 7 Sep 1814 - Place where: Fort Erie - Of what ship or corps: Land forces - Whether man of war, privateer or merchant vessel: Taken on shore - Time when received into custody: 1 Nov 1814 - From what ship or whence received: Montreal - Exchanged, discharged, died, or escape: Discharged - Time when: 8 Nov 1814 - Whither, and by what order, or number or re-entry: S. George No. 575 for Halifax by order of Sir George Provost

Hill, William   Prisoner 1086.   Rank: Private - By what ship or how taken: Troops - Time when: 24 Aug 1813 - Place where: Fort George - Of what ship or corps: Land forces - Whether man of war, privateer or merchant vessel: Taken on shore - Time when received into custody: 10 Oct 1813 - From what ship or whence received: Steamboat - Exchanged, discharged, died, or escape: Discharged - Time when: 31 Oct 1813 - Whither, and by what order, or number or re-entry: Malabar Transport

Hince, John   Prisoner 1301.   Rank: Private - By what ship or how taken: Troops - Time when: 19 Dec 1813 - Place where: Fort Niagara - Of what ship or corps: Land forces - Whether man of war, privateer or merchant vessel: Taken on shore - Time when received into custody: 29 Jan 1814 - From what ship or whence received: Montreal by land carriage - Exchanged, discharged, died, or escape: Discharged - Time when: 11 Mar 1814 - Whither, and by what order, or number or re-entry: Volunteered for New Brunswick Fencibles

Hind, Nathaniel   Prisoner 1298.   Rank: Private - By what ship or how taken: Troops - Time when: 19 Dec 1813 - Place where: Fort Niagara - Of what ship or corps: Land forces - Whether man of war, privateer or merchant vessel: Taken on shore - Time when received into custody: 29 Jan 1814 - From what ship or whence received: Montreal by land carriage - Exchanged, discharged, died, or escape: Discharged - Time when: 27 Feb 1814 - Whither, and by what order, or number or re-entry: Volunteered for New Brunswick Fencibles

Hix, Comfort   Prisoner 1776.   Rank: Private - By what ship or how taken: Troops - Time when: 7 Sep 1814 - Place where: Fort Erie - Of what ship or corps: Land forces - Whether man of war, privateer or merchant vessel: Taken on shore - Time when received into custody: 1 Nov 1814 - From what ship or whence received: Montreal - Exchanged, discharged, died, or escape: Discharged - Time when: 8 Nov 1814 - Whither, and by what order, or number or re-entry: S. George No. 575 for Halifax by order of Sir George Provost

Hodge, Benjamin   Prisoner 1655.   Rank: Citizen - By what ship or how taken: Troops - Time when: 1 Jan 1814 - Place where: Buffalo - Of what ship or corps: Land forces - Whether man of war, privateer or merchant vessel: Taken on shore - Time when received into custody: 5 Oct 1814 - From what ship or whence received: Montreal - Exchanged, discharged, died, or escape: Discharged - Time when: 8 Oct 1814 - Whither, and by what order, or number or re-entry: H.M. Ship Ceylon

Hogg, George   Prisoner 492.   Rank: Private - By what ship or how taken: Troops - Time when: 24 Jun 1813 - Place where: Beaver Dam - Of what ship or corps: Land forces - Whether man of war, privateer or merchant vessel: Taken on shore - Time when received into custody: 7 Jul 1813 - From what ship or whence received: Steamboat - Exchanged, discharged, died, or escape: Discharged - Time when: 10 Aug 1813 - Whither, and by what order, or number or re-entry: HM Ship Regulius by order of Sir George Provost

Holcolm, L.   Prisoner 1638.   Rank: Private - By what ship or how taken: Troops - Time when: 6 Sep 1814 - Place where: Plattsburg - Of what ship or corps: Land forces - Whether man of war, privateer or merchant vessel: Taken on shore - Time when received into custody: 5 Oct 1814 - From what ship or whence received: Montreal - Exchanged, discharged,

American Prisoners of War held at Quebec during the War of 1812

died, or escape: Discharged - Time when: 8 Oct 1814 - Whither, and by what order, or number or re-entry: H.M. Ship Ceylon

Holford, Elijah   Prisoner 1477. Rank: Private - By what ship or how taken: Troops - Time when: 15 Jul 1814 - Place where: St. Davids - Of what ship or corps: Land forces - Whether man of war, privateer or merchant vessel: Taken on shore - Time when received into custody: 12 Aug 1814 - From what ship or whence received: Royal Seaman No. 289 Transport - Exchanged, discharged, died, or escape: Discharged - Time when: 10 Nov 1814 - Whither, and by what order, or number or re-entry: Soverign Transport No. 628 to Halifax by orders of Sir George Provost

Hollister, P. F.   Prisoner 1947. Rank: Sergeant - By what ship or how taken: Troops - Time when: 17 Sep 1814 - Place where: Fort Erie - Of what ship or corps: Land forces - Whether man of war, privateer or merchant vessel: Taken on shore - Time when received into custody: 1 Nov 1814 - From what ship or whence received: Montreal - Exchanged, discharged, died, or escape: Discharged - Time when: 13 Mar 1815 - Whither, and by what order, or number or re-entry: United States

Holloby, John   Prisoner 1424. Rank: Private - By what ship or how taken: Troops - Time when: 19 Dec 1813 - Place where: Fort Niagara - Of what ship or corps: Land forces - Whether man of war, privateer or merchant vessel: Taken on shore - Time when received into custody: 29 Jan 1814 - From what ship or whence received: Montreal by land carriage - Exchanged, discharged, died, or escape: Discharged - Time when: 4 May 1814 - Whither, and by what order, or number or re-entry: United States

Holloway, John   Prisoner 559. Rank: Private - By what ship or how taken: Troops - Time when: 26 Jun 1813 - Place where: Beaver Dam - Of what ship or corps: Land forces - Whether man of war, privateer or merchant vessel: Taken on shore - Time when received into custody: 13 Jul 1813 - From what ship or whence received: Steamboat - Exchanged, discharged, died, or escape: Discharged - Time when: 31 Oct 1813 - Whither, and by what order, or number or re-entry: Malabar Transport

Hollville, Robert   Prisoner 1428. Rank: Private - By what ship or how taken: Troops - Time when: 19 Dec 1813 - Place where: Fort Niagara - Of what ship or corps: Land forces - Whether man of war, privateer or merchant vessel: Taken on shore - Time when received into custody: 29 Jan 1814 - From what ship or whence received: Montreal by land carriage - Exchanged, discharged, died, or escape: Discharged - Time when: 4 May 1814 - Whither, and by what order, or number or re-entry: United States

Holmes, Charles   Prisoner 1398. Rank: Private - By what ship or how taken: Troops - Time when: 19 Dec 1813 - Place where: Fort Niagara - Of what ship or corps: Land forces - Whether man of war, privateer or merchant vessel: Taken on shore - Time when received into custody: 29 Jan 1814 - From what ship or whence received: Montreal by land carriage - Exchanged, discharged, died, or escape: Discharged - Time when: 4 May 1814 - Whither, and by what order, or number or re-entry: United States

Holmes, Thomas   Prisoner 1325. Rank: Private - By what ship or how taken: Troops - Time when: 19 Dec 1813 - Place where: Fort Niagara - Of what ship or corps: Land forces - Whether man of war, privateer or merchant vessel: Taken on shore - Time when received into custody: 29 Jan 1814 - From what ship or whence received: Montreal by land carriage - Exchanged, discharged, died, or escape: Discharged - Time when: 4 May 1814 - Whither, and by what order, or number or re-entry: United States

Holson, James   Prisoner 615. Rank: Private - By what ship or how taken: Troops - Time when: 26 Jun 1813 - Place where: Stoney Point - Of what ship or corps: Land forces - Whether man of war, privateer or merchant vessel: Taken on shore - Time when received into custody: 7 Jul 1813 - From what ship or whence received: Steamboat - Exchanged, discharged, died, or escape: Discharged - Time when: 10 Aug 1813 - Whither, and by what order, or number or re-entry: HM Ship Regulius by order of Sir George Provost

Honeywell, Encoh   Prisoner 601. Rank: Private - By what ship or how taken: Troops - Time when: 26 Jun 1813 - Place where: Stoney Point - Of what ship or corps: Land forces - Whether man of war, privateer or merchant vessel: Taken on shore - Time when received into custody: 7 Jul 1813 - From what ship or whence received: Steamboat - Exchanged, discharged, died, or escape: Discharged - Time when: 10 Aug 1813 - Whither, and by what order, or number or re-entry: HM Ship Regulius by order of Sir George Provost

Hooke, Thomas   Prisoner 1429. Rank: Able seaman - By what ship or how taken: Nymph - Time when: 1 Feb 1814 - Place where: Off Bermuda - Of what ship or corps: Ebe - Whether man of war, privateer or merchant vessel: Letter of Marque - Time when received into custody: 24 May 1814 - From what ship or whence received: Mary Transport No. 360 Halifax - Exchanged, discharged, died, or escape: Discharged - Time when: 4 May 1814 - Whither, and by what order, or number or re-entry: United States

American Prisoners of War held at Quebec during the War of 1812

Hooker, Oris   Prisoner 344.   Rank: Private - By what ship or how taken: Boats & Troops - Time when: 22 Feb 1813 - Place where: Hedgesburgh - Of what ship or corps: Land forces - Whether man of war, privateer or merchant vessel: Taken on shore - Time when received into custody: 28 Jun 1813 - From what ship or whence received: Mary of Quebec - Exchanged, discharged, died, or escape: Died - Time when: 9 Sep 1813 - Whither, and by what order, or number or re-entry: Dysentery

Hooper, John   Prisoner 56.   Rank: Private - By what ship or how taken: Boats & Troops - Time when: 28 May 1813 - Place where: Stoney Point, Henderson Harbor - Of what ship or corps: Land forces - Whether man of war, privateer or merchant vessel: Taken on shore - Time when received into custody: 8 Jun 1813 - From what ship or whence received: Batteaux - Exchanged, discharged, died, or escape: Discharged - Time when: 31 Oct 1813 - Whither, and by what order, or number or re-entry: Malabar Transport

Hooper, Simon   Prisoner 86.   Rank: Private - By what ship or how taken: Boats & Troops - Time when: 28 May 1813 - Place where: Stoney Point, Henderson Harbor - Of what ship or corps: Land forces - Whether man of war, privateer or merchant vessel: Taken on shore - Time when received into custody: 8 Jun 1813 - From what ship or whence received: Batteaux - Exchanged, discharged, died, or escape: Died - Time when: 26 Jul 1813 - Whither, and by what order, or number or re-entry:

Hoopman, Philip   Prisoner 933.   Rank: Private - By what ship or how taken: Troops - Time when: 26 Jun 1813 - Place where: Beaver Dam   Of what ship or corps: Land forces   Whether man of war, privateer or merchant vessel: Taken on shore   Time when received into custody: 21 Jul 1813 - From what ship or whence received: Steamboat - Exchanged, discharged, died, or escape: Discharged - Time when: 10 Aug 1813 - Whither, and by what order, or number or re-entry: HM Ship Malpomena

Hope. Levi   Prisoner 1069.   Rank: Steward - By what ship or how taken: Lord Melvin - Time when: 10 Aug 1813 - Place where: Lake Ontario - Of what ship or corps: Growler - Whether man of war, privateer or merchant vessel: Man of War - Time when received into custody: 5 Sep 1813 - From what ship or whence received: Steamboat - Exchanged, discharged, died, or escape: Discharged - Time when: 4 May 1814 - Whither, and by what order, or number or re-entry: United States

Hopkins, John   Prisoner 1333.   Rank: Musician - By what ship or how taken: Troops - Time when: 19 Dec 1813 - Place where: Fort Niagara - Of what ship or corps: Land forces - Whether man of war, privateer or merchant vessel: Taken on shore - Time when received into custody: 29 Jan 1814 - From what ship or whence received: Montreal by land carriage - Exchanged, discharged, died, or escape: Discharged - Time when: 27 Feb 1814 - Whither, and by what order, or number or re-entry: Volunteered for New Brunswick Fencibles

Hopkinson, Caleb   Prisoner 1873.   Rank: Private - By what ship or how taken: Troops - Time when: 17 Sep 1814 - Place where: Fort Erie - Of what ship or corps: Land forces - Whether man of war, privateer or merchant vessel: Taken on shore - Time when received into custody: 1 Nov 1814 - From what ship or whence received: Montreal - Exchanged, discharged, died, or escape: Discharged - Time when: 8 Nov 1814 - Whither, and by what order, or number or re-entry: S. George No. 575 for Halifax

Horn, Andrew   Prisoner 73.   Rank: Private - By what ship or how taken: Boats & Troops - Time when: 28 May 1813 - Place where: Stoney Point, Henderson Harbor - Of what ship or corps: Land forces - Whether man of war, privateer or merchant vessel: Taken on shore - Time when received into custody: 8 Jun 1813 - From what ship or whence received: Batteaux - Exchanged, discharged, died, or escape: Discharged - Time when: 31 Oct 1813 - Whither, and by what order, or number or re-entry: Malabar Transport

Horn, Wentworth   Prisoner 70.   Rank: Drummer - By what ship or how taken: Boats & Troops - Time when: 28 May 1813 - Place where: Stoney Point, Henderson Harbor - Of what ship or corps: Land forces - Whether man of war, privateer or merchant vessel: Taken on shore - Time when received into custody: 8 Jun 1813 - From what ship or whence received: Batteaux - Exchanged, discharged, died, or escape: Discharged - Time when: 31 Oct 1813 - Whither, and by what order, or number or re-entry: Malabar Transport

Horney, David   Prisoner 389.   Rank: Private - By what ship or how taken: Troops - Time when: 6 Jun 1813 - Place where: Stoney Point - Of what ship or corps: Land forces - Whether man of war, privateer or merchant vessel: Taken on shore - Time when received into custody: 28 Jun 1813 - From what ship or whence received: Mary of Quebec - Exchanged, discharged, died, or escape: Discharged - Time when: 31 Oct 1813 - Whither, and by what order, or number or re-entry: Malabar Transport

Horton, Barnebus   Prisoner 1535.   Rank: Private - By what ship or how taken: Troops - Time when: 25 Jul 1814 - Place where: Lundy's Lane - Of what ship or corps: Land forces - Whether man of war, privateer or merchant vessel: Taken on shore - Time when received into custody: 30 Aug 1814 - From what ship or whence received: Lady Delaval Schooner 578 -

American Prisoners of War held at Quebec during the War of 1812

Exchanged, discharged, died, or escape: Discharged - Time when: 8 Oct 1814 - Whither, and by what order, or number or re-entry: Queen No. 415

Horton, Cyrus   Prisoner 1880. Rank: Private - By what ship or how taken: Troops - Time when: 17 Sep 1814 - Place where: Fort Erie - Of what ship or corps: Land forces - Whether man of war, privateer or merchant vessel: Taken on shore - Time when received into custody: 1 Nov 1814 - From what ship or whence received: Montreal - Exchanged, discharged, died, or escape: Discharged - Time when: 8 Nov 1814 - Whither, and by what order, or number or re-entry: S. George No. 575 for Halifax by order of Sir George Provost

Hose, Jacob   Prisoner 715. Rank: Private - By what ship or how taken: Troops - Time when: 26 Jun 1813 - Place where: Beaver Dam - Of what ship or corps: Land forces - Whether man of war, privateer or merchant vessel: Taken on shore - Time when received into custody: 7 Jul 1813 - From what ship or whence received: Steamboat - Exchanged, discharged, died, or escape: Discharged - Time when: 10 Aug 1813 - Whither, and by what order, or number or re-entry: HM Ship Regulius by order of Sir George Provost

Houndshell, John   Prisoner 1338. Rank: Private - By what ship or how taken: Troops - Time when: 19 Dec 1813 - Place where: Fort Niagara - Of what ship or corps: Land forces - Whether man of war, privateer or merchant vessel: Taken on shore - Time when received into custody: 29 Jan 1814 - From what ship or whence received: Montreal by land carriage - Exchanged, discharged, died, or escape: Discharged - Time when: 22 Feb 1814 - Whither, and by what order, or number or re-entry: Volunteered for New Brunswick Fencibles

House, Frederick   Prisoner 679. Rank: Sergeant - By what ship or how taken: Troops - Time when: 26 Jun 1813 - Place where: Beaver Dam - Of what ship or corps: Land forces - Whether man of war, privateer or merchant vessel: Taken on shore - Time when received into custody: 7 Jul 1813 - From what ship or whence received: Steamboat - Exchanged, discharged, died, or escape: Discharged - Time when: 10 Aug 1813 - Whither, and by what order, or number or re-entry: HM Ship Regulius by order of Sir George Provost

House, Isaac   Prisoner 1498. Rank: Private - By what ship or how taken: Troops - Time when: 24 Jul 1814 - Place where: Lundy's Lane - Of what ship or corps: Land forces - Whether man of war, privateer or merchant vessel: Taken on shore - Time when received into custody: 19 Aug 1814 - From what ship or whence received: Triton No. 438 Transport - Exchanged, discharged, died, or escape: Escaped - Time when: 1 Oct 1814 - Whither, and by what order, or number or re-entry:

Hovel, Nathaniel   Prisoner 1187. Rank: Private - By what ship or how taken: Troops - Time when: 5 May 1813 - Place where: Rapids - Of what ship or corps: Land forces - Whether man of war, privateer or merchant vessel: Taken on shore - Time when received into custody: 25 Nov 1813 - From what ship or whence received: Town Goal - Exchanged, discharged, died, or escape: Discharged - Time when: 4 May 1814 - Whither, and by what order, or number or re-entry: United States

Hover, George   Prisoner 900. Rank: Private - By what ship or how taken: Troops - Time when: 26 Jun 1813 - Place where: Beaver Dam - Of what ship or corps: Land forces - Whether man of war, privateer or merchant vessel: Taken on shore - Time when received into custody: 21 Jul 1813 - From what ship or whence received: Steamboat - Exchanged, discharged, died, or escape: Discharged - Time when: 10 Aug 1813 - Whither, and by what order, or number or re-entry: HM Ship Malpomena

How, John   Prisoner 123. Rank: Private - By what ship or how taken: Boats & Troops - Time when: 28 May 1813 - Place where: Stoney Point, Henderson Harbor - Of what ship or corps: Land forces - Whether man of war, privateer or merchant vessel: Taken on shore - Time when received into custody: 8 Jun 1813 - From what ship or whence received: Batteaux - Exchanged, discharged, died, or escape: Discharged - Time when: 31 Oct 1813 - Whither, and by what order, or number or re-entry: Malabar Transport

Howard, Aron   Prisoner 1941. Rank: Private - By what ship or how taken: Troops - Time when: 17 Sep 1814 - Place where: Fort Erie - Of what ship or corps: Land forces - Whether man of war, privateer or merchant vessel: Taken on shore - Time when received into custody: 1 Nov 1814 - From what ship or whence received: Montreal - Exchanged, discharged, died, or escape: Discharged - Time when: 13 Mar 1815 - Whither, and by what order, or number or re-entry: United States

Howard, Edward   Prisoner 1305. Rank: Private - By what ship or how taken: Troops - Time when: 19 Dec 1813 - Place where: Fort Niagara - Of what ship or corps: Land forces - Whether man of war, privateer or merchant vessel: Taken on shore - Time when received into custody: 29 Jan 1814 - From what ship or whence received: Montreal by land carriage - Exchanged, discharged, died, or escape: Discharged - Time when: 4 May 1814 - Whither, and by what order, or number or re-entry: United States

American Prisoners of War held at Quebec during the War of 1812

Howard, Joseph   Prisoner 89.   Rank: Private - By what ship or how taken: Boats & Troops - Time when: 28 May 1813 - Place where: Stoney Point, Henderson Harbor - Of what ship or corps: Land forces - Whether man of war, privateer or merchant vessel: Taken on shore - Time when received into custody: 8 Jun 1813 - From what ship or whence received: Batteaux - Exchanged, discharged, died, or escape: Died - Time when: 3 Jul 1813 - Whither, and by what order, or number or re-entry: Dysentery

Howard, Josiah   Prisoner 58.   Rank: Private - By what ship or how taken: Boats & Troops - Time when: 28 May 1813 - Place where: Stoney Point, Henderson Harbor - Of what ship or corps: Land forces - Whether man of war, privateer or merchant vessel: Taken on shore - Time when received into custody: 8 Jun 1813 - From what ship or whence received: Batteaux - Exchanged, discharged, died, or escape: Discharged - Time when: 31 Oct 1813 - Whither, and by what order, or number or re-entry: Malabar Transport

Howard, Lewis   Prisoner 87.   Rank: Private - By what ship or how taken: Boats & Troops - Time when: 28 May 1813 - Place where: Stoney Point, Henderson Harbor - Of what ship or corps: Land forces - Whether man of war, privateer or merchant vessel: Taken on shore - Time when received into custody: 8 Jun 1813 - From what ship or whence received: Batteaux - Exchanged, discharged, died, or escape: Discharged - Time when: 2 Nov 1813 - Whither, and by what order, or number or re-entry: Malabar Transport

Howard, Ralph   Prisoner 1865.   Rank: Private - By what ship or how taken: Troops - Time when: 17 Sep 1814 - Place where: Fort Erie - Of what ship or corps: Land forces - Whether man of war, privateer or merchant vessel: Taken on shore - Time when received into custody: 1 Nov 1814 - From what ship or whence received: Montreal - Exchanged, discharged, died, or escape: Discharged - Time when: 8 Nov 1814 - Whither, and by what order, or number or re-entry: S. George No. 575 for Halifax

Howe, Calvin   Prisoner 15.   Rank: Sergeant - By what ship or how taken: Boats & Troops - Time when: 28 May 1813 - Place where: Stoney Point, Henderson Harbor - Of what ship or corps: Land forces - Whether man of war, privateer or merchant vessel: Taken on shore - Time when received into custody: 8 Jun 1813 - From what ship or whence received: Batteaux - Exchanged, discharged, died, or escape: Discharged - Time when: 31 Oct 1813 - Whither, and by what order, or number or re-entry: Malabar Transport

Howe, William   Prisoner 6.   Rank: Private - By what ship or how taken: Boats & Troops - Time when: 28 May 1813 - Place where: Stoney Point, Henderson Harbor - Of what ship or corps: Land forces - Whether man of war, privateer or merchant vessel: Taken on shore - Time when received into custody: 8 Jun 1813 - From what ship or whence received: Batteaux - Exchanged, discharged, died, or escape: Discharged - Time when: 18 Sep 1813 - Whither, and by what order, or number or re-entry: Dick Transport

Howe, Willis   Prisoner 1559.   Rank: Private - By what ship or how taken: Troops - Time when: 25 Jul 1814 - Place where: Lundy's Lane - Of what ship or corps: Land forces - Whether man of war, privateer or merchant vessel: Taken on shore - Time when received into custody: 30 Aug 1814 - From what ship or whence received: Lady Delaval Schooner 578 - Exchanged, discharged, died, or escape: Discharged - Time when: 8 Oct 1814 - Whither, and by what order, or number or re-entry: H.M. Ship Ceylon

Howley, Comfort   Prisoner 1882.   Rank: Private - By what ship or how taken: Troops - Time when: 17 Sep 1814 - Place where: Fort Erie - Of what ship or corps: Land forces - Whether man of war, privateer or merchant vessel: Taken on shore - Time when received into custody: 1 Nov 1814 - From what ship or whence received: Montreal - Exchanged, discharged, died, or escape: Discharged - Time when: 8 Nov 1814 - Whither, and by what order, or number or re-entry: S. George No. 575 for Halifax by order of Sir George Provost

Hoy, Barney   Prisoner 318.   Rank: Private - By what ship or how taken: Boats & Troops - Time when: 6 Jun 1813 - Place where: Stoney Point - Of what ship or corps: Land forces - Whether man of war, privateer or merchant vessel: Taken on shore - Time when received into custody: 28 Jun 1813 - From what ship or whence received: Quebec of Quebec - Exchanged, discharged, died, or escape: Discharged - Time when: 7 Aug 1813 - Whither, and by what order, or number or re-entry: H.M. Ship Cievare

Hubbard, Joseph   Prisoner 1579.   Rank: Seaman - By what ship or how taken: Gun Boats - Time when: 12 Aug 1814 - Place where: Fort Erie - Of what ship or corps: Somers - Whether man of war, privateer or merchant vessel: Man of War - Time when received into custody: 5 Oct 1814 - From what ship or whence received: Montreal - Exchanged, discharged, died, or escape: Discharged - Time when: 10 Nov 1814 - Whither, and by what order, or number or re-entry: Freedom No. 582

Hubbard, Thomas   Prisoner 84.   Rank: Private - By what ship or how taken: Boats & Troops - Time when: 28 May 1813 - Place where: Stoney Point, Henderson Harbor - Of what ship or corps: Land forces - Whether man of war, privateer or merchant vessel: Taken on shore - Time when received into custody: 8 Jun 1813 - From what ship or whence received:

American Prisoners of War held at Quebec during the War of 1812

Batteaux - Exchanged, discharged, died, or escape: Discharged - Time when: 31 Oct 1813 - Whither, and by what order, or number or re-entry: Malabar Transport

Hubbell, William   Prisoner 1962. Rank: Private - By what ship or how taken: Troops - Time when: 17 Sep 1814 - Place where: Fort Erie - Of what ship or corps: Land forces - Whether man of war, privateer or merchant vessel: Taken on shore - Time when received into custody: 11 Dec 1814 - From what ship or whence received: Montreal - Exchanged, discharged, died, or escape: Discharged - Time when: 13 Mar 1815 - Whither, and by what order, or number or re-entry: United States

Hugh, Michael   Prisoner 850. Rank: Corporal - By what ship or how taken: Troops - Time when: 26 Jun 1813 - Place where: Beaver Dam - Of what ship or corps: Land forces - Whether man of war, privateer or merchant vessel: Taken on shore - Time when received into custody: 7 Jul 1813 - From what ship or whence received: Steamboat - Exchanged, discharged, died, or escape: Discharged - Time when: 10 Aug 1813 - Whither, and by what order, or number or re-entry: HM Ship Malpomena

Huie, John   Prisoner 1707. Rank: Captain - By what ship or how taken: Troops - Time when: 17 Sep 1814 - Place where: Fort Erie - Of what ship or corps: Land forces - Whether man of war, privateer or merchant vessel: Taken on shore - Time when received into custody: 28 Oct 1814 - From what ship or whence received: Montreal - Exchanged, discharged, died, or escape: Discharged - Time when: 13 Mar 1815 - Whither, and by what order, or number or re-entry: United States

Huit, John   Prisoner 1706. Rank: Captain - By what ship or how taken: Troops - Time when: 17 Sep 1814 - Place where: Fort Erie - Of what ship or corps: Land forces - Whether man of war, privateer or merchant vessel: Taken on shore - Time when received into custody: 28 Oct 1814 - From what ship or whence received: Montreal - Exchanged, discharged, died, or escape: Discharged - Time when: 13 Mar 1815 - Whither, and by what order, or number or re-entry: United States

Hunt, John   Prisoner 1508. Rank: Captain - By what ship or how taken: Troops - Time when: 25 Jul 1814 - Place where: Lundy's Lane - Of what ship or corps: Land forces - Whether man of war, privateer or merchant vessel: Taken on shore - Time when received into custody: 25 Aug 1814 - From what ship or whence received: Steamboat - Exchanged, discharged, died, or escape: Discharged - Time when: 15 Nov 1814 - Whither, and by what order, or number or re-entry: Wolga No. 377

Hunt, John   Prisoner 166. Rank: Able seaman - By what ship or how taken: Boats & Troops - Time when: 3 Jun 1813 - Place where: Lake Champlain - Of what ship or corps: Eagle - Whether man of war, privateer or merchant vessel: Man of War - Time when received into custody: 9 Jun 1813 - From what ship or whence received: Batteaux - Exchanged, discharged, died, or escape: Discharged - Time when: 31 Oct 1813 - Whither, and by what order, or number or re-entry: Malabar Transport

Hunt, Soloman   Prisoner 118. Rank: Private - By what ship or how taken: Boats & Troops - Time when: 28 May 1813 - Place where: Stoney Point, Henderson Harbor - Of what ship or corps: Land forces - Whether man of war, privateer or merchant vessel: Taken on shore - Time when received into custody: 8 Jun 1813 - From what ship or whence received: Batteaux - Exchanged, discharged, died, or escape: Died - Time when: 4 Aug 1813 - Whither, and by what order, or number or re-entry:

Hunter, James   Prisoner 871. Rank: Private - By what ship or how taken: Troops - Time when: 26 Jun 1813 - Place where: Beaver Dam - Of what ship or corps: Land forces - Whether man of war, privateer or merchant vessel: Taken on shore - Time when received into custody: 7 Jul 1813 - From what ship or whence received: Steamboat - Exchanged, discharged, died, or escape: Discharged - Time when: 10 Aug 1813 - Whither, and by what order, or number or re-entry: HM Ship Malpomena

Hunter, James   Prisoner 594. Rank: Private - By what ship or how taken: Troops - Time when: 26 Jun 1813 - Place where: Stoney Point - Of what ship or corps: Land forces - Whether man of war, privateer or merchant vessel: Taken on shore - Time when received into custody: 7 Jul 1813 - From what ship or whence received: Steamboat - Exchanged, discharged, died, or escape: Discharged - Time when: 10 Aug 1813 - Whither, and by what order, or number or re-entry: HM Ship Regulius by order of Sir George Provost

Hunter, Joseph   Prisoner 431. Rank: Private - By what ship or how taken: Troops - Time when: 24 Jun 1813 - Place where: Beaver Dam - Of what ship or corps: Land forces - Whether man of war, privateer or merchant vessel: Taken on shore - Time when received into custody: 7 Jul 1813 - From what ship or whence received: Steamboat - Exchanged, discharged, died, or escape: Discharged - Time when: 10 Aug 1813 - Whither, and by what order, or number or re-entry: HM Ship Regulius by order of Sir George Provost

American Prisoners of War held at Quebec during the War of 1812

Hurd, John   Prisoner 567. Rank: Private - By what ship or how taken: Troops - Time when: 26 Jun 1813 - Place where: Beaver Dam - Of what ship or corps: Land forces - Whether man of war, privateer or merchant vessel: Taken on shore - Time when received into custody: 13 Jul 1813 - From what ship or whence received: Steamboat - Exchanged, discharged, died, or escape: Discharged - Time when: 10 Aug 1813 - Whither, and by what order, or number or re-entry: HM Ship Regulius by order of Sir George Provost

Huss, John   Prisoner 1635. Rank: Private - By what ship or how taken: Troops - Time when: 5 Jul 1814 - Place where: Chippewa - Of what ship or corps: Land forces - Whether man of war, privateer or merchant vessel: Taken on shore - Time when received into custody: 5 Oct 1814 - From what ship or whence received: Montreal - Exchanged, discharged, died, or escape: Discharged - Time when: 8 Oct 1814 - Whither, and by what order, or number or re-entry: H.M. Ship Ceylon

Hutchins, A.   Prisoner 1515. Rank: Private - By what ship or how taken: Troops - Time when: 25 Jul 1814 - Place where: Lundy's Lane - Of what ship or corps: Land forces - Whether man of war, privateer or merchant vessel: Taken on shore - Time when received into custody: 30 Aug 1814 - From what ship or whence received: Lady Delaval Schooner 578 - Exchanged, discharged, died, or escape: Escaped - Time when: 1 Oct 1814 - Whither, and by what order, or number or re-entry:

Hutchins, Eraoh   Prisoner 129. Rank: Private - By what ship or how taken: Boats & Troops - Time when: 28 May 1813 - Place where: Stoney Point, Henderson Harbor - Of what ship or corps: Land forces - Whether man of war, privateer or merchant vessel: Taken on shore - Time when received into custody: 8 Jun 1813 - From what ship or whence received: Batteaux - Exchanged, discharged, died, or escape: Escaped - Time when: 3 Sep 1813 - Whither, and by what order, or number or re-entry:

Hutchinson, Elihu   Prisoner 965. Rank: Private - By what ship or how taken: Troops - Time when: 5 Jul 1813 - Place where: Fort Schisher - Of what ship or corps: Land forces - Whether man of war, privateer or merchant vessel: Taken on shore - Time when received into custody: 5 Sep 1813 - From what ship or whence received: Steamboat - Exchanged, discharged, died, or escape: - Time when: - Whither, and by what order, or number or re-entry:

Hutchison, David   Prisoner 1271. Rank: Privateer - By what ship or how taken: Troops - Time when: 19 Dec 1813 - Place where: Fort Niagara - Of what ship or corps: Land forces - Whether man of war, privateer or merchant vessel: Taken on shore - Time when received into custody: 29 Jan 1814 - From what ship or whence received: Montreal by land carriage - Exchanged, discharged, died, or escape: Discharged - Time when: 4 May 1814 - Whither, and by what order, or number or re-entry: United States

Hutchison, Robert B.   Prisoner 1856. Rank: Private - By what ship or how taken: Troops - Time when: 17 Sep 1814 - Place where: Fort Erie - Of what ship or corps: Land forces - Whether man of war, privateer or merchant vessel: Taken on shore - Time when received into custody: 1 Nov 1814 - From what ship or whence received: Montreal - Exchanged, discharged, died, or escape: Discharged - Time when: 8 Nov 1814 - Whither, and by what order, or number or re-entry: S. George No. 575 for Halifax

Hyde , Nathan   Prisoner 1146. Rank: Private - By what ship or how taken: Troops - Time when: 27 Oct 1812 - Place where: Rapids Prince Reason - Of what ship or corps: Land forces - Whether man of war, privateer or merchant vessel: Taken on shore - Time when received into custody: 25 Nov 1813 - From what ship or whence received: Town Goal - Exchanged, discharged, died, or escape: Discharged - Time when: 21 Apr 1814 - Whither, and by what order, or number or re-entry: United States

Hydendry, Henry   Prisoner 1094. Rank: Private - By what ship or how taken: Troops - Time when: 24 Aug 1813 - Place where: Fort George - Of what ship or corps: Land forces - Whether man of war, privateer or merchant vessel: Taken on shore - Time when received into custody: 10 Oct 1813 - From what ship or whence received: Steamboat - Exchanged, discharged, died, or escape: Discharged - Time when: 31 Oct 1813 - Whither, and by what order, or number or re-entry: Malabar Transport

Hyett, Joseph   Prisoner 972. Rank: Private - By what ship or how taken: Troops - Time when: 5 Jul 1813 - Place where: Fort Schisher - Of what ship or corps: Land forces - Whether man of war, privateer or merchant vessel: Taken on shore - Time when received into custody: 5 Sep 1813 - From what ship or whence received: Steamboat - Exchanged, discharged, died, or escape: Discharged - Time when: 31 Oct 1813 - Whither, and by what order, or number or re-entry: Malabar Transport

Ingalls, Jonathan   Prisoner 133. Rank: Private - By what ship or how taken: Boats & Troops - Time when: 28 May 1813 - Place where: Stoney Point, Henderson Harbor - Of what ship or corps: Land forces - Whether man of war, privateer or merchant vessel: Taken on shore - Time when received into custody: 8 Jul 1813 - From what ship or whence received: Batteaux - Exchanged, discharged, died, or escape: Died - Time when: 14 Aug 1813 - Whither, and by what order, or

American Prisoners of War held at Quebec during the War of 1812

number or re-entry:

Ingham, Nathaniel   Prisoner 1806. Rank: Private - By what ship or how taken: Troops - Time when: 17 Sep 1814 - Place where: Fort Erie - Of what ship or corps: Land forces - Whether man of war, privateer or merchant vessel: Taken on shore - Time when received into custody: 1 Nov 1814 - From what ship or whence received: Montreal - Exchanged, discharged, died, or escape: Discharged - Time when: 8 Nov 1814 - Whither, and by what order, or number or re-entry: S. George No. 575 for Halifax by order of Sir George Provost

Inghram, Benjamin   Prisoner 1076. Rank: Private - By what ship or how taken: Troops - Time when: 24 Aug 1813 - Place where: Fort George - Of what ship or corps: Land forces - Whether man of war, privateer or merchant vessel: Taken on shore - Time when received into custody: 10 Oct 1813 - From what ship or whence received: Steamboat - Exchanged, discharged, died, or escape: Discharged - Time when: 31 Oct 1813 - Whither, and by what order, or number or re-entry: Malabar Transport

Ireland, Jonas   Prisoner 74. Rank: Private - By what ship or how taken: Boats & Troops - Time when: 28 May 1813 - Place where: Stoney Point, Henderson Harbor - Of what ship or corps: Land forces - Whether man of war, privateer or merchant vessel: Taken on shore - Time when received into custody: 8 Jun 1813 - From what ship or whence received: Batteaux - Exchanged, discharged, died, or escape: Discharged - Time when: 31 Oct 1813 - Whither, and by what order, or number or re-entry: Malabar Transport

Ireland, Jonathan   Prisoner 580. Rank: Private - By what ship or how taken: Troops - Time when: 26 Jun 1813 - Place where: Beaver Dam - Of what ship or corps: Land forces - Whether man of war, privateer or merchant vessel: Taken on shore - Time when received into custody: 13 Jul 1813 - From what ship or whence received: Steamboat - Exchanged, discharged, died, or escape: Discharged - Time when: 10 Aug 1813 - Whither, and by what order, or number or re-entry: HM Ship Regulius by order of Sir George Provost

Irwin, John   Prisoner 1435. Rank: Private - By what ship or how taken: Troops - Time when: 5 Jul 1814 - Place where: Chippewa - Of what ship or corps: Land forces - Whether man of war, privateer or merchant vessel: Taken on shore - Time when received into custody: 12 Aug 1814 - From what ship or whence received: Royal Seaman No. 289 Transport - Exchanged, discharged, died, or escape: Discharged - Time when: 8 Oct 1814 - Whither, and by what order, or number or re-entry: Queen No. 415

Ives, Amos   Prisoner 1505. Rank: Private - By what ship or how taken: Troops - Time when: 25 Jul 1814 - Place where: Lundy's Lane - Of what ship or corps: Land forces - Whether man of war, privateer or merchant vessel: Taken on shore - Time when received into custody: 19 Aug 1814 - From what ship or whence received: Triton No. 438 Transport - Exchanged, discharged, died, or escape: Discharged - Time when: 8 Oct 1814 - Whither, and by what order, or number or re-entry: Queen No. 415

Jack, Andrew   Prisoner 1148. Rank: Private - By what ship or how taken: Troops - Time when: 5 May 1813 - Place where: Rapids Prince Reason - Of what ship or corps: Land forces - Whether man of war, privateer or merchant vessel: Taken on shore - Time when received into custody: 25 Nov 1813 - From what ship or whence received: Town Goal - Exchanged, discharged, died, or escape: Discharged - Time when: 21 Apr 1814 - Whither, and by what order, or number or re-entry: United States

Jackson, Barnaby   Prisoner 1750. Rank: Private - By what ship or how taken: Gun Boats - Time when: 3 Sep 1814 - Place where: Lake Huron - Of what ship or corps: Tigress - Whether man of war, privateer or merchant vessel: Man of War - Time when received into custody: 1 Nov 1814 - From what ship or whence received: Montreal - Exchanged, discharged, died, or escape: Discharged - Time when: 8 Nov 1814 - Whither, and by what order, or number or re-entry: S. George No. 575 for Halifax by order of Sir George Provost

Jackson, Enoch   Prisoner 122. Rank: Private - By what ship or how taken: Boats & Troops - Time when: 28 May 1813 - Place where: Stoney Point, Henderson Harbor - Of what ship or corps: Land forces - Whether man of war, privateer or merchant vessel: Taken on shore - Time when received into custody: 8 Jun 1813 - From what ship or whence received: Batteaux - Exchanged, discharged, died, or escape: Discharged - Time when: 31 Oct 1813 - Whither, and by what order, or number or re-entry: Malabar Transport

Jennings, Noah   Prisoner 1300. Rank: Private - By what ship or how taken: Troops - Time when: 19 Dec 1813 - Place where: Fort Niagara - Of what ship or corps: Land forces - Whether man of war, privateer or merchant vessel: Taken on shore - Time when received into custody: 29 Jan 1814 - From what ship or whence received: Montreal by land carriage - Exchanged, discharged, died, or escape: Discharged - Time when: 4 May 1814 - Whither, and by what order, or number or re-entry: United States

Johnson, Benjamin   Prisoner 1460. Rank: Private - By what ship or how taken: Troops - Time when: 6 May 1814 - Place where: Oswago - Of what ship or corps: Land forces - Whether man of war, privateer or merchant vessel: Taken on shore - Time when received into custody: 12 Aug 1814 - From what ship or whence received: Royal Seaman No. 289 Transport - Exchanged, discharged, died, or escape: Discharged - Time when: 8 Oct 1814 - Whither, and by what order, or number or re-entry: Queen No. 415

Johnson, Daniel   Prisoner 1688. Rank: Private - By what ship or how taken: Troops - Time when: 27 Aug 1814 - Place where: Fort Erie - Of what ship or corps: Land forces - Whether man of war, privateer or merchant vessel: Taken on shore - Time when received into custody: 23 Oct 1814 - From what ship or whence received: Montreal - Exchanged, discharged, died, or escape: Discharged - Time when: 8 Nov 1814 - Whither, and by what order, or number or re-entry: S. George No. 575 for Halifax

Johnson, David   Prisoner 60. Rank: Private - By what ship or how taken: Boats & Troops - Time when: 28 May 1813 - Place where: Stoney Point, Henderson Harbor - Of what ship or corps: Land forces - Whether man of war, privateer or merchant vessel: Taken on shore - Time when received into custody: 8 Jun 1813 - From what ship or whence received: Batteaux - Exchanged, discharged, died, or escape: Discharged - Time when: 31 Oct 1813 - Whither, and by what order, or number or re-entry: Malabar Transport

Johnson, David   Prisoner 1456. Rank: Private - By what ship or how taken: Troops - Time when: 6 May 1814 - Place where: Oswago - Of what ship or corps: Land forces - Whether man of war, privateer or merchant vessel: Taken on shore - Time when received into custody: 12 Aug 1814 - From what ship or whence received: Royal Seaman No. 289 Transport - Exchanged, discharged, died, or escape: Discharged - Time when: 8 Nov 1814 - Whither, and by what order, or number or re-entry: George No. 575 for Halifax by orders of Sir George Provost

Johnson, Hugh   Prisoner 636. Rank: Private - By what ship or how taken: Troops - Time when: 24 Jun 1813 - Place where: Stoney Point - Of what ship or corps: Land forces - Whether man of war, privateer or merchant vessel: Taken on shore - Time when received into custody: 7 Jul 1813 - From what ship or whence received: Steamboat - Exchanged, discharged, died, or escape: Discharged - Time when: 10 Aug 1813 - Whither, and by what order, or number or re-entry: HM Ship Regulius by order of Sir George Provost

Johnson, Isaac   Prisoner 625. Rank: Private - By what ship or how taken: Troops - Time when: 24 Jun 1813 - Place where: Stoney Point - Of what ship or corps: Land forces - Whether man of war, privateer or merchant vessel: Taken on shore - Time when received into custody: 7 Jul 1813 - From what ship or whence received: Steamboat - Exchanged, discharged, died, or escape: Discharged - Time when: 10 Aug 1813 - Whither, and by what order, or number or re-entry: HM Ship Regulius by order of Sir George Provost

Johnson, Jason   Prisoner 587. Rank: Private - By what ship or how taken: Troops - Time when: 26 Jun 1813 - Place where: Beaver Dam - Of what ship or corps: Land forces - Whether man of war, privateer or merchant vessel: Taken on shore - Time when received into custody: 13 Jul 1813 - From what ship or whence received: Steamboat - Exchanged, discharged, died, or escape: Discharged - Time when: 31 Oct 1813 - Whither, and by what order, or number or re-entry: Malabar Transport

Johnson, John   Prisoner 59. Rank: Private - By what ship or how taken: Boats & Troops - Time when: 28 May 1813 - Place where: Stoney Point, Henderson Harbor - Of what ship or corps: Land forces - Whether man of war, privateer or merchant vessel: Taken on shore - Time when received into custody: 8 Jun 1813 - From what ship or whence received: Batteaux - Exchanged, discharged, died, or escape: Discharged - Time when: 31 Oct 1813 - Whither, and by what order, or number or re-entry: Malabar Transport

Johnson, John   Prisoner 411. Rank: Sergeant - By what ship or how taken: Troops - Time when: 24 Jun 1813 - Place where: Beaver Dam - Of what ship or corps: Land forces - Whether man of war, privateer or merchant vessel: Taken on shore - Time when received into custody: 7 Jul 1813 - From what ship or whence received: Steamboat - Exchanged, discharged, died, or escape: Discharged - Time when: 22 Aug 1813 - Whither, and by what order, or number or re-entry: Lord Cartheart Transport

Johnson, John   Prisoner 849. Rank: Private - By what ship or how taken: Troops - Time when: 26 Jun 1813 - Place where: Beaver Dam - Of what ship or corps: Land forces - Whether man of war, privateer or merchant vessel: Taken on shore - Time when received into custody: 7 Jul 1813 - From what ship or whence received: Steamboat - Exchanged, discharged, died, or escape: Discharged - Time when: 10 Aug 1813 - Whither, and by what order, or number or re-entry: HM Ship Malpomena

Johnson, Mark   Prisoner 1571. Rank: Gunner - By what ship or how taken: Gun Boats - Time when: 12 Aug 1814 - Place where: Fort Erie - Of what ship or corps: Somers - Whether man of war, privateer or merchant vessel: Man of War - Time when received into custody: 5 Oct 1814 - From what ship or whence received: Montreal - Exchanged, discharged, died, or escape: Discharged - Time when: 10 Nov 1814 - Whither, and by what order, or number or re-entry: Freedom

American Prisoners of War held at Quebec during the War of 1812

No. 582

Johnson, Noble   Prisoner 654. Rank: Private - By what ship or how taken: Troops - Time when: 24 Jun 1813 - Place where: Stoney Point - Of what ship or corps: Land forces - Whether man of war, privateer or merchant vessel: Taken on shore - Time when received into custody: 7 Jul 1813 - From what ship or whence received: Steamboat - Exchanged, discharged, died, or escape: Discharged - Time when: 31 Oct 1813 - Whither, and by what order, or number or re-entry: Malabar Transport

Johnson, Ross   Prisoner 1197. Rank: Citizen - By what ship or how taken: - Time when: - Place where: - Of what ship or corps: - Whether man of war, privateer or merchant vessel: - Time when received into custody: 12 Dec 1813 - From what ship or whence received: Town Goal - Exchanged, discharged, died, or escape: Discharged - Time when: 4 May 1814 - Whither, and by what order, or number or re-entry: United States

Johnson, Thomas   Prisoner 1137. Rank: Private - By what ship or how taken: Troops - Time when: 22 Jan 1812 - Place where: Rapids Prince Reason - Of what ship or corps: Land forces - Whether man of war, privateer or merchant vessel: Taken on shore - Time when received into custody: 25 Nov 1813 - From what ship or whence received: Town Goal - Exchanged, discharged, died, or escape: Discharged - Time when: 4 May 1814 - Whither, and by what order, or number or re-entry: United States

Johnson, Truman   Prisoner 284. Rank: Private - By what ship or how taken: Troops - Time when: 6 Jun 1813 - Place where: Stoney Point - Of what ship or corps: Land forces - Whether man of war, privateer or merchant vessel: Taken on shore - Time when received into custody: 28 Jun 1813 - From what ship or whence received: Batteaux - Exchanged, discharged, died, or escape: Discharged - Time when: 31 Oct 1813 - Whither, and by what order, or number or re-entry: Malabar Transport

Johnson, William   Prisoner 1854. Rank: Private - By what ship or how taken: Troops - Time when: 17 Sep 1814 - Place where: Fort Erie - Of what ship or corps: Land forces - Whether man of war, privateer or merchant vessel: Taken on shore - Time when received into custody: 1 Nov 1814 - From what ship or whence received: Montreal - Exchanged, discharged, died, or escape: Discharged - Time when: 8 Nov 1814 - Whither, and by what order, or number or re-entry: S. George No. 575 for Halifax

Johnson, William   Prisoner 1510. Rank: Cornet - By what ship or how taken: Troops - Time when: 17 Jul 1814 - Place where: St. Davids - Of what ship or corps: Land forces - Whether man of war, privateer or merchant vessel: Taken on shore - Time when received into custody: 25 Aug 1814 - From what ship or whence received: Steamboat - Exchanged, discharged, died, or escape: Discharged - Time when: 10 Nov 1814 - Whither, and by what order, or number or re-entry: Transport Stately No. 408 for Halifax

Johnson, William   Prisoner 560. Rank: Private - By what ship or how taken: Troops - Time when: 26 Jun 1813 - Place where: Beaver Dam - Of what ship or corps: Land forces - Whether man of war, privateer or merchant vessel: Taken on shore - Time when received into custody: 13 Jul 1813 - From what ship or whence received: Steamboat - Exchanged, discharged, died, or escape: Discharged - Time when: 10 Aug 1813 - Whither, and by what order, or number or re-entry: HM Ship Regulius by order of Sir George Provost

Johnson, William   Prisoner 990. Rank: Seaman - By what ship or how taken: Lord Melvin - Time when: 10 Aug 1813 - Place where: Lake Ontario - Of what ship or corps: Growler - Whether man of war, privateer or merchant vessel: Man of War - Time when received into custody: 5 Sep 1813 - From what ship or whence received: Steamboat - Exchanged, discharged, died, or escape: Discharged - Time when: 18 Sep 1813 - Whither, and by what order, or number or re-entry: To the Regulius Transport by order of Major General Glasgow

Johnson, William   Prisoner 1208. Rank: Ensign - By what ship or how taken: Troops - Time when: 19 Dec 1813 - Place where: Fort Niagara - Of what ship or corps: Land forces - Whether man of war, privateer or merchant vessel: Taken on shore - Time when received into custody: 18 Jan 1814 - From what ship or whence received: Montreal by land carriage - Exchanged, discharged, died, or escape: Discharged - Time when: 4 May 1814 - Whither, and by what order, or number or re-entry: United States

Johnston, Assa   Prisoner 1289. Rank: Private - By what ship or how taken: Troops - Time when: 19 Dec 1813 - Place where: Fort Niagara - Of what ship or corps: Land forces - Whether man of war, privateer or merchant vessel: Taken on shore - Time when received into custody: 29 Jan 1814 - From what ship or whence received: Montreal by land carriage - Exchanged, discharged, died, or escape: Discharged - Time when: 4 May 1814 - Whither, and by what order, or number or re-entry: United States

American Prisoners of War held at Quebec during the War of 1812

Johnston, James   Prisoner 1287. Rank: Private - By what ship or how taken: Troops - Time when: 19 Dec 1813 - Place where: Fort Niagara - Of what ship or corps: Land forces - Whether man of war, privateer or merchant vessel: Taken on shore - Time when received into custody: 29 Jan 1814 - From what ship or whence received: Montreal by land carriage - Exchanged, discharged, died, or escape: Discharged - Time when: 4 May 1814 - Whither, and by what order, or number or re-entry: United States

Johnston, James H.   Prisoner 1942. Rank: Private - By what ship or how taken: Troops - Time when: 17 Sep 1814 - Place where: Fort Erie - Of what ship or corps: Land forces - Whether man of war, privateer or merchant vessel: Taken on shore - Time when received into custody: 1 Nov 1814 - From what ship or whence received: Montreal - Exchanged, discharged, died, or escape: Discharged - Time when: 16 Mar 1815 - Whither, and by what order, or number or re-entry: United States

Johnston, Littleton   Prisoner 1205. Rank: Lieutenant - By what ship or how taken: Troops - Time when: 19 Dec 1813 - Place where: Fort Niagara - Of what ship or corps: Land forces - Whether man of war, privateer or merchant vessel: Taken on shore - Time when received into custody: 18 Jan 1814 - From what ship or whence received: Montreal by land carriage - Exchanged, discharged, died, or escape: Discharged - Time when: 4 May 1814 - Whither, and by what order, or number or re-entry: United States

Johnston, Richard   Prisoner 1352. Rank: Private - By what ship or how taken: Troops - Time when: 19 Dec 1813 - Place where: Fort Niagara - Of what ship or corps: Land forces - Whether man of war, privateer or merchant vessel: Taken on shore - Time when received into custody: 29 Jan 1814 - From what ship or whence received: Montreal by land carriage - Exchanged, discharged, died, or escape: Discharged - Time when: 4 May 1814 - Whither, and by what order, or number or re-entry: United States

Johnston, William   Prisoner 1354. Rank: Sergeant - By what ship or how taken: Troops - Time when: 19 Dec 1813 - Place where: Fort Niagara - Of what ship or corps: Land forces - Whether man of war, privateer or merchant vessel: Taken on shore - Time when received into custody: 29 Jan 1814 - From what ship or whence received: Montreal by land carriage - Exchanged, discharged, died, or escape: Discharged - Time when: 21 Feb 1814 - Whither, and by what order, or number or re-entry: Volunteered for New Brunswick Fencibles

Jones, Henry   Prisoner 342. Rank: Private - By what ship or how taken: Boats & Troops - Time when: 22 Feb 1813 - Place where: Hedgesburgh - Of what ship or corps: Land forces - Whether man of war, privateer or merchant vessel: Taken on shore - Time when received into custody: 28 Jun 1813 - From what ship or whence received: Mary of Quebec - Exchanged, discharged, died, or escape: Discharged - Time when: 31 Oct 1813 - Whither, and by what order, or number or re-entry: Malabar Transport

Jones, John   Prisoner 1136. Rank: Private - By what ship or how taken: Troops - Time when: 5 May 1813 - Place where: Rapids Prince Reason - Of what ship or corps: Land forces - Whether man of war, privateer or merchant vessel: Taken on shore - Time when received into custody: 25 Nov 1813 - From what ship or whence received: Town Goal - Exchanged, discharged, died, or escape: Discharged - Time when: 4 May 1814 - Whither, and by what order, or number or re-entry: United States

Jones, Leroy   Prisoner 1139. Rank: Private - By what ship or how taken: Troops - Time when: 22 Jan 1812 - Place where: Rapids Prince Reason - Of what ship or corps: Land forces - Whether man of war, privateer or merchant vessel: Taken on shore - Time when received into custody: 25 Nov 1813 - From what ship or whence received: Town Goal - Exchanged, discharged, died, or escape: Discharged - Time when: 4 May 1814 - Whither, and by what order, or number or re-entry: United States

Jones, Martin   Prisoner 1001. Rank: Seaman - By what ship or how taken: Earl Moria - Time when: 10 Aug 1813 - Place where: Lake Ontario - Of what ship or corps: Julia - Whether man of war, privateer or merchant vessel: Man of War - Time when received into custody: 5 Sep 1813 - From what ship or whence received: Steamboat - Exchanged, discharged, died, or escape: Discharged - Time when: 7 Oct 1813 - Whither, and by what order, or number or re-entry: General Kempt Transport

Jones, Nathan   Prisoner 17. Rank: Corporal - By what ship or how taken: Boats & Troops - Time when: 28 May 1813 - Place where: Stoney Point, Henderson Harbor - Of what ship or corps: Land forces - Whether man of war, privateer or merchant vessel: Taken on shore - Time when received into custody: 8 Jun 1813 - From what ship or whence received: Batteaux - Exchanged, discharged, died, or escape: Discharged - Time when: 8 Oct 1814 - Whither, and by what order, or number or re-entry: H.M. Ship Ceylon

Jones, Samuel   Prisoner 1254. Rank: Private - By what ship or how taken: Troops - Time when: 19 Dec 1813 - Place where: Fort Niagara - Of what ship or corps: Land forces - Whether man of war, privateer or merchant vessel: Taken on shore - Time when received into custody: 29 Jan 1814 - From what ship or whence received: Montreal by land carriage -

American Prisoners of War held at Quebec during the War of 1812

Exchanged, discharged, died, or escape: Discharged - Time when: 27 Feb 1814 - Whither, and by what order, or number or re-entry: Volunteered for New Brunswick Fencibles

Jones, Thomas   Prisoner 928. Rank: Private - By what ship or how taken: Troops - Time when: 26 Jun 1813 - Place where: Beaver Dam - Of what ship or corps: Land forces - Whether man of war, privateer or merchant vessel: Taken on shore - Time when received into custody: 21 Jul 1813 - From what ship or whence received: Steamboat - Exchanged, discharged, died, or escape: Discharged - Time when: 10 Aug 1813 - Whither, and by what order, or number or re-entry: HM Ship Malpomena

Jones, William   Prisoner 575. Rank: Private - By what ship or how taken: Troops - Time when: 26 Jun 1813 - Place where: Beaver Dam - Of what ship or corps: Land forces - Whether man of war, privateer or merchant vessel: Taken on shore - Time when received into custody: 13 Jul 1813 - From what ship or whence received: Steamboat - Exchanged, discharged, died, or escape: Discharged - Time when: 10 Aug 1813 - Whither, and by what order, or number or re-entry: HM Ship Regulius by order of Sir George Provost

Jones, William   Prisoner 286. Rank: Private - By what ship or how taken: Troops - Time when: 6 Jun 1813 - Place where: Stoney Point - Of what ship or corps: Land forces - Whether man of war, privateer or merchant vessel: Taken on shore - Time when received into custody: 28 Jun 1813 - From what ship or whence received: Batteaux - Exchanged, discharged, died, or escape: Discharged - Time when: 31 Oct 1813 - Whither, and by what order, or number or re-entry: Malabar Transport

Jones, William   Prisoner 1698. Rank: Private - By what ship or how taken: Troops - Time when: 1 Aug 1814 - Place where: Fort Erie - Of what ship or corps: Land forces - Whether man of war, privateer or merchant vessel: Taken on shore - Time when received into custody: 23 Oct 1814 - From what ship or whence received: Montreal - Exchanged, discharged, died, or escape: Discharged - Time when: 8 Nov 1814 - Whither, and by what order, or number or re-entry: S. George No. 575 for Halifax

Jones, William L.   Prisoner 550. Rank: Sergeant - By what ship or how taken: Troops - Time when: 26 Jun 1813 - Place where: Beaver Dam - Of what ship or corps: Land forces - Whether man of war, privateer or merchant vessel: Taken on shore - Time when received into custody: 13 Jul 1813 - From what ship or whence received: Steamboat - Exchanged, discharged, died, or escape: - Time when: - Whither, and by what order, or number or re-entry:

Joseph, John   Prisoner 1016. Rank: Marine Private - By what ship or how taken: Earl Moria - Time when: 10 Aug 1813 - Place where: Lake Ontario - Of what ship or corps: Julia - Whether man of war, privateer or merchant vessel: Man of War - Time when received into custody: 5 Sep 1813 - From what ship or whence received: Steamboat - Exchanged, discharged, died, or escape: Discharged - Time when: 31 Oct 1813 - Whither, and by what order, or number or re-entry: Malabar Transport

Joy, Bennett   Prisoner 1976. Rank: Private - By what ship or how taken: Troops - Time when: 2 Nov 1814 - Place where: Fort Erie - Of what ship or corps: Land forces - Whether man of war, privateer or merchant vessel: Taken on shore - Time when received into custody: 11 Dec 1814 - From what ship or whence received: Montreal - Exchanged, discharged, died, or escape: Discharged - Time when: 13 Mar 1815 - Whither, and by what order, or number or re-entry: United States

Judd, William   Prisoner 1936. Rank: Private - By what ship or how taken: Troops - Time when: 17 Sep 1814 - Place where: Fort Erie - Of what ship or corps: Land forces - Whether man of war, privateer or merchant vessel: Taken on shore - Time when received into custody: - From what ship or whence received: - Exchanged, discharged, died, or escape: Died - Time when: 7 Nov 1814 - Whither, and by what order, or number or re-entry: Dysentry

Kain, John   Prisoner 864. Rank: Private - By what ship or how taken: Troops - Time when: 26 Jun 1813 - Place where: Beaver Dam - Of what ship or corps: Land forces - Whether man of war, privateer or merchant vessel: Taken on shore - Time when received into custody: 7 Jul 1813 - From what ship or whence received: Steamboat - Exchanged, discharged, died, or escape: Discharged - Time when: 31 Oct 1813 - Whither, and by what order, or number or re-entry: Malabar Transport

Karney, Thomas   Prisoner 526. Rank: Lieutenant - By what ship or how taken: Troops - Time when: 24 Jun 1813 - Place where: Beaver Dam - Of what ship or corps: Land forces - Whether man of war, privateer or merchant vessel: Taken on shore - Time when received into custody: 13 Jul 1813 - From what ship or whence received: Steamboat - Exchanged, discharged, died, or escape: Discharged - Time when: 13 Dec 1813 - Whither, and by what order, or number or re-entry: United States

Kehae, John   Prisoner 1772. Rank: Corporal - By what ship or how taken: Troops - Time when: 7 Sep 1814 - Place where: Fort Erie - Of what ship or corps: Land forces - Whether man of war, privateer or merchant vessel: Taken on shore - Time

American Prisoners of War held at Quebec during the War of 1812

when received into custody: 1 Nov 1814 - From what ship or whence received: Montreal - Exchanged, discharged, died, or escape: Discharged - Time when: 8 Nov 1814 - Whither, and by what order, or number or re-entry: S. George No. 575 for Halifax by order of Sir George Provost

Keith, Lephlmiah   Prisoner 34. Rank: Private - By what ship or how taken: Boats & Troops - Time when: 28 May 1813 - Place where: Stoney Point, Henderson Harbor - Of what ship or corps: Land forces - Whether man of war, privateer or merchant vessel: Taken on shore - Time when received into custody: 8 Jun 1813 - From what ship or whence received: Batteaux - Exchanged, discharged, died, or escape: Discharged - Time when: 31 Oct 1813 - Whither, and by what order, or number or re-entry: Malabar Transport

Kelley, James   Prisoner 1085. Rank: Private - By what ship or how taken: Troops - Time when: 24 Aug 1813 - Place where: Fort George - Of what ship or corps: Land forces - Whether man of war, privateer or merchant vessel: Taken on shore - Time when received into custody: 10 Oct 1813 - From what ship or whence received: Steamboat - Exchanged, discharged, died, or escape: Discharged - Time when: 31 Oct 1813 - Whither, and by what order, or number or re-entry: Malabar Transport

Kellog, Tsar   Prisoner 728. Rank: Corporal - By what ship or how taken: Troops - Time when: 26 Jun 1813 - Place where: Beaver Dam - Of what ship or corps: Land forces - Whether man of war, privateer or merchant vessel: Taken on shore - Time when received into custody: 7 Jul 1813 - From what ship or whence received: Steamboat - Exchanged, discharged, died, or escape: Discharged - Time when: 10 Aug 1813 - Whither, and by what order, or number or re-entry: HM Ship Regulius by order of Sir George Provost

Kelly, Charles   Prisoner 760. Rank: Private - By what ship or how taken: Troops - Time when: 26 Jun 1813 - Place where: Beaver Dam - Of what ship or corps: Land forces - Whether man of war, privateer or merchant vessel: Taken on shore - Time when received into custody: 7 Jul 1813 - From what ship or whence received: Steamboat - Exchanged, discharged, died, or escape: Discharged - Time when: 10 Aug 1813 - Whither, and by what order, or number or re-entry: HM Ship Regulius by order of Sir George Provost

Kelly, William   Prisoner 925. Rank: Private - By what ship or how taken: Troops - Time when: 26 Jun 1813 - Place where: Beaver Dam - Of what ship or corps: Land forces - Whether man of war, privateer or merchant vessel: Taken on shore - Time when received into custody: 21 Jul 1813 - From what ship or whence received: Steamboat - Exchanged, discharged, died, or escape: Discharged - Time when: 10 Aug 1813 - Whither, and by what order, or number or re-entry: HM Ship Malpomena

Kelly, William   Prisoner 390. Rank: Private - By what ship or how taken: Troops - Time when: 6 Jun 1813 - Place where: Stoney Point - Of what ship or corps: Land forces - Whether man of war, privateer or merchant vessel: Taken on shore - Time when received into custody: 28 Jun 1813 - From what ship or whence received: Mary of Quebec - Exchanged, discharged, died, or escape: Discharged - Time when: 31 Oct 1813 - Whither, and by what order, or number or re-entry: Malabar Transport

Kennedy, William   Prisoner 1409. Rank: Corporal - By what ship or how taken: Troops - Time when: 19 Dec 1813 - Place where: Fort Niagara - Of what ship or corps: Land forces - Whether man of war, privateer or merchant vessel: Taken on shore - Time when received into custody: 29 Jan 1814 - From what ship or whence received: Montreal by land carriage - Exchanged, discharged, died, or escape: Discharged - Time when: 4 May 1814 - Whither, and by what order, or number or re-entry: United States

Kenyon, J.   Prisoner 1594. Rank: Corporal - By what ship or how taken: Troops - Time when: 12 Aug 1814 - Place where: Fort Erie - Of what ship or corps: Land forces - Whether man of war, privateer or merchant vessel: Taken on shore - Time when received into custody: 5 Oct 1814 - From what ship or whence received: Montreal - Exchanged, discharged, died, or escape: Discharged - Time when: 8 Oct 1814 - Whither, and by what order, or number or re-entry: H.M. Ship Ceylon

Kerrington, Esakel   Prisoner 769. Rank: Private - By what ship or how taken: Troops - Time when: 26 Jun 1813 - Place where: Beaver Dam - Of what ship or corps: Land forces - Whether man of war, privateer or merchant vessel: Taken on shore - Time when received into custody: 7 Jul 1813 - From what ship or whence received: Steamboat - Exchanged, discharged, died, or escape: Discharged - Time when: 10 Aug 1813 - Whither, and by what order, or number or re-entry: HM Ship Malpomena

Kimball, Abel   Prisoner 5. Rank: Private - By what ship or how taken: Boats & Troops - Time when: 28 May 1813 - Place where: Stoney Point, Henderson Harbor - Of what ship or corps: Land forces - Whether man of war, privateer or merchant vessel: Taken on shore - Time when received into custody: 8 Jun 1813 - From what ship or whence received: Batteaux - Exchanged, discharged, died, or escape: Discharged - Time when: 4 May 1814 - Whither, and by what order, or number or re-entry: United States

American Prisoners of War held at Quebec during the War of 1812

Kimball, Benjamin W.   Prisoner 35.   Rank: Private - By what ship or how taken: Boats & Troops - Time when: 28 May 1813 - Place where: Stoney Point, Henderson Harbor - Of what ship or corps: Land forces - Whether man of war, privateer or merchant vessel: Taken on shore - Time when received into custody: 8 Jun 1813 - From what ship or whence received: Batteaux - Exchanged, discharged, died, or escape: Died - Time when: 6 Aug 1813 - Whither, and by what order, or number or re-entry:

Kimball, Hannibal   Prisoner 88.   Rank: Private - By what ship or how taken: Boats & Troops - Time when: 28 May 1813 - Place where: Stoney Point, Henderson Harbor - Of what ship or corps: Land forces - Whether man of war, privateer or merchant vessel: Taken on shore - Time when received into custody: 8 Jun 1813 - From what ship or whence received: Batteaux - Exchanged, discharged, died, or escape: Discharged - Time when: 4 May 1814 - Whither, and by what order, or number or re-entry: United States

Kimball, Nathaniel   Prisoner 90.   Rank: Private - By what ship or how taken: Boats & Troops - Time when: 28 May 1813 - Place where: Stoney Point, Henderson Harbor - Of what ship or corps: Land forces - Whether man of war, privateer or merchant vessel: Taken on shore - Time when received into custody: 8 Jun 1813 - From what ship or whence received: Batteaux - Exchanged, discharged, died, or escape: Discharged - Time when: 31 Oct 1813 - Whither, and by what order, or number or re-entry: Malabar Transport

Kindle, Rezin   Prisoner 1142.   Rank: Private - By what ship or how taken: Troops - Time when: 22 Jan 1812 - Place where: Rapids Prince Reason - Of what ship or corps: Land forces - Whether man of war, privateer or merchant vessel: Taken on shore - Time when received into custody: 25 Nov 1813 - From what ship or whence received: Town Goal - Exchanged, discharged, died, or escape: Discharged - Time when: 21 Apr 1814 - Whither, and by what order, or number or re-entry: United States

King, Elijhu   Prisoner 1892.   Rank: Corporal - By what ship or how taken: Troops - Time when: 17 Sep 1814 - Place where: Fort Erie - Of what ship or corps: Land forces - Whether man of war, privateer or merchant vessel: Taken on shore - Time when received into custody: 1 Nov 1814 - From what ship or whence received: Montreal - Exchanged, discharged, died, or escape: Discharged - Time when: 8 Nov 1814 - Whither, and by what order, or number or re-entry: S. George No. 575 for Halifax by order of Sir George Provost

King, Robert   Prisoner 1944.   Rank: Private - By what ship or how taken: Troops - Time when: 17 Sep 1814 - Place where: Fort Erie - Of what ship or corps: Land forces - Whether man of war, privateer or merchant vessel: Taken on shore - Time when received into custody: 1 Nov 1814 - From what ship or whence received: Montreal - Exchanged, discharged, died, or escape: Discharged - Time when: 13 Mar 1815 - Whither, and by what order, or number or re-entry: United States

King, William   Prisoner 451.   Rank: Private - By what ship or how taken: Troops - Time when: 24 Jun 1813 - Place where: Beaver Dam - Of what ship or corps: Malabar & Hydia - Whether man of war, privateer or merchant vessel: Taken on shore - Time when received into custody: 7 Jul 1813 - From what ship or whence received: Steamboat - Exchanged, discharged, died, or escape: Discharged - Time when: 10 Aug 1813 - Whither, and by what order, or number or re-entry: HM Ship Regulius by order of Sir George Provost

Kingman, Ebin.   Prisoner 91.   Rank: Private - By what ship or how taken: Boats & Troops - Time when: 28 May 1813 - Place where: Stoney Point, Henderson Harbor - Of what ship or corps: Land forces - Whether man of war, privateer or merchant vessel: Taken on shore - Time when received into custody: 8 Jun 1813 - From what ship or whence received: Batteaux - Exchanged, discharged, died, or escape: Discharged - Time when: 31 Oct 1813 - Whither, and by what order, or number or re-entry: Malabar Transport

Kingsland, Joseph   Prisoner 558.   Rank: Private - By what ship or how taken: Troops - Time when: 26 Jun 1813 - Place where: Beaver Dam - Of what ship or corps: Land forces - Whether man of war, privateer or merchant vessel: Taken on shore - Time when received into custody: 13 Jul 1813 - From what ship or whence received: Steamboat - Exchanged, discharged, died, or escape: Discharged - Time when: 31 Oct 1813 - Whither, and by what order, or number or re-entry: Malabar Transport

Kirk, John   Prisoner 1521.   Rank: Corporal - By what ship or how taken: Troops - Time when: 25 Jul 1814 - Place where: Lundy's Lane - Of what ship or corps: Land forces - Whether man of war, privateer or merchant vessel: Taken on shore - Time when received into custody: 30 Aug 1814 - From what ship or whence received: Lady Delaval Schooner 578 - Exchanged, discharged, died, or escape: Discharged - Time when: 8 Oct 1814 - Whither, and by what order, or number or re-entry: Queen No. 415

American Prisoners of War held at Quebec during the War of 1812

Knags, Witmore   Prisoner 1191. Rank: Citizen - By what ship or how taken: - Time when: - Place where: - Of what ship or corps: - Whether man of war, privateer or merchant vessel: - Time when received into custody: 12 Dec 1813 - From what ship or whence received: Town Goal - Exchanged, discharged, died, or escape: Discharged - Time when: 4 May 1814 - Whither, and by what order, or number or re-entry: United States

Knight, Andrew   Prisoner 92. Rank: Private - By what ship or how taken: Boats & Troops - Time when: 28 May 1813 - Place where: Stoney Point, Henderson Harbor - Of what ship or corps: Land forces - Whether man of war, privateer or merchant vessel: Taken on shore - Time when received into custody: 8 Jun 1813 - From what ship or whence received: Batteaux - Exchanged, discharged, died, or escape: Died - Time when: 27 Aug 1813 - Whither, and by what order, or number or re-entry: Typhus Fever

Knight, Hudson   Prisoner 71. Rank: Fifer - By what ship or how taken: Boats & Troops - Time when: 28 May 1813 - Place where: Stoney Point, Henderson Harbor - Of what ship or corps: Land forces - Whether man of war, privateer or merchant vessel: Taken on shore - Time when received into custody: 8 Jun 1813 - From what ship or whence received: Batteaux - Exchanged, discharged, died, or escape: Discharged - Time when: 31 Oct 1813 - Whither, and by what order, or number or re-entry: Malabar Transport

Knight, William   Prisoner 279. Rank: Boy - By what ship or how taken: Troops - Time when: 6 Jun 1813 - Place where: Stoney Point - Of what ship or corps: Land forces - Whether man of war, privateer or merchant vessel: Taken on shore - Time when received into custody: 28 Jun 1813 - From what ship or whence received: Batteaux - Exchanged, discharged, died, or escape: Discharged - Time when: 31 Oct 1813 - Whither, and by what order, or number or re-entry: Malabar Transport

Knowles, Joseph   Prisoner 1159. Rank: Corporal - By what ship or how taken: Troops - Time when: 5 May 1813 - Place where: Rapids Prince Reason - Of what ship or corps: Land forces - Whether man of war, privateer or merchant vessel: Taken on shore - Time when received into custody: 25 Nov 1813 - From what ship or whence received: Town Goal - Exchanged, discharged, died, or escape: Discharged - Time when: 12 Mar 1814 - Whither, and by what order, or number or re-entry: New Brunswick Fencibles

Knowles, Seth   Prisoner 975. Rank: Private - By what ship or how taken: Troops - Time when: 5 Jul 1813 - Place where: Fort Schisher - Of what ship or corps: Land forces - Whether man of war, privateer or merchant vessel: Taken on shore - Time when received into custody: 5 Sep 1813 - From what ship or whence received: Steamboat - Exchanged, discharged, died, or escape: Discharged - Time when: 31 Oct 1813 - Whither, and by what order, or number or re-entry: Malabar Transport

Knowlton, Ebenezer   Prisoner 709. Rank: Private - By what ship or how taken: Troops - Time when: 26 Jun 1813 - Place where: Beaver Dam - Of what ship or corps: Land forces - Whether man of war, privateer or merchant vessel: Taken on shore - Time when received into custody: 7 Jul 1813 - From what ship or whence received: Steamboat - Exchanged, discharged, died, or escape: Discharged - Time when: 10 Aug 1813 - Whither, and by what order, or number or re-entry: HM Ship Regulius by order of Sir George Provost

Kolley, J. W.   Prisoner 1701. Rank: Citizen - By what ship or how taken: - Time when: 25 Jul 1814 - Place where: Nifriepepis Bay - Of what ship or corps: - Whether man of war, privateer or merchant vessel: - Time when received into custody: 23 Oct 1814 - From what ship or whence received: Montreal - Exchanged, discharged, died, or escape: Exchanged - Time when: 14 Dec 1814 - Whither, and by what order, or number or re-entry: United States

Konnell, Thomas   Prisoner 151. Rank: Ensign - By what ship or how taken: Boats & Troops - Time when: 3 Jun 1813 - Place where: Lake Champlain - Of what ship or corps: Growler - Whether man of war, privateer or merchant vessel: Man of War - Time when received into custody: 8 Jul 1813 - From what ship or whence received: Batteaux - Exchanged, discharged, died, or escape: Discharged - Time when: 18 Sep 1813 - Whither, and by what order, or number or re-entry: Dick Transport

Koontz, Jacob   Prisoner 1228. Rank: Private - By what ship or how taken: Troops - Time when: 19 Dec 1813 - Place where: Fort Niagara - Of what ship or corps: Land forces - Whether man of war, privateer or merchant vessel: Taken on shore - Time when received into custody: 29 Jan 1814 - From what ship or whence received: Montreal by land carriage - Exchanged, discharged, died, or escape: Discharged - Time when: 4 May 1814 - Whither, and by what order, or number or re-entry: United States

Kronnengie, John   Prisoner 281. Rank: Private - By what ship or how taken: Troops - Time when: 6 Jun 1813 - Place where: Stoney Point - Of what ship or corps: Land forces - Whether man of war, privateer or merchant vessel: Taken on shore - Time when received into custody: 28 Jun 1813 - From what ship or whence received: Batteaux - Exchanged, discharged, died, or escape: Discharged - Time when: 31 Oct 1813 - Whither, and by what order, or number or re-entry: Malabar Transport

American Prisoners of War held at Quebec during the War of 1812

Kuber, Jacob   Prisoner 423. Rank: Corporal - By what ship or how taken: Troops - Time when: 24 Jun 1813 - Place where: Beaver Dam - Of what ship or corps: Land forces - Whether man of war, privateer or merchant vessel: Taken on shore - Time when received into custody: 7 Jul 1813 - From what ship or whence received: Steamboat - Exchanged, discharged, died, or escape: Discharged - Time when: 8 Oct 1813 - Whither, and by what order, or number or re-entry: H.M. Ship Ceylon

Kuntz, David   Prisoner 775. Rank: Private - By what ship or how taken: Troops - Time when: 26 Jun 1813 - Place where: Beaver Dam - Of what ship or corps: Land forces - Whether man of war, privateer or merchant vessel: Taken on shore - Time when received into custody: 7 Jul 1813 - From what ship or whence received: Steamboat - Exchanged, discharged, died, or escape: Discharged - Time when: 10 Aug 1813 - Whither, and by what order, or number or re-entry: HM Ship Malpomena

La Bonte, Francis   Prisoner 1198. Rank: Citizen - By what ship or how taken: - Time when: - Place where: - Of what ship or corps: - Whether man of war, privateer or merchant vessel: - Time when received into custody: 1 Dec 1813 - From what ship or whence received: Town Goal - Exchanged, discharged, died, or escape: Discharged - Time when: 3 Jan 1814 - Whither, and by what order, or number or re-entry: To Town Goal

Labrey, Stephen   Prisoner 1809. Rank: Private - By what ship or how taken: Troops - Time when: 17 Sep 1814 - Place where: Fort Erie - Of what ship or corps: Land forces - Whether man of war, privateer or merchant vessel: Taken on shore - Time when received into custody: 1 Nov 1814 - From what ship or whence received: Montreal - Exchanged, discharged, died, or escape: Discharged - Time when: 8 Nov 1814 - Whither, and by what order, or number or re-entry: S. George No. 575 for Halifax by order of Sir George Provost

Lackey, Amasa   Prisoner 368. Rank: Private - By what ship or how taken: Troops - Time when: 6 Jun 1813 - Place where: Stoney Point - Of what ship or corps: Land forces - Whether man of war, privateer or merchant vessel: Taken on shore - Time when received into custody: 28 Jun 1813 - From what ship or whence received: Mary of Quebec - Exchanged, discharged, died, or escape: Died - Time when: 2 Apr 1814 - Whither, and by what order, or number or re-entry: Debility

Lackey, Hugh   Prisoner 1246. Rank: Sergeant - By what ship or how taken: Troops - Time when: 19 Dec 1813 - Place where: Fort Niagara - Of what ship or corps: Land forces - Whether man of war, privateer or merchant vessel: Taken on shore - Time when received into custody: 29 Jan 1814 - From what ship or whence received: Montreal by land carriage - Exchanged, discharged, died, or escape: Discharged - Time when: 27 Feb 1814 - Whither, and by what order, or number or re-entry: Volunteered for New Brunswick Fencibles

Lain, Benjamin   Prisoner 515. Rank: Private - By what ship or how taken: Troops - Time when: 24 Jun 1813 - Place where: Beaver Dam - Of what ship or corps: Land forces - Whether man of war, privateer or merchant vessel: Taken on shore - Time when received into custody: 7 Jul 1813 - From what ship or whence received: Steamboat - Exchanged, discharged, died, or escape: Died - Time when: 23 Jul 1813 - Whither, and by what order, or number or re-entry: Dysentery

Lainge, Isaac   Prisoner 1404. Rank: Private - By what ship or how taken: Troops - Time when: 19 Dec 1813 - Place where: Fort Niagara - Of what ship or corps: Land forces - Whether man of war, privateer or merchant vessel: Taken on shore - Time when received into custody: 29 Jan 1814 - From what ship or whence received: Montreal by land carriage - Exchanged, discharged, died, or escape: Discharged - Time when: 4 May 1814 - Whither, and by what order, or number or re-entry: United States

Lainn, J.   Prisoner 1617. Rank: Private - By what ship or how taken: Gun Boats - Time when: 15 Aug 1814 - Place where: Fort Erie - Of what ship or corps: Land forces - Whether man of war, privateer or merchant vessel: Taken on shore - Time when received into custody: 5 Oct 1814 - From what ship or whence received: Montreal - Exchanged, discharged, died, or escape: Discharged - Time when: 8 Oct 1814 - Whither, and by what order, or number or re-entry: H.M. Ship Ceylon

Lake, Elishua   Prisoner 1867. Rank: Private - By what ship or how taken: Troops - Time when: 17 Sep 1814 - Place where: Fort Erie - Of what ship or corps: Land forces - Whether man of war, privateer or merchant vessel: Taken on shore - Time when received into custody: 1 Nov 1814 - From what ship or whence received: Montreal - Exchanged, discharged, died, or escape: Discharged - Time when: 8 Nov 1814 - Whither, and by what order, or number or re-entry: S. George No. 575 for Halifax

Lamb, Josiah P.   Prisoner 68. Rank: Corporal - By what ship or how taken: Boats & Troops - Time when: 28 May 1813 - Place where: Stoney Point, Henderson Harbor - Of what ship or corps: Land forces - Whether man of war, privateer or merchant vessel: Taken on shore - Time when received into custody: 8 Jun 1813 - From what ship or whence received:

American Prisoners of War held at Quebec during the War of 1812

Batteaux - Exchanged, discharged, died, or escape: Died - Time when: 14 Feb 1814 - Whither, and by what order, or number or re-entry: Dysentery

Lamb, William   Prisoner 792. Rank: Private - By what ship or how taken: Troops - Time when: 26 Jun 1813 - Place where: Beaver Dam - Of what ship or corps: Land forces - Whether man of war, privateer or merchant vessel: Taken on shore - Time when received into custody: 7 Jul 1813 - From what ship or whence received: Steamboat - Exchanged, discharged, died, or escape: Discharged - Time when: 10 Aug 1813 - Whither, and by what order, or number or re-entry: HM Ship Malpomena

Lamson, John   Prisoner 69. Rank: Corporal - By what ship or how taken: Boats & Troops - Time when: 28 May 1813 - Place where: Stoney Point, Henderson Harbor - Of what ship or corps: Land forces - Whether man of war, privateer or merchant vessel: Taken on shore - Time when received into custody: 8 Jun 1813 - From what ship or whence received: Batteaux - Exchanged, discharged, died, or escape: Discharged - Time when: 8 Oct 1813 - Whither, and by what order, or number or re-entry: H.M. Ship Ceylon

Lancaster, W.   Prisoner 1620. Rank: Private - By what ship or how taken: Gun Boats - Time when: 15 Aug 1814 - Place where: Fort Erie - Of what ship or corps: Land forces - Whether man of war, privateer or merchant vessel: Taken on shore - Time when received into custody: 5 Oct 1814 - From what ship or whence received: Montreal - Exchanged, discharged, died, or escape: Discharged - Time when: 8 Oct 1814 - Whither, and by what order, or number or re-entry: H.M. Ship Ceylon

Land, Joseph   Prisoner 1470. Rank: Private - By what ship or how taken: Gun Boats - Time when: 29 May 1814 - Place where: Sandy Creek - Of what ship or corps: Land forces - Whether man of war, privateer or merchant vessel: Taken on shore - Time when received into custody: 12 Aug 1814 - From what ship or whence received: Royal Seaman No. 289 Transport - Exchanged, discharged, died, or escape: Discharged - Time when: 8 Oct 1814 - Whither, and by what order, or number or re-entry: Queen No. 415

Lander, Charles   Prisoner 119. Rank: Private - By what ship or how taken: Boats & Troops - Time when: 28 May 1813 - Place where: Stoney Point, Henderson Harbor - Of what ship or corps: Land forces - Whether man of war, privateer or merchant vessel: Taken on shore - Time when received into custody: 8 Jun 1813 - From what ship or whence received: Batteaux - Exchanged, discharged, died, or escape: Died - Time when: 22 Jul 1813 - Whither, and by what order, or number or re-entry: Dysentery

Landers, John   Prisoner 1951. Rank: Private - By what ship or how taken: Troops - Time when: 23 Oct 1814 - Place where: Fort Erie - Of what ship or corps: Land forces - Whether man of war, privateer or merchant vessel: Taken on shore - Time when received into custody: 11 Dec 1814 - From what ship or whence received: Montreal - Exchanged, discharged, died, or escape: Discharged - Time when: 13 Mar 1815 - Whither, and by what order, or number or re-entry: United States

Lane, Jobe   Prisoner 974. Rank: Private - By what ship or how taken: Troops - Time when: 5 Jul 1813 - Place where: Fort Schisher - Of what ship or corps: Land forces - Whether man of war, privateer or merchant vessel: Taken on shore - Time when received into custody: 5 Sep 1813 - From what ship or whence received: Steamboat - Exchanged, discharged, died, or escape: Discharged - Time when: 31 Oct 1813 - Whither, and by what order, or number or re-entry: Malabar Transport

Lanton, Peory   Prisoner 21. Rank: Private - By what ship or how taken: Boats & Troops - Time when: 28 May 1813 - Place where: Stoney Point, Henderson Harbor - Of what ship or corps: Land forces - Whether man of war, privateer or merchant vessel: Taken on shore - Time when received into custody: 8 Jun 1813 - From what ship or whence received: Batteaux - Exchanged, discharged, died, or escape: Died - Time when: 20 Jul 1813 - Whither, and by what order, or number or re-entry: Dysentery

Lanunsbery, Lemuel   Prisoner 1104. Rank: Private - By what ship or how taken: Troops - Time when: 24 Aug 1813 - Place where: Fort George - Of what ship or corps: Land forces - Whether man of war, privateer or merchant vessel: Taken on shore - Time when received into custody: 12 Oct 1813 - From what ship or whence received: Steamboat - Exchanged, discharged, died, or escape: Discharged - Time when: 31 Oct 1813 - Whither, and by what order, or number or re-entry: Malabar Transport

Lark, Joseph   Prisoner 1367. Rank: Private - By what ship or how taken: Troops - Time when: 19 Dec 1813 - Place where: Fort Niagara - Of what ship or corps: Land forces - Whether man of war, privateer or merchant vessel: Taken on shore - Time when received into custody: 29 Jan 1814 - From what ship or whence received: Montreal by land carriage - Exchanged, discharged, died, or escape: Discharged - Time when: 4 May 1814 - Whither, and by what order, or number or re-entry: United States

American Prisoners of War held at Quebec during the War of 1812

Larkins, Thomas   Prisoner 1316. Rank: Private - By what ship or how taken: Troops - Time when: 19 Dec 1813 - Place where: Fort Niagara - Of what ship or corps: Land forces - Whether man of war, privateer or merchant vessel: Taken on shore - Time when received into custody: 29 Jan 1814 - From what ship or whence received: Montreal by land carriage - Exchanged, discharged, died, or escape: Discharged - Time when: 22 Feb 1814 - Whither, and by what order, or number or re-entry: Volunteered for New Brunswick Fencibles

Larney, Joseph P.   Prisoner 1090. Rank: Private - By what ship or how taken: Troops - Time when: 24 Aug 1813 - Place where: Fort George - Of what ship or corps: Land forces - Whether man of war, privateer or merchant vessel: Taken on shore - Time when received into custody: 10 Oct 1813 - From what ship or whence received: Steamboat - Exchanged, discharged, died, or escape: Discharged - Time when: 31 Oct 1813 - Whither, and by what order, or number or re-entry: Malabar Transport

Lash, Jeremiah   Prisoner 686. Rank: Private - By what ship or how taken: Troops - Time when: 26 Jun 1813 - Place where: Beaver Dam - Of what ship or corps: Land forces - Whether man of war, privateer or merchant vessel: Taken on shore - Time when received into custody: 7 Jul 1813 - From what ship or whence received: Steamboat - Exchanged, discharged, died, or escape: Discharged - Time when: 10 Aug 1813 - Whither, and by what order, or number or re-entry: HM Ship Regulius by order of Sir George Provost

Latham, John   Prisoner 1443. Rank: Private - By what ship or how taken: Troops - Time when: 6 May 1814 - Place where: Oswago - Of what ship or corps: Land forces - Whether man of war, privateer or merchant vessel: Taken on shore - Time when received into custody: 12 Aug 1814 - From what ship or whence received: Royal Seaman No. 289 Transport - Exchanged, discharged, died, or escape: Discharged - Time when: 8 Oct 1814 - Whither, and by what order, or number or re-entry: Queen No. 415

Latimer, Arthur   Prisoner 1711. Rank: Midshipman - By what ship or how taken: Troops - Time when: 17 Sep 1814 - Place where: Fort Erie - Of what ship or corps: Jack - Whether man of war, privateer or merchant vessel: Man of War - Time when received into custody: 28 Oct 1814 - From what ship or whence received: Montreal - Exchanged, discharged, died, or escape: Discharged - Time when: 10 Nov 1814 - Whither, and by what order, or number or re-entry: Lord Cartheart No. 161 for Halifax

Latroop, Beniah   Prisoner 1696. Rank: Private - By what ship or how taken: Troops - Time when: 10 Sep 1814 - Place where: Plattsburg - Of what ship or corps: Land forces - Whether man of war, privateer or merchant vessel: Taken on shore - Time when received into custody: 23 Oct 1814 - From what ship or whence received: Montreal - Exchanged, discharged, died, or escape: Discharged - Time when: 8 Nov 1814 - Whither, and by what order, or number or re-entry: S. George No. 575 for Halifax

Laundrough, Andrew   Prisoner 1756. Rank: Private - By what ship or how taken: Gun Boats - Time when: 6 Sep 1814 - Place where: Lake Huron - Of what ship or corps: Scorpion - Whether man of war, privateer or merchant vessel: Man of War - Time when received into custody: 1 Nov 1814 - From what ship or whence received: Montreal - Exchanged, discharged, died, or escape: Discharged - Time when: 8 Nov 1814 - Whither, and by what order, or number or re-entry: S. George No. 575 for Halifax by order of Sir George Provost

Laurie, Thomas   Prisoner 1532. Rank: Private - By what ship or how taken: Troops - Time when: 25 Jul 1814 - Place where: Lundy's Lane - Of what ship or corps: Land forces - Whether man of war, privateer or merchant vessel: Taken on shore - Time when received into custody: 30 Aug 1814 - From what ship or whence received: Lady Delaval Schooner 578 - Exchanged, discharged, died, or escape: Discharged - Time when: 8 Nov 1814 - Whither, and by what order, or number or re-entry: George No. 575 for Halifax by orders of Sir George Provost

Lawrence, Abel   Prisoner 29. Rank: Sergeant - By what ship or how taken: Boats & Troops - Time when: 28 May 1813 - Place where: Stoney Point, Henderson Harbor - Of what ship or corps: Land forces - Whether man of war, privateer or merchant vessel: Taken on shore - Time when received into custody: 8 Jun 1813 - From what ship or whence received: Batteaux - Exchanged, discharged, died, or escape: Discharged - Time when: 8 Oct 1813 - Whither, and by what order, or number or re-entry: H.M. Ship Ceylon

Lawton, John   Prisoner 1722. Rank: Carpenter's Mate - By what ship or how taken: Gun Boats - Time when: 6 Sep 1814 - Place where: Lake Huron - Of what ship or corps: Scorpion - Whether man of war, privateer or merchant vessel: Man of War - Time when received into custody: 28 Oct 1814 - From what ship or whence received: Montreal - Exchanged, discharged, died, or escape: Discharged - Time when: 7 Nov 1814 - Whither, and by what order, or number or re-entry: Transport Freedom No. 582 by orders of his Excellency Sir George Provost

American Prisoners of War held at Quebec during the War of 1812

Lawton, John   Prisoner 1006. Rank: Seaman - By what ship or how taken: Earl Moria - Time when: 10 Aug 1813 - Place where: Lake Ontario - Of what ship or corps: Julia - Whether man of war, privateer or merchant vessel: Man of War - Time when received into custody: 5 Sep 1813 - From what ship or whence received: Steamboat - Exchanged, discharged, died, or escape: Discharged - Time when: 31 Oct 1813 - Whither, and by what order, or number or re-entry: Malabar Transport

Lazelaeu, Benjamin   Prisoner 766. Rank: Private - By what ship or how taken: Troops - Time when: 26 Jun 1813 - Place where: Beaver Dam - Of what ship or corps: Land forces - Whether man of war, privateer or merchant vessel: Taken on shore - Time when received into custody: 7 Jul 1813 - From what ship or whence received: Steamboat - Exchanged, discharged, died, or escape: Discharged - Time when: 10 Aug 1813 - Whither, and by what order, or number or re-entry: HM Ship Malpomena

Le Due, P.   Prisoner 1659. Rank: Private - By what ship or how taken: - Time when: - Place where: - Of what ship or corps: - Whether man of war, privateer or merchant vessel: - Time when received into custody: 5 Oct 1814 - From what ship or whence received: Montreal - Exchanged, discharged, died, or escape: Discharged - Time when: 8 Oct 1814 - Whither, and by what order, or number or re-entry: H.M. Ship Ceylon

Leach, George W.   Prisoner 1800. Rank: Private - By what ship or how taken: Troops - Time when: 17 Sep 1814 - Place where: Fort Erie - Of what ship or corps: Land forces - Whether man of war, privateer or merchant vessel: Taken on shore - Time when received into custody: 1 Nov 1814 - From what ship or whence received: Montreal - Exchanged, discharged, died, or escape: Discharged - Time when: 8 Nov 1814 - Whither, and by what order, or number or re-entry: S. George No. 575 for Halifax by order of Sir George Provost

Learned, Henry   Prisoner 668. Rank: Private - By what ship or how taken: Troops - Time when: 24 Jun 1813 - Place where: Stoney Point - Of what ship or corps: Land forces - Whether man of war, privateer or merchant vessel: Taken on shore - Time when received into custody: 7 Jul 1813 - From what ship or whence received: Steamboat - Exchanged, discharged, died, or escape: Discharged - Time when: 10 Aug 1813 - Whither, and by what order, or number or re-entry: HM Ship Regulius by order of Sir George Provost

Leazier, Elisha   Prisoner 552. Rank: Corporal - By what ship or how taken: Troops - Time when: 26 Jun 1813 - Place where: Beaver Dam - Of what ship or corps: Land forces - Whether man of war, privateer or merchant vessel: Taken on shore - Time when received into custody: 13 Jul 1813 - From what ship or whence received: Steamboat - Exchanged, discharged, died, or escape: Discharged - Time when: 10 Aug 1813 - Whither, and by what order, or number or re-entry: HM Ship Regulius by order of Sir George Provost

LeCount, William   Prisoner 906. Rank: Private - By what ship or how taken: Troops - Time when: 26 Jun 1813 - Place where: Beaver Dam - Of what ship or corps: Land forces - Whether man of war, privateer or merchant vessel: Taken on shore - Time when received into custody: 21 Jul 1813 - From what ship or whence received: Steamboat - Exchanged, discharged, died, or escape: Discharged - Time when: 10 Aug 1813 - Whither, and by what order, or number or re-entry: HM Ship Malpomena

Ledieu, Amable   Prisoner 1702. Rank: Private - By what ship or how taken: Troops - Time when: 3 Aug 1814 - Place where: Fort Erie - Of what ship or corps: Land forces - Whether man of war, privateer or merchant vessel: Taken on shore - Time when received into custody: 23 Oct 1814 - From what ship or whence received: Montreal - Exchanged, discharged, died, or escape: Discharged - Time when: 8 Nov 1814 - Whither, and by what order, or number or re-entry: S. George No. 575 for Halifax

Ledman, Francis   Prisoner 312. Rank: Private - By what ship or how taken: Boats & Troops - Time when: 6 Jun 1813 - Place where: Stoney Point - Of what ship or corps: Land forces - Whether man of war, privateer or merchant vessel: Taken on shore - Time when received into custody: 28 Jun 1813 - From what ship or whence received: Quebec of Quebec - Exchanged, discharged, died, or escape: Discharged - Time when: 31 Oct 1813 - Whither, and by what order, or number or re-entry: Malabar Transport

Legg, Daniel   Prisoner 306. Rank: Private - By what ship or how taken: Boats & Troops - Time when: 6 Jun 1813 - Place where: Stoney Point - Of what ship or corps: Land forces - Whether man of war, privateer or merchant vessel: Taken on shore - Time when received into custody: 28 Jun 1813 - From what ship or whence received: Quebec of Quebec - Exchanged, discharged, died, or escape: Discharged - Time when: 31 Oct 1813 - Whither, and by what order, or number or re-entry: Malabar Transport

Lejuny, Anthony   Prisoner 1902. Rank: Servant - By what ship or how taken: Troops - Time when: 17 Sep 1814 - Place where: Fort Erie - Of what ship or corps: Land forces - Whether man of war, privateer or merchant vessel: Taken on shore - Time when received into custody: 1 Nov 1814 - From what ship or whence received: Montreal - Exchanged, discharged, died, or escape: Discharged - Time when: 13 Mar 1815 - Whither, and by what order, or number or re-

American Prisoners of War held at Quebec during the War of 1812

entry: United States

Leonard, Isaac   Prisoner 1158.   Rank: Corporal - By what ship or how taken: Troops - Time when: 5 May 1813 - Place where: Rapids Prince Reason - Of what ship or corps: Land forces - Whether man of war, privateer or merchant vessel: Taken on shore - Time when received into custody: 25 Nov 1813 - From what ship or whence received: Town Goal - Exchanged, discharged, died, or escape: Discharged - Time when: 12 Mar 1814 - Whither, and by what order, or number or re-entry: New Brunswick Fencibles

Leonard, Nathaniel   Prisoner 1215.   Rank: Non-Constition - By what ship or how taken: Troops - Time when: 19 Dec 1813 - Place where: Fort Niagara - Of what ship or corps: Land forces - Whether man of war, privateer or merchant vessel: Taken on shore - Time when received into custody: 28 Jan 1814 - From what ship or whence received: Montreal by land carriage - Exchanged, discharged, died, or escape: Discharged - Time when: 4 May 1814 - Whither, and by what order, or number or re-entry: United States

Leonard, Nathaniel   Prisoner 1212.   Rank: Captain - By what ship or how taken: Troops - Time when: 19 Dec 1813 - Place where: Fort Niagara - Of what ship or corps: Land forces - Whether man of war, privateer or merchant vessel: Taken on shore - Time when received into custody: 28 Jan 1814 - From what ship or whence received: Montreal by land carriage - Exchanged, discharged, died, or escape: Discharged - Time when: 4 May 1814 - Whither, and by what order, or number or re-entry: United States

Leping, Noel   Prisoner 1909.   Rank: Private - By what ship or how taken: Troops - Time when: 17 Sep 1814 - Place where: Fort Erie - Of what ship or corps: Land forces - Whether man of war, privateer or merchant vessel: Taken on shore - Time when received into custody: 1 Nov 1814 - From what ship or whence received: Montreal - Exchanged, discharged, died, or escape: Discharged - Time when: 8 Nov 1814 - Whither, and by what order, or number or re-entry: S. George No. 575 for Halifax by orderof Sir George Provost

Levi, Henry   Prisoner 718.   Rank: Corporal - By what ship or how taken: Troops - Time when: 26 Jun 1813 - Place where: Beaver Dam - Of what ship or corps: Land forces - Whether man of war, privateer or merchant vessel: Taken on shore - Time when received into custody: 7 Jul 1813 - From what ship or whence received: Steamboat - Exchanged, discharged, died, or escape: Discharged - Time when: 10 Aug 1813 - Whither, and by what order, or number or re-entry: HM Ship Regulius by order of Sir George Provost

Lewis, Dudley   Prisoner 588.   Rank: Private - By what ship or how taken: Troops - Time when: 26 Jun 1813 - Place where: Beaver Dam - Of what ship or corps: Land forces - Whether man of war, privateer or merchant vessel: Taken on shore - Time when received into custody: 13 Jul 1813 - From what ship or whence received: Steamboat - Exchanged, discharged, died, or escape: Discharged - Time when: 10 Aug 1813 - Whither, and by what order, or number or re-entry: HM Ship Regulius by order of Sir George Provost

Lewis, John   Prisoner 30.   Rank: Private - By what ship or how taken: Boats & Troops - Time when: 28 May 1813 - Place where: Stoney Point, Henderson Harbor - Of what ship or corps: Land forces - Whether man of war, privateer or merchant vessel: Taken on shore - Time when received into custody: 8 Jun 1813 - From what ship or whence received: Batteaux - Exchanged, discharged, died, or escape: Died - Time when: 7 Sep 1813 - Whither, and by what order, or number or re-entry: Deanhuar

Lewis, Leonard   Prisoner 1008.   Rank: Seaman - By what ship or how taken: Earl Moria - Time when: 10 Aug 1813 - Place where: Lake Ontario - Of what ship or corps: Julia - Whether man of war, privateer or merchant vessel: Man of War - Time when received into custody: 5 Sep 1813 - From what ship or whence received: Steamboat - Exchanged, discharged, died, or escape: Discharged - Time when: 31 Oct 1813 - Whither, and by what order, or number or re-entry: Malabar Transport

Lewis, Samuel   Prisoner 1890.   Rank: Private - By what ship or how taken: Troops - Time when: 17 Sep 1814 - Place where: Fort Erie - Of what ship or corps: Land forces - Whether man of war, privateer or merchant vessel: Taken on shore - Time when received into custody: 1 Nov 1814 - From what ship or whence received: Montreal - Exchanged, discharged, died, or escape: Discharged - Time when: 8 Nov 1814 - Whither, and by what order, or number or re-entry: S. George No. 575 for Halifax by order of Sir George Provost

Lewis, William   Prisoner 1567.   Rank: Servant - By what ship or how taken: Gun Boats - Time when: 12 Aug 1814 - Place where: Fort Erie - Of what ship or corps: Land forces - Whether man of war, privateer or merchant vessel: Taken on shore - Time when received into custody: 16 Sep 1814 - From what ship or whence received: Steamboat - Exchanged, discharged, died, or escape: Discharged - Time when: 8 Nov 1814 - Whither, and by what order, or number or re-entry: George No. 575 for Halifax

Lewis, William   Prisoner 247.   Rank: Lieutenant Colonel - By what ship or how taken: Boats & Troops - Time when: 24 Jun

American Prisoners of War held at Quebec during the War of 1812

1813 - Place where: Rec in charge of Beauport - Of what ship or corps: Land forces - Whether man of war, privateer or merchant vessel: Taken on shore - Time when received into custody: 24 Jun 1813 - From what ship or whence received: At Beauport - Exchanged, discharged, died, or escape: Discharged - Time when: 29 Mar 1814 - Whither, and by what order, or number or re-entry: United States

Lias, Nathaniel   Prisoner 1239. Rank: Private - By what ship or how taken: Troops - Time when: 19 Dec 1813 - Place where: Fort Niagara - Of what ship or corps: Land forces - Whether man of war, privateer or merchant vessel: Taken on shore - Time when received into custody: 29 Jan 1814 - From what ship or whence received: Montreal by land carriage - Exchanged, discharged, died, or escape: Discharged - Time when: 27 Feb 1814 - Whither, and by what order, or number or re-entry: Volunteered for New Brunswick Fencibles

Libby, Thadedus   Prisoner 1188. Rank: Private - By what ship or how taken: Troops - Time when: 5 May 1813 - Place where: Rapids - Of what ship or corps: Land forces - Whether man of war, privateer or merchant vessel: Taken on shore - Time when received into custody: 25 Nov 1813 - From what ship or whence received: Town Goal - Exchanged, discharged, died, or escape: Died - Time when: 25 Feb 1814 - Whither, and by what order, or number or re-entry: Gun shot wounds in the head

Liei, John   Prisoner 872. Rank: Private - By what ship or how taken: Troops - Time when: 26 Jun 1813 - Place where: Beaver Dam - Of what ship or corps: Land forces - Whether man of war, privateer or merchant vessel: Taken on shore - Time when received into custody: 7 Jul 1813 - From what ship or whence received: Steamboat - Exchanged, discharged, died, or escape: Discharged - Time when: 10 Aug 1813 - Whither, and by what order, or number or re-entry: HM Ship Malpomena

Lighter, Jacob   Prisoner 410. Rank: Sergeant - By what ship or how taken: Troops - Time when: 24 Jun 1813 - Place where: Beaver Dam - Of what ship or corps: Land forces - Whether man of war, privateer or merchant vessel: Taken on shore - Time when received into custody: 7 Jul 1813 - From what ship or whence received: Steamboat - Exchanged, discharged, died, or escape: Discharged - Time when: 31 Oct 1813 - Whither, and by what order, or number or re-entry: Malabar Transport

Liles, James   Prisoner 1904. Rank: Private - By what ship or how taken: Troops - Time when: 17 Sep 1814 - Place where: Fort Erie - Of what ship or corps: Land forces - Whether man of war, privateer or merchant vessel: Taken on shore - Time when received into custody: 1 Nov 1814 - From what ship or whence received: Montreal - Exchanged, discharged, died, or escape: Discharged - Time when: 8 Nov 1814 - Whither, and by what order, or number or re-entry: S. George No. 575 for Halifax by order of Sir George Provost

Limoners, Peter D.   Prisoner 1057. Rank: Private - By what ship or how taken: Troops - Time when: 24 Jun 1813 - Place where: Beaver Dam - Of what ship or corps: Land forces - Whether man of war, privateer or merchant vessel: Taken on shore - Time when received into custody: 5 Sep 1813 - From what ship or whence received: Steamboat - Exchanged, discharged, died, or escape: Discharged - Time when: 31 Oct 1813 - Whither, and by what order, or number or re-entry: Malabar Transport

Lindsey, William   Prisoner 294. Rank: Private - By what ship or how taken: Boats & Troops - Time when: 6 Jun 1813 - Place where: Stoney Point - Of what ship or corps: Land forces - Whether man of war, privateer or merchant vessel: Taken on shore - Time when received into custody: 28 Jun 1813 - From what ship or whence received: Quebec of Quebec - Exchanged, discharged, died, or escape: Discharged - Time when: 31 Oct 1813 - Whither, and by what order, or number or re-entry: HM Ship Success

Linel, Samuel   Prisoner 136. Rank: Private - By what ship or how taken: Boats & Troops - Time when: 28 May 1813 - Place where: Stoney Point, Henderson Harbor - Of what ship or corps: Land forces - Whether man of war, privateer or merchant vessel: Taken on shore - Time when received into custody: 8 Jul 1813 - From what ship or whence received: Batteaux - Exchanged, discharged, died, or escape: Discharged - Time when: 31 Oct 1813 - Whither, and by what order, or number or re-entry: Malabar Transport

Lines, John   Prisoner 1189. Rank: Private - By what ship or how taken: Troops - Time when: 5 May 1813 - Place where: Rapids - Of what ship or corps: Land forces - Whether man of war, privateer or merchant vessel: Taken on shore - Time when received into custody: 25 Nov 1813 - From what ship or whence received: Town Goal - Exchanged, discharged, died, or escape: Discharged - Time when: 4 May 1814 - Whither, and by what order, or number or re-entry: United States

Lingie, John   Prisoner 1123. Rank: Private - By what ship or how taken: Troops - Time when: 17 Oct 1813 - Place where: Red Mills - Of what ship or corps: Land forces - Whether man of war, privateer or merchant vessel: Taken on shore - Time when received into custody: 12 Oct 1813 - From what ship or whence received: Steamboat - Exchanged, discharged, died, or escape: Discharged - Time when: 31 Oct 1813 - Whither, and by what order, or number or re-entry: Malabar

American Prisoners of War held at Quebec during the War of 1812

Transport

Linnerd, Alfred   Prisoner 609. Rank: Private - By what ship or how taken: Troops - Time when: 26 Jun 1813 - Place where: Stoney Point - Of what ship or corps: Land forces - Whether man of war, privateer or merchant vessel: Taken on shore - Time when received into custody: 7 Jul 1813 - From what ship or whence received: Steamboat - Exchanged, discharged, died, or escape: Discharged - Time when: 10 Aug 1813 - Whither, and by what order, or number or re-entry: HM Ship Regulius by order of Sir George Provost

Lipperket, William   Prisoner 788. Rank: Private - By what ship or how taken: Troops - Time when: 26 Jun 1813 - Place where: Beaver Dam - Of what ship or corps: Land forces - Whether man of war, privateer or merchant vessel: Taken on shore - Time when received into custody: 7 Jul 1813 - From what ship or whence received: Steamboat - Exchanged, discharged, died, or escape: Discharged - Time when: 10 Aug 1813 - Whither, and by what order, or number or re-entry: HM Ship Malpomena

Little, Peter   Prisoner 735. Rank: Private - By what ship or how taken: Troops - Time when: 26 Jun 1813 - Place where: Beaver Dam - Of what ship or corps: Land forces - Whether man of war, privateer or merchant vessel: Taken on shore - Time when received into custody: 7 Jul 1813 - From what ship or whence received: Steamboat - Exchanged, discharged, died, or escape: Discharged - Time when: 10 Aug 1813 - Whither, and by what order, or number or re-entry: HM Ship Regulius by order of Sir George Provost

Little, Salmon   Prisoner 268. Rank: Sergeant - By what ship or how taken: Boats & Troops - Time when: 8 Jun 1813 - Place where: 40 Mile Creek - Of what ship or corps: Batteaux - Whether man of war, privateer or merchant vessel: Boat - Time when received into custody: 28 Jun 1813 - From what ship or whence received: Batteaux - Exchanged, discharged, died, or escape: Discharged - Time when: - Whither, and by what order, or number or re-entry: HM Ship Success

Little, Samuel   Prisoner 266. Rank: Sergeant - By what ship or how taken: Boats & Troops - Time when: 24 Jun 1813 - Place where: Stoney Point - Of what ship or corps: Batteaux - Whether man of war, privateer or merchant vessel: Boat - Time when received into custody: 24 Jun 1813 - From what ship or whence received: Quebec of Quebec - Exchanged, discharged, died, or escape: Discharged - Time when: - Whither, and by what order, or number or re-entry: HM Ship Success

Littlefield, John   Prisoner 922. Rank: Private - By what ship or how taken: Troops - Time when: 26 Jun 1813 - Place where: Beaver Dam - Of what ship or corps: Land forces - Whether man of war, privateer or merchant vessel: Taken on shore - Time when received into custody: 21 Jul 1813 - From what ship or whence received: Steamboat - Exchanged, discharged, died, or escape: Discharged - Time when: 10 Aug 1813 - Whither, and by what order, or number or re-entry: HM Ship Malpomena

Lloyd, Thompson C.   Prisoner 1343. Rank: Sergeant - By what ship or how taken: Troops - Time when: 19 Dec 1813 - Place where: Fort Niagara - Of what ship or corps: Land forces - Whether man of war, privateer or merchant vessel: Taken on shore - Time when received into custody: 29 Jan 1814 - From what ship or whence received: Montreal by land carriage - Exchanged, discharged, died, or escape: Discharged - Time when: 4 May 1814 - Whither, and by what order, or number or re-entry: United States

Lloyd, William   Prisoner 958. Rank: Private - By what ship or how taken: Troops - Time when: 5 Jul 1813 - Place where: Fort Schisher - Of what ship or corps: Land forces - Whether man of war, privateer or merchant vessel: Taken on shore - Time when received into custody: 5 Sep 1813 - From what ship or whence received: Steamboat - Exchanged, discharged, died, or escape: Discharged - Time when: 31 Oct 1813 - Whither, and by what order, or number or re-entry: Malabar Transport

Lochard, Thomas   Prisoner 1402. Rank: Private - By what ship or how taken: Troops - Time when: 19 Dec 1813 - Place where: Fort Niagara - Of what ship or corps: Land forces - Whether man of war, privateer or merchant vessel: Taken on shore - Time when received into custody: 29 Jan 1814 - From what ship or whence received: Montreal by land carriage - Exchanged, discharged, died, or escape: Discharged - Time when: 4 May 1814 - Whither, and by what order, or number or re-entry: United States

Logan, Timothy   Prisoner 635. Rank: Private - By what ship or how taken: Troops - Time when: 24 Jun 1813 - Place where: Stoney Point - Of what ship or corps: Land forces - Whether man of war, privateer or merchant vessel: Taken on shore - Time when received into custody: 7 Jul 1813 - From what ship or whence received: Steamboat - Exchanged, discharged, died, or escape: Discharged - Time when: 10 Aug 1813 - Whither, and by what order, or number or re-entry: HM Ship Regulius by order of Sir George Provost

American Prisoners of War held at Quebec during the War of 1812

Long, Peter W.   Prisoner 1682. Rank: Sergeant - By what ship or how taken: Troops - Time when: 25 Jul 1814 - Place where: Niagara - Of what ship or corps: Land forces - Whether man of war, privateer or merchant vessel: Taken on shore - Time when received into custody: 23 Oct 1814 - From what ship or whence received: Montreal - Exchanged, discharged, died, or escape: Discharged - Time when: 8 Nov 1814 - Whither, and by what order, or number or re-entry: S. George No. 575 for Halifax

Loomes, Jaires   Prisoner 143. Rank: Sailing Mate - By what ship or how taken: Boats & Troops - Time when: 3 Jun 1813 - Place where: Lake Champlain - Of what ship or corps: Eagle - Whether man of war, privateer or merchant vessel: Man of War - Time when received into custody: 8 Jul 1813 - From what ship or whence received: Batteaux - Exchanged, discharged, died, or escape: Discharged - Time when: 4 May 1814 - Whither, and by what order, or number or re-entry: United States

Loomis, Daniel   Prisoner 380. Rank: Corporal - By what ship or how taken: Troops - Time when: 6 Jun 1813 - Place where: Stoney Point - Of what ship or corps: Land forces - Whether man of war, privateer or merchant vessel: Taken on shore - Time when received into custody: 28 Jun 1813 - From what ship or whence received: Mary of Quebec - Exchanged, discharged, died, or escape: Discharged - Time when: 31 Oct 1813 - Whither, and by what order, or number or re-entry: HM Ship Success

Loomis, Gustaves   Prisoner 1202. Rank: Lieutenant - By what ship or how taken: Troops - Time when: 19 Dec 1813 - Place where: Fort Niagara - Of what ship or corps: Land forces - Whether man of war, privateer or merchant vessel: Taken on shore - Time when received into custody: 18 Jan 1814 - From what ship or whence received: Montreal by land carriage - Exchanged, discharged, died, or escape: Discharged - Time when: 4 May 1814 - Whither, and by what order, or number or re-entry: United States

Lord, Horatio   Prisoner 1255. Rank: Private - By what ship or how taken: Troops - Time when: 19 Dec 1813 - Place where: Fort Niagara - Of what ship or corps: Land forces - Whether man of war, privateer or merchant vessel: Taken on shore - Time when received into custody: 29 Jan 1814 - From what ship or whence received: Montreal by land carriage - Exchanged, discharged, died, or escape: Discharged - Time when: 27 Feb 1814 - Whither, and by what order, or number or re-entry: Volunteered for New Brunswick Fencibles

Lord, Samuel   Prisoner 1732. Rank: Seaman - By what ship or how taken: Gun Boats - Time when: 6 Sep 1814 - Place where: Lake Huron - Of what ship or corps: Scorpion - Whether man of war, privateer or merchant vessel: Man of War - Time when received into custody: 1 Nov 1814 - From what ship or whence received: Montreal - Exchanged, discharged, died, or escape: Discharged - Time when: 7 Nov 1814 - Whither, and by what order, or number or re-entry: Transport Freedom No. 582 by orders of his Excellency Sir George Provost

Losier, Abraham   Prisoner 355. Rank: Private - By what ship or how taken: Troops - Time when: 6 Jun 1813 - Place where: Stoney Point - Of what ship or corps: Land forces - Whether man of war, privateer or merchant vessel: Taken on shore - Time when received into custody: 28 Jun 1813 - From what ship or whence received: Mary of Quebec - Exchanged, discharged, died, or escape: Discharged - Time when: 31 Oct 1813 - Whither, and by what order, or number or re-entry: HM Ship Success

Lou, Samuel   Prisoner 680. Rank: Private - By what ship or how taken: Troops - Time when: 26 Jun 1813 - Place where: Beaver Dam - Of what ship or corps: Land forces - Whether man of war, privateer or merchant vessel: Taken on shore - Time when received into custody: 7 Jul 1813 - From what ship or whence received: Steamboat - Exchanged, discharged, died, or escape: Discharged - Time when: 31 Oct 1813 - Whither, and by what order, or number or re-entry: Malabar Transport

Love, Thomas C.   Prisoner 1946. Rank: Sergeant - By what ship or how taken: Troops - Time when: 17 Sep 1814 - Place where: Fort Erie - Of what ship or corps: Land forces - Whether man of war, privateer or merchant vessel: Taken on shore - Time when received into custody: 1 Nov 1814 - From what ship or whence received: Montreal - Exchanged, discharged, died, or escape: Discharged - Time when: 13 Mar 1815 - Whither, and by what order, or number or re-entry: United States

Lovejoy, Jacob   Prisoner 210. Rank: Private - By what ship or how taken: Boats & Troops - Time when: 3 Jun 1813 - Place where: Lake Champlain - Of what ship or corps: Growler - Whether man of war, privateer or merchant vessel: Man of War - Time when received into custody: 9 Jun 1813 - From what ship or whence received: Batteaux - Exchanged, discharged, died, or escape: Discharged - Time when: 31 Oct 1813 - Whither, and by what order, or number or re-entry: Malabar Transport

Lovell, S.   Prisoner 1520. Rank: Private - By what ship or how taken: Troops - Time when: 25 Jul 1814 - Place where: Lundy's Lane - Of what ship or corps: Land forces - Whether man of war, privateer or merchant vessel: Taken on shore - Time when received into custody: 30 Aug 1814 - From what ship or whence received: Lady Delaval Schooner 578 -

American Prisoners of War held at Quebec during the War of 1812

Exchanged, discharged, died, or escape: Discharged - Time when: 8 Oct 1814 - Whither, and by what order, or number or re-entry: Queen No. 415

Lovland, Charles   Prisoner 1537. Rank: Citizen - By what ship or how taken: Troops - Time when: 25 Jul 1814 - Place where: Lundy's Lane - Of what ship or corps: Land forces - Whether man of war, privateer or merchant vessel: Taken on shore - Time when received into custody: 30 Aug 1814 - From what ship or whence received: Lady Delaval Schooner 578 - Exchanged, discharged, died, or escape: Escaped - Time when: 15 Oct 1814 - Whither, and by what order, or number or re-entry:

Lowell, Nicholas   Prisoner 1834. Rank: Private - By what ship or how taken: Troops - Time when: 17 Sep 1814 - Place where: Fort Erie - Of what ship or corps: Land forces - Whether man of war, privateer or merchant vessel: Taken on shore - Time when received into custody: 1 Nov 1814 - From what ship or whence received: Montreal - Exchanged, discharged, died, or escape: Discharged - Time when: 8 Nov 1814 - Whither, and by what order, or number or re-entry: S. George No. 575 for Halifax by order of Sir George Provost

Lucas, Ephraim   Prisoner 113. Rank: Private - By what ship or how taken: Boats & Troops - Time when: 28 May 1813 - Place where: Stoney Point, Henderson Harbor - Of what ship or corps: Land forces - Whether man of war, privateer or merchant vessel: Taken on shore - Time when received into custody: 8 Jun 1813 - From what ship or whence received: Batteaux - Exchanged, discharged, died, or escape: Discharged - Time when: 31 Oct 1813 - Whither, and by what order, or number or re-entry: Malabar Transport

Luce, Aaron   Prisoner 1284. Rank: Private - By what ship or how taken: Troops - Time when: 19 Dec 1813 - Place where: Fort Niagara - Of what ship or corps: Land forces - Whether man of war, privateer or merchant vessel: Taken on shore - Time when received into custody: 29 Jan 1814 - From what ship or whence received: Montreal by land carriage - Exchanged, discharged, died, or escape: Discharged - Time when: 4 May 1814 - Whither, and by what order, or number or re-entry: United States

Luce, Robert   Prisoner 1815. Rank: Private - By what ship or how taken: Troops - Time when: 17 Sep 1814 - Place where: Fort Erie - Of what ship or corps: Land forces - Whether man of war, privateer or merchant vessel: Taken on shore - Time when received into custody: 1 Nov 1814 - From what ship or whence received: Montreal - Exchanged, discharged, died, or escape: Discharged - Time when: 8 Nov 1814 - Whither, and by what order, or number or re-entry: S. George No. 575 for Halifax by order of Sir George Provost

Luckey, Samuel   Prisoner 767. Rank: Private - By what ship or how taken: Troops - Time when: 26 Jun 1813 - Place where: Beaver Dam - Of what ship or corps: Land forces - Whether man of war, privateer or merchant vessel: Taken on shore - Time when received into custody: 7 Jul 1813 - From what ship or whence received: Steamboat - Exchanged, discharged, died, or escape: Discharged - Time when: 10 Aug 1813 - Whither, and by what order, or number or re-entry: HM Ship Malpomena

Lyles, William   Prisoner 1015. Rank: Marine Sergeant - By what ship or how taken: Earl Moria - Time when: 10 Aug 1813 - Place where: Lake Ontario - Of what ship or corps: Julia - Whether man of war, privateer or merchant vessel: Man of War - Time when received into custody: 5 Sep 1813 - From what ship or whence received: Steamboat - Exchanged, discharged, died, or escape: - Time when: - Whither, and by what order, or number or re-entry:

Lynch, John   Prisoner 303. Rank: Private - By what ship or how taken: Boats & Troops - Time when: 6 Jun 1813 - Place where: Stoney Point - Of what ship or corps: Land forces - Whether man of war, privateer or merchant vessel: Taken on shore - Time when received into custody: 28 Jun 1813 - From what ship or whence received: Quebec of Quebec - Exchanged, discharged, died, or escape: Discharged - Time when: 7 Aug 1813 - Whither, and by what order, or number or re-entry: H.M. Ship Cievare

Lytle, Daniel   Prisoner 1092. Rank: Private - By what ship or how taken: Troops - Time when: 24 Aug 1813 - Place where: Fort George - Of what ship or corps: Land forces - Whether man of war, privateer or merchant vessel: Taken on shore - Time when received into custody: 10 Oct 1813 - From what ship or whence received: Steamboat - Exchanged, discharged, died, or escape: Discharged - Time when: 31 Oct 1813 - Whither, and by what order, or number or re-entry: Malabar Transport

Machesney, John   Prisoner 949. Rank: Captain - By what ship or how taken: Troops - Time when: 26 Jun 1813 - Place where: Beaver Dam - Of what ship or corps: Land forces - Whether man of war, privateer or merchant vessel: Taken on shore - Time when received into custody: 21 Jul 1813 - From what ship or whence received: Steamboat - Exchanged, discharged, died, or escape: Discharged - Time when: 4 May 1814 - Whither, and by what order, or number or re-entry: United States

Mack, Abner   Prisoner 132. Rank: Private - By what ship or how taken: Boats & Troops - Time when: 28 May 1813 - Place

American Prisoners of War held at Quebec during the War of 1812

where: Stoney Point, Henderson Harbor - Of what ship or corps: Land forces - Whether man of war, privateer or merchant vessel: Taken on shore - Time when received into custody: 8 Jul 1813 - From what ship or whence received: Batteaux - Exchanged, discharged, died, or escape: Discharged - Time when: 31 Oct 1813 - Whither, and by what order, or number or re-entry: Malabar Transport

Mackelfresh, Joseph H.   Prisoner 916.   Rank: Private - By what ship or how taken: Troops - Time when: 26 Jun 1813 - Place where: Beaver Dam - Of what ship or corps: Land forces - Whether man of war, privateer or merchant vessel: Taken on shore - Time when received into custody: 21 Jul 1813 - From what ship or whence received: Steamboat - Exchanged, discharged, died, or escape: Discharged - Time when: 10 Aug 1813 - Whither, and by what order, or number or re-entry: HM Ship Malpomena

Mackey, John   Prisoner 581.   Rank: Private - By what ship or how taken: Troops - Time when: 26 Jun 1813 - Place where: Beaver Dam - Of what ship or corps: Land forces - Whether man of war, privateer or merchant vessel: Taken on shore - Time when received into custody: 13 Jul 1813 - From what ship or whence received: Steamboat - Exchanged, discharged, died, or escape: Discharged - Time when: 9 Aug 1813 - Whither, and by what order, or number or re-entry: HM Ship Wasp

Macnalley, John   Prisoner 1306.   Rank: Private - By what ship or how taken: Troops - Time when: 19 Dec 1813 - Place where: Fort Niagara - Of what ship or corps: Land forces - Whether man of war, privateer or merchant vessel: Taken on shore - Time when received into custody: 29 Jan 1814 - From what ship or whence received: Montreal by land carriage - Exchanged, discharged, died, or escape: Discharged - Time when: 24 Feb 1814 - Whither, and by what order, or number or re-entry: Volunteered for New Brunswick Fencibles

Madder, Thomas   Prisoner 191.   Rank: Private - By what ship or how taken: Boats & Troops - Time when: 3 Jun 1813 - Place where: Lake Champlain - Of what ship or corps: Growler - Whether man of war, privateer or merchant vessel: Man of War - Time when received into custody: 9 Jun 1813 - From what ship or whence received: Batteaux - Exchanged, discharged, died, or escape: Discharged - Time when: 4 May 1814 - Whither, and by what order, or number or re-entry: United States

Madison, George   Prisoner 248.   Rank: Major - By what ship or how taken: Boats & Troops - Time when: 24 Jun 1813 - Place where: Rec in charge of Beauport - Of what ship or corps: Land forces - Whether man of war, privateer or merchant vessel: Taken on shore - Time when received into custody: 24 Jun 1813 - From what ship or whence received: At Beauport - Exchanged, discharged, died, or escape: Discharged - Time when: 29 Mar 1814 - Whither, and by what order, or number or re-entry: United States

Mager, Robert   Prisoner 877.   Rank: Private - By what ship or how taken: Troops - Time when: 26 Jun 1813 - Place where: Beaver Dam - Of what ship or corps: Land forces - Whether man of war, privateer or merchant vessel: Taken on shore - Time when received into custody: 7 Jul 1813 - From what ship or whence received: Steamboat - Exchanged, discharged, died, or escape: Discharged - Time when: 10 Aug 1813 - Whither, and by what order, or number or re-entry: HM Ship Malpomena

Mahan, Francis   Prisoner 1138.   Rank: Private - By what ship or how taken: Troops - Time when: 22 Jan 1812 - Place where: Rapids Prince Reason - Of what ship or corps: Land forces - Whether man of war, privateer or merchant vessel: Taken on shore - Time when received into custody: 25 Nov 1813 - From what ship or whence received: Town Goal - Exchanged, discharged, died, or escape: Discharged - Time when: 4 May 1814 - Whither, and by what order, or number or re-entry: United States

Maher, Samuel   Prisoner 748.   Rank: Private - By what ship or how taken: Troops - Time when: 26 Jun 1813 - Place where: Beaver Dam - Of what ship or corps: Land forces - Whether man of war, privateer or merchant vessel: Taken on shore - Time when received into custody: 7 Jul 1813 - From what ship or whence received: Steamboat - Exchanged, discharged, died, or escape: Discharged - Time when: 10 Aug 1813 - Whither, and by what order, or number or re-entry: HM Ship Malpomena

Mallet, John   Prisoner 984.   Rank: Seaman - By what ship or how taken: Earl Moria - Time when: 10 Aug 1813 - Place where: Lake Ontario - Of what ship or corps: Julia - Whether man of war, privateer or merchant vessel: Man of War - Time when received into custody: 5 Sep 1813 - From what ship or whence received: Steamboat - Exchanged, discharged, died, or escape: Discharged - Time when: 18 Sep 1813 - Whither, and by what order, or number or re-entry: To the Regulus Transport by order of Major General Glasgow

Manchester, Noah   Prisoner 1281.   Rank: Private - By what ship or how taken: Troops - Time when: 19 Dec 1813 - Place where: Fort Niagara - Of what ship or corps: Land forces - Whether man of war, privateer or merchant vessel: Taken on shore - Time when received into custody: 29 Jan 1814 - From what ship or whence received: Montreal by land carriage - Exchanged, discharged, died, or escape: Discharged - Time when: 11 Mar 1814 - Whither, and by what order, or number or re-entry: Volunteered for New Brunswick Fencibles

Mandeville, Peter   Prisoner 1119. Rank: Private - By what ship or how taken: Troops - Time when: 17 Oct 1813 - Place where: Red Mills - Of what ship or corps: Land forces - Whether man of war, privateer or merchant vessel: Taken on shore - Time when received into custody: 12 Oct 1813 - From what ship or whence received: Steamboat - Exchanged, discharged, died, or escape: Discharged - Time when: 31 Oct 1813 - Whither, and by what order, or number or re-entry: Malabar Transport

Manuel, John   Prisoner 1585. Rank: Seaman - By what ship or how taken: Gun Boats - Time when: 12 Aug 1814 - Place where: Fort Erie - Of what ship or corps: Ohio - Whether man of war, privateer or merchant vessel: Man of War - Time when received into custody: 5 Oct 1814 - From what ship or whence received: Montreal - Exchanged, discharged, died, or escape: Discharged - Time when: 10 Nov 1814 - Whither, and by what order, or number or re-entry: Freedom No. 582

March, Hosea   Prisoner 1860. Rank: Private - By what ship or how taken: Troops - Time when: 17 Sep 1814 - Place where: Fort Erie - Of what ship or corps: Land forces - Whether man of war, privateer or merchant vessel: Taken on shore - Time when received into custody: 1 Nov 1814 - From what ship or whence received: Montreal - Exchanged, discharged, died, or escape: Discharged - Time when: 8 Nov 1814 - Whither, and by what order, or number or re-entry: S. George No. 575 for Halifax

March, William   Prisoner 703. Rank: Private - By what ship or how taken: Troops - Time when: 26 Jun 1813 - Place where: Beaver Dam - Of what ship or corps: Land forces - Whether man of war, privateer or merchant vessel: Taken on shore - Time when received into custody: 7 Jul 1813 - From what ship or whence received: Steamboat - Exchanged, discharged, died, or escape: Discharged - Time when: 10 Aug 1813 - Whither, and by what order, or number or re-entry: HM Ship Regulius by order of Sir George Provost

Marker, Benjamin   Prisoner 1345. Rank: Private - By what ship or how taken: Troops - Time when: 19 Dec 1813 - Place where: Fort Niagara - Of what ship or corps: Land forces - Whether man of war, privateer or merchant vessel: Taken on shore - Time when received into custody: 29 Jan 1814 - From what ship or whence received: Montreal by land carriage - Exchanged, discharged, died, or escape: Discharged - Time when: 4 May 1814 - Whither, and by what order, or number or re-entry: United States

Marks, Henry   Prisoner 1244. Rank: Private - By what ship or how taken: Troops - Time when: 19 Dec 1813 - Place where: Fort Niagara - Of what ship or corps: Land forces - Whether man of war, privateer or merchant vessel: Taken on shore - Time when received into custody: 29 Jan 1814 - From what ship or whence received: Montreal by land carriage - Exchanged, discharged, died, or escape: Discharged - Time when: 27 Feb 1814 - Whither, and by what order, or number or re-entry: Volunteered for New Brunswick Fencibles

Marks, Ira   Prisoner 67. Rank: Sergeant - By what ship or how taken: Boats & Troops - Time when: 28 May 1813 - Place where: Stoney Point, Henderson Harbor - Of what ship or corps: Land forces - Whether man of war, privateer or merchant vessel: Taken on shore - Time when received into custody: 8 Jun 1813 - From what ship or whence received: Batteaux - Exchanged, discharged, died, or escape: Discharged - Time when: 8 Oct 1813 - Whither, and by what order, or number or re-entry: H.M. Ship Ceylon

Marlin, William   Prisoner 624. Rank: Private - By what ship or how taken: Troops - Time when: 24 Jun 1813 - Place where: Stoney Point - Of what ship or corps: Land forces - Whether man of war, privateer or merchant vessel: Taken on shore - Time when received into custody: 7 Jul 1813 - From what ship or whence received: Steamboat - Exchanged, discharged, died, or escape: Discharged - Time when: 10 Aug 1813 - Whither, and by what order, or number or re-entry: HM Ship Regulius by order of Sir George Provost

Marshall, Joseph   Prisoner 525. Rank: Lieutenant - By what ship or how taken: Troops - Time when: 24 Jun 1813 - Place where: Beaver Dam - Of what ship or corps: Land forces - Whether man of war, privateer or merchant vessel: Taken on shore - Time when received into custody: 13 Jul 1813 - From what ship or whence received: Steamboat - Exchanged, discharged, died, or escape: Discharged - Time when: 10 Aug 1813 - Whither, and by what order, or number or re-entry: HM Ship Regulius by order of Sir George Provost

Marshall, William   Prisoner 675. Rank: Private - By what ship or how taken: Troops - Time when: 26 Jun 1813 - Place where: Beaver Dam - Of what ship or corps: Land forces - Whether man of war, privateer or merchant vessel: Taken on shore - Time when received into custody: 7 Jul 1813 - From what ship or whence received: Steamboat - Exchanged, discharged, died, or escape: Discharged - Time when: 10 Aug 1813 - Whither, and by what order, or number or re-entry: HM Ship Regulius by order of Sir George Provost

American Prisoners of War held at Quebec during the War of 1812

Martin, Byron   Prisoner 660. Rank: Private - By what ship or how taken: Troops - Time when: 24 Jun 1813 - Place where: Stoney Point - Of what ship or corps: Land forces - Whether man of war, privateer or merchant vessel: Taken on shore - Time when received into custody: 7 Jul 1813 - From what ship or whence received: Steamboat - Exchanged, discharged, died, or escape: Discharged - Time when: 10 Aug 1813 - Whither, and by what order, or number or re-entry: HM Ship Regulius by order of Sir George Provost

Martin, James   Prisoner 1739. Rank: Seaman - By what ship or how taken: Gun Boats - Time when: 3 Sep 1814 - Place where: Lake Huron - Of what ship or corps: Tigress - Whether man of war, privateer or merchant vessel: Man of War - Time when received into custody: 1 Nov 1814 - From what ship or whence received: Montreal - Exchanged, discharged, died, or escape: Discharged - Time when: 7 Nov 1814 - Whither, and by what order, or number or re-entry: Transport Freedom No. 582 by orders of his Excellency Sir George Provost

Martin, Silvanus   Prisoner 46. Rank: Private - By what ship or how taken: Boats & Troops - Time when: 28 May 1813 - Place where: Stoney Point, Henderson Harbor - Of what ship or corps: Land forces - Whether man of war, privateer or merchant vessel: Taken on shore - Time when received into custody: 8 Jun 1813 - From what ship or whence received: Batteaux - Exchanged, discharged, died, or escape: Died - Time when: 3 Aug 1813 - Whither, and by what order, or number or re-entry:

Marvel, Joseph   Prisoner 1010. Rank: Seaman - By what ship or how taken: Earl Moria - Time when: 10 Aug 1813 - Place where: Lake Ontario - Of what ship or corps: Julia - Whether man of war, privateer or merchant vessel: Man of War - Time when received into custody: 5 Sep 1813 - From what ship or whence received: Steamboat - Exchanged, discharged, died, or escape: Discharged - Time when: 31 Oct 1813 - Whither, and by what order, or number or re-entry: Malabar Transport

Mason, Ira   Prisoner 824. Rank: Private - By what ship or how taken: Troops - Time when: 26 Jun 1813 - Place where: Beaver Dam - Of what ship or corps: Land forces - Whether man of war, privateer or merchant vessel: Taken on shore - Time when received into custody: 7 Jul 1813 - From what ship or whence received: Steamboat - Exchanged, discharged, died, or escape: Discharged - Time when: 10 Aug 1813 - Whither, and by what order, or number or re-entry: HM Ship Malpomena

Masters, John   Prisoner 1172. Rank: Private - By what ship or how taken: Troops - Time when: 5 May 1813 - Place where: Rapids Prince Reason - Of what ship or corps: Land forces - Whether man of war, privateer or merchant vessel: Taken on shore - Time when received into custody: 25 Nov 1813 - From what ship or whence received: Town Goal - Exchanged, discharged, died, or escape: Discharged - Time when: 12 Mar 1814 - Whither, and by what order, or number or re-entry: New Brunswick Fencibles

Mathews, Daniel   Prisoner 722. Rank: Private - By what ship or how taken: Troops - Time when: 26 Jun 1813 - Place where: Beaver Dam - Of what ship or corps: Land forces - Whether man of war, privateer or merchant vessel: Taken on shore - Time when received into custody: 7 Jul 1813 - From what ship or whence received: Steamboat - Exchanged, discharged, died, or escape: Discharged - Time when: 10 Aug 1813 - Whither, and by what order, or number or re-entry: HM Ship Regulius by order of Sir George Provost

Matill, Francis   Prisoner 1757. Rank: Private - By what ship or how taken: Gun Boats - Time when: 6 Sep 1814 - Place where: Lake Huron - Of what ship or corps: Scorpion - Whether man of war, privateer or merchant vessel: Man of War - Time when received into custody: 1 Nov 1814 - From what ship or whence received: Montreal - Exchanged, discharged, died, or escape: Discharged - Time when: 8 Nov 1814 - Whither, and by what order, or number or re-entry: S. George No. 575 for Halifax by order of Sir George Provost

Matlock, Joseph   Prisoner 480. Rank: Private - By what ship or how taken: Troops - Time when: 24 Jun 1813 - Place where: Beaver Dam - Of what ship or corps: Land forces - Whether man of war, privateer or merchant vessel: Taken on shore - Time when received into custody: 7 Jul 1813 - From what ship or whence received: Steamboat - Exchanged, discharged, died, or escape: Discharged - Time when: 10 Aug 1813 - Whither, and by what order, or number or re-entry: HM Ship Regulius by order of Sir George Provost

Matthews, John   Prisoner 653. Rank: Private - By what ship or how taken: Troops - Time when: 24 Jun 1813 - Place where: Stoney Point - Of what ship or corps: Land forces - Whether man of war, privateer or merchant vessel: Taken on shore - Time when received into custody: 7 Jul 1813 - From what ship or whence received: Steamboat - Exchanged, discharged, died, or escape: Discharged - Time when: 10 Aug 1813 - Whither, and by what order, or number or re-entry: HM Ship Regulius by order of Sir George Provost

Maxwell, Robert   Prisoner 620. Rank: Private - By what ship or how taken: Troops - Time when: 24 Jun 1813 - Place where: Stoney Point - Of what ship or corps: Land forces - Whether man of war, privateer or merchant vessel: Taken on shore - Time when received into custody: 7 Jul 1813 - From what ship or whence received: Steamboat - Exchanged,

American Prisoners of War held at Quebec during the War of 1812

discharged, died, or escape: Discharged - Time when: 9 Aug 1813 - Whither, and by what order, or number or re-entry: HM Ship Wasp

Maxwell, Thomas   Prisoner 1977. Rank: Private - By what ship or how taken: Troops - Time when: 2 Nov 1814 - Place where: Fort Erie - Of what ship or corps: Land forces - Whether man of war, privateer or merchant vessel: Taken on shore - Time when received into custody: 11 Dec 1814 - From what ship or whence received: Montreal - Exchanged, discharged, died, or escape: Discharged - Time when: - Whither, and by what order, or number or re-entry:

Maxwell, Thompson   Prisoner 1957. Rank: Forage Master - By what ship or how taken: Troops - Time when: 23 Oct 1814 - Place where: Fort Erie - Of what ship or corps: Land forces - Whether man of war, privateer or merchant vessel: Taken on shore - Time when received into custody: 11 Dec 1814 - From what ship or whence received: Montreal - Exchanged, discharged, died, or escape: Discharged - Time when: 13 Mar 1815 - Whither, and by what order, or number or re-entry: United States

Maybe, Jacob   Prisoner 822. Rank: Private - By what ship or how taken: Troops - Time when: 26 Jun 1813 - Place where: Beaver Dam - Of what ship or corps: Land forces - Whether man of war, privateer or merchant vessel: Taken on shore - Time when received into custody: 7 Jul 1813 - From what ship or whence received: Steamboat - Exchanged, discharged, died, or escape: Discharged - Time when: 10 Aug 1813 - Whither, and by what order, or number or re-entry: HM Ship Malpomena

McAubrory, William   Prisoner 376. Rank: Private - By what ship or how taken: Troops - Time when: 6 Jun 1813 - Place where: Stoney Point - Of what ship or corps: Land forces - Whether man of war, privateer or merchant vessel: Taken on shore - Time when received into custody: 28 Jun 1813 - From what ship or whence received: Mary of Quebec - Exchanged, discharged, died, or escape: Discharged - Time when: 7 Aug 1813 - Whither, and by what order, or number or re-entry: H.M. Ship Cievare

McAvery alias McAvor, John   Prisoner 1036. Rank: Seaman - By what ship or how taken: Lord Melvin - Time when: 10 Aug 1813 - Place where: Lake Ontario - Of what ship or corps: Growler - Whether man of war, privateer or merchant vessel: Man of War - Time when received into custody: 5 Sep 1813 - From what ship or whence received: Steamboat - Exchanged, discharged, died, or escape: Discharged - Time when: - Whither, and by what order, or number or re-entry: HM Ship Success

McCaller, Benjamin   Prisoner 726. Rank: Private - By what ship or how taken: Troops - Time when: 26 Jun 1813 - Place where: Beaver Dam - Of what ship or corps: Land forces - Whether man of war, privateer or merchant vessel: Taken on shore - Time when received into custody: 7 Jul 1813 - From what ship or whence received: Steamboat - Exchanged, discharged, died, or escape: Discharged - Time when: 10 Aug 1813 - Whither, and by what order, or number or re-entry: HM Ship Regulius by order of Sir George Provost

McCann, Robert   Prisoner 332. Rank: Private - By what ship or how taken: Boats & Troops - Time when: 6 Jun 1813 - Place where: Stoney Point - Of what ship or corps: Land forces - Whether man of war, privateer or merchant vessel: Taken on shore - Time when received into custody: 28 Jun 1813 - From what ship or whence received: Quebec of Quebec - Exchanged, discharged, died, or escape: Discharged - Time when: 31 Oct 1813 - Whither, and by what order, or number or re-entry: HM Ship Success

McCardall, Jacob   Prisoner 1423. Rank: Private - By what ship or how taken: Troops - Time when: 19 Dec 1813 - Place where: Fort Niagara - Of what ship or corps: Land forces - Whether man of war, privateer or merchant vessel: Taken on shore - Time when received into custody: 29 Jan 1814 - From what ship or whence received: Montreal by land carriage - Exchanged, discharged, died, or escape: Discharged - Time when: 4 May 1814 - Whither, and by what order, or number or re-entry: United States

McCarthy, Charles   Prisoner 1058. Rank: Private - By what ship or how taken: Troops - Time when: 24 Jun 1813 - Place where: Beaver Dam - Of what ship or corps: Land forces - Whether man of war, privateer or merchant vessel: Taken on shore - Time when received into custody: 5 Sep 1813 - From what ship or whence received: Steamboat - Exchanged, discharged, died, or escape: Discharged - Time when: 31 Oct 1813 - Whither, and by what order, or number or re-entry: Malabar Transport

McChristie, J.   Prisoner 1643. Rank: Private - By what ship or how taken: Troops - Time when: 19 Dec 1813 - Place where: Niagara - Of what ship or corps: Land forces - Whether man of war, privateer or merchant vessel: Taken on shore - Time when received into custody: 5 Oct 1814 - From what ship or whence received: Montreal - Exchanged, discharged, died, or escape: Discharged - Time when: 8 Oct 1814 - Whither, and by what order, or number or re-entry: H.M. Ship Ceylon

McCirchar, Stephen   Prisoner 433. Rank: Private - By what ship or how taken: Troops - Time when: 24 Jun 1813 - Place where: Beaver Dam - Of what ship or corps: Land forces - Whether man of war, privateer or merchant vessel: Taken on shore - Time when received into custody: 7 Jul 1813 - From what ship or whence received: Steamboat - Exchanged, discharged, died, or escape: Discharged - Time when: 10 Aug 1813 - Whither, and by what order, or number or re-entry: HM Ship Regulius by order of Sir George Provost

McClary, James   Prisoner 1804. Rank: Private - By what ship or how taken: Troops - Time when: 17 Sep 1814 - Place where: Fort Erie - Of what ship or corps: Land forces - Whether man of war, privateer or merchant vessel: Taken on shore - Time when received into custody: 1 Nov 1814 - From what ship or whence received: Montreal - Exchanged, discharged, died, or escape: Discharged - Time when: 8 Nov 1814 - Whither, and by what order, or number or re-entry: S. George No. 575 for Halifax by order of Sir George Provost

McClure, John   Prisoner 892. Rank: Private - By what ship or how taken: Troops - Time when: 26 Jun 1813 - Place where: Beaver Dam - Of what ship or corps: Land forces - Whether man of war, privateer or merchant vessel: Taken on shore - Time when received into custody: 7 Jul 1813 - From what ship or whence received: Steamboat - Exchanged, discharged, died, or escape: Discharged - Time when: 10 Aug 1813 - Whither, and by what order, or number or re-entry: HM Ship Malpomena

McConaghey, Benjamin   Prisoner 672. Rank: Private - By what ship or how taken: Troops - Time when: 26 Jun 1813 - Place where: Beaver Dam - Of what ship or corps: Land forces - Whether man of war, privateer or merchant vessel: Taken on shore - Time when received into custody: 7 Jul 1813 - From what ship or whence received: Steamboat - Exchanged, discharged, died, or escape: Discharged - Time when: 10 Aug 1813 - Whither, and by what order, or number or re-entry: HM Ship Regulius by order of Sir George Provost

McConoly, H.   Prisoner 1614. Rank: Private - By what ship or how taken: Gun Boats - Time when: 12 Aug 1814 - Place where: Fort Erie - Of what ship or corps: Land forces - Whether man of war, privateer or merchant vessel: Taken on shore - Time when received into custody: 5 Oct 1814 - From what ship or whence received: Montreal - Exchanged, discharged, died, or escape: Discharged - Time when: 8 Oct 1814 - Whither, and by what order, or number or re-entry: H.M. Ship Ceylon

McCroy, Thomas   Prisoner 1362. Rank: Sergeant - By what ship or how taken: Troops - Time when: 19 Dec 1813 - Place where: Fort Niagara - Of what ship or corps: Land forces - Whether man of war, privateer or merchant vessel: Taken on shore - Time when received into custody: 29 Jan 1814 - From what ship or whence received: Montreal by land carriage - Exchanged, discharged, died, or escape: Discharged - Time when: 4 May 1814 - Whither, and by what order, or number or re-entry: United States

McCullock, Samuel   Prisoner 1536. Rank: Private - By what ship or how taken: Troops - Time when: 25 Jul 1814 - Place where: Lundy's Lane - Of what ship or corps: Land forces - Whether man of war, privateer or merchant vessel: Taken on shore - Time when received into custody: 30 Aug 1814 - From what ship or whence received: Lady Delaval Schooner 578 - Exchanged, discharged, died, or escape: Discharged - Time when: 8 Oct 1814 - Whither, and by what order, or number or re-entry: Queen No. 415

McCurdy, Robert   Prisoner 1182. Rank: Private - By what ship or how taken: Troops - Time when: 5 May 1813 - Place where: Rapids - Of what ship or corps: Land forces - Whether man of war, privateer or merchant vessel: Taken on shore - Time when received into custody: 25 Nov 1813 - From what ship or whence received: Town Goal - Exchanged, discharged, died, or escape: Discharged - Time when: 4 May 1814 - Whither, and by what order, or number or re-entry: United States

McCurl, Isaac   Prisoner 1295. Rank: Private - By what ship or how taken: Troops - Time when: 19 Dec 1813 - Place where: Fort Niagara - Of what ship or corps: Land forces - Whether man of war, privateer or merchant vessel: Taken on shore - Time when received into custody: 29 Jan 1814 - From what ship or whence received: Montreal by land carriage - Exchanged, discharged, died, or escape: Discharged - Time when: 4 May 1814 - Whither, and by what order, or number or re-entry: United States

McDoan, J,   Prisoner 1541. Rank: Private - By what ship or how taken: Troops - Time when: 25 Jul 1814 - Place where: Lundy's Lane - Of what ship or corps: Land forces - Whether man of war, privateer or merchant vessel: Taken on shore - Time when received into custody: 30 Aug 1814 - From what ship or whence received: Lady Delaval Schooner 578 - Exchanged, discharged, died, or escape: Discharged - Time when: 8 Oct 1814 - Whither, and by what order, or number or re-entry: Queen No. 415

McDonald, Francis   Prisoner 1089. Rank: Private - By what ship or how taken: Troops - Time when: 24 Aug 1813 - Place where: Fort George - Of what ship or corps: Land forces - Whether man of war, privateer or merchant vessel: Taken on shore - Time when received into custody: 10 Oct 1813 - From what ship or whence received: Steamboat - Exchanged, discharged, died, or escape: Discharged - Time when: 31 Oct 1813 - Whither, and by what order, or number or re-entry:

American Prisoners of War held at Quebec during the War of 1812

Malabar Transport

McDonald, Peter   Prisoner 405. Rank: Private - By what ship or how taken: Troops - Time when: 24 Jun 1813 - Place where: Beaver Dam - Of what ship or corps: Land forces - Whether man of war, privateer or merchant vessel: Taken on shore - Time when received into custody: 7 Jul 1813 - From what ship or whence received: Steamboat - Exchanged, discharged, died, or escape: Discharged - Time when: 31 Oct 1813 - Whither, and by what order, or number or re-entry: Malabar Transport

McDonald, Theophilus   Prisoner 576. Rank: Private - By what ship or how taken: Troops - Time when: 26 Jun 1813 - Place where: Beaver Dam - Of what ship or corps: Land forces - Whether man of war, privateer or merchant vessel: Taken on shore - Time when received into custody: 13 Jul 1813 - From what ship or whence received: Steamboat - Exchanged, discharged, died, or escape: Discharged - Time when: 10 Aug 1813 - Whither, and by what order, or number or re-entry: HM Ship Regulius by order of Sir George Provost

McDowell, Andrew   Prisoner 402. Rank: Captain - By what ship or how taken: Troops - Time when: 24 Jun 1813 - Place where: Beaver Dam - Of what ship or corps: Land forces - Whether man of war, privateer or merchant vessel: Taken on shore - Time when received into custody: 7 Jul 1813 - From what ship or whence received: Steamboat - Exchanged, discharged, died, or escape: Discharged - Time when: 10 Aug 1813 - Whither, and by what order, or number or re-entry: Per order His Exellency Sir George Prevost

McDune, William   Prisoner 311. Rank: Corporal - By what ship or how taken: Boats & Troops - Time when: 6 Jun 1813 - Place where: Stoney Point - Of what ship or corps: Land forces - Whether man of war, privateer or merchant vessel: Taken on shore - Time when received into custody: 28 Jun 1813 - From what ship or whence received: Quebec of Quebec - Exchanged, discharged, died, or escape: Discharged - Time when: 8 Oct 1813 - Whither, and by what order, or number or re-entry: H.M. Ship Ceylon

McEver, William   Prisoner 689. Rank: Private - By what ship or how taken: Troops - Time when: 26 Jun 1813 - Place where: Beaver Dam - Of what ship or corps: Land forces - Whether man of war, privateer or merchant vessel: Taken on shore - Time when received into custody: 7 Jul 1813 - From what ship or whence received: Steamboat - Exchanged, discharged, died, or escape: Discharged - Time when: 10 Aug 1813 - Whither, and by what order, or number or re-entry: HM Ship Regulius by order of Sir George Provost

McEwen, Alexander   Prisoner 259. Rank: Captain - By what ship or how taken: Boats & Troops - Time when: 24 Jun 1813 - Place where: Stoney Point - Of what ship or corps: Land forces - Whether man of war, privateer or merchant vessel: Taken on shore - Time when received into custody: 24 Jun 1813 - From what ship or whence received: Steamboat - Exchanged, discharged, died, or escape: Discharged - Time when: 13 Dec 1813 - Whither, and by what order, or number or re-entry: United States

McGee, George   Prisoner 1115. Rank: Private - By what ship or how taken: Troops - Time when: 17 Oct 1813 - Place where: Red Mills - Of what ship or corps: Land forces - Whether man of war, privateer or merchant vessel: Taken on shore - Time when received into custody: 12 Oct 1813 - From what ship or whence received: Steamboat - Exchanged, discharged, died, or escape: Discharged - Time when: 31 Oct 1813 - Whither, and by what order, or number or re-entry: Malabar Transport

McGee, William   Prisoner 1046. Rank: Private - By what ship or how taken: Lord Melvin - Time when: 10 Aug 1813 - Place where: Lake Ontario - Of what ship or corps: Growler - Whether man of war, privateer or merchant vessel: Man of War - Time when received into custody: 5 Sep 1813 - From what ship or whence received: Steamboat - Exchanged, discharged, died, or escape: Discharged - Time when: 31 Oct 1813 - Whither, and by what order, or number or re-entry: Malabar Transport

McGlathay, Thomas   Prisoner 1433. Rank: Able seaman - By what ship or how taken: Prometheus - Time when: 5 Mar 1814 - Place where: Off Halifax - Of what ship or corps: Lizard - Whether man of war, privateer or merchant vessel: Privateer - Time when received into custody: 24 May 1814 - From what ship or whence received: Mary Transport No. 360 Halifax - Exchanged, discharged, died, or escape: Discharged - Time when: 4 May 1814 - Whither, and by what order, or number or re-entry: United States

McGoud, John   Prisoner 505. Rank: Private - By what ship or how taken: Troops - Time when: 24 Jun 1813 - Place where: Beaver Dam - Of what ship or corps: Land forces - Whether man of war, privateer or merchant vessel: Taken on shore - Time when received into custody: 7 Jul 1813 - From what ship or whence received: Steamboat - Exchanged, discharged, died, or escape: Discharged - Time when: 9 Aug 1813 - Whither, and by what order, or number or re-entry: HM Ship Wasp

McGowen, Patrick   Prisoner 1920. Rank: Private - By what ship or how taken: Troops - Time when: 17 Sep 1814 - Place where: Fort Erie - Of what ship or corps: Land forces - Whether man of war, privateer or merchant vessel: Taken on shore - Time when received into custody: 1 Nov 1814 - From what ship or whence received: Montreal - Exchanged, discharged, died, or escape: Discharged - Time when: 14 Nov 1814 - Whither, and by what order, or number or re-entry: Soverign No. 628 for Halifax

McGregor, R.   Prisoner 1580. Rank: Seaman - By what ship or how taken: Gun Boats - Time when: 12 Aug 1814 - Place where: Fort Erie - Of what ship or corps: Somers - Whether man of war, privateer or merchant vessel: Man of War - Time when received into custody: 5 Oct 1814 - From what ship or whence received: Montreal - Exchanged, discharged, died, or escape: Discharged - Time when: 10 Nov 1814 - Whither, and by what order, or number or re-entry: Freedom No. 582

McGuire, Hugh   Prisoner 665. Rank: Private - By what ship or how taken: Troops - Time when: 24 Jun 1813 - Place where: Stoney Point - Of what ship or corps: Land forces - Whether man of war, privateer or merchant vessel: Taken on shore - Time when received into custody: 7 Jul 1813 - From what ship or whence received: Steamboat - Exchanged, discharged, died, or escape: Discharged - Time when: 9 Aug 1813 - Whither, and by what order, or number or re-entry: HM Ship Wasp

McGunnell, Michael   Prisoner 1242. Rank: Private - By what ship or how taken: Troops - Time when: 19 Dec 1813 - Place where: Fort Niagara - Of what ship or corps: Land forces - Whether man of war, privateer or merchant vessel: Taken on shore - Time when received into custody: 29 Jan 1814 - From what ship or whence received: Montreal by land carriage - Exchanged, discharged, died, or escape: Discharged - Time when: 27 Feb 1814 - Whither, and by what order, or number or re-entry: Volunteered for New Brunswick Fencibles

McIlroy, James   Prisoner 1130. Rank: Private - By what ship or how taken: Troops - Time when: 5 May 1813 - Place where: Rapids Prince Reason - Of what ship or corps: Land forces - Whether man of war, privateer or merchant vessel: Taken on shore - Time when received into custody: 25 Nov 1813 - From what ship or whence received: Town Goal - Exchanged, discharged, died, or escape: Discharged - Time when: 4 May 1814 - Whither, and by what order, or number or re-entry: United States

McIntyre, James   Prisoner 1933. Rank: Private - By what ship or how taken: Troops - Time when: 17 Sep 1814 - Place where: Fort Erie - Of what ship or corps: Land forces - Whether man of war, privateer or merchant vessel: Taken on shore - Time when received into custody: - From what ship or whence received: - Exchanged, discharged, died, or escape: Died - Time when: 23 Dec 1814 - Whither, and by what order, or number or re-entry: Dysentery

McKee, Edward   Prisoner 848. Rank: Private - By what ship or how taken: Troops - Time when: 26 Jun 1813 - Place where: Beaver Dam - Of what ship or corps: Land forces - Whether man of war, privateer or merchant vessel: Taken on shore - Time when received into custody: 7 Jul 1813 - From what ship or whence received: Steamboat - Exchanged, discharged, died, or escape: Discharged - Time when: 10 Aug 1813 - Whither, and by what order, or number or re-entry: HM Ship Malpomena

McKeever, Charles   Prisoner 406. Rank: Private - By what ship or how taken: Troops - Time when: 24 Jun 1813 - Place where: Beaver Dam - Of what ship or corps: Land forces - Whether man of war, privateer or merchant vessel: Taken on shore - Time when received into custody: 7 Jul 1813 - From what ship or whence received: Steamboat - Exchanged, discharged, died, or escape: Discharged - Time when: 7 Aug 1813 - Whither, and by what order, or number or re-entry: H.M. Ship Cievare

McKenney, John   Prisoner 938. Rank: Private - By what ship or how taken: Troops - Time when: 26 Jun 1813 - Place where: Beaver Dam - Of what ship or corps: Land forces - Whether man of war, privateer or merchant vessel: Taken on shore - Time when received into custody: 21 Jul 1813 - From what ship or whence received: Steamboat - Exchanged, discharged, died, or escape: Discharged - Time when: 10 Aug 1813 - Whither, and by what order, or number or re-entry: HM Ship Malpomena

McKenzie, David   Prisoner 810. Rank: Private - By what ship or how taken: Troops - Time when: 26 Jun 1813 - Place where: Beaver Dam - Of what ship or corps: Land forces - Whether man of war, privateer or merchant vessel: Taken on shore - Time when received into custody: 7 Jul 1813 - From what ship or whence received: Steamboat - Exchanged, discharged, died, or escape: Discharged - Time when: 10 Aug 1813 - Whither, and by what order, or number or re-entry: HM Ship Malpomena

McKenzie, Kenneth   Prisoner 401. Rank: Captain - By what ship or how taken: Troops - Time when: 24 Jun 1813 - Place where: Beaver Dam - Of what ship or corps: Land forces - Whether man of war, privateer or merchant vessel: Taken on shore - Time when received into custody: 7 Jul 1813 - From what ship or whence received: Steamboat - Exchanged, discharged, died, or escape: Discharged - Time when: 10 Aug 1813 - Whither, and by what order, or number or re-

American Prisoners of War held at Quebec during the War of 1812

entry: Per order His Exellency Sir George Prevost

McKenzie, Thomas   Prisoner 1083. Rank: Private - By what ship or how taken: Troops - Time when: 24 Aug 1813 - Place where: Fort George - Of what ship or corps: Land forces - Whether man of war, privateer or merchant vessel: Taken on shore - Time when received into custody: 10 Oct 1813 - From what ship or whence received: Steamboat - Exchanged, discharged, died, or escape: Discharged - Time when: 31 Oct 1813 - Whither, and by what order, or number or re-entry: Malabar Transport

McLaghlan, Mark   Prisoner 1291. Rank: Private - By what ship or how taken: Troops - Time when: 19 Dec 1813 - Place where: Fort Niagara - Of what ship or corps: Land forces - Whether man of war, privateer or merchant vessel: Taken on shore - Time when received into custody: 29 Jan 1814 - From what ship or whence received: Montreal by land carriage - Exchanged, discharged, died, or escape: Discharged - Time when: 4 May 1814 - Whither, and by what order, or number or re-entry: United States

McMillen, Archibald   Prisoner 48. Rank: Private - By what ship or how taken: Boats & Troops - Time when: 28 May 1813 - Place where: Stoney Point, Henderson Harbor - Of what ship or corps: Land forces - Whether man of war, privateer or merchant vessel: Taken on shore - Time when received into custody: 8 Jun 1813 - From what ship or whence received: Batteaux - Exchanged, discharged, died, or escape: Died - Time when: 12 Aug 1813 - Whither, and by what order, or number or re-entry:

McMillin, George   Prisoner 745. Rank: Private - By what ship or how taken: Troops - Time when: 26 Jun 1813 - Place where: Beaver Dam - Of what ship or corps: Land forces - Whether man of war, privateer or merchant vessel: Taken on shore - Time when received into custody: 7 Jul 1813 - From what ship or whence received: Steamboat - Exchanged, discharged, died, or escape: Discharged - Time when: 10 Aug 1813 - Whither, and by what order, or number or re-entry: HM Ship Malpomena

McMillin, William   Prisoner 1132. Rank: Private - By what ship or how taken: Troops - Time when: 5 May 1813 - Place where: Rapids Prince Reason - Of what ship or corps: Land forces - Whether man of war, privateer or merchant vessel: Taken on shore - Time when received into custody: 25 Nov 1813 - From what ship or whence received: Town Goal - Exchanged, discharged, died, or escape: Discharged - Time when: 4 May 1814 - Whither, and by what order, or number or re-entry: United States

McNutt, J.   Prisoner 1478. Rank: Private - By what ship or how taken: Troops - Time when: 15 Jul 1814 - Place where: 4 Mile Creek - Of what ship or corps: Land forces - Whether man of war, privateer or merchant vessel: Taken on shore - Time when received into custody: 12 Aug 1814 - From what ship or whence received: Royal Seaman No. 289 Transport - Exchanged, discharged, died, or escape: Discharged - Time when: 8 Oct 1814 - Whither, and by what order, or number or re-entry: Queen No. 415

McQuaid, Edward   Prisoner 1351. Rank: Private - By what ship or how taken: Troops - Time when: 19 Dec 1813 - Place where: Fort Niagara - Of what ship or corps: Land forces - Whether man of war, privateer or merchant vessel: Taken on shore - Time when received into custody: 29 Jan 1814 - From what ship or whence received: Montreal by land carriage - Exchanged, discharged, died, or escape: Discharged - Time when: 4 May 1814 - Whither, and by what order, or number or re-entry: United States

McQueen, Donald   Prisoner 944. Rank: Corporal - By what ship or how taken: Troops - Time when: 26 Jun 1813 - Place where: Beaver Dam - Of what ship or corps: Land forces - Whether man of war, privateer or merchant vessel: Taken on shore - Time when received into custody: 21 Jul 1813 - From what ship or whence received: Steamboat - Exchanged, discharged, died, or escape: Discharged - Time when: 10 Aug 1813 - Whither, and by what order, or number or re-entry: HM Ship Malpomena

McQuestion, H,   Prisoner 1560. Rank: Sergeant - By what ship or how taken: Troops - Time when: 25 Jul 1814 - Place where: Lundy's Lane - Of what ship or corps: Land forces - Whether man of war, privateer or merchant vessel: Taken on shore - Time when received into custody: 30 Aug 1814 - From what ship or whence received: Lady Delaval Schooner 578 - Exchanged, discharged, died, or escape: Discharged - Time when: 8 Oct 1814 - Whither, and by what order, or number or re-entry: Queen No. 415

McWaters, James   Prisoner 779. Rank: Private - By what ship or how taken: Troops - Time when: 26 Jun 1813 - Place where: Beaver Dam - Of what ship or corps: Land forces - Whether man of war, privateer or merchant vessel: Taken on shore - Time when received into custody: 7 Jul 1813 - From what ship or whence received: Steamboat - Exchanged, discharged, died, or escape: Discharged - Time when: 10 Aug 1813 - Whither, and by what order, or number or re-entry: HM Ship Malpomena

Mead, William   Prisoner 1959. Rank: Private - By what ship or how taken: Troops - Time when: 23 Oct 1814 - Place where:

American Prisoners of War held at Quebec during the War of 1812

Fort Erie - Of what ship or corps: Land forces - Whether man of war, privateer or merchant vessel: Taken on shore - Time when received into custody: 11 Dec 1814 - From what ship or whence received: Montreal - Exchanged, discharged, died, or escape: Discharged - Time when: 16 Mar 1815 - Whither, and by what order, or number or re-entry: United States

Mears, Michael   Prisoner 823. Rank: Private - By what ship or how taken: Troops - Time when: 26 Jun 1813 - Place where: Beaver Dam - Of what ship or corps: Land forces - Whether man of war, privateer or merchant vessel: Taken on shore - Time when received into custody: 7 Jul 1813 - From what ship or whence received: Steamboat - Exchanged, discharged, died, or escape: Discharged - Time when: 10 Aug 1813 - Whither, and by what order, or number or re-entry: HM Ship Malpomena

Mecham, Jesse   Prisoner 976. Rank: Private - By what ship or how taken: Troops - Time when: 5 Jul 1813 - Place where: Fort Schisher - Of what ship or corps: Land forces - Whether man of war, privateer or merchant vessel: Taken on shore - Time when received into custody: 5 Sep 1813 - From what ship or whence received: Steamboat - Exchanged, discharged, died, or escape: Discharged - Time when: 31 Oct 1813 - Whither, and by what order, or number or re-entry: Malabar Transport

Mechame, Almond   Prisoner 772. Rank: Private - By what ship or how taken: Troops - Time when: 26 Jun 1813 - Place where: Beaver Dam - Of what ship or corps: Land forces - Whether man of war, privateer or merchant vessel: Taken on shore - Time when received into custody: 7 Jul 1813 - From what ship or whence received: Steamboat - Exchanged, discharged, died, or escape: Discharged - Time when: 10 Aug 1813 - Whither, and by what order, or number or re-entry: HM Ship Malpomena

Meintere, Tedeck   Prisoner 364. Rank: Private - By what ship or how taken: Troops - Time when: 6 Jun 1813 - Place where: Stoney Point - Of what ship or corps: Land forces - Whether man of war, privateer or merchant vessel: Taken on shore - Time when received into custody: 28 Jun 1813 - From what ship or whence received: Mary of Quebec - Exchanged, discharged, died, or escape: Discharged - Time when: 31 Oct 1813 - Whither, and by what order, or number or re-entry: Malabar Transport

Melage, P.   Prisoner 1660. Rank: Citizen - By what ship or how taken: - Time when: - Place where: - Of what ship or corps: - Whether man of war, privateer or merchant vessel: - Time when received into custody: 5 Oct 1814 - From what ship or whence received: Montreal - Exchanged, discharged, died, or escape: Discharged - Time when: 8 Oct 1814 - Whither, and by what order, or number or re-entry: H.M. Ship Ceylon

Melone, John   Prisoner 1411. Rank: Private - By what ship or how taken: Troops - Time when: 19 Dec 1813 - Place where: Fort Niagara - Of what ship or corps: Land forces - Whether man of war, privateer or merchant vessel: Taken on shore - Time when received into custody: 29 Jan 1814 - From what ship or whence received: Montreal by land carriage - Exchanged, discharged, died, or escape: Discharged - Time when: 4 May 1814 - Whither, and by what order, or number or re-entry: United States

Melony, Simeon   Prisoner 1893. Rank: Private - By what ship or how taken: Troops - Time when: 17 Sep 1814 - Place where: Fort Erie - Of what ship or corps: Land forces - Whether man of war, privateer or merchant vessel: Taken on shore - Time when received into custody: 1 Nov 1814 - From what ship or whence received: Montreal - Exchanged, discharged, died, or escape: Discharged - Time when: 8 Nov 1814 - Whither, and by what order, or number or re-entry: S. George No. 575 for Halifax by order of Sir George Provost

Melvin, William   Prisoner 361. Rank: Private - By what ship or how taken: Troops - Time when: 6 Jun 1813 - Place where: Stoney Point - Of what ship or corps: Land forces - Whether man of war, privateer or merchant vessel: Taken on shore - Time when received into custody: 28 Jun 1813 - From what ship or whence received: Mary of Quebec - Exchanged, discharged, died, or escape: Discharged - Time when: 7 Aug 1813 - Whither, and by what order, or number or re-entry: H.M. Ship Cievare

Menard, P.   Prisoner 1656. Rank: Private - By what ship or how taken: Troops - Time when: 3 Aug 1814 - Place where: Plattsburg - Of what ship or corps: Land forces - Whether man of war, privateer or merchant vessel: Taken on shore - Time when received into custody: 5 Oct 1814 - From what ship or whence received: Montreal - Exchanged, discharged, died, or escape: Discharged - Time when: 8 Oct 1814 - Whither, and by what order, or number or re-entry: H.M. Ship Ceylon

Mendell, Alden   Prisoner 1534. Rank: Private - By what ship or how taken: Troops - Time when: 25 Jul 1814 - Place where: Lundy's Lane - Of what ship or corps: Land forces - Whether man of war, privateer or merchant vessel: Taken on shore - Time when received into custody: 30 Aug 1814 - From what ship or whence received: Lady Delaval Schooner 578 - Exchanged, discharged, died, or escape: Discharged - Time when: 8 Oct 1814 - Whither, and by what order, or number or re-entry: Queen No. 415

American Prisoners of War held at Quebec during the War of 1812

Merrell, Abraham   Prisoner 1180. Rank: Private - By what ship or how taken: Troops - Time when: 5 May 1813 - Place where: Rapids - Of what ship or corps: Land forces - Whether man of war, privateer or merchant vessel: Taken on shore - Time when received into custody: 25 Nov 1813 - From what ship or whence received: Town Goal - Exchanged, discharged, died, or escape: Discharged - Time when: 4 May 1814 - Whither, and by what order, or number or re-entry: United States

Merrill, Charles   Prisoner 1843. Rank: Private - By what ship or how taken: Troops - Time when: 17 Sep 1814 - Place where: Fort Erie - Of what ship or corps: Land forces - Whether man of war, privateer or merchant vessel: Taken on shore - Time when received into custody: 1 Nov 1814 - From what ship or whence received: Montreal - Exchanged, discharged, died, or escape: Discharged - Time when: 8 Nov 1814 - Whither, and by what order, or number or re-entry: S. George No. 575 for Halifax by order of Sir George Provost

Merrill, Eli   Prisoner 12. Rank: Private - By what ship or how taken: Boats & Troops - Time when: 28 May 1813 - Place where: Stoney Point, Henderson Harbor - Of what ship or corps: Land forces - Whether man of war, privateer or merchant vessel: Taken on shore - Time when received into custody: 8 Jun 1813 - From what ship or whence received: Batteaux - Exchanged, discharged, died, or escape: Died - Time when: 26 Sep 1813 - Whither, and by what order, or number or re-entry: Dysentery

Merrill, Jacob   Prisoner 93. Rank: Private - By what ship or how taken: Boats & Troops - Time when: 28 May 1813 - Place where: Stoney Point, Henderson Harbor - Of what ship or corps: Land forces - Whether man of war, privateer or merchant vessel: Taken on shore - Time when received into custody: 8 Jun 1813 - From what ship or whence received: Batteaux - Exchanged, discharged, died, or escape: Discharged - Time when: 31 Oct 1813 - Whither, and by what order, or number or re-entry: Malabar Transport

Merrill, Jacob   Prisoner 215. Rank: Private - By what ship or how taken: Boats & Troops - Time when: 3 Jun 1813 - Place where: Lake Champlain - Of what ship or corps: Growler - Whether man of war, privateer or merchant vessel: Man of War - Time when received into custody: 9 Jun 1813 - From what ship or whence received: Batteaux - Exchanged, discharged, died, or escape: Discharged - Time when: 31 Oct 1813 - Whither, and by what order, or number or re-entry: Malabar Transport

Merrill, M.   Prisoner 1313. Rank: Private - By what ship or how taken: Troops - Time when: 19 Dec 1813 - Place where: Fort Niagara - Of what ship or corps: Land forces - Whether man of war, privateer or merchant vessel: Taken on shore - Time when received into custody: 29 Jan 1814 - From what ship or whence received: Montreal by land carriage - Exchanged, discharged, died, or escape: Discharged - Time when: 4 May 1814 - Whither, and by what order, or number or re-entry: United States

Merrill, Nathaniel   Prisoner 1979. Rank: Private - By what ship or how taken: Troops - Time when: 2 Nov 1814 - Place where: Fort Erie - Of what ship or corps: Land forces - Whether man of war, privateer or merchant vessel: Taken on shore - Time when received into custody: 30 Dec 1814 - From what ship or whence received: Montreal - Exchanged, discharged, died, or escape: Discharged - Time when: 13 Mar 1815 - Whither, and by what order, or number or re-entry: United States

Merrill, Thedorias   Prisoner 221. Rank: Private - By what ship or how taken: Boats & Troops - Time when: 3 Jun 1813 - Place where: Lake Champlain - Of what ship or corps: Growler - Whether man of war, privateer or merchant vessel: Man of War - Time when received into custody: 9 Jun 1813 - From what ship or whence received: Batteaux - Exchanged, discharged, died, or escape: Discharged - Time when: 31 Oct 1813 - Whither, and by what order, or number or re-entry: Malabar Transport

Merritt, Jonathan   Prisoner 187. Rank: Private - By what ship or how taken: Boats & Troops - Time when: 3 Jun 1813 - Place where: Lake Champlain - Of what ship or corps: Growler - Whether man of war, privateer or merchant vessel: Man of War - Time when received into custody: 9 Jun 1813 - From what ship or whence received: Batteaux - Exchanged, discharged, died, or escape: Discharged - Time when: 31 Oct 1813 - Whither, and by what order, or number or re-entry: Malabar Transport

Messinger, W. S.   Prisoner 1486. Rank: Private - By what ship or how taken: Troops - Time when: 25 Jul 1814 - Place where: Lundy's Lane - Of what ship or corps: Land forces - Whether man of war, privateer or merchant vessel: Taken on shore - Time when received into custody: 12 Aug 1814 - From what ship or whence received: Royal Seaman No. 289 Transport - Exchanged, discharged, died, or escape: Discharged - Time when: 8 Oct 1814 - Whither, and by what order, or number or re-entry: Queen No. 415

American Prisoners of War held at Quebec during the War of 1812

Meticham, Seth   Prisoner 770. Rank: Private - By what ship or how taken: Troops - Time when: 26 Jun 1813 - Place where: Beaver Dam - Of what ship or corps: Land forces - Whether man of war, privateer or merchant vessel: Taken on shore - Time when received into custody: 7 Jul 1813 - From what ship or whence received: Steamboat - Exchanged, discharged, died, or escape: Discharged - Time when: 10 Aug 1813 - Whither, and by what order, or number or re-entry: HM Ship Malpomena

Miles, John   Prisoner 733. Rank: Private - By what ship or how taken: Troops - Time when: 26 Jun 1813 - Place where: Beaver Dam - Of what ship or corps: Land forces - Whether man of war, privateer or merchant vessel: Taken on shore - Time when received into custody: 7 Jul 1813 - From what ship or whence received: Steamboat - Exchanged, discharged, died, or escape: Discharged - Time when: 10 Aug 1813 - Whither, and by what order, or number or re-entry: HM Ship Regulius by order of Sir George Provost

Millan, George   Prisoner 1945. Rank: Private - By what ship or how taken: Troops - Time when: 17 Sep 1814 - Place where: Fort Erie - Of what ship or corps: Land forces - Whether man of war, privateer or merchant vessel: Taken on shore - Time when received into custody: 7 Dec 1814 - From what ship or whence received: Montreal - Exchanged, discharged, died, or escape: Discharged - Time when: 13 Mar 1815 - Whither, and by what order, or number or re-entry: United States

Millbanks, David   Prisoner 1910. Rank: Private - By what ship or how taken: Troops - Time when: 17 Sep 1814 - Place where: Fort Erie - Of what ship or corps: Land forces - Whether man of war, privateer or merchant vessel: Taken on shore - Time when received into custody: 1 Nov 1814 - From what ship or whence received: Montreal - Exchanged, discharged, died, or escape: Discharged - Time when: 8 Nov 1814 - Whither, and by what order, or number or re-entry: S. George No. 575 for Halifax by order of Sir George Provost

Miller, Garrett   Prisoner 475. Rank: Private - By what ship or how taken: Troops - Time when: 24 Jun 1813 - Place where: Beaver Dam - Of what ship or corps: Land forces - Whether man of war, privateer or merchant vessel: Taken on shore - Time when received into custody: 7 Jul 1813 - From what ship or whence received: Steamboat - Exchanged, discharged, died, or escape: Discharged - Time when: 10 Aug 1813 - Whither, and by what order, or number or re-entry: HM Ship Regulius by order of Sir George Provost

Miller, James   Prisoner 1753. Rank: Private - By what ship or how taken: Gun Boats - Time when: 6 Sep 1814 - Place where: Lake Huron - Of what ship or corps: Scorpion - Whether man of war, privateer or merchant vessel: Man of War - Time when received into custody: 1 Nov 1814 - From what ship or whence received: Montreal - Exchanged, discharged, died, or escape: Discharged - Time when: 8 Nov 1814 - Whither, and by what order, or number or re-entry: S. George No. 575 for Halifax by order of Sir George Provost

Miller, James   Prisoner 1332. Rank: Private - By what ship or how taken: Troops - Time when: 19 Dec 1813 - Place where: Fort Niagara - Of what ship or corps: Land forces - Whether man of war, privateer or merchant vessel: Taken on shore - Time when received into custody: 29 Jan 1814 - From what ship or whence received: Montreal by land carriage - Exchanged, discharged, died, or escape: Discharged - Time when: 4 May 1814 - Whither, and by what order, or number or re-entry: United States

Miller, Rubin   Prisoner 1294. Rank: Private - By what ship or how taken: Troops - Time when: 19 Dec 1813 - Place where: Fort Niagara - Of what ship or corps: Land forces - Whether man of war, privateer or merchant vessel: Taken on shore - Time when received into custody: 29 Jan 1814 - From what ship or whence received: Montreal by land carriage - Exchanged, discharged, died, or escape: Discharged - Time when: 4 May 1814 - Whither, and by what order, or number or re-entry: United States

Milless, Stephen   Prisoner 556. Rank: Private - By what ship or how taken: Troops - Time when: 26 Jun 1813 - Place where: Beaver Dam - Of what ship or corps: Land forces - Whether man of war, privateer or merchant vessel: Taken on shore - Time when received into custody: 13 Jul 1813 - From what ship or whence received: Steamboat - Exchanged, discharged, died, or escape: Discharged - Time when: 10 Aug 1813 - Whither, and by what order, or number or re-entry: HM Ship Regulius by order of Sir George Provost

Million, Rodney   Prisoner 1141. Rank: Private - By what ship or how taken: Troops - Time when: 22 Jan 1812 - Place where: Rapids Prince Reason - Of what ship or corps: Land forces - Whether man of war, privateer or merchant vessel: Taken on shore - Time when received into custody: 25 Nov 1813 - From what ship or whence received: Town Goal - Exchanged, discharged, died, or escape: Discharged - Time when: 21 Apr 1814 - Whither, and by what order, or number or re-entry: United States

Mills, Ellias   Prisoner 1160. Rank: Corporal - By what ship or how taken: Troops - Time when: 5 May 1813 - Place where: Rapids Prince Reason - Of what ship or corps: Land forces - Whether man of war, privateer or merchant vessel: Taken on shore - Time when received into custody: 25 Nov 1813 - From what ship or whence received: Town Goal -

American Prisoners of War held at Quebec during the War of 1812

Exchanged, discharged, died, or escape: Discharged - Time when: 12 Mar 1814 - Whither, and by what order, or number or re-entry: New Brunswick Fencibles

Minger, Joseph   Prisoner 1469. Rank: Private - By what ship or how taken: Troops - Time when: 5 Jul 1814 - Place where: Gibonsee - Of what ship or corps: Land forces - Whether man of war, privateer or merchant vessel: Taken on shore - Time when received into custody: 12 Aug 1814 - From what ship or whence received: Royal Seaman No. 289 Transport - Exchanged, discharged, died, or escape: Discharged - Time when: 8 Oct 1814 - Whither, and by what order, or number or re-entry: Queen No. 415

Minor, Harris   Prisoner 1612. Rank: Private - By what ship or how taken: Gun Boats - Time when: 12 Aug 1814 - Place where: Fort Erie - Of what ship or corps: Land forces - Whether man of war, privateer or merchant vessel: Taken on shore - Time when received into custody: 5 Oct 1814 - From what ship or whence received: Montreal - Exchanged, discharged, died, or escape: Discharged - Time when: 8 Oct 1814 - Whither, and by what order, or number or re-entry: H.M. Ship Ceylon

Minor, Lewis   Prisoner 338. Rank: Private - By what ship or how taken: Boats & Troops - Time when: 22 Feb 1813 - Place where: Hedgesburgh - Of what ship or corps: Land forces - Whether man of war, privateer or merchant vessel: Taken on shore - Time when received into custody: 28 Jun 1813 - From what ship or whence received: Mary of Quebec - Exchanged, discharged, died, or escape: Discharged - Time when: 31 Oct 1813 - Whither, and by what order, or number or re-entry: Malabar Transport

Mitchell, Charles   Prisoner 663. Rank: Private - By what ship or how taken: Troops - Time when: 24 Jun 1813 - Place where: Stoney Point - Of what ship or corps: Land forces - Whether man of war, privateer or merchant vessel: Taken on shore - Time when received into custody: 7 Jul 1813 - From what ship or whence received: Steamboat - Exchanged, discharged, died, or escape: Discharged - Time when: 10 Aug 1813 - Whither, and by what order, or number or re-entry: HM Ship Regulius by order of Sir George Provost

Mitchell, Hugh   Prisoner 1549. Rank: Private - By what ship or how taken: Troops - Time when: 25 Jul 1814 - Place where: Lundy's Lane - Of what ship or corps: Land forces - Whether man of war, privateer or merchant vessel: Taken on shore - Time when received into custody: 30 Aug 1814 - From what ship or whence received: Lady Delaval Schooner 578 - Exchanged, discharged, died, or escape: Discharged - Time when: 8 Oct 1814 - Whither, and by what order, or number or re-entry: Queen No. 415

Mitchell, William   Prisoner 95. Rank: Private - By what ship or how taken: Boats & Troops - Time when: 28 May 1813 - Place where: Stoney Point, Henderson Harbor - Of what ship or corps: Land forces - Whether man of war, privateer or merchant vessel: Taken on shore - Time when received into custody: 8 Jun 1813 - From what ship or whence received: Batteaux - Exchanged, discharged, died, or escape: Died - Time when: 4 Aug 1813 - Whither, and by what order, or number or re-entry:

Monaham, David   Prisoner 891. Rank: Private - By what ship or how taken: Troops - Time when: 26 Jun 1813 - Place where: Beaver Dam - Of what ship or corps: Land forces - Whether man of war, privateer or merchant vessel: Taken on shore - Time when received into custody: 7 Jul 1813 - From what ship or whence received: Steamboat - Exchanged, discharged, died, or escape: Discharged - Time when: 10 Aug 1813 - Whither, and by what order, or number or re-entry: HM Ship Malpomena

Monteath, Walter Noel   Prisoner 147. Rank: Midshipman - By what ship or how taken: Boats & Troops - Time when: 3 Jun 1813 - Place where: Lake Champlain - Of what ship or corps: Growler - Whether man of war, privateer or merchant vessel: Man of War - Time when received into custody: 8 Jul 1813 - From what ship or whence received: Batteaux - Exchanged, discharged, died, or escape: Discharged - Time when: 4 May 1814 - Whither, and by what order, or number or re-entry: United States

Moody, John   Prisoner 202. Rank: Corporal - By what ship or how taken: Boats & Troops - Time when: 3 Jun 1813 - Place where: Lake Champlain - Of what ship or corps: Growler - Whether man of war, privateer or merchant vessel: Man of War - Time when received into custody: 9 Jun 1813 - From what ship or whence received: Batteaux - Exchanged, discharged, died, or escape: Died - Time when: 30 Jul 1813 - Whither, and by what order, or number or re-entry: Dysentery

Moones, Green   Prisoner 1156. Rank: Private - By what ship or how taken: Troops - Time when: 5 May 1813 - Place where: Rapids Prince Reason - Of what ship or corps: Land forces - Whether man of war, privateer or merchant vessel: Taken on shore - Time when received into custody: 25 Nov 1813 - From what ship or whence received: Town Goal - Exchanged, discharged, died, or escape: Discharged - Time when: 12 Mar 1814 - Whither, and by what order, or number or re-entry: New Brunswick Fencibles

American Prisoners of War held at Quebec during the War of 1812

Moore, Abel   Prisoner 1224. Rank: Private - By what ship or how taken: Troops - Time when: 19 Dec 1813 - Place where: Fort Niagara - Of what ship or corps: Land forces - Whether man of war, privateer or merchant vessel: Taken on shore - Time when received into custody: 29 Jan 1814 - From what ship or whence received: Montreal by land carriage - Exchanged, discharged, died, or escape: Discharged - Time when: 4 May 1814 - Whither, and by what order, or number or re-entry: United States

Moore, Abraham   Prisoner 1897. Rank: Private - By what ship or how taken: Troops - Time when: 17 Sep 1814 - Place where: Fort Erie - Of what ship or corps: Land forces - Whether man of war, privateer or merchant vessel: Taken on shore - Time when received into custody: 1 Nov 1814 - From what ship or whence received: Montreal - Exchanged, discharged, died, or escape: Discharged - Time when: 8 Nov 1814 - Whither, and by what order, or number or re-entry: S. George No. 575 for Halifax by order of Sir George Provost

Moore, John   Prisoner 561. Rank: Private - By what ship or how taken: Troops - Time when: 26 Jun 1813 - Place where: Beaver Dam - Of what ship or corps: Land forces - Whether man of war, privateer or merchant vessel: Taken on shore - Time when received into custody: 13 Jul 1813 - From what ship or whence received: Steamboat - Exchanged, discharged, died, or escape: Discharged - Time when: 10 Aug 1813 - Whither, and by what order, or number or re-entry: HM Ship Regulius by order of Sir George Provost

Moore, Jonas   Prisoner 336. Rank: Private - By what ship or how taken: Boats & Troops - Time when: 6 Jun 1813 - Place where: Stoney Point - Of what ship or corps: Land forces - Whether man of war, privateer or merchant vessel: Taken on shore - Time when received into custody: 28 Jun 1813 - From what ship or whence received: Quebec of Quebec - Exchanged, discharged, died, or escape: Died - Time when: 11 Sep 1813 - Whither, and by what order, or number or re-entry:

Moore, Joseph   Prisoner 1552. Rank: Private - By what ship or how taken: Troops - Time when: 25 Jul 1814 - Place where: Lundy's Lane - Of what ship or corps: Land forces - Whether man of war, privateer or merchant vessel: Taken on shore - Time when received into custody: 30 Aug 1814 - From what ship or whence received: Lady Delaval Schooner 578 - Exchanged, discharged, died, or escape: Discharged - Time when: 8 Oct 1814 - Whither, and by what order, or number or re-entry: Queen No. 415

Moore, Lemond   Prisoner 422. Rank: Corporal - By what ship or how taken: Troops - Time when: 24 Jun 1813 - Place where: Beaver Dam - Of what ship or corps: Land forces - Whether man of war, privateer or merchant vessel: Taken on shore - Time when received into custody: 7 Jul 1813 - From what ship or whence received: Steamboat - Exchanged, discharged, died, or escape: Discharged - Time when: 31 Oct 1813 - Whither, and by what order, or number or re-entry: Malabar Transport

Moore, Mathew   Prisoner 1808. Rank: Private - By what ship or how taken: Troops - Time when: 17 Sep 1814 - Place where: Fort Erie - Of what ship or corps: Land forces - Whether man of war, privateer or merchant vessel: Taken on shore - Time when received into custody: 1 Nov 1814 - From what ship or whence received: Montreal - Exchanged, discharged, died, or escape: Discharged - Time when: 8 Nov 1814 - Whither, and by what order, or number or re-entry: S. George No. 575 for Halifax by order of Sir George Provost

Moren, John   Prisoner 1611. Rank: Private - By what ship or how taken: Troops - Time when: 6 Sep 1814 - Place where: Plattsburg - Of what ship or corps: Land forces - Whether man of war, privateer or merchant vessel: Taken on shore - Time when received into custody: 5 Oct 1814 - From what ship or whence received: Montreal - Exchanged, discharged, died, or escape: Discharged - Time when: 8 Oct 1814 - Whither, and by what order, or number or re-entry: H.M. Ship Ceylon

Morgan, William   Prisoner 1726. Rank: Seaman - By what ship or how taken: Gun Boats - Time when: 6 Sep 1814 - Place where: Lake Huron - Of what ship or corps: Scorpion - Whether man of war, privateer or merchant vessel: Man of War - Time when received into custody: 1 Nov 1814 - From what ship or whence received: Montreal - Exchanged, discharged, died, or escape: Discharged - Time when: 7 Nov 1814 - Whither, and by what order, or number or re-entry: Transport Freedom No. 582 by orders of his Excellency Sir George Provost

Morrice, Samuel H.   Prisoner 1432. Rank: Able seaman - By what ship or how taken: Emblis - Time when: 15 Feb 1814 - Place where: St. Johns - Of what ship or corps: Corsack - Whether man of war, privateer or merchant vessel: Privateer - Time when received into custody: 24 May 1814 - From what ship or whence received: Mary Transport No. 360 Halifax - Exchanged, discharged, died, or escape: Discharged - Time when: 4 May 1814 - Whither, and by what order, or number or re-entry: United States

Morris, John N.   Prisoner 532. Rank: Lieutenant - By what ship or how taken: Troops - Time when: 24 Jun 1813 - Place where: Beaver Dam - Of what ship or corps: Land forces - Whether man of war, privateer or merchant vessel: Taken on shore - Time when received into custody: 13 Jul 1813 - From what ship or whence received: Steamboat - Exchanged,

discharged, died, or escape: Discharged - Time when: 10 Aug 1813 - Whither, and by what order, or number or re-entry: HM Ship Regulius by order of Sir George Provost

Morris, Morris   Prisoner 397. Rank: Private - By what ship or how taken: Troops - Time when: 6 Jun 1813 - Place where: Stoney Point - Of what ship or corps: Land forces - Whether man of war, privateer or merchant vessel: Taken on shore - Time when received into custody: 28 Jun 1813 - From what ship or whence received: Mary of Quebec - Exchanged, discharged, died, or escape: Discharged - Time when: 31 Oct 1813 - Whither, and by what order, or number or re-entry: Malabar Transport

Morris, Peter   Prisoner 296. Rank: Private - By what ship or how taken: Boats & Troops - Time when: 6 Jun 1813 - Place where: Stoney Point - Of what ship or corps: Land forces - Whether man of war, privateer or merchant vessel: Taken on shore - Time when received into custody: 28 Jun 1813 - From what ship or whence received: Quebec of Quebec - Exchanged, discharged, died, or escape: Discharged - Time when: 22 Aug 1813 - Whither, and by what order, or number or re-entry: Rotta Transport

Morrison, Alexander   Prisoner 1969. Rank: Private - By what ship or how taken: Troops - Time when: 17 Oct 1814 - Place where: Chippawa - Of what ship or corps: Land forces - Whether man of war, privateer or merchant vessel: Taken on shore - Time when received into custody: 11 Dec 1814 - From what ship or whence received: Montreal - Exchanged, discharged, died, or escape: Discharged - Time when: 13 Mar 1815 - Whither, and by what order, or number or re-entry: United States

Morrison, James   Prisoner 1405. Rank: Private - By what ship or how taken: Troops - Time when: 19 Dec 1813 - Place where: Fort Niagara - Of what ship or corps: Land forces - Whether man of war, privateer or merchant vessel: Taken on shore - Time when received into custody: 29 Jan 1814 - From what ship or whence received: Montreal by land carriage - Exchanged, discharged, died, or escape: Discharged - Time when: 4 May 1814 - Whither, and by what order, or number or re-entry: United States

Morrison, Joseph   Prisoner 1504. Rank: Private - By what ship or how taken: Troops - Time when: 25 Jul 1814 - Place where: Lundy's Lane - Of what ship or corps: Land forces - Whether man of war, privateer or merchant vessel: Taken on shore - Time when received into custody: 19 Aug 1814 - From what ship or whence received: Triton No. 438 Transport - Exchanged, discharged, died, or escape: Discharged - Time when: 13 Mar 1815 - Whither, and by what order, or number or re-entry: United States

Morrison, William   Prisoner 1339. Rank: Private - By what ship or how taken: Troops - Time when: 19 Dec 1813 - Place where: Fort Niagara - Of what ship or corps: Land forces - Whether man of war, privateer or merchant vessel: Taken on shore - Time when received into custody: 29 Jan 1814 - From what ship or whence received: Montreal by land carriage - Exchanged, discharged, died, or escape: Discharged - Time when: 4 May 1814 - Whither, and by what order, or number or re-entry: United States

Morrow, Edward   Prisoner 1500. Rank: Private - By what ship or how taken: Troops - Time when: 25 Jul 1814 - Place where: Lundy's Lane - Of what ship or corps: Land forces - Whether man of war, privateer or merchant vessel: Taken on shore - Time when received into custody: 19 Aug 1814 - From what ship or whence received: Triton No. 438 Transport - Exchanged, discharged, died, or escape: Discharged - Time when: 8 Oct 1814 - Whither, and by what order, or number or re-entry: Queen No. 415

Morse, Jacob   Prisoner 155. Rank: ? - By what ship or how taken: Boats & Troops - Time when: 3 Jun 1813 - Place where: Lake Champlain - Of what ship or corps: Growler - Whether man of war, privateer or merchant vessel: Man of War - Time when received into custody: 8 Jul 1813 - From what ship or whence received: Batteaux - Exchanged, discharged, died, or escape: Discharged - Time when: 31 Oct 1813 - Whither, and by what order, or number or re-entry: Malabar Transport

Morse, Joshua   Prisoner 237. Rank: Private - By what ship or how taken: Boats & Troops - Time when: 3 Jun 1813 - Place where: Lake Champlain - Of what ship or corps: Growler - Whether man of war, privateer or merchant vessel: Man of War - Time when received into custody: 9 Jun 1813 - From what ship or whence received: Batteaux - Exchanged, discharged, died, or escape: Discharged - Time when: 31 Oct 1813 - Whither, and by what order, or number or re-entry: Malabar Transport

Mortimore, Thomas   Prisoner 1031. Rank: Seaman - By what ship or how taken: Lord Melvin - Time when: 10 Aug 1813 - Place where: Lake Ontario - Of what ship or corps: Growler - Whether man of war, privateer or merchant vessel: Man of War - Time when received into custody: 5 Sep 1813 - From what ship or whence received: Steamboat - Exchanged, discharged, died, or escape: Discharged - Time when: 4 May 1814 - Whither, and by what order, or number or re-entry: United States

American Prisoners of War held at Quebec during the War of 1812

Morton, Sethu   Prisoner 1781. Rank: Private - By what ship or how taken: Troops - Time when: 7 Sep 1814 - Place where: Fort Erie - Of what ship or corps: Land forces - Whether man of war, privateer or merchant vessel: Taken on shore - Time when received into custody: 1 Nov 1814 - From what ship or whence received: Montreal - Exchanged, discharged, died, or escape: Discharged - Time when: 8 Nov 1814 - Whither, and by what order, or number or re-entry: S. George No. 575 for Halifax by order of Sir George Provost

Moses, Charles   Prisoner 830. Rank: Drummer - By what ship or how taken: Troops - Time when: 26 Jun 1813 - Place where: Beaver Dam - Of what ship or corps: Land forces - Whether man of war, privateer or merchant vessel: Taken on shore - Time when received into custody: 7 Jul 1813 - From what ship or whence received: Steamboat - Exchanged, discharged, died, or escape: Discharged - Time when: 10 Aug 1813 - Whither, and by what order, or number or re-entry: HM Ship Malpomena

Moses, John   Prisoner 1529. Rank: Private - By what ship or how taken: Troops - Time when: 25 Jul 1814 - Place where: Lundy's Lane - Of what ship or corps: Land forces - Whether man of war, privateer or merchant vessel: Taken on shore - Time when received into custody: 30 Aug 1814 - From what ship or whence received: Lady Delaval Schooner 578 - Exchanged, discharged, died, or escape: Discharged - Time when: 8 Oct 1814 - Whither, and by what order, or number or re-entry: Queen No. 415

Mount, James   Prisoner 1922. Rank: Private - By what ship or how taken: Troops - Time when: 17 Sep 1814 - Place where: Fort Erie - Of what ship or corps: Land forces - Whether man of war, privateer or merchant vessel: Taken on shore - Time when received into custody: 1 Nov 1814 - From what ship or whence received: Montreal - Exchanged, discharged, died, or escape: Discharged - Time when: 14 Nov 1814 - Whither, and by what order, or number or re-entry: Soverign No. 628 for Halifax

Mudd, Massom   Prisoner 539. Rank: Lieutenant - By what ship or how taken: Troops - Time when: 24 Jun 1813 - Place where: Beaver Dam - Of what ship or corps: Land forces - Whether man of war, privateer or merchant vessel: Taken on shore - Time when received into custody: 13 Jul 1813 - From what ship or whence received: Steamboat - Exchanged, discharged, died, or escape: Discharged - Time when: 13 Dec 1813 - Whither, and by what order, or number or re-entry: United States

Mudge, Ebenezer   Prisoner 185. Rank: Private - By what ship or how taken: Boats & Troops - Time when: 3 Jun 1813 - Place where: Lake Champlain - Of what ship or corps: Growler - Whether man of war, privateer or merchant vessel: Man of War - Time when received into custody: 9 Jun 1813 - From what ship or whence received: Batteaux - Exchanged, discharged, died, or escape: Discharged - Time when: 31 Oct 1813 - Whither, and by what order, or number or re-entry: Malabar Transport

Muller, Jesse   Prisoner 1939. Rank: Private - By what ship or how taken: Troops - Time when: 17 Sep 1814 - Place where: Fort Erie - Of what ship or corps: Land forces - Whether man of war, privateer or merchant vessel: Taken on shore - Time when received into custody: 1 Nov 1814 - From what ship or whence received: Montreal - Exchanged, discharged, died, or escape: Discharged - Time when: 13 Mar 1815 - Whither, and by what order, or number or re-entry: United States

Mullett, William   Prisoner 1038. Rank: Seaman - By what ship or how taken: Lord Melvin - Time when: 10 Aug 1813 - Place where: Lake Ontario - Of what ship or corps: Growler - Whether man of war, privateer or merchant vessel: Man of War - Time when received into custody: 5 Sep 1813 - From what ship or whence received: Steamboat - Exchanged, discharged, died, or escape: Discharged - Time when: 31 Oct 1813 - Whither, and by what order, or number or re-entry: Malabar Transport

Mullinex, Thomas   Prisoner 901. Rank: Private - By what ship or how taken: Troops - Time when: 26 Jun 1813 - Place where: Beaver Dam - Of what ship or corps: Land forces - Whether man of war, privateer or merchant vessel: Taken on shore - Time when received into custody: 21 Jul 1813 - From what ship or whence received: Steamboat - Exchanged, discharged, died, or escape: - Time when: - Whither, and by what order, or number or re-entry:

Munger, Haace   Prisoner 959. Rank: Private - By what ship or how taken: Troops - Time when: 5 Jul 1813 - Place where: Fort Schisher - Of what ship or corps: Land forces - Whether man of war, privateer or merchant vessel: Taken on shore - Time when received into custody: 5 Sep 1813 - From what ship or whence received: Steamboat - Exchanged, discharged, died, or escape: Discharged - Time when: 31 Oct 1813 - Whither, and by what order, or number or re-entry: Malabar Transport

Munroe, E.   Prisoner 1639. Rank: Private - By what ship or how taken: Troops - Time when: 6 Sep 1814 - Place where: Plattsburg - Of what ship or corps: Land forces - Whether man of war, privateer or merchant vessel: Taken on shore - Time when received into custody: 5 Oct 1814 - From what ship or whence received: Montreal - Exchanged, discharged, died, or escape: Discharged - Time when: 8 Oct 1814 - Whither, and by what order, or number or re-entry: H.M. Ship

American Prisoners of War held at Quebec during the War of 1812

Ceylon

Munrow, John   Prisoner 11. Rank: Private - By what ship or how taken: Boats & Troops - Time when: 28 May 1813 - Place where: Stoney Point, Henderson Harbor - Of what ship or corps: Land forces - Whether man of war, privateer or merchant vessel: Taken on shore - Time when received into custody: 8 Jun 1813 - From what ship or whence received: Batteaux - Exchanged, discharged, died, or escape: Discharged - Time when: 31 Oct 1813 - Whither, and by what order, or number or re-entry: Malabar Transport

Murdock, George   Prisoner 530. Rank: Lieutenant - By what ship or how taken: Troops - Time when: 24 Jun 1813 - Place where: Beaver Dam - Of what ship or corps: Land forces - Whether man of war, privateer or merchant vessel: Taken on shore - Time when received into custody: 13 Jul 1813 - From what ship or whence received: Steamboat - Exchanged, discharged, died, or escape: Discharged - Time when: 13 Dec 1813 - Whither, and by what order, or number or re-entry: United States

Murphy, George   Prisoner 674. Rank: Corporal - By what ship or how taken: Troops - Time when: 26 Jun 1813 - Place where: Beaver Dam - Of what ship or corps: Land forces - Whether man of war, privateer or merchant vessel: Taken on shore - Time when received into custody: 7 Jul 1813 - From what ship or whence received: Steamboat - Exchanged, discharged, died, or escape: Discharged - Time when: 10 Aug 1813 - Whither, and by what order, or number or re-entry: HM Ship Regulius by order of Sir George Provost

Murphy, John   Prisoner 932. Rank: Private - By what ship or how taken: Troops - Time when: 26 Jun 1813 - Place where: Beaver Dam - Of what ship or corps: Land forces - Whether man of war, privateer or merchant vessel: Taken on shore - Time when received into custody: 21 Jul 1813 - From what ship or whence received: Steamboat - Exchanged, discharged, died, or escape: Discharged - Time when: 10 Aug 1813 - Whither, and by what order, or number or re-entry: HM Ship Malpomena

Murphy, William   Prisoner 1886. Rank: Private - By what ship or how taken: Troops - Time when: 17 Sep 1814 - Place where: Fort Erie - Of what ship or corps: Land forces - Whether man of war, privateer or merchant vessel: Taken on shore - Time when received into custody: 1 Nov 1814 - From what ship or whence received: Montreal - Exchanged, discharged, died, or escape: Discharged - Time when: 8 Nov 1814 - Whither, and by what order, or number or re-entry: S. George No. 575 for Halifax by order of Sir George Provost

Murry, James   Prisoner 234. Rank: Private - By what ship or how taken: Boats & Troops - Time when: 3 Jun 1813 - Place where: Lake Champlain - Of what ship or corps: Eagle - Whether man of war, privateer or merchant vessel: Man of War - Time when received into custody: 9 Jun 1813 - From what ship or whence received: Batteaux - Exchanged, discharged, died, or escape: Discharged - Time when: 31 Oct 1813 - Whither, and by what order, or number or re-entry: Malabar Transport

Mus, Abraham   Prisoner 782. Rank: Private - By what ship or how taken: Troops - Time when: 26 Jun 1813 - Place where: Beaver Dam - Of what ship or corps: Land forces - Whether man of war, privateer or merchant vessel: Taken on shore - Time when received into custody: 7 Jul 1813 - From what ship or whence received: Steamboat - Exchanged, discharged, died, or escape: Discharged - Time when: 10 Aug 1813 - Whither, and by what order, or number or re-entry: HM Ship Malpomena

Mustain, Lewis   Prisoner 1379. Rank: Sergeant - By what ship or how taken: Troops - Time when: 19 Dec 1813 - Place where: Fort Niagara - Of what ship or corps: Land forces - Whether man of war, privateer or merchant vessel: Taken on shore - Time when received into custody: 29 Jan 1814 - From what ship or whence received: Montreal by land carriage - Exchanged, discharged, died, or escape: Discharged - Time when: 4 May 1814 - Whither, and by what order, or number or re-entry: United States

Myer, Michael   Prisoner 1908. Rank: Private - By what ship or how taken: Troops - Time when: 17 Sep 1814 - Place where: Fort Erie - Of what ship or corps: Land forces - Whether man of war, privateer or merchant vessel: Taken on shore - Time when received into custody: 1 Nov 1814 - From what ship or whence received: Montreal - Exchanged, discharged, died, or escape: Discharged - Time when: 8 Nov 1814 - Whither, and by what order, or number or re-entry: S. George No. 575 for Halifax by order of Sir George Provost

Myers, Edward   Prisoner 999. Rank: Seaman - By what ship or how taken: Earl Moria - Time when: 10 Aug 1813 - Place where: Lake Ontario - Of what ship or corps: Julia - Whether man of war, privateer or merchant vessel: Man of War - Time when received into custody: 5 Sep 1813 - From what ship or whence received: Steamboat - Exchanged, discharged, died, or escape: Discharged - Time when: 18 Sep 1813 - Whither, and by what order, or number or re-entry: Regulius Transport

Myers, Joseph   Prisoner 1988. Rank: Seaman - By what ship or how taken: Troops - Time when: - Place where: - Of what ship

American Prisoners of War held at Quebec during the War of 1812

or corps: George - Whether man of war, privateer or merchant vessel: Man of War - Time when received into custody: - From what ship or whence received: - Exchanged, discharged, died, or escape: Discharged - Time when: 13 Mar 1815 - Whither, and by what order, or number or re-entry: United States

Napernery, John   Prisoner 359. Rank: Private - By what ship or how taken: Troops - Time when: 6 Jun 1813 - Place where: Stoney Point - Of what ship or corps: Land forces - Whether man of war, privateer or merchant vessel: Taken on shore - Time when received into custody: 28 Jun 1813 - From what ship or whence received: Mary of Quebec - Exchanged, discharged, died, or escape: Discharged - Time when: 7 Aug 1813 - Whither, and by what order, or number or re-entry: H.M. Ship Cievare

Neighbors, John   Prisoner 1335. Rank: Private - By what ship or how taken: Troops - Time when: 19 Dec 1813 - Place where: Fort Niagara - Of what ship or corps: Land forces - Whether man of war, privateer or merchant vessel: Taken on shore - Time when received into custody: 29 Jan 1814 - From what ship or whence received: Montreal by land carriage - Exchanged, discharged, died, or escape: Discharged - Time when: 4 May 1814 - Whither, and by what order, or number or re-entry: United States

Neils, Nathaniel W.   Prisoner 780. Rank: Private - By what ship or how taken: Troops - Time when: 26 Jun 1813 - Place where: Beaver Dam - Of what ship or corps: Land forces - Whether man of war, privateer or merchant vessel: Taken on shore - Time when received into custody: 7 Jul 1813 - From what ship or whence received: Steamboat - Exchanged, discharged, died, or escape: Discharged - Time when: 10 Aug 1813 - Whither, and by what order, or number or re-entry: HM Ship Malpomena

Nelson, James   Prisoner 1110. Rank: Private - By what ship or how taken: Troops - Time when: 17 Oct 1813 - Place where: Red Mills - Of what ship or corps: Land forces - Whether man of war, privateer or merchant vessel: Taken on shore - Time when received into custody: 12 Oct 1813 - From what ship or whence received: Steamboat - Exchanged, discharged, died, or escape: Discharged - Time when: 31 Oct 1813 - Whither, and by what order, or number or re-entry: Malabar Transport

Nelson, Timothy   Prisoner 1948. Rank: Sergeant - By what ship or how taken: Troops - Time when: 17 Sep 1814 - Place where: Fort Erie - Of what ship or corps: Land forces - Whether man of war, privateer or merchant vessel: Taken on shore - Time when received into custody: 1 Nov 1814 - From what ship or whence received: Montreal - Exchanged, discharged, died, or escape: Discharged - Time when: 13 Mar 1815 - Whither, and by what order, or number or re-entry: United States

Nesbett, John   Prisoner 1419. Rank: Sergeant - By what ship or how taken: Troops - Time when: 19 Dec 1813 - Place where: Fort Niagara - Of what ship or corps: Land forces - Whether man of war, privateer or merchant vessel: Taken on shore - Time when received into custody: 29 Jan 1814 - From what ship or whence received: Montreal by land carriage - Exchanged, discharged, died, or escape: Discharged - Time when: 4 May 1814 - Whither, and by what order, or number or re-entry: United States

Newland, Thomas S.   Prisoner 280. Rank: Private - By what ship or how taken: Troops - Time when: 6 Jun 1813 - Place where: Stoney Point - Of what ship or corps: Land forces - Whether man of war, privateer or merchant vessel: Taken on shore - Time when received into custody: 28 Jun 1813 - From what ship or whence received: Batteaux - Exchanged, discharged, died, or escape: Discharged - Time when: 7 Aug 1813 - Whither, and by what order, or number or re-entry: H.M. Ship Cievare

Newman, Henry   Prisoner 330. Rank: Private - By what ship or how taken: Boats & Troops - Time when: 6 Jun 1813 - Place where: Stoney Point - Of what ship or corps: Land forces - Whether man of war, privateer or merchant vessel: Taken on shore - Time when received into custody: 28 Jun 1813 - From what ship or whence received: Quebec of Quebec - Exchanged, discharged, died, or escape: Discharged - Time when: 4 May 1814 - Whither, and by what order, or number or re-entry: United States

Newman, J.   Prisoner 1578. Rank: Seaman - By what ship or how taken: Gun Boats - Time when: 12 Aug 1814 - Place where: Fort Erie - Of what ship or corps: Somers - Whether man of war, privateer or merchant vessel: Man of War - Time when received into custody: 5 Oct 1814 - From what ship or whence received: Montreal - Exchanged, discharged, died, or escape: Discharged - Time when: 10 Nov 1814 - Whither, and by what order, or number or re-entry: Freedom No. 582

Newman, Stokely   Prisoner 962. Rank: Private - By what ship or how taken: Troops - Time when: 5 Jul 1813 - Place where: Fort Schisher - Of what ship or corps: Land forces - Whether man of war, privateer or merchant vessel: Taken on shore - Time when received into custody: 5 Sep 1813 - From what ship or whence received: Steamboat - Exchanged, discharged, died, or escape: Discharged - Time when: 31 Oct 1813 - Whither, and by what order, or number or re-entry: Malabar Transport

American Prisoners of War held at Quebec during the War of 1812

Newton, John   Prisoner 648. Rank: Private - By what ship or how taken: Troops - Time when: 24 Jun 1813 - Place where: Stoney Point - Of what ship or corps: Land forces - Whether man of war, privateer or merchant vessel: Taken on shore - Time when received into custody: 7 Jul 1813 - From what ship or whence received: Steamboat - Exchanged, discharged, died, or escape: Discharged - Time when: 10 Aug 1813 - Whither, and by what order, or number or re-entry: HM Ship Regulius by order of Sir George Provost

Nicholson, John   Prisoner 1312. Rank: Private - By what ship or how taken: Troops - Time when: 19 Dec 1813 - Place where: Fort Niagara - Of what ship or corps: Land forces - Whether man of war, privateer or merchant vessel: Taken on shore - Time when received into custody: 29 Jan 1814 - From what ship or whence received: Montreal by land carriage - Exchanged, discharged, died, or escape: Discharged - Time when: 4 May 1814 - Whither, and by what order, or number or re-entry: United States

Nicholson, Soloman   Prisoner 114. Rank: Private - By what ship or how taken: Boats & Troops - Time when: 28 May 1813 - Place where: Stoney Point, Henderson Harbor - Of what ship or corps: Land forces - Whether man of war, privateer or merchant vessel: Taken on shore - Time when received into custody: 8 Jun 1813 - From what ship or whence received: Batteaux - Exchanged, discharged, died, or escape: Discharged - Time when: 31 Oct 1813 - Whither, and by what order, or number or re-entry: Malabar Transport

Nicholson, William   Prisoner 163. Rank: Able seaman - By what ship or how taken: Boats & Troops - Time when: 3 Jun 1813 - Place where: Lake Champlain - Of what ship or corps: Eagle - Whether man of war, privateer or merchant vessel: Man of War - Time when received into custody: 9 Jun 1813 - From what ship or whence received: Batteaux - Exchanged, discharged, died, or escape: Discharged - Time when: 31 Oct 1813 - Whither, and by what order, or number or re-entry: Malabar Transport

Nigh, George   Prisoner 1457. Rank: Private - By what ship or how taken: Troops - Time when: 6 May 1814 - Place where: Oswago - Of what ship or corps: Land forces - Whether man of war, privateer or merchant vessel: Taken on shore - Time when received into custody: 12 Aug 1814 - From what ship or whence received: Royal Seaman No. 289 Transport - Exchanged, discharged, died, or escape: Discharged - Time when: 8 Oct 1814 - Whither, and by what order, or number or re-entry: Queen No. 415

Nixon, William   Prisoner 589. Rank: Private - By what ship or how taken: Troops - Time when: 26 Jun 1813 - Place where: Beaver Dam - Of what ship or corps: Land forces - Whether man of war, privateer or merchant vessel: Taken on shore - Time when received into custody: 13 Jul 1813 - From what ship or whence received: Steamboat - Exchanged, discharged, died, or escape: Discharged - Time when: 10 Aug 1813 - Whither, and by what order, or number or re-entry: HM Ship Regulius by order of Sir George Provost

Nobles, Stephen   Prisoner 1533. Rank: Private - By what ship or how taken: Troops - Time when: 25 Jul 1814 - Place where: Lundy's Lane - Of what ship or corps: Land forces - Whether man of war, privateer or merchant vessel: Taken on shore - Time when received into custody: 30 Aug 1814 - From what ship or whence received: Lady Delaval Schooner 578 - Exchanged, discharged, died, or escape: Discharged - Time when: 8 Oct 1814 - Whither, and by what order, or number or re-entry: Queen No. 415

Norbry, James   Prisoner 152. Rank: Ensign - By what ship or how taken: Boats & Troops - Time when: 3 Jun 1813 - Place where: Lake Champlain - Of what ship or corps: Growler - Whether man of war, privateer or merchant vessel: Man of War - Time when received into custody: 8 Jul 1813 - From what ship or whence received: Batteaux - Exchanged, discharged, died, or escape: Discharged - Time when: 7 Oct 1813 - Whither, and by what order, or number or re-entry: General Kempt Transport

North, Joseph E.   Prisoner 1929. Rank: Private - By what ship or how taken: Troops - Time when: 17 Sep 1814 - Place where: Fort Erie - Of what ship or corps: Land forces - Whether man of war, privateer or merchant vessel: Taken on shore - Time when received into custody: 1 Nov 1814 - From what ship or whence received: Montreal - Exchanged, discharged, died, or escape: Discharged - Time when: 13 Mar 1815 - Whither, and by what order, or number or re-entry: United States

Northup, Thomas   Prisoner 1812. Rank: Private - By what ship or how taken: Troops - Time when: 17 Sep 1814 - Place where: Fort Erie - Of what ship or corps: Land forces - Whether man of war, privateer or merchant vessel: Taken on shore - Time when received into custody: 1 Nov 1814 - From what ship or whence received: Montreal - Exchanged, discharged, died, or escape: Discharged - Time when: 8 Nov 1814 - Whither, and by what order, or number or re-entry: S. George No. 575 for Halifax by order of Sir George Provost

American Prisoners of War held at Quebec during the War of 1812

Norton, Andrew   Prisoner 1744. Rank: Seaman - By what ship or how taken: Gun Boats - Time when: 3 Sep 1814 - Place where: Lake Huron - Of what ship or corps: Tigress - Whether man of war, privateer or merchant vessel: Man of War - Time when received into custody: 1 Nov 1814 - From what ship or whence received: Montreal - Exchanged, discharged, died, or escape: Discharged - Time when: 7 Nov 1814 - Whither, and by what order, or number or re-entry: Transport Freedom No. 582 by orders of his Excellency Sir George Provost

Norton, D. B.   Prisoner 1539. Rank: Private - By what ship or how taken: Troops - Time when: 25 Jul 1814 - Place where: Lundy's Lane - Of what ship or corps: Land forces - Whether man of war, privateer or merchant vessel: Taken on shore - Time when received into custody: 30 Aug 1814 - From what ship or whence received: Lady Delaval Schooner 578 - Exchanged, discharged, died, or escape: Discharged - Time when: 8 Oct 1814 - Whither, and by what order, or number or re-entry: Queen No. 415

Norton, Lewis   Prisoner 1718. Rank: Private - By what ship or how taken: Gun Boats - Time when: 6 Sep 1814 - Place where: Lake Huron - Of what ship or corps: Scorpion - Whether man of war, privateer or merchant vessel: Man of War - Time when received into custody: 28 Oct 1814 - From what ship or whence received: Montreal - Exchanged, discharged, died, or escape: Discharged - Time when: 10 Nov 1814 - Whither, and by what order, or number or re-entry: Transport Stately No. 408 for Halifax

Norton, Robert   Prisoner 857. Rank: Private - By what ship or how taken: Troops - Time when: 26 Jun 1813 - Place where: Beaver Dam - Of what ship or corps: Land forces - Whether man of war, privateer or merchant vessel: Taken on shore - Time when received into custody: 7 Jul 1813 - From what ship or whence received: Steamboat - Exchanged, discharged, died, or escape: Discharged - Time when: 10 Aug 1813 - Whither, and by what order, or number or re-entry: HM Ship Malpomena

Nourse, Thomas B. W.   Prisoner 1175. Rank: Private - By what ship or how taken: Troops - Time when: 5 May 1813 - Place where: Rapids Prince Reason - Of what ship or corps: Land forces - Whether man of war, privateer or merchant vessel: Taken on shore - Time when received into custody: 25 Nov 1813 - From what ship or whence received: Town Goal - Exchanged, discharged, died, or escape: Discharged - Time when: 12 Mar 1814 - Whither, and by what order, or number or re-entry: New Brunswick Fencibles

Nunn, Jonathan   Prisoner 1386. Rank: Private - By what ship or how taken: Troops - Time when: 19 Dec 1813 - Place where: Fort Niagara - Of what ship or corps: Land forces - Whether man of war, privateer or merchant vessel: Taken on shore - Time when received into custody: 29 Jan 1814 - From what ship or whence received: Montreal by land carriage - Exchanged, discharged, died, or escape: Discharged - Time when: 4 May 1814 - Whither, and by what order, or number or re-entry: United States

Nute, Jonathan   Prisoner 96. Rank: Private - By what ship or how taken: Boats & Troops - Time when: 28 May 1813 - Place where: Stoney Point, Henderson Harbor - Of what ship or corps: Land forces - Whether man of war, privateer or merchant vessel: Taken on shore - Time when received into custody: 8 Jun 1813 - From what ship or whence received: Batteaux - Exchanged, discharged, died, or escape: Discharged - Time when: 4 May 1814 - Whither, and by what order, or number or re-entry: United States

Nutter, John   Prisoner 1780. Rank: Private - By what ship or how taken: Troops - Time when: 7 Sep 1814 - Place where: Fort Erie - Of what ship or corps: Land forces - Whether man of war, privateer or merchant vessel: Taken on shore - Time when received into custody: 1 Nov 1814 - From what ship or whence received: Montreal - Exchanged, discharged, died, or escape: Discharged - Time when: 8 Nov 1814 - Whither, and by what order, or number or re-entry: S. George No. 575 for Halifax by order of Sir George Provost

Nybro, Godfred   Prisoner 596. Rank: Private - By what ship or how taken: Troops - Time when: 26 Jun 1813 - Place where: Stoney Point - Of what ship or corps: Land forces - Whether man of war, privateer or merchant vessel: Taken on shore - Time when received into custody: 7 Jul 1813 - From what ship or whence received: Steamboat - Exchanged, discharged, died, or escape: Discharged - Time when: 10 Aug 1813 - Whither, and by what order, or number or re-entry: HM Ship Regulius by order of Sir George Provost

Oates, John   Prisoner 457. Rank: Private - By what ship or how taken: Troops - Time when: 24 Jun 1813 - Place where: Beaver Dam - Of what ship or corps: Malabar & Hydia - Whether man of war, privateer or merchant vessel: Taken on shore - Time when received into custody: 7 Jul 1813 - From what ship or whence received: Steamboat - Exchanged, discharged, died, or escape: Discharged - Time when: 10 Aug 1813 - Whither, and by what order, or number or re-entry: HM Ship Regulius by order of Sir George Provost

O'Conner, Michael   Prisoner 1247. Rank: Private - By what ship or how taken: Troops - Time when: 19 Dec 1813 - Place where: Fort Niagara - Of what ship or corps: Land forces - Whether man of war, privateer or merchant vessel: Taken on shore - Time when received into custody: 29 Jan 1814 - From what ship or whence received: Montreal by land carriage

American Prisoners of War held at Quebec during the War of 1812

- Exchanged, discharged, died, or escape: Discharged - Time when: 27 Feb 1814 - Whither, and by what order, or number or re-entry: Volunteered for New Brunswick Fencibles

Oddly, John   Prisoner 945. Rank: Private - By what ship or how taken: Troops - Time when: 26 Jun 1813 - Place where: Beaver Dam - Of what ship or corps: Land forces - Whether man of war, privateer or merchant vessel: Taken on shore - Time when received into custody: 21 Jul 1813 - From what ship or whence received: Steamboat - Exchanged, discharged, died, or escape: Discharged - Time when: 10 Aug 1813 - Whither, and by what order, or number or re-entry: HM Ship Malpomena

Ogle, Howard   Prisoner 1122. Rank: Private - By what ship or how taken: Troops - Time when: 17 Oct 1813 - Place where: Red Mills - Of what ship or corps: Land forces - Whether man of war, privateer or merchant vessel: Taken on shore - Time when received into custody: 12 Oct 1813 - From what ship or whence received: Steamboat - Exchanged, discharged, died, or escape: Discharged - Time when: 31 Oct 1813 - Whither, and by what order, or number or re-entry: Malabar Transport

Oiler, George   Prisoner 565. Rank: Private - By what ship or how taken: Troops - Time when: 26 Jun 1813 - Place where: Beaver Dam - Of what ship or corps: Land forces - Whether man of war, privateer or merchant vessel: Taken on shore - Time when received into custody: 13 Jul 1813 - From what ship or whence received: Steamboat - Exchanged, discharged, died, or escape: Discharged - Time when: 10 Aug 1813 - Whither, and by what order, or number or re-entry: HM Ship Regulius by order of Sir George Provost

Oin, Ebenezer   Prisoner 1260. Rank: Private - By what ship or how taken: Troops - Time when: 19 Dec 1813 - Place where: Fort Niagara - Of what ship or corps: Land forces - Whether man of war, privateer or merchant vessel: Taken on shore - Time when received into custody: 29 Jan 1814 - From what ship or whence received: Montreal by land carriage - Exchanged, discharged, died, or escape: Discharged - Time when: 4 May 1814 - Whither, and by what order, or number or re-entry: United States

Oin, Joseph   Prisoner 1259. Rank: Private - By what ship or how taken: Troops - Time when: 19 Dec 1813 - Place where: Fort Niagara - Of what ship or corps: Land forces - Whether man of war, privateer or merchant vessel: Taken on shore - Time when received into custody: 29 Jan 1814 - From what ship or whence received: Montreal by land carriage - Exchanged, discharged, died, or escape: Discharged - Time when: 4 May 1814 - Whither, and by what order, or number or re-entry: United States

Oliver, Grifin   Prisoner 1671. Rank: Seaman - By what ship or how taken: Gun Boats - Time when: 25 Aug 1814 - Place where: Lake Ontario - Of what ship or corps: Taken on a gigg - Whether man of war, privateer or merchant vessel: Man of War - Time when received into custody: 23 Oct 1814 - From what ship or whence received: Montreal - Exchanged, discharged, died, or escape: Discharged - Time when: 7 Nov 1814 - Whither, and by what order, or number or re-entry: Transport Freedom No. 582 by orders of his Excellency Sir George Provost

Olstender, Gabriel   Prisoner 753. Rank: Private - By what ship or how taken: Troops - Time when: 26 Jun 1813 - Place where: Beaver Dam - Of what ship or corps: Land forces - Whether man of war, privateer or merchant vessel: Taken on shore - Time when received into custody: 7 Jul 1813 - From what ship or whence received: Steamboat - Exchanged, discharged, died, or escape: Discharged - Time when: 10 Aug 1813 - Whither, and by what order, or number or re-entry: HM Ship Malpomena

O'Neil, Con.   Prisoner 667. Rank: Private - By what ship or how taken: Troops - Time when: 24 Jun 1813 - Place where: Stoney Point - Of what ship or corps: Land forces - Whether man of war, privateer or merchant vessel: Taken on shore - Time when received into custody: 7 Jul 1813 - From what ship or whence received: Steamboat - Exchanged, discharged, died, or escape: Discharged - Time when: 10 Aug 1813 - Whither, and by what order, or number or re-entry: HM Ship Regulius by order of Sir George Provost

Orcutt, Rufus   Prisoner 1765. Rank: Sergeant - By what ship or how taken: Troops - Time when: 7 Sep 1814 - Place where: Fort Erie - Of what ship or corps: Land forces - Whether man of war, privateer or merchant vessel: Taken on shore - Time when received into custody: 1 Nov 1814 - From what ship or whence received: Montreal - Exchanged, discharged, died, or escape: Discharged - Time when: 8 Nov 1814 - Whither, and by what order, or number or re-entry: S. George No. 575 for Halifax by order of Sir George Provost

Orstunoser, Jones   Prisoner 360. Rank: Private - By what ship or how taken: Troops - Time when: 6 Jun 1813 - Place where: Stoney Point - Of what ship or corps: Land forces - Whether man of war, privateer or merchant vessel: Taken on shore - Time when received into custody: 28 Jun 1813 - From what ship or whence received: Mary of Quebec - Exchanged, discharged, died, or escape: Discharged - Time when: 31 Oct 1813 - Whither, and by what order, or number or re-entry: Malabar Transport

American Prisoners of War held at Quebec during the War of 1812

Osbourn, Thomas   Prisoner 771. Rank: Sergeant - By what ship or how taken: Troops - Time when: 26 Jun 1813 - Place where: Beaver Dam - Of what ship or corps: Land forces - Whether man of war, privateer or merchant vessel: Taken on shore - Time when received into custody: 7 Jul 1813 - From what ship or whence received: Steamboat - Exchanged, discharged, died, or escape: Discharged - Time when: 10 Aug 1813 - Whither, and by what order, or number or re-entry: HM Ship Malpomena

Osgood, Richard   Prisoner 245. Rank: Private - By what ship or how taken: Boats & Troops - Time when: 24 Jun 1813 - Place where: Rec in charge of Beauport - Of what ship or corps: Land forces - Whether man of war, privateer or merchant vessel: Taken on shore - Time when received into custody: 9 Jun 1813 - From what ship or whence received: Steamboat - Exchanged, discharged, died, or escape: Discharged - Time when: 31 Oct 1813 - Whither, and by what order, or number or re-entry: Malabar Transport

Osten, Charles   Prisoner 1586. Rank: Seaman - By what ship or how taken: Gun Boats - Time when: 12 Aug 1814 - Place where: Fort Erie - Of what ship or corps: Somers - Whether man of war, privateer or merchant vessel: Man of War - Time when received into custody: 5 Oct 1814 - From what ship or whence received: Montreal - Exchanged, discharged, died, or escape: Discharged - Time when: 10 Nov 1814 - Whither, and by what order, or number or re-entry: Freedom No. 582

Ostrander, R.   Prisoner 1603. Rank: Private - By what ship or how taken: Troops - Time when: 12 Aug 1814 - Place where: Fort Erie - Of what ship or corps: Land forces - Whether man of war, privateer or merchant vessel: Taken on shore - Time when received into custody: 5 Oct 1814 - From what ship or whence received: Montreal - Exchanged, discharged, died, or escape: Discharged - Time when: 8 Oct 1814 - Whither, and by what order, or number or re-entry: H.M. Ship Ceylon

Owen, Amasa   Prisoner 1265. Rank: Corporal - By what ship or how taken: Troops - Time when: 19 Dec 1813 - Place where: Fort Niagara - Of what ship or corps: Land forces - Whether man of war, privateer or merchant vessel: Taken on shore - Time when received into custody: 29 Jan 1814 - From what ship or whence received: Montreal by land carriage - Exchanged, discharged, died, or escape: Discharged - Time when: 11 Mar 1814 - Whither, and by what order, or number or re-entry: Volunteered for New Brunswick Fencibles

Owen, Frederick   Prisoner 1785. Rank: Private - By what ship or how taken: Troops - Time when: 7 Sep 1814 - Place where: Fort Erie - Of what ship or corps: Land forces - Whether man of war, privateer or merchant vessel: Taken on shore - Time when received into custody: 1 Nov 1814 - From what ship or whence received: Montreal - Exchanged, discharged, died, or escape: Discharged - Time when: 8 Nov 1814 - Whither, and by what order, or number or re-entry: S. George No. 575 for Halifax by order of Sir George Provost

Owen, Jeremiah   Prisoner 1358. Rank: Private - By what ship or how taken: Troops - Time when: 19 Dec 1813 - Place where: Fort Niagara - Of what ship or corps: Land forces - Whether man of war, privateer or merchant vessel: Taken on shore - Time when received into custody: 29 Jan 1814 - From what ship or whence received: Montreal by land carriage - Exchanged, discharged, died, or escape: Discharged - Time when: 4 May 1814 - Whither, and by what order, or number or re-entry: United States

Oweritt, John   Prisoner 729. Rank: Private - By what ship or how taken: Troops - Time when: 26 Jun 1813 - Place where: Beaver Dam - Of what ship or corps: Land forces - Whether man of war, privateer or merchant vessel: Taken on shore - Time when received into custody: 7 Jul 1813 - From what ship or whence received: Steamboat - Exchanged, discharged, died, or escape: Discharged - Time when: 10 Aug 1813 - Whither, and by what order, or number or re-entry: HM Ship Regulius by order of Sir George Provost

Pace, Jonathan   Prisoner 354. Rank: Private - By what ship or how taken: Troops - Time when: 6 Jun 1813 - Place where: Stoney Point - Of what ship or corps: Land forces - Whether man of war, privateer or merchant vessel: Taken on shore - Time when received into custody: 28 Jun 1813 - From what ship or whence received: Mary of Quebec - Exchanged, discharged, died, or escape: Discharged - Time when: 31 Oct 1813 - Whither, and by what order, or number or re-entry: Malabar Transport

Pack, Luther   Prisoner 183. Rank: Corporal - By what ship or how taken: Boats & Troops - Time when: 3 Jun 1813 - Place where: Lake Champlain - Of what ship or corps: Growler - Whether man of war, privateer or merchant vessel: Man of War - Time when received into custody: 9 Jun 1813 - From what ship or whence received: Batteaux - Exchanged, discharged, died, or escape: Discharged - Time when: 31 Oct 1813 - Whither, and by what order, or number or re-entry: Malabar Transport

Packhard, Joseph   Prisoner 1978. Rank: Private - By what ship or how taken: Troops - Time when: 2 Nov 1814 - Place where: Fort Erie - Of what ship or corps: Land forces - Whether man of war, privateer or merchant vessel: Taken on shore - Time when received into custody: 30 Dec 1814 - From what ship or whence received: Montreal - Exchanged,

American Prisoners of War held at Quebec during the War of 1812

discharged, died, or escape: Discharged - Time when: 13 Mar 1815 - Whither, and by what order, or number or re-entry: United States

Pactaolt, Henry   Prisoner 1017. Rank: Marine Private - By what ship or how taken: Earl Moria - Time when: 10 Aug 1813 - Place where: Lake Ontario - Of what ship or corps: Julia - Whether man of war, privateer or merchant vessel: Man of War - Time when received into custody: 5 Sep 1813 - From what ship or whence received: Steamboat - Exchanged, discharged, died, or escape: Discharged - Time when: 31 Oct 1813 - Whither, and by what order, or number or re-entry: Malabar Transport

Page, John   Prisoner 1609. Rank: Private - By what ship or how taken: Troops - Time when: 6 Sep 1814 - Place where: Plattsburg - Of what ship or corps: Land forces - Whether man of war, privateer or merchant vessel: Taken on shore - Time when received into custody: 5 Oct 1814 - From what ship or whence received: Montreal - Exchanged, discharged, died, or escape: Discharged - Time when: 8 Oct 1814 - Whither, and by what order, or number or re-entry: H.M. Ship Ceylon

Paine, Richard   Prisoner 768. Rank: Private - By what ship or how taken: Troops - Time when: 26 Jun 1813 - Place where: Beaver Dam - Of what ship or corps: Land forces - Whether man of war, privateer or merchant vessel: Taken on shore - Time when received into custody: 7 Jul 1813 - From what ship or whence received: Steamboat - Exchanged, discharged, died, or escape: Discharged - Time when: 10 Aug 1813 - Whither, and by what order, or number or re-entry: HM Ship Malpomena

Paine, William   Prisoner 943. Rank: Private - By what ship or how taken: Troops - Time when: 26 Jun 1813 - Place where: Beaver Dam - Of what ship or corps: Land forces - Whether man of war, privateer or merchant vessel: Taken on shore - Time when received into custody: 21 Jul 1813 - From what ship or whence received: Steamboat - Exchanged, discharged, died, or escape: Discharged - Time when: 10 Aug 1813 - Whither, and by what order, or number or re-entry: HM Ship Malpomena

Palishaw, Mathew   Prisoner 1927. Rank: Private - By what ship or how taken: Troops - Time when: 17 Sep 1814 - Place where: Fort Erie - Of what ship or corps: Land forces - Whether man of war, privateer or merchant vessel: Taken on shore - Time when received into custody: 1 Nov 1814 - From what ship or whence received: Montreal - Exchanged, discharged, died, or escape: Discharged - Time when: 10 Nov 1814 - Whither, and by what order, or number or re-entry: Transport Stately No. 408 for Halifax

Palmer, Gordon   Prisoner 1024. Rank: Quarter Gunner - By what ship or how taken: Earl Moria - Time when: 10 Aug 1813 - Place where: Lake Ontario - Of what ship or corps: Julia - Whether man of war, privateer or merchant vessel: Man of War - Time when received into custody: 5 Sep 1813 - From what ship or whence received: Steamboat - Exchanged, discharged, died, or escape: Discharged - Time when: 31 Oct 1813 - Whither, and by what order, or number or re-entry: Malabar Transport

Palmer, J. B.   Prisoner 950. Rank: Lieutenant - By what ship or how taken: Troops - Time when: 26 Jun 1813 - Place where: Beaver Dam - Of what ship or corps: Land forces - Whether man of war, privateer or merchant vessel: Taken on shore - Time when received into custody: 21 Jul 1813 - From what ship or whence received: Steamboat - Exchanged, discharged, died, or escape: Discharged - Time when: 4 May 1814 - Whither, and by what order, or number or re-entry: United States

Palmer, John William   Prisoner 1666. Rank: Master's Mate - By what ship or how taken: Gun Boats - Time when: 6 Sep 1814 - Place where: Lake Huron - Of what ship or corps: Scorpion - Whether man of war, privateer or merchant vessel: Man of War - Time when received into custody: 23 Oct 1814 - From what ship or whence received: Montreal - Exchanged, discharged, died, or escape: Discharged - Time when: 10 Nov 1814 - Whither, and by what order, or number or re-entry: Lord Cartheart No. 161 for Halifax

Palmer, Nicholas   Prisoner 719. Rank: Private - By what ship or how taken: Troops - Time when: 26 Jun 1813 - Place where: Beaver Dam - Of what ship or corps: Land forces - Whether man of war, privateer or merchant vessel: Taken on shore - Time when received into custody: 7 Jul 1813 - From what ship or whence received: Steamboat - Exchanged, discharged, died, or escape: Discharged - Time when: 4 May 1814 - Whither, and by what order, or number or re-entry: United States

Palmer, Thomas   Prisoner 1741. Rank: Seaman - By what ship or how taken: Gun Boats - Time when: 3 Sep 1814 - Place where: Lake Huron - Of what ship or corps: Tigress - Whether man of war, privateer or merchant vessel: Man of War - Time when received into custody: 1 Nov 1814 - From what ship or whence received: Montreal - Exchanged, discharged, died, or escape: Discharged - Time when: 7 Nov 1814 - Whither, and by what order, or number or re-entry: Transport Freedom No. 582 by orders of his Excellency Sir George Provost

American Prisoners of War held at Quebec during the War of 1812

Palmer, William   Prisoner 1012. Rank: Seaman - By what ship or how taken: Earl Moria - Time when: 10 Aug 1813 - Place where: Lake Ontario - Of what ship or corps: Julia - Whether man of war, privateer or merchant vessel: Man of War - Time when received into custody: 5 Sep 1813 - From what ship or whence received: Steamboat - Exchanged, discharged, died, or escape: Discharged - Time when: 31 Oct 1813 - Whither, and by what order, or number or re-entry: Malabar Transport

Paradise, John   Prisoner 759. Rank: Private - By what ship or how taken: Troops - Time when: 26 Jun 1813 - Place where: Beaver Dam - Of what ship or corps: Land forces - Whether man of war, privateer or merchant vessel: Taken on shore - Time when received into custody: 7 Jul 1813 - From what ship or whence received: Steamboat - Exchanged, discharged, died, or escape: Discharged - Time when: 10 Aug 1813 - Whither, and by what order, or number or re-entry: HM Ship Malpomena

Parcel, James H.   Prisoner 1317. Rank: Sergeant - By what ship or how taken: Troops - Time when: 19 Dec 1813 - Place where: Fort Niagara - Of what ship or corps: Land forces - Whether man of war, privateer or merchant vessel: Taken on shore - Time when received into custody: 29 Jan 1814 - From what ship or whence received: Montreal by land carriage - Exchanged, discharged, died, or escape: Discharged - Time when: 4 May 1814 - Whither, and by what order, or number or re-entry: United States

Park, Roger   Prisoner 973. Rank: Private - By what ship or how taken: Troops - Time when: 5 Jul 1813 - Place where: Fort Schisher - Of what ship or corps: Land forces - Whether man of war, privateer or merchant vessel: Taken on shore - Time when received into custody: 5 Sep 1813 - From what ship or whence received: Steamboat - Exchanged, discharged, died, or escape: - Time when: - Whither, and by what order, or number or re-entry:

Parker, Edward   Prisoner 224. Rank: Private - By what ship or how taken: Boats & Troops - Time when: 3 Jun 1813 - Place where: Lake Champlain - Of what ship or corps: Growler - Whether man of war, privateer or merchant vessel: Man of War - Time when received into custody: 9 Jun 1813 - From what ship or whence received: Batteaux - Exchanged, discharged, died, or escape: Died - Time when: 19 Sep 1813 - Whither, and by what order, or number or re-entry: Typhus Fever

Parker, John   Prisoner 1740. Rank: Seaman - By what ship or how taken: Gun Boats - Time when: 3 Sep 1814 - Place where: Lake Huron - Of what ship or corps: Tigress - Whether man of war, privateer or merchant vessel: Man of War - Time when received into custody: 1 Nov 1814 - From what ship or whence received: Montreal - Exchanged, discharged, died, or escape: Discharged - Time when: 7 Nov 1814 - Whither, and by what order, or number or re-entry: Transport Freedom No. 582 by orders of his Excellency Sir George Provost

Parkinson, James   Prisoner 1876. Rank: Private - By what ship or how taken: Troops - Time when: 17 Sep 1814 - Place where: Fort Erie - Of what ship or corps: Land forces - Whether man of war, privateer or merchant vessel: Taken on shore - Time when received into custody: 1 Nov 1814 - From what ship or whence received: Montreal - Exchanged, discharged, died, or escape: Discharged - Time when: 8 Nov 1814 - Whither, and by what order, or number or re-entry: S. George No. 575 for Halifax by order of Sir George Provost

Parks, Henry   Prisoner 1938. Rank: Private - By what ship or how taken: Troops - Time when: 17 Sep 1814 - Place where: Fort Erie - Of what ship or corps: Land forces - Whether man of war, privateer or merchant vessel: Taken on shore - Time when received into custody: 1 Nov 1814 - From what ship or whence received: Montreal - Exchanged, discharged, died, or escape: Discharged - Time when: 13 Mar 1815 - Whither, and by what order, or number or re-entry: United States

Parks, J.   Prisoner 1596. Rank: Private - By what ship or how taken: Troops - Time when: 12 Aug 1814 - Place where: Fort Erie - Of what ship or corps: Land forces - Whether man of war, privateer or merchant vessel: Taken on shore - Time when received into custody: 5 Oct 1814 - From what ship or whence received: Montreal - Exchanged, discharged, died, or escape: Discharged - Time when: 8 Oct 1814 - Whither, and by what order, or number or re-entry: H.M. Ship Ceylon

Parks, Selvy   Prisoner 486. Rank: Private - By what ship or how taken: Troops - Time when: 24 Jun 1813 - Place where: Beaver Dam - Of what ship or corps: Land forces - Whether man of war, privateer or merchant vessel: Taken on shore - Time when received into custody: 7 Jul 1813 - From what ship or whence received: Steamboat - Exchanged, discharged, died, or escape: Discharged - Time when: 10 Aug 1813 - Whither, and by what order, or number or re-entry: HM Ship Regulius by order of Sir George Provost

Parsons, Samuel   Prisoner 388. Rank: Private - By what ship or how taken: Troops - Time when: 6 Jun 1813 - Place where: Stoney Point - Of what ship or corps: Land forces - Whether man of war, privateer or merchant vessel: Taken on shore - Time when received into custody: 28 Jun 1813 - From what ship or whence received: Mary of Quebec - Exchanged, discharged, died, or escape: Discharged - Time when: 10 Oct 1813 - Whither, and by what order, or number or re-entry:

American Prisoners of War held at Quebec during the War of 1812

    Jane Transport

Patch, D.   Prisoner 1555. Rank: Corporal - By what ship or how taken: Troops - Time when: 25 Jul 1814 - Place where: Lundy's Lane - Of what ship or corps: Land forces - Whether man of war, privateer or merchant vessel: Taken on shore - Time when received into custody: 30 Aug 1814 - From what ship or whence received: Lady Delaval Schooner 578 - Exchanged, discharged, died, or escape: Discharged - Time when: 8 Oct 1814 - Whither, and by what order, or number or re-entry: Queen No. 415

Patterson, John   Prisoner 1935. Rank: Private - By what ship or how taken: Troops - Time when: 17 Sep 1814 - Place where: Fort Erie - Of what ship or corps: Land forces - Whether man of war, privateer or merchant vessel: Taken on shore - Time when received into custody: - From what ship or whence received: - Exchanged, discharged, died, or escape: Died - Time when: 7 Dec 1814 - Whither, and by what order, or number or re-entry: Phrenitis

Patterson, John   Prisoner 1248. Rank: Private - By what ship or how taken: Troops - Time when: 19 Dec 1813 - Place where: Fort Niagara - Of what ship or corps: Land forces - Whether man of war, privateer or merchant vessel: Taken on shore - Time when received into custody: 29 Jan 1814 - From what ship or whence received: Montreal by land carriage - Exchanged, discharged, died, or escape: Discharged - Time when: 27 Feb 1814 - Whither, and by what order, or number or re-entry: Volunteered for New Brunswick Fencibles

Patterson, Thomas   Prisoner 1793. Rank: Private - By what ship or how taken: Troops - Time when: 7 Sep 1814 - Place where: Fort Erie - Of what ship or corps: Land forces - Whether man of war, privateer or merchant vessel: Taken on shore - Time when received into custody: 1 Nov 1814 - From what ship or whence received: Montreal - Exchanged, discharged, died, or escape: Discharged - Time when: 8 Nov 1814 - Whither, and by what order, or number or re-entry: S. George No. 575 for Halifax by order of Sir George Provost

Pattison, Thomas   Prisoner 868. Rank: Private - By what ship or how taken: Troops - Time when: 26 Jun 1813 - Place where: Beaver Dam - Of what ship or corps: Land forces - Whether man of war, privateer or merchant vessel: Taken on shore - Time when received into custody: 7 Jul 1813 - From what ship or whence received: Steamboat - Exchanged, discharged, died, or escape: Discharged - Time when: 10 Aug 1813 - Whither, and by what order, or number or re-entry: HM Ship Malpomena

Patton, David   Prisoner 597. Rank: Private - By what ship or how taken: Troops - Time when: 26 Jun 1813 - Place where: Stoney Point - Of what ship or corps: Land forces - Whether man of war, privateer or merchant vessel: Taken on shore - Time when received into custody: 7 Jul 1813 - From what ship or whence received: Steamboat - Exchanged, discharged, died, or escape: Discharged - Time when: 10 Aug 1813 - Whither, and by what order, or number or re-entry: HM Ship Regulius by order of Sir George Provost

Paul, Simeon   Prisoner 227. Rank: Private - By what ship or how taken: Boats & Troops - Time when: 3 Jun 1813 - Place where: Lake Champlain - Of what ship or corps: Eagle - Whether man of war, privateer or merchant vessel: Man of War - Time when received into custody: 9 Jun 1813 - From what ship or whence received: Batteaux - Exchanged, discharged, died, or escape: Died - Time when: 25 Aug 1813 - Whither, and by what order, or number or re-entry: Synochus

Paulling, William K.   Prisoner 1209. Rank: Ensign - By what ship or how taken: Troops - Time when: 19 Dec 1813 - Place where: Fort Niagara - Of what ship or corps: Land forces - Whether man of war, privateer or merchant vessel: Taken on shore - Time when received into custody: 18 Jan 1814 - From what ship or whence received: Montreal by land carriage - Exchanged, discharged, died, or escape: Discharged - Time when: 4 May 1814 - Whither, and by what order, or number or re-entry: United States

Payne, Rubin   Prisoner 186. Rank: Private - By what ship or how taken: Boats & Troops - Time when: 3 Jun 1813 - Place where: Lake Champlain - Of what ship or corps: Eagle - Whether man of war, privateer or merchant vessel: Man of War - Time when received into custody: 9 Jun 1813 - From what ship or whence received: Batteaux - Exchanged, discharged, died, or escape: Discharged - Time when: 31 Oct 1813 - Whither, and by what order, or number or re-entry: Malabar Transport

Peak, John   Prisoner 1646. Rank: Private - By what ship or how taken: Troops - Time when: 19 Dec 1813 - Place where: Niagara - Of what ship or corps: Land forces - Whether man of war, privateer or merchant vessel: Taken on shore - Time when received into custody: 5 Oct 1814 - From what ship or whence received: Montreal - Exchanged, discharged, died, or escape: Discharged - Time when: 8 Oct 1814 - Whither, and by what order, or number or re-entry: H.M. Ship Ceylon

Pearl, John   Prisoner 1598. Rank: Private - By what ship or how taken: Troops - Time when: 12 Aug 1814 - Place where: Fort Erie - Of what ship or corps: Land forces - Whether man of war, privateer or merchant vessel: Taken on shore - Time

American Prisoners of War held at Quebec during the War of 1812

when received into custody: 5 Oct 1814 - From what ship or whence received: Montreal - Exchanged, discharged, died, or escape: Discharged - Time when: 8 Oct 1814 - Whither, and by what order, or number or re-entry: H.M. Ship Ceylon

Pearl, John   Prisoner 28.   Rank: Private - By what ship or how taken: Boats & Troops - Time when: 28 May 1813 - Place where: Stoney Point, Henderson Harbor - Of what ship or corps: Land forces - Whether man of war, privateer or merchant vessel: Taken on shore - Time when received into custody: 8 Jun 1813 - From what ship or whence received: Batteaux - Exchanged, discharged, died, or escape: Discharged - Time when: 31 Oct 1813 - Whither, and by what order, or number or re-entry: Malabar Transport

Pearson, John   Prisoner 1037.   Rank: Seaman - By what ship or how taken: Lord Melvin - Time when: 10 Aug 1813 - Place where: Lake Ontario - Of what ship or corps: Growler - Whether man of war, privateer or merchant vessel: Man of War - Time when received into custody: 5 Sep 1813 - From what ship or whence received: Steamboat - Exchanged, discharged, died, or escape: Discharged - Time when: 31 Oct 1813 - Whither, and by what order, or number or re-entry: Malabar Transport

Peck, Ollus   Prisoner 1288.   Rank: Private - By what ship or how taken: Troops - Time when: 19 Dec 1813 - Place where: Fort Niagara - Of what ship or corps: Land forces - Whether man of war, privateer or merchant vessel: Taken on shore - Time when received into custody: 29 Jan 1814 - From what ship or whence received: Montreal by land carriage - Exchanged, discharged, died, or escape: Discharged - Time when: 4 May 1814 - Whither, and by what order, or number or re-entry: United States

Penly, Joseph   Prisoner 212.   Rank: Private - By what ship or how taken: Boats & Troops - Time when: 3 Jun 1813 - Place where: Lake Champlain - Of what ship or corps: Growler - Whether man of war, privateer or merchant vessel: Man of War - Time when received into custody: 9 Jun 1813 - From what ship or whence received: Batteaux - Exchanged, discharged, died, or escape: Discharged - Time when: 31 Oct 1813 - Whither, and by what order, or number or re-entry: Malabar Transport

Pennell, Samuel   Prisoner 97.   Rank: Private - By what ship or how taken: Boats & Troops - Time when: 28 May 1813 - Place where: Stoney Point, Henderson Harbor - Of what ship or corps: Land forces - Whether man of war, privateer or merchant vessel: Taken on shore - Time when received into custody: 8 Jun 1813 - From what ship or whence received: Batteaux - Exchanged, discharged, died, or escape: Discharged - Time when: 31 Oct 1813 - Whither, and by what order, or number or re-entry: Malabar Transport

Pennington, L.   Prisoner 1601.   Rank: Private - By what ship or how taken: Troops - Time when: 12 Aug 1814 - Place where: Fort Erie - Of what ship or corps: Land forces - Whether man of war, privateer or merchant vessel: Taken on shore - Time when received into custody: 5 Oct 1814 - From what ship or whence received: Montreal - Exchanged, discharged, died, or escape: Discharged - Time when: 8 Oct 1814 - Whither, and by what order, or number or re-entry: H.M. Ship Ceylon

Penny, Nicholas   Prisoner 813.   Rank: Private - By what ship or how taken: Troops - Time when: 26 Jun 1813 - Place where: Beaver Dam - Of what ship or corps: Land forces - Whether man of war, privateer or merchant vessel: Taken on shore - Time when received into custody: 7 Jul 1813 - From what ship or whence received: Steamboat - Exchanged, discharged, died, or escape: Discharged - Time when: 10 Aug 1813 - Whither, and by what order, or number or re-entry: HM Ship Malpomena

Perell, Jacob   Prisoner 1102.   Rank: Private - By what ship or how taken: Troops - Time when: 24 Aug 1813 - Place where: Fort George - Of what ship or corps: Land forces - Whether man of war, privateer or merchant vessel: Taken on shore - Time when received into custody: 12 Oct 1813 - From what ship or whence received: Steamboat - Exchanged, discharged, died, or escape: Discharged - Time when: 31 Oct 1813 - Whither, and by what order, or number or re-entry: Malabar Transport

Perkins, John   Prisoner 1143.   Rank: Private - By what ship or how taken: Troops - Time when: 5 May 1813 - Place where: Rapids Prince Reason - Of what ship or corps: Land forces - Whether man of war, privateer or merchant vessel: Taken on shore - Time when received into custody: 25 Nov 1813 - From what ship or whence received: Town Goal - Exchanged, discharged, died, or escape: Discharged - Time when: 21 Apr 1814 - Whither, and by what order, or number or re-entry: United States

Perkins, Rufas   Prisoner 905.   Rank: Private - By what ship or how taken: Troops - Time when: 26 Jun 1813 - Place where: Beaver Dam - Of what ship or corps: Land forces - Whether man of war, privateer or merchant vessel: Taken on shore - Time when received into custody: 21 Jul 1813 - From what ship or whence received: Steamboat - Exchanged, discharged, died, or escape: Discharged - Time when: 10 Aug 1813 - Whither, and by what order, or number or re-entry: HM Ship Malpomena

American Prisoners of War held at Quebec during the War of 1812

Perkins, Thomas   Prisoner 1450. Rank: Private - By what ship or how taken: Troops - Time when: 6 May 1814 - Place where: Oswago - Of what ship or corps: Land forces - Whether man of war, privateer or merchant vessel: Taken on shore - Time when received into custody: 12 Aug 1814 - From what ship or whence received: Royal Seaman No. 289 Transport - Exchanged, discharged, died, or escape: Discharged - Time when: 8 Oct 1814 - Whither, and by what order, or number or re-entry: Queen No. 415

Permerline, Johan   Prisoner 555. Rank: Private - By what ship or how taken: Troops - Time when: 26 Jun 1813 - Place where: Beaver Dam - Of what ship or corps: Land forces - Whether man of war, privateer or merchant vessel: Taken on shore - Time when received into custody: 13 Jul 1813 - From what ship or whence received: Steamboat - Exchanged, discharged, died, or escape: - Time when: - Whither, and by what order, or number or re-entry:

Perrique, James   Prisoner 705. Rank: Corporal - By what ship or how taken: Troops - Time when: 26 Jun 1813 - Place where: Beaver Dam - Of what ship or corps: Land forces - Whether man of war, privateer or merchant vessel: Taken on shore - Time when received into custody: 7 Jul 1813 - From what ship or whence received: Steamboat - Exchanged, discharged, died, or escape: Discharged - Time when: 10 Aug 1813 - Whither, and by what order, or number or re-entry: HM Ship Regulius by order of Sir George Provost

Perry, David   Prisoner 1506. Rank: Sergeant - By what ship or how taken: Troops - Time when: 25 Jul 1814 - Place where: Lundy's Lane - Of what ship or corps: Land forces - Whether man of war, privateer or merchant vessel: Taken on shore - Time when received into custody: 25 Aug 1814 - From what ship or whence received: Steamboat - Exchanged, discharged, died, or escape: Discharged - Time when: 10 Nov 1814 - Whither, and by what order, or number or re-entry: Soverign Transport No. 628 to Halifax by orders of Sir George Provost

Petare, John   Prisoner 825. Rank: Private - By what ship or how taken: Troops - Time when: 26 Jun 1813 - Place where: Beaver Dam - Of what ship or corps: Land forces - Whether man of war, privateer or merchant vessel: Taken on shore - Time when received into custody: 7 Jul 1813 - From what ship or whence received: Steamboat - Exchanged, discharged, died, or escape: Discharged - Time when: 4 May 1814 - Whither, and by what order, or number or re-entry: United States

Peters , J.   Prisoner 1591. Rank: Seaman - By what ship or how taken: Gun Boats - Time when: 12 Aug 1814 - Place where: Fort Erie - Of what ship or corps: Somers - Whether man of war, privateer or merchant vessel: Man of War - Time when received into custody: 5 Oct 1814 - From what ship or whence received: Montreal - Exchanged, discharged, died, or escape: Discharged - Time when: 10 Nov 1814 - Whither, and by what order, or number or re-entry: Freedom No. 582

Petersen, J.   Prisoner 1589. Rank: Seaman - By what ship or how taken: Gun Boats - Time when: 12 Aug 1814 - Place where: Fort Erie - Of what ship or corps: Somers - Whether man of war, privateer or merchant vessel: Man of War - Time when received into custody: 5 Oct 1814 - From what ship or whence received: Montreal - Exchanged, discharged, died, or escape: Discharged - Time when: 10 Nov 1814 - Whither, and by what order, or number or re-entry: Freedom No. 582

Peterson, James   Prisoner 1045. Rank: Seaman - By what ship or how taken: Earl Moria - Time when: 10 Aug 1813 - Place where: Lake Ontario - Of what ship or corps: Julia - Whether man of war, privateer or merchant vessel: Man of War - Time when received into custody: 5 Sep 1813 - From what ship or whence received: Steamboat - Exchanged, discharged, died, or escape: Discharged - Time when: 21 Sep 1813 - Whither, and by what order, or number or re-entry: Mersey Transport

Peterson, Lemuel   Prisoner 1967. Rank: Private - By what ship or how taken: Troops - Time when: 17 Oct 1814 - Place where: Chippawa - Of what ship or corps: Land forces - Whether man of war, privateer or merchant vessel: Taken on shore - Time when received into custody: 11 Dec 1814 - From what ship or whence received: Montreal - Exchanged, discharged, died, or escape: Discharged - Time when: 13 Mar 1815 - Whither, and by what order, or number or re-entry: United States

Peterson, Peter   Prisoner 61. Rank: Private - By what ship or how taken: Boats & Troops - Time when: 28 May 1813 - Place where: Stoney Point, Henderson Harbor - Of what ship or corps: Land forces - Whether man of war, privateer or merchant vessel: Taken on shore - Time when received into custody: 8 Jun 1813 - From what ship or whence received: Batteaux - Exchanged, discharged, died, or escape: Discharged - Time when: 31 Oct 1813 - Whither, and by what order, or number or re-entry: Malabar Transport

American Prisoners of War held at Quebec during the War of 1812

Pettit, John   Prisoner 1917. Rank: Private - By what ship or how taken: Troops - Time when: 17 Sep 1814 - Place where: Fort Erie - Of what ship or corps: Land forces - Whether man of war, privateer or merchant vessel: Taken on shore - Time when received into custody: 1 Nov 1814 - From what ship or whence received: Montreal - Exchanged, discharged, died, or escape: Discharged - Time when: 16 Mar 1815 - Whither, and by what order, or number or re-entry: United States

Philips, Samuel   Prisoner 437. Rank: Private - By what ship or how taken: Troops - Time when: 24 Jun 1813 - Place where: Beaver Dam - Of what ship or corps: Land forces - Whether man of war, privateer or merchant vessel: Taken on shore - Time when received into custody: 7 Jul 1813 - From what ship or whence received: Steamboat - Exchanged, discharged, died, or escape: Discharged - Time when: 10 Aug 1813 - Whither, and by what order, or number or re-entry: HM Ship Regulius by order of Sir George Provost

Phillips, Augustus   Prisoner 1747. Rank: Seaman - By what ship or how taken: Gun Boats - Time when: 3 Sep 1814 - Place where: Lake Huron - Of what ship or corps: Tigress - Whether man of war, privateer or merchant vessel: Man of War - Time when received into custody: 1 Nov 1814 - From what ship or whence received: Montreal - Exchanged, discharged, died, or escape: Discharged - Time when: 7 Nov 1814 - Whither, and by what order, or number or re-entry: Transport Freedom No. 582 by orders of his Excellency Sir George Provost

Phillips, John Capen   Prisoner 1. Rank: Private - By what ship or how taken: Boats & Troops - Time when: 28 May 1813 - Place where: Stoney Point, Henderson Harbor - Of what ship or corps: Land forces - Whether man of war, privateer or merchant vessel: Taken on shore - Time when received into custody: 8 Jun 1813 - From what ship or whence received: Batteaux - Exchanged, discharged, died, or escape: Discharged - Time when: 31 Oct 1813 - Whither, and by what order, or number or re-entry: Malabar Transport

Phillips, Joseph   Prisoner 1825. Rank: Private - By what ship or how taken: Troops - Time when: 17 Sep 1814 - Place where: Fort Erie - Of what ship or corps: Land forces - Whether man of war, privateer or merchant vessel: Taken on shore - Time when received into custody: 1 Nov 1814 - From what ship or whence received: Montreal - Exchanged, discharged, died, or escape: Discharged - Time when: 8 Nov 1814 - Whither, and by what order, or number or re-entry: S. George No. 575 for Halifax by order of Sir George Provost

Phoenix, John   Prisoner 1004. Rank: Cabin Boy - By what ship or how taken: Earl Moria - Time when: 10 Aug 1813 - Place where: Lake Ontario - Of what ship or corps: Julia - Whether man of war, privateer or merchant vessel: Man of War - Time when received into custody: 5 Sep 1813 - From what ship or whence received: Steamboat - Exchanged, discharged, died, or escape: Discharged - Time when: 31 Oct 1813 - Whither, and by what order, or number or re-entry: Malabar Transport

Pichevin, Anthony   Prisoner 1437. Rank: Private - By what ship or how taken: Troops - Time when: 6 May 1814 - Place where: Oswago - Of what ship or corps: Land forces - Whether man of war, privateer or merchant vessel: Taken on shore - Time when received into custody: 12 Aug 1814 - From what ship or whence received: Royal Seaman No. 289 Transport - Exchanged, discharged, died, or escape: Discharged - Time when: 8 Oct 1814 - Whither, and by what order, or number or re-entry: Queen No. 415

Picket, Lester   Prisoner 1628. Rank: Private - By what ship or how taken: Troops - Time when: 6 Sep 1814 - Place where: Plattsburg - Of what ship or corps: Land forces - Whether man of war, privateer or merchant vessel: Taken on shore - Time when received into custody: 5 Oct 1814 - From what ship or whence received: Montreal - Exchanged, discharged, died, or escape: Discharged - Time when: 8 Oct 1814 - Whither, and by what order, or number or re-entry: H.M. Ship Ceylon

Pickle, Balhe   Prisoner 785. Rank: Private - By what ship or how taken: Troops - Time when: 26 Jun 1813 - Place where: Beaver Dam - Of what ship or corps: Land forces - Whether man of war, privateer or merchant vessel: Taken on shore - Time when received into custody: 7 Jul 1813 - From what ship or whence received: Steamboat - Exchanged, discharged, died, or escape: Discharged - Time when: 10 Aug 1813 - Whither, and by what order, or number or re-entry: HM Ship Malpomena

Pier, Henry   Prisoner 1857. Rank: Private - By what ship or how taken: Troops - Time when: 17 Sep 1814 - Place where: Fort Erie - Of what ship or corps: Land forces - Whether man of war, privateer or merchant vessel: Taken on shore - Time when received into custody: 1 Nov 1814 - From what ship or whence received: Montreal - Exchanged, discharged, died, or escape: Discharged - Time when: 8 Nov 1814 - Whither, and by what order, or number or re-entry: S. George No. 575 for Halifax

Pierce, Henry   Prisoner 1926. Rank: Private - By what ship or how taken: Troops - Time when: 17 Sep 1814 - Place where: Fort Erie - Of what ship or corps: Land forces - Whether man of war, privateer or merchant vessel: Taken on shore - Time when received into custody: 1 Nov 1814 - From what ship or whence received: Montreal - Exchanged, discharged, died, or escape: Discharged - Time when: 14 Nov 1814 - Whither, and by what order, or number or re-entry: Soverign No. 628 for Halifax

Pierce, Thomas   Prisoner 1219. Rank: Private - By what ship or how taken: Troops - Time when: 19 Dec 1813 - Place where: Fort Niagara - Of what ship or corps: Land forces - Whether man of war, privateer or merchant vessel: Taken on shore - Time when received into custody: 29 Jan 1814 - From what ship or whence received: Montreal by land carriage - Exchanged, discharged, died, or escape: Discharged - Time when: 4 May 1814 - Whither, and by what order, or number or re-entry: United States

Pitcher, Jacob   Prisoner 897. Rank: Private - By what ship or how taken: Troops - Time when: 26 Jun 1813 - Place where: Beaver Dam - Of what ship or corps: Land forces - Whether man of war, privateer or merchant vessel: Taken on shore - Time when received into custody: 7 Jul 1813 - From what ship or whence received: Steamboat - Exchanged, discharged, died, or escape: Discharged - Time when: 10 Aug 1813 - Whither, and by what order, or number or re-entry: HM Ship Malpomena

Pitcher, Jacob   Prisoner 1858. Rank: Private - By what ship or how taken: Troops - Time when: 17 Sep 1814 - Place where: Fort Erie - Of what ship or corps: Land forces - Whether man of war, privateer or merchant vessel: Taken on shore - Time when received into custody: 1 Nov 1814 - From what ship or whence received: Montreal - Exchanged, discharged, died, or escape: Discharged - Time when: 8 Nov 1814 - Whither, and by what order, or number or re-entry: S. George No. 575 for Halifax

Plainloir, John   Prisoner 196. Rank: Private - By what ship or how taken: Boats & Troops - Time when: 3 Jun 1813 - Place where: Lake Champlain - Of what ship or corps: Growler - Whether man of war, privateer or merchant vessel: Man of War - Time when received into custody: 9 Jun 1813 - From what ship or whence received: Batteaux - Exchanged, discharged, died, or escape: Died - Time when: 14 Aug 1813 - Whither, and by what order, or number or re-entry:

Plants, Edward T.   Prisoner 302. Rank: Private - By what ship or how taken: Boats & Troops - Time when: 6 Jun 1813 - Place where: Stoney Point - Of what ship or corps: Land forces - Whether man of war, privateer or merchant vessel: Taken on shore - Time when received into custody: 28 Jun 1813 - From what ship or whence received: Quebec of Quebec - Exchanged, discharged, died, or escape: Discharged - Time when: 31 Oct 1813 - Whither, and by what order, or number or re-entry: Malabar Transport

Platenburgh, Jacob   Prisoner 1078. Rank: Private - By what ship or how taken: Troops - Time when: 24 Aug 1813 - Place where: Fort George - Of what ship or corps: Land forces - Whether man of war, privateer or merchant vessel: Taken on shore - Time when received into custody: 10 Oct 1813 - From what ship or whence received: Steamboat - Exchanged, discharged, died, or escape: Discharged - Time when: 31 Oct 1813 - Whither, and by what order, or number or re-entry: Malabar Transport

Plott, John   Prisoner 1087. Rank: Private - By what ship or how taken: Troops - Time when: 24 Aug 1813 - Place where: Fort George - Of what ship or corps: Land forces - Whether man of war, privateer or merchant vessel: Taken on shore - Time when received into custody: 10 Oct 1813 - From what ship or whence received: Steamboat - Exchanged, discharged, died, or escape: Discharged - Time when: 31 Oct 1813 - Whither, and by what order, or number or re-entry: Malabar Transport

Plumer, Isaac   Prisoner 207. Rank: Private - By what ship or how taken: Boats & Troops - Time when: 3 Jun 1813 - Place where: Lake Champlain - Of what ship or corps: Growler - Whether man of war, privateer or merchant vessel: Man of War - Time when received into custody: 9 Jun 1813 - From what ship or whence received: Batteaux - Exchanged, discharged, died, or escape: Discharged - Time when: 31 Oct 1813 - Whither, and by what order, or number or re-entry: Malabar Transport

Poff, Peter   Prisoner 1217. Rank: Private - By what ship or how taken: Troops - Time when: 19 Dec 1813 - Place where: Fort Niagara - Of what ship or corps: Land forces - Whether man of war, privateer or merchant vessel: Taken on shore - Time when received into custody: 29 Jan 1814 - From what ship or whence received: Montreal by land carriage - Exchanged, discharged, died, or escape: Discharged - Time when: 27 Feb 1814 - Whither, and by what order, or number or re-entry: Volunteered for New Brunswick Fencibles

Pollard, Martin   Prisoner 540. Rank: Private - By what ship or how taken: Troops - Time when: 24 Jun 1813 - Place where: Beaver Dam - Of what ship or corps: Land forces - Whether man of war, privateer or merchant vessel: Taken on shore - Time when received into custody: 13 Jul 1813 - From what ship or whence received: Steamboat - Exchanged, discharged, died, or escape: Discharged - Time when: 10 Aug 1813 - Whither, and by what order, or number or re-entry: HM Ship Regulius by order of Sir George Provost

Potts, Jeremiah   Prisoner 1388. Rank: Private - By what ship or how taken: Troops - Time when: 19 Dec 1813 - Place where:

Fort Niagara - Of what ship or corps: Land forces - Whether man of war, privateer or merchant vessel: Taken on shore - Time when received into custody: 29 Jan 1814 - From what ship or whence received: Montreal by land carriage - Exchanged, discharged, died, or escape: Discharged - Time when: 4 May 1814 - Whither, and by what order, or number or re-entry: United States

Poulston, J.   Prisoner 1576. Rank: Seaman - By what ship or how taken: Gun Boats - Time when: 12 Aug 1814 - Place where: Fort Erie - Of what ship or corps: Somers - Whether man of war, privateer or merchant vessel: Man of War - Time when received into custody: 5 Oct 1814 - From what ship or whence received: Montreal - Exchanged, discharged, died, or escape: Discharged - Time when: 10 Nov 1814 - Whither, and by what order, or number or re-entry: Freedom No. 582

Powell, Puley   Prisoner 1528. Rank: Private - By what ship or how taken: Troops - Time when: 25 Jul 1814 - Place where: Lundy's Lane - Of what ship or corps: Land forces - Whether man of war, privateer or merchant vessel: Taken on shore - Time when received into custody: 30 Aug 1814 - From what ship or whence received: Lady Delaval Schooner 578 - Exchanged, discharged, died, or escape: Discharged - Time when: 8 Nov 1814 - Whither, and by what order, or number or re-entry: George No. 575 for Halifax by orders of Sir George Provost

Powers, Joseph   Prisoner 476. Rank: Private - By what ship or how taken: Troops - Time when: 24 Jun 1813 - Place where: Beaver Dam - Of what ship or corps: Land forces - Whether man of war, privateer or merchant vessel: Taken on shore - Time when received into custody: 7 Jul 1813 - From what ship or whence received: Steamboat - Exchanged, discharged, died, or escape: Discharged - Time when: 10 Aug 1813 - Whither, and by what order, or number or re-entry: HM Ship Regulius by order of Sir George Provost

Powers, William   Prisoner 1901. Rank: Private - By what ship or how taken: Troops - Time when: 17 Sep 1814 - Place where: Fort Erie - Of what ship or corps: Land forces - Whether man of war, privateer or merchant vessel: Taken on shore - Time when received into custody: 1 Nov 1814 - From what ship or whence received: Montreal - Exchanged, discharged, died, or escape: Discharged - Time when: 8 Nov 1814 - Whither, and by what order, or number or re-entry: S. George No. 575 for Halifax by order of Sir George Provost

Pratt, Charles   Prisoner 226. Rank: Private - By what ship or how taken: Boats & Troops - Time when: 3 Jun 1813 - Place where: Lake Champlain - Of what ship or corps: Eagle - Whether man of war, privateer or merchant vessel: Man of War - Time when received into custody: 9 Jun 1813 - From what ship or whence received: Batteaux - Exchanged, discharged, died, or escape: Discharged - Time when: 31 Oct 1813 - Whither, and by what order, or number or re-entry: Malabar Transport

Pratt, Nathaniel   Prisoner 117. Rank: Private - By what ship or how taken: Boats & Troops - Time when: 28 May 1813 - Place where: Stoney Point, Henderson Harbor - Of what ship or corps: Land forces - Whether man of war, privateer or merchant vessel: Taken on shore - Time when received into custody: 8 Jun 1813 - From what ship or whence received: Batteaux - Exchanged, discharged, died, or escape: Died - Time when: 23 Jul 1813 - Whither, and by what order, or number or re-entry: Dysentery

Pratt, Walter   Prisoner 220. Rank: Private - By what ship or how taken: Boats & Troops - Time when: 3 Jun 1813 - Place where: Lake Champlain - Of what ship or corps: Eagle - Whether man of war, privateer or merchant vessel: Man of War - Time when received into custody: 9 Jun 1813 - From what ship or whence received: Batteaux - Exchanged, discharged, died, or escape: Died - Time when: 15 Sep 1813 - Whither, and by what order, or number or re-entry: Typhus Fever

Prentice, James   Prisoner 1237. Rank: Private - By what ship or how taken: Troops - Time when: 19 Dec 1813 - Place where: Fort Niagara - Of what ship or corps: Land forces - Whether man of war, privateer or merchant vessel: Taken on shore - Time when received into custody: 29 Jan 1814 - From what ship or whence received: Montreal by land carriage - Exchanged, discharged, died, or escape: Discharged - Time when: 27 Feb 1814 - Whither, and by what order, or number or re-entry: Volunteered for New Brunswick Fencibles

Preston, Ormond   Prisoner 880. Rank: Private - By what ship or how taken: Troops - Time when: 26 Jun 1813 - Place where: Beaver Dam - Of what ship or corps: Land forces - Whether man of war, privateer or merchant vessel: Taken on shore - Time when received into custody: 7 Jul 1813 - From what ship or whence received: Steamboat - Exchanged, discharged, died, or escape: Discharged - Time when: 10 Aug 1813 - Whither, and by what order, or number or re-entry: HM Ship Malpomena

Preutts, Gabriel   Prisoner 1414. Rank: Private - By what ship or how taken: Troops - Time when: 19 Dec 1813 - Place where: Fort Niagara - Of what ship or corps: Land forces - Whether man of war, privateer or merchant vessel: Taken on shore - Time when received into custody: 29 Jan 1814 - From what ship or whence received: Montreal by land carriage - Exchanged, discharged, died, or escape: Discharged - Time when: 4 May 1814 - Whither, and by what order, or

American Prisoners of War held at Quebec during the War of 1812

number or re-entry: United States

Price, George   Prisoner 652. Rank: Private - By what ship or how taken: Troops - Time when: 24 Jun 1813 - Place where: Stoney Point - Of what ship or corps: Land forces - Whether man of war, privateer or merchant vessel: Taken on shore - Time when received into custody: 7 Jul 1813 - From what ship or whence received: Steamboat - Exchanged, discharged, died, or escape: Discharged - Time when: 10 Aug 1813 - Whither, and by what order, or number or re-entry: HM Ship Regulius by order of Sir George Provost

Price, Job   Prisoner 656. Rank: Private - By what ship or how taken: Troops - Time when: 24 Jun 1813 - Place where: Stoney Point - Of what ship or corps: Land forces - Whether man of war, privateer or merchant vessel: Taken on shore - Time when received into custody: 7 Jul 1813 - From what ship or whence received: Steamboat - Exchanged, discharged, died, or escape: Discharged - Time when: 10 Aug 1813 - Whither, and by what order, or number or re-entry: HM Ship Regulius by order of Sir George Provost

Price, Meritt   Prisoner 509. Rank: Private - By what ship or how taken: Troops - Time when: 24 Jun 1813 - Place where: Beaver Dam - Of what ship or corps: Land forces - Whether man of war, privateer or merchant vessel: Taken on shore - Time when received into custody: 7 Jul 1813 - From what ship or whence received: Steamboat - Exchanged, discharged, died, or escape: Discharged - Time when: 10 Aug 1813 - Whither, and by what order, or number or re-entry: HM Ship Regulius by order of Sir George Provost

Price, Robert   Prisoner 319. Rank: Private - By what ship or how taken: Boats & Troops - Time when: 6 Jun 1813 - Place where: Stoney Point - Of what ship or corps: Land forces - Whether man of war, privateer or merchant vessel: Taken on shore - Time when received into custody: 28 Jun 1813 - From what ship or whence received: Quebec of Quebec - Exchanged, discharged, died, or escape: Discharged - Time when: 31 Oct 1813 - Whither, and by what order, or number or re-entry: Malabar Transport

Price, William   Prisoner 112. Rank: Sergeant - By what ship or how taken: Boats & Troops - Time when: 28 May 1813 - Place where: Stoney Point, Henderson Harbor - Of what ship or corps: Land forces - Whether man of war, privateer or merchant vessel: Taken on shore - Time when received into custody: 8 Jun 1813 - From what ship or whence received: Batteaux - Exchanged, discharged, died, or escape: Discharged - Time when: 8 Oct 1813 - Whither, and by what order, or number or re-entry: H.M. Ship Ceylon

Prince, John   Prisoner 605. Rank: Private - By what ship or how taken: Troops - Time when: 26 Jun 1813 - Place where: Stoney Point - Of what ship or corps: Land forces - Whether man of war, privateer or merchant vessel: Taken on shore - Time when received into custody: 7 Jul 1813 - From what ship or whence received: Steamboat - Exchanged, discharged, died, or escape: Discharged - Time when: 31 Oct 1813 - Whither, and by what order, or number or re-entry: Malabar Transport

Prouth, Jacob   Prisoner 172. Rank: Able seaman - By what ship or how taken: Boats & Troops - Time when: 3 Jun 1813 - Place where: Lake Champlain - Of what ship or corps: Growler - Whether man of war, privateer or merchant vessel: Man of War - Time when received into custody: 9 Jun 1813 - From what ship or whence received: Batteaux - Exchanged, discharged, died, or escape: Discharged - Time when: 10 Oct 1813 - Whither, and by what order, or number or re-entry: Orlando Transport

Pudehour, Conduit   Prisoner 971. Rank: Private - By what ship or how taken: Troops - Time when: 5 Jul 1813 - Place where: Fort Schisher - Of what ship or corps: Land forces - Whether man of war, privateer or merchant vessel: Taken on shore - Time when received into custody: 5 Sep 1813 - From what ship or whence received: Steamboat - Exchanged, discharged, died, or escape: Discharged - Time when: 31 Oct 1813 - Whither, and by what order, or number or re-entry: Malabar Transport

Purse, John   Prisoner 1461. Rank: Private - By what ship or how taken: Troops - Time when: 6 May 1814 - Place where: Oswago - Of what ship or corps: Land forces - Whether man of war, privateer or merchant vessel: Taken on shore - Time when received into custody: 12 Aug 1814 - From what ship or whence received: Royal Seaman No. 289 Transport - Exchanged, discharged, died, or escape: Discharged - Time when: 8 Oct 1814 - Whither, and by what order, or number or re-entry: Queen No. 415

Purse, William   Prisoner 815. Rank: Private - By what ship or how taken: Troops - Time when: 26 Jun 1813 - Place where: Beaver Dam - Of what ship or corps: Land forces - Whether man of war, privateer or merchant vessel: Taken on shore - Time when received into custody: 7 Jul 1813 - From what ship or whence received: Steamboat - Exchanged, discharged, died, or escape: Discharged - Time when: 10 Aug 1813 - Whither, and by what order, or number or re-entry: HM Ship Malpomena

American Prisoners of War held at Quebec during the War of 1812

Quick, Jacob   Prisoner 300. Rank: Sergeant - By what ship or how taken: Boats & Troops - Time when: 6 Jun 1813 - Place where: Stoney Point - Of what ship or corps: Land forces - Whether man of war, privateer or merchant vessel: Taken on shore - Time when received into custody: 28 Jun 1813 - From what ship or whence received: Quebec of Quebec - Exchanged, discharged, died, or escape: Discharged - Time when: 22 Aug 1813 - Whither, and by what order, or number or re-entry: Rotta Transport

Quin, Patrick   Prisoner 1292. Rank: Private - By what ship or how taken: Troops - Time when: 19 Dec 1813 - Place where: Fort Niagara - Of what ship or corps: Land forces - Whether man of war, privateer or merchant vessel: Taken on shore - Time when received into custody: 29 Jan 1814 - From what ship or whence received: Montreal by land carriage - Exchanged, discharged, died, or escape: Discharged - Time when: 22 Feb 1814 - Whither, and by what order, or number or re-entry: Volunteered for New Brunswick Fencibles

Quonilrouly, Henry   Prisoner 479. Rank: Private - By what ship or how taken: Troops - Time when: 24 Jun 1813 - Place where: Beaver Dam - Of what ship or corps: Land forces - Whether man of war, privateer or merchant vessel: Taken on shore - Time when received into custody: 7 Jul 1813 - From what ship or whence received: Steamboat - Exchanged, discharged, died, or escape: Discharged - Time when: 10 Aug 1813 - Whither, and by what order, or number or re-entry: HM Ship Regulius by order of Sir George Provost

Ramsey, N.   Prisoner 1657. Rank: Citizen - By what ship or how taken: Troops - Time when: 20 Jul 1814 - Place where: Queenstown - Of what ship or corps: Land forces - Whether man of war, privateer or merchant vessel: Taken on shore - Time when received into custody: 5 Oct 1814 - From what ship or whence received: Montreal - Exchanged, discharged, died, or escape: Discharged - Time when: 8 Oct 1814 - Whither, and by what order, or number or re-entry: H.M. Ship Ceylon

Rand, D.   Prisoner 1546. Rank: Private - By what ship or how taken: Troops - Time when: 25 Jul 1814 - Place where: Lundy's Lane - Of what ship or corps: Land forces - Whether man of war, privateer or merchant vessel: Taken on shore - Time when received into custody: 30 Aug 1814 - From what ship or whence received: Lady Delaval Schooner 578 - Exchanged, discharged, died, or escape: Discharged - Time when: 8 Oct 1814 - Whither, and by what order, or number or re-entry: Queen No. 415

Randall, Greif   Prisoner 1382. Rank: Private - By what ship or how taken: Troops - Time when: 19 Dec 1813 - Place where: Fort Niagara - Of what ship or corps: Land forces - Whether man of war, privateer or merchant vessel: Taken on shore - Time when received into custody: 29 Jan 1814 - From what ship or whence received: Montreal by land carriage - Exchanged, discharged, died, or escape: Discharged - Time when: 4 May 1814 - Whither, and by what order, or number or re-entry: United States

Randall, Isaac   Prisoner 1905. Rank: Private - By what ship or how taken: Troops - Time when: 17 Sep 1814 - Place where: Fort Erie - Of what ship or corps: Land forces - Whether man of war, privateer or merchant vessel: Taken on shore - Time when received into custody: 1 Nov 1814 - From what ship or whence received: Montreal - Exchanged, discharged, died, or escape: Discharged - Time when: 8 Nov 1814 - Whither, and by what order, or number or re-entry: S. George No. 575 for Halifax by order of Sir George Provost

Randall, Joseph   Prisoner 1442. Rank: Private - By what ship or how taken: Troops - Time when: 6 May 1814 - Place where: Oswago - Of what ship or corps: Land forces - Whether man of war, privateer or merchant vessel: Taken on shore - Time when received into custody: 12 Aug 1814 - From what ship or whence received: Royal Seaman No. 289 Transport - Exchanged, discharged, died, or escape: Discharged - Time when: 8 Oct 1814 - Whither, and by what order, or number or re-entry: Queen No. 415

Randall, Thomas   Prisoner 950. Rank: Lieutenant - By what ship or how taken: Troops - Time when: 26 Jun 1813 - Place where: Beaver Dam - Of what ship or corps: Land forces - Whether man of war, privateer or merchant vessel: Taken on shore - Time when received into custody: 21 Jul 1813 - From what ship or whence received: Steamboat - Exchanged, discharged, died, or escape: Discharged - Time when: 4 May 1814 - Whither, and by what order, or number or re-entry: United States

Ranger, Benjamin   Prisoner 1686. Rank: Private - By what ship or how taken: Troops - Time when: 12 Aug 1814 - Place where: Fort Erie - Of what ship or corps: Land forces - Whether man of war, privateer or merchant vessel: Taken on shore - Time when received into custody: 23 Oct 1814 - From what ship or whence received: Montreal - Exchanged, discharged, died, or escape: Discharged - Time when: 8 Nov 1814 - Whither, and by what order, or number or re-entry: S. George No. 575 for Halifax

Ranney, Julias   Prisoner 1695. Rank: Corporal - By what ship or how taken: Troops - Time when: 4 Aug 1814 - Place where: Fort Erie - Of what ship or corps: Land forces - Whether man of war, privateer or merchant vessel: Taken on shore - Time when received into custody: 23 Oct 1814 - From what ship or whence received: Montreal - Exchanged, discharged, died, or escape: Discharged - Time when: 8 Nov 1814 - Whither, and by what order, or number or re-entry: S. George No. 575 for Halifax

Ransom, Owen   Prisoner 1108. Rank: Lieutenant - By what ship or how taken: Troops - Time when: 17 Oct 1813 - Place where: Red Mills - Of what ship or corps: Land forces - Whether man of war, privateer or merchant vessel: Taken on shore - Time when received into custody: 12 Oct 1813 - From what ship or whence received: Steamboat - Exchanged, discharged, died, or escape: - Time when: - Whither, and by what order, or number or re-entry:

Rathboun, Jeremiah   Prisoner 325. Rank: Private - By what ship or how taken: Boats & Troops - Time when: 6 Jun 1813 - Place where: Stoney Point - Of what ship or corps: Land forces - Whether man of war, privateer or merchant vessel: Taken on shore - Time when received into custody: 28 Jun 1813 - From what ship or whence received: Quebec of Quebec - Exchanged, discharged, died, or escape: Discharged - Time when: 31 Oct 1813 - Whither, and by what order, or number or re-entry: Malabar Transport

Rathburn, Jeremiah   Prisoner 1844. Rank: Private - By what ship or how taken: Troops - Time when: 17 Sep 1814 - Place where: Fort Erie - Of what ship or corps: Land forces - Whether man of war, privateer or merchant vessel: Taken on shore - Time when received into custody: 1 Nov 1814 - From what ship or whence received: Montreal - Exchanged, discharged, died, or escape: Discharged - Time when: 8 Nov 1814 - Whither, and by what order, or number or re-entry: S. George No. 575 for Halifax by order of Sir George Provost

Ray, George   Prisoner 1801. Rank: Private - By what ship or how taken: Troops - Time when: 17 Sep 1814 - Place where: Fort Erie - Of what ship or corps: Land forces - Whether man of war, privateer or merchant vessel: Taken on shore - Time when received into custody: 1 Nov 1814 - From what ship or whence received: Montreal - Exchanged, discharged, died, or escape: Discharged - Time when: 8 Nov 1814 - Whither, and by what order, or number or re-entry: S. George No. 575 for Halifax by order of Sir George Provost

Ray, Robert   Prisoner 1439. Rank: Private - By what ship or how taken: Troops - Time when: 6 May 1814 - Place where: Oswago - Of what ship or corps: Land forces - Whether man of war, privateer or merchant vessel: Taken on shore - Time when received into custody: 12 Aug 1814 - From what ship or whence received: Royal Seaman No. 289 Transport - Exchanged, discharged, died, or escape: Discharged - Time when: 8 Oct 1814 - Whither, and by what order, or number or re-entry: Queen No. 415

Rea, Charles   Prisoner 1729. Rank: Seaman - By what ship or how taken: Gun Boats - Time when: 6 Sep 1814 - Place where: Lake Huron - Of what ship or corps: Scorpion - Whether man of war, privateer or merchant vessel: Man of War - Time when received into custody: 1 Nov 1814 - From what ship or whence received: Montreal - Exchanged, discharged, died, or escape: Discharged - Time when: 7 Nov 1814 - Whither, and by what order, or number or re-entry: Transport Freedom No. 582 by orders of his Excellency Sir George Provost

Rea , John   Prisoner 504. Rank: Private - By what ship or how taken: Troops - Time when: 24 Jun 1813 - Place where: Beaver Dam - Of what ship or corps: Land forces - Whether man of war, privateer or merchant vessel: Taken on shore - Time when received into custody: 7 Jul 1813 - From what ship or whence received: Steamboat - Exchanged, discharged, died, or escape: Discharged - Time when: 10 Aug 1813 - Whither, and by what order, or number or re-entry: HM Ship Regulius by order of Sir George Provost

Read, James   Prisoner 356. Rank: Private - By what ship or how taken: Troops - Time when: 6 Jun 1813 - Place where: Stoney Point - Of what ship or corps: Land forces - Whether man of war, privateer or merchant vessel: Taken on shore - Time when received into custody: 28 Jun 1813 - From what ship or whence received: Mary of Quebec - Exchanged, discharged, died, or escape: Discharged - Time when: 31 Oct 1813 - Whither, and by what order, or number or re-entry: Malabar Transport

Read, Joseph P.   Prisoner 200. Rank: Sergeant - By what ship or how taken: Boats & Troops - Time when: 3 Jun 1813 - Place where: Lake Champlain - Of what ship or corps: Growler - Whether man of war, privateer or merchant vessel: Man of War - Time when received into custody: 9 Jun 1813 - From what ship or whence received: Batteaux - Exchanged, discharged, died, or escape: Discharged - Time when: 31 Oct 1813 - Whither, and by what order, or number or re-entry: Malabar Transport

Read, Samuel R.   Prisoner 201. Rank: Corporal - By what ship or how taken: Boats & Troops - Time when: 3 Jun 1813 - Place where: Lake Champlain - Of what ship or corps: Growler - Whether man of war, privateer or merchant vessel: Man of War - Time when received into custody: 9 Jun 1813 - From what ship or whence received: Batteaux - Exchanged, discharged, died, or escape: Discharged - Time when: 8 Oct 1813 - Whither, and by what order, or number or re-entry: H.M. Ship Ceylon

Reade, Thomas   Prisoner 1730. Rank: Seaman - By what ship or how taken: Gun Boats - Time when: 6 Sep 1814 - Place

American Prisoners of War held at Quebec during the War of 1812

where: Lake Huron - Of what ship or corps: Scorpion - Whether man of war, privateer or merchant vessel: Man of War - Time when received into custody: 1 Nov 1814 - From what ship or whence received: Montreal - Exchanged, discharged, died, or escape: Discharged - Time when: 7 Nov 1814 - Whither, and by what order, or number or re-entry: Transport Freedom No. 582 by orders of his Excellency Sir George Provost

Reagan, James   Prisoner 1964. Rank: Sergeant - By what ship or how taken: Troops - Time when: 19 Dec 1813 - Place where: Fort Niagara - Of what ship or corps: Land forces - Whether man of war, privateer or merchant vessel: Taken on shore - Time when received into custody: 11 Dec 1814 - From what ship or whence received: Montreal - Exchanged, discharged, died, or escape: Discharged - Time when: 13 Mar 1815 - Whither, and by what order, or number or re-entry: United States

Reardon, T.   Prisoner 1476. Rank: Private - By what ship or how taken: Troops - Time when: 15 Jul 1814 - Place where: St. Davids - Of what ship or corps: Land forces - Whether man of war, privateer or merchant vessel: Taken on shore - Time when received into custody: 12 Aug 1814 - From what ship or whence received: Royal Seaman No. 289 Transport - Exchanged, discharged, died, or escape: Discharged - Time when: 8 Oct 1814 - Whither, and by what order, or number or re-entry: Queen No. 415

Redfield, Anthony C.   Prisoner 1245. Rank: Private - By what ship or how taken: Troops - Time when: 19 Dec 1813 - Place where: Fort Niagara - Of what ship or corps: Land forces - Whether man of war, privateer or merchant vessel: Taken on shore - Time when received into custody: 29 Jan 1814 - From what ship or whence received: Montreal by land carriage - Exchanged, discharged, died, or escape: Discharged - Time when: 27 Feb 1814 - Whither, and by what order, or number or re-entry: Volunteered for New Brunswick Fencibles

Redman, Martin   Prisoner 467. Rank: Private - By what ship or how taken: Troops - Time when: 24 Jun 1813 - Place where: Beaver Dam - Of what ship or corps: Malabar & Hydia - Whether man of war, privateer or merchant vessel: Taken on shore - Time when received into custody: 7 Jul 1813 - From what ship or whence received: Steamboat - Exchanged, discharged, died, or escape: Discharged - Time when: 10 Aug 1813 - Whither, and by what order, or number or re-entry: HM Ship Regulius by order of Sir George Provost

Reed, C. W.   Prisoner 1513. Rank: Sergeant Major - By what ship or how taken: Troops - Time when: 25 Jul 1814 - Place where: Lundy's Lane - Of what ship or corps: Land forces - Whether man of war, privateer or merchant vessel: Taken on shore - Time when received into custody: 30 Aug 1814 - From what ship or whence received: Lady Delaval Schooner 578 - Exchanged, discharged, died, or escape: Discharged - Time when: 8 Oct 1814 - Whither, and by what order, or number or re-entry: Queen No. 415

Reed, Isaac   Prisoner 43. Rank: Private - By what ship or how taken: Boats & Troops - Time when: 28 May 1813 - Place where: Stoney Point, Henderson Harbor - Of what ship or corps: Land forces - Whether man of war, privateer or merchant vessel: Taken on shore - Time when received into custody: 8 Jun 1813 - From what ship or whence received: Batteaux - Exchanged, discharged, died, or escape: Died - Time when: 4 Aug 1813 - Whither, and by what order, or number or re-entry:

Reed, James   Prisoner 1551. Rank: Private - By what ship or how taken: Troops - Time when: 25 Jul 1814 - Place where: Lundy's Lane - Of what ship or corps: Land forces - Whether man of war, privateer or merchant vessel: Taken on shore - Time when received into custody: 30 Aug 1814 - From what ship or whence received: Lady Delaval Schooner 578 - Exchanged, discharged, died, or escape: Discharged - Time when: 8 Oct 1814 - Whither, and by what order, or number or re-entry: Queen No. 415

Reed, William   Prisoner 1011. Rank: Seaman - By what ship or how taken: Earl Moria - Time when: 10 Aug 1813 - Place where: Lake Ontario - Of what ship or corps: Julia - Whether man of war, privateer or merchant vessel: Man of War - Time when received into custody: 5 Sep 1813 - From what ship or whence received: Steamboat - Exchanged, discharged, died, or escape: Discharged - Time when: 31 Oct 1813 - Whither, and by what order, or number or re-entry: Malabar Transport

Reese, Henry   Prisoner 953. Rank: Private - By what ship or how taken: Troops - Time when: 5 Jul 1813 - Place where: Fort Schisher - Of what ship or corps: Land forces - Whether man of war, privateer or merchant vessel: Taken on shore - Time when received into custody: 5 Sep 1813 - From what ship or whence received: Steamboat - Exchanged, discharged, died, or escape: Discharged - Time when: 10 Sep 1813 - Whither, and by what order, or number or re-entry: Volunteered for the army

Rehuhard, Thomas   Prisoner 291. Rank: Private - By what ship or how taken: Boats & Troops - Time when: 6 Jun 1813 - Place where: Stoney Point - Of what ship or corps: Land forces - Whether man of war, privateer or merchant vessel: Taken on shore - Time when received into custody: 28 Jun 1813 - From what ship or whence received: Quebec of Quebec - Exchanged, discharged, died, or escape: Discharged - Time when: 31 Oct 1813 - Whither, and by what order, or

American Prisoners of War held at Quebec during the War of 1812

number or re-entry: Malabar Transport

Reithner, J.   Prisoner 1488. Rank: Private - By what ship or how taken: Troops - Time when: 25 Jul 1814 - Place where: Lundy's Lane - Of what ship or corps: Land forces - Whether man of war, privateer or merchant vessel: Taken on shore - Time when received into custody: 12 Aug 1814 - From what ship or whence received: Royal Seaman No. 289 Transport - Exchanged, discharged, died, or escape: Discharged - Time when: 8 Oct 1814 - Whither, and by what order, or number or re-entry: Queen No. 415

Remington, Ira   Prisoner 1553. Rank: Private - By what ship or how taken: Troops - Time when: 25 Jul 1814 - Place where: Lundy's Lane - Of what ship or corps: Land forces - Whether man of war, privateer or merchant vessel: Taken on shore - Time when received into custody: 30 Aug 1814 - From what ship or whence received: Lady Delaval Schooner 578 - Exchanged, discharged, died, or escape: Discharged - Time when: 8 Oct 1814 - Whither, and by what order, or number or re-entry: Queen No. 415

Reynolds, Gilbert   Prisoner 1064. Rank: Private - By what ship or how taken: Troops - Time when: 24 Jun 1813 - Place where: Beaver Dam - Of what ship or corps: Land forces - Whether man of war, privateer or merchant vessel: Taken on shore - Time when received into custody: 5 Sep 1813 - From what ship or whence received: Steamboat - Exchanged, discharged, died, or escape: Discharged - Time when: 31 Oct 1813 - Whither, and by what order, or number or re-entry: Malabar Transport

Reynolds, John C.   Prisoner 264. Rank: Sergeant - By what ship or how taken: Boats & Troops - Time when: 24 Jun 1813 - Place where: Stoney Point - Of what ship or corps: Land forces - Whether man of war, privateer or merchant vessel: Taken on shore - Time when received into custody: 24 Jun 1813 - From what ship or whence received: Steamboat - Exchanged, discharged, died, or escape: Discharged - Time when: 26 Feb 1814 - Whither, and by what order, or number or re-entry: Volunteered for New Brunswick Fencibles

Reynolds, William   Prisoner 1389. Rank: Private - By what ship or how taken: Troops - Time when: 19 Dec 1813 - Place where: Fort Niagara - Of what ship or corps: Land forces - Whether man of war, privateer or merchant vessel: Taken on shore - Time when received into custody: 29 Jan 1814 - From what ship or whence received: Montreal by land carriage - Exchanged, discharged, died, or escape: Discharged - Time when: 4 May 1814 - Whither, and by what order, or number or re-entry: United States

Rhodes, Henry   Prisoner 1894. Rank: Private - By what ship or how taken: Troops - Time when: 17 Sep 1814 - Place where: Fort Erie - Of what ship or corps: Land forces - Whether man of war, privateer or merchant vessel: Taken on shore - Time when received into custody: 1 Nov 1814 - From what ship or whence received: Montreal - Exchanged, discharged, died, or escape: Discharged - Time when: 8 Nov 1814 - Whither, and by what order, or number or re-entry: S. George No. 575 for Halifax by order of Sir George Provost

Rice, John   Prisoner 1269. Rank: Privateer - By what ship or how taken: Troops - Time when: 19 Dec 1813 - Place where: Fort Niagara - Of what ship or corps: Land forces - Whether man of war, privateer or merchant vessel: Taken on shore - Time when received into custody: 29 Jan 1814 - From what ship or whence received: Montreal by land carriage - Exchanged, discharged, died, or escape: Discharged - Time when: 4 May 1814 - Whither, and by what order, or number or re-entry: United States

Rice, Nathaniel   Prisoner 1861. Rank: Private - By what ship or how taken: Troops - Time when: 17 Sep 1814 - Place where: Fort Erie - Of what ship or corps: Land forces - Whether man of war, privateer or merchant vessel: Taken on shore - Time when received into custody: 1 Nov 1814 - From what ship or whence received: Montreal - Exchanged, discharged, died, or escape: Discharged - Time when: 8 Nov 1814 - Whither, and by what order, or number or re-entry: S. George No. 575 for Halifax

Rice, Nathaniel   Prisoner 239. Rank: Private - By what ship or how taken: Boats & Troops - Time when: 3 Jun 1813 - Place where: Lake Champlain - Of what ship or corps: Eagle - Whether man of war, privateer or merchant vessel: Man of War - Time when received into custody: 9 Jun 1813 - From what ship or whence received: Batteaux - Exchanged, discharged, died, or escape: Discharged - Time when: 31 Oct 1813 - Whither, and by what order, or number or re-entry: Malabar Transport

Rice, Samuel   Prisoner 190. Rank: Private - By what ship or how taken: Boats & Troops - Time when: 3 Jun 1813 - Place where: Lake Champlain - Of what ship or corps: Growler - Whether man of war, privateer or merchant vessel: Man of War - Time when received into custody: 9 Jun 1813 - From what ship or whence received: Batteaux - Exchanged, discharged, died, or escape: Discharged - Time when: 31 Oct 1813 - Whither, and by what order, or number or re-entry: Malabar Transport

American Prisoners of War held at Quebec during the War of 1812

Richards, F. Prisoner 1542. Rank: Private - By what ship or how taken: Troops - Time when: 25 Jul 1814 - Place where: Lundy's Lane - Of what ship or corps: Land forces - Whether man of war, privateer or merchant vessel: Taken on shore - Time when received into custody: 30 Aug 1814 - From what ship or whence received: Lady Delaval Schooner 578 - Exchanged, discharged, died, or escape: Discharged - Time when: 8 Oct 1814 - Whither, and by what order, or number or re-entry: Queen No. 415

Richards, John Prisoner 926. Rank: Private - By what ship or how taken: Troops - Time when: 26 Jun 1813 - Place where: Beaver Dam - Of what ship or corps: Land forces - Whether man of war, privateer or merchant vessel: Taken on shore - Time when received into custody: 21 Jul 1813 - From what ship or whence received: Steamboat - Exchanged, discharged, died, or escape: Discharged - Time when: 10 Aug 1813 - Whither, and by what order, or number or re-entry: HM Ship Malpomena

Richards, Stephem Prisoner 1070. Rank: Steward - By what ship or how taken: Troops - Time when: 24 Aug 1813 - Place where: Fort George - Of what ship or corps: Land forces - Whether man of war, privateer or merchant vessel: Taken on shore - Time when received into custody: 10 Oct 1813 - From what ship or whence received: Steamboat - Exchanged, discharged, died, or escape: Discharged - Time when: 31 Oct 1813 - Whither, and by what order, or number or re-entry: Malabar Transport

Richards, Stephen Prisoner 161. Rank: Able seaman - By what ship or how taken: Boats & Troops - Time when: 3 Jun 1813 - Place where: Lake Champlain - Of what ship or corps: Eagle - Whether man of war, privateer or merchant vessel: Man of War - Time when received into custody: 9 Jun 1813 - From what ship or whence received: Batteaux - Exchanged, discharged, died, or escape: Discharged - Time when: 10 Oct 1813 - Whither, and by what order, or number or re-entry: Jane Transport

Richardson, Jason Prisoner 1328. Rank: Sergeant - By what ship or how taken: Troops - Time when: 19 Dec 1813 - Place where: Fort Niagara - Of what ship or corps: Land forces - Whether man of war, privateer or merchant vessel: Taken on shore - Time when received into custody: 29 Jan 1814 - From what ship or whence received: Montreal by land carriage - Exchanged, discharged, died, or escape: Discharged - Time when: 4 May 1814 - Whither, and by what order, or number or re-entry: United States

Richardson, John Prisoner 1054. Rank: Private - By what ship or how taken: Lord Melvin - Time when: 10 Aug 1813 - Place where: Lake Ontario - Of what ship or corps: Growler - Whether man of war, privateer or merchant vessel: Man of War - Time when received into custody: 5 Sep 1813 - From what ship or whence received: Steamboat - Exchanged, discharged, died, or escape: Discharged - Time when: 31 Oct 1813 - Whither, and by what order, or number or re-entry: Malabar Transport

Richardson, Simeon Prisoner 236. Rank: Private - By what ship or how taken: Boats & Troops - Time when: 3 Jun 1813 - Place where: Lake Champlain - Of what ship or corps: Growler - Whether man of war, privateer or merchant vessel: Man of War - Time when received into custody: 9 Jun 1813 - From what ship or whence received: Batteaux - Exchanged, discharged, died, or escape: Discharged - Time when: 4 May 1814 - Whither, and by what order, or number or re-entry: United States

Richardson, William Prisoner 1280. Rank: Private - By what ship or how taken: Troops - Time when: 19 Dec 1813 - Place where: Fort Niagara - Of what ship or corps: Land forces - Whether man of war, privateer or merchant vessel: Taken on shore - Time when received into custody: 29 Jan 1814 - From what ship or whence received: Montreal by land carriage - Exchanged, discharged, died, or escape: Discharged - Time when: 4 May 1814 - Whither, and by what order, or number or re-entry: United States

Richie, Allen Prisoner 649. Rank: Private - By what ship or how taken: Troops - Time when: 24 Jun 1813 - Place where: Stoney Point - Of what ship or corps: Land forces - Whether man of war, privateer or merchant vessel: Taken on shore - Time when received into custody: 7 Jul 1813 - From what ship or whence received: Steamboat - Exchanged, discharged, died, or escape: Discharged - Time when: 10 Aug 1813 - Whither, and by what order, or number or re-entry: HM Ship Regulius by order of Sir George Provost

Ridden, John Prisoner 1675. Rank: Seaman - By what ship or how taken: Gun Boats - Time when: 25 Aug 1814 - Place where: Lake Ontario - Of what ship or corps: Taken on a gigg - Whether man of war, privateer or merchant vessel: Man of War - Time when received into custody: 23 Oct 1814 - From what ship or whence received: Montreal - Exchanged, discharged, died, or escape: Discharged - Time when: 7 Nov 1814 - Whither, and by what order, or number or re-entry: Transport Freedom No. 582 by orders of his Excellency Sir George Provost

Riddle, E. Prisoner 1531. Rank: Private - By what ship or how taken: Troops - Time when: 25 Jul 1814 - Place where: Lundy's Lane - Of what ship or corps: Land forces - Whether man of war, privateer or merchant vessel: Taken on shore - Time when received into custody: 30 Aug 1814 - From what ship or whence received: Lady Delaval Schooner 578 -

American Prisoners of War held at Quebec during the War of 1812

Exchanged, discharged, died, or escape: Discharged - Time when: 8 Oct 1814 - Whither, and by what order, or number or re-entry: Queen No. 415

Riddle, Robert   Prisoner 826. Rank: Private - By what ship or how taken: Troops - Time when: 26 Jun 1813 - Place where: Beaver Dam - Of what ship or corps: Land forces - Whether man of war, privateer or merchant vessel: Taken on shore - Time when received into custody: 7 Jul 1813 - From what ship or whence received: Steamboat - Exchanged, discharged, died, or escape: Discharged - Time when: 10 Aug 1813 - Whither, and by what order, or number or re-entry: HM Ship Malpomena

Ridge, William   Prisoner 1408. Rank: Private - By what ship or how taken: Troops - Time when: 19 Dec 1813 - Place where: Fort Niagara - Of what ship or corps: Land forces - Whether man of war, privateer or merchant vessel: Taken on shore - Time when received into custody: 29 Jan 1814 - From what ship or whence received: Montreal by land carriage - Exchanged, discharged, died, or escape: Discharged - Time when: 4 May 1814 - Whither, and by what order, or number or re-entry: United States

Rigden, James   Prisoner 1199. Rank: Citizen - By what ship or how taken: - Time when: - Place where: - Of what ship or corps: - Whether man of war, privateer or merchant vessel: - Time when received into custody: 12 Dec 1813 - From what ship or whence received: Town Goal - Exchanged, discharged, died, or escape: Discharged - Time when: 1 Dec 1814 - Whither, and by what order, or number or re-entry: To Town Goal

Riggan, Labon   Prisoner 756. Rank: Private - By what ship or how taken: Troops - Time when: 26 Jun 1813 - Place where: Beaver Dam - Of what ship or corps: Land forces - Whether man of war, privateer or merchant vessel: Taken on shore - Time when received into custody: 7 Jul 1813 - From what ship or whence received: Steamboat - Exchanged, discharged, died, or escape: Discharged - Time when: 10 Aug 1813 - Whither, and by what order, or number or re-entry: HM Ship Malpomena

Riley, Pursey   Prisoner 1855. Rank: Private - By what ship or how taken: Troops - Time when: 17 Sep 1814 - Place where: Fort Erie - Of what ship or corps: Land forces - Whether man of war, privateer or merchant vessel: Taken on shore - Time when received into custody: 1 Nov 1814 - From what ship or whence received: Montreal - Exchanged, discharged, died, or escape: Discharged - Time when: 8 Nov 1814 - Whither, and by what order, or number or re-entry: S. George No. 575 for Halifax

Rilley, James   Prisoner 1002. Rank: Seaman - By what ship or how taken: Earl Moria - Time when: 10 Aug 1813 - Place where: Lake Ontario - Of what ship or corps: Julia - Whether man of war, privateer or merchant vessel: Man of War - Time when received into custody: 5 Sep 1813 - From what ship or whence received: Steamboat - Exchanged, discharged, died, or escape: Discharged - Time when: 18 Sep 1813 - Whither, and by what order, or number or re-entry: Regulius Transport

Rimsey, Joseph   Prisoner 563. Rank: Private - By what ship or how taken: Troops - Time when: 26 Jun 1813 - Place where: Beaver Dam - Of what ship or corps: Land forces - Whether man of war, privateer or merchant vessel: Taken on shore - Time when received into custody: 13 Jul 1813 - From what ship or whence received: Steamboat - Exchanged, discharged, died, or escape: Discharged - Time when: 10 Aug 1813 - Whither, and by what order, or number or re-entry: HM Ship Regulius by order of Sir George Provost

Rindle, Samuel   Prisoner 838. Rank: Corporal - By what ship or how taken: Troops - Time when: 26 Jun 1813 - Place where: Beaver Dam - Of what ship or corps: Land forces - Whether man of war, privateer or merchant vessel: Taken on shore - Time when received into custody: 7 Jul 1813 - From what ship or whence received: Steamboat - Exchanged, discharged, died, or escape: Discharged - Time when: 10 Aug 1813 - Whither, and by what order, or number or re-entry: HM Ship Malpomena

Rine, Joseph   Prisoner 1003. Rank: Seaman - By what ship or how taken: Earl Moria - Time when: 10 Aug 1813 - Place where: Lake Ontario - Of what ship or corps: Julia - Whether man of war, privateer or merchant vessel: Man of War - Time when received into custody: 5 Sep 1813 - From what ship or whence received: Steamboat - Exchanged, discharged, died, or escape: Discharged - Time when: 18 Sep 1813 - Whither, and by what order, or number or re-entry: Edward Allice Transport

Roach, Isaac   Prisoner 403. Rank: Captain - By what ship or how taken: Troops - Time when: 24 Jun 1813 - Place where: Beaver Dam - Of what ship or corps: Land forces - Whether man of war, privateer or merchant vessel: Taken on shore - Time when received into custody: 7 Jul 1813 - From what ship or whence received: Steamboat - Exchanged, discharged, died, or escape: Discharged - Time when: 13 Dec 1813 - Whither, and by what order, or number or re-entry: United States

Robb, James   Prisoner 1881. Rank: Private - By what ship or how taken: Troops - Time when: 17 Sep 1814 - Place where: Fort

American Prisoners of War held at Quebec during the War of 1812

Erie - Of what ship or corps: Land forces - Whether man of war, privateer or merchant vessel: Taken on shore - Time when received into custody: 1 Nov 1814 - From what ship or whence received: Montreal - Exchanged, discharged, died, or escape: Discharged - Time when: 8 Nov 1814 - Whither, and by what order, or number or re-entry: S. George No. 575 for Halifax by order of Sir George Provost

Roberts, Aaron   Prisoner 1399. Rank: Private - By what ship or how taken: Troops - Time when: 19 Dec 1813 - Place where: Fort Niagara - Of what ship or corps: Land forces - Whether man of war, privateer or merchant vessel: Taken on shore - Time when received into custody: 29 Jan 1814 - From what ship or whence received: Montreal by land carriage - Exchanged, discharged, died, or escape: Discharged - Time when: 4 May 1814 - Whither, and by what order, or number or re-entry: United States

Roberts, Henry   Prisoner 514. Rank: Private - By what ship or how taken: Troops - Time when: 24 Jun 1813 - Place where: Beaver Dam - Of what ship or corps: Land forces - Whether man of war, privateer or merchant vessel: Taken on shore - Time when received into custody: 7 Jul 1813 - From what ship or whence received: Steamboat - Exchanged, discharged, died, or escape: Discharged - Time when: 10 Aug 1813 - Whither, and by what order, or number or re-entry: HM Ship Regulius by order of Sir George Provost

Roberts, Joel   Prisoner 1025. Rank: Quartermaster - By what ship or how taken: Lord Melvin - Time when: 10 Aug 1813 - Place where: Lake Ontario - Of what ship or corps: Growler - Whether man of war, privateer or merchant vessel: Man of War - Time when received into custody: 5 Sep 1813 - From what ship or whence received: Steamboat - Exchanged, discharged, died, or escape: Discharged - Time when: 1 Nov 1813 - Whither, and by what order, or number or re-entry: The Hero for England

Roberts, John   Prisoner 1509. Rank: Captain - By what ship or how taken: Troops - Time when: 25 Jul 1814 - Place where: Lundy's Lane - Of what ship or corps: Land forces - Whether man of war, privateer or merchant vessel: Taken on shore - Time when received into custody: 25 Aug 1814 - From what ship or whence received: Steamboat - Exchanged, discharged, died, or escape: Discharged - Time when: 10 Nov 1814 - Whither, and by what order, or number or re-entry: Transport Stately No. 408 for Halifax

Roberts, William   Prisoner 721. Rank: Private - By what ship or how taken: Troops - Time when: 26 Jun 1813 - Place where: Beaver Dam - Of what ship or corps: Land forces - Whether man of war, privateer or merchant vessel: Taken on shore - Time when received into custody: 7 Jul 1813 - From what ship or whence received: Steamboat - Exchanged, discharged, died, or escape: Discharged - Time when: 10 Aug 1813 - Whither, and by what order, or number or re-entry: HM Ship Regulius by order of Sir George Provost

Robins, Toram   Prisoner 814. Rank: Private - By what ship or how taken: Troops - Time when: 26 Jun 1813 - Place where: Beaver Dam - Of what ship or corps: Land forces - Whether man of war, privateer or merchant vessel: Taken on shore - Time when received into custody: 7 Jul 1813 - From what ship or whence received: Steamboat - Exchanged, discharged, died, or escape: Discharged - Time when: 31 Oct 1813 - Whither, and by what order, or number or re-entry: Malabar Transport

Robinson, Daniel   Prisoner 682. Rank: Private - By what ship or how taken: Troops - Time when: 26 Jun 1813 - Place where: Beaver Dam - Of what ship or corps: Land forces - Whether man of war, privateer or merchant vessel: Taken on shore - Time when received into custody: 7 Jul 1813 - From what ship or whence received: Steamboat - Exchanged, discharged, died, or escape: Discharged - Time when: 10 Aug 1813 - Whither, and by what order, or number or re-entry: HM Ship Regulius by order of Sir George Provost

Robinson, James   Prisoner 1273. Rank: Privateer - By what ship or how taken: Troops - Time when: 19 Dec 1813 - Place where: Fort Niagara - Of what ship or corps: Land forces - Whether man of war, privateer or merchant vessel: Taken on shore - Time when received into custody: 29 Jan 1814 - From what ship or whence received: Montreal by land carriage - Exchanged, discharged, died, or escape: Discharged - Time when: 26 Feb 1814 - Whither, and by what order, or number or re-entry: Volunteered for New Brunswick Fencibles

Robinson, Nathan   Prisoner 387. Rank: Private - By what ship or how taken: Troops - Time when: 6 Jun 1813 - Place where: Stoney Point - Of what ship or corps: Land forces - Whether man of war, privateer or merchant vessel: Taken on shore - Time when received into custody: 28 Jun 1813 - From what ship or whence received: Mary of Quebec - Exchanged, discharged, died, or escape: Died - Time when: 29 Jul 1813 - Whither, and by what order, or number or re-entry: Dysentery

Robinson, Nicholas   Prisoner 947. Rank: Sergeant - By what ship or how taken: Troops - Time when: 26 Jun 1813 - Place where: Beaver Dam - Of what ship or corps: Land forces - Whether man of war, privateer or merchant vessel: Taken on shore - Time when received into custody: 21 Jul 1813 - From what ship or whence received: Steamboat - Exchanged, discharged, died, or escape: Discharged - Time when: 10 Aug 1813 - Whither, and by what order, or number or re-

American Prisoners of War held at Quebec during the War of 1812

entry: HM Ship Malpomena

Robinson, Nicholas N.   Prisoner 534. Rank: Lieutenant - By what ship or how taken: Troops - Time when: 24 Jun 1813 - Place where: Beaver Dam - Of what ship or corps: Land forces - Whether man of war, privateer or merchant vessel: Taken on shore - Time when received into custody: 13 Jul 1813 - From what ship or whence received: Steamboat - Exchanged, discharged, died, or escape: Discharged - Time when: 13 Dec 1813 - Whither, and by what order, or number or re-entry: HM Ship Regulius by order of Sir George Provost

Rockway, J.   Prisoner 1483. Rank: Private - By what ship or how taken: Troops - Time when: 6 May 1814 - Place where: Oswago - Of what ship or corps: Land forces - Whether man of war, privateer or merchant vessel: Taken on shore - Time when received into custody: 12 Aug 1814 - From what ship or whence received: Royal Seaman No. 289 Transport - Exchanged, discharged, died, or escape: Discharged - Time when: 8 Oct 1814 - Whither, and by what order, or number or re-entry: Queen No. 415

Roderick, John   Prisoner 1743. Rank: Seaman - By what ship or how taken: Gun Boats - Time when: 3 Sep 1814 - Place where: Lake Huron - Of what ship or corps: Tigress - Whether man of war, privateer or merchant vessel: Man of War - Time when received into custody: 1 Nov 1814 - From what ship or whence received: Montreal - Exchanged, discharged, died, or escape: Discharged - Time when: 7 Nov 1814 - Whither, and by what order, or number or re-entry: Transport Freedom No. 582 by orders of his Excellency Sir George Provost

Rogers, Clement F.   Prisoner 1569. Rank: Midshipman - By what ship or how taken: Gun Boats - Time when: 12 Aug 1814 - Place where: Fort Erie - Of what ship or corps: Somers - Whether man of war, privateer or merchant vessel: Man of War - Time when received into custody: 16 Sep 1814 - From what ship or whence received: Steamboat - Exchanged, discharged, died, or escape: Discharged - Time when: 10 Nov 1814 - Whither, and by what order, or number or re-entry: Lord Cartheart No. 161 for Halifax

Rogers, Robert   Prisoner 1330. Rank: Private - By what ship or how taken: Troops - Time when: 19 Dec 1813 - Place where: Fort Niagara - Of what ship or corps: Land forces - Whether man of war, privateer or merchant vessel: Taken on shore - Time when received into custody: 29 Jan 1814 - From what ship or whence received: Montreal by land carriage - Exchanged, discharged, died, or escape: Discharged - Time when: 4 May 1814 - Whither, and by what order, or number or re-entry: United States

Roles, Rezin   Prisoner 428. Rank: Private - By what ship or how taken: Troops - Time when: 24 Jun 1813 - Place where: Beaver Dam - Of what ship or corps: Land forces - Whether man of war, privateer or merchant vessel: Taken on shore - Time when received into custody: 7 Jul 1813 - From what ship or whence received: Steamboat - Exchanged, discharged, died, or escape: Discharged - Time when: 31 Oct 1813 - Whither, and by what order, or number or re-entry: Malabar Transport

Rollins, Thomas   Prisoner 630. Rank: Private - By what ship or how taken: Troops - Time when: 24 Jun 1813 - Place where: Stoney Point - Of what ship or corps: Land forces - Whether man of war, privateer or merchant vessel: Taken on shore - Time when received into custody: 7 Jul 1813 - From what ship or whence received: Steamboat - Exchanged, discharged, died, or escape: Discharged - Time when: 4 May 1814 - Whither, and by what order, or number or re-entry: United States

Romley, Eliza   Prisoner 240. Rank: Women - By what ship or how taken: Boats & Troops - Time when: 3 Jun 1813 - Place where: Lake Champlain - Of what ship or corps: Growler - Whether man of war, privateer or merchant vessel: Man of War - Time when received into custody: 9 Jun 1813 - From what ship or whence received: Batteaux - Exchanged, discharged, died, or escape: Discharged - Time when: 25 Jun 1813 - Whither, and by what order, or number or re-entry:

Roney, M.   Prisoner 1441. Rank: Private - By what ship or how taken: Troops - Time when: 6 May 1814 - Place where: Oswago - Of what ship or corps: Land forces - Whether man of war, privateer or merchant vessel: Taken on shore - Time when received into custody: 12 Aug 1814 - From what ship or whence received: Royal Seaman No. 289 Transport - Exchanged, discharged, died, or escape: Discharged - Time when: 8 Oct 1814 - Whither, and by what order, or number or re-entry: Queen No. 415

Root, A. L.   Prisoner 1783. Rank: Private - By what ship or how taken: Troops - Time when: 7 Sep 1814 - Place where: Fort Erie - Of what ship or corps: Land forces - Whether man of war, privateer or merchant vessel: Taken on shore - Time when received into custody: 1 Nov 1814 - From what ship or whence received: Montreal - Exchanged, discharged, died, or escape: Discharged - Time when: 8 Nov 1814 - Whither, and by what order, or number or re-entry: S. George No. 575 for Halifax by order of Sir George Provost

Root, John   Prisoner 429. Rank: Private - By what ship or how taken: Troops - Time when: 24 Jun 1813 - Place where: Beaver Dam - Of what ship or corps: Land forces - Whether man of war, privateer or merchant vessel: Taken on shore - Time when received into custody: 7 Jul 1813 - From what ship or whence received: Steamboat - Exchanged, discharged, died, or escape: Died - Time when: 23 Aug 1813 - Whither, and by what order, or number or re-entry:

Rose, Henry S.   Prisoner 921. Rank: Private - By what ship or how taken: Troops - Time when: 26 Jun 1813 - Place where: Beaver Dam - Of what ship or corps: Land forces - Whether man of war, privateer or merchant vessel: Taken on shore - Time when received into custody: 21 Jul 1813 - From what ship or whence received: Steamboat - Exchanged, discharged, died, or escape: Discharged - Time when: 10 Aug 1813 - Whither, and by what order, or number or re-entry: HM Ship Malpomena

Rose, John   Prisoner 518. Rank: Private - By what ship or how taken: Troops - Time when: 24 Jun 1813 - Place where: Beaver Dam - Of what ship or corps: Land forces - Whether man of war, privateer or merchant vessel: Taken on shore - Time when received into custody: 7 Jul 1813 - From what ship or whence received: Steamboat - Exchanged, discharged, died, or escape: Discharged - Time when: 10 Aug 1813 - Whither, and by what order, or number or re-entry: HM Ship Regulius by order of Sir George Provost

Rose, Jonathan   Prisoner 744. Rank: Private - By what ship or how taken: Troops - Time when: 26 Jun 1813 - Place where: Beaver Dam - Of what ship or corps: Land forces - Whether man of war, privateer or merchant vessel: Taken on shore - Time when received into custody: 7 Jul 1813 - From what ship or whence received: Steamboat - Exchanged, discharged, died, or escape: Discharged - Time when: 10 Aug 1813 - Whither, and by what order, or number or re-entry: HM Ship Regulius by order of Sir George Provost

Rose, Nathaniel   Prisoner 455. Rank: Private - By what ship or how taken: Troops - Time when: 24 Jun 1813 - Place where: Beaver Dam - Of what ship or corps: Malabar & Hydia - Whether man of war, privateer or merchant vessel: Taken on shore - Time when received into custody: 7 Jul 1813 - From what ship or whence received: Steamboat - Exchanged, discharged, died, or escape: Discharged - Time when: 10 Aug 1813 - Whither, and by what order, or number or re-entry: HM Ship Regulius by order of Sir George Provost

Roseman, E.   Prisoner 1496. Rank: Private - By what ship or how taken: Troops - Time when: 25 Jul 1814 - Place where: Niagara - Of what ship or corps: Land forces - Whether man of war, privateer or merchant vessel: Taken on shore - Time when received into custody: 19 Aug 1814 - From what ship or whence received: Triton No. 438 Transport - Exchanged, discharged, died, or escape: Discharged - Time when: 8 Oct 1814 - Whither, and by what order, or number or re-entry: Queen No. 415

Ross, Batman   Prisoner 1777. Rank: Private - By what ship or how taken: Troops - Time when: 7 Sep 1814 - Place where: Fort Erie - Of what ship or corps: Land forces - Whether man of war, privateer or merchant vessel: Taken on shore - Time when received into custody: 1 Nov 1814 - From what ship or whence received: Montreal - Exchanged, discharged, died, or escape: Discharged - Time when: 8 Nov 1814 - Whither, and by what order, or number or re-entry: S. George No. 575 for Halifax by order of Sir George Provost

Ross, David   Prisoner 622. Rank: Private - By what ship or how taken: Troops - Time when: 24 Jun 1813 - Place where: Stoney Point - Of what ship or corps: Land forces - Whether man of war, privateer or merchant vessel: Taken on shore - Time when received into custody: 7 Jul 1813 - From what ship or whence received: Steamboat - Exchanged, discharged, died, or escape: Discharged - Time when: 10 Aug 1813 - Whither, and by what order, or number or re-entry: HM Ship Regulius by order of Sir George Provost

Ross, Ely H.   Prisoner 1803. Rank: Private - By what ship or how taken: Troops - Time when: 17 Sep 1814 - Place where: Fort Erie - Of what ship or corps: Land forces - Whether man of war, privateer or merchant vessel: Taken on shore - Time when received into custody: 1 Nov 1814 - From what ship or whence received: Montreal - Exchanged, discharged, died, or escape: Discharged - Time when: 8 Nov 1814 - Whither, and by what order, or number or re-entry: S. George No. 575 for Halifax by order of Sir George Provost

Ross, Joseph N.   Prisoner 889. Rank: Private - By what ship or how taken: Troops - Time when: 26 Jun 1813 - Place where: Beaver Dam - Of what ship or corps: Land forces - Whether man of war, privateer or merchant vessel: Taken on shore - Time when received into custody: 7 Jul 1813 - From what ship or whence received: Steamboat - Exchanged, discharged, died, or escape: Discharged - Time when: 10 Aug 1813 - Whither, and by what order, or number or re-entry: HM Ship Malpomena

Rothworth, John   Prisoner 1693. Rank: Private - By what ship or how taken: Troops - Time when: 4 Aug 1814 - Place where: Fort Erie - Of what ship or corps: Land forces - Whether man of war, privateer or merchant vessel: Taken on shore - Time when received into custody: 23 Oct 1814 - From what ship or whence received: Montreal - Exchanged, discharged, died, or escape: Discharged - Time when: 8 Nov 1814 - Whither, and by what order, or number or re-entry: S. George No. 575 for Halifax

American Prisoners of War held at Quebec during the War of 1812

Round, Amos   Prisoner 37. Rank: Private - By what ship or how taken: Boats & Troops - Time when: 28 May 1813 - Place where: Stoney Point, Henderson Harbor - Of what ship or corps: Land forces - Whether man of war, privateer or merchant vessel: Taken on shore - Time when received into custody: 8 Jun 1813 - From what ship or whence received: Batteaux - Exchanged, discharged, died, or escape: Escaped - Time when: 6 Jul 1813 - Whither, and by what order, or number or re-entry:

Round, Rubin   Prisoner 495. Rank: Private - By what ship or how taken: Troops - Time when: 24 Jun 1813 - Place where: Beaver Dam - Of what ship or corps: Land forces - Whether man of war, privateer or merchant vessel: Taken on shore - Time when received into custody: 7 Jul 1813 - From what ship or whence received: Steamboat - Exchanged, discharged, died, or escape: Discharged - Time when: 10 Aug 1813 - Whither, and by what order, or number or re-entry: HM Ship Regulius by order of Sir George Provost

Roupough, Corneilus   Prisoner 372. Rank: Private - By what ship or how taken: Troops - Time when: 6 Jun 1813 - Place where: Stoney Point - Of what ship or corps: Land forces - Whether man of war, privateer or merchant vessel: Taken on shore - Time when received into custody: 28 Jun 1813 - From what ship or whence received: Mary of Quebec - Exchanged, discharged, died, or escape: Discharged - Time when: 13 Dec 1813 - Whither, and by what order, or number or re-entry: United States

Rowe, Benjamin   Prisoner 197. Rank: Private - By what ship or how taken: Boats & Troops - Time when: 3 Jun 1813 - Place where: Lake Champlain - Of what ship or corps: Eagle - Whether man of war, privateer or merchant vessel: Man of War - Time when received into custody: 9 Jun 1813 - From what ship or whence received: Batteaux - Exchanged, discharged, died, or escape: Discharged - Time when: 31 Oct 1813 - Whither, and by what order, or number or re-entry: Malabar Transport

Rowe, Benjamin   Prisoner 100. Rank: Private - By what ship or how taken: Boats & Troops - Time when: 28 May 1813 - Place where: Stoney Point, Henderson Harbor - Of what ship or corps: Land forces - Whether man of war, privateer or merchant vessel: Taken on shore - Time when received into custody: 8 Jun 1813 - From what ship or whence received: Batteaux - Exchanged, discharged, died, or escape: Discharged - Time when: 31 Oct 1813 - Whither, and by what order, or number or re-entry: Malabar Transport

Rowe, Jonathan   Prisoner 20. Rank: Private - By what ship or how taken: Boats & Troops - Time when: 28 May 1813 - Place where: Stoney Point, Henderson Harbor - Of what ship or corps: Land forces - Whether man of war, privateer or merchant vessel: Taken on shore - Time when received into custody: 8 Jun 1813 - From what ship or whence received: Batteaux - Exchanged, discharged, died, or escape: Discharged - Time when: 31 Oct 1813 - Whither, and by what order, or number or re-entry: Malabar Transport

Rowe, Michael   Prisoner 375. Rank: Private - By what ship or how taken: Troops - Time when: 6 Jun 1813 - Place where: Stoney Point - Of what ship or corps: Land forces - Whether man of war, privateer or merchant vessel: Taken on shore - Time when received into custody: 28 Jun 1813 - From what ship or whence received: Mary of Quebec - Exchanged, discharged, died, or escape: Discharged - Time when: 31 Oct 1813 - Whither, and by what order, or number or re-entry: Malabar Transport

Rowe, William   Prisoner 1727. Rank: Seaman - By what ship or how taken: Gun Boats - Time when: 6 Sep 1814 - Place where: Lake Huron - Of what ship or corps: Scorpion - Whether man of war, privateer or merchant vessel: Man of War - Time when received into custody: 1 Nov 1814 - From what ship or whence received: Montreal - Exchanged, discharged, died, or escape: Discharged - Time when: 7 Nov 1814 - Whither, and by what order, or number or re-entry: Transport Freedom No. 582 by orders of his Excellency Sir George Provost

Rowland, Alexander   Prisoner 1114. Rank: D Mast Sergeant - By what ship or how taken: Troops - Time when: 17 Oct 1813 - Place where: Red Mills - Of what ship or corps: Land forces - Whether man of war, privateer or merchant vessel: Taken on shore - Time when received into custody: 12 Oct 1813 - From what ship or whence received: Steamboat - Exchanged, discharged, died, or escape: Discharged - Time when: 31 Oct 1813 - Whither, and by what order, or number or re-entry: Malabar Transport

Rowley, Charles   Prisoner 1852. Rank: Private - By what ship or how taken: Troops - Time when: 17 Sep 1814 - Place where: Fort Erie - Of what ship or corps: Land forces - Whether man of war, privateer or merchant vessel: Taken on shore - Time when received into custody: 1 Nov 1814 - From what ship or whence received: Montreal - Exchanged, discharged, died, or escape: Discharged - Time when: 8 Nov 1814 - Whither, and by what order, or number or re-entry: S. George No. 575 for Halifax

Rowley, Nathan   Prisoner 631. Rank: Private - By what ship or how taken: Troops - Time when: 24 Jun 1813 - Place where: Stoney Point - Of what ship or corps: Land forces - Whether man of war, privateer or merchant vessel: Taken on shore - Time when received into custody: 7 Jul 1813 - From what ship or whence received: Steamboat - Exchanged,

American Prisoners of War held at Quebec during the War of 1812

discharged, died, or escape: Discharged - Time when: 10 Aug 1813 - Whither, and by what order, or number or re-entry: HM Ship Regulius by order of Sir George Provost

Rowsey, Ralph   Prisoner 1485. Rank: Private - By what ship or how taken: Troops - Time when: 25 Jul 1814 - Place where: Lundy's Lane - Of what ship or corps: Land forces - Whether man of war, privateer or merchant vessel: Taken on shore - Time when received into custody: 12 Aug 1814 - From what ship or whence received: Royal Seaman No. 289 Transport - Exchanged, discharged, died, or escape: Discharged - Time when: 8 Nov 1814 - Whither, and by what order, or number or re-entry: George No. 575 for Halifax by orders of Sir George Provost

Rudd, Levi   Prisoner 1610. Rank: Private - By what ship or how taken: Troops - Time when: 6 Sep 1814 - Place where: Plattsburg - Of what ship or corps: Land forces - Whether man of war, privateer or merchant vessel: Taken on shore - Time when received into custody: 5 Oct 1814 - From what ship or whence received: Montreal - Exchanged, discharged, died, or escape: Discharged - Time when: 8 Oct 1814 - Whither, and by what order, or number or re-entry: H.M. Ship Ceylon

Runyan, Francis   Prisoner 1163. Rank: Corporal - By what ship or how taken: Troops - Time when: 5 May 1813 - Place where: Fort Maggie - Of what ship or corps: Land forces - Whether man of war, privateer or merchant vessel: Taken on shore - Time when received into custody: 25 Nov 1813 - From what ship or whence received: Town Goal - Exchanged, discharged, died, or escape: Discharged - Time when: 12 Mar 1814 - Whither, and by what order, or number or re-entry: New Brunswick Fencibles

Runyan, Thomas   Prisoner 1344. Rank: Private - By what ship or how taken: Troops - Time when: 19 Dec 1813 - Place where: Fort Niagara - Of what ship or corps: Land forces - Whether man of war, privateer or merchant vessel: Taken on shore - Time when received into custody: 29 Jan 1814 - From what ship or whence received: Montreal by land carriage - Exchanged, discharged, died, or escape: Discharged - Time when: 4 May 1814 - Whither, and by what order, or number or re-entry: United States

Russell, Benjamin   Prisoner 1431. Rank: Able seaman - By what ship or how taken: Purveyor - Time when: 15 Feb 1814 - Place where: Browns Brook ? - Of what ship or corps: Alfred - Whether man of war, privateer or merchant vessel: Privateer - Time when received into custody: 24 May 1814 - From what ship or whence received: Mary Transport No. 360 Halifax - Exchanged, discharged, died, or escape: Discharged - Time when: 4 May 1814 - Whither, and by what order, or number or re-entry: United States

Rust, Richard H.   Prisoner 1233. Rank: Sergeant - By what ship or how taken: Troops - Time when: 19 Dec 1813 - Place where: Fort Niagara - Of what ship or corps: Land forces - Whether man of war, privateer or merchant vessel: Taken on shore - Time when received into custody: 29 Jan 1814 - From what ship or whence received: Montreal by land carriage - Exchanged, discharged, died, or escape: Discharged - Time when: 24 Feb 1814 - Whither, and by what order, or number or re-entry: Volunteered for New Brunswick Fencibles

Rust, William   Prisoner 1550. Rank: Private - By what ship or how taken: Troops - Time when: 25 Jul 1814 - Place where: Lundy's Lane - Of what ship or corps: Land forces - Whether man of war, privateer or merchant vessel: Taken on shore - Time when received into custody: 30 Aug 1814 - From what ship or whence received: Lady Delaval Schooner 578 - Exchanged, discharged, died, or escape: Discharged - Time when: 8 Oct 1814 - Whither, and by what order, or number or re-entry: Queen No. 415

Rutter, Thomas   Prisoner 1665. Rank: Sailing Master - By what ship or how taken: Gun Boats - Time when: 6 Sep 1814 - Place where: Lake Huron - Of what ship or corps: Scorpion - Whether man of war, privateer or merchant vessel: Man of War - Time when received into custody: 23 Oct 1814 - From what ship or whence received: Montreal - Exchanged, discharged, died, or escape: Discharged - Time when: 10 Nov 1814 - Whither, and by what order, or number or re-entry: Lord Cartheart No. 161 for Halifax

Rutter, William   Prisoner 1728. Rank: Seaman - By what ship or how taken: Gun Boats - Time when: 6 Sep 1814 - Place where: Lake Huron - Of what ship or corps: Scorpion - Whether man of war, privateer or merchant vessel: Man of War - Time when received into custody: 1 Nov 1814 - From what ship or whence received: Montreal - Exchanged, discharged, died, or escape: Discharged - Time when: 7 Nov 1814 - Whither, and by what order, or number or re-entry: Transport Freedom No. 582 by orders of his Excellency Sir George Provost

Sage, Harlety   Prisoner 1878. Rank: Private - By what ship or how taken: Troops - Time when: 17 Sep 1814 - Place where: Fort Erie - Of what ship or corps: Land forces - Whether man of war, privateer or merchant vessel: Taken on shore - Time when received into custody: 1 Nov 1814 - From what ship or whence received: Montreal - Exchanged, discharged, died, or escape: Discharged - Time when: 8 Nov 1814 - Whither, and by what order, or number or re-entry: S. George No. 575 for Halifax by order of Sir George Provost

American Prisoners of War held at Quebec during the War of 1812

Sanborn, John L.   Prisoner 179.   Rank: Sergeant - By what ship or how taken: Boats & Troops - Time when: 3 Jun 1813 - Place where: Lake Champlain - Of what ship or corps: Growler - Whether man of war, privateer or merchant vessel: Man of War - Time when received into custody: 9 Jun 1813 - From what ship or whence received: Batteaux - Exchanged, discharged, died, or escape: Died - Time when: 23 Jul 1813 - Whither, and by what order, or number or re-entry: Dysentery

Sasse, John   Prisoner 1018.   Rank: Marine Private - By what ship or how taken: Lord Melvin - Time when: 10 Aug 1813 - Place where: Lake Ontario - Of what ship or corps: Growler - Whether man of war, privateer or merchant vessel: Man of War - Time when received into custody: 5 Sep 1813 - From what ship or whence received: Steamboat - Exchanged, discharged, died, or escape: Discharged - Time when: 31 Oct 1813 - Whither, and by what order, or number or re-entry: Malabar Transport

Saunders, William G.   Prisoner 536.   Rank: Lieutenant - By what ship or how taken: Troops - Time when: 24 Jun 1813 - Place where: Beaver Dam - Of what ship or corps: Land forces - Whether man of war, privateer or merchant vessel: Taken on shore - Time when received into custody: 13 Jul 1813 - From what ship or whence received: Steamboat - Exchanged, discharged, died, or escape: Discharged - Time when: 10 Aug 1813 - Whither, and by what order, or number or re-entry: HM Ship Regulius by order of Sir George Provost

Saunderson, John   Prisoner 273.   Rank: Private - By what ship or how taken: Troops - Time when: 6 Jun 1813 - Place where: Stoney Point - Of what ship or corps: Land forces - Whether man of war, privateer or merchant vessel: Taken on shore - Time when received into custody: 28 Jun 1813 - From what ship or whence received: Batteaux - Exchanged, discharged, died, or escape: Discharged - Time when: 31 Oct 1813 - Whither, and by what order, or number or re-entry: Malabar Transport

Sawyer, Charles W.   Prisoner 1101.   Rank: Private - By what ship or how taken: Troops - Time when: 24 Aug 1813 - Place where: Fort George - Of what ship or corps: Land forces - Whether man of war, privateer or merchant vessel: Taken on shore - Time when received into custody: 12 Oct 1813 - From what ship or whence received: Steamboat - Exchanged, discharged, died, or escape: Discharged - Time when: 31 Oct 1813 - Whither, and by what order, or number or re-entry: Malabar Transport

Sawyer, Horace B.   Prisoner 145.   Rank: Midshipman - By what ship or how taken: Boats & Troops - Time when: 3 Jun 1813 - Place where: Lake Champlain - Of what ship or corps: Eagle - Whether man of war, privateer or merchant vessel: Man of War - Time when received into custody: 8 Jul 1813 - From what ship or whence received: Batteaux - Exchanged, discharged, died, or escape: Discharged - Time when: 10 Aug 1813 - Whither, and by what order, or number or re-entry: Per order His Exellency Sir George Prevost

Scarles, William   Prisoner 1538.   Rank: Private - By what ship or how taken: Troops - Time when: 25 Jul 1814 - Place where: Lundy's Lane - Of what ship or corps: Land forces - Whether man of war, privateer or merchant vessel: Taken on shore - Time when received into custody: 30 Aug 1814 - From what ship or whence received: Lady Delaval Schooner 578 - Exchanged, discharged, died, or escape: Discharged - Time when: 8 Oct 1814 - Whither, and by what order, or number or re-entry: Queen No. 415

Schooley, William   Prisoner 1084.   Rank: Private - By what ship or how taken: Troops - Time when: 24 Aug 1813 - Place where: Fort George - Of what ship or corps: Land forces - Whether man of war, privateer or merchant vessel: Taken on shore - Time when received into custody: 10 Oct 1813 - From what ship or whence received: Steamboat - Exchanged, discharged, died, or escape: Discharged - Time when: 31 Oct 1813 - Whither, and by what order, or number or re-entry: Malabar Transport

Schoolman, William   Prisoner 717.   Rank: Private - By what ship or how taken: Troops - Time when: 26 Jun 1813 - Place where: Beaver Dam - Of what ship or corps: Land forces - Whether man of war, privateer or merchant vessel: Taken on shore - Time when received into custody: 7 Jul 1813 - From what ship or whence received: Steamboat - Exchanged, discharged, died, or escape: Discharged - Time when: 10 Aug 1813 - Whither, and by what order, or number or re-entry: HM Ship Regulius by order of Sir George Provost

Schultz, John   Prisoner 404.   Rank: Private - By what ship or how taken: Troops - Time when: 24 Jun 1813 - Place where: Beaver Dam - Of what ship or corps: Land forces - Whether man of war, privateer or merchant vessel: Taken on shore - Time when received into custody: 7 Jul 1813 - From what ship or whence received: Steamboat - Exchanged, discharged, died, or escape: Discharged - Time when: 10 Aug 1813 - Whither, and by what order, or number or re-entry: Per order His Exellency Sir George Prevost

American Prisoners of War held at Quebec during the War of 1812

Scisso, Thomas   Prisoner 173. Rank: Able seaman - By what ship or how taken: Boats & Troops - Time when: 3 Jun 1813 - Place where: Lake Champlain - Of what ship or corps: Growler - Whether man of war, privateer or merchant vessel: Man of War - Time when received into custody: 9 Jun 1813 - From what ship or whence received: Batteaux - Exchanged, discharged, died, or escape: Discharged - Time when: 31 Oct 1813 - Whither, and by what order, or number or re-entry: Malabar Transport

Scott, Abraham   Prisoner 125. Rank: Private - By what ship or how taken: Boats & Troops - Time when: 28 May 1813 - Place where: Stoney Point, Henderson Harbor - Of what ship or corps: Land forces - Whether man of war, privateer or merchant vessel: Taken on shore - Time when received into custody: 8 Jun 1813 - From what ship or whence received: Batteaux - Exchanged, discharged, died, or escape: Discharged - Time when: 31 Oct 1813 - Whither, and by what order, or number or re-entry: Malabar Transport

Scott, James   Prisoner 664. Rank: Private - By what ship or how taken: Troops - Time when: 24 Jun 1813 - Place where: Stoney Point - Of what ship or corps: Land forces - Whether man of war, privateer or merchant vessel: Taken on shore - Time when received into custody: 7 Jul 1813 - From what ship or whence received: Steamboat - Exchanged, discharged, died, or escape: Discharged - Time when: 9 Aug 1813 - Whither, and by what order, or number or re-entry: HM Ship Wasp

Scott, John   Prisoner 482. Rank: Private - By what ship or how taken: Troops - Time when: 24 Jun 1813 - Place where: Beaver Dam - Of what ship or corps: Land forces - Whether man of war, privateer or merchant vessel: Taken on shore - Time when received into custody: 7 Jul 1813 - From what ship or whence received: Steamboat - Exchanged, discharged, died, or escape: Discharged - Time when: 10 Aug 1813 - Whither, and by what order, or number or re-entry: HM Ship Regulius by order of Sir George Provost

Scott, Joseph M.   Prisoner 1416. Rank: Private - By what ship or how taken: Troops - Time when: 19 Dec 1813 - Place where: Fort Niagara - Of what ship or corps: Land forces - Whether man of war, privateer or merchant vessel: Taken on shore - Time when received into custody: 29 Jan 1814 - From what ship or whence received: Montreal by land carriage - Exchanged, discharged, died, or escape: Discharged - Time when: 4 May 1814 - Whither, and by what order, or number or re-entry: United States

Scott, Silar   Prisoner 982. Rank: Private - By what ship or how taken: Troops - Time when: 5 Jul 1813 - Place where: Fort Schisher - Of what ship or corps: Land forces - Whether man of war, privateer or merchant vessel: Taken on shore - Time when received into custody: 5 Sep 1813 - From what ship or whence received: Steamboat - Exchanged, discharged, died, or escape: Discharged - Time when: 31 Oct 1813 - Whither, and by what order, or number or re-entry: Malabar Transport

Scott, Soloman   Prisoner 391. Rank: Private - By what ship or how taken: Troops - Time when: 6 Jun 1813 - Place where: Stoney Point - Of what ship or corps: Land forces - Whether man of war, privateer or merchant vessel: Taken on shore - Time when received into custody: 28 Jun 1813 - From what ship or whence received: Mary of Quebec - Exchanged, discharged, died, or escape: Discharged - Time when: 31 Oct 1813 - Whither, and by what order, or number or re-entry: Malabar Transport

Scott, William   Prisoner 1190. Rank: Citizen - By what ship or how taken: - Time when: - Place where: - Of what ship or corps: - Whether man of war, privateer or merchant vessel: - Time when received into custody: 12 Dec 1813 - From what ship or whence received: Town Goal - Exchanged, discharged, died, or escape: Discharged - Time when: 4 May 1814 - Whither, and by what order, or number or re-entry: United States

Scott, William   Prisoner 851. Rank: Private - By what ship or how taken: Troops - Time when: 26 Jun 1813 - Place where: Beaver Dam - Of what ship or corps: Land forces - Whether man of war, privateer or merchant vessel: Taken on shore - Time when received into custody: 7 Jul 1813 - From what ship or whence received: Steamboat - Exchanged, discharged, died, or escape: Discharged - Time when: 10 Aug 1813 - Whither, and by what order, or number or re-entry: HM Ship Malpomena

Scott MD, William   Prisoner 1186. Rank: Doctor - By what ship or how taken: Troops - Time when: 5 May 1813 - Place where: Rapids - Of what ship or corps: Land forces - Whether man of war, privateer or merchant vessel: Taken on shore - Time when received into custody: 25 Nov 1813 - From what ship or whence received: Town Goal - Exchanged, discharged, died, or escape: Discharged - Time when: 31 Jan 1814 - Whither, and by what order, or number or re-entry: To United States

Scudder, Stephen   Prisoner 333. Rank: Private - By what ship or how taken: Boats & Troops - Time when: 6 Jun 1813 - Place where: Stoney Point - Of what ship or corps: Land forces - Whether man of war, privateer or merchant vessel: Taken on shore - Time when received into custody: 28 Jun 1813 - From what ship or whence received: Quebec of Quebec - Exchanged, discharged, died, or escape: Discharged - Time when: 31 Oct 1813 - Whither, and by what order, or number or re-entry: Malabar Transport

Scuving, Joel   Prisoner 1272. Rank: Privateer - By what ship or how taken: Troops - Time when: 19 Dec 1813 - Place where: Fort Niagara - Of what ship or corps: Land forces - Whether man of war, privateer or merchant vessel: Taken on shore - Time when received into custody: 29 Jan 1814 - From what ship or whence received: Montreal by land carriage - Exchanged, discharged, died, or escape: Discharged - Time when: 4 May 1814 - Whither, and by what order, or number or re-entry: United States

See, Daniel   Prisoner 327. Rank: Private - By what ship or how taken: Boats & Troops - Time when: 6 Jun 1813 - Place where: Stoney Point - Of what ship or corps: Land forces - Whether man of war, privateer or merchant vessel: Taken on shore - Time when received into custody: 28 Jun 1813 - From what ship or whence received: Quebec of Quebec - Exchanged, discharged, died, or escape: Discharged - Time when: 31 Oct 1813 - Whither, and by what order, or number or re-entry: Malabar Transport

Sellock, Henry   Prisoner 899. Rank: Sergeant - By what ship or how taken: Troops - Time when: 26 Jun 1813 - Place where: Beaver Dam - Of what ship or corps: Land forces - Whether man of war, privateer or merchant vessel: Taken on shore - Time when received into custody: 7 Jul 1813 - From what ship or whence received: Steamboat - Exchanged, discharged, died, or escape: Discharged - Time when: 10 Aug 1813 - Whither, and by what order, or number or re-entry: HM Ship Malpomena

Seriven, Richard   Prisoner 547. Rank: Private - By what ship or how taken: Troops - Time when: 26 Jun 1813 - Place where: Beaver Dam - Of what ship or corps: Land forces - Whether man of war, privateer or merchant vessel: Taken on shore - Time when received into custody: 13 Jul 1813 - From what ship or whence received: Steamboat - Exchanged, discharged, died, or escape: Discharged - Time when: 10 Aug 1813 - Whither, and by what order, or number or re-entry: HM Ship Regulius by order of Sir George Provost

Serviss, William   Prisoner 1668. Rank: Lieutenant - By what ship or how taken: Troops - Time when: 31 Aug 1814 - Place where: Fort Erie - Of what ship or corps: Land forces - Whether man of war, privateer or merchant vessel: Taken on shore - Time when received into custody: 23 Oct 1814 - From what ship or whence received: Montreal - Exchanged, discharged, died, or escape: Discharged - Time when: 13 Mar 1815 - Whither, and by what order, or number or re-entry: United States

Shaddock, John   Prisoner 120. Rank: Private - By what ship or how taken: Boats & Troops - Time when: 28 May 1813 - Place where: Stoney Point, Henderson Harbor - Of what ship or corps: Land forces - Whether man of war, privateer or merchant vessel: Taken on shore - Time when received into custody: 8 Jun 1813 - From what ship or whence received: Batteaux - Exchanged, discharged, died, or escape: Discharged - Time when: 31 Oct 1813 - Whither, and by what order, or number or re-entry: Malabar Transport

Shaffer, Valentine   Prisoner 700. Rank: Private - By what ship or how taken: Troops - Time when: 26 Jun 1813 - Place where: Beaver Dam - Of what ship or corps: Land forces - Whether man of war, privateer or merchant vessel: Taken on shore - Time when received into custody: 7 Jul 1813 - From what ship or whence received: Steamboat - Exchanged, discharged, died, or escape: Discharged - Time when: 10 Aug 1813 - Whither, and by what order, or number or re-entry: HM Ship Regulius by order of Sir George Provost

Shafter, Jacob   Prisoner 1216. Rank: Private - By what ship or how taken: Troops - Time when: 19 Dec 1813 - Place where: Fort Niagara - Of what ship or corps: Land forces - Whether man of war, privateer or merchant vessel: Taken on shore - Time when received into custody: 28 Jan 1814 - From what ship or whence received: Montreal by land carriage - Exchanged, discharged, died, or escape: Discharged - Time when: 4 May 1814 - Whither, and by what order, or number or re-entry: United States

Sharpe, Soloman   Prisoner 192. Rank: Private - By what ship or how taken: Boats & Troops - Time when: 3 Jun 1813 - Place where: Lake Champlain - Of what ship or corps: Growler - Whether man of war, privateer or merchant vessel: Man of War - Time when received into custody: 9 Jun 1813 - From what ship or whence received: Batteaux - Exchanged, discharged, died, or escape: Discharged - Time when: 31 Oct 1813 - Whither, and by what order, or number or re-entry: Malabar Transport

Shaver, Frederick   Prisoner 1984. Rank: Citizen - By what ship or how taken: Troops - Time when: 31 Oct 1814 - Place where: Fort Niagara - Of what ship or corps: Land forces - Whether man of war, privateer or merchant vessel: Taken on shore - Time when received into custody: 30 Dec 1814 - From what ship or whence received: Montreal - Exchanged, discharged, died, or escape: Discharged - Time when: 13 Mar 1815 - Whither, and by what order, or number or re-entry: United States

Shaver, George   Prisoner 137. Rank: Private - By what ship or how taken: Boats & Troops - Time when: 28 May 1813 - Place

American Prisoners of War held at Quebec during the War of 1812

where: Stoney Point, Henderson Harbor - Of what ship or corps: Land forces - Whether man of war, privateer or merchant vessel: Taken on shore - Time when received into custody: 8 Jul 1813 - From what ship or whence received: Batteaux - Exchanged, discharged, died, or escape: Died - Time when: 26 Jul 1813 - Whither, and by what order, or number or re-entry: Dysentery

Sheaves, Thomas   Prisoner 843.   Rank: Private - By what ship or how taken: Troops - Time when: 26 Jun 1813 - Place where: Beaver Dam - Of what ship or corps: Land forces - Whether man of war, privateer or merchant vessel: Taken on shore - Time when received into custody: 7 Jul 1813 - From what ship or whence received: Steamboat - Exchanged, discharged, died, or escape: Discharged - Time when: 10 Aug 1813 - Whither, and by what order, or number or re-entry: HM Ship Malpomena

Sheeps, David   Prisoner 378.   Rank: Private - By what ship or how taken: Troops - Time when: 6 Jun 1813 - Place where: Stoney Point - Of what ship or corps: Land forces - Whether man of war, privateer or merchant vessel: Taken on shore - Time when received into custody: 28 Jun 1813 - From what ship or whence received: Mary of Quebec - Exchanged, discharged, died, or escape: Discharged - Time when: 31 Oct 1813 - Whither, and by what order, or number or re-entry: Malabar Transport

Sheffield, Henry   Prisoner 885.   Rank: Private - By what ship or how taken: Troops - Time when: 26 Jun 1813 - Place where: Beaver Dam - Of what ship or corps: Land forces - Whether man of war, privateer or merchant vessel: Taken on shore - Time when received into custody: 7 Jul 1813 - From what ship or whence received: Steamboat - Exchanged, discharged, died, or escape: Discharged - Time when: 10 Aug 1813 - Whither, and by what order, or number or re-entry: HM Ship Malpomena

Shell, Henry   Prisoner 528.   Rank: Lieutenant - By what ship or how taken: Troops - Time when: 24 Jun 1813 - Place where: Beaver Dam - Of what ship or corps: Land forces - Whether man of war, privateer or merchant vessel: Taken on shore - Time when received into custody: 13 Jul 1813 - From what ship or whence received: Steamboat - Exchanged, discharged, died, or escape: Discharged - Time when: 10 Aug 1813 - Whither, and by what order, or number or re-entry: HM Ship Regulius by order of Sir George Provost

Shepheard, Christian   Prisoner 1826.   Rank: Private - By what ship or how taken: Troops - Time when: 17 Sep 1814 - Place where: Fort Erie - Of what ship or corps: Land forces - Whether man of war, privateer or merchant vessel: Taken on shore - Time when received into custody: 1 Nov 1814 - From what ship or whence received: Montreal - Exchanged, discharged, died, or escape: Discharged - Time when: 8 Nov 1814 - Whither, and by what order, or number or re-entry: S. George No. 575 for Halifax by order of Sir George Provost

Shepheard, Samuel   Prisoner 1170.   Rank: Private - By what ship or how taken: Troops - Time when: 5 May 1813 - Place where: Rapids Prince Reason - Of what ship or corps: Land forces - Whether man of war, privateer or merchant vessel: Taken on shore - Time when received into custody: 25 Nov 1813 - From what ship or whence received: Town Goal - Exchanged, discharged, died, or escape: Discharged - Time when: 12 Mar 1814 - Whither, and by what order, or number or re-entry: New Brunswick Fencibles

Shrater, Anthony   Prisoner 702.   Rank: Private - By what ship or how taken: Troops - Time when: 26 Jun 1813 - Place where: Beaver Dam - Of what ship or corps: Land forces - Whether man of war, privateer or merchant vessel: Taken on shore - Time when received into custody: 7 Jul 1813 - From what ship or whence received: Steamboat - Exchanged, discharged, died, or escape: Discharged - Time when: 31 Oct 1813 - Whither, and by what order, or number or re-entry: Malabar Transport

Shute, John   Prisoner 8.   Rank: Private - By what ship or how taken: Boats & Troops - Time when: 28 May 1813 - Place where: Stoney Point, Henderson Harbor - Of what ship or corps: Land forces - Whether man of war, privateer or merchant vessel: Taken on shore - Time when received into custody: 8 Jun 1813 - From what ship or whence received: Batteaux - Exchanged, discharged, died, or escape: Discharged - Time when: 4 May 1814 - Whither, and by what order, or number or re-entry: United States

Shutt, Henry   Prisoner 1390.   Rank: Corporal - By what ship or how taken: Troops - Time when: 19 Dec 1813 - Place where: Fort Niagara - Of what ship or corps: Land forces - Whether man of war, privateer or merchant vessel: Taken on shore - Time when received into custody: 29 Jan 1814 - From what ship or whence received: Montreal by land carriage - Exchanged, discharged, died, or escape: Discharged - Time when: 4 May 1814 - Whither, and by what order, or number or re-entry: United States

Sickles, James   Prisoner 1871.   Rank: Private - By what ship or how taken: Troops - Time when: 17 Sep 1814 - Place where: Fort Erie - Of what ship or corps: Land forces - Whether man of war, privateer or merchant vessel: Taken on shore - Time when received into custody: 1 Nov 1814 - From what ship or whence received: Montreal - Exchanged, discharged, died, or escape: Discharged - Time when: 8 Nov 1814 - Whither, and by what order, or number or re-entry:

American Prisoners of War held at Quebec during the War of 1812

S. George No. 575 for Halifax

Sickles, Michael   Prisoner 557. Rank: Private - By what ship or how taken: Troops - Time when: 26 Jun 1813 - Place where: Beaver Dam - Of what ship or corps: Land forces - Whether man of war, privateer or merchant vessel: Taken on shore - Time when received into custody: 13 Jul 1813 - From what ship or whence received: Steamboat - Exchanged, discharged, died, or escape: Discharged - Time when: 10 Aug 1813 - Whither, and by what order, or number or re-entry: HM Ship Regulius by order of Sir George Provost

Silence, Nicholas   Prisoner 692. Rank: Private - By what ship or how taken: Troops - Time when: 26 Jun 1813 - Place where: Beaver Dam - Of what ship or corps: Land forces - Whether man of war, privateer or merchant vessel: Taken on shore - Time when received into custody: 7 Jul 1813 - From what ship or whence received: Steamboat - Exchanged, discharged, died, or escape: Discharged - Time when: 10 Aug 1813 - Whither, and by what order, or number or re-entry: HM Ship Regulius by order of Sir George Provost

Simmons, Levi   Prisoner 1624. Rank: Private - By what ship or how taken: Troops - Time when: 9 Sep 1814 - Place where: Plattsburg - Of what ship or corps: Land forces - Whether man of war, privateer or merchant vessel: Taken on shore - Time when received into custody: 5 Oct 1814 - From what ship or whence received: Montreal - Exchanged, discharged, died, or escape: Discharged - Time when: 8 Oct 1814 - Whither, and by what order, or number or re-entry: H.M. Ship Ceylon

Simpson, Mark   Prisoner 548. Rank: Sergeant - By what ship or how taken: Troops - Time when: 26 Jun 1813 - Place where: Beaver Dam - Of what ship or corps: Land forces - Whether man of war, privateer or merchant vessel: Taken on shore - Time when received into custody: 13 Jul 1813 - From what ship or whence received: Steamboat - Exchanged, discharged, died, or escape: Discharged - Time when: 10 Aug 1813 - Whither, and by what order, or number or re-entry: HM Ship Regulius by order of Sir George Provost

Sinclair, Jacob   Prisoner 219. Rank: Private - By what ship or how taken: Boats & Troops - Time when: 3 Jun 1813 - Place where: Lake Champlain - Of what ship or corps: Growler - Whether man of war, privateer or merchant vessel: Man of War - Time when received into custody: 9 Jun 1813 - From what ship or whence received: Batteaux - Exchanged, discharged, died, or escape: Died - Time when: 19 Sep 1813 - Whither, and by what order, or number or re-entry: Typhus Fever

Skinner, Benjamin   Prisoner 1494. Rank: Private - By what ship or how taken: Troops - Time when: 25 Jul 1814 - Place where: Lundy's Lane - Of what ship or corps: Land forces - Whether man of war, privateer or merchant vessel: Taken on shore - Time when received into custody: 19 Aug 1814 - From what ship or whence received: Triton No. 438 Transport - Exchanged, discharged, died, or escape: Discharged - Time when: 8 Oct 1814 - Whither, and by what order, or number or re-entry: Queen No. 415

Slaughter, George   Prisoner 415. Rank: Sergeant - By what ship or how taken: Troops - Time when: 24 Jun 1813 - Place where: Beaver Dam - Of what ship or corps: Land forces - Whether man of war, privateer or merchant vessel: Taken on shore - Time when received into custody: 7 Jul 1813 - From what ship or whence received: Steamboat - Exchanged, discharged, died, or escape: Discharged - Time when: 31 Oct 1813 - Whither, and by what order, or number or re-entry: HM Ship Success

Sloan, Ebenezer   Prisoner 1193. Rank: Citizen - By what ship or how taken: - Time when: - Place where: - Of what ship or corps: - Whether man of war, privateer or merchant vessel: - Time when received into custody: 12 Dec 1813 - From what ship or whence received: Town Goal - Exchanged, discharged, died, or escape: Discharged - Time when: 4 May 1814 - Whither, and by what order, or number or re-entry: United States

Sloin, William   Prisoner 469. Rank: Private - By what ship or how taken: Troops - Time when: 24 Jun 1813 - Place where: Beaver Dam - Of what ship or corps: Malabar & Hydia - Whether man of war, privateer or merchant vessel: Taken on shore - Time when received into custody: 7 Jul 1813 - From what ship or whence received: Steamboat - Exchanged, discharged, died, or escape: Discharged - Time when: 7 Aug 1813 - Whither, and by what order, or number or re-entry: H.M. Ship Cievare

Sly, Thomas   Prisoner 713. Rank: Drummer - By what ship or how taken: Troops - Time when: 26 Jun 1813 - Place where: Beaver Dam - Of what ship or corps: Land forces - Whether man of war, privateer or merchant vessel: Taken on shore - Time when received into custody: 7 Jul 1813 - From what ship or whence received: Steamboat - Exchanged, discharged, died, or escape: Discharged - Time when: 10 Aug 1813 - Whither, and by what order, or number or re-entry: HM Ship Regulius by order of Sir George Provost

American Prisoners of War held at Quebec during the War of 1812

Smiley, John   Prisoner 741. Rank: Private - By what ship or how taken: Troops - Time when: 26 Jun 1813 - Place where: Beaver Dam - Of what ship or corps: Land forces - Whether man of war, privateer or merchant vessel: Taken on shore - Time when received into custody: 7 Jul 1813 - From what ship or whence received: Steamboat - Exchanged, discharged, died, or escape: Discharged - Time when: 10 Aug 1813 - Whither, and by what order, or number or re-entry: HM Ship Regulius by order of Sir George Provost

Smilley, Thomas   Prisoner 707. Rank: Private - By what ship or how taken: Troops - Time when: 26 Jun 1813 - Place where: Beaver Dam - Of what ship or corps: Land forces - Whether man of war, privateer or merchant vessel: Taken on shore - Time when received into custody: 7 Jul 1813 - From what ship or whence received: Steamboat - Exchanged, discharged, died, or escape: Discharged - Time when: 31 Oct 1813 - Whither, and by what order, or number or re-entry: Malabar Transport

Smith, Benjamin   Prisoner 749. Rank: Private - By what ship or how taken: Troops - Time when: 26 Jun 1813 - Place where: Beaver Dam - Of what ship or corps: Land forces - Whether man of war, privateer or merchant vessel: Taken on shore - Time when received into custody: 7 Jul 1813 - From what ship or whence received: Steamboat - Exchanged, discharged, died, or escape: Discharged - Time when: 10 Aug 1813 - Whither, and by what order, or number or re-entry: HM Ship Malpomena

Smith, Corneilus   Prisoner 126. Rank: Private - By what ship or how taken: Boats & Troops - Time when: 28 May 1813 - Place where: Stoney Point, Henderson Harbor - Of what ship or corps: Land forces - Whether man of war, privateer or merchant vessel: Taken on shore - Time when received into custody: 8 Jun 1813 - From what ship or whence received: Batteaux - Exchanged, discharged, died, or escape: Discharged - Time when: 31 Oct 1813 - Whither, and by what order, or number or re-entry: Malabar Transport

Smith, Daniel   Prisoner 208. Rank: Boy - By what ship or how taken: Boats & Troops - Time when: 3 Jun 1813 - Place where: Lake Champlain - Of what ship or corps: Eagle - Whether man of war, privateer or merchant vessel: Man of War - Time when received into custody: 9 Jun 1813 - From what ship or whence received: Batteaux - Exchanged, discharged, died, or escape: Discharged - Time when: 31 Oct 1813 - Whither, and by what order, or number or re-entry: Malabar Transport

Smith, Elijah   Prisoner 274. Rank: Private - By what ship or how taken: Troops - Time when: 6 Jun 1813 - Place where: Stoney Point - Of what ship or corps: Land forces - Whether man of war, privateer or merchant vessel: Taken on shore - Time when received into custody: 28 Jun 1813 - From what ship or whence received: Batteaux - Exchanged, discharged, died, or escape: Discharged - Time when: 31 Oct 1813 - Whither, and by what order, or number or re-entry: Malabar Transport

Smith, Frederick   Prisoner 1091. Rank: Private - By what ship or how taken: Troops - Time when: 24 Aug 1813 - Place where: Fort George - Of what ship or corps: Land forces - Whether man of war, privateer or merchant vessel: Taken on shore - Time when received into custody: 10 Oct 1813 - From what ship or whence received: Steamboat - Exchanged, discharged, died, or escape: Discharged - Time when: 31 Oct 1813 - Whither, and by what order, or number or re-entry: Malabar Transport

Smith, Henry   Prisoner 1689. Rank: Private - By what ship or how taken: Troops - Time when: 19 Sep 1814 - Place where: Lole of Noire - Of what ship or corps: Land forces - Whether man of war, privateer or merchant vessel: Taken on shore - Time when received into custody: 23 Oct 1814 - From what ship or whence received: Montreal - Exchanged, discharged, died, or escape: Discharged - Time when: 8 Nov 1814 - Whither, and by what order, or number or re-entry: S. George No. 575 for Halifax

Smith, Ira   Prisoner 1683. Rank: Sergeant - By what ship or how taken: Troops - Time when: 4 Aug 1814 - Place where: Fort Erie - Of what ship or corps: Land forces - Whether man of war, privateer or merchant vessel: Taken on shore - Time when received into custody: 23 Oct 1814 - From what ship or whence received: Montreal - Exchanged, discharged, died, or escape: Discharged - Time when: 8 Nov 1814 - Whither, and by what order, or number or re-entry: S. George No. 575 for Halifax

Smith, Jacob   Prisoner 611. Rank: Private - By what ship or how taken: Troops - Time when: 26 Jun 1813 - Place where: Stoney Point - Of what ship or corps: Land forces - Whether man of war, privateer or merchant vessel: Taken on shore - Time when received into custody: 7 Jul 1813 - From what ship or whence received: Steamboat - Exchanged, discharged, died, or escape: Discharged - Time when: 10 Aug 1813 - Whither, and by what order, or number or re-entry: HM Ship Regulius by order of Sir George Provost

Smith, James   Prisoner 931. Rank: Lieutenant - By what ship or how taken: Troops - Time when: 26 Jun 1813 - Place where: Beaver Dam - Of what ship or corps: Land forces - Whether man of war, privateer or merchant vessel: Taken on shore - Time when received into custody: 21 Jul 1813 - From what ship or whence received: Steamboat - Exchanged,

discharged, died, or escape: Discharged - Time when: 10 Aug 1813 - Whither, and by what order, or number or re-entry: HM Ship Regulius by order of Sir George Provost

Smith, John   Prisoner 988. Rank: Seaman - By what ship or how taken: Earl Moria - Time when: 10 Aug 1813 - Place where: Lake Ontario - Of what ship or corps: Julia - Whether man of war, privateer or merchant vessel: Man of War - Time when received into custody: 5 Sep 1813 - From what ship or whence received: Steamboat - Exchanged, discharged, died, or escape: Discharged - Time when: 18 Sep 1813 - Whither, and by what order, or number or re-entry: To the Regulius Transport by order of Major General Glasgow

Smith, John   Prisoner 1912. Rank: Private - By what ship or how taken: Troops - Time when: 17 Sep 1814 - Place where: Fort Erie - Of what ship or corps: Land forces - Whether man of war, privateer or merchant vessel: Taken on shore - Time when received into custody: 1 Nov 1814 - From what ship or whence received: Montreal - Exchanged, discharged, died, or escape: Discharged - Time when: 8 Nov 1814 - Whither, and by what order, or number or re-entry: S. George No. 575 for Halifax by order of Sir George Provost

Smith, John   Prisoner 742. Rank: Private - By what ship or how taken: Troops - Time when: 26 Jun 1813 - Place where: Beaver Dam - Of what ship or corps: Land forces - Whether man of war, privateer or merchant vessel: Taken on shore - Time when received into custody: 7 Jul 1813 - From what ship or whence received: Steamboat - Exchanged, discharged, died, or escape: Discharged - Time when: 10 Aug 1813 - Whither, and by what order, or number or re-entry: HM Ship Malpomena

Smith, John   Prisoner 808. Rank: Private - By what ship or how taken: Troops - Time when: 26 Jun 1813 - Place where: Beaver Dam - Of what ship or corps: Land forces - Whether man of war, privateer or merchant vessel: Taken on shore - Time when received into custody: 7 Jul 1813 - From what ship or whence received: Steamboat - Exchanged, discharged, died, or escape: Discharged - Time when: 10 Aug 1813 - Whither, and by what order, or number or re-entry: HM Ship Malpomena

Smith, John   Prisoner 1043. Rank: Seaman - By what ship or how taken: Earl Moria - Time when: 10 Aug 1813 - Place where: Lake Ontario - Of what ship or corps: Julia - Whether man of war, privateer or merchant vessel: Man of War - Time when received into custody: 5 Sep 1813 - From what ship or whence received: Steamboat - Exchanged, discharged, died, or escape: Discharged - Time when: 1 Nov 1813 - Whither, and by what order, or number or re-entry: Lord Cartheart Transport

Smith, John   Prisoner 381. Rank: Corporal - By what ship or how taken: Troops - Time when: 6 Jun 1813 - Place where: Stoney Point - Of what ship or corps: Land forces - Whether man of war, privateer or merchant vessel: Taken on shore - Time when received into custody: 28 Jun 1813 - From what ship or whence received: Mary of Quebec - Exchanged, discharged, died, or escape: Discharged - Time when: 22 Aug 1813 - Whither, and by what order, or number or re-entry: Rotta Transport

Smith, John C.   Prisoner 1987. Rank: Citizen - By what ship or how taken: Troops - Time when: 9 Nov 1814 - Place where: Chippawa - Of what ship or corps: Land forces - Whether man of war, privateer or merchant vessel: Taken on shore - Time when received into custody: 30 Dec 1814 - From what ship or whence received: Montreal - Exchanged, discharged, died, or escape: Discharged - Time when: 13 Mar 1815 - Whither, and by what order, or number or re-entry: United States

Smith, Jonathan   Prisoner 1184. Rank: Private - By what ship or how taken: Troops - Time when: 5 May 1813 - Place where: Rappids - Of what ship or corps: Land forces - Whether man of war, privateer or merchant vessel: Taken on shore - Time when received into custody: 25 Nov 1813 - From what ship or whence received: Town Goal - Exchanged, discharged, died, or escape: Died - Time when: 28 Apr 1814 - Whither, and by what order, or number or re-entry: Hematemesis

Smith, Joseph   Prisoner 62. Rank: Private - By what ship or how taken: Boats & Troops - Time when: 28 May 1813 - Place where: Stoney Point, Henderson Harbor - Of what ship or corps: Land forces - Whether man of war, privateer or merchant vessel: Taken on shore - Time when received into custody: 8 Jun 1813 - From what ship or whence received: Batteaux - Exchanged, discharged, died, or escape: Discharged - Time when: 31 Oct 1813 - Whither, and by what order, or number or re-entry: Malabar Transport

Smith, Noah   Prisoner 1548. Rank: Private - By what ship or how taken: Troops - Time when: 25 Jul 1814 - Place where: Lundy's Lane - Of what ship or corps: Land forces - Whether man of war, privateer or merchant vessel: Taken on shore - Time when received into custody: 30 Aug 1814 - From what ship or whence received: Lady Delaval Schooner 578 - Exchanged, discharged, died, or escape: Discharged - Time when: 8 Oct 1814 - Whither, and by what order, or number or re-entry: Queen No. 415

American Prisoners of War held at Quebec during the War of 1812

Smith, Richard   Prisoner 98. Rank: Private - By what ship or how taken: Boats & Troops - Time when: 28 May 1813 - Place where: Stoney Point, Henderson Harbor - Of what ship or corps: Land forces - Whether man of war, privateer or merchant vessel: Taken on shore - Time when received into custody: 8 Jun 1813 - From what ship or whence received: Batteaux - Exchanged, discharged, died, or escape: Discharged - Time when: 31 Oct 1813 - Whither, and by what order, or number or re-entry: Malabar Transport

Smith, Sidney   Prisoner 243. Rank: Lieutenant - By what ship or how taken: Boats & Troops - Time when: 24 Jun 1813 - Place where: Rec in charge of Beauport - Of what ship or corps: Land forces - Whether man of war, privateer or merchant vessel: Taken on shore - Time when received into custody: 9 Jun 1813 - From what ship or whence received: Steamboat - Exchanged, discharged, died, or escape: Discharged - Time when: 10 Dec 1813 - Whither, and by what order, or number or re-entry: United States

Smith, Stephen   Prisoner 36. Rank: Private - By what ship or how taken: Boats & Troops - Time when: 28 May 1813 - Place where: Stoney Point, Henderson Harbor - Of what ship or corps: Land forces - Whether man of war, privateer or merchant vessel: Taken on shore - Time when received into custody: 8 Jun 1813 - From what ship or whence received: Batteaux - Exchanged, discharged, died, or escape: Died - Time when: 5 Aug 1813 - Whither, and by what order, or number or re-entry: Typhus Fever

Smith, Thomas   Prisoner 1690. Rank: Private - By what ship or how taken: Troops - Time when: 25 Jul 1814 - Place where: Lundy's Lane - Of what ship or corps: Land forces - Whether man of war, privateer or merchant vessel: Taken on shore - Time when received into custody: 23 Oct 1814 - From what ship or whence received: Montreal - Exchanged, discharged, died, or escape: Discharged - Time when: 8 Nov 1814 - Whither, and by what order, or number or re-entry: S. George No. 575 for Halifax

Smith, Thomas   Prisoner 170. Rank: Able seaman - By what ship or how taken: Boats & Troops - Time when: 3 Jun 1813 - Place where: Lake Champlain - Of what ship or corps: Growler - Whether man of war, privateer or merchant vessel: Man of War - Time when received into custody: 9 Jun 1813 - From what ship or whence received: Batteaux - Exchanged, discharged, died, or escape: Discharged - Time when: 10 Oct 1813 - Whither, and by what order, or number or re-entry: Orlando Transport

Smith, Thomas   Prisoner 128. Rank: Private - By what ship or how taken: Boats & Troops - Time when: 28 May 1813 - Place where: Stoney Point, Henderson Harbor - Of what ship or corps: Land forces - Whether man of war, privateer or merchant vessel: Taken on shore - Time when received into custody: 8 Jun 1813 - From what ship or whence received: Batteaux - Exchanged, discharged, died, or escape: Escaped - Time when: 3 Sep 1813 - Whither, and by what order, or number or re-entry:

Smith, William   Prisoner 502. Rank: Private - By what ship or how taken: Troops - Time when: 24 Jun 1813 - Place where: Beaver Dam - Of what ship or corps: Land forces - Whether man of war, privateer or merchant vessel: Taken on shore - Time when received into custody: 7 Jul 1813 - From what ship or whence received: Steamboat - Exchanged, discharged, died, or escape: Died - Time when: 16 Jul 1813 - Whither, and by what order, or number or re-entry: Dysentery

Smith, William   Prisoner 1044. Rank: Seaman - By what ship or how taken: Earl Moria - Time when: 10 Aug 1813 - Place where: Lake Ontario - Of what ship or corps: Julia - Whether man of war, privateer or merchant vessel: Man of War - Time when received into custody: 5 Sep 1813 - From what ship or whence received: Steamboat - Exchanged, discharged, died, or escape: Discharged - Time when: 31 Oct 1813 - Whither, and by what order, or number or re-entry: Malabar Transport

Smith, William   Prisoner 1641. Rank: Private - By what ship or how taken: Troops - Time when: 10 Sep 1814 - Place where: Plattsburg - Of what ship or corps: Land forces - Whether man of war, privateer or merchant vessel: Taken on shore - Time when received into custody: 5 Oct 1814 - From what ship or whence received: Montreal - Exchanged, discharged, died, or escape: Discharged - Time when: 8 Oct 1814 - Whither, and by what order, or number or re-entry: H.M. Ship Ceylon

Smith, William   Prisoner 1862. Rank: Private - By what ship or how taken: Troops - Time when: 17 Sep 1814 - Place where: Fort Erie - Of what ship or corps: Land forces - Whether man of war, privateer or merchant vessel: Taken on shore - Time when received into custody: 1 Nov 1814 - From what ship or whence received: Montreal - Exchanged, discharged, died, or escape: Discharged - Time when: 8 Nov 1814 - Whither, and by what order, or number or re-entry: S. George No. 575 for Halifax

Smith, William H.   Prisoner 1763. Rank: Sergeant - By what ship or how taken: Troops - Time when: 7 Sep 1814 - Place where: Fort Erie - Of what ship or corps: Land forces - Whether man of war, privateer or merchant vessel: Taken on shore - Time when received into custody: 1 Nov 1814 - From what ship or whence received: Montreal - Exchanged, discharged, died, or escape: Discharged - Time when: 8 Nov 1814 - Whither, and by what order, or number or re-entry: S. George No. 575 for Halifax by order of Sir George Provost

Smith, William Henry   Prisoner 1283. Rank: Sergeant - By what ship or how taken: Troops - Time when: 19 Dec 1813 - Place where: Fort Niagara - Of what ship or corps: Land forces - Whether man of war, privateer or merchant vessel: Taken on shore - Time when received into custody: 29 Jan 1814 - From what ship or whence received: Montreal by land carriage - Exchanged, discharged, died, or escape: Discharged - Time when: 4 May 1814 - Whither, and by what order, or number or re-entry: United States

Sneed, Leakle   Prisoner 1842. Rank: Private - By what ship or how taken: Troops - Time when: 17 Sep 1814 - Place where: Fort Erie - Of what ship or corps: Land forces - Whether man of war, privateer or merchant vessel: Taken on shore - Time when received into custody: 1 Nov 1814 - From what ship or whence received: Montreal - Exchanged, discharged, died, or escape: Discharged - Time when: 8 Nov 1814 - Whither, and by what order, or number or re-entry: S. George No. 575 for Halifax by order of Sir George Provost

Snell, Shedrick   Prisoner 1691. Rank: Musician - By what ship or how taken: Troops - Time when: 7 Sep 1814 - Place where: Plattsburg - Of what ship or corps: Land forces - Whether man of war, privateer or merchant vessel: Taken on shore - Time when received into custody: 23 Oct 1814 - From what ship or whence received: Montreal - Exchanged, discharged, died, or escape: Discharged - Time when: 14 Nov 1814 - Whither, and by what order, or number or re-entry: Soverign Transport No. 628 to Halifax

Snow, Assa   Prisoner 669. Rank: Private - By what ship or how taken: Troops - Time when: 24 Jun 1813 - Place where: Stoney Point - Of what ship or corps: Land forces - Whether man of war, privateer or merchant vessel: Taken on shore - Time when received into custody: 7 Jul 1813 - From what ship or whence received: Steamboat - Exchanged, discharged, died, or escape: Discharged - Time when: 10 Aug 1813 - Whither, and by what order, or number or re-entry: HM Ship Regulius by order of Sir George Provost

Snyder, George   Prisoner 694. Rank: Private - By what ship or how taken: Troops - Time when: 26 Jun 1813 - Place where: Beaver Dam - Of what ship or corps: Land forces - Whether man of war, privateer or merchant vessel: Taken on shore - Time when received into custody: 7 Jul 1813 - From what ship or whence received: Steamboat - Exchanged, discharged, died, or escape: Discharged - Time when: 10 Aug 1813 - Whither, and by what order, or number or re-entry: HM Ship Regulius by order of Sir George Provost

Sonnet, Charles   Prisoner 939. Rank: Private - By what ship or how taken: Troops - Time when: 26 Jun 1813 - Place where: Beaver Dam - Of what ship or corps: Land forces - Whether man of war, privateer or merchant vessel: Taken on shore - Time when received into custody: 21 Jul 1813 - From what ship or whence received: Steamboat - Exchanged, discharged, died, or escape: Discharged - Time when: 10 Aug 1813 - Whither, and by what order, or number or re-entry: HM Ship Malpomena

Southards, William   Prisoner 1377. Rank: Private - By what ship or how taken: Troops - Time when: 19 Dec 1813 - Place where: Fort Niagara - Of what ship or corps: Land forces - Whether man of war, privateer or merchant vessel: Taken on shore - Time when received into custody: 29 Jan 1814 - From what ship or whence received: Montreal by land carriage - Exchanged, discharged, died, or escape: Discharged - Time when: 4 May 1814 - Whither, and by what order, or number or re-entry: United States

Southwick, J.   Prisoner 1637. Rank: Private - By what ship or how taken: Troops - Time when: 6 Sep 1814 - Place where: Plattsburg - Of what ship or corps: Land forces - Whether man of war, privateer or merchant vessel: Taken on shore - Time when received into custody: 5 Oct 1814 - From what ship or whence received: Montreal - Exchanged, discharged, died, or escape: Discharged - Time when: 8 Oct 1814 - Whither, and by what order, or number or re-entry: H.M. Ship Ceylon

Sowder, Jacob   Prisoner 684. Rank: Private - By what ship or how taken: Troops - Time when: 26 Jun 1813 - Place where: Beaver Dam - Of what ship or corps: Land forces - Whether man of war, privateer or merchant vessel: Taken on shore - Time when received into custody: 7 Jul 1813 - From what ship or whence received: Steamboat - Exchanged, discharged, died, or escape: Discharged - Time when: 10 Aug 1813 - Whither, and by what order, or number or re-entry: HM Ship Regulius by order of Sir George Provost

Spalding, William   Prisoner 497. Rank: Private - By what ship or how taken: Troops - Time when: 24 Jun 1813 - Place where: Beaver Dam - Of what ship or corps: Land forces - Whether man of war, privateer or merchant vessel: Taken on shore - Time when received into custody: 7 Jul 1813 - From what ship or whence received: Steamboat - Exchanged, discharged, died, or escape: Discharged - Time when: 10 Aug 1813 - Whither, and by what order, or number or re-entry: HM Ship Regulius by order of Sir George Provost

American Prisoners of War held at Quebec during the War of 1812

Sparks, William   Prisoner 1196. Rank: Citizen - By what ship or how taken: - Time when: - Place where: - Of what ship or corps: - Whether man of war, privateer or merchant vessel: - Time when received into custody: 12 Dec 1813 - From what ship or whence received: Town Goal - Exchanged, discharged, died, or escape: Discharged - Time when: 4 May 1814 - Whither, and by what order, or number or re-entry: United States

Spencer, Andrew   Prisoner 99. Rank: Private - By what ship or how taken: Boats & Troops - Time when: 28 May 1813 - Place where: Stoney Point, Henderson Harbor - Of what ship or corps: Land forces - Whether man of war, privateer or merchant vessel: Taken on shore - Time when received into custody: 8 Jun 1813 - From what ship or whence received: Batteaux - Exchanged, discharged, died, or escape: Discharged - Time when: 31 Oct 1813 - Whither, and by what order, or number or re-entry: Malabar Transport

Spencer, Nathan   Prisoner 308. Rank: Fifer - By what ship or how taken: Boats & Troops - Time when: 6 Jun 1813 - Place where: Stoney Point - Of what ship or corps: Land forces - Whether man of war, privateer or merchant vessel: Taken on shore - Time when received into custody: 28 Jun 1813 - From what ship or whence received: Quebec of Quebec - Exchanged, discharged, died, or escape: Discharged - Time when: 31 Oct 1813 - Whither, and by what order, or number or re-entry: Malabar Transport

Sperry, Jacob   Prisoner 189. Rank: Private - By what ship or how taken: Boats & Troops - Time when: 3 Jun 1813 - Place where: Lake Champlain - Of what ship or corps: Eagle - Whether man of war, privateer or merchant vessel: Man of War - Time when received into custody: 9 Jun 1813 - From what ship or whence received: Batteaux - Exchanged, discharged, died, or escape: Discharged - Time when: 31 Oct 1813 - Whither, and by what order, or number or re-entry: Malabar Transport

Spink, Anthony   Prisoner 377. Rank: Private - By what ship or how taken: Troops - Time when: 6 Jun 1813 - Place where: Stoney Point - Of what ship or corps: Land forces - Whether man of war, privateer or merchant vessel: Taken on shore - Time when received into custody: 28 Jun 1813 - From what ship or whence received: Mary of Quebec - Exchanged, discharged, died, or escape: Discharged - Time when: 31 Oct 1813 - Whither, and by what order, or number or re-entry: Malabar Transport

Sprigs, George   Prisoner 997. Rank: Seaman - By what ship or how taken: Earl Moria - Time when: 10 Aug 1813 - Place where: Lake Ontario - Of what ship or corps: Julia - Whether man of war, privateer or merchant vessel: Man of War - Time when received into custody: 5 Sep 1813 - From what ship or whence received: Steamboat - Exchanged, discharged, died, or escape: Discharged - Time when: 21 Sep 1813 - Whither, and by what order, or number or re-entry: Mersey Transport

Spunier, Lott   Prisoner 549. Rank: Sergeant - By what ship or how taken: Troops - Time when: 26 Jun 1813 - Place where: Beaver Dam - Of what ship or corps: Land forces - Whether man of war, privateer or merchant vessel: Taken on shore - Time when received into custody: 13 Jul 1813 - From what ship or whence received: Steamboat - Exchanged, discharged, died, or escape: Discharged - Time when: 10 Aug 1813 - Whither, and by what order, or number or re-entry: HM Ship Regulius by order of Sir George Provost

Spurgeion, Nathaniel   Prisoner 1762. Rank: Private - By what ship or how taken: Gun Boats - Time when: 6 Sep 1814 - Place where: Lake Huron - Of what ship or corps: Scorpion - Whether man of war, privateer or merchant vessel: Man of War - Time when received into custody: 1 Nov 1814 - From what ship or whence received: Montreal - Exchanged, discharged, died, or escape: Discharged - Time when: 8 Nov 1814 - Whither, and by what order, or number or re-entry: S. George No. 575 for Halifax by order of Sir George Provost

Stacy, L.   Prisoner 1588. Rank: Seaman - By what ship or how taken: Gun Boats - Time when: 12 Aug 1814 - Place where: Fort Erie - Of what ship or corps: Ohio - Whether man of war, privateer or merchant vessel: Man of War - Time when received into custody: 5 Oct 1814 - From what ship or whence received: Montreal - Exchanged, discharged, died, or escape: Discharged - Time when: 10 Nov 1814 - Whither, and by what order, or number or re-entry: Freedom No. 582

Staind, Isaac   Prisoner 1934. Rank: Private - By what ship or how taken: Troops - Time when: 17 Sep 1814 - Place where: Fort Erie - Of what ship or corps: Land forces - Whether man of war, privateer or merchant vessel: Taken on shore - Time when received into custody: 1 Nov 1814 - From what ship or whence received: Montreal - Exchanged, discharged, died, or escape: - Time when: - Whither, and by what order, or number or re-entry:

Stamford, Nathaniel   Prisoner 1737. Rank: Seaman - By what ship or how taken: Gun Boats - Time when: 3 Sep 1814 - Place where: Lake Huron - Of what ship or corps: Tigress - Whether man of war, privateer or merchant vessel: Man of War - Time when received into custody: 1 Nov 1814 - From what ship or whence received: Montreal - Exchanged, discharged, died, or escape: Discharged - Time when: 7 Nov 1814 - Whither, and by what order, or number or re-entry: Transport Freedom No. 582 by orders of his Excellency Sir George Provost

American Prisoners of War held at Quebec during the War of 1812

Stanbury, John   Prisoner 1685. Rank: Private - By what ship or how taken: Troops - Time when: 15 Aug 1814 - Place where: Fort Erie - Of what ship or corps: Land forces - Whether man of war, privateer or merchant vessel: Taken on shore - Time when received into custody: 23 Oct 1814 - From what ship or whence received: Montreal - Exchanged, discharged, died, or escape: Discharged - Time when: 8 Nov 1814 - Whither, and by what order, or number or re-entry: S. George No. 575 for Halifax

Stanbury, Samuel   Prisoner 285. Rank: Private - By what ship or how taken: Troops - Time when: 6 Jun 1813 - Place where: Stoney Point - Of what ship or corps: Land forces - Whether man of war, privateer or merchant vessel: Taken on shore - Time when received into custody: 28 Jun 1813 - From what ship or whence received: Batteaux - Exchanged, discharged, died, or escape: Discharged - Time when: 31 Oct 1813 - Whither, and by what order, or number or re-entry: Malabar Transport

Stanhope, C. L.   Prisoner 267. Rank: Lieutenant - By what ship or how taken: Boats & Troops - Time when: 24 Jun 1813 - Place where: Stoney Point - Of what ship or corps: Land forces - Whether man of war, privateer or merchant vessel: Taken on shore - Time when received into custody: 24 Jun 1813 - From what ship or whence received: Quebec of Quebec - Exchanged, discharged, died, or escape: Discharged - Time when: 31 Oct 1813 - Whither, and by what order, or number or re-entry: Malabar Transport

Stanhope, Curtis L.   Prisoner 269. Rank: Private - By what ship or how taken: Troops - Time when: 6 Jun 1813 - Place where: Stoney Point - Of what ship or corps: Land forces - Whether man of war, privateer or merchant vessel: Taken on shore - Time when received into custody: 28 Jun 1813 - From what ship or whence received: Batteaux - Exchanged, discharged, died, or escape: Discharged - Time when: 31 Oct 1813 - Whither, and by what order, or number or re-entry: Malabar Transport

Stanley, L.   Prisoner 1465. Rank: Private - By what ship or how taken: Gun Boats - Time when: 29 May 1814 - Place where: Sandy Creek - Of what ship or corps: Land forces - Whether man of war, privateer or merchant vessel: Taken on shore - Time when received into custody: 12 Aug 1814 - From what ship or whence received: Royal Seaman No. 289 Transport - Exchanged, discharged, died, or escape: Discharged - Time when: 8 Oct 1814 - Whither, and by what order, or number or re-entry: Queen No. 415

Stansburgh, Jonathan   Prisoner 407. Rank: Private - By what ship or how taken: Troops - Time when: 24 Jun 1813 - Place where: Beaver Dam - Of what ship or corps: Land forces - Whether man of war, privateer or merchant vessel: Taken on shore - Time when received into custody: 7 Jul 1813 - From what ship or whence received: Steamboat - Exchanged, discharged, died, or escape: Discharged - Time when: 22 Aug 1813 - Whither, and by what order, or number or re-entry: Hydra No. 434

Stanton, Phineas   Prisoner 1507. Rank: Major - By what ship or how taken: Troops - Time when: 25 Jul 1814 - Place where: Lundy's Lane - Of what ship or corps: Land forces - Whether man of war, privateer or merchant vessel: Taken on shore - Time when received into custody: 25 Jul 1814 - From what ship or whence received: Steamboat - Exchanged, discharged, died, or escape: Discharged - Time when: 10 Nov 1814 - Whither, and by what order, or number or re-entry: Soverign Transport No. 628 to Halifax by orders of Sir George Provost

Stearns, Nathan   Prisoner 194. Rank: Private - By what ship or how taken: Boats & Troops - Time when: 3 Jun 1813 - Place where: Lake Champlain - Of what ship or corps: Eagle - Whether man of war, privateer or merchant vessel: Man of War - Time when received into custody: 9 Jun 1813 - From what ship or whence received: Batteaux - Exchanged, discharged, died, or escape: Discharged - Time when: 31 Oct 1813 - Whither, and by what order, or number or re-entry: Malabar Transport

Steele, G. D.   Prisoner 1623. Rank: Citizen - By what ship or how taken: Troops - Time when: 22 Apr 1814 - Place where: Mosisco Bay - Of what ship or corps: Land forces - Whether man of war, privateer or merchant vessel: Taken on shore - Time when received into custody: 5 Oct 1814 - From what ship or whence received: Montreal - Exchanged, discharged, died, or escape: Discharged - Time when: 8 Oct 1814 - Whither, and by what order, or number or re-entry: H.M. Ship Ceylon

Steele, George G.   Prisoner 258. Rank: Captain - By what ship or how taken: Boats & Troops - Time when: 24 Jun 1813 - Place where: Stoney Point - Of what ship or corps: Land forces - Whether man of war, privateer or merchant vessel: Taken on shore - Time when received into custody: 24 Jun 1813 - From what ship or whence received: Steamboat - Exchanged, discharged, died, or escape: Discharged - Time when: 10 Aug 1813 - Whither, and by what order, or number or re-entry: Per order His Exellency Sir George Prevost

Stephens, John   Prisoner 883. Rank: Private - By what ship or how taken: Troops - Time when: 26 Jun 1813 - Place where: Beaver Dam - Of what ship or corps: Land forces - Whether man of war, privateer or merchant vessel: Taken on shore - Time when received into custody: 7 Jul 1813 - From what ship or whence received: Steamboat - Exchanged,

American Prisoners of War held at Quebec during the War of 1812

discharged, died, or escape: Discharged - Time when: 10 Aug 1813 - Whither, and by what order, or number or re-entry: HM Ship Malpomena

Sternburg, Christian   Prisoner 1982. Rank: Private - By what ship or how taken: Troops - Time when: 19 Dec 1813 - Place where: Fort Niagara - Of what ship or corps: Land forces - Whether man of war, privateer or merchant vessel: Taken on shore - Time when received into custody: 30 Dec 1814 - From what ship or whence received: Montreal - Exchanged, discharged, died, or escape: Discharged - Time when: 13 Mar 1815 - Whither, and by what order, or number or re-entry: United States

Stevens, Benjamin W.   Prisoner 2. Rank: Sergeant - By what ship or how taken: Boats & Troops - Time when: 28 May 1813 - Place where: Stoney Point, Henderson Harbor - Of what ship or corps: Land forces - Whether man of war, privateer or merchant vessel: Taken on shore - Time when received into custody: 8 Jun 1813 - From what ship or whence received: Batteaux - Exchanged, discharged, died, or escape: Discharged - Time when: 8 Oct 1813 - Whither, and by what order, or number or re-entry: H.M. Ship Ceylon

Stevens, Jephthah   Prisoner 1357. Rank: Private - By what ship or how taken: Troops - Time when: 19 Dec 1813 - Place where: Fort Niagara - Of what ship or corps: Land forces - Whether man of war, privateer or merchant vessel: Taken on shore - Time when received into custody: 29 Jan 1814 - From what ship or whence received: Montreal by land carriage - Exchanged, discharged, died, or escape: Discharged - Time when: 4 May 1814 - Whither, and by what order, or number or re-entry: United States

Stevens, John   Prisoner 1931. Rank: Private - By what ship or how taken: Troops - Time when: 17 Sep 1814 - Place where: Fort Erie - Of what ship or corps: Land forces - Whether man of war, privateer or merchant vessel: Taken on shore - Time when received into custody: 1 Nov 1814 - From what ship or whence received: Montreal - Exchanged, discharged, died, or escape: Discharged - Time when: 13 Mar 1815 - Whither, and by what order, or number or re-entry: United States

Stevens, Josiah   Prisoner 1353. Rank: Private - By what ship or how taken: Troops - Time when: 19 Dec 1813 - Place where: Fort Niagara - Of what ship or corps: Land forces - Whether man of war, privateer or merchant vessel: Taken on shore - Time when received into custody: 29 Jan 1814 - From what ship or whence received: Montreal by land carriage - Exchanged, discharged, died, or escape: Discharged - Time when: 4 May 1814 - Whither, and by what order, or number or re-entry: United States

Stevens, William   Prisoner 66. Rank: Sergeant - By what ship or how taken: Boats & Troops - Time when: 28 May 1813 - Place where: Stoney Point, Henderson Harbor - Of what ship or corps: Land forces - Whether man of war, privateer or merchant vessel: Taken on shore - Time when received into custody: 8 Jun 1813 - From what ship or whence received: Batteaux - Exchanged, discharged, died, or escape: Discharged - Time when: 31 Oct 1813 - Whither, and by what order, or number or re-entry: Malabar Transport

Stewart, James   Prisoner 1185. Rank: Ensign - By what ship or how taken: Troops - Time when: 5 May 1813 - Place where: Rapids - Of what ship or corps: Land forces - Whether man of war, privateer or merchant vessel: Taken on shore - Time when received into custody: 25 Nov 1813 - From what ship or whence received: Town Goal - Exchanged, discharged, died, or escape: Discharged - Time when: 4 May 1814 - Whither, and by what order, or number or re-entry: United States

Stewart, James   Prisoner 1201. Rank: Lieutenant - By what ship or how taken: Troops - Time when: 19 Dec 1813 - Place where: Fort Niagara - Of what ship or corps: Land forces - Whether man of war, privateer or merchant vessel: Taken on shore - Time when received into custody: 18 Jan 1814 - From what ship or whence received: Montreal by land carriage - Exchanged, discharged, died, or escape: Discharged - Time when: 4 May 1814 - Whither, and by what order, or number or re-entry: United States

Stewart, John   Prisoner 1527. Rank: Private - By what ship or how taken: Troops - Time when: 25 Jul 1814 - Place where: Lundy's Lane - Of what ship or corps: Land forces - Whether man of war, privateer or merchant vessel: Taken on shore - Time when received into custody: 30 Aug 1814 - From what ship or whence received: Lady Delaval Schooner 578 - Exchanged, discharged, died, or escape: Discharged - Time when: 8 Oct 1814 - Whither, and by what order, or number or re-entry: Queen No. 415

Stickney, Abijah   Prisoner 1418. Rank: Private - By what ship or how taken: Troops - Time when: 19 Dec 1813 - Place where: Fort Niagara - Of what ship or corps: Land forces - Whether man of war, privateer or merchant vessel: Taken on shore - Time when received into custody: 29 Jan 1814 - From what ship or whence received: Montreal by land carriage - Exchanged, discharged, died, or escape: Discharged - Time when: 4 May 1814 - Whither, and by what order, or number or re-entry: United States

American Prisoners of War held at Quebec during the War of 1812

Stocker, Jesse L.   Prisoner 413. Rank: Sergeant - By what ship or how taken: Troops - Time when: 24 Jun 1813 - Place where: Beaver Dam - Of what ship or corps: Land forces - Whether man of war, privateer or merchant vessel: Taken on shore - Time when received into custody: 7 Jul 1813 - From what ship or whence received: Steamboat - Exchanged, discharged, died, or escape: Discharged - Time when: 8 Oct 1813 - Whither, and by what order, or number or re-entry: H.M. Ship Ceylon

Stockwell, L. L.   Prisoner 1558. Rank: Private - By what ship or how taken: Troops - Time when: 25 Jul 1814 - Place where: Lundy's Lane - Of what ship or corps: Land forces - Whether man of war, privateer or merchant vessel: Taken on shore - Time when received into custody: 30 Aug 1814 - From what ship or whence received: Lady Delaval Schooner 578 - Exchanged, discharged, died, or escape: Discharged - Time when: - Whither, and by what order, or number or re-entry: H.M. Ship Ceylon

Store, Stephen   Prisoner 1279. Rank: Private - By what ship or how taken: Troops - Time when: 19 Dec 1813 - Place where: Fort Niagara - Of what ship or corps: Land forces - Whether man of war, privateer or merchant vessel: Taken on shore - Time when received into custody: 29 Jan 1814 - From what ship or whence received: Montreal by land carriage - Exchanged, discharged, died, or escape: Discharged - Time when: 4 May 1814 - Whither, and by what order, or number or re-entry: United States

Storey, Pliney   Prisoner 271. Rank: Private - By what ship or how taken: Troops - Time when: 6 Jun 1813 - Place where: Stoney Point - Of what ship or corps: Land forces - Whether man of war, privateer or merchant vessel: Taken on shore - Time when received into custody: 28 Jun 1813 - From what ship or whence received: Batteaux - Exchanged, discharged, died, or escape: Discharged - Time when: 31 Oct 1813 - Whither, and by what order, or number or re-entry: Malabar Transport

Stottle, George   Prisoner 1940. Rank: Private - By what ship or how taken: Troops - Time when: 17 Sep 1814 - Place where: Fort Erie - Of what ship or corps: Land forces - Whether man of war, privateer or merchant vessel: Taken on shore - Time when received into custody: 1 Nov 1814 - From what ship or whence received: Montreal - Exchanged, discharged, died, or escape: Discharged - Time when: 13 Mar 1815 - Whither, and by what order, or number or re-entry: United States

Stout, Jonathan   Prisoner 1870. Rank: Private - By what ship or how taken: Troops - Time when: 17 Sep 1814 - Place where: Fort Erie - Of what ship or corps: Land forces - Whether man of war, privateer or merchant vessel: Taken on shore - Time when received into custody: 1 Nov 1814 - From what ship or whence received: Montreal - Exchanged, discharged, died, or escape: Discharged - Time when: 8 Nov 1814 - Whither, and by what order, or number or re-entry: S. George No. 575 for Halifax

Stowner, Henry   Prisoner 1303. Rank: Private - By what ship or how taken: Troops - Time when: 19 Dec 1813 - Place where: Fort Niagara - Of what ship or corps: Land forces - Whether man of war, privateer or merchant vessel: Taken on shore - Time when received into custody: 29 Jan 1814 - From what ship or whence received: Montreal by land carriage - Exchanged, discharged, died, or escape: Discharged - Time when: 24 Feb 1814 - Whither, and by what order, or number or re-entry: Volunteered for New Brunswick Fencibles

Streback, J. M.   Prisoner 1583. Rank: Seaman - By what ship or how taken: Gun Boats - Time when: 12 Aug 1814 - Place where: Fort Erie - Of what ship or corps: Ohio - Whether man of war, privateer or merchant vessel: Man of War - Time when received into custody: 5 Oct 1814 - From what ship or whence received: Montreal - Exchanged, discharged, died, or escape: Discharged - Time when: 10 Nov 1814 - Whither, and by what order, or number or re-entry: Freedom No. 582

Street, Ishemail   Prisoner 424. Rank: Corporal - By what ship or how taken: Troops - Time when: 24 Jun 1813 - Place where: Beaver Dam - Of what ship or corps: Land forces - Whether man of war, privateer or merchant vessel: Taken on shore - Time when received into custody: 7 Jul 1813 - From what ship or whence received: Steamboat - Exchanged, discharged, died, or escape: Discharged - Time when: 31 Oct 1813 - Whither, and by what order, or number or re-entry: Malabar Transport

Strickland, Richard   Prisoner 980. Rank: Private - By what ship or how taken: Troops - Time when: 5 Jul 1813 - Place where: Fort Schisher - Of what ship or corps: Land forces - Whether man of war, privateer or merchant vessel: Taken on shore - Time when received into custody: 5 Sep 1813 - From what ship or whence received: Steamboat - Exchanged, discharged, died, or escape: Discharged - Time when: 31 Oct 1813 - Whither, and by what order, or number or re-entry: Malabar Transport

American Prisoners of War held at Quebec during the War of 1812

Stroud, John   Prisoner 430. Rank: Private - By what ship or how taken: Troops - Time when: 24 Jun 1813 - Place where: Beaver Dam - Of what ship or corps: Land forces - Whether man of war, privateer or merchant vessel: Taken on shore - Time when received into custody: 7 Jul 1813 - From what ship or whence received: Steamboat - Exchanged, discharged, died, or escape: Discharged - Time when: 10 Aug 1813 - Whither, and by what order, or number or re-entry: HM Ship Regulius by order of Sir George Provost

Stuard, Thomas   Prisoner 613. Rank: Private - By what ship or how taken: Troops - Time when: 26 Jun 1813 - Place where: Stoney Point - Of what ship or corps: Land forces - Whether man of war, privateer or merchant vessel: Taken on shore - Time when received into custody: 7 Jul 1813 - From what ship or whence received: Steamboat - Exchanged, discharged, died, or escape: Discharged - Time when: 10 Aug 1813 - Whither, and by what order, or number or re-entry: HM Ship Regulius by order of Sir George Provost

Stubbs, Henry   Prisoner 1530. Rank: Private - By what ship or how taken: Troops - Time when: 25 Jul 1814 - Place where: Lundy's Lane - Of what ship or corps: Land forces - Whether man of war, privateer or merchant vessel: Taken on shore - Time when received into custody: 30 Aug 1814 - From what ship or whence received: Lady Delaval Schooner 578 - Exchanged, discharged, died, or escape: Discharged - Time when: 8 Oct 1814 - Whither, and by what order, or number or re-entry: Queen No. 415

Stutevant, Thomas   Prisoner 865. Rank: Private - By what ship or how taken: Troops - Time when: 26 Jun 1813 - Place where: Beaver Dam - Of what ship or corps: Land forces - Whether man of war, privateer or merchant vessel: Taken on shore - Time when received into custody: 7 Jul 1813 - From what ship or whence received: Steamboat - Exchanged, discharged, died, or escape: Discharged - Time when: 10 Aug 1813 - Whither, and by what order, or number or re-entry: HM Ship Malpomena

Stymets, John   Prisoner 1041. Rank: Seaman - By what ship or how taken: Lord Melvin - Time when: 10 Aug 1813 - Place where: Lake Ontario - Of what ship or corps: Growler - Whether man of war, privateer or merchant vessel: Man of War - Time when received into custody: 5 Sep 1813 - From what ship or whence received: Steamboat - Exchanged, discharged, died, or escape: Discharged - Time when: 31 Oct 1813 - Whither, and by what order, or number or re-entry: HM Ship Success

Sulivan, David   Prisoner 1331. Rank: Private - By what ship or how taken: Troops - Time when: 19 Dec 1813 - Place where: Fort Niagara - Of what ship or corps: Land forces - Whether man of war, privateer or merchant vessel: Taken on shore - Time when received into custody: 29 Jan 1814 - From what ship or whence received: Montreal by land carriage - Exchanged, discharged, died, or escape: Discharged - Time when: 4 May 1814 - Whither, and by what order, or number or re-entry: United States

Summers, William   Prisoner 272. Rank: Private - By what ship or how taken: Troops - Time when: 6 Jun 1813 - Place where: Stoney Point - Of what ship or corps: Land forces - Whether man of war, privateer or merchant vessel: Taken on shore - Time when received into custody: 28 Jun 1813 - From what ship or whence received: Batteaux - Exchanged, discharged, died, or escape: Discharged - Time when: 4 May 1814 - Whither, and by what order, or number or re-entry: United States

Sutherly, Joseph   Prisoner 797. Rank: Private - By what ship or how taken: Troops - Time when: 26 Jun 1813 - Place where: Beaver Dam - Of what ship or corps: Land forces - Whether man of war, privateer or merchant vessel: Taken on shore - Time when received into custody: 7 Jul 1813 - From what ship or whence received: Steamboat - Exchanged, discharged, died, or escape: Discharged - Time when: 10 Aug 1813 - Whither, and by what order, or number or re-entry: HM Ship Malpomena

Swan, Samuel   Prisoner 517. Rank: Private - By what ship or how taken: Troops - Time when: 24 Jun 1813 - Place where: Beaver Dam - Of what ship or corps: Land forces - Whether man of war, privateer or merchant vessel: Taken on shore - Time when received into custody: 7 Jul 1813 - From what ship or whence received: Steamboat - Exchanged, discharged, died, or escape: Discharged - Time when: 31 Oct 1813 - Whither, and by what order, or number or re-entry: Malabar Transport

Swartwort, Augustus   Prisoner 1708. Rank: Private - By what ship or how taken: Gun Boats - Time when: 6 Sep 1814 - Place where: Lake Huron - Of what ship or corps: Scorpion - Whether man of war, privateer or merchant vessel: Man of War - Time when received into custody: 28 Oct 1814 - From what ship or whence received: Montreal - Exchanged, discharged, died, or escape: Discharged - Time when: 10 Nov 1814 - Whither, and by what order, or number or re-entry: Lord Cartheart No. 161 for Halifax

Swatewood, Jacob   Prisoner 773. Rank: Private - By what ship or how taken: Troops - Time when: 26 Jun 1813 - Place where: Beaver Dam - Of what ship or corps: Land forces - Whether man of war, privateer or merchant vessel: Taken on shore - Time when received into custody: 7 Jul 1813 - From what ship or whence received: Steamboat - Exchanged,

American Prisoners of War held at Quebec during the War of 1812

discharged, died, or escape: Discharged - Time when: 10 Aug 1813 - Whither, and by what order, or number or re-entry: HM Ship Malpomena

Sweet, Abraham   Prisoner 1960. Rank: Private - By what ship or how taken: Troops - Time when: 17 Sep 1814 - Place where: Fort Erie - Of what ship or corps: Land forces - Whether man of war, privateer or merchant vessel: Taken on shore - Time when received into custody: 11 Dec 1814 - From what ship or whence received: Montreal - Exchanged, discharged, died, or escape: Discharged - Time when: 13 Mar 1815 - Whither, and by what order, or number or re-entry: United States

Tabott, Benjamin   Prisoner 607. Rank: Private - By what ship or how taken: Troops - Time when: 26 Jun 1813 - Place where: Stoney Point - Of what ship or corps: Land forces - Whether man of war, privateer or merchant vessel: Taken on shore - Time when received into custody: 7 Jul 1813 - From what ship or whence received: Steamboat - Exchanged, discharged, died, or escape: Discharged - Time when: 10 Aug 1813 - Whither, and by what order, or number or re-entry: HM Ship Regulius by order of Sir George Provost

Tabvery, Ephraim   Prisoner 63. Rank: Private - By what ship or how taken: Boats & Troops - Time when: 28 May 1813 - Place where: Stoney Point, Henderson Harbor - Of what ship or corps: Land forces - Whether man of war, privateer or merchant vessel: Taken on shore - Time when received into custody: 8 Jun 1813 - From what ship or whence received: Batteaux - Exchanged, discharged, died, or escape: Discharged - Time when: 31 Oct 1813 - Whither, and by what order, or number or re-entry: Malabar Transport

Taggent, Archibald   Prisoner 893. Rank: Private - By what ship or how taken: Troops - Time when: 26 Jun 1813 - Place where: Beaver Dam - Of what ship or corps: Land forces - Whether man of war, privateer or merchant vessel: Taken on shore - Time when received into custody: 7 Jul 1813 - From what ship or whence received: Steamboat - Exchanged, discharged, died, or escape: Discharged - Time when: 10 Aug 1813 - Whither, and by what order, or number or re-entry: HM Ship Malpomena

Taggert, Thomas   Prisoner 1863. Rank: Corporal - By what ship or how taken: Troops - Time when: 17 Sep 1814 - Place where: Fort Erie - Of what ship or corps: Land forces - Whether man of war, privateer or merchant vessel: Taken on shore - Time when received into custody: 1 Nov 1814 - From what ship or whence received: Montreal - Exchanged, discharged, died, or escape: Discharged - Time when: 8 Nov 1814 - Whither, and by what order, or number or re-entry: S. George No. 575 for Halifax

Talbott, Elijah   Prisoner 490. Rank: Private - By what ship or how taken: Troops - Time when: 24 Jun 1813 - Place where: Beaver Dam - Of what ship or corps: Land forces - Whether man of war, privateer or merchant vessel: Taken on shore - Time when received into custody: 7 Jul 1813 - From what ship or whence received: Steamboat - Exchanged, discharged, died, or escape: Discharged - Time when: 10 Aug 1813 - Whither, and by what order, or number or re-entry: HM Ship Regulius by order of Sir George Provost

Talbott, John H.   Prisoner 489. Rank: Private - By what ship or how taken: Troops - Time when: 24 Jun 1813 - Place where: Beaver Dam - Of what ship or corps: Land forces - Whether man of war, privateer or merchant vessel: Taken on shore - Time when received into custody: 7 Jul 1813 - From what ship or whence received: Steamboat - Exchanged, discharged, died, or escape: Discharged - Time when: 10 Aug 1813 - Whither, and by what order, or number or re-entry: HM Ship Regulius by order of Sir George Provost

Tanner, Asa   Prisoner 1467. Rank: Private - By what ship or how taken: Gun Boats - Time when: 29 May 1814 - Place where: Sandy Creek - Of what ship or corps: Land forces - Whether man of war, privateer or merchant vessel: Taken on shore - Time when received into custody: 12 Aug 1814 - From what ship or whence received: Royal Seaman No. 289 Transport - Exchanged, discharged, died, or escape: Discharged - Time when: 8 Nov 1814 - Whither, and by what order, or number or re-entry: George No. 575 for Halifax

Tanning, John C.   Prisoner 1014. Rank: Seaman - By what ship or how taken: Earl Moria - Time when: 10 Aug 1813 - Place where: Lake Ontario - Of what ship or corps: Julia - Whether man of war, privateer or merchant vessel: Man of War - Time when received into custody: 5 Sep 1813 - From what ship or whence received: Steamboat - Exchanged, discharged, died, or escape: Discharged - Time when: 31 Oct 1813 - Whither, and by what order, or number or re-entry: Malabar Transport

Tardon, Thomas   Prisoner 911. Rank: Private - By what ship or how taken: Troops - Time when: 26 Jun 1813 - Place where: Beaver Dam - Of what ship or corps: Land forces - Whether man of war, privateer or merchant vessel: Taken on shore - Time when received into custody: 21 Jul 1813 - From what ship or whence received: Steamboat - Exchanged, discharged, died, or escape: Discharged - Time when: 10 Aug 1813 - Whither, and by what order, or number or re-entry: HM Ship Malpomena

American Prisoners of War held at Quebec during the War of 1812

Tarrehill, Zem.   Prisoner 1407.   Rank: Private - By what ship or how taken: Troops - Time when: 19 Dec 1813 - Place where: Fort Niagara - Of what ship or corps: Land forces - Whether man of war, privateer or merchant vessel: Taken on shore - Time when received into custody: 29 Jan 1814 - From what ship or whence received: Montreal by land carriage - Exchanged, discharged, died, or escape: Discharged - Time when: 4 May 1814 - Whither, and by what order, or number or re-entry: United States

Taylor, Isaac M.   Prisoner 1144.   Rank: Private - By what ship or how taken: Troops - Time when: 5 May 1813 - Place where: Rapids Prince Reason - Of what ship or corps: Land forces - Whether man of war, privateer or merchant vessel: Taken on shore - Time when received into custody: 25 Nov 1813 - From what ship or whence received: Town Goal - Exchanged, discharged, died, or escape: Discharged - Time when: 21 Apr 1814 - Whither, and by what order, or number or re-entry: United States

Taylor, John   Prisoner 1039.   Rank: Seaman - By what ship or how taken: Lord Melvin - Time when: 10 Aug 1813 - Place where: Lake Ontario - Of what ship or corps: Growler - Whether man of war, privateer or merchant vessel: Man of War - Time when received into custody: 5 Sep 1813 - From what ship or whence received: Steamboat - Exchanged, discharged, died, or escape: Discharged - Time when: 31 Oct 1813 - Whither, and by what order, or number or re-entry: Malabar Transport

Taylor, John   Prisoner 1455.   Rank: Private - By what ship or how taken: Troops - Time when: 6 May 1814 - Place where: Oswago - Of what ship or corps: Land forces - Whether man of war, privateer or merchant vessel: Taken on shore - Time when received into custody: 12 Aug 1814 - From what ship or whence received: Royal Seaman No. 289 Transport - Exchanged, discharged, died, or escape: Discharged - Time when: 8 Oct 1814 - Whither, and by what order, or number or re-entry: Queen No. 415

Taylor, Lewis L.   Prisoner 400.   Rank: Major - By what ship or how taken: Troops - Time when: 24 Jun 1813 - Place where: Beaver Dam - Of what ship or corps: Land forces - Whether man of war, privateer or merchant vessel: Taken on shore - Time when received into custody: 7 Jul 1813 - From what ship or whence received: Steamboat - Exchanged, discharged, died, or escape: Discharged - Time when: 10 Aug 1813 - Whither, and by what order, or number or re-entry: Per order His Exellency Sir George Prevost

Taylor, Richard   Prisoner 427.   Rank: Private - By what ship or how taken: Troops - Time when: 24 Jun 1813 - Place where: Beaver Dam - Of what ship or corps: Land forces - Whether man of war, privateer or merchant vessel: Taken on shore - Time when received into custody: 7 Jul 1813 - From what ship or whence received: Steamboat - Exchanged, discharged, died, or escape: Discharged - Time when: 4 May 1814 - Whither, and by what order, or number or re-entry: United States

Taylor, Samuel   Prisoner 1687.   Rank: Private - By what ship or how taken: Troops - Time when: 12 Aug 1814 - Place where: Fort Erie - Of what ship or corps: Somers - Whether man of war, privateer or merchant vessel: Man of War - Time when received into custody: 23 Oct 1814 - From what ship or whence received: Montreal - Exchanged, discharged, died, or escape: Discharged - Time when: 8 Nov 1814 - Whither, and by what order, or number or re-entry: S. George No. 575 for Halifax

Taylor, Thomas   Prisoner 216.   Rank: Private - By what ship or how taken: Boats & Troops - Time when: 3 Jun 1813 - Place where: Lake Champlain - Of what ship or corps: Eagle - Whether man of war, privateer or merchant vessel: Man of War - Time when received into custody: 9 Jun 1813 - From what ship or whence received: Batteaux - Exchanged, discharged, died, or escape: Discharged - Time when: 31 Oct 1813 - Whither, and by what order, or number or re-entry: Malabar Transport

Taylor, Thomas   Prisoner 1270.   Rank: Privateer - By what ship or how taken: Troops - Time when: 19 Dec 1813 - Place where: Fort Niagara - Of what ship or corps: Land forces - Whether man of war, privateer or merchant vessel: Taken on shore - Time when received into custody: 29 Jan 1814 - From what ship or whence received: Montreal by land carriage - Exchanged, discharged, died, or escape: Discharged - Time when: 4 May 1814 - Whither, and by what order, or number or re-entry: United States

Taylor, William   Prisoner 1415.   Rank: Private - By what ship or how taken: Troops - Time when: 19 Dec 1813 - Place where: Fort Niagara - Of what ship or corps: Land forces - Whether man of war, privateer or merchant vessel: Taken on shore - Time when received into custody: 29 Jan 1814 - From what ship or whence received: Montreal by land carriage - Exchanged, discharged, died, or escape: Discharged - Time when: 4 May 1814 - Whither, and by what order, or number or re-entry: United States

Taylor, William   Prisoner 292.   Rank: Private - By what ship or how taken: Boats & Troops - Time when: 6 Jun 1813 - Place where: Stoney Point - Of what ship or corps: Land forces - Whether man of war, privateer or merchant vessel: Taken on shore - Time when received into custody: 28 Jun 1813 - From what ship or whence received: Quebec of Quebec -

American Prisoners of War held at Quebec during the War of 1812

Exchanged, discharged, died, or escape: Discharged - Time when: 31 Oct 1813 - Whither, and by what order, or number or re-entry: Malabar Transport

Temple, William   Prisoner 1111. Rank: Private - By what ship or how taken: Troops - Time when: 17 Oct 1813 - Place where: Red Mills - Of what ship or corps: Land forces - Whether man of war, privateer or merchant vessel: Taken on shore - Time when received into custody: 12 Oct 1813 - From what ship or whence received: Steamboat - Exchanged, discharged, died, or escape: Discharged - Time when: 31 Oct 1813 - Whither, and by what order, or number or re-entry: Malabar Transport

Templin, John   Prisoner 1109. Rank: Private - By what ship or how taken: Troops - Time when: 17 Oct 1813 - Place where: Red Mills - Of what ship or corps: Land forces - Whether man of war, privateer or merchant vessel: Taken on shore - Time when received into custody: 12 Oct 1813 - From what ship or whence received: Steamboat - Exchanged, discharged, died, or escape: Discharged - Time when: 31 Oct 1813 - Whither, and by what order, or number or re-entry: Malabar Transport

Tenney, John   Prisoner 460. Rank: Private - By what ship or how taken: Troops - Time when: 24 Jun 1813 - Place where: Beaver Dam - Of what ship or corps: Malabar & Hydia - Whether man of war, privateer or merchant vessel: Taken on shore - Time when received into custody: 7 Jul 1813 - From what ship or whence received: Steamboat - Exchanged, discharged, died, or escape: Discharged - Time when: 10 Aug 1813 - Whither, and by what order, or number or re-entry: HM Ship Regulius by order of Sir George Provost

Thayer, A.   Prisoner 1545. Rank: Private - By what ship or how taken: Troops - Time when: 25 Jul 1814 - Place where: Lundy's Lane - Of what ship or corps: Land forces - Whether man of war, privateer or merchant vessel: Taken on shore - Time when received into custody: 30 Aug 1814 - From what ship or whence received: Lady Delaval Schooner 578 - Exchanged, discharged, died, or escape: Discharged - Time when: 8 Oct 1814 - Whither, and by what order, or number or re-entry: Queen No. 415

Thead, Isaac   Prisoner 14. Rank: Private - By what ship or how taken: Boats & Troops - Time when: 28 May 1813 - Place where: Stoney Point, Henderson Harbor - Of what ship or corps: Land forces - Whether man of war, privateer or merchant vessel: Taken on shore - Time when received into custody: 8 Jun 1813 - From what ship or whence received: Batteaux - Exchanged, discharged, died, or escape: Discharged - Time when: 31 Oct 1813 - Whither, and by what order, or number or re-entry: Malabar Transport

Thipelwood, Charles   Prisoner 572. Rank: Private - By what ship or how taken: Troops - Time when: 26 Jun 1813 - Place where: Beaver Dam - Of what ship or corps: Land forces - Whether man of war, privateer or merchant vessel: Taken on shore - Time when received into custody: 13 Jul 1813 - From what ship or whence received: Steamboat - Exchanged, discharged, died, or escape: Discharged - Time when: 10 Aug 1813 - Whither, and by what order, or number or re-entry: HM Ship Regulius by order of Sir George Provost

Thomas, John   Prisoner 1678. Rank: Seaman - By what ship or how taken: Gun Boats - Time when: 4 Aug 1814 - Place where: Lake Ontario - Of what ship or corps: Jack - Whether man of war, privateer or merchant vessel: Man of War - Time when received into custody: 23 Oct 1814 - From what ship or whence received: Montreal - Exchanged, discharged, died, or escape: Discharged - Time when: 7 Nov 1814 - Whither, and by what order, or number or re-entry: Transport Freedom No. 582 by orders of his Excellency Sir George Provost

Thomas, Samuel   Prisoner 732. Rank: Private - By what ship or how taken: Troops - Time when: 26 Jun 1813 - Place where: Beaver Dam - Of what ship or corps: Land forces - Whether man of war, privateer or merchant vessel: Taken on shore - Time when received into custody: 7 Jul 1813 - From what ship or whence received: Steamboat - Exchanged, discharged, died, or escape: Discharged - Time when: 10 Aug 1813 - Whither, and by what order, or number or re-entry: HM Ship Regulius by order of Sir George Provost

Thomas, William   Prisoner 765. Rank: Private - By what ship or how taken: Troops - Time when: 26 Jun 1813 - Place where: Beaver Dam - Of what ship or corps: Land forces - Whether man of war, privateer or merchant vessel: Taken on shore - Time when received into custody: 7 Jul 1813 - From what ship or whence received: Steamboat - Exchanged, discharged, died, or escape: Discharged - Time when: 10 Aug 1813 - Whither, and by what order, or number or re-entry: HM Ship Malpomena

Thompson, James   Prisoner 1514. Rank: Sergeant - By what ship or how taken: Troops - Time when: 25 Jul 1814 - Place where: Lundy's Lane - Of what ship or corps: Land forces - Whether man of war, privateer or merchant vessel: Taken on shore - Time when received into custody: 30 Aug 1814 - From what ship or whence received: Lady Delaval Schooner 578 - Exchanged, discharged, died, or escape: Discharged - Time when: 8 Oct 1814 - Whither, and by what order, or number or re-entry: Queen No. 415

American Prisoners of War held at Quebec during the War of 1812

Thompson, John   Prisoner 1103.   Rank: Private - By what ship or how taken: Troops - Time when: 24 Aug 1813 - Place where: Fort George - Of what ship or corps: Land forces - Whether man of war, privateer or merchant vessel: Taken on shore - Time when received into custody: 12 Oct 1813 - From what ship or whence received: Steamboat - Exchanged, discharged, died, or escape: Discharged - Time when: 31 Oct 1813 - Whither, and by what order, or number or re-entry: Malabar Transport

Thompson, John T.   Prisoner 1153.   Rank: Private - By what ship or how taken: Troops - Time when: 5 May 1813 - Place where: Rapids Prince Reason - Of what ship or corps: Land forces - Whether man of war, privateer or merchant vessel: Taken on shore - Time when received into custody: 25 Nov 1813 - From what ship or whence received: Town Goal - Exchanged, discharged, died, or escape: Discharged - Time when: 4 May 1814 - Whither, and by what order, or number or re-entry: United States

Thompson, John W.   Prisoner 531.   Rank: Lieutenant - By what ship or how taken: Troops - Time when: 24 Jun 1813 - Place where: Beaver Dam - Of what ship or corps: Land forces - Whether man of war, privateer or merchant vessel: Taken on shore - Time when received into custody: 13 Jul 1813 - From what ship or whence received: Steamboat - Exchanged, discharged, died, or escape: Discharged - Time when: 13 Dec 1813 - Whither, and by what order, or number or re-entry: United States

Thompson, Jonathan   Prisoner 869.   Rank: Private - By what ship or how taken: Troops - Time when: 26 Jun 1813 - Place where: Beaver Dam - Of what ship or corps: Land forces - Whether man of war, privateer or merchant vessel: Taken on shore - Time when received into custody: 7 Jul 1813 - From what ship or whence received: Steamboat - Exchanged, discharged, died, or escape: Discharged - Time when: 10 Aug 1813 - Whither, and by what order, or number or re-entry: HM Ship Malpomena

Thompson, William   Prisoner 1810.   Rank: Private - By what ship or how taken: Troops - Time when: 17 Sep 1814 - Place where: Fort Erie - Of what ship or corps: Land forces - Whether man of war, privateer or merchant vessel: Taken on shore - Time when received into custody: 1 Nov 1814 - From what ship or whence received: Montreal - Exchanged, discharged, died, or escape: Discharged - Time when: 8 Nov 1814 - Whither, and by what order, or number or re-entry: S. George No. 575 for Halifax by order of Sir George Provost

Thorn, Jonathan   Prisoner 1779.   Rank: Private - By what ship or how taken: Troops - Time when: 7 Sep 1814 - Place where: Fort Erie - Of what ship or corps: Land forces - Whether man of war, privateer or merchant vessel: Taken on shore - Time when received into custody: 1 Nov 1814 - From what ship or whence received: Montreal - Exchanged, discharged, died, or escape: Discharged - Time when: 8 Nov 1814 - Whither, and by what order, or number or re-entry: S. George No. 575 for Halifax by order of Sir George Provost

Thorn, William   Prisoner 1932.   Rank: Private - By what ship or how taken: Troops - Time when: 17 Sep 1814 - Place where: Fort Erie - Of what ship or corps: Land forces - Whether man of war, privateer or merchant vessel: Taken on shore - Time when received into custody: 1 Nov 1814 - From what ship or whence received: Montreal - Exchanged, discharged, died, or escape: Discharged - Time when: 13 Mar 1815 - Whither, and by what order, or number or re-entry: United States

Thornberg, Thomas   Prisoner 1649.   Rank: Private - By what ship or how taken: Troops - Time when: 19 Dec 1813 - Place where: Niagara - Of what ship or corps: Land forces - Whether man of war, privateer or merchant vessel: Taken on shore - Time when received into custody: 5 Oct 1814 - From what ship or whence received: Montreal - Exchanged, discharged, died, or escape: Discharged - Time when: 8 Oct 1814 - Whither, and by what order, or number or re-entry: H.M. Ship Ceylon

Thornburgh, John   Prisoner 1334.   Rank: Sergeant - By what ship or how taken: Troops - Time when: 19 Dec 1813 - Place where: Fort Niagara - Of what ship or corps: Land forces - Whether man of war, privateer or merchant vessel: Taken on shore - Time when received into custody: 29 Jan 1814 - From what ship or whence received: Montreal by land carriage - Exchanged, discharged, died, or escape: Discharged - Time when: 4 May 1814 - Whither, and by what order, or number or re-entry: United States

Thornning, Thomas   Prisoner 1035.   Rank: Seaman - By what ship or how taken: Lord Melvin - Time when: 10 Aug 1813 - Place where: Lake Ontario - Of what ship or corps: Growler - Whether man of war, privateer or merchant vessel: Man of War - Time when received into custody: 5 Sep 1813 - From what ship or whence received: Steamboat - Exchanged, discharged, died, or escape: Discharged - Time when: 1 Nov 1813 - Whither, and by what order, or number or re-entry: Lord Cartheart Transport

Thornton, William   Prisoner 1026.   Rank: Seaman - By what ship or how taken: Lord Melvin - Time when: 10 Aug 1813 - Place where: Lake Ontario - Of what ship or corps: Growler - Whether man of war, privateer or merchant vessel: Man of War - Time when received into custody: 5 Sep 1813 - From what ship or whence received: Steamboat - Exchanged,

American Prisoners of War held at Quebec during the War of 1812

discharged, died, or escape: Discharged - Time when: 1 Nov 1813 - Whither, and by what order, or number or re-entry: The Hero for England

Thristy, Joel   Prisoner 720. Rank: Private - By what ship or how taken: Troops - Time when: 26 Jun 1813 - Place where: Beaver Dam - Of what ship or corps: Land forces - Whether man of war, privateer or merchant vessel: Taken on shore - Time when received into custody: 7 Jul 1813 - From what ship or whence received: Steamboat - Exchanged, discharged, died, or escape: Discharged - Time when: 10 Aug 1813 - Whither, and by what order, or number or re-entry: HM Ship Regulius by order of Sir George Provost

Thundersville, John   Prisoner 725. Rank: Private - By what ship or how taken: Troops - Time when: 26 Jun 1813 - Place where: Beaver Dam - Of what ship or corps: Land forces - Whether man of war, privateer or merchant vessel: Taken on shore - Time when received into custody: 7 Jul 1813 - From what ship or whence received: Steamboat - Exchanged, discharged, died, or escape: Discharged - Time when: 10 Aug 1813 - Whither, and by what order, or number or re-entry: HM Ship Regulius by order of Sir George Provost

Tiemell, William   Prisoner 4. Rank: Sergeant - By what ship or how taken: Boats & Troops - Time when: 28 May 1813 - Place where: Stoney Point, Henderson Harbor - Of what ship or corps: Land forces - Whether man of war, privateer or merchant vessel: Taken on shore - Time when received into custody: 8 Jun 1813 - From what ship or whence received: Batteaux - Exchanged, discharged, died, or escape: Discharged - Time when: 8 Oct 1813 - Whither, and by what order, or number or re-entry: H.M. Ship Ceylon

Tilden, Lemiah   Prisoner 1179. Rank: Private - By what ship or how taken: Troops - Time when: 5 May 1813 - Place where: Rapids - Of what ship or corps: Land forces - Whether man of war, privateer or merchant vessel: Taken on shore - Time when received into custody: 25 Nov 1813 - From what ship or whence received: Town Goal - Exchanged, discharged, died, or escape: Discharged - Time when: 4 May 1814 - Whither, and by what order, or number or re-entry: United States

Till, James   Prisoner 573. Rank: Private - By what ship or how taken: Troops - Time when: 26 Jun 1813 - Place where: Beaver Dam - Of what ship or corps: Land forces - Whether man of war, privateer or merchant vessel: Taken on shore - Time when received into custody: 13 Jul 1813 - From what ship or whence received: Steamboat - Exchanged, discharged, died, or escape: Died - Time when: 31 Aug 1813 - Whither, and by what order, or number or re-entry: Typhus Fever

Timson, Peter   Prisoner 1768. Rank: Corporal - By what ship or how taken: Troops - Time when: 7 Sep 1814 - Place where: Fort Erie - Of what ship or corps: Land forces - Whether man of war, privateer or merchant vessel: Taken on shore - Time when received into custody: 1 Nov 1814 - From what ship or whence received: Montreal - Exchanged, discharged, died, or escape: Discharged - Time when: 8 Nov 1814 - Whither, and by what order, or number or re-entry: S. George No. 575 for Halifax by order of Sir George Provost

Titus, George   Prisoner 24. Rank: Private - By what ship or how taken: Boats & Troops - Time when: 28 May 1813 - Place where: Stoney Point, Henderson Harbor - Of what ship or corps: Land forces - Whether man of war, privateer or merchant vessel: Taken on shore - Time when received into custody: 8 Jun 1813 - From what ship or whence received: Batteaux - Exchanged, discharged, died, or escape: Discharged - Time when: 4 May 1814 - Whither, and by what order, or number or re-entry: United States

Todd, John   Prisoner 513. Rank: Private - By what ship or how taken: Troops - Time when: 24 Jun 1813 - Place where: Beaver Dam - Of what ship or corps: Land forces - Whether man of war, privateer or merchant vessel: Taken on shore - Time when received into custody: 7 Jul 1813 - From what ship or whence received: Steamboat - Exchanged, discharged, died, or escape: Discharged - Time when: 10 Aug 1813 - Whither, and by what order, or number or re-entry: HM Ship Wasp

Tomlinson, John   Prisoner 796. Rank: Private - By what ship or how taken: Troops - Time when: 26 Jun 1813 - Place where: Beaver Dam - Of what ship or corps: Land forces - Whether man of war, privateer or merchant vessel: Taken on shore - Time when received into custody: 7 Jul 1813 - From what ship or whence received: Steamboat - Exchanged, discharged, died, or escape: Discharged - Time when: 10 Aug 1813 - Whither, and by what order, or number or re-entry: HM Ship Malpomena

Tonnier, Joshua   Prisoner 746. Rank: Private - By what ship or how taken: Troops - Time when: 26 Jun 1813 - Place where: Beaver Dam - Of what ship or corps: Land forces - Whether man of war, privateer or merchant vessel: Taken on shore - Time when received into custody: 7 Jul 1813 - From what ship or whence received: Steamboat - Exchanged, discharged, died, or escape: Discharged - Time when: 10 Aug 1813 - Whither, and by what order, or number or re-entry: HM Ship Malpomena

Torer, Jon   Prisoner 439. Rank: Private - By what ship or how taken: Troops - Time when: 24 Jun 1813 - Place where: Beaver

American Prisoners of War held at Quebec during the War of 1812

Dam - Of what ship or corps: Land forces - Whether man of war, privateer or merchant vessel: Taken on shore - Time when received into custody: 7 Jul 1813 - From what ship or whence received: Steamboat - Exchanged, discharged, died, or escape: Discharged - Time when: 10 Aug 1813 - Whither, and by what order, or number or re-entry: HM Ship Regulius by order of Sir George Provost

Torrey, Joseph   Prisoner 1050. Rank: Private - By what ship or how taken: Lord Melvin - Time when: 10 Aug 1813 - Place where: Lake Ontario - Of what ship or corps: Growler - Whether man of war, privateer or merchant vessel: Man of War - Time when received into custody: 5 Sep 1813 - From what ship or whence received: Steamboat - Exchanged, discharged, died, or escape: Discharged - Time when: 2 Nov 1813 - Whither, and by what order, or number or re-entry: Malabar Transport

Town, G. C.   Prisoner 1489. Rank: Sergeant - By what ship or how taken: Troops - Time when: 25 Jul 1814 - Place where: Lundy's Lane - Of what ship or corps: Land forces - Whether man of war, privateer or merchant vessel: Taken on shore - Time when received into custody: 12 Aug 1814 - From what ship or whence received: Royal Seaman No. 289 Transport - Exchanged, discharged, died, or escape: Discharged - Time when: 8 Oct 1814 - Whither, and by what order, or number or re-entry: Queen No. 415

Townsend, Jeremiah   Prisoner 1851. Rank: Private - By what ship or how taken: Troops - Time when: 17 Sep 1814 - Place where: Fort Erie - Of what ship or corps: Land forces - Whether man of war, privateer or merchant vessel: Taken on shore - Time when received into custody: 1 Nov 1814 - From what ship or whence received: Montreal - Exchanged, discharged, died, or escape: Discharged - Time when: 14 Nov 1814 - Whither, and by what order, or number or re-entry: Soverign No. 628 for Halifax

Tracey, William   Prisoner 493. Rank: Private - By what ship or how taken: Troops - Time when: 24 Jun 1813 - Place where: Beaver Dam - Of what ship or corps: Land forces - Whether man of war, privateer or merchant vessel: Taken on shore - Time when received into custody: 7 Jul 1813 - From what ship or whence received: Steamboat - Exchanged, discharged, died, or escape: Discharged - Time when: 10 Aug 1813 - Whither, and by what order, or number or re-entry: HM Ship Regulius by order of Sir George Provost

Trant, James   Prisoner 1068. Rank: Sailing Master - By what ship or how taken: Earl Moria - Time when: 10 Aug 1813 - Place where: Lake Ontario - Of what ship or corps: Julia - Whether man of war, privateer or merchant vessel: Man of War - Time when received into custody: 5 Sep 1813 - From what ship or whence received: Steamboat - Exchanged, discharged, died, or escape: Discharged - Time when: 4 May 1814 - Whither, and by what order, or number or re-entry: United States

Treefry, Joel   Prisoner 1672. Rank: Seaman - By what ship or how taken: Gun Boats - Time when: 25 Aug 1814 - Place where: Lake Ontario - Of what ship or corps: Taken on a gigg - Whether man of war, privateer or merchant vessel: Man of War - Time when received into custody: 23 Oct 1814 - From what ship or whence received: Montreal - Exchanged, discharged, died, or escape: Discharged - Time when: 7 Nov 1814 - Whither, and by what order, or number or re-entry: Transport Freedom No. 582 by orders of his Excellency Sir George Provost

Tribe, Benjamin   Prisoner 1007. Rank: Seaman - By what ship or how taken: Earl Moria - Time when: 10 Aug 1813 - Place where: Lake Ontario - Of what ship or corps: Julia - Whether man of war, privateer or merchant vessel: Man of War - Time when received into custody: 5 Sep 1813 - From what ship or whence received: Steamboat - Exchanged, discharged, died, or escape: Discharged - Time when: 7 Oct 1813 - Whither, and by what order, or number or re-entry: General Kempt Transport

Trimble, Carey A.   Prisoner 1425. Rank: Lieutenant - By what ship or how taken: Troops - Time when: 19 Dec 1813 - Place where: Fort Niagara - Of what ship or corps: Land forces - Whether man of war, privateer or merchant vessel: Taken on shore - Time when received into custody: 29 Jan 1814 - From what ship or whence received: Montreal by land carriage - Exchanged, discharged, died, or escape: Discharged - Time when: 4 May 1814 - Whither, and by what order, or number or re-entry: United States

Troop, James   Prisoner 1220. Rank: Private - By what ship or how taken: Troops - Time when: 19 Dec 1813 - Place where: Fort Niagara - Of what ship or corps: Land forces - Whether man of war, privateer or merchant vessel: Taken on shore - Time when received into custody: 29 Jan 1814 - From what ship or whence received: Montreal by land carriage - Exchanged, discharged, died, or escape: Discharged - Time when: 4 May 1814 - Whither, and by what order, or number or re-entry: United States

Trott, Thomas   Prisoner 463. Rank: Private - By what ship or how taken: Troops - Time when: 24 Jun 1813 - Place where: Beaver Dam - Of what ship or corps: Malabar & Hydia - Whether man of war, privateer or merchant vessel: Taken on shore - Time when received into custody: 7 Jul 1813 - From what ship or whence received: Steamboat - Exchanged, discharged, died, or escape: Discharged - Time when: 21 Apr 1814 - Whither, and by what order, or number or re-

American Prisoners of War held at Quebec during the War of 1812

entry: United States

Truby, Samuel   Prisoner 1981. Rank: Private - By what ship or how taken: Troops - Time when: 17 Sep 1814 - Place where: Fort Erie - Of what ship or corps: Land forces - Whether man of war, privateer or merchant vessel: Taken on shore - Time when received into custody: 30 Dec 1814 - From what ship or whence received: Montreal - Exchanged, discharged, died, or escape: Discharged - Time when: 13 Mar 1815 - Whither, and by what order, or number or re-entry: United States

Truebridge, T.   Prisoner 583. Rank: Private - By what ship or how taken: Troops - Time when: 26 Jun 1813 - Place where: Beaver Dam - Of what ship or corps: Land forces - Whether man of war, privateer or merchant vessel: Taken on shore - Time when received into custody: 13 Jul 1813 - From what ship or whence received: Steamboat - Exchanged, discharged, died, or escape: Discharged - Time when: 10 Aug 1813 - Whither, and by what order, or number or re-entry: HM Ship Regulius by order of Sir George Provost

Tubbs, Samuel F.   Prisoner 1839. Rank: Private - By what ship or how taken: Troops - Time when: 17 Sep 1814 - Place where: Fort Erie - Of what ship or corps: Land forces - Whether man of war, privateer or merchant vessel: Taken on shore - Time when received into custody: 1 Nov 1814 - From what ship or whence received: Montreal - Exchanged, discharged, died, or escape: Discharged - Time when: 8 Nov 1814 - Whither, and by what order, or number or re-entry: S. George No. 575 for Halifax by order of Sir George Provost

Tucker, Benjamin   Prisoner 470. Rank: Private - By what ship or how taken: Troops - Time when: 24 Jun 1813 - Place where: Beaver Dam - Of what ship or corps: Malabar & Hydia - Whether man of war, privateer or merchant vessel: Taken on shore - Time when received into custody: 7 Jul 1813 - From what ship or whence received: Steamboat - Exchanged, discharged, died, or escape: Discharged - Time when: 10 Aug 1813 - Whither, and by what order, or number or re-entry: HM Ship Regulius by order of Sir George Provost

Tucker, Joseph   Prisoner 730. Rank: Private - By what ship or how taken: Troops - Time when: 26 Jun 1813 - Place where: Beaver Dam - Of what ship or corps: Land forces - Whether man of war, privateer or merchant vessel: Taken on shore - Time when received into custody: 7 Jul 1813 - From what ship or whence received: Steamboat - Exchanged, discharged, died, or escape: Discharged - Time when: 10 Aug 1813 - Whither, and by what order, or number or re-entry: HM Ship Regulius by order of Sir George Provost

Tuffs, William   Prisoner 384. Rank: Private - By what ship or how taken: Troops - Time when: 6 Jun 1813 - Place where: Stoney Point - Of what ship or corps: Land forces - Whether man of war, privateer or merchant vessel: Taken on shore - Time when received into custody: 28 Jun 1813 - From what ship or whence received: Mary of Quebec - Exchanged, discharged, died, or escape: Died - Time when: 22 Mar 1815 - Whither, and by what order, or number or re-entry: Pneumonia

Tulley, Thomas   Prisoner 1113. Rank: Private - By what ship or how taken: Troops - Time when: 17 Oct 1813 - Place where: Red Mills - Of what ship or corps: Land forces - Whether man of war, privateer or merchant vessel: Taken on shore - Time when received into custody: 12 Oct 1813 - From what ship or whence received: Steamboat - Exchanged, discharged, died, or escape: Discharged - Time when: 31 Oct 1813 - Whither, and by what order, or number or re-entry: Malabar Transport

Tuner, Daniel   Prisoner 1664. Rank: Lieutenant - By what ship or how taken: Gun Boats - Time when: 6 Sep 1814 - Place where: Lake Huron - Of what ship or corps: Scorpion - Whether man of war, privateer or merchant vessel: Man of War - Time when received into custody: 23 Oct 1814 - From what ship or whence received: Montreal - Exchanged, discharged, died, or escape: Discharged - Time when: 14 Nov 1814 - Whither, and by what order, or number or re-entry: Soverign Transport No. 628 to Halifax

Turnbull, John   Prisoner 146. Rank: Master's Mate - By what ship or how taken: Boats & Troops - Time when: 3 Jun 1813 - Place where: Lake Champlain - Of what ship or corps: Growler - Whether man of war, privateer or merchant vessel: Man of War - Time when received into custody: 8 Jul 1813 - From what ship or whence received: Batteaux - Exchanged, discharged, died, or escape: Discharged - Time when: 4 May 1814 - Whither, and by what order, or number or re-entry: United States

Turner, Henry   Prisoner 169. Rank: Cook - By what ship or how taken: Boats & Troops - Time when: 3 Jun 1813 - Place where: Lake Champlain - Of what ship or corps: Growler - Whether man of war, privateer or merchant vessel: Man of War - Time when received into custody: 9 Jun 1813 - From what ship or whence received: Batteaux - Exchanged, discharged, died, or escape: Discharged - Time when: 31 Oct 1813 - Whither, and by what order, or number or re-entry: Malabar Transport

American Prisoners of War held at Quebec during the War of 1812

Turner, Isaac   Prisoner 1384. Rank: Private - By what ship or how taken: Troops - Time when: 19 Dec 1813 - Place where: Fort Niagara - Of what ship or corps: Land forces - Whether man of war, privateer or merchant vessel: Taken on shore - Time when received into custody: 29 Jan 1814 - From what ship or whence received: Montreal by land carriage - Exchanged, discharged, died, or escape: Discharged - Time when: 4 May 1814 - Whither, and by what order, or number or re-entry: United States

Turner, John   Prisoner 1135. Rank: Private - By what ship or how taken: Troops - Time when: 5 May 1813 - Place where: Rapids Prince Reason - Of what ship or corps: Land forces - Whether man of war, privateer or merchant vessel: Taken on shore - Time when received into custody: 25 Nov 1813 - From what ship or whence received: Town Goal - Exchanged, discharged, died, or escape: Discharged - Time when: 4 May 1814 - Whither, and by what order, or number or re-entry: United States

Turner, S.   Prisoner 1491. Rank: Corporal - By what ship or how taken: Troops - Time when: 25 Jul 1814 - Place where: Lundy's Lane - Of what ship or corps: Land forces - Whether man of war, privateer or merchant vessel: Taken on shore - Time when received into custody: 19 Aug 1814 - From what ship or whence received: Triton No. 438 Transport - Exchanged, discharged, died, or escape: Discharged - Time when: 8 Oct 1814 - Whither, and by what order, or number or re-entry: Queen No. 415

Turner, Walter   Prisoner 847. Rank: Private - By what ship or how taken: Troops - Time when: 26 Jun 1813 - Place where: Beaver Dam - Of what ship or corps: Land forces - Whether man of war, privateer or merchant vessel: Taken on shore - Time when received into custody: 7 Jul 1813 - From what ship or whence received: Steamboat - Exchanged, discharged, died, or escape: Discharged - Time when: 10 Aug 1813 - Whither, and by what order, or number or re-entry: HM Ship Malpomena

Updegrass, Jesse   Prisoner 554. Rank: Corporal - By what ship or how taken: Troops - Time when: 26 Jun 1813 - Place where: Beaver Dam - Of what ship or corps: Land forces - Whether man of war, privateer or merchant vessel: Taken on shore - Time when received into custody: 13 Jul 1813 - From what ship or whence received: Steamboat - Exchanged, discharged, died, or escape: Discharged - Time when: 10 Aug 1813 - Whither, and by what order, or number or re-entry: HM Ship Regulius by order of Sir George Provost

Usher, Edward   Prisoner 468. Rank: Private - By what ship or how taken: Troops - Time when: 24 Jun 1813 - Place where: Beaver Dam - Of what ship or corps: Malabar & Hydia - Whether man of war, privateer or merchant vessel: Taken on shore - Time when received into custody: 7 Jul 1813 - From what ship or whence received: Steamboat - Exchanged, discharged, died, or escape: Discharged - Time when: 10 Aug 1813 - Whither, and by what order, or number or re-entry: HM Ship Regulius by order of Sir George Provost

Ustelburgh, Philip   Prisoner 856. Rank: Private - By what ship or how taken: Troops - Time when: 26 Jun 1813 - Place where: Beaver Dam - Of what ship or corps: Land forces - Whether man of war, privateer or merchant vessel: Taken on shore - Time when received into custody: 7 Jul 1813 - From what ship or whence received: Steamboat - Exchanged, discharged, died, or escape: Discharged - Time when: 10 Aug 1813 - Whither, and by what order, or number or re-entry: HM Ship Malpomena

Vail, William W.   Prisoner 1966. Rank: Private - By what ship or how taken: Troops - Time when: 19 Jul 1814 - Place where: Queenstown - Of what ship or corps: Land forces - Whether man of war, privateer or merchant vessel: Taken on shore - Time when received into custody: 11 Dec 1814 - From what ship or whence received: Montreal - Exchanged, discharged, died, or escape: Discharged - Time when: 13 Mar 1815 - Whither, and by what order, or number or re-entry: United States

Valentine, Elisha   Prisoner 1385. Rank: Private - By what ship or how taken: Troops - Time when: 19 Dec 1813 - Place where: Fort Niagara - Of what ship or corps: Land forces - Whether man of war, privateer or merchant vessel: Taken on shore - Time when received into custody: 29 Jan 1814 - From what ship or whence received: Montreal by land carriage - Exchanged, discharged, died, or escape: Discharged - Time when: 21 Feb 1814 - Whither, and by what order, or number or re-entry: Volunteered for New Brunswick Fencibles

Valients, William   Prisoner 651. Rank: Private - By what ship or how taken: Troops - Time when: 24 Jun 1813 - Place where: Stoney Point - Of what ship or corps: Land forces - Whether man of war, privateer or merchant vessel: Taken on shore - Time when received into custody: 7 Jul 1813 - From what ship or whence received: Steamboat - Exchanged, discharged, died, or escape: Discharged - Time when: 10 Aug 1813 - Whither, and by what order, or number or re-entry: HM Ship Regulius by order of Sir George Provost

Van Bibbar, Isaac   Prisoner 691. Rank: Private - By what ship or how taken: Troops - Time when: 26 Jun 1813 - Place where: Beaver Dam - Of what ship or corps: Land forces - Whether man of war, privateer or merchant vessel: Taken on shore - Time when received into custody: 7 Jul 1813 - From what ship or whence received: Steamboat - Exchanged,

discharged, died, or escape: Discharged - Time when: 10 Aug 1813 - Whither, and by what order, or number or re-entry: HM Ship Regulius by order of Sir George Provost

Van Buren, Edward   Prisoner 1502. Rank: Private - By what ship or how taken: Troops - Time when: 19 Jul 1814 - Place where: 4 Mile Creek - Of what ship or corps: Land forces - Whether man of war, privateer or merchant vessel: Taken on shore - Time when received into custody: 19 Aug 1814 - From what ship or whence received: Triton No. 438 Transport - Exchanged, discharged, died, or escape: Discharged - Time when: 8 Oct 1814 - Whither, and by what order, or number or re-entry: Queen No. 415

Van De Venter, Christopher   Prisoner 256. Rank: Major - By what ship or how taken: Boats & Troops - Time when: 24 Jun 1813 - Place where: Stoney Point - Of what ship or corps: Land forces - Whether man of war, privateer or merchant vessel: Taken on shore - Time when received into custody: 24 Jun 1813 - From what ship or whence received: Steamboat - Exchanged, discharged, died, or escape: Discharged - Time when: 13 Dec 1813 - Whither, and by what order, or number or re-entry: United States

Van Frankling, Isaac   Prisoner 1846. Rank: Private - By what ship or how taken: Troops - Time when: 17 Sep 1814 - Place where: Fort Erie - Of what ship or corps: Land forces - Whether man of war, privateer or merchant vessel: Taken on shore - Time when received into custody: 1 Nov 1814 - From what ship or whence received: Montreal - Exchanged, discharged, died, or escape: Discharged - Time when: 8 Nov 1814 - Whither, and by what order, or number or re-entry: S. George No. 575 for Halifax by order of Sir George Provost

Van Kuven, Abraham   Prisoner 1807. Rank: Citizen - By what ship or how taken: Troops - Time when: 17 Sep 1814 - Place where: Fort Erie - Of what ship or corps: Land forces - Whether man of war, privateer or merchant vessel: Taken on shore - Time when received into custody: 1 Nov 1814 - From what ship or whence received: Montreal - Exchanged, discharged, died, or escape: Discharged - Time when: 8 Nov 1814 - Whither, and by what order, or number or re-entry: S. George No. 575 for Halifax by order of Sir George Provost

Van Suraringen, H. J.   Prisoner 260. Rank: Lieutenant - By what ship or how taken: Boats & Troops - Time when: 24 Jun 1813 - Place where: Stoney Point - Of what ship or corps: Land forces - Whether man of war, privateer or merchant vessel: Taken on shore - Time when received into custody: 24 Jun 1813 - From what ship or whence received: Steamboat - Exchanged, discharged, died, or escape: Discharged - Time when: 10 Aug 1813 - Whither, and by what order, or number or re-entry: Per order His Exellency Sir George Prevost

Van Veghten, Derck   Prisoner 257. Rank: Captain - By what ship or how taken: Boats & Troops - Time when: 24 Jun 1813 - Place where: Stoney Point - Of what ship or corps: Land forces - Whether man of war, privateer or merchant vessel: Taken on shore - Time when received into custody: 24 Jun 1813 - From what ship or whence received: Steamboat - Exchanged, discharged, died, or escape: Discharged - Time when: 13 Dec 1813 - Whither, and by what order, or number or re-entry: United States

Vanderherle, Samuel   Prisoner 641. Rank: Private - By what ship or how taken: Troops - Time when: 24 Jun 1813 - Place where: Stoney Point - Of what ship or corps: Land forces - Whether man of war, privateer or merchant vessel: Taken on shore - Time when received into custody: 7 Jul 1813 - From what ship or whence received: Steamboat - Exchanged, discharged, died, or escape: Discharged - Time when: 10 Aug 1813 - Whither, and by what order, or number or re-entry: HM Ship Regulius by order of Sir George Provost

Vanhorn, James   Prisoner 1149. Rank: Private - By what ship or how taken: Troops - Time when: 5 May 1813 - Place where: Rapids Prince Reason - Of what ship or corps: Land forces - Whether man of war, privateer or merchant vessel: Taken on shore - Time when received into custody: 25 Nov 1813 - From what ship or whence received: Town Goal - Exchanged, discharged, died, or escape: Discharged - Time when: 21 Apr 1814 - Whither, and by what order, or number or re-entry: United States

Vanhouton, Garrett   Prisoner 1877. Rank: Private - By what ship or how taken: Troops - Time when: 17 Sep 1814 - Place where: Fort Erie - Of what ship or corps: Land forces - Whether man of war, privateer or merchant vessel: Taken on shore - Time when received into custody: 1 Nov 1814 - From what ship or whence received: Montreal - Exchanged, discharged, died, or escape: Discharged - Time when: 8 Nov 1814 - Whither, and by what order, or number or re-entry: S. George No. 575 for Halifax by order of Sir George Provost

Vanrecker, Cornelius   Prisoner 1223. Rank: Private - By what ship or how taken: Troops - Time when: 19 Dec 1813 - Place where: Fort Niagara - Of what ship or corps: Land forces - Whether man of war, privateer or merchant vessel: Taken on shore - Time when received into custody: 29 Jan 1814 - From what ship or whence received: Montreal by land carriage - Exchanged, discharged, died, or escape: Discharged - Time when: 26 Feb 1814 - Whither, and by what order, or number or re-entry: Volunteered for New Brunswick Fencibles

American Prisoners of War held at Quebec during the War of 1812

Vanslyck, Cornelius   Prisoner 1166. Rank: Private - By what ship or how taken: Troops - Time when: 5 May 1813 - Place where: Rapids Prince Reason - Of what ship or corps: Land forces - Whether man of war, privateer or merchant vessel: Taken on shore - Time when received into custody: 25 Nov 1813 - From what ship or whence received: Town Goal - Exchanged, discharged, died, or escape: Discharged - Time when: 12 Mar 1814 - Whither, and by what order, or number or re-entry: New Brunswick Fencibles

Vazure, Jove   Prisoner 1448. Rank: Private - By what ship or how taken: Troops - Time when: 6 May 1814 - Place where: Oswago - Of what ship or corps: Land forces - Whether man of war, privateer or merchant vessel: Taken on shore - Time when received into custody: 12 Aug 1814 - From what ship or whence received: Royal Seaman No. 289 Transport - Exchanged, discharged, died, or escape: Discharged - Time when: 8 Oct 1814 - Whither, and by what order, or number or re-entry: Queen No. 415

Vinten, Ezekial   Prisoner 957. Rank: Private - By what ship or how taken: Troops - Time when: 5 Jul 1813 - Place where: Fort Schisher - Of what ship or corps: Land forces - Whether man of war, privateer or merchant vessel: Taken on shore - Time when received into custody: 5 Sep 1813 - From what ship or whence received: Steamboat - Exchanged, discharged, died, or escape: Discharged - Time when: 31 Oct 1813 - Whither, and by what order, or number or re-entry: Malabar Transport

Virgin, Levet   Prisoner 101. Rank: Private - By what ship or how taken: Boats & Troops - Time when: 28 May 1813 - Place where: Stoney Point, Henderson Harbor - Of what ship or corps: Land forces - Whether man of war, privateer or merchant vessel: Taken on shore - Time when received into custody: 8 Jun 1813 - From what ship or whence received: Batteaux - Exchanged, discharged, died, or escape: Discharged - Time when: 31 Oct 1813 - Whither, and by what order, or number or re-entry: Malabar Transport

Voigh, Thomas   Prisoner 1274. Rank: Privateer - By what ship or how taken: Troops - Time when: 19 Dec 1813 - Place where: Fort Niagara - Of what ship or corps: Land forces - Whether man of war, privateer or merchant vessel: Taken on shore - Time when received into custody: 29 Jan 1814 - From what ship or whence received: Montreal by land carriage - Exchanged, discharged, died, or escape: Discharged - Time when: 27 Feb 1814 - Whither, and by what order, or number or re-entry: Volunteered for New Brunswick Fencibles

Von, Samuel   Prisoner 316. Rank: Private - By what ship or how taken: Boats & Troops - Time when: 6 Jun 1813 - Place where: Stoney Point - Of what ship or corps: Land forces - Whether man of war, privateer or merchant vessel: Taken on shore - Time when received into custody: 28 Jun 1813 - From what ship or whence received: Quebec of Quebec - Exchanged, discharged, died, or escape: Discharged - Time when: 31 Oct 1813 - Whither, and by what order, or number or re-entry: Malabar Transport

Wade, Nathan   Prisoner 1738. Rank: Seaman - By what ship or how taken: Gun Boats - Time when: 3 Sep 1814 - Place where: Lake Huron - Of what ship or corps: Tigress - Whether man of war, privateer or merchant vessel: Man of War - Time when received into custody: 1 Nov 1814 - From what ship or whence received: Montreal - Exchanged, discharged, died, or escape: Discharged - Time when: 7 Nov 1814 - Whither, and by what order, or number or re-entry: Transport Freedom No. 582 by orders of his Excellency Sir George Provost

Wadon, L.   Prisoner 1517. Rank: Private - By what ship or how taken: Troops - Time when: 25 Jul 1814 - Place where: Lundy's Lane - Of what ship or corps: Land forces - Whether man of war, privateer or merchant vessel: Taken on shore - Time when received into custody: 30 Aug 1814 - From what ship or whence received: Lady Delaval Schooner 578 - Exchanged, discharged, died, or escape: Discharged - Time when: 8 Oct 1814 - Whither, and by what order, or number or re-entry: Queen No. 415

Wager, Joseph   Prisoner 1814. Rank: Private - By what ship or how taken: Troops - Time when: 17 Sep 1814 - Place where: Fort Erie - Of what ship or corps: Land forces - Whether man of war, privateer or merchant vessel: Taken on shore - Time when received into custody: 1 Nov 1814 - From what ship or whence received: Montreal - Exchanged, discharged, died, or escape: Discharged - Time when: 8 Nov 1814 - Whither, and by what order, or number or re-entry: S. George No. 575 for Halifax by order of Sir George Provost

Waite, Brunsey   Prisoner 1986. Rank: Citizen - By what ship or how taken: Troops - Time when: 7 Dec 1814 - Place where: Fort Erie - Of what ship or corps: Land forces - Whether man of war, privateer or merchant vessel: Taken on shore - Time when received into custody: 30 Dec 1814 - From what ship or whence received: Montreal - Exchanged, discharged, died, or escape: Discharged - Time when: 13 Mar 1815 - Whither, and by what order, or number or re-entry: United States

Wakeman, Bradley   Prisoner 1971. Rank: Private - By what ship or how taken: Troops - Time when: 17 Oct 1814 - Place where: Chippawa - Of what ship or corps: Land forces - Whether man of war, privateer or merchant vessel: Taken on shore - Time when received into custody: 11 Dec 1814 - From what ship or whence received: Montreal - Exchanged, discharged, died, or escape: Discharged - Time when: 13 Mar 1815 - Whither, and by what order, or number or re-entry: United States

Walker, Colman   Prisoner 1131. Rank: Private - By what ship or how taken: Troops - Time when: 5 May 1813 - Place where: Rapids Prince Reason - Of what ship or corps: Land forces - Whether man of war, privateer or merchant vessel: Taken on shore - Time when received into custody: 25 Nov 1813 - From what ship or whence received: Town Goal - Exchanged, discharged, died, or escape: Discharged - Time when: 4 May 1814 - Whither, and by what order, or number or re-entry: United States

Walker, John   Prisoner 1066. Rank: Private - By what ship or how taken: Troops - Time when: 24 Jun 1813 - Place where: Beaver Dam - Of what ship or corps: Land forces - Whether man of war, privateer or merchant vessel: Taken on shore - Time when received into custody: 5 Sep 1813 - From what ship or whence received: Steamboat - Exchanged, discharged, died, or escape: Discharged - Time when: 10 Sep 1813 - Whither, and by what order, or number or re-entry: Volunteered for the army

Walker, Samuel   Prisoner 912. Rank: Private - By what ship or how taken: Troops - Time when: 26 Jun 1813 - Place where: Beaver Dam - Of what ship or corps: Land forces - Whether man of war, privateer or merchant vessel: Taken on shore - Time when received into custody: 21 Jul 1813 - From what ship or whence received: Steamboat - Exchanged, discharged, died, or escape: Discharged - Time when: 10 Aug 1813 - Whither, and by what order, or number or re-entry: HM Ship Malpomena

Walker, Simeon   Prisoner 640. Rank: Private - By what ship or how taken: Troops - Time when: 24 Jun 1813 - Place where: Stoney Point - Of what ship or corps: Land forces - Whether man of war, privateer or merchant vessel: Taken on shore - Time when received into custody: 7 Jul 1813 - From what ship or whence received: Steamboat - Exchanged, discharged, died, or escape: Discharged - Time when: 10 Aug 1813 - Whither, and by what order, or number or re-entry: HM Ship Regulius by order of Sir George Provost

Walker, William   Prisoner 1234. Rank: Private - By what ship or how taken: Troops - Time when: 19 Dec 1813 - Place where: Fort Niagara - Of what ship or corps: Land forces - Whether man of war, privateer or merchant vessel: Taken on shore - Time when received into custody: 29 Jan 1814 - From what ship or whence received: Montreal by land carriage - Exchanged, discharged, died, or escape: Discharged - Time when: 4 May 1814 - Whither, and by what order, or number or re-entry: United States

Walker, William   Prisoner 3. Rank: Sergeant - By what ship or how taken: Boats & Troops - Time when: 28 May 1813 - Place where: Stoney Point, Henderson Harbor - Of what ship or corps: Land forces - Whether man of war, privateer or merchant vessel: Taken on shore - Time when received into custody: 8 Jun 1813 - From what ship or whence received: Batteaux - Exchanged, discharged, died, or escape: Discharged - Time when: 31 Oct 1813 - Whither, and by what order, or number or re-entry: Malabar Transport

Wallace, Abel   Prisoner 1836. Rank: Private - By what ship or how taken: Troops - Time when: 17 Sep 1814 - Place where: Fort Erie - Of what ship or corps: Land forces - Whether man of war, privateer or merchant vessel: Taken on shore - Time when received into custody: 1 Nov 1814 - From what ship or whence received: Montreal - Exchanged, discharged, died, or escape: Discharged - Time when: 8 Nov 1814 - Whither, and by what order, or number or re-entry: S. George No. 575 for Halifax by order of Sir George Provost

Wallace, Samuel   Prisoner 1410. Rank: Private - By what ship or how taken: Troops - Time when: 19 Dec 1813 - Place where: Fort Niagara - Of what ship or corps: Land forces - Whether man of war, privateer or merchant vessel: Taken on shore - Time when received into custody: 29 Jan 1814 - From what ship or whence received: Montreal by land carriage - Exchanged, discharged, died, or escape: Discharged - Time when: 4 May 1814 - Whither, and by what order, or number or re-entry: United States

Wallis, James   Prisoner 1161. Rank: Corporal - By what ship or how taken: Troops - Time when: 5 May 1813 - Place where: Fort Maggie - Of what ship or corps: Land forces - Whether man of war, privateer or merchant vessel: Taken on shore - Time when received into custody: 25 Nov 1813 - From what ship or whence received: Town Goal - Exchanged, discharged, died, or escape: Discharged - Time when: 12 Mar 1814 - Whither, and by what order, or number or re-entry: New Brunswick Fencibles

Walter, Abraham   Prisoner 148. Rank: Pilot - By what ship or how taken: Boats & Troops - Time when: 3 Jun 1813 - Place where: Lake Champlain - Of what ship or corps: Growler - Whether man of war, privateer or merchant vessel: Man of War - Time when received into custody: 8 Jul 1813 - From what ship or whence received: Batteaux - Exchanged, discharged, died, or escape: Escaped - Time when: 6 Nov 1813 - Whither, and by what order, or number or re-entry:

American Prisoners of War held at Quebec during the War of 1812

Walton, Edward   Prisoner 731. Rank: Private - By what ship or how taken: Troops - Time when: 26 Jun 1813 - Place where: Beaver Dam - Of what ship or corps: Land forces - Whether man of war, privateer or merchant vessel: Taken on shore - Time when received into custody: 7 Jul 1813 - From what ship or whence received: Steamboat - Exchanged, discharged, died, or escape: Discharged - Time when: 31 Oct 1813 - Whither, and by what order, or number or re-entry: Malabar Transport

Ward, John   Prisoner 1127. Rank: Private - By what ship or how taken: Troops - Time when: 5 May 1813 - Place where: Rapids Prince Reason - Of what ship or corps: Land forces - Whether man of war, privateer or merchant vessel: Taken on shore - Time when received into custody: 25 Nov 1813 - From what ship or whence received: Town Goal - Exchanged, discharged, died, or escape: Discharged - Time when: 4 May 1814 - Whither, and by what order, or number or re-entry: United States

Ward, Lewis   Prisoner 1524. Rank: Private - By what ship or how taken: Troops - Time when: 25 Jul 1814 - Place where: Lundy's Lane - Of what ship or corps: Land forces - Whether man of war, privateer or merchant vessel: Taken on shore - Time when received into custody: 30 Aug 1814 - From what ship or whence received: Lady Delaval Schooner 578 - Exchanged, discharged, died, or escape: Discharged - Time when: 8 Oct 1814 - Whither, and by what order, or number or re-entry: Queen No. 415

Wardle, Linnard   Prisoner 881. Rank: Private - By what ship or how taken: Troops - Time when: 26 Jun 1813 - Place where: Beaver Dam - Of what ship or corps: Land forces - Whether man of war, privateer or merchant vessel: Taken on shore - Time when received into custody: 7 Jul 1813 - From what ship or whence received: Steamboat - Exchanged, discharged, died, or escape: Discharged - Time when: 10 Aug 1813 - Whither, and by what order, or number or re-entry: HM Ship Malpomena

Waring, John   Prisoner 529. Rank: Lieutenant - By what ship or how taken: Troops - Time when: 24 Jun 1813 - Place where: Beaver Dam - Of what ship or corps: Land forces - Whether man of war, privateer or merchant vessel: Taken on shore - Time when received into custody: 13 Jul 1813 - From what ship or whence received: Steamboat - Exchanged, discharged, died, or escape: Discharged - Time when: 13 Dec 1813 - Whither, and by what order, or number or re-entry: United States

Waring, Jonathan   Prisoner 1121. Rank: Private - By what ship or how taken: Troops - Time when: 17 Oct 1813 - Place where: Red Mills - Of what ship or corps: Land forces - Whether man of war, privateer or merchant vessel: Taken on shore - Time when received into custody: 12 Oct 1813 - From what ship or whence received: Steamboat - Exchanged, discharged, died, or escape: Discharged - Time when: 31 Oct 1813 - Whither, and by what order, or number or re-entry: Malabar Transport

Warley, Joseph   Prisoner 1120. Rank: Private - By what ship or how taken: Troops - Time when: 17 Oct 1813 - Place where: Red Mills - Of what ship or corps: Land forces - Whether man of war, privateer or merchant vessel: Taken on shore - Time when received into custody: 12 Oct 1813 - From what ship or whence received: Steamboat - Exchanged, discharged, died, or escape: Discharged - Time when: 31 Oct 1813 - Whither, and by what order, or number or re-entry: Malabar Transport

Warmsly, Richard   Prisoner 1669. Rank: Seaman - By what ship or how taken: Gun Boats - Time when: 25 Aug 1814 - Place where: Lake Ontario - Of what ship or corps: Taken on a gigg - Whether man of war, privateer or merchant vessel: Man of War - Time when received into custody: 23 Oct 1814 - From what ship or whence received: Montreal - Exchanged, discharged, died, or escape: Discharged - Time when: 7 Nov 1814 - Whither, and by what order, or number or re-entry: Transport Freedom No. 582 by orders of his Excellency Sir George Provost

Warren, Martin   Prisoner 1557. Rank: Private - By what ship or how taken: Troops - Time when: 25 Jul 1814 - Place where: Lundy's Lane - Of what ship or corps: Land forces - Whether man of war, privateer or merchant vessel: Taken on shore - Time when received into custody: 30 Aug 1814 - From what ship or whence received: Lady Delaval Schooner 578 - Exchanged, discharged, died, or escape: Discharged - Time when: 8 Oct 1814 - Whither, and by what order, or number or re-entry: Queen No. 415

Warren, Thomas L.   Prisoner 1985. Rank: Citizen - By what ship or how taken: Troops - Time when: 31 Oct 1814 - Place where: Fort Niagara - Of what ship or corps: Land forces - Whether man of war, privateer or merchant vessel: Taken on shore - Time when received into custody: 30 Dec 1814 - From what ship or whence received: Montreal - Exchanged, discharged, died, or escape: Discharged - Time when: 13 Mar 1815 - Whither, and by what order, or number or re-entry: United States

Warren, W. H.   Prisoner 1033. Rank: Seaman - By what ship or how taken: Lord Melvin - Time when: 10 Aug 1813 - Place where: Lake Ontario - Of what ship or corps: Growler - Whether man of war, privateer or merchant vessel: Man of War - Time when received into custody: 5 Sep 1813 - From what ship or whence received: Steamboat - Exchanged,

American Prisoners of War held at Quebec during the War of 1812

discharged, died, or escape: Discharged - Time when: 21 Sep 1813 - Whither, and by what order, or number or re-entry: Mersey Transport

Waterman, Elisha   Prisoner 1381.   Rank: Private - By what ship or how taken: Troops - Time when: 19 Dec 1813 - Place where: Fort Niagara - Of what ship or corps: Land forces - Whether man of war, privateer or merchant vessel: Taken on shore - Time when received into custody: 29 Jan 1814 - From what ship or whence received: Montreal by land carriage - Exchanged, discharged, died, or escape: Discharged - Time when: 4 May 1814 - Whither, and by what order, or number or re-entry: United States

Watlas, Burton   Prisoner 456.   Rank: Private - By what ship or how taken: Troops - Time when: 24 Jun 1813 - Place where: Beaver Dam - Of what ship or corps: Malabar & Hydia - Whether man of war, privateer or merchant vessel: Taken on shore - Time when received into custody: 7 Jul 1813 - From what ship or whence received: Steamboat - Exchanged, discharged, died, or escape: Discharged - Time when: 10 Aug 1813 - Whither, and by what order, or number or re-entry: HM Ship Regulius by order of Sir George Provost

Watson, David   Prisoner 1042.   Rank: Seaman - By what ship or how taken: Lord Melvin - Time when: 10 Aug 1813 - Place where: Lake Ontario - Of what ship or corps: Growler - Whether man of war, privateer or merchant vessel: Man of War - Time when received into custody: 5 Sep 1813 - From what ship or whence received: Steamboat - Exchanged, discharged, died, or escape: Discharged - Time when: 1 Nov 1813 - Whither, and by what order, or number or re-entry: Lord Cartheart Transport

Watson, Major   Prisoner 341.   Rank: Private - By what ship or how taken: Boats & Troops - Time when: 22 Feb 1813 - Place where: Hedgesburgh - Of what ship or corps: Land forces - Whether man of war, privateer or merchant vessel: Taken on shore - Time when received into custody: 28 Jun 1813 - From what ship or whence received: Mary of Quebec - Exchanged, discharged, died, or escape: Discharged - Time when: 7 Aug 1813 - Whither, and by what order, or number or re-entry: H.M. Ship Cievare

Watson, William   Prisoner 762.   Rank: Private - By what ship or how taken: Troops - Time when: 26 Jun 1813 - Place where: Beaver Dam - Of what ship or corps: Land forces - Whether man of war, privateer or merchant vessel: Taken on shore - Time when received into custody: 7 Jul 1813 - From what ship or whence received: Steamboat - Exchanged, discharged, died, or escape: Discharged - Time when: 10 Aug 1813 - Whither, and by what order, or number or re-entry: HM Ship Malpomena

Waugham, James   Prisoner 736.   Rank: Private - By what ship or how taken: Troops - Time when: 26 Jun 1813 - Place where: Beaver Dam - Of what ship or corps: Land forces - Whether man of war, privateer or merchant vessel: Taken on shore - Time when received into custody: 7 Jul 1813 - From what ship or whence received: Steamboat - Exchanged, discharged, died, or escape: Discharged - Time when: 10 Aug 1813 - Whither, and by what order, or number or re-entry: HM Ship Regulius by order of Sir George Provost

Wavern, Elisha   Prisoner 379.   Rank: Sergeant Major - By what ship or how taken: Troops - Time when: 6 Jun 1813 - Place where: Stoney Point - Of what ship or corps: Land forces - Whether man of war, privateer or merchant vessel: Taken on shore - Time when received into custody: 28 Jun 1813 - From what ship or whence received: Mary of Quebec - Exchanged, discharged, died, or escape: Discharged - Time when: 8 Oct 1813 - Whither, and by what order, or number or re-entry: H.M. Ship Ceylon

Wayne, Michael   Prisoner 301.   Rank: Private - By what ship or how taken: Boats & Troops - Time when: 6 Jun 1813 - Place where: Stoney Point - Of what ship or corps: Land forces - Whether man of war, privateer or merchant vessel: Taken on shore - Time when received into custody: 28 Jun 1813 - From what ship or whence received: Quebec of Quebec - Exchanged, discharged, died, or escape: Discharged - Time when: 7 Aug 1813 - Whither, and by what order, or number or re-entry: H.M. Ship Cievare

Webber, Nathan   Prisoner 127.   Rank: Private - By what ship or how taken: Boats & Troops - Time when: 28 May 1813 - Place where: Stoney Point, Henderson Harbor - Of what ship or corps: Land forces - Whether man of war, privateer or merchant vessel: Taken on shore - Time when received into custody: 8 Jun 1813 - From what ship or whence received: Batteaux - Exchanged, discharged, died, or escape: Escaped - Time when: 3 Sep 1813 - Whither, and by what order, or number or re-entry:

Webster, R.   Prisoner 1661.   Rank: Private - By what ship or how taken: - Time when: - Place where: - Of what ship or corps: - Whether man of war, privateer or merchant vessel: - Time when received into custody: 5 Oct 1814 - From what ship or whence received: Montreal - Exchanged, discharged, died, or escape: Discharged - Time when: 8 Oct 1814 - Whither, and by what order, or number or re-entry: H.M. Ship Ceylon

Weiant, Peter   Prisoner 1958.   Rank: Private - By what ship or how taken: Troops - Time when: 23 Oct 1814 - Place where: Fort

American Prisoners of War held at Quebec during the War of 1812

Erie - Of what ship or corps: Land forces - Whether man of war, privateer or merchant vessel: Taken on shore - Time when received into custody: 11 Dec 1814 - From what ship or whence received: Montreal - Exchanged, discharged, died, or escape: Discharged - Time when: 13 Mar 1815 - Whither, and by what order, or number or re-entry: United States

Weiman, Lawrence   Prisoner 115. Rank: Private - By what ship or how taken: Boats & Troops - Time when: 28 May 1813 - Place where: Stoney Point, Henderson Harbor - Of what ship or corps: Land forces - Whether man of war, privateer or merchant vessel: Taken on shore - Time when received into custody: 8 Jun 1813 - From what ship or whence received: Batteaux - Exchanged, discharged, died, or escape: Discharged - Time when: 22 Aug 1813 - Whither, and by what order, or number or re-entry: Cartheart Transport

Welch, Henry   Prisoner 673. Rank: Sergeant - By what ship or how taken: Troops - Time when: 26 Jun 1813 - Place where: Beaver Dam - Of what ship or corps: Land forces - Whether man of war, privateer or merchant vessel: Taken on shore - Time when received into custody: 7 Jul 1813 - From what ship or whence received: Steamboat - Exchanged, discharged, died, or escape: Discharged - Time when: 10 Aug 1813 - Whither, and by what order, or number or re-entry: HM Ship Regulius by order of Sir George Provost

Welch, Rupel   Prisoner 383. Rank: Private - By what ship or how taken: Troops - Time when: 6 Jun 1813 - Place where: Stoney Point - Of what ship or corps: Land forces - Whether man of war, privateer or merchant vessel: Taken on shore - Time when received into custody: 28 Jun 1813 - From what ship or whence received: Mary of Quebec - Exchanged, discharged, died, or escape: Discharged - Time when: 4 May 1814 - Whither, and by what order, or number or re-entry: United States

Weldon, Ira   Prisoner 1697. Rank: Private - By what ship or how taken: Troops - Time when: 25 Jul 1814 - Place where: Lundy's Lane - Of what ship or corps: Land forces - Whether man of war, privateer or merchant vessel: Taken on shore - Time when received into custody: 23 Oct 1814 - From what ship or whence received: Montreal - Exchanged, discharged, died, or escape: Discharged - Time when: 8 Nov 1814 - Whither, and by what order, or number or re-entry: S. George No. 575 for Halifax

Wells, Caleb   Prisoner 386. Rank: Private - By what ship or how taken: Troops - Time when: 6 Jun 1813 - Place where: Stoney Point - Of what ship or corps: Land forces - Whether man of war, privateer or merchant vessel: Taken on shore - Time when received into custody: 28 Jun 1813 - From what ship or whence received: Mary of Quebec - Exchanged, discharged, died, or escape: Discharged - Time when: 31 Oct 1813 - Whither, and by what order, or number or re-entry: Malabar Transport

Wells, Elijah   Prisoner 917. Rank: Private - By what ship or how taken: Troops - Time when: 26 Jun 1813 - Place where: Beaver Dam - Of what ship or corps: Land forces - Whether man of war, privateer or merchant vessel: Taken on shore - Time when received into custody: 21 Jul 1813 - From what ship or whence received: Steamboat - Exchanged, discharged, died, or escape: Discharged - Time when: 10 Aug 1813 - Whither, and by what order, or number or re-entry: HM Ship Malpomena

Went, George   Prisoner 1463. Rank: Private - By what ship or how taken: Troops - Time when: 5 Jul 1814 - Place where: Chippewa - Of what ship or corps: Land forces - Whether man of war, privateer or merchant vessel: Taken on shore - Time when received into custody: 12 Aug 1814 - From what ship or whence received: Royal Seaman No. 289 Transport - Exchanged, discharged, died, or escape: Discharged - Time when: 10 Nov 1814 - Whither, and by what order, or number or re-entry: Soverign Transport No. 628 to Halifax by orders of Sir George Provost

Werman, Edward   Prisoner 1282. Rank: Sergeant - By what ship or how taken: Troops - Time when: 19 Dec 1813 - Place where: Fort Niagara - Of what ship or corps: Land forces - Whether man of war, privateer or merchant vessel: Taken on shore - Time when received into custody: 29 Jan 1814 - From what ship or whence received: Montreal by land carriage - Exchanged, discharged, died, or escape: Discharged - Time when: 4 May 1814 - Whither, and by what order, or number or re-entry: United States

West, Abia   Prisoner 1921. Rank: Private - By what ship or how taken: Troops - Time when: 17 Sep 1814 - Place where: Fort Erie - Of what ship or corps: Land forces - Whether man of war, privateer or merchant vessel: Taken on shore - Time when received into custody: 1 Nov 1814 - From what ship or whence received: Montreal - Exchanged, discharged, died, or escape: Discharged - Time when: 14 Nov 1814 - Whither, and by what order, or number or re-entry: Soverign No. 628 for Halifax

West, Abraham   Prisoner 642. Rank: Private - By what ship or how taken: Troops - Time when: 24 Jun 1813 - Place where: Stoney Point - Of what ship or corps: Land forces - Whether man of war, privateer or merchant vessel: Taken on shore - Time when received into custody: 7 Jul 1813 - From what ship or whence received: Steamboat - Exchanged, discharged, died, or escape: Discharged - Time when: 10 Aug 1813 - Whither, and by what order, or number or re-

American Prisoners of War held at Quebec during the War of 1812

entry: HM Ship Regulius by order of Sir George Provost

West, Charles   Prisoner 409. Rank: Sergeant - By what ship or how taken: Troops - Time when: 24 Jun 1813 - Place where: Beaver Dam - Of what ship or corps: Land forces - Whether man of war, privateer or merchant vessel: Taken on shore - Time when received into custody: 7 Jul 1813 - From what ship or whence received: Steamboat - Exchanged, discharged, died, or escape: Discharged - Time when: 8 Oct 1813 - Whither, and by what order, or number or re-entry: H.M. Ship Ceylon

West, Hugh S.   Prisoner 289. Rank: Private - By what ship or how taken: Boats & Troops - Time when: 6 Jun 1813 - Place where: Stoney Point - Of what ship or corps: Land forces - Whether man of war, privateer or merchant vessel: Taken on shore - Time when received into custody: 28 Jun 1813 - From what ship or whence received: Quebec of Quebec - Exchanged, discharged, died, or escape: Discharged - Time when: 31 Oct 1813 - Whither, and by what order, or number or re-entry: Malabar Transport

Westbrooks, Abraham   Prisoner 1088. Rank: Private - By what ship or how taken: Troops - Time when: 24 Aug 1813 - Place where: Fort George - Of what ship or corps: Land forces - Whether man of war, privateer or merchant vessel: Taken on shore - Time when received into custody: 10 Oct 1813 - From what ship or whence received: Steamboat - Exchanged, discharged, died, or escape: Discharged - Time when: 31 Oct 1813 - Whither, and by what order, or number or re-entry: Malabar Transport

Whagerman, Jeremiah   Prisoner 590. Rank: Private - By what ship or how taken: Troops - Time when: 26 Jun 1813 - Place where: Stoney Point - Of what ship or corps: Land forces - Whether man of war, privateer or merchant vessel: Taken on shore - Time when received into custody: 7 Jul 1813 - From what ship or whence received: Steamboat - Exchanged, discharged, died, or escape: Discharged - Time when: 10 Aug 1813 - Whither, and by what order, or number or re-entry: HM Ship Regulius by order of Sir George Provost

Wharf, Andrew   Prisoner 1434. Rank: Able seaman - By what ship or how taken: Prometheus - Time when: 5 Mar 1814 - Place where: Off Halifax - Of what ship or corps: Lizard - Whether man of war, privateer or merchant vessel: Privateer - Time when received into custody: 24 May 1814 - From what ship or whence received: Mary Transport No. 360 Halifax - Exchanged, discharged, died, or escape: Discharged - Time when: 4 May 1814 - Whither, and by what order, or number or re-entry: United States

Wheedon, Charles   Prisoner 1581. Rank: Seaman - By what ship or how taken: Gun Boats - Time when: 12 Aug 1814 - Place where: Fort Erie - Of what ship or corps: Ohio - Whether man of war, privateer or merchant vessel: Man of War - Time when received into custody: 5 Oct 1814 - From what ship or whence received: Montreal - Exchanged, discharged, died, or escape: Discharged - Time when: 10 Nov 1814 - Whither, and by what order, or number or re-entry: Freedom No. 582

Wheeler, Enoch   Prisoner 1875. Rank: Corporal - By what ship or how taken: Troops - Time when: 17 Sep 1814 - Place where: Fort Erie - Of what ship or corps: Land forces - Whether man of war, privateer or merchant vessel: Taken on shore - Time when received into custody: 1 Nov 1814 - From what ship or whence received: Montreal - Exchanged, discharged, died, or escape: Discharged - Time when: 8 Nov 1814 - Whither, and by what order, or number or re-entry: S. George No. 575 for Halifax by order of Sir George Provost

Wheeler, Nathaniel   Prisoner 1195. Rank: Citizen - By what ship or how taken: - Time when: - Place where: - Of what ship or corps: - Whether man of war, privateer or merchant vessel: - Time when received into custody: 12 Dec 1813 - From what ship or whence received: Town Goal - Exchanged, discharged, died, or escape: Discharged - Time when: 4 May 1814 - Whither, and by what order, or number or re-entry: United States

Wheeler, Stephen   Prisoner 47. Rank: Private - By what ship or how taken: Boats & Troops - Time when: 28 May 1813 - Place where: Stoney Point, Henderson Harbor - Of what ship or corps: Land forces - Whether man of war, privateer or merchant vessel: Taken on shore - Time when received into custody: 8 Jun 1813 - From what ship or whence received: Batteaux - Exchanged, discharged, died, or escape: Discharged - Time when: 31 Oct 1813 - Whither, and by what order, or number or re-entry: Malabar Transport

Wheeler, Willison   Prisoner 288. Rank: Private - By what ship or how taken: Boats & Troops - Time when: 6 Jun 1813 - Place where: Stoney Point - Of what ship or corps: Land forces - Whether man of war, privateer or merchant vessel: Taken on shore - Time when received into custody: 28 Jun 1813 - From what ship or whence received: Quebec of Quebec - Exchanged, discharged, died, or escape: Discharged - Time when: 31 Oct 1813 - Whither, and by what order, or number or re-entry: Malabar Transport

American Prisoners of War held at Quebec during the War of 1812

Wheelock, Abel   Prisoner 241. Rank: Lieutenant - By what ship or how taken: Boats & Troops - Time when: 24 Jun 1813 - Place where: Rec in charge of Beauport - Of what ship or corps: Land forces - Whether man of war, privateer or merchant vessel: Taken on shore - Time when received into custody: 9 Jun 1813 - From what ship or whence received: Steamboat - Exchanged, discharged, died, or escape: Discharged - Time when: 10 Aug 1813 - Whither, and by what order, or number or re-entry: Per order His Exellency Sir George Prevost

Wheller, Anthony   Prisoner 614. Rank: Private - By what ship or how taken: Troops - Time when: 26 Jun 1813 - Place where: Stoney Point - Of what ship or corps: Land forces - Whether man of war, privateer or merchant vessel: Taken on shore - Time when received into custody: 7 Jul 1813 - From what ship or whence received: Steamboat - Exchanged, discharged, died, or escape: Discharged - Time when: 10 Aug 1813 - Whither, and by what order, or number or re-entry: HM Ship Regulius by order of Sir George Provost

Whellock, James   Prisoner 658. Rank: Private - By what ship or how taken: Troops - Time when: 24 Jun 1813 - Place where: Stoney Point - Of what ship or corps: Land forces - Whether man of war, privateer or merchant vessel: Taken on shore - Time when received into custody: 7 Jul 1813 - From what ship or whence received: Steamboat - Exchanged, discharged, died, or escape: Discharged - Time when: 31 Oct 1813 - Whither, and by what order, or number or re-entry: Malabar Transport

Whilington, Robert   Prisoner 177. Rank: Private - By what ship or how taken: Boats & Troops - Time when: 3 Jun 1813 - Place where: Lake Champlain - Of what ship or corps: Growler - Whether man of war, privateer or merchant vessel: Man of War - Time when received into custody: 9 Jun 1813 - From what ship or whence received: Batteaux - Exchanged, discharged, died, or escape: Discharged - Time when: 31 Oct 1813 - Whither, and by what order, or number or re-entry: Malabar Transport

White, Cornelius   Prisoner 1518. Rank: Private - By what ship or how taken: Troops - Time when: 25 Jul 1814 - Place where: Lundy's Lane - Of what ship or corps: Land forces - Whether man of war, privateer or merchant vessel: Taken on shore - Time when received into custody: 30 Aug 1814 - From what ship or whence received: Lady Delaval Schooner 578 - Exchanged, discharged, died, or escape: Discharged - Time when: 8 Oct 1814 - Whither, and by what order, or number or re-entry: Queen No. 415

White, George   Prisoner 1961. Rank: Private - By what ship or how taken: Troops - Time when: 28 Oct 1814 - Place where: Fort Erie - Of what ship or corps: Land forces - Whether man of war, privateer or merchant vessel: Taken on shore - Time when received into custody: 11 Dec 1814 - From what ship or whence received: Montreal - Exchanged, discharged, died, or escape: Discharged - Time when: 13 Mar 1815 - Whither, and by what order, or number or re-entry: United States

White, Isaac   Prisoner 1329. Rank: Sergeant - By what ship or how taken: Troops - Time when: 19 Dec 1813 - Place where: Fort Niagara - Of what ship or corps: Land forces - Whether man of war, privateer or merchant vessel: Taken on shore - Time when received into custody: 29 Jan 1814 - From what ship or whence received: Montreal by land carriage - Exchanged, discharged, died, or escape: Discharged - Time when: 4 May 1814 - Whither, and by what order, or number or re-entry: United States

White, John   Prisoner 449. Rank: Private - By what ship or how taken: Troops - Time when: 24 Jun 1813 - Place where: Beaver Dam - Of what ship or corps: Land forces - Whether man of war, privateer or merchant vessel: Taken on shore - Time when received into custody: 7 Jul 1813 - From what ship or whence received: Steamboat - Exchanged, discharged, died, or escape: Discharged - Time when: 10 Aug 1813 - Whither, and by what order, or number or re-entry: HM Ship Regulius by order of Sir George Provost

White, Joshua   Prisoner 218. Rank: Private - By what ship or how taken: Boats & Troops - Time when: 3 Jun 1813 - Place where: Lake Champlain - Of what ship or corps: Eagle - Whether man of war, privateer or merchant vessel: Man of War - Time when received into custody: 9 Jun 1813 - From what ship or whence received: Batteaux - Exchanged, discharged, died, or escape: Discharged - Time when: 31 Oct 1813 - Whither, and by what order, or number or re-entry: Malabar Transport

White, Richard   Prisoner 1462. Rank: Citizen - By what ship or how taken: Troops - Time when: 14 May 1814 - Place where: Pattonville - Of what ship or corps: Land forces - Whether man of war, privateer or merchant vessel: Taken on shore - Time when received into custody: 12 Aug 1814 - From what ship or whence received: Royal Seaman No. 289 Transport - Exchanged, discharged, died, or escape: Discharged - Time when: 8 Oct 1814 - Whither, and by what order, or number or re-entry: Queen No. 415

White, Samuel   Prisoner 1663. Rank: Captain - By what ship or how taken: Troops - Time when: - Place where: - Of what ship or corps: Land forces - Whether man of war, privateer or merchant vessel: - Time when received into custody: 13 Oct 1814 - From what ship or whence received: Montreal - Exchanged, discharged, died, or escape: Discharged - Time

American Prisoners of War held at Quebec during the War of 1812

when: 10 Nov 1814 - Whither, and by what order, or number or re-entry: Transport Stately No. 408 for Halifax

White, William   Prisoner 1074. Rank: Private - By what ship or how taken: Troops - Time when: 24 Aug 1813 - Place where: Fort George - Of what ship or corps: Land forces - Whether man of war, privateer or merchant vessel: Taken on shore - Time when received into custody: 10 Oct 1813 - From what ship or whence received: Steamboat - Exchanged, discharged, died, or escape: Discharged - Time when: 4 May 1814 - Whither, and by what order, or number or re-entry: United States

Whitley, David R.   Prisoner 374. Rank: Private - By what ship or how taken: Troops - Time when: 6 Jun 1813 - Place where: Stoney Point - Of what ship or corps: Land forces - Whether man of war, privateer or merchant vessel: Taken on shore - Time when received into custody: 28 Jun 1813 - From what ship or whence received: Mary of Quebec - Exchanged, discharged, died, or escape: Discharged - Time when: 31 Oct 1813 - Whither, and by what order, or number or re-entry: Malabar Transport

Whitman, Stephen   Prisoner 612. Rank: Private - By what ship or how taken: Troops - Time when: 26 Jun 1813 - Place where: Stoney Point - Of what ship or corps: Land forces - Whether man of war, privateer or merchant vessel: Taken on shore - Time when received into custody: 7 Jul 1813 - From what ship or whence received: Steamboat - Exchanged, discharged, died, or escape: Discharged - Time when: 10 Aug 1813 - Whither, and by what order, or number or re-entry: HM Ship Regulius by order of Sir George Provost

Whitney, Isaac   Prisoner 1173. Rank: Private - By what ship or how taken: Troops - Time when: 5 May 1813 - Place where: Rapids Prince Reason - Of what ship or corps: Land forces - Whether man of war, privateer or merchant vessel: Taken on shore - Time when received into custody: 25 Nov 1813 - From what ship or whence received: Town Goal - Exchanged, discharged, died, or escape: Discharged - Time when: 12 Mar 1814 - Whither, and by what order, or number or re-entry: New Brunswick Fencibles

Whitney, Jeremiah   Prisoner 106. Rank: Private - By what ship or how taken: Boats & Troops - Time when: 28 May 1813 - Place where: Stoney Point, Henderson Harbor - Of what ship or corps: Land forces - Whether man of war, privateer or merchant vessel: Taken on shore - Time when received into custody: 8 Jun 1813 - From what ship or whence received: Batteaux - Exchanged, discharged, died, or escape: Discharged - Time when: 4 May 1814 - Whither, and by what order, or number or re-entry: United States

Whitney, Joseph   Prisoner 65. Rank: Sergeant - By what ship or how taken: Boats & Troops - Time when: 28 May 1813 - Place where: Stoney Point, Henderson Harbor - Of what ship or corps: Land forces - Whether man of war, privateer or merchant vessel: Taken on shore - Time when received into custody: 8 Jun 1813 - From what ship or whence received: Batteaux - Exchanged, discharged, died, or escape: Discharged - Time when: 31 Oct 1813 - Whither, and by what order, or number or re-entry: Malabar Transport

Whitten, George   Prisoner 1652. Rank: Private - By what ship or how taken: Troops - Time when: 11 Nov 1813 - Place where: Williamsburg - Of what ship or corps: Land forces - Whether man of war, privateer or merchant vessel: Taken on shore - Time when received into custody: 5 Oct 1814 - From what ship or whence received: Montreal - Exchanged, discharged, died, or escape: Discharged - Time when: 8 Oct 1814 - Whither, and by what order, or number or re-entry: H.M. Ship Ceylon

Whitton, John   Prisoner 798. Rank: Private - By what ship or how taken: Troops - Time when: 26 Jun 1813 - Place where: Beaver Dam - Of what ship or corps: Land forces - Whether man of war, privateer or merchant vessel: Taken on shore - Time when received into custody: 7 Jul 1813 - From what ship or whence received: Steamboat - Exchanged, discharged, died, or escape: Discharged - Time when: 10 Aug 1813 - Whither, and by what order, or number or re-entry: HM Ship Malpomena

Wilay, Thomas   Prisoner 1700. Rank: Private - By what ship or how taken: Troops - Time when: 20 Jul 1814 - Place where: French Mills - Of what ship or corps: Land forces - Whether man of war, privateer or merchant vessel: Taken on shore - Time when received into custody: 23 Oct 1814 - From what ship or whence received: Montreal - Exchanged, discharged, died, or escape: Discharged - Time when: 8 Nov 1814 - Whither, and by what order, or number or re-entry: S. George No. 575 for Halifax

Wilay, William   Prisoner 1403. Rank: Private - By what ship or how taken: Troops - Time when: 19 Dec 1813 - Place where: Fort Niagara - Of what ship or corps: Land forces - Whether man of war, privateer or merchant vessel: Taken on shore - Time when received into custody: 29 Jan 1814 - From what ship or whence received: Montreal by land carriage - Exchanged, discharged, died, or escape: Discharged - Time when: 4 May 1814 - Whither, and by what order, or number or re-entry: United States

Wilcox, Almeron   Prisoner 1788. Rank: Private - By what ship or how taken: Troops - Time when: 7 Sep 1814 - Place where:

American Prisoners of War held at Quebec during the War of 1812

Fort Erie - Of what ship or corps: Land forces - Whether man of war, privateer or merchant vessel: Taken on shore - Time when received into custody: 1 Nov 1814 - From what ship or whence received: Montreal - Exchanged, discharged, died, or escape: Discharged - Time when: 8 Nov 1814 - Whither, and by what order, or number or re-entry: S. George No. 575 for Halifax by order of Sir George Provost

Wilcox, Burton   Prisoner 1719. Rank: Private - By what ship or how taken: Gun Boats - Time when: 6 Sep 1814 - Place where: Lake Huron - Of what ship or corps: Scorpion - Whether man of war, privateer or merchant vessel: Man of War - Time when received into custody: 28 Oct 1814 - From what ship or whence received: Montreal - Exchanged, discharged, died, or escape: Discharged - Time when: 10 Nov 1814 - Whither, and by what order, or number or re-entry: Transport Stately No. 408 for Halifax

Wilcox, David   Prisoner 1169. Rank: Private - By what ship or how taken: Troops - Time when: 5 May 1813 - Place where: Rapids Prince Reason - Of what ship or corps: Land forces - Whether man of war, privateer or merchant vessel: Taken on shore - Time when received into custody: 25 Nov 1813 - From what ship or whence received: Town Goal - Exchanged, discharged, died, or escape: Discharged - Time when: 12 Mar 1814 - Whither, and by what order, or number or re-entry: New Brunswick Fencibles

Wilcox, John   Prisoner 956. Rank: Private - By what ship or how taken: Troops - Time when: 5 Jul 1813 - Place where: Fort Schisher - Of what ship or corps: Land forces - Whether man of war, privateer or merchant vessel: Taken on shore - Time when received into custody: 5 Sep 1813 - From what ship or whence received: Steamboat - Exchanged, discharged, died, or escape: Discharged - Time when: 31 Oct 1813 - Whither, and by what order, or number or re-entry: Malabar Transport

Wilcox, Oliver   Prisoner 1710. Rank: Quartermaster - By what ship or how taken: Troops - Time when: 17 Sep 1814 - Place where: Fort Erie - Of what ship or corps: Land forces - Whether man of war, privateer or merchant vessel: Taken on shore - Time when received into custody: 28 Oct 1814   From what ship or whence received: Montreal   Exchanged, discharged, died, or escape: Discharged - Time when: 10 Nov 1814 - Whither, and by what order, or number or re-entry: Transport Stately No. 408 for Halifax

Wilcox, William   Prisoner 985. Rank: Purser Steward - By what ship or how taken: Earl Moria - Time when: 10 Aug 1813 - Place where: Lake Ontario - Of what ship or corps: Julia - Whether man of war, privateer or merchant vessel: Man of War - Time when received into custody: 5 Sep 1813 - From what ship or whence received: Steamboat - Exchanged, discharged, died, or escape: Discharged - Time when: 18 Sep 1813 - Whither, and by what order, or number or re-entry: To the Regulius Transport by order of Major General Glasgow

Wilder, Elihu   Prisoner 18. Rank: Corporal - By what ship or how taken: Boats & Troops - Time when: 28 May 1813 - Place where: Stoney Point, Henderson Harbor - Of what ship or corps: Land forces - Whether man of war, privateer or merchant vessel: Taken on shore - Time when received into custody: 8 Jun 1813 - From what ship or whence received: Batteaux - Exchanged, discharged, died, or escape: Discharged - Time when: 31 Oct 1813 - Whither, and by what order, or number or re-entry: Malabar Transport

Wilder, Ezra   Prisoner 1937. Rank: Sergeant - By what ship or how taken: Troops - Time when: 17 Sep 1814 - Place where: Fort Erie - Of what ship or corps: Land forces - Whether man of war, privateer or merchant vessel: Taken on shore - Time when received into custody: 1 Nov 1814 - From what ship or whence received: Montreal - Exchanged, discharged, died, or escape: Discharged - Time when: 13 Mar 1815 - Whither, and by what order, or number or re-entry: United States

Wilder, Titus   Prisoner 820. Rank: Private - By what ship or how taken: Troops - Time when: 26 Jun 1813 - Place where: Beaver Dam - Of what ship or corps: Land forces - Whether man of war, privateer or merchant vessel: Taken on shore - Time when received into custody: 7 Jul 1813 - From what ship or whence received: Steamboat - Exchanged, discharged, died, or escape: Discharged - Time when: 10 Aug 1813 - Whither, and by what order, or number or re-entry: HM Ship Malpomena

Wildon, John   Prisoner 996. Rank: Seaman - By what ship or how taken: Earl Moria - Time when: 10 Aug 1813 - Place where: Lake Ontario - Of what ship or corps: Julia - Whether man of war, privateer or merchant vessel: Man of War - Time when received into custody: 5 Sep 1813 - From what ship or whence received: Steamboat - Exchanged, discharged, died, or escape: Discharged - Time when: 18 Sep 1813 - Whither, and by what order, or number or re-entry: HM Ship Success

Wilhelmi, Daniel   Prisoner 1268. Rank: Privateer - By what ship or how taken: Troops - Time when: 19 Dec 1813 - Place where: Fort Niagara - Of what ship or corps: Land forces - Whether man of war, privateer or merchant vessel: Taken on shore - Time when received into custody: 29 Jan 1814 - From what ship or whence received: Montreal by land carriage - Exchanged, discharged, died, or escape: Discharged - Time when: 4 May 1814 - Whither, and by what order, or

American Prisoners of War held at Quebec during the War of 1812

number or re-entry: United States

Wilkins, Aaron   Prisoner 64. Rank: Private - By what ship or how taken: Boats & Troops - Time when: 28 May 1813 - Place where: Stoney Point, Henderson Harbor - Of what ship or corps: Land forces - Whether man of war, privateer or merchant vessel: Taken on shore - Time when received into custody: 8 Jun 1813 - From what ship or whence received: Batteaux - Exchanged, discharged, died, or escape: Discharged - Time when: 31 Oct 1813 - Whither, and by what order, or number or re-entry: Malabar Transport

Wilkins, Edward   Prisoner 1183. Rank: Private - By what ship or how taken: Troops - Time when: 5 May 1813 - Place where: Rapids - Of what ship or corps: Land forces - Whether man of war, privateer or merchant vessel: Taken on shore - Time when received into custody: 25 Nov 1813 - From what ship or whence received: Town Goal - Exchanged, discharged, died, or escape: Discharged - Time when: 4 May 1814 - Whither, and by what order, or number or re-entry: United States

Wilkins, James   Prisoner 783. Rank: Private - By what ship or how taken: Troops - Time when: 26 Jun 1813 - Place where: Beaver Dam - Of what ship or corps: Land forces - Whether man of war, privateer or merchant vessel: Taken on shore - Time when received into custody: 7 Jul 1813 - From what ship or whence received: Steamboat - Exchanged, discharged, died, or escape: Discharged - Time when: 10 Aug 1813 - Whither, and by what order, or number or re-entry: HM Ship Malpomena

Wilkins , John   Prisoner 619. Rank: Private - By what ship or how taken: Troops - Time when: 24 Jun 1813 - Place where: Stoney Point - Of what ship or corps: Land forces - Whether man of war, privateer or merchant vessel: Taken on shore - Time when received into custody: 7 Jul 1813 - From what ship or whence received: Steamboat - Exchanged, discharged, died, or escape: Discharged - Time when: 10 Aug 1813 - Whither, and by what order, or number or re-entry: HM Ship Regulius by order of Sir George Provost

Wilkinson, Andrew   Prisoner 103. Rank: Private - By what ship or how taken: Boats & Troops - Time when: 28 May 1813 - Place where: Stoney Point, Henderson Harbor - Of what ship or corps: Land forces - Whether man of war, privateer or merchant vessel: Taken on shore - Time when received into custody: 8 Jun 1813 - From what ship or whence received: Batteaux - Exchanged, discharged, died, or escape: Discharged - Time when: 4 May 1814 - Whither, and by what order, or number or re-entry: United States

Wilkinson, James   Prisoner 434. Rank: Private - By what ship or how taken: Troops - Time when: 24 Jun 1813 - Place where: Beaver Dam - Of what ship or corps: Land forces - Whether man of war, privateer or merchant vessel: Taken on shore - Time when received into custody: 7 Jul 1813 - From what ship or whence received: Steamboat - Exchanged, discharged, died, or escape: Discharged - Time when: 10 Aug 1813 - Whither, and by what order, or number or re-entry: HM Ship Regulius by order of Sir George Provost

Wilkinson, Oliver   Prisoner 328. Rank: Private - By what ship or how taken: Boats & Troops - Time when: 6 Jun 1813 - Place where: Stoney Point - Of what ship or corps: Land forces - Whether man of war, privateer or merchant vessel: Taken on shore - Time when received into custody: 28 Jun 1813 - From what ship or whence received: Quebec of Quebec - Exchanged, discharged, died, or escape: Discharged - Time when: 31 Oct 1813 - Whither, and by what order, or number or re-entry: Malabar Transport

Willets, Joseph   Prisoner 1060. Rank: Private - By what ship or how taken: Troops - Time when: 24 Jun 1813 - Place where: Beaver Dam - Of what ship or corps: Land forces - Whether man of war, privateer or merchant vessel: Taken on shore - Time when received into custody: 5 Sep 1813 - From what ship or whence received: Steamboat - Exchanged, discharged, died, or escape: Discharged - Time when: 31 Oct 1813 - Whither, and by what order, or number or re-entry: Malabar Transport

Willett, Phil   Prisoner 1095. Rank: Private - By what ship or how taken: Troops - Time when: 24 Aug 1813 - Place where: Fort George - Of what ship or corps: Land forces - Whether man of war, privateer or merchant vessel: Taken on shore - Time when received into custody: 10 Oct 1813 - From what ship or whence received: Steamboat - Exchanged, discharged, died, or escape: Discharged - Time when: 31 Oct 1813 - Whither, and by what order, or number or re-entry: Malabar Transport

Williams, Andrew   Prisoner 553. Rank: Private - By what ship or how taken: Troops - Time when: 26 Jun 1813 - Place where: Beaver Dam - Of what ship or corps: Land forces - Whether man of war, privateer or merchant vessel: Taken on shore - Time when received into custody: 13 Jul 1813 - From what ship or whence received: Steamboat - Exchanged, discharged, died, or escape: Discharged - Time when: 10 Aug 1813 - Whither, and by what order, or number or re-entry: HM Ship Regulius by order of Sir George Provost

American Prisoners of War held at Quebec during the War of 1812

Williams, Benjamin   Prisoner 1005. Rank: Seaman - By what ship or how taken: Earl Moria - Time when: 10 Aug 1813 - Place where: Lake Ontario - Of what ship or corps: Julia - Whether man of war, privateer or merchant vessel: Man of War - Time when received into custody: 5 Sep 1813 - From what ship or whence received: Steamboat - Exchanged, discharged, died, or escape: Discharged - Time when: 31 Oct 1813 - Whither, and by what order, or number or re-entry: Malabar Transport

Williams, Calvin   Prisoner 1022. Rank: Boats'n - By what ship or how taken: Lord Melvin - Time when: 10 Aug 1813 - Place where: Lake Ontario - Of what ship or corps: Growler - Whether man of war, privateer or merchant vessel: Man of War - Time when received into custody: 5 Sep 1813 - From what ship or whence received: Steamboat - Exchanged, discharged, died, or escape: Discharged - Time when: 21 Sep 1813 - Whither, and by what order, or number or re-entry: Mersey Transport

Williams, Elijah   Prisoner 1490. Rank: Sergeant - By what ship or how taken: Troops - Time when: 25 Jul 1814 - Place where: Lundy's Lane - Of what ship or corps: Land forces - Whether man of war, privateer or merchant vessel: Taken on shore - Time when received into custody: 19 Aug 1814 - From what ship or whence received: Triton No. 438 Transport - Exchanged, discharged, died, or escape: Discharged - Time when: 13 Mar 1815 - Whither, and by what order, or number or re-entry: United States

Williams, Henry   Prisoner 992. Rank: Seaman - By what ship or how taken: Earl Moria - Time when: 10 Aug 1813 - Place where: Lake Ontario - Of what ship or corps: Julia - Whether man of war, privateer or merchant vessel: Man of War - Time when received into custody: 5 Sep 1813 - From what ship or whence received: Steamboat - Exchanged, discharged, died, or escape: Discharged - Time when: 31 Oct 1813 - Whither, and by what order, or number or re-entry: Malabar Transport

Williams, Jack   Prisoner 1989. Rank: Seaman - By what ship or how taken: Troops - Time when: - Place where: - Of what ship or corps: Armline - Whether man of war, privateer or merchant vessel: Man of War - Time when received into custody: - From what ship or whence received: - Exchanged, discharged, died, or escape: Discharged - Time when: 13 Mar 1815 - Whither, and by what order, or number or re-entry: United States

Williams, Jesse   Prisoner 1734. Rank: Seaman - By what ship or how taken: Gun Boats - Time when: 6 Sep 1814 - Place where: Lake Huron - Of what ship or corps: Scorpion - Whether man of war, privateer or merchant vessel: Man of War - Time when received into custody: 1 Nov 1814 - From what ship or whence received: Montreal - Exchanged, discharged, died, or escape: Discharged - Time when: 7 Nov 1814 - Whither, and by what order, or number or re-entry: Transport Freedom No. 582 by orders of his Excellency Sir George Provost

Williams, John W.   Prisoner 1766. Rank: Sergeant - By what ship or how taken: Troops - Time when: 7 Sep 1814 - Place where: Fort Erie - Of what ship or corps: Land forces - Whether man of war, privateer or merchant vessel: Taken on shore - Time when received into custody: 1 Nov 1814 - From what ship or whence received: Montreal - Exchanged, discharged, died, or escape: Discharged - Time when: 8 Nov 1814 - Whither, and by what order, or number or re-entry: S. George No. 575 for Halifax by order of Sir George Provost

Williams, P.   Prisoner 1590. Rank: Seaman - By what ship or how taken: Gun Boats - Time when: 12 Aug 1814 - Place where: Fort Erie - Of what ship or corps: Ohio - Whether man of war, privateer or merchant vessel: Man of War - Time when received into custody: 5 Oct 1814 - From what ship or whence received: Montreal - Exchanged, discharged, died, or escape: Discharged - Time when: 10 Nov 1814 - Whither, and by what order, or number or re-entry: Freedom No. 582

Williams, Robert   Prisoner 1492. Rank: Private - By what ship or how taken: Troops - Time when: 25 Jul 1814 - Place where: Lundy's Lane - Of what ship or corps: Land forces - Whether man of war, privateer or merchant vessel: Taken on shore - Time when received into custody: 19 Aug 1814 - From what ship or whence received: Triton No. 438 Transport - Exchanged, discharged, died, or escape: Discharged - Time when: 8 Oct 1814 - Whither, and by what order, or number or re-entry: Queen No. 415

Williams, Samuel   Prisoner 94. Rank: Private - By what ship or how taken: Boats & Troops - Time when: 28 May 1813 - Place where: Stoney Point, Henderson Harbor - Of what ship or corps: Land forces - Whether man of war, privateer or merchant vessel: Taken on shore - Time when received into custody: 8 Jun 1813 - From what ship or whence received: Batteaux - Exchanged, discharged, died, or escape: Discharged - Time when: 31 Oct 1813 - Whither, and by what order, or number or re-entry: Malabar Transport

Williams, Samuel   Prisoner 1725. Rank: Seaman - By what ship or how taken: Gun Boats - Time when: 6 Sep 1814 - Place where: Lake Huron - Of what ship or corps: Scorpion - Whether man of war, privateer or merchant vessel: Man of War - Time when received into custody: 1 Nov 1814 - From what ship or whence received: Montreal - Exchanged, discharged, died, or escape: Discharged - Time when: 7 Nov 1814 - Whither, and by what order, or number or re-entry: Transport Freedom No. 582 by orders of his Excellency Sir George Provost

American Prisoners of War held at Quebec during the War of 1812

Williams, Thomas   Prisoner 853. Rank: Private - By what ship or how taken: Troops - Time when: 26 Jun 1813 - Place where: Beaver Dam - Of what ship or corps: Land forces - Whether man of war, privateer or merchant vessel: Taken on shore - Time when received into custody: 7 Jul 1813 - From what ship or whence received: Steamboat - Exchanged, discharged, died, or escape: Discharged - Time when: 10 Aug 1813 - Whither, and by what order, or number or re-entry: HM Ship Malpomena

Williams, Thomas   Prisoner 1767. Rank: Sergeant - By what ship or how taken: Troops - Time when: 7 Sep 1814 - Place where: Fort Erie - Of what ship or corps: Land forces - Whether man of war, privateer or merchant vessel: Taken on shore - Time when received into custody: 1 Nov 1814 - From what ship or whence received: Montreal - Exchanged, discharged, died, or escape: Discharged - Time when: 8 Nov 1814 - Whither, and by what order, or number or re-entry: S. George No. 575 for Halifax by order of Sir George Provost

Williamson, John F.   Prisoner 1206. Rank: Lieutenant - By what ship or how taken: Troops - Time when: 19 Dec 1813 - Place where: Fort Niagara - Of what ship or corps: Land forces - Whether man of war, privateer or merchant vessel: Taken on shore - Time when received into custody: 18 Jan 1814 - From what ship or whence received: Montreal by land carriage - Exchanged, discharged, died, or escape: Discharged - Time when: 4 May 1814 - Whither, and by what order, or number or re-entry: United States

Williby, George   Prisoner 357. Rank: Captain - By what ship or how taken: Troops - Time when: 6 Jun 1813 - Place where: Stoney Point - Of what ship or corps: Land forces - Whether man of war, privateer or merchant vessel: Taken on shore - Time when received into custody: 28 Jun 1813 - From what ship or whence received: Mary of Quebec - Exchanged, discharged, died, or escape: Discharged - Time when: 31 Oct 1813 - Whither, and by what order, or number or re-entry: Malabar Transport

Willinea, John N.   Prisoner 866. Rank: Private - By what ship or how taken: Troops - Time when: 26 Jun 1813 - Place where: Beaver Dam - Of what ship or corps: Land forces - Whether man of war, privateer or merchant vessel: Taken on shore - Time when received into custody: 7 Jul 1813 - From what ship or whence received: Steamboat - Exchanged, discharged, died, or escape: Discharged - Time when: 10 Aug 1813 - Whither, and by what order, or number or re-entry: HM Ship Malpomena

Willis, Alfred   Prisoner 661. Rank: Private - By what ship or how taken: Troops - Time when: 24 Jun 1813 - Place where: Stoney Point - Of what ship or corps: Land forces - Whether man of war, privateer or merchant vessel: Taken on shore - Time when received into custody: 7 Jul 1813 - From what ship or whence received: Steamboat - Exchanged, discharged, died, or escape: Discharged - Time when: 10 Aug 1813 - Whither, and by what order, or number or re-entry: HM Ship Regulius by order of Sir George Provost

Willis, Austin   Prisoner 1613. Rank: Private - By what ship or how taken: Gun Boats - Time when: 12 Aug 1814 - Place where: Fort Erie - Of what ship or corps: Land forces - Whether man of war, privateer or merchant vessel: Taken on shore - Time when received into custody: 5 Oct 1814 - From what ship or whence received: Montreal - Exchanged, discharged, died, or escape: Discharged - Time when: 8 Oct 1814 - Whither, and by what order, or number or re-entry: H.M. Ship Ceylon

Willis, John   Prisoner 903. Rank: Sergeant - By what ship or how taken: Troops - Time when: 26 Jun 1813 - Place where: Beaver Dam - Of what ship or corps: Land forces - Whether man of war, privateer or merchant vessel: Taken on shore - Time when received into custody: 21 Jul 1813 - From what ship or whence received: Steamboat - Exchanged, discharged, died, or escape: Discharged - Time when: 10 Aug 1813 - Whither, and by what order, or number or re-entry: HM Ship Malpomena

Wilson, Alexander   Prisoner 909. Rank: Private - By what ship or how taken: Troops - Time when: 26 Jun 1813 - Place where: Beaver Dam - Of what ship or corps: Land forces - Whether man of war, privateer or merchant vessel: Taken on shore - Time when received into custody: 21 Jul 1813 - From what ship or whence received: Steamboat - Exchanged, discharged, died, or escape: Discharged - Time when: 10 Aug 1813 - Whither, and by what order, or number or re-entry: HM Ship Malpomena

Wilson, Daniel   Prisoner 774. Rank: Private - By what ship or how taken: Troops - Time when: 26 Jun 1813 - Place where: Beaver Dam - Of what ship or corps: Land forces - Whether man of war, privateer or merchant vessel: Taken on shore - Time when received into custody: 7 Jul 1813 - From what ship or whence received: Steamboat - Exchanged, discharged, died, or escape: Discharged - Time when: 10 Aug 1813 - Whither, and by what order, or number or re-entry: HM Ship Malpomena

Wilson, Ebenezer   Prisoner 1709. Rank: Major - By what ship or how taken: Troops - Time when: 17 Sep 1814 - Place where: Fort Erie - Of what ship or corps: Land forces - Whether man of war, privateer or merchant vessel: Taken on shore -

American Prisoners of War held at Quebec during the War of 1812

Time when received into custody: 28 Oct 1814 - From what ship or whence received: Montreal - Exchanged, discharged, died, or escape: Discharged - Time when: 10 Nov 1814 - Whither, and by what order, or number or re-entry: Transport Stately No. 408 for Halifax

Wilson, Horace   Prisoner 1837. Rank: Private - By what ship or how taken: Troops - Time when: 17 Sep 1814 - Place where: Fort Erie - Of what ship or corps: Land forces - Whether man of war, privateer or merchant vessel: Taken on shore - Time when received into custody: 1 Nov 1814 - From what ship or whence received: Montreal - Exchanged, discharged, died, or escape: Discharged - Time when: 8 Nov 1814 - Whither, and by what order, or number or re-entry: S. George No. 575 for Halifax by order of Sir George Provost

Wilson, James   Prisoner 562. Rank: Private - By what ship or how taken: Troops - Time when: 26 Jun 1813 - Place where: Beaver Dam - Of what ship or corps: Land forces - Whether man of war, privateer or merchant vessel: Taken on shore - Time when received into custody: 13 Jul 1813 - From what ship or whence received: Steamboat - Exchanged, discharged, died, or escape: Discharged - Time when: 10 Aug 1813 - Whither, and by what order, or number or re-entry: HM Ship Regulius by order of Sir George Provost

Wilson, W. H.   Prisoner 1631. Rank: Private - By what ship or how taken: Troops - Time when: 6 Sep 1814 - Place where: Plattsburg - Of what ship or corps: Land forces - Whether man of war, privateer or merchant vessel: Taken on shore - Time when received into custody: 5 Oct 1814 - From what ship or whence received: Montreal - Exchanged, discharged, died, or escape: Discharged - Time when: 8 Oct 1814 - Whither, and by what order, or number or re-entry: H.M. Ship Ceylon

Wilson, Warren   Prisoner 908. Rank: Private - By what ship or how taken: Troops - Time when: 26 Jun 1813 - Place where: Beaver Dam - Of what ship or corps: Land forces - Whether man of war, privateer or merchant vessel: Taken on shore - Time when received into custody: 21 Jul 1813 - From what ship or whence received: Steamboat - Exchanged, discharged, died, or escape: Discharged - Time when: 10 Aug 1813 - Whither, and by what order, or number or re-entry: HM Ship Malpomena

Wilson, William   Prisoner 1128. Rank: Private - By what ship or how taken: Troops - Time when: 5 May 1813 - Place where: Rapids Prince Reason - Of what ship or corps: Land forces - Whether man of war, privateer or merchant vessel: Taken on shore - Time when received into custody: 25 Nov 1813 - From what ship or whence received: Town Goal - Exchanged, discharged, died, or escape: Discharged - Time when: 4 May 1814 - Whither, and by what order, or number or re-entry: United States

Wilson, William   Prisoner 1145. Rank: Private - By what ship or how taken: Troops - Time when: 5 May 1813 - Place where: Rapids Prince Reason - Of what ship or corps: Land forces - Whether man of war, privateer or merchant vessel: Taken on shore - Time when received into custody: 25 Nov 1813 - From what ship or whence received: Town Goal - Exchanged, discharged, died, or escape: Discharged - Time when: 21 Apr 1814 - Whither, and by what order, or number or re-entry: United States

Wimiss, Daniel   Prisoner 608. Rank: Private - By what ship or how taken: Troops - Time when: 26 Jun 1813 - Place where: Stoney Point - Of what ship or corps: Land forces - Whether man of war, privateer or merchant vessel: Taken on shore - Time when received into custody: 7 Jul 1813 - From what ship or whence received: Steamboat - Exchanged, discharged, died, or escape: Discharged - Time when: 31 Oct 1813 - Whither, and by what order, or number or re-entry: Malabar Transport

Winchester, James   Prisoner 246. Rank: Brigadier General - By what ship or how taken: Boats & Troops - Time when: 24 Jun 1813 - Place where: Rec in charge of Beauport - Of what ship or corps: Land forces - Whether man of war, privateer or merchant vessel: Taken on shore - Time when received into custody: 24 Jun 1813 - From what ship or whence received: At Beauport - Exchanged, discharged, died, or escape: Discharged - Time when: 21 Apr 1814 - Whither, and by what order, or number or re-entry: United States

Winder, William H.   Prisoner 255. Rank: Brigadier General - By what ship or how taken: Boats & Troops - Time when: 24 Jun 1813 - Place where: Stoney Point - Of what ship or corps: Land forces - Whether man of war, privateer or merchant vessel: Taken on shore - Time when received into custody: 24 Jun 1813 - From what ship or whence received: Steamboat - Exchanged, discharged, died, or escape: Discharged - Time when: 3 Apr 1814 - Whither, and by what order, or number or re-entry: United States

Winder, William H.   Prisoner 1426. Rank: Brigadier General - By what ship or how taken: Troops - Time when: 19 Dec 1813 - Place where: Fort Niagara - Of what ship or corps: Land forces - Whether man of war, privateer or merchant vessel: Taken on shore - Time when received into custody: 29 Jan 1814 - From what ship or whence received: Montreal by land carriage - Exchanged, discharged, died, or escape: - Time when: - Whither, and by what order, or number or re-entry:

American Prisoners of War held at Quebec during the War of 1812

Winn, Clement   Prisoner 481. Rank: Private - By what ship or how taken: Troops - Time when: 24 Jun 1813 - Place where: Beaver Dam - Of what ship or corps: Land forces - Whether man of war, privateer or merchant vessel: Taken on shore - Time when received into custody: 7 Jul 1813 - From what ship or whence received: Steamboat - Exchanged, discharged, died, or escape: Discharged - Time when: 10 Aug 1813 - Whither, and by what order, or number or re-entry: HM Ship Regulius by order of Sir George Provost

Winnet, George   Prisoner 1471. Rank: Private - By what ship or how taken: Troops - Time when: 5 Jul 1814 - Place where: Chippewa - Of what ship or corps: Land forces - Whether man of war, privateer or merchant vessel: Taken on shore - Time when received into custody: 12 Aug 1814 - From what ship or whence received: Royal Seaman No. 289 Transport - Exchanged, discharged, died, or escape: Discharged - Time when: 8 Oct 1814 - Whither, and by what order, or number or re-entry: Queen No. 415

Winter, Christian   Prisoner 1360. Rank: Private - By what ship or how taken: Troops - Time when: 19 Dec 1813 - Place where: Fort Niagara - Of what ship or corps: Land forces - Whether man of war, privateer or merchant vessel: Taken on shore - Time when received into custody: 29 Jan 1814 - From what ship or whence received: Montreal by land carriage - Exchanged, discharged, died, or escape: Discharged - Time when: 4 May 1814 - Whither, and by what order, or number or re-entry: United States

Winters, J.   Prisoner 1605. Rank: Private - By what ship or how taken: Troops - Time when: 6 Sep 1814 - Place where: Plattsburg - Of what ship or corps: Land forces - Whether man of war, privateer or merchant vessel: Taken on shore - Time when received into custody: 5 Oct 1814 - From what ship or whence received: Montreal - Exchanged, discharged, died, or escape: Discharged - Time when: 8 Oct 1814 - Whither, and by what order, or number or re-entry: H.M. Ship Ceylon

Winters, Stephen   Prisoner 1493. Rank: Corporal - By what ship or how taken: Troops - Time when: 25 Jul 1814 - Place where: Lundy's Lane - Of what ship or corps: Land forces - Whether man of war, privateer or merchant vessel: Taken on shore - Time when received into custody: 19 Aug 1814 - From what ship or whence received: Triton No. 438 Transport - Exchanged, discharged, died, or escape: Discharged - Time when: 8 Oct 1814 - Whither, and by what order, or number or re-entry: Queen No. 415

Winton, James   Prisoner 353. Rank: Private - By what ship or how taken: Troops - Time when: 6 Jun 1813 - Place where: Stoney Point - Of what ship or corps: Land forces - Whether man of war, privateer or merchant vessel: Taken on shore - Time when received into custody: 28 Jun 1813 - From what ship or whence received: Mary of Quebec - Exchanged, discharged, died, or escape: Discharged - Time when: 31 Oct 1813 - Whither, and by what order, or number or re-entry: Malabar Transport

Witherall, Gerrard   Prisoner 343. Rank: Private - By what ship or how taken: Boats & Troops - Time when: 22 Feb 1813 - Place where: Hedgesburgh - Of what ship or corps: Land forces - Whether man of war, privateer or merchant vessel: Taken on shore - Time when received into custody: 28 Jun 1813 - From what ship or whence received: Mary of Quebec - Exchanged, discharged, died, or escape: Discharged - Time when: 31 Oct 1813 - Whither, and by what order, or number or re-entry: Malabar Transport

Withington, Thomas   Prisoner 1150. Rank: Private - By what ship or how taken: Troops - Time when: 5 May 1813 - Place where: Rapids Prince Reason - Of what ship or corps: Land forces - Whether man of war, privateer or merchant vessel: Taken on shore - Time when received into custody: 25 Nov 1813 - From what ship or whence received: Town Goal - Exchanged, discharged, died, or escape: Discharged - Time when: 21 Apr 1814 - Whither, and by what order, or number or re-entry: United States

Wittum, Reiford   Prisoner 1965. Rank: Private - By what ship or how taken: Troops - Time when: 25 Jul 1814 - Place where: Lundy's Lane - Of what ship or corps: Land forces - Whether man of war, privateer or merchant vessel: Taken on shore - Time when received into custody: 11 Dec 1814 - From what ship or whence received: Montreal - Exchanged, discharged, died, or escape: Discharged - Time when: 13 Mar 1815 - Whither, and by what order, or number or re-entry: United States

Wolffrom, William   Prisoner 628. Rank: Private - By what ship or how taken: Troops - Time when: 24 Jun 1813 - Place where: Stoney Point - Of what ship or corps: Land forces - Whether man of war, privateer or merchant vessel: Taken on shore - Time when received into custody: 7 Jul 1813 - From what ship or whence received: Steamboat - Exchanged, discharged, died, or escape: Discharged - Time when: 10 Aug 1813 - Whither, and by what order, or number or re-entry: HM Ship Regulius by order of Sir George Provost

American Prisoners of War held at Quebec during the War of 1812

Wood, Amory   Prisoner 979. Rank: Private - By what ship or how taken: Troops - Time when: 5 Jul 1813 - Place where: Fort Schisher - Of what ship or corps: Land forces - Whether man of war, privateer or merchant vessel: Taken on shore - Time when received into custody: 5 Sep 1813 - From what ship or whence received: Steamboat - Exchanged, discharged, died, or escape: Discharged - Time when: 31 Oct 1813 - Whither, and by what order, or number or re-entry: Malabar Transport

Wood, Andrew   Prisoner 1523. Rank: Private - By what ship or how taken: Troops - Time when: 25 Jul 1814 - Place where: Lundy's Lane - Of what ship or corps: Land forces - Whether man of war, privateer or merchant vessel: Taken on shore - Time when received into custody: 30 Aug 1814 - From what ship or whence received: Lady Delaval Schooner 578 - Exchanged, discharged, died, or escape: Discharged - Time when: 8 Oct 1814 - Whither, and by what order, or number or re-entry: Queen No. 415

Wood, Emery   Prisoner 1773. Rank: Private - By what ship or how taken: Troops - Time when: 7 Sep 1814 - Place where: Fort Erie - Of what ship or corps: Land forces - Whether man of war, privateer or merchant vessel: Taken on shore - Time when received into custody: 1 Nov 1814 - From what ship or whence received: Montreal - Exchanged, discharged, died, or escape: Discharged - Time when: 8 Nov 1814 - Whither, and by what order, or number or re-entry: S. George No. 575 for Halifax by order of Sir George Provost

Wood, Frederick   Prisoner 970. Rank: Private - By what ship or how taken: Troops - Time when: 5 Jul 1813 - Place where: Fort Schisher - Of what ship or corps: Land forces - Whether man of war, privateer or merchant vessel: Taken on shore - Time when received into custody: 5 Sep 1813 - From what ship or whence received: Steamboat - Exchanged, discharged, died, or escape: Discharged - Time when: 31 Oct 1813 - Whither, and by what order, or number or re-entry: Malabar Transport

Wood, George W.   Prisoner 1249. Rank: Private - By what ship or how taken: Troops - Time when: 19 Dec 1813 - Place where: Fort Niagara - Of what ship or corps: Land forces - Whether man of war, privateer or merchant vessel: Taken on shore - Time when received into custody: 29 Jan 1814 - From what ship or whence received: Montreal by land carriage - Exchanged, discharged, died, or escape: Discharged - Time when: 27 Feb 1814 - Whither, and by what order, or number or re-entry: Volunteered for New Brunswick Fencibles

Wood, Isarrel   Prisoner 102. Rank: Private - By what ship or how taken: Boats & Troops - Time when: 28 May 1813 - Place where: Stoney Point, Henderson Harbor - Of what ship or corps: Land forces - Whether man of war, privateer or merchant vessel: Taken on shore - Time when received into custody: 8 Jun 1813 - From what ship or whence received: Batteaux - Exchanged, discharged, died, or escape: Discharged - Time when: 31 Oct 1813 - Whither, and by what order, or number or re-entry: Malabar Transport

Wood , Pratt   Prisoner 582. Rank: Private - By what ship or how taken: Troops - Time when: 26 Jun 1813 - Place where: Beaver Dam - Of what ship or corps: Land forces - Whether man of war, privateer or merchant vessel: Taken on shore - Time when received into custody: 13 Jul 1813 - From what ship or whence received: Steamboat - Exchanged, discharged, died, or escape: Discharged - Time when: 10 Aug 1813 - Whither, and by what order, or number or re-entry: HM Ship Regulius by order of Sir George Provost

Woodland, Lebai   Prisoner 396. Rank: Private - By what ship or how taken: Troops - Time when: 6 Jun 1813 - Place where: Stoney Point - Of what ship or corps: Land forces - Whether man of war, privateer or merchant vessel: Taken on shore - Time when received into custody: 28 Jun 1813 - From what ship or whence received: Mary of Quebec - Exchanged, discharged, died, or escape: Discharged - Time when: 31 Oct 1813 - Whither, and by what order, or number or re-entry: Malabar Transport

Woodlowe, Charles   Prisoner 1625. Rank: Private - By what ship or how taken: Troops - Time when: 11 Sep 1814 - Place where: Plattsburg - Of what ship or corps: Land forces - Whether man of war, privateer or merchant vessel: Taken on shore - Time when received into custody: 5 Oct 1814 - From what ship or whence received: Montreal - Exchanged, discharged, died, or escape: Discharged - Time when: 8 Oct 1814 - Whither, and by what order, or number or re-entry: H.M. Ship Ceylon

Woodman, Benjamin   Prisoner 238. Rank: Private - By what ship or how taken: Boats & Troops - Time when: 3 Jun 1813 - Place where: Lake Champlain - Of what ship or corps: Eagle - Whether man of war, privateer or merchant vessel: Man of War - Time when received into custody: 9 Jun 1813 - From what ship or whence received: Batteaux - Exchanged, discharged, died, or escape: Discharged - Time when: 31 Oct 1813 - Whither, and by what order, or number or re-entry: Malabar Transport

Woodman, Jeremiah   Prisoner 1775. Rank: Private - By what ship or how taken: Troops - Time when: 7 Sep 1814 - Place where: Fort Erie - Of what ship or corps: Land forces - Whether man of war, privateer or merchant vessel: Taken on shore - Time when received into custody: 1 Nov 1814 - From what ship or whence received: Montreal - Exchanged,

American Prisoners of War held at Quebec during the War of 1812

discharged, died, or escape: Discharged - Time when: 8 Nov 1814 - Whither, and by what order, or number or re-entry: S. George No. 575 for Halifax by order of Sir George Provost

Woolfriet, John   Prisoner 828.   Rank: Private - By what ship or how taken: Troops - Time when: 26 Jun 1813 - Place where: Beaver Dam - Of what ship or corps: Land forces - Whether man of war, privateer or merchant vessel: Taken on shore - Time when received into custody: 7 Jul 1813 - From what ship or whence received: Steamboat - Exchanged, discharged, died, or escape: Discharged - Time when: 10 Aug 1813 - Whither, and by what order, or number or re-entry: HM Ship Malpomena

Woolworth, Elijah   Prisoner 1654.   Rank: Private - By what ship or how taken: Troops - Time when: 11 Nov 1813 - Place where: Williamsburg - Of what ship or corps: Land forces - Whether man of war, privateer or merchant vessel: Taken on shore - Time when received into custody: 5 Oct 1814 - From what ship or whence received: Montreal - Exchanged, discharged, died, or escape: Discharged - Time when: 8 Oct 1814 - Whither, and by what order, or number or re-entry: H.M. Ship Ceylon

Wright, Jonas   Prisoner 1458.   Rank: Private - By what ship or how taken: Troops - Time when: 6 May 1814 - Place where: Oswago - Of what ship or corps: Land forces - Whether man of war, privateer or merchant vessel: Taken on shore - Time when received into custody: 12 Aug 1814 - From what ship or whence received: Royal Seaman No. 289 Transport - Exchanged, discharged, died, or escape: Discharged - Time when: 8 Oct 1814 - Whither, and by what order, or number or re-entry: Queen No. 415

Wright, Oliver   Prisoner 178.   Rank: Private - By what ship or how taken: Boats & Troops - Time when: 3 Jun 1813 - Place where: Lake Champlain - Of what ship or corps: Growler - Whether man of war, privateer or merchant vessel: Man of War - Time when received into custody: 9 Jun 1813 - From what ship or whence received: Batteaux - Exchanged, discharged, died, or escape: Discharged - Time when: 31 Oct 1813 - Whither, and by what order, or number or re-entry: Malabar Transport

Wright, Terick   Prisoner 846.   Rank: Sergeant - By what ship or how taken: Troops - Time when: 26 Jun 1813 - Place where: Beaver Dam - Of what ship or corps: Land forces - Whether man of war, privateer or merchant vessel: Taken on shore - Time when received into custody: 7 Jul 1813 - From what ship or whence received: Steamboat - Exchanged, discharged, died, or escape: Discharged - Time when: 10 Aug 1813 - Whither, and by what order, or number or re-entry: HM Ship Malpomena

Wright, William   Prisoner 1293.   Rank: Private - By what ship or how taken: Troops - Time when: 19 Dec 1813 - Place where: Fort Niagara - Of what ship or corps: Land forces - Whether man of war, privateer or merchant vessel: Taken on shore - Time when received into custody: 29 Jan 1814 - From what ship or whence received: Montreal by land carriage - Exchanged, discharged, died, or escape: Discharged - Time when: 9 Mar 1814 - Whither, and by what order, or number or re-entry: Volunteered for New Brunswick Fencibles

Wrights, Henry   Prisoner 902.   Rank: Private - By what ship or how taken: Troops - Time when: 26 Jun 1813 - Place where: Beaver Dam - Of what ship or corps: Land forces - Whether man of war, privateer or merchant vessel: Taken on shore - Time when received into custody: 21 Jul 1813 - From what ship or whence received: Steamboat - Exchanged, discharged, died, or escape: Discharged - Time when: 31 Oct 1813 - Whither, and by what order, or number or re-entry: Malabar Transport

Wyon, John M.   Prisoner 75.   Rank: Private - By what ship or how taken: Boats & Troops - Time when: 28 May 1813 - Place where: Stoney Point, Henderson Harbor - Of what ship or corps: Land forces - Whether man of war, privateer or merchant vessel: Taken on shore - Time when received into custody: 8 Jun 1813 - From what ship or whence received: Batteaux - Exchanged, discharged, died, or escape: Escaped - Time when: 11 Sep 1813 - Whither, and by what order, or number or re-entry:

Yarrington, Avah   Prisoner 655.   Rank: Drummer - By what ship or how taken: Troops - Time when: 24 Jun 1813 - Place where: Stoney Point - Of what ship or corps: Land forces - Whether man of war, privateer or merchant vessel: Taken on shore - Time when received into custody: 7 Jul 1813 - From what ship or whence received: Steamboat - Exchanged, discharged, died, or escape: Discharged - Time when: 10 Aug 1813 - Whither, and by what order, or number or re-entry: HM Ship Regulius by order of Sir George Provost

Yates, Francis   Prisoner 1629.   Rank: Private - By what ship or how taken: Troops - Time when: 6 Sep 1814 - Place where: Plattsburg - Of what ship or corps: Land forces - Whether man of war, privateer or merchant vessel: Taken on shore - Time when received into custody: 5 Oct 1814 - From what ship or whence received: Montreal - Exchanged, discharged, died, or escape: Discharged - Time when: 8 Oct 1814 - Whither, and by what order, or number or re-entry: H.M. Ship Ceylon

American Prisoners of War held at Quebec during the War of 1812

Yates, Francis   Prisoner 1267. Rank: Privateer - By what ship or how taken: Troops - Time when: 19 Dec 1813 - Place where: Fort Niagara - Of what ship or corps: Land forces - Whether man of war, privateer or merchant vessel: Taken on shore - Time when received into custody: 29 Jan 1814 - From what ship or whence received: Montreal by land carriage - Exchanged, discharged, died, or escape: Discharged - Time when: 4 May 1814 - Whither, and by what order, or number or re-entry: United States

Yates, Henry D.   Prisoner 412. Rank: Sergeant - By what ship or how taken: Troops - Time when: 24 Jun 1813 - Place where: Beaver Dam - Of what ship or corps: Land forces - Whether man of war, privateer or merchant vessel: Taken on shore - Time when received into custody: 7 Jul 1813 - From what ship or whence received: Steamboat - Exchanged, discharged, died, or escape: Discharged - Time when: 8 Oct 1813 - Whither, and by what order, or number or re-entry: H.M. Ship Ceylon

Young, Christian   Prisoner 1903. Rank: Private - By what ship or how taken: Troops - Time when: 17 Sep 1814 - Place where: Fort Erie - Of what ship or corps: Land forces - Whether man of war, privateer or merchant vessel: Taken on shore - Time when received into custody: 1 Nov 1814 - From what ship or whence received: Montreal - Exchanged, discharged, died, or escape: Discharged - Time when: 8 Nov 1814 - Whither, and by what order, or number or re-entry: S. George No. 575 for Halifax by order of Sir George Provost

Young, David   Prisoner 1866. Rank: Private - By what ship or how taken: Troops - Time when: 17 Sep 1814 - Place where: Fort Erie - Of what ship or corps: Land forces - Whether man of war, privateer or merchant vessel: Taken on shore - Time when received into custody: 1 Nov 1814 - From what ship or whence received: Montreal - Exchanged, discharged, died, or escape: Discharged - Time when: 8 Nov 1814 - Whither, and by what order, or number or re-entry: S. George No. 575 for Halifax

Young, Thomas   Prisoner 1963. Rank: Sergeant - By what ship or how taken: Troops - Time when: 17 Sep 1814 - Place where: Fort Erie - Of what ship or corps: Land forces - Whether man of war, privateer or merchant vessel: Taken on shore - Time when received into custody: 11 Dec 1814 - From what ship or whence received: Montreal - Exchanged, discharged, died, or escape: Discharged - Time when: 13 Mar 1815 - Whither, and by what order, or number or re-entry: United States

Young, Thomas   Prisoner 1449. Rank: Private - By what ship or how taken: Troops - Time when: 6 May 1814 - Place where: Oswago - Of what ship or corps: Land forces - Whether man of war, privateer or merchant vessel: Taken on shore - Time when received into custody: 12 Aug 1814 - From what ship or whence received: Royal Seaman No. 289 Transport - Exchanged, discharged, died, or escape: Discharged - Time when: 8 Oct 1814 - Whither, and by what order, or number or re-entry: Queen No. 415

Young, William   Prisoner 637. Rank: Private - By what ship or how taken: Troops - Time when: 24 Jun 1813 - Place where: Stoney Point - Of what ship or corps: Land forces - Whether man of war, privateer or merchant vessel: Taken on shore - Time when received into custody: 7 Jul 1813 - From what ship or whence received: Steamboat - Exchanged, discharged, died, or escape: Discharged - Time when: 10 Aug 1813 - Whither, and by what order, or number or re-entry: HM Ship Regulius by order of Sir George Provost

American Prisoners of War held in Quebec during the War of 1812

1	Phillips, John Capen		64	Wilkins, Aaron
2	Stevens, Benjamin W.		65	Whitney, Joseph
3	Walker, William		66	Stevens, William
4	Tiemell, William		67	Marks, Ira
5	Kimball, Abel		68	Lamb, Josiah P.
6	Howe, William		69	Lamson, John
7	Hagar, Henry		70	Horn, Wentworth
8	Shute, John		71	Knight, Hudson
9	Heath, John		72	Cook, Robert
10	Field, Eli		73	Horn, Andrew
11	Munrow, John		74	Ireland, Jonas
12	Merrill, Eli		75	Wyon, John M.
13	Goodnow, Elisha		76	Clark, Benjamin
14	Thead, Isaac		77	Missing name
15	Howe, Calvin		78	Missing name
16	Belcher, Joseph		79	Churchill, Oliver
17	Jones, Nathan		80	Dearborn, Soloman
18	Wilder, Elihu		81	Davis, Stephen
19	Harvey, Luther		82	Dearing, John
20	Rowe, Jonathan		83	Fobes, Quen
21	Lanton, Peory		84	Hubbard, Thomas
22	Boyce, John		85	Hall, Lot
23	Davis, Moses		86	Hooper, Simon
24	Titus, George		87	Howard, Lewis
25	Missing name		88	Kimball, Hannibal
26	Missing name		89	Howard, Joseph
27	Missing name		90	Kimball, Nathaniel
28	Pearl, John		91	Kingman, Ebin.
29	Lawrence, Abel		92	Knight, Andrew
30	Lewis, John		93	Merrill, Jacob
31	Daggett, Lewis		94	Williams, Samuel
32	Carver, William		95	Mitchell, William
33	Ella, John		96	Nute, Jonathan
34	Keith, Lephlmiah		97	Pennell, Samuel
35	Kimball, Benjamin W.		98	Smith, Richard
36	Smith, Stephen		99	Spencer, Andrew
37	Round, Amos		100	Rowe, Benjamin
38	Daggett, Josiah		101	Virgin, Levet
39	Bonney, William		102	Wood, Isarrel
40	Bacon, Jabbec		103	Wilkinson, Andrew
41	Bangs, Seth		104	Missing name
42	Harrodon, Elisha		105	Missing name
43	Reed, Isaac		106	Whitney, Jeremiah
44	Booth, Richard		107	Finney, Samuel
45	Easter, Stephen		108	Alfen, John
46	Martin, Silvanus		109	Fitzgerald, Aaron
47	Wheeler, Stephen		110	Finney, Elihu
48	McMillen, Archibald		111	Blancet, Levy
49	Ames, Oliver		112	Price, William
50	Batehelor, Orsen		113	Lucas, Ephraim
51	Missing name		114	Nicholson, Soloman
52	Missing name		115	Weiman, Lawrence
53	Evans, Thomas		116	Bosson, Thaddius
54	Foster, John		117	Pratt, Nathaniel
55	Green, Eli		118	Hunt, Soloman
56	Hooper, John		119	Lander, Charles
57	Hayway, Archibald		120	Shaddock, John
58	Howard, Josiah		121	Cory, Asa
59	Johnson, John		122	Jackson, Enoch
60	Johnson, David		123	How, John
61	Peterson, Peter		124	Hamwood, George
62	Smith, Joseph		125	Scott, Abraham
63	Tabvery, Ephraim		126	Smith, Corneilus

#	Name	#	Name
127	Webber, Nathan	190	Rice, Samuel
128	Smith, Thomas	191	Madder, Thomas
129	Hutchins, Eraoh	192	Sharpe, Soloman
130	Missing name	193	Danforth, Joseph F.
131	Missing name	194	Stearns, Nathan
132	Mack, Abner	195	Harvey, William
133	Ingalls, Jonathan	196	Plainloir, John
134	Cottes, Edward	197	Rowe, Benjamin
135	Cook, Joseph	198	Campbell, James
136	Linel, Samuel	199	Bridge, Franklin
137	Shaver, George	200	Read, Joseph P.
138	Ayers, John	201	Read, Samuel R.
139	Havwood, Abijah	202	Moody, John
140	Drew, Ira	203	Herrick, Eli
141	Cranson, John H.	204	Missing name
142	Graves, Abraham	205	Missing name
143	Loomes, Jaires	206	Missing name
144	Freeborne, John	207	Plumer, Isaac
145	Sawyer, Horace B.	208	Smith, Daniel
146	Turnbull, John	209	Haines, Daniel
147	Monteath, Walter Noel	210	Lovejoy, Jacob
148	Walter, Abraham	211	Ham, Rufus
149	Herrick, Oliver	212	Penly, Joseph
150	Dennison, Washington	213	Allen, Isaac
151	Konnell, Thomas	214	Dresser, Thomas
152	Norbry, James	215	Merrill, Jacob
153	Batty, Joseph	216	Taylor, Thomas
154	Duncan, Mathew	217	Campbell, William
155	Morse, Jacob	218	White, Joshua
156	Missing name	219	Sinclair, Jacob
157	Missing name	220	Pratt, Walter
158	Boston, Daniel	221	Merrill, Thedorias
159	Carnes, Joseph	222	Frost, Phineas
160	Green, William	223	Drake, Eliasha
161	Richards, Stephen	224	Parker, Edward
162	Furbush, Joshua	225	Ham, Robert
163	Nicholson, William	226	Pratt, Charles
164	Gitchell, Josiah	227	Paul, Simeon
165	Dyer, Isaac	228	Missing name
166	Hunt, John	229	Missing name
167	Dyer, Daniel	230	Missing name
168	Emmins, Phillip	231	Foster, Nathaniel
169	Turner, Henry	232	Gibson, Ebenezer
170	Smith, Thomas	233	Estes, Edward
171	Barber, William	234	Murry, James
172	Prouth, Jacob	235	Cobb, John
173	Scisso, Thomas	236	Richardson, Simeon
174	Frickes, John	237	Morse, Joshua
175	Harris, James	238	Woodman, Benjamin
176	Green, James	239	Rice, Nathaniel
177	Whilington, Robert	240	Romley, Eliza
178	Wright, Oliver	241	Wheelock, Abel
179	Sanborn, John L.	242	Bradford, Samuel
180	Brink, Orson	243	Smith, Sidney
181	Missing name	244	Colman, Charles
182	Missing name	245	Osgood, Richard
183	Pack, Luther	246	Winchester, James
184	Butman, Benjamin	247	Lewis, William
185	Mudge, Ebenezer	248	Madison, George
186	Payne, Rubin	249	Conkey, Joshua
187	Merritt, Jonathan	250	Godard, Lewis
188	Ballard, John	251	Beard, William C.
189	Sperry, Jacob	252	Missing name

253	Missing name	316	Von, Samuel
254	Chandler, John	317	Evans, James
255	Winder, William H.	318	Hoy, Barney
256	Van De Venter, Christopher	319	Price, Robert
257	Van Veghten, Derck	320	Guton, Thomas
258	Steele, George G.	321	Missing name
259	McEwen, Alexander	322	Missing name
260	Van Suraringen, H. J.	323	Doughty, Elias
261	Hemmick, George	324	Defriend, John
262	Draper, Francis	325	Rathboun, Jeremiah
263	Chase, Joshua	326	Davis, Elnathan
264	Reynolds, John C.	327	See, Daniel
265	Doyle, James	328	Wilkinson, Oliver
266	Little, Samuel	329	Foot, Henry
267	Stanhope, C. L.	330	Newman, Henry
268	Little, Salmon	331	Goodwin, Richard
269	Stanhope, Curtis L.	332	McCann, Robert
270	Ervin, James B.	333	Scudder, Stephen
271	Storey, Pliney	334	Baker, Daniel B.
272	Summers, William	335	Countryman, Elias
273	Saunderson, John	336	Moore, Jonas
274	Smith, Elijah	337	Cox, John
275	Missing name	338	Minor, Lewis
276	Missing name	339	Barnes, Seth
277	Frayman, James	340	Conkey, Tebena
278	Beck, Andrew	341	Watson, Major
279	Knight, William	342	Jones, Henry
280	Newland, Thomas S.	343	Witherall, Gerrard
281	Kronnengie, John	344	Hooker, Oris
282	Allen, John	345	Missing name
283	Bowen, Thomas	346	Missing name
284	Johnson, Truman	347	Missing name
285	Stanbury, Samuel	348	Berg, Lawrence
286	Jones, William	349	Carry, Daniel
287	Hedderick, George	350	Brown, James
288	Wheeler, Willison	351	Fisher, Anthony
289	West, Hugh S.	352	Boarmaster, Henry
290	Bays, Jacob	353	Winton, James
291	Rehuhard, Thomas	354	Pace, Jonathan
292	Taylor, William	355	Losier, Abraham
293	Bear, Henry	356	Read, James
294	Lindsey, William	357	Williby, George
295	Fitzgerald, John	358	Campbell, Mathew
296	Morris, Peter	359	Napernery, John
297	Missing name	360	Orstunoser, Jones
298	Missing name	361	Melvin, William
299	Missing name	362	Bradford, John
300	Quick, Jacob	363	Barttey, William
301	Wayne, Michael	364	Meintere, Tedeck
302	Plants, Edward T.	365	Dungan, Benjamin
303	Lynch, John	366	Barron, John
304	Bowyer, George	367	Flemmings, Joseph
305	Clayton, Thomas	368	Lackey, Amasa
306	Legg, Daniel	369	Missing name
307	Clay, Elijah	370	Missing name
308	Spencer, Nathan	371	Missing name
309	Ervin, John	372	Roupough, Corneilus
310	Celley, Paul	373	Gosset, Stephen
311	McDune, William	374	Whitley, David R.
312	Ledman, Francis	375	Rowe, Michael
313	Emery, Stephen	376	McAubrory, William
314	Evener, Christian	377	Spink, Anthony
315	Freeman, James	378	Sheeps, David

#	Name	#	Name
379	Wavern, Elisha	442	Garland, Levy
380	Loomis, Daniel	443	Count, Levin
381	Smith, John	444	Broadist, Moses
382	Crayton, William	445	Missing name
383	Welch, Rupel	446	Missing name
384	Tuffs, William	447	Missing name
385	Boyd, Samuel	448	Denmade, Edward
386	Wells, Caleb	449	White, John
387	Robinson, Nathan	450	Carpenter, John
388	Parsons, Samuel	451	King, William
389	Horney, David	452	Ackley, William
390	Kelly, William	453	Faunce, Peter
391	Scott, Soloman	454	Burrell, John
392	Corkins, Joel	455	Rose, Nathaniel
393	Missing name	456	Watlas, Burton
394	Missing name	457	Oates, John
395	Missing name	458	Andrews, David
396	Woodland, Lebai	459	Duguenom, Charles
397	Morris, Morris	460	Tenney, John
398	Evans, Edward	461	Clark, Stephen
399	Hardy, Elisha	462	Clark, James
400	Taylor, Lewis L.	463	Trott, Thomas
401	McKenzie, Kenneth	464	Batch, George
402	McDowell, Andrew	465	Courtney, George
403	Roach, Isaac	466	Armstrong, William
404	Schultz, John	467	Redman, Martin
405	McDonald, Peter	468	Usher, Edward
406	McKeever, Charles	469	Sloin, William
407	Stansburgh, Jonathan	470	Tucker, Benjamin
408	Conway, Michael	471	Beals, John
409	West, Charles	472	Missing name
410	Lighter, Jacob	473	Missing name
411	Johnson, John	474	Missing name
412	Yates, Henry D.	475	Miller, Garrett
413	Stocker, Jesse L.	476	Powers, Joseph
414	Boggs, Lyman	477	Davis, Thomas
415	Slaughter, George	478	Boohm, Joseph
416	Hassar, George	479	Quonilrouly, Henry
417	Dunning, Jesse	480	Matlock, Joseph
418	Missing name	481	Winn, Clement
419	Missing name	482	Scott, John
420	Missing name	483	Davisson, John
421	Denton, Charles	484	Daggert, Thomas
422	Moore, Lemond	485	Griffin, John
423	Kuber, Jacob	486	Parks, Selvy
424	Street, Ishemail	487	Blogs, Mordericke
425	Dixon, James	488	Halted, John
426	Bradshaw, Edward	489	Talbott, John H.
427	Taylor, Richard	490	Talbott, Elijah
428	Roles, Rezin	491	Artis, John
429	Root, John	492	Hogg, George
430	Stroud, John	493	Tracey, William
431	Hunter, Joseph	494	Herring, John
432	Bowen, William	495	Round, Rubin
433	McCirchar, Stephen	496	Booth, George
434	Wilkinson, James	497	Spalding, William
435	Brison, James	498	Missing name
436	Beard, Richard	499	Missing name
437	Philips, Samuel	500	Missing name
438	Frasel, Hubbard	501	Doud, John
439	Torer, Jon	502	Smith, William
440	Christopher, Samuel	503	Cune, Thomas
441	Grouse, Frederick	504	Rea, John

505	McGoud, John	568	Missing name
506	Brown, John	569	Missing name
507	Doughtery, Hamilton	570	Missing name
508	Black, John	571	Caknary, James
509	Price, Meritt	572	Thipelwood, Charles
510	Henry, James	573	Till, James
511	Beard, John	574	Davis, Benjamin
512	Carmody, Dalby	575	Jones, William
513	Todd, John	576	McDonald, Theophilus
514	Roberts, Henry	577	English, John
515	Lain, Benjamin	578	Eaton, William
516	Green, John	579	Anderson, Henry
517	Swan, Samuel	580	Ireland, Jonathan
518	Rose, John	581	Mackey, John
519	Capatity, William	582	Wood, Pratt
520	Cavry, James	583	Truebridge, T.
521	Givin, James	584	Arthur, James
522	Missing name	585	Boyer, Nelson
523	Missing name	586	Chapman, Eliphea
524	Fleming, Henry	587	Johnson, Jason
525	Marshall, Joseph	588	Lewis, Dudley
526	Karney, Thomas	589	Nixon, William
527	Arell, Richard	590	Whagerman, Jeremiah
528	Shell, Henry	591	Cook, William
529	Waring, John	592	Missing name
530	Murdock, George	593	Missing name
531	Thompson, John W.	594	Hunter, James
532	Morris, John N.	595	Fullerton, William
533	Godwin, Kimmel	596	Nybro, Godfred
534	Robinson, Nicholas N.	597	Patton, David
535	Burd, Benjamin E.	598	Davis, Ezra
536	Saunders, William G.	599	Henry, George
537	Griswold, Samuel B.	600	Filkins, John F.
538	Clark, Abraham	601	Honeywell, Encoh
539	Mudd, Massom	602	Davis, Theddeck
540	Pollard, Martin	603	Conwell, John
541	Birk, John	604	Cunningham, Kellup
542	Cerkhill, James W.	605	Prince, John
543	Dill, Peter	606	Davidson, John
544	Blanch, James	607	Tabott, Benjamin
545	Missing name	608	Wimiss, Daniel
546	Missing name	609	Linnerd, Alfred
547	Seriven, Richard	610	Bishop, Jesse
548	Simpson, Mark	611	Smith, Jacob
549	Spunier, Lott	612	Whitman, Stephen
550	Jones, William L.	613	Stuard, Thomas
551	Gunies, Michael	614	Wheller, Anthony
552	Leazier, Elisha	615	Holson, James
553	Williams, Andrew	616	Missing name
554	Updegrass, Jesse	617	Missing name
555	Permerline, Johan	618	Missing name
556	Milless, Stephen	619	Wilkins, John
557	Sickles, Michael	620	Maxwell, Robert
558	Kingsland, Joseph	621	Carr, William
559	Holloway, John	622	Ross, David
560	Johnson, William	623	Hagherty, Mathew
561	Moore, John	624	Marlin, William
562	Wilson, James	625	Johnson, Isaac
563	Rimsey, Joseph	626	Fisher, Jacob
564	Crarmey, Edward	627	Ervin, Lewis
565	Oiler, George	628	Wolffrom, William
566	Cole, Andrew	629	Cook, Haz.
567	Hurd, John	630	Rollins, Thomas

631	Rowley, Nathan	694	Snyder, George
632	Bacon, Nathan	695	Missing name
633	Burns, Andrew	696	Missing name
634	Forrest, Arthur	697	Missing name
635	Logan, Timothy	698	Hargood, George
636	Johnson, Hugh	699	Dubois, David
637	Young, William	700	Shaffer, Valentine
638	Agen, John	701	Frank, Christian F.
639	Hale, William	702	Shrater, Anthony
640	Walker, Simeon	703	March, William
641	Vanderherle, Samuel	704	Grey, James
642	West, Abraham	705	Perrique, James
643	Missing name	706	Cann, John
644	Missing name	707	Smilley, Thomas
645	Missing name	708	Francisco, John
646	Bull, William	709	Knowlton, Ebenezer
647	Andrews, Stephen	710	Collins, Robert
648	Newton, John	711	Dellaghon, George
649	Richie, Allen	712	Evertson, Benjamin
650	Haynes, Clement	713	Sly, Thomas
651	Valients, William	714	Fitz, Charles
652	Price, George	715	Hose, Jacob
653	Matthews, John	716	Donaldson, Thomas
654	Johnson, Noble	717	Schoolman, William
655	Yarrington, Avah	718	Levi, Henry
656	Price, Job	719	Palmer, Nicholas
657	Harkness, James	720	Thristy, Joel
658	Whellock, James	721	Roberts, William
659	Bryce, James	722	Mathews, Daniel
660	Martin, Byron	723	Missing name
661	Willis, Alfred	724	Missing name
662	Crocker, Benjamin	725	Thundersville, John
663	Mitchell, Charles	726	McCaller, Benjamin
664	Scott, James	727	Andrews, Edward
665	McGuire, Hugh	728	Kellog, Tsar
666	Dennis, Patrick M.	729	Oweritt, John
667	O'Neil, Con.	730	Tucker, Joseph
668	Learned, Henry	731	Walton, Edward
669	Snow, Assa	732	Thomas, Samuel
670	Missing name	733	Miles, John
671	Missing name	734	Barnes, Thomas
672	McConaghey, Benjamin	735	Little, Peter
673	Welch, Henry	736	Waugham, James
674	Murphy, George	737	Elmore, Philip
675	Marshall, William	738	Crabtree, John
676	Dandridge, Richard	739	Dougherty, William
677	Davis, John	740	Hagar, John
678	Baker, John	741	Smiley, John
679	House, Frederick	742	Smith, John
680	Lou, Samuel	743	Ansol, Philip
681	Goodwin, Joseph	744	Rose, Jonathan
682	Robinson, Daniel	745	McMillin, George
683	Carroll, Isaac	746	Tonnier, Joshua
684	Sowder, Jacob	747	Brown, Perry W.
685	Henry, Samuel	748	Maher, Samuel
686	Lash, Jeremiah	749	Smith, Benjamin
687	Batts, James	750	Missing name
688	Heddon, Amas	751	Missing name
689	McEver, William	752	Missing name
690	Cord, Jacob	753	Olstender, Gabriel
691	Van Bibbar, Isaac	754	Burlue, Gilbert
692	Silence, Nicholas	755	Dervalt, Alvin
693	Clement, Daniel	756	Riggan, Labon

#	Name	#	Name
757	Brown, Michael	819	Befarr, Leonard
758	Bartlett, James	820	Wilder, Titus
759	Paradise, John	821	Chambers, Henry
760	Kelly, Charles	822	Maybe, Jacob
761	Booth, John	823	Mears, Michael
762	Watson, William	824	Mason, Ira
763	Graves, Darius	825	Petare, John
764	Gray, Samuel	826	Riddle, Robert
765	Thomas, William	827	Clarke, John
766	Lazelaeu, Benjamin	828	Woolfriet, John
767	Luckey, Samuel	829	Curtis, Uria
768	Paine, Richard	830	Moses, Charles
769	Kerrington, Esakel	831	Missing name
770	Meticham, Seth	832	Missing name
771	Osbourn, Thomas	833	Missing name
772	Mechame, Almond	834	Fairfield, Soloman
773	Swatewood, Jacob	835	Bogea, John
774	Wilson, Daniel	836	Hately, John
775	Kuntz, David	837	Farrell, Michael
776	Eton, Ambrose	838	Rindle, Samuel
777	Missing name	839	Hervey, John
778	Missing name	840	Haidy, Amos
779	McWaters, James	841	Barker, John
780	Neils, Nathaniel W.	842	Barber, John
781	Fuller, James	843	Sheaves, Thomas
782	Mus, Abraham	844	Cook, John H.
783	Wilkins, James	845	Heding, Henry
784	Calkins, Eliphel	846	Wright, Terick
785	Pickle, Balhe	847	Turner, Walter
786	Barto, Selis	848	McKee, Edward
787	Clauts, William	849	Johnson, John
788	Lipperket, William	850	Hugh, Michael
789	Brown, Francis	851	Scott, William
790	Carter, Marthil	852	Delshaven, Michael
791	Brownhill, John	853	Williams, Thomas
792	Lamb, William	854	Clark, Sheldren
792	Cravertson, George	855	Hanyan, Elihu
793	Gates, Jacob	856	Ustelburgh, Philip
794	Haydon, Daniel	857	Norton, Robert
795	Cashman, William	858	Emmins, Henry
796	Tomlinson, John	859	Gorman, Edward
797	Sutherly, Joseph	860	Missing name
798	Whitton, John	861	Missing name
799	Henry, George	862	Aberts, Michael
800	Drummin, John	863	Gruet, James
801	Childers, Joseph	864	Kain, John
802	Missing name	865	Stutevant, Thomas
803	Missing name	866	Willinea, John N.
804	Missing name	867	Cannon, Dominick
805	Missing name	868	Pattison, Thomas
806	Haggerty, Leve	869	Thompson, Jonathan
807	Davis, Hugh	870	Gruet, William
808	Smith, John	871	Hunter, James
809	Desheates, Peter	872	Liei, John
810	McKenzie, David	873	Griner, George
811	Goodrich, Henry C.	874	Dulman, George
812	Bull, Benjamin S.	875	Baninstine, John
813	Penny, Nicholas	876	Fields, Thomas
814	Robins, Toram	877	Mager, Robert
815	Purse, William	878	Gray, John D.
816	Grimes, John	879	Bay, John
817	Belluite, Leve	880	Preston, Ormond
818	Hartman, Andrew	881	Wardle, Linnard

882	Carr, James		945	Oddly, John
883	Stephens, John		946	Bowe, Artemus
884	Chrise, John		947	Robinson, Nicholas
885	Sheffield, Henry		948	Brown, James
886	Missing name		949	Machesney, John
887	Missing name		950	Randall, Thomas
888	Missing name		950 a	Palmer, J. B.
889	Ross, Joseph N.		951	Harrington, Estes
890	Dempsey, George		952	Baker, George
891	Monaham, David		953	Reese, Henry
892	McClure, John		954	Green, Thomas
893	Taggent, Archibald		955	Furguson, John
894	Blue, Henry		956	Wilcox, John
895	Bowers, Jesse		957	Vinten, Ezekial
896	Barnes, Samuel		958	Lloyd, William
897	Pitcher, Jacob		959	Munger, Haace
898	Gilbert, Abique		960	Clyne, Isaac
899	Sellock, Henry		961	Cranstone, John
900	Hover, George		962	Newman, Stokely
901	Mullinex, Thomas		963	Avery, Richard
902	Wrights, Henry		964	Avery, Matlass
903	Willis, John		965	Hutchinson, Elihu
904	Bowice, Joseph		966	Henon, James
905	Perkins, Rufas		967	Bertel, Edward
906	LeCount, William		968	Missing name
907	Barlow, John		969	Missing name
908	Wilson, Warren		970	Wood, Frederick
909	Wilson, Alexander		971	Pudehour, Conduit
910	Hamilton, James		972	Hyett, Joseph
911	Tardon, Thomas		973	Park, Roger
912	Walker, Samuel		974	Lane, Jobe
913	Doddson, Thomas S.		975	Knowles, Seth
914	Missing name		976	Mecham, Jesse
915	Missing name		977	Cady, Daniel G.
916	Mackelfresh, Joseph H.		978	Ames, Thomas
917	Wells, Elijah		979	Wood, Amory
918	Christian, Humphrey		980	Strickland, Richard
919	Decker, Joseph		981	Brine, Thomas
920	Hickins, Francis		982	Scott, Silar
921	Rose, Henry S.		983	Green, Thomas
922	Littlefield, John		984	Mallet, John
923	Bissure, Theodore		985	Wilcox, William
924	Frink, Rupel		986	Clawson, Henry
925	Kelly, William		987	Buel, Jeremiah
926	Richards, John		988	Smith, John
927	Asher, Frederick		989	Dours, William
928	Jones, Thomas		990	Johnson, William
929	Boersther, Charles G.		991	Corsey, John
930	Cummings, David		992	Williams, Henry
931	Smith, James		993	Blosea, Nathaniel
932	Murphy, John		994	Missing name
933	Hoopman, Philip		995	Missing name
934	Badger, Ephraim T.		996	Wildon, John
935	Davis, Richard		997	Sprigs, George
936	Hall, Aug. C.		998	Fistock, Thomas
937	Brakeman, Lodowick		999	Myers, Edward
938	McKenney, John		1000	Blank, Samuel
939	Sonnet, Charles		1001	Jones, Martin
940	Missing name		1002	Rilley, James
941	Missing name		1003	Rine, Joseph
942	Missing name		1004	Phoenix, John
943	Paine, William		1005	Williams, Benjamin
944	McQueen, Donald		1006	Lawton, John

1007	Tribe, Benjamin	1070	Richards, Stephem
1008	Lewis, Leonard	1071	Brown, Henry
1009	Headman, Charles	1072	Missing name
1010	Marvel, Joseph	1073	Missing name
1011	Reed, William	1074	White, William
1012	Palmer, William	1075	Gready, Martin
1013	Duffy, Ebenezer	1076	Inghram, Benjamin
1014	Tanning, John C.	1077	Free, Almond
1015	Lyles, William	1078	Platenburgh, Jacob
1016	Joseph, John	1079	Crosby, James
1017	Pactaolt, Henry	1080	Beckford, John
1018	Sasse, John	1081	Campbell, Joseph
1019	Missing name	1082	Hallz or Hall, Orin or Horace
1020	Missing name	1083	McKenzie, Thomas
1021	Missing name	1084	Schooley, William
1022	Williams, Calvin	1085	Kelley, James
1023	Gibbs, John	1086	Hill, William
1024	Palmer, Gordon	1087	Plott, John
1025	Roberts, Joel	1088	Westbrooks, Abraham
1026	Thornton, William	1089	McDonald, Francis
1027	Harvey, Peter	1090	Larney, Joseph P.
1028	Brown, Thomas	1091	Smith, Frederick
1029	Dunn, William	1092	Lytle, Daniel
1030	Baker, Samuel	1093	Banger, Thomas
1031	Mortimore, Thomas	1094	Hydendry, Henry
1032	Harris, Robert	1095	Willett, Phil
1033	Warren, W. H.	1096	Davis, John
1034	Baker, Philip	1097	Gilllispie, William
1035	Thornning, Thomas	1098	Missing name
1036	McAvery alias McAvor, John	1099	Missing name
1037	Pearson, John	1100	Hendricks, John
1038	Mullett, William	1101	Sawyer, Charles W.
1039	Taylor, John	1102	Perell, Jacob
1040	Everett, John	1103	Thompson, John
1041	Stymets, John	1104	Lanunsbery, Lemuel
1042	Watson, David	1105	Decker, Zeli
1043	Smith, John	1106	Bilby, Henry
1044	Smith, William	1107	Hard, Daniel
1045	Peterson, James	1108	Ransom, Owen
1046	McGee, William	1109	Templin, John
1047	Missing name	1110	Nelson, James
1048	Davis, Thomas	1111	Temple, William
1049	Connor, John	1112	Fairchild, Cyrus
1050	Torrey, Joseph	1113	Tulley, Thomas
1051	Chambers, Samuel	1114	Rowland, Alexander
1052	Hicks, Isaac	1115	McGee, George
1053	Christie, John	1116	Beech, James
1054	Richardson, John	1117	Goodwin, Simeon
1055	Guynnup, John	1118	Gunison, James
1056	Goodwin, James	1119	Mandeville, Peter
1057	Limoners, Peter D.	1120	Warley, Joseph
1058	McCarthy, Charles	1121	Waring, Jonathan
1059	Frehen, Edward	1122	Ogle, Howard
1060	Willets, Joseph	1123	Lingie, John
1061	Ferrish, Barney	1124	Missing name
1062	Gibson, Fortune	1125	Missing name
1063	Diver, David	1126	Bingham, Isaac
1064	Reynolds, Gilbert	1127	Ward, John
1065	Barker, Robert	1128	Wilson, William
1066	Walker, John	1129	Byrn, Phillip
1067	Deason, David	1130	McIlroy, James
1068	Trant, James	1131	Walker, Colman
1069	Hope, Levi	1132	McMillin, William

#	Name	#	Name
1133	Bronaugh, Thomas	1196	Sparks, William
1134	Cawthorn, Eleazer	1197	Johnson, Ross
1135	Turner, John	1198	La Bonte, Francis
1136	Jones, John	1199	Rigden, James
1137	Johnson, Thomas	1200	Gazlir, John
1138	Mahan, Francis	1201	Stewart, James
1139	Jones, Leroy	1202	Loomis, Gustaves
1140	Armstrong, Thomas	1203	Frederick, Henry
1141	Million, Rodney	1204	Missing name
1142	Kindle, Rezin	1205	Johnston, Littleton
1143	Perkins, John	1206	Williamson, John F.
1144	Taylor, Isaac M.	1207	Gilbreath, John
1145	Wilson, William	1208	Johnson, William
1146	Hyde, Nathan	1209	Paulling, William K.
1147	Greemo, Paul	1210	Heron, James E.
1148	Jack, Andrew	1211	Calliham, Francis
1149	Vanhorn, James	1212	Leonard, Nathaniel
1150	Withington, Thomas	1213	Chapin, Cyrenius
1151	Missing name	1214	Davis, Peter
1152	Brace, Stephen	1215	Leonard, Nathaniel
1153	Thompson, John T.	1216	Shafter, Jacob
1154	Fleming, William	1217	Poff, Peter
1155	Bowen, Joseph	1218	Guest, Charles
1156	Moones, Green	1219	Pierce, Thomas
1157	Atherton, William	1220	Troop, James
1158	Leonard, Isaac	1221	Chase, John
1159	Knowles, Joseph	1222	Bascomb, Samuel
1160	Mills, Ellias	1223	Vanrecker, Cornelius
1161	Wallis, James	1224	Moore, Abel
1162	Groomes, Richard	1225	Harper, William
1163	Runyan, Francis	1226	Burees, Viris
1164	Corbin, James	1227	Forrester, Peter
1165	Hewins, Thomas	1228	Koontz, Jacob
1166	Vanslyck, Cornelius	1229	Coaswell, Allanson
1167	Crocker, John	1230	Missing name
1168	Eaton, Moses	1231	Missing name
1169	Wilcox, David	1232	Briggs, William
1170	Shepheard, Samuel	1233	Rust, Richard H.
1171	Hall, Allen	1234	Walker, William
1172	Masters, John	1235	Bennett, James W.
1173	Whitney, Isaac	1236	Banker, Christian
1174	Erwing, Patrick	1237	Prentice, James
1175	Nourse, Thomas B. W.	1238	Bowlett, Nathaniel
1176	Gilchrist, James	1239	Lias, Nathaniel
1177	Missing name	1240	Gibbs, Eusebais
1178	Missing name	1241	Greaves, Philander
1179	Tilden, Lemiah	1242	McGunnell, Michael
1180	Merrell, Abraham	1243	Hamilton, John
1181	Edson, Nathan	1244	Marks, Henry
1182	McCurdy, Robert	1245	Redfield, Anthony C.
1183	Wilkins, Edward	1246	Lackey, Hugh
1184	Smith, Jonathan	1247	O'Conner, Michael
1185	Stewart, James	1248	Patterson, John
1186	Scott MD, William	1249	Wood, George W.
1187	Hovel, Nathaniel	1250	Brandon, Samuel
1188	Libby, Thadedus	1251	Day, John
1189	Lines, John	1252	Halison, Jacob
1190	Scott, William	1253	Brown, William
1191	Knags, Witmore	1254	Jones, Samuel
1192	Beals, William	1255	Lord, Horatio
1193	Sloan, Ebenezer	1256	Brauntsman, Daniel
1194	Gilbert, John C.	1257	Missing name
1195	Wheeler, Nathaniel	1258	Missing name

1259	Oin, Joseph	1322	Cermour, Robert
1260	Oin, Ebenezer	1323	Number unassigned
1261	Coates, Elizha	1324	Craft, George B.
1262	Clarke, Norman	1325	Holmes, Thomas
1263	Coalbough, Michael	1326	Harvey, Charles
1264	Dogherty, Jared	1327	Bishop, Josiah
1265	Owen, Amasa	1328	Richardson, Jason
1266	George, John	1329	White, Isaac
1267	Yates, Francis	1330	Rogers, Robert
1268	Wilhelmi, Daniel	1331	Sulivan, David
1269	Rice, John	1332	Miller, James
1270	Taylor, Thomas	1333	Hopkins, John
1271	Hutchison, David	1334	Thornburgh, John
1272	Scuving, Joel	1335	Neighbors, John
1273	Robinson, James	1336	Hansel, William
1274	Voigh, Thomas	1337	Hall, William
1275	Farmham, Gauis	1338	Houndshell, John
1276	Bossell, John	1339	Morrison, William
1277	Gifford, Francis	1340	Missing name
1278	Anderson, Peter	1341	Missing name
1279	Store, Stephen	1342	Missing name
1280	Richardson, William	1343	Lloyd, Thompson C.
1281	Manchester, Noah	1344	Runyan, Thomas
1282	Werman, Edward	1345	Marker, Benjamin
1283	Smith, William Henry	1346	Boyd, William
1284	Luce, Aaron	1347	Brown, Joseph
1285	Missing name	1348	Amyets, John
1286	Missing name	1349	Hagan, Thomas
1287	Johnston, James	1350	Atchley, Joseph
1288	Peck, Ollus	1351	McQuaid, Edward
1289	Johnston, Assa	1352	Johnston, Richard
1290	Groves, George	1353	Stevens, Josiah
1291	McLaghlan, Mark	1354	Johnston, William
1292	Quin, Patrick	1355	Berwick, George W.
1293	Wright, William	1356	Arnold, James
1294	Miller, Rubin	1357	Stevens, Jephthah
1295	McCurl, Isaac	1358	Owen, Jeremiah
1296	Bishop, James	1359	Greenley, William
1297	Fincher, Jesse	1360	Winter, Christian
1298	Hind, Nathaniel	1361	Barnes, Jacob
1299	Handing, Amasa	1362	McCroy, Thomas
1300	Jennings, Noah	1363	Ewings, James
1301	Hince, John	1364	Head, William
1302	Bromley, Salmon	1365	Number unassigned
1303	Stowner, Henry	1366	Number unassigned
1304	Gates, Horatio	1367	Lark, Joseph
1305	Howard, Edward	1368	Missing name
1306	Macnalley, John	1369	Missing name
1307	Haines, Joel	1370	Missing name
1308	Harley, George	1371	Hankins, Gilbreath
1309	Green, Jeremiah N.	1372	Clark, Henry
1310	Darling, Thomas	1373	Hill, Allen
1311	Draton, Joseph	1374	Drake, George William
1312	Nicholson, John	1375	Eades, Thomas
1313	Merrill, M.	1376	Curtis, Morgan
1314	Missing name	1377	Southards, William
1315	Missing name	1378	Cross, Barnebus
1316	Larkins, Thomas	1379	Mustain, Lewis
1317	Parcel, James H.	1380	Buchanan, John
1318	Burtsell, David	1381	Waterman, Elisha
1319	Grayson, John	1382	Randall, Greif
1320	Fenning, Charles	1383	Farrard, Michael
1321	Hayes, Patrick	1384	Turner, Isaac

#	Name	#	Name
1385	Valentine, Elisha	1448	Vazure, Jove
1386	Nunn, Jonathan	1449	Young, Thomas
1387	Gentry, John	1450	Perkins, Thomas
1388	Potts, Jeremiah	1451	Hammond, Jed.
1389	Reynolds, William	1452	Folks, John
1390	Shutt, Henry	1453	Dolf, Joseph
1391	Diffenderffer, Henry	1454	Feders, Jacob
1392	Glenn, James	1455	Taylor, John
1393	Chick, Nathaniel	1456	Johnson, David
1394	Missing name	1457	Nigh, George
1395	Missing name	1458	Wright, Jonas
1396	Archer, Robert	1459	Bowers, Joseph
1397	Elton, Moses	1460	Johnson, Benjamin
1398	Holmes, Charles	1461	Purse, John
1399	Roberts, Aaron	1462	White, Richard
1400	Buskerk, Garrett	1463	Went, George
1401	Cheek, William	1464	Campbell, Jesse
1402	Lochard, Thomas	1465	Stanley, L.
1403	Wilay, William	1466	Dover, D.
1404	Lainge, Isaac	1467	Tanner, Asa
1405	Morrison, James	1468	Gill, William
1406	Atchley, Daniel	1469	Minger, Joseph
1407	Tarrehill, Zem.	1470	Land, Joseph
1408	Ridge, William	1471	Winnet, George
1409	Kennedy, William	1472	Missing name
1410	Wallace, Samuel	1473	Dearborn, D.
1411	Melone, John	1474	Allen, J.
1412	Clark, Charles	1475	Bradley, S.
1413	Blyth, John	1476	Reardon, T.
1414	Preutts, Gabriel	1477	Holford, Elijah
1415	Taylor, William	1478	McNutt, J.
1416	Scott, Joseph M.	1479	Barnes, E.
1417	Dogherty, James	1480	Comfort, R.
1418	Stickney, Abijah	1481	Cotton, Seth
1419	Nesbett, John	1482	Drake, W.
1420	Missing name	1483	Rockway, J.
1421	Missing name	1484	Davis, William
1422	Harris, James	1485	Rowsey, Ralph
1423	McCardall, Jacob	1486	Messinger, W. S.
1424	Holloby, John	1487	Bridgeman, W.
1425	Trimble, Carey A.	1488	Reithner, J.
1426	Winder, William H.	1489	Town, G. C.
1427	Creighton, Hugh	1490	Williams, Elijah
1428	Hollville, Robert	1491	Turner, S.
1429	Hooke, Thomas	1492	Williams, Robert
1430	Brett, Francis	1493	Winters, Stephen
1431	Russell, Benjamin	1494	Skinner, Benjamin
1432	Morrice, Samuel H.	1495	Crawford, William
1433	McGlathay, Thomas	1496	Roseman, E.
1434	Wharf, Andrew	1497	Missing name
1435	Irwin, John	1498	House, Isaac
1436	de Masters, Foster	1499	Copner, J.
1437	Pichevin, Anthony	1500	Morrow, Edward
1438	Bush, Hollower	1501	Bruce, William
1439	Ray, Robert	1502	Van Buren, Edward
1440	Cutler, Leonard	1503	Brown, Thomas
1441	Roney, M.	1504	Morrison, Joseph
1442	Randall, Joseph	1505	Ives, Amos
1443	Latham, John	1506	Perry, David
1444	Halbert, Lotha	1507	Stanton, Phineas
1445	Brown, John	1508	Hunt, John
1446	Fry, Jacob	1509	Roberts, John
1447	Missing name	1510	Johnson, William

1511	Galloway, Samuel	1574	Cornell, G.
1512	Barnes, William	1575	Devenus, J.
1513	Reed, C. W.	1576	Poulston, J.
1514	Thompson, James	1577	Dabine, J.
1515	Hutchins, A.	1578	Newman, J.
1516	Hammond, S.	1579	Hubbard, Joseph
1517	Wadon, L.	1580	McGregor, R.
1518	White, Cornelius	1581	Wheedon, Charles
1519	Hardy, Andrew H.	1582	Bryan, J.
1520	Lovell, S.	1583	Streback, J. M.
1521	Kirk, John	1584	Denning, J.
1522	Missing name	1585	Manuel, John
1523	Wood, Andrew	1586	Osten, Charles
1524	Ward, Lewis	1587	Atwood, E.
1525	Cushing, William	1588	Stacy, L.
1526	Allen, Ira	1589	Petersen, J.
1527	Stewart, John	1590	Williams, P.
1528	Powell, Puley	1591	Peters, J.
1529	Moses, John	1592	Black, C.
1530	Stubbs, Henry	1593	Bowtell, H.
1531	Riddle, E.	1594	Kenyon, J.
1532	Laurie, Thomas	1595	Fowler, James
1533	Nobles, Stephen	1596	Parks, J.
1534	Mendell, Alden	1597	Missing name
1535	Horton, Barnebus	1598	Pearl, John
1536	McCullock, Samuel	1599	Giles, John
1537	Lovland, Charles	1600	Bussell, D.
1538	Scarles, William	1601	Pennington, L.
1539	Norton, D. B.	1602	Beers, James
1540	Eaton, H. P.	1603	Ostrander, R.
1541	McDoan, J.	1604	Duvall, J.
1542	Richards, F.	1605	Winters, J.
1543	Dallas, D.	1606	Douay, H.
1544	Dunklebury, J.	1607	Dennison, J.
1545	Thayer, A.	1608	Curtis, Zeba
1546	Rand, D.	1609	Page, John
1547	Missing name	1610	Rudd, Levi
1548	Smith, Noah	1611	Moren, John
1549	Mitchell, Hugh	1612	Minor, Harris
1550	Rust, William	1613	Willis, Austin
1551	Reed, James	1614	McConoly, H.
1552	Moore, Joseph	1615	Butsman, D.
1553	Remington, Ira	1616	Goodall, J.
1554	Allen, Samuel	1617	Lainn, J.
1555	Patch, D.	1618	Gale, J. G.
1556	Gordon, John	1619	Eaton, George
1557	Warren, Martin	1620	Lancaster, W.
1558	Stockwell, L. L.	1621	Brown, R.
1559	Howe, Willis	1622	Missing name
1560	McQuestion, H.	1623	Steele, G. D.
1561	Fuller, Chester	1624	Simmons, Levi
1562	Grant, A. T.	1625	Woodlowe, Charles
1563	German, J.	1626	Dodge, John
1564	Fontaine, John J.	1627	Avery, A.
1565	Cronkling, Henry M.	1628	Picket, Lester
1566	Cummings, John L.	1629	Yates, Francis
1567	Lewis, William	1630	Fay, Hey.
1568	Darling, Gamaliel	1631	Wilson, W. H.
1569	Rogers, Clement F.	1632	Douglas, Caleb
1570	Bird, John D.	1633	Brownwell, D.
1571	Johnson, Mark	1634	Bowers, George
1572	Missing name	1635	Huss, John
1573	Griffiths, William	1636	Edging, M.

1637	Southwick, J.	1700	Wilay, Thomas
1638	Holcolm, L.	1701	Kolley, J. W.
1639	Munroe, E.	1702	Ledieu, Amable
1640	Gillmore, John	1703	Armstrong, Earl
1641	Smith, William	1704	Brown, John
1642	Carrall, T.	1705	Churchill, Worthy L.
1643	McChristie, J.	1706	Huit, John
1644	Dickenson, J.	1707	Huie, John
1645	Cahall, E.	1708	Swartwort, Augustus
1646	Peak, John	1709	Wilson, Ebenezer
1647	Missing name	1710	Wilcox, Oliver
1648	Missing name	1711	Latimer, Arthur
1649	Thornberg, Thomas	1712	Crouch, Henry
1650	Hart, John	1713	Church, Jesse
1651	Gowan, Thomas	1714	Case, John
1652	Whitten, George	1715	Clark, Joseph
1653	Campbell, Frederick	1716	Gregory, Francis H.
1654	Woolworth, Elijah	1717	Chambers, James
1655	Hodge, Benjamin	1718	Norton, Lewis
1656	Menard, P.	1719	Wilcox, Burton
1657	Ramsey, N.	1720	Burtle, Dovis
1658	Bell, J. H.	1721	Felton, John
1659	Le Due, P.	1722	Lawton, John
1660	Melage, P.	1723	Bunnell, David C.
1661	Webster, R.	1724	Missing name
1662	Gillies, James	1725	Williams, Samuel
1663	White, Samuel	1726	Morgan, William
1664	Tuner, Daniel	1727	Rowe, William
1665	Rutter, Thomas	1728	Rutter, William
1666	Palmer, John William	1729	Rea, Charles
1667	Ballard, James H.	1730	Reade, Thomas
1668	Serviss, William	1731	Bourdineou, Elijhua
1669	Warmsly, Richard	1732	Lord, Samuel
1670	Atkins, Henry	1733	Boyley, Moses
1671	Oliver, Grifin	1734	Williams, Jesse
1672	Treefry, Joel	1735	Brown, Henry
1673	Missing name	1736	Farrell, Richard
1674	Missing name	1737	Stamford, Nathaniel
1675	Ridden, John	1738	Wade, Nathan
1676	Clews, Thomas	1739	Martin, James
1677	Gustavas, John	1740	Parker, John
1678	Thomas, John	1741	Palmer, Thomas
1679	Gillis, Walter	1742	Ely, Daniel
1680	Christian, Charles P.	1743	Roderick, John
1681	Eastman, Henry	1744	Norton, Andrew
1682	Long, Peter W.	1745	Griffin, William
1683	Smith, Ira	1746	Cedus, Francis
1684	Crundle, Joshua	1747	Phillips, Augustus
1685	Stanbury, John	1748	Galispie, Martin
1686	Ranger, Benjamin	1749	Missing name
1687	Taylor, Samuel	1750	Jackson, Barnaby
1688	Johnson, Daniel	1751	Carr, John
1689	Smith, Henry	1752	Baldwyn, John
1690	Smith, Thomas	1753	Miller, James
1691	Snell, Shedrick	1754	Green, Samuel
1692	Brown, William	1755	Denenberg, William
1693	Rothworth, John	1756	Laundrough, Andrew
1694	Grisold, James	1757	Matill, Francis
1695	Ranney, Julias	1758	Falcon, John
1696	Latroop, Beniah	1759	Flury, Francis
1697	Weldon, Ira	1760	Carthwright, George
1698	Jones, William	1761	Gill, Emauel
1699	Missing name	1762	Spurgeion, Nathaniel

1763	Smith, William H.	1826	Shepheard, Christian
1764	Adney, William D.	1827	Cole, Henry
1765	Orcutt, Rufus	1828	Frankling, G.
1766	Williams, John W.	1829	Goble, Daniel
1767	Williams, Thomas	1830	Douglass, Luther
1768	Timson, Peter	1831	Bacon, Moses
1769	Blancet, Levi	1832	Abbett, John
1770	Coalbath, John F.	1833	Hickling, William
1771	Bishop, Job	1834	Lowell, Nicholas
1772	Kehae, John	1835	Burns, John E.
1773	Wood, Emery	1836	Wallace, Abel
1774	Missing name	1837	Wilson, Horace
1775	Woodman, Jeremiah	1838	Benton, John
1776	Hix, Comfort	1839	Tubbs, Samuel F.
1777	Ross, Batman	1840	Carroll, Martin
1778	Baker, Samuel	1841	Herley, John
1779	Thorn, Jonathan	1842	Sneed, Leakle
1780	Nutter, John	1843	Merrill, Charles
1781	Morton, Sethu	1844	Rathburn, Jeremiah
1782	Austin, William	1845	Denison, John
1783	Root, A. L.	1846	Van Frankling, Isaac
1784	Gardner, Hiram	1847	Doti, Ambrose
1785	Owen, Frederick	1848	Gonsolby, Samuel
1786	Baptise, John	1849	Missing name
1787	Grinder, John	1850	Edgets, Horan
1788	Wilcox, Almeron	1851	Townsend, Jeremiah
1789	Denison, Luther	1852	Rowley, Charles
1790	Bowen, Pearce	1853	Farr, Chester W.
1791	Baker, Lloyd	1854	Johnson, William
1792	Barrett, Dyer	1855	Riley, Pursey
1793	Patterson, Thomas	1856	Hutchison, Robert B.
1794	Claffin, George	1857	Pier, Henry
1795	Estty, Israel	1858	Pitcher, Jacob
1796	Hill, Valentine	1859	Hiler, Peter
1797	Benedick, Henry	1860	March, Hosea
1798	Day, Andrew D.	1861	Rice, Nathaniel
1799	Missing name	1862	Smith, William
1800	Leach, George W.	1863	Taggert, Thomas
1801	Ray, George	1864	Higgins, Hiram
1802	Cheney, Elijhua	1865	Howard, Ralph
1803	Ross, Ely H.	1866	Young, David
1804	McClary, James	1867	Lake, Elishua
1805	Haddard, Whitman	1868	Dyke, Elijhua
1806	Ingham, Nathaniel	1869	Henry, John
1807	Van Kuven, Abraham	1870	Stout, Jonathan
1808	Moore, Mathew	1871	Sickles, James
1809	Labrey, Stephen	1872	de Fredrick, Peter
1810	Thompson, William	1873	Hopkinson, Caleb
1811	Brown, Rufus	1874	Missing name
1812	Northup, Thomas	1875	Wheeler, Enoch
1813	Ginning, Stephen	1876	Parkinson, James
1814	Wager, Joseph	1877	Vanhouton, Garrett
1815	Luce, Robert	1878	Sage, Harlety
1816	Clayton, Fariner	1879	Gulintine, James
1817	Gillet, Eleazer	1880	Horton, Cyrus
1818	Butterfield, Abraham	1881	Robb, James
1819	Brenhard, Arnold	1882	Howley, Comfort
1820	Edy, Charles	1883	Buckley, Elis
1821	Campbell, Oliver	1884	Hagerty, Thomas
1822	Bevins, John H.	1885	Garland, John
1823	Caldwell, Nathaniel	1886	Murphy, William
1824	Missing name	1887	Hall, Daniel
1825	Phillips, Joseph	1888	Connor, William

American Prisoners of War held in Quebec during the War of 1812

1889	French, Thomas		1952	Fagan, Phillip
1890	Lewis, Samuel		1953	Folson, John
1891	Dalyrumple, John		1954	Henderson, Amos
1892	King, Elijhu		1955	Blake, William
1893	Melony, Simeon		1956	Adams, George
1894	Rhodes, Henry		1957	Maxwell, Thompson
1895	Abby, Horace B.		1958	Weiant, Peter
1896	Dunn, Joel		1959	Mead, William
1897	Moore, Abraham		1960	Sweet, Abraham
1898	Crossby, William		1961	White, George
1899	Missing name		1962	Hubbell, William
1900	Davis, Thomas		1963	Young, Thomas
1901	Powers, William		1964	Reagan, James
1902	Lejuny, Anthony		1965	Wittum, Reiford
1903	Young, Christian		1966	Vail, William W.
1904	Liles, James		1967	Peterson, Lemuel
1905	Randall, Isaac		1968	Burch, Levi
1906	Bell, Orling		1969	Morrison, Alexander
1907	Ayrus, Samuel		1970	Clarey, Timothy
1908	Myer, Michael		1971	Wakeman, Bradley
1909	Leping, Noel		1972	Bennett, John
1910	Millbanks, David		1973	Cole, Benjamin
1911	Dodd, Moses		1974	Missing name
1912	Smith, John		1975	Coombe, Isaac
1913	Burk, Edward		1976	Joy, Bennett
1914	Brookes, Joseph		1977	Maxwell, Thomas
1915	Armstrong, Isaac		1978	Packhard, Joseph
1916	Armstrong, George		1979	Merrill, Nathaniel
1917	Pettit, John		1980	Enas, Abner
1918	Doolittle, William		1981	Truby, Samuel
1919	Conklin, John F.		1982	Sternburg, Christian
1920	McGowen, Patrick		1983	Gouldsmith, Thomas
1921	West, Abia		1984	Shaver, Frederick
1922	Mount, James		1985	Warren, Thomas L.
1923	Blairdie, Phillip		1986	Waite, Brunsey
1924	Missing name		1987	Smith, John C.
1925	Henderson, George W.		1988	Myers, Joseph
1926	Pierce, Henry		1989	Williams, Jack
1927	Palishaw, Mathew		1990	Gibson, Samuel
1928	Fuller, John B.			
1929	North, Joseph E.			
1930	Hartwell, Calvin			
1931	Stevens, John			
1932	Thorn, William			
1933	McIntyre, James			
1934	Staind, Isaac			
1935	Patterson, John			
1936	Judd, William			
1937	Wilder, Ezra			
1938	Parks, Henry			
1939	Muller, Jesse			
1940	Stottle, George			
1941	Howard, Aron			
1942	Johnston, James H.			
1943	Harris, James			
1944	King, Robert			
1945	Millan, George			
1946	Love, Thomas C.			
1947	Hollister, P. F.			
1948	Nelson, Timothy			
1949	Missing name			
1950	Blake, Jonathan			
1951	Landers, John			

American Prisoners of War held in Quebec during the War of 1812

Sailors listing by ship

Alfred	Russell, Benjamin	Ebe	Hooke, Thomas
Armline	Williams, Jack	Forsyth	Clews, Thomas
			Gustavas, John
Batteaux	Little, Salmon		
	Foot, Henry	George	Gibson, Samuel
	Little, Samuel		Myers, Joseph
Corsack	Morrice, Samuel H.	US Sloop Growler	Allen, Isaac
			Ballard, John
US Sloop Eagle	Boston, Daniel		Barber, William
	Bridge, Franklin		Batty, Joseph
	Butman, Benjamin		Berg, Lawrence
	Carnes, Joseph		Brink, Orson
	Danforth, Joseph F.		Campbell, James
	Dyer, Daniel		Campbell, William
	Dyer, Isaac		Carry, Daniel
	Emmins, Phillip		Cobb, John
	Estes, Edward		Dennison, Washington
	Foster, Nathaniel		Drake, Eliasha
	Freeborne, John		Dresser, Thomas
	Furbush, Joshua		Duncan, Mathew
	Gitchell, Josiah		Frickes, John
	Goodwin, James		Frost, Phineas
	Green, William		Gibson, Ebenezer
	Haines, Daniel		Green, James
	Ham, Robert		Ham, Rufus
	Harvey, William		Harris, James
	Hunt, John		Herrick, Eli
	Loomes, Jaires		Herrick, Oliver
	Murry, James		Konnell, Thomas
	Nicholson, William		Lovejoy, Jacob
	Paul, Simeon		Madder, Thomas
	Payne, Rubin		Merrill, Jacob
	Pratt, Charles		Merrill, Thedorias
	Pratt, Walter		Merritt, Jonathan
	Rice, Nathaniel		Monteath, Walter Noel
	Richards, Stephen		Moody, John
	Rowe, Benjamin		Morse, Jacob
	Sawyer, Horace B.		Morse, Joshua
	Smith, Daniel		Mudge, Ebenezer
	Sperry, Jacob		Norbry, James
	Stearns, Nathan		Pack, Luther
	Taylor, Thomas		Parker, Edward
	White, Joshua		Penly, Joseph
	Woodman, Benjamin		Plainloir, John
			Plumer, Isaac

American Prisoners of War held in Quebec during the War of 1812

Sailors listing by ship

US Sloop Growler	Prouth, Jacob	US Schooner Growler	Thornton, William
	Read, Joseph P.		Torrey, Joseph
	Read, Samuel R.		Warren, W. H.
	Rice, Samuel		Watson, David
	Richardson, Simeon		Williams, Calvin
	Romley, Eliza		
	Sanborn, John L.	Jack (Fort Erie)	Latimer, Arthur
	Scisso, Thomas		
	Sharpe, Soloman	Jack (Lake Ontario)	Gillis, Walter
	Sinclair, Jacob		Thomas, John
	Smith, Thomas		
	Turnbull, John	US Schooner Julia	Blank, Samuel
	Turner, Henry		Blosea, Nathaniel
	Walter, Abraham		Clawson, Henry
	Whilington, Robert		Corsey, John
	Wright, Oliver		Duffy, Ebenezer
			Fistock, Thomas
US Schooner Growler	Baker, Philip		Headman, Charles
	Baker, Samuel		Jones, Martin
	Brown, Thomas		Joseph, John
	Buel, Jeremiah		Lawton, John
	Chambers, Samuel		Lewis, Leonard
	Christie, John		Lyles, William
	Connor, John		Mallet, John
	Davis, Thomas		Marvel, Joseph
	Deason, David		Myers, Edward
	Dours, William		Pactaolt, Henry
	Dunn, William		Palmer, Gordon
	Everett, John		Palmer, William
	Gibbs, John		Peterson, James
	Guynnup, John		Phoenix, John
	Harris, Robert		Reed, William
	Harvey, Peter		Rilley, James
	Hicks, Isaac		Rine, Joseph
	Hope, Levi		Smith, John
	Johnson, William		Smith, William
	McAvery alias McAvor, John		Sprigs, George
	McGee, William		Tanning, John C.
	Mortimore, Thomas		Trant, James
	Mullett, William		Tribe, Benjamin
	Pearson, John		Wilcox, William
	Richardson, John		Wildon, John
	Roberts, Joel		Williams, Benjamin
	Sasse, John		Williams, Henry
	Stymets, John		
	Taylor, John	Lizard	McGlathay, Thomas
	Thornning, Thomas		Wharf, Andrew

American Prisoners of War held in Quebec during the War of 1812

Sailors listing by ship

Malabar & Hydia	Ackley, William		Gregory, Francis H.
	Andrews, David		Laundrough, Andrew
	Armstrong, William		Lawton, John
	Batch, George		Lord, Samuel
	Beals, John		Matill, Francis
	Burrell, John		Miller, James
	Carpenter, John		Morgan, William
	Clark, James		Norton, Lewis
	Clark, Stephen		Palmer, John William
	Courtney, George		Rea, Charles
	Duguenom, Charles		Reade, Thomas
	Faunce, Peter		Rowe, William
	King, William		Rutter, Thomas
	Oates, John		Rutter, William
	Redman, Martin		Spurgeion, Nathaniel
	Rose, Nathaniel		Swartwort, Augustus
	Sloin, William		Tuner, Daniel
	Tenney, John		Wilcox, Burton
	Trott, Thomas		Williams, Jesse
	Tucker, Benjamin		Williams, Samuel
	Usher, Edward		
	Watlas, Burton	US Schooner Somers	Bird, John D.
			Black, C.
US Sloop Ohio	Atwood, E.		Bryan, J.
	Cornell, G.		Dabine, J.
	Cronkling, Henry M.		Darling, Gamaliel
	Cummings, John L.		Griffiths, William
	Denning, J.		Hubbard, Joseph
	Devenus, J.		Johnson, Mark
	Manuel, John		McGregor, R.
	Stacy, L.		Newman, J.
	Streback, J. M.		Osten, Charles
	Wheedon, Charles		Peters , J.
	Williams, P.		Petersen, J.
			Poulston, J.
Posheu	Brett, Francis		Rogers, Clement F.
			Taylor, Samuel
US Schooner Scorpion	Bourdineou, Elijhua		
	Boyley, Moses	Taken on a gigg	Atkins, Henry
	Brown, Henry		Oliver, Grifin
	Bunnell, David C.		Ridden, John
	Burtle, Dovis		Treefry, Joel
	Carr, John		Warmsly, Richard
	Chambers, James		
	Felton, John	US Schooner Tigress	Baldwyn, John
	Galispie, Martin		Carthwright, George
	Gill, Emauel		Cedus, Francis

Sailors listing by ship

US Schooner Tigress

- Denenberg, William
- Ely, Daniel
- Enas, Abner
- Falcon, John
- Farrell, Richard
- Flury, Francis
- Green, Samuel
- Griffin, William
- Jackson, Barnaby
- Martin, James
- Norton, Andrew
- Palmer, Thomas
- Parker, John
- Phillips, Augustus
- Roderick, John
- Stamford, Nathaniel
- Wade, Nathan

American Prisoners of War held in Quebec during the War of 1812

Soldiers listed by battles

Not listed	White, Samuel	Battle of Beaver Dams	Boyer, Nelson
			Bradshaw, Edward
4 Mile Creek	Brown, Thomas		Brakeman, Lodowick
	McNutt, J.		Brison, James
	Van Buren, Edward		Broadist, Moses
			Brown, Francis
Battle of Beaver Dams	Aberts, Michael		Brown, James
	Anderson, Henry		Brown, John
	Andrews, Edward		Brown, Michael
	Ansol, Philip		Brown, Perry W.
	Arell, Richard		Brownhill, John
	Arthur, James		Bull, Benjamin S.
	Artis, John		Burd, Benjamin E.
	Asher, Frederick		Burlue, Gilbert
	Badger, Ephraim T.		Caknary, James
	Baker, John		Calkins, Eliphel
	Baninstine, John		Cann, John
	Barber, John		Cannon, Dominick
	Barker, John		Capatity, William
	Barker, Robert		Carmody, Dalby
	Barlow, John		Carr, James
	Barnes, Samuel		Carroll, Isaac
	Barnes, Thomas		Carter, Marthil
	Bartlett, James		Cashman, William
	Barto, Selis		Cavry, James
	Batts, James		Cerkhill, James W.
	Bay, John		Chambers, Henry
	Beard, John		Chapman, Eliphea
	Beard, Richard		Childers, Joseph
	Befarr, Leonard		Chrise, John
	Belluite, Leve		Christian, Humphrey
	Birk, John		Christopher, Samuel
	Bissure, Theodore		Clark, Abraham
	Black, John		Clark, Sheldren
	Blanch, James		Clarke, John
	Blogs, Mordericke		Clauts, William
	Blue, Henry		Clement, Daniel
	Boersther, Charles G.		Cole, Andrew
	Bogea, John		Collins, Robert
	Boggs, Lyman		Conway, Michael
	Boohm, Joseph		Cook, John H.
	Booth, George		Cord, Jacob
	Booth, John		Count, Levin
	Bowe, Artemus		Crabtree, John
	Bowen, William		Crarmey, Edward
	Bowers, Jesse		Cravertson, George
	Bowice, Joseph		Cummings, David

American Prisoners of War held in Quebec during the War of 1812

Soldiers listed by battles

Battle of Beaver Dams	Battle of Beaver Dams
Cune, Thomas	Fuller, James
Curtis, Uria	Garland, Levy
Daggert, Thomas	Gates, Jacob
Dandridge, Richard	Gibson, Fortune
Davis, Benjamin	Gilbert, Abique
Davis, Hugh	Givin, James
Davis, John	Godwin, Kimmel
Davis, Richard	Goodrich, Henry C.
Davis, Thomas	Goodwin, Joseph
Davisson, John	Gorman, Edward
Decker, Joseph	Graves, Darius
Dellaghon, George	Gray, John D.
Delshaven, Michael	Gray, Samuel
Dempsey, George	Green, John
Denmade, Edward	Grey, James
Denton, Charles	Griffin, John
Dervalt, Alvin	Grimes, John
Desheates, Peter	Griner, George
Dill, Peter	Griswold, Samuel B.
Diver, David	Grouse, Frederick
Dixon, James	Gruet, James
Doddson, Thomas S.	Gruet, William
Donaldson, Thomas	Gunies, Michael
Doud, John	Hagar, John
Dougherty, William	Haggerty, Leve
Doughtery, Hamilton	Haidy, Amos
Drummin, John	Hall, Aug. C.
Dubois, David	Halted, John
Dulman, George	Hamilton, James
Dunning, Jesse	Hanyan, Elihu
Eaton, William	Hargood, George
Elmore, Philip	Hartman, Andrew
Emmins, Henry	Hassar, George
English, John	Hately, John
Eton, Ambrose	Haydon, Daniel
Evertson, Benjamin	Heddon, Amas
Fairfield, Soloman	Heding, Henry
Farrell, Michael	Henry, George
Ferrish, Barney	Henry, James
Fields, Thomas	Henry, Samuel
Fitz, Charles	Herring, John
Fleming, Henry	Hervey, John
Francisco, John	Hickins, Francis
Frank, Christian F.	Hogg, George
Frasel, Hubbard	Holloway, John
Frehen, Edward	Hoopman, Philip
Frink, Rupel	Hose, Jacob

American Prisoners of War held in Quebec during the War of 1812

Soldiers listed by battles

Battle of Beaver Dams

House, Frederick
Hover, George
Hugh, Michael
Hunter, James
Hunter, Joseph
Hurd, John
Ireland, Jonathan
Johnson, Jason
Johnson, John
Johnson, William
Jones, Thomas
Jones, William
Jones, William L.
Kain, John
Karney, Thomas
Kellog, Tsar
Kelly, Charles
Kelly, William
Kerrington, Esakel
Kingsland, Joseph
Knowlton, Ebenezer
Kuber, Jacob
Kuntz, David
Lain, Benjamin
Lamb, William
Lash, Jeremiah
Lazelaeu, Benjamin
Leazier, Elisha
LeCount, William
Levi, Henry
Lewis, Dudley
Liei, John
Lighter, Jacob
Limoners, Peter D.
Lipperket, William
Little, Peter
Littlefield, John
Lou, Samuel
Luckey, Samuel
Machesney, John
Mackelfresh, Joseph H.
Mackey, John
Mager, Robert
Maher, Samuel
March, William
Marshall, Joseph
Marshall, William

Battle of Beaver Dams

Mason, Ira
Mathews, Daniel
Matlock, Joseph
Maybe, Jacob
McCaller, Benjamin
McCarthy, Charles
McCirchar, Stephen
McClure, John
McConaghey, Benjamin
McDonald, Peter
McDonald, Theophilus
McDowell, Andrew
McEver, William
McGoud, John
McKee, Edward
McKeever, Charles
McKenney, John
McKenzie, David
McKenzie, Kenneth
McMillin, George
McQueen, Donald
McWaters, James
Mears, Michael
Mechame, Almond
Meticham, Seth
Miles, John
Miller, Garrett
Milless, Stephen
Monaham, David
Moore, John
Moore, Lemond
Morris, John N.
Moses, Charles
Mudd, Massom
Mullinex, Thomas
Murdock, George
Murphy, George
Murphy, John
Mus, Abraham
Neils, Nathaniel W.
Nixon, William
Norton, Robert
Oddly, John
Oiler, George
Olstender, Gabriel
Osbourn, Thomas
Oweritt, John

American Prisoners of War held in Quebec during the War of 1812

Soldiers listed by battles

Battle of Beaver Dams		Battle of Beaver Dams	
	Paine, Richard		Scott, William
	Paine, William		Sellock, Henry
	Palmer, J. B.		Seriven, Richard
	Palmer, Nicholas		Shaffer, Valentine
	Paradise, John		Sheaves, Thomas
	Parks, Selvy		Sheffield, Henry
	Pattison, Thomas		Shell, Henry
	Penny, Nicholas		Shrater, Anthony
	Perkins, Rufas		Sickles, Michael
	Permerline, Johan		Silence, Nicholas
	Perrique, James		Simpson, Mark
	Petare, John		Slaughter, George
	Philips, Samuel		Sly, Thomas
	Pickle, Balhe		Smiley, John
	Pitcher, Jacob		Smilley, Thomas
	Pollard, Martin		Smith, Benjamin
	Powers, Joseph		Smith, James
	Preston, Ormond		Smith, John
	Price, Meritt		Smith, William
	Purse, William		Snyder, George
	Quonilrouly, Henry		Sonnet, Charles
	Randall, Thomas		Sowder, Jacob
	Rea, John		Spalding, William
	Reynolds, Gilbert		Spunier, Lott
	Richards, John		Stansburgh, Jonathan
	Riddle, Robert		Stephens, John
	Riggan, Labon		Stocker, Jesse L.
	Rimsey, Joseph		Street, Ishemail
	Rindle, Samuel		Stroud, John
	Roach, Isaac		Stutevant, Thomas
	Roberts, Henry		Sutherly, Joseph
	Roberts, William		Swan, Samuel
	Robins, Toram		Swatewood, Jacob
	Robinson, Daniel		Taggent, Archibald
	Robinson, Nicholas		Talbott, Elijah
	Robinson, Nicholas N.		Talbott, John H.
	Roles, Rezin		Tardon, Thomas
	Root, John		Taylor, Lewis L.
	Rose, Henry S.		Taylor, Richard
	Rose, John		Thipelwood, Charles
	Rose, Jonathan		Thomas, Samuel
	Ross, Joseph N.		Thomas, William
	Round, Rubin		Thompson, John W.
	Saunders, William G.		Thompson, Jonathan
	Schoolman, William		Thristy, Joel
	Schultz, John		Thundersville, John
	Scott, John		Till, James

American Prisoners of War held in Quebec during the War of 1812

Soldiers listed by battles

Battle of Beaver Dams	Todd, John	Battle of Chippawa	Morrison, Alexander
	Tomlinson, John		Peterson, Lemuel
	Tonnier, Joshua		Smith, John C.
	Torer, Jon		Wakeman, Bradley
	Tracey, William		Dearborn, D.
	Truebridge, T.		Galloway, Samuel
	Tucker, Joseph		Grisold, James
	Turner, Walter		Huss, John
	Updegrass, Jesse		Irwin, John
	Ustelburgh, Philip		Went, George
	Van Bibbar, Isaac		Winnet, George
	Walker, John		
	Walker, Samuel	Detroit	Crundle, Joshua
	Walton, Edward		
	Wardle, Linnard	Battle of Fort Dearborn	Corbin, James
	Waring, John		
	Watson, William	Battle of Fort Erie	Abbett, John
	Waugham, James		Abby, Horace B.
	Welch, Henry		Adams, George
	Wells, Elijah		Adney, William D.
	West, Charles		Armstrong, George
	White, John		Armstrong, Isaac
	Whitton, John		Austin, William
	Wilder, Titus		Ayrus, Samuel
	Wilkins, James		Bacon, Moses
	Wilkinson, James		Baker, Lloyd
	Willets, Joseph		Baker, Samuel
	Williams, Andrew		Ballard, James H.
	Williams, Thomas		Baptise, John
	Willinea, John N.		Barrett, Dyer
	Willis, John		Beers, James
	Wilson, Alexander		Bell, Orling
	Wilson, Daniel		Benedick, Henry
	Wilson, James		Benton, John
	Wilson, Warren		Bevins, John H.
	Winn, Clement		Bishop, Job
	Wood, Pratt		Blairdie, Phillip
	Woolfriet, John		Blake, Jonathan
	Wright, Terick		Blake, William
	Wrights, Henry		Blancet, Levi
	Yates, Henry D.		Bowen, Pearce
			Bowtell, H.
Buffalo	Brown, William		Brenhard, Arnold
	Hodge, Benjamin		Brookes, Joseph
			Brown, R.
Battle of Chippawa	Burch, Levi		Brown, Rufus
	Clarey, Timothy		Buckley, Elis

American Prisoners of War held in Quebec during the War of 1812

Soldiers listed by battles

Battle of Fort Erie

Burk, Edward
Burns, John E.
Bussell, D.
Butsman, D.
Butterfield, Abraham
Caldwell, Nathaniel
Campbell, Oliver
Carroll, Martin
Case, John
Cheney, Elijhua
Christian, Charles P.
Church, Jesse
Churchill, Worthy L.
Claffin, George
Clark, Joseph
Clayton, Fariner
Coalbath, John F.
Cole, Henry
Conklin, John F.
Connor, William
Coombe, Isaac
Crossby, William
Crouch, Henry
Dalyrumple, John
Davis, Thomas
Day, Andrew D.
de Fredrick, Peter
Denison, John
Denison, Luther
Dodd, Moses
Doolittle, William
Doti, Ambrose
Douglass, Luther
Dunn, Joel
Duvall, J.
Dyke, Elijhua
Eastman, Henry
Eaton, George
Edgets, Horan
Edging, M.
Edy, Charles
Estty, Israel
Fagan, Phillip
Farr, Chester W.
Fontaine, John J.
Fowler, James
Frankling, G.

Battle of Fort Erie

French, Thomas
Fuller, John B.
Gale, J. G.
Gardner, Hiram
Garland, John
Giles, John
Gillet, Eleazer
Ginning, Stephen
Goble, Daniel
Gonsolby, Samuel
Goodall, J.
Grinder, John
Gulintine, James
Haddard, Whitman
Hagerty, Thomas
Hall, Daniel
Harris, James
Hartwell, Calvin
Henderson, Amos
Henderson, George W.
Henry, John
Herley, John
Hickling, William
Higgins, Hiram
Hiler, Peter
Hill, Valentine
Hix, Comfort
Hollister, P. F.
Hopkinson, Caleb
Horton, Cyrus
Howard, Aron
Howard, Ralph
Howley, Comfort
Hubbell, William
Huie, John
Huit, John
Hutchison, Robert B.
Ingham, Nathaniel
Johnson, Daniel
Johnson, William
Johnston, James H.
Jones, William
Joy, Bennett
Judd, William
Kehae, John
Kenyon, J.
King, Elijhu

American Prisoners of War held in Quebec during the War of 1812

Soldiers listed by battles

Battle of Fort Erie

King, Robert
Labrey, Stephen
Lainn, J.
Lake, Elishua
Lancaster, W.
Landers, John
Leach, George W.
Ledieu, Amable
Lejuny, Anthony
Leping, Noel
Lewis, Samuel
Lewis, William
Liles, James
Love, Thomas C.
Lowell, Nicholas
Luce, Robert
March, Hosea
Maxwell, Thomas
Maxwell, Thompson
McClary, James
McConoly, H.
McGowen, Patrick
McIntyre, James
Mead, William
Melony, Simeon
Merrill, Charles
Merrill, Nathaniel
Millan, George
Millbanks, David
Minor, Harris
Moore, Abraham
Moore, Mathew
Morton, Sethu
Mount, James
Muller, Jesse
Murphy, William
Myer, Michael
Nelson, Timothy
North, Joseph E.
Northup, Thomas
Nutter, John
Orcutt, Rufus
Ostrander, R.
Owen, Frederick
Packhard, Joseph
Palishaw, Mathew
Parkinson, James

Battle of Fort Erie

Parks, Henry
Parks, J.
Patterson, John
Patterson, Thomas
Pearl, John
Pennington, L.
Pettit, John
Phillips, Joseph
Pier, Henry
Pierce, Henry
Pitcher, Jacob
Powers, William
Randall, Isaac
Ranger, Benjamin
Ranney, Julias
Rathburn, Jeremiah
Ray, George
Rhodes, Henry
Rice, Nathaniel
Riley, Pursey
Robb, James
Root, A. L.
Ross, Batman
Ross, Ely H.
Rothworth, John
Rowley, Charles
Sage, Harlety
Serviss, William
Shepheard, Christian
Sickles, James
Smith, Ira
Smith, John
Smith, William
Smith, William H.
Sneed, Leakle
Staind, Isaac
Stanbury, John
Stevens, John
Stottle, George
Stout, Jonathan
Sweet, Abraham
Taggert, Thomas
Thompson, William
Thorn, Jonathan
Thorn, William
Timson, Peter
Townsend, Jeremiah

202

American Prisoners of War held in Quebec during the War of 1812

Soldiers listed by battles

Battle of Fort Erie	Truby, Samuel	Battle of Fort George	Perell, Jacob
	Tubbs, Samuel F.		Platenburgh, Jacob
	Van Frankling, Isaac		Plott, John
	Van Kuven, Abraham		Richards, Stephem
	Vanhouton, Garrett		Sawyer, Charles W.
	Wager, Joseph		Schooley, William
	Waite, Brunsey		Smith, Frederick
	Wallace, Abel		Thompson, John
	Weiant, Peter		Westbrooks, Abraham
	West, Abia		White, William
	Wheeler, Enoch		Willett, Phil
	White, George		
	Wilcox, Almeron	Fort Maggie	Groomes, Richard
	Wilcox, Oliver		Runyan, Francis
	Wilder, Ezra		Wallis, James
	Williams, John W.		
	Williams, Thomas	Battle of Fort Niagara	Amyets, John
	Willis, Austin		Anderson, Peter
	Wilson, Ebenezer		Archer, Robert
	Wilson, Horace		Arnold, James
	Wood, Emery		Atchley, Daniel
	Woodman, Jeremiah		Atchley, Joseph
	Young, Christian		Banker, Christian
	Young, David		Barnes, Jacob
	Young, Thomas		Bascomb, Samuel
			Bennett, James W.
Battle of Fort George	Banger, Thomas		Berwick, George W.
	Beckford, John		Bishop, James
	Brown, Henry		Bishop, Josiah
	Campbell, Joseph		Blyth, John
	Crosby, James		Bossell, John
	Davis, John		Bowlett, Nathaniel
	Decker, Zeli		Boyd, William
	Free, Almond		Brandon, Samuel
	Gilllispie, William		Brauntsman, Daniel
	Gready, Martin		Briggs, William
	Hallz or Hall, Orin or Horace		Bromley, Salmon
	Hendricks, John		Brown, Joseph
	Hill, William		Brown, William
	Hydendry, Henry		Buchanan, John
	Inghram, Benjamin		Burees, Viris
	Kelley, James		Burtsell, David
	Lanunsbery, Lemuel		Buskerk, Garrett
	Larney, Joseph P.		Cahall, E.
	Lytle, Daniel		Calliham, Francis
	McDonald, Francis		Cermour, Robert
	McKenzie, Thomas		Chapin, Cyrenius

American Prisoners of War held in Quebec during the War of 1812

Soldiers listed by battles

Battle of Fort Niagara		Battle of Fort Niagara	
	Chase, John		Halison, Jacob
	Cheek, William		Hall, William
	Chick, Nathaniel		Hamilton, John
	Clark, Charles		Handing, Amasa
	Clark, Henry		Hankins, Gilbreath
	Clarke, Norman		Hansel, William
	Coalbough, Michael		Harley, George
	Coaswell, Allanson		Harper, William
	Coates, Elizha		Harris, James
	Craft, George B.		Hart, John
	Creighton, Hugh		Harvey, Charles
	Cross, Barnebus		Hayes, Patrick
	Curtis, Morgan		Head, William
	Darling, Thomas		Heron, James E.
	Davis, Peter		Hill, Allen
	Day, John		Hince, John
	Dickenson, J.		Hind, Nathaniel
	Diffenderffer, Henry		Holloby, John
	Dogherty, James		Hollville, Robert
	Dogherty, Jared		Holmes, Charles
	Drake, George William		Holmes, Thomas
	Draton, Joseph		Hopkins, John
	Eades, Thomas		Houndshell, John
	Elton, Moses		Howard, Edward
	Ewings, James		Hutchison, David
	Farmham, Gauis		Jennings, Noah
	Farrard, Michael		Johnson, William
	Fenning, Charles		Johnston, Assa
	Fincher, Jesse		Johnston, James
	Forrester, Peter		Johnston, Littleton
	Frederick, Henry		Johnston, Richard
	Gates, Horatio		Johnston, William
	Gentry, John		Jones, Samuel
	George, John		Kennedy, William
	Gibbs, Eusebais		Koontz, Jacob
	Gifford, Francis		Lackey, Hugh
	Gilbreath, John		Lainge, Isaac
	Glenn, James		Lark, Joseph
	Gowan, Thomas		Larkins, Thomas
	Grayson, John		Leonard, Nathaniel
	Greaves, Philander		Lias, Nathaniel
	Green, Jeremiah N.		Lloyd, Thompson C.
	Greenley, William		Lochard, Thomas
	Groves, George		Long, Peter W.
	Guest, Charles		Loomis, Gustaves
	Hagan, Thomas		Lord, Horatio
	Haines, Joel		Luce, Aaron

American Prisoners of War held in Quebec during the War of 1812

Soldiers listed by battles

Battle of Fort Niagara

Macnalley, John
Manchester, Noah
Marker, Benjamin
Marks, Henry
McCardall, Jacob
McChristie, J.
McCroy, Thomas
McCurl, Isaac
McGunnell, Michael
McLaghlan, Mark
McQuaid, Edward
Melone, John
Merrill, M.
Miller, James
Miller, Rubin
Moore, Abel
Morrison, James
Morrison, William
Mustain, Lewis
Neighbors, John
Nesbett, John
Nicholson, John
Nunn, Jonathan
O'Conner, Michael
Oin, Ebenezer
Oin, Joseph
Owen, Amasa
Owen, Jeremiah
Parcel, James H.
Patterson, John
Paulling, William K.
Peak, John
Peck, Ollus
Pierce, Thomas
Poff, Peter
Potts, Jeremiah
Prentice, James
Preutts, Gabriel
Quin, Patrick
Randall, Greif
Reagan, James
Redfield, Anthony C.
Reynolds, William
Rice, John
Richardson, Jason
Richardson, William
Ridge, William

Battle of Fort Niagara

Roberts, Aaron
Robinson, James
Rogers, Robert
Roseman, E.
Runyan, Thomas
Rust, Richard H.
Scott, Joseph M.
Scuving, Joel
Shafter, Jacob
Shaver, Frederick
Shutt, Henry
Smith, William Henry
Southards, William
Sternburg, Christian
Stevens, Jephthah
Stevens, Josiah
Stewart, James
Stickney, Abijah
Store, Stephen
Stowner, Henry
Sulivan, David
Tarrehill, Zem.
Taylor, Thomas
Taylor, William
Thornberg, Thomas
Thornburgh, John
Trimble, Carey A.
Troop, James
Turner, Isaac
Valentine, Elisha
Vanrecker, Cornelius
Voigh, Thomas
Walker, William
Wallace, Samuel
Warren, Thomas L.
Waterman, Elisha
Werman, Edward
White, Isaac
Wilay, William
Wilhelmi, Daniel
Williamson, John F.
Winder, William H.
Winter, Christian
Wood, George W.
Wright, William
Yates, Francis

American Prisoners of War held in Quebec during the War of 1812

Soldiers listed by battles

Fort Schisher	Ames, Thomas	Battle of Lundy's Lane	Allen, Ira
	Avery, Matlass		Allen, Samuel
	Avery, Richard		Armstrong, Earl
	Baker, George		Barnes, William
	Bertel, Edward		Bowers, George
	Brine, Thomas		Bridgeman, W.
	Cady, Daniel G.		Brownwell, D.
	Clyne, Isaac		Bruce, William
	Cranstone, John		Copner, J.
	Furguson, John		Crawford, William
	Green, Thomas		Cushing, William
	Harrington, Estes		Dallas, D.
	Henon, James		Davis, William
	Hutchinson, Elihu		Dunklebury, J.
	Hyett, Joseph		Eaton, H. P.
	Knowles, Seth		Fuller, Chester
	Lane, Jobe		German, J.
	Lloyd, William		Gordon, John
	Mecham, Jesse		Grant, A. T.
	Munger, Haace		Hammond, S.
	Newman, Stokely		Hardy, Andrew H.
	Park, Roger		Horton, Barnebus
	Pudehour, Conduit		House, Isaac
	Reese, Henry		Howe, Willis
	Scott, Silar		Hunt, John
	Strickland, Richard		Hutchins, A.
	Vinten, Ezekial		Ives, Amos
	Wilcox, John		Kirk, John
	Wood, Amory		Laurie, Thomas
	Wood, Frederick		Lovell, S.
French Mills	Wilay, Thomas		Lovland, Charles
			McCullock, Samuel
Gibonsee	Minger, Joseph		McDoan, J.
			McQuestion, H.
Hedgesburgh	Barnes, Seth		Mendell, Alden
	Conkey, Tebena		Messinger, W. S.
	Hooker, Oris		Mitchell, Hugh
	Jones, Henry		Moore, Joseph
	Minor, Lewis		Morrison, Joseph
	Watson, Major		Morrow, Edward
	Witherall, Gerrard		Moses, John
			Nobles, Stephen
Lake Ontario	Gouldsmith, Thomas		Norton, D. B.
			Patch, D.
Lole of Noire	Smith, Henry		Perry, David
			Powell, Puley

Soldiers listed by battles

Battle of Lundy's Lane

- Rand, D.
- Reed, C. W.
- Reed, James
- Reithner, J.
- Remington, Ira
- Richards, F.
- Riddle, E.
- Roberts, John
- Rowsey, Ralph
- Rust, William
- Scarles, William
- Skinner, Benjamin
- Smith, Noah
- Smith, Thomas
- Stanton, Phincas
- Stewart, John
- Stockwell, L. L.
- Stubbs, Henry
- Thayer, A.
- Thompson, James
- Town, G. C.
- Turner, S.
- Wadon, L.
- Ward, Lewis
- Warren, Martin
- Weldon, Ira
- White, Cornelius
- Williams, Elijah
- Williams, Robert
- Winters, Stephen
- Wittum, Reiford
- Wood, Andrew

Skirmish at Lyons Creek

- Folson, John

Mosisco Bay

- Steele, G. D.

Battle of Oswago

- Bowers, Joseph
- Brown, John
- Cutler, Leonard
- Dolf, Joseph
- Feders, Jacob
- Folks, John
- Fry, Jacob
- Halbert, Lotha
- Hammond, Jed.

Battle of Oswago (cont.)

- Johnson, Benjamin
- Johnson, David
- Latham, John
- Nigh, George
- Perkins, Thomas
- Pichevin, Anthony
- Purse, John
- Randall, Joseph
- Ray, Robert
- Rockway, J.
- Roney, M.
- Taylor, John
- Vazure, Jove
- Wright, Jonas
- Young, Thomas

Pattonville

- White, Richard

Battle of Plattsburg

- Avery, A.
- Brown, John
- Carrall, T.
- Curtis, Zeba
- Dennison, J.
- Dodge, John
- Douay, H.
- Douglas, Caleb
- Fay, Hey.
- Gillmore, John
- Holcolm, L.
- Latroop, Beniah
- Menard, P.
- Moren, John
- Munroe, E.
- Page, John
- Picket, Lester
- Rudd, Levi
- Simmons, Levi
- Smith, William
- Snell, Shedrick
- Southwick, J.
- Wilson, W. H.
- Winters, J.
- Woodlowe, Charles
- Yates, Francis

Battle of Queenstown

- Allen, J.
- Ramsey, N.

American Prisoners of War held in Quebec during the War of 1812

Soldiers listed by battles

Battle of Queenstown	Vail, William W.	Rapids Prince Reason	Shepheard, Samuel
			Taylor, Isaac M.
Rapids	Edson, Nathan		Thompson, John T.
	Hewins, Thomas		Turner, John
	Hovel, Nathaniel		Vanhorn, James
	Libby, Thadedus		Vanslyck, Cornelius
	Lines, John		Walker, Colman
	McCurdy, Robert		Ward, John
	Merrell, Abraham		Whitney, Isaac
	Scott MD, William		Wilcox, David
	Smith, Jonathan		Wilson, William
	Stewart, James		Withington, Thomas
	Tilden, Lemiah		
	Wilkins, Edward	Rec in charge of Beauport	Beard, William C.
			Bradford, Samuel
Rapids Prince Reason	Armstrong, Thomas		Colman, Charles
	Atherton, William		Conkey, Joshua
	Bingham, Isaac		Godard, Lewis
	Bowen, Joseph		Lewis, William
	Brace, Stephen		Madison, George
	Bronaugh, Thomas		Osgood, Richard
	Byrn, Phillip		Smith, Sidney
	Cawthorn, Eleazer		Wheelock, Abel
	Crocker, John		Winchester, James
	Eaton, Moses		
	Erwing, Patrick	Red Mills	Beech, James
	Fleming, William		Bilby, Henry
	Gilchrist, James		Fairchild, Cyrus
	Greemo, Paul		Goodwin, Simeon
	Hall, Allen		Gunison, James
	Hyde, Nathan		Hard, Daniel
	Jack, Andrew		Lingie, John
	Johnson, Thomas		Mandeville, Peter
	Jones, John		McGee, George
	Jones, Leroy		Nelson, James
	Kindle, Rezin		Ogle, Howard
	Knowles, Joseph		Ransom, Owen
	Leonard, Isaac		Rowland, Alexander
	Mahan, Francis		Temple, William
	Masters, John		Templin, John
	McIlroy, James		Tulley, Thomas
	McMillin, William		Waring, Jonathan
	Million, Rodney		Warley, Joseph
	Mills, Ellias		
	Moones, Green	Battle of the River Raisin	Bell, J. H.
	Nourse, Thomas B. W.		
	Perkins, John	Sacketts Harbor	Bush, Hollower

American Prisoners of War held in Quebec during the War of 1812

Soldiers listed by battles

Sacketts Harbor	de Masters, Foster	Battle of Stoney Point	Conwell, John
			Cook, Haz.
Saint Lawrence	Bennett, John		Cook, William
	Cole, Benjamin		Corkins, Joel
			Countryman, Elias
Skirmish of Sandy Creek	Campbell, Jesse		Cox, John
	Dover, D.		Crayton, William
	Gill, William		Crocker, Benjamin
	Land, Joseph		Cunningham, Kellup
	Stanley, L.		Davidson, John
	Tanner, Asa		Davis, Elnathan
			Davis, Ezra
St. Davids	Barnes, E.		Davis, Theddeck
	Bradley, S.		Defriend, John
	Comfort, R.		Dennis, Patrick M.
	Cotton, Seth		Doughty, Elias
	Drake, W.		Doyle, James
	Holford, Elijah		Draper, Francis
	Johnson, William		Dungan, Benjamin
	Reardon, T.		Emery, Stephen
Battle of Stoney Point	Agen, John		Ervin, James B.
	Allen, John		Ervin, John
	Andrews, Stephen		Ervin, Lewis
	Bacon, Nathan		Evans, Edward
	Baker, Daniel B.		Evans, James
	Barron, John		Evener, Christian
	Barttey, William		Filkins, John F.
	Bays, Jacob		Fisher, Anthony
	Bear, Henry		Fisher, Jacob
	Beck, Andrew		Fitzgerald, John
	Bishop, Jesse		Flemmings, Joseph
	Boarmaster, Henry		Forrest, Arthur
	Bowen, Thomas		Frayman, James
	Bowyer, George		Freeman, James
	Boyd, Samuel		Fullerton, William
	Bradford, John		Goodwin, Richard
	Brown, James		Gosset, Stephen
	Bryce, James		Guton, Thomas
	Bull, William		Hagherty, Mathew
	Burns, Andrew		Hale, William
	Campbell, Mathew		Hardy, Elisha
	Carr, William		Harkness, James
	Celley, Paul		Haynes, Clement
	Chandler, John		Hedderick, George
	Chase, Joshua		Hemmick, George
	Clay, Elijah		Henry, George
	Clayton, Thomas		Holson, James

American Prisoners of War held in Quebec during the War of 1812

Soldiers listed by battles

Battle of Stoney Point

Honeywell, Encoh
Horney, David
Hoy, Barney
Hunter, James
Johnson, Hugh
Johnson, Isaac
Johnson, Noble
Johnson, Truman
Jones, William
Kelly, William
Knight, William
Kronnengie, John
Lackey, Amasa
Learned, Henry
Ledman, Francis
Legg, Daniel
Lindsey, William
Linnerd, Alfred
Logan, Timothy
Loomis, Daniel
Losier, Abraham
Lynch, John
Marlin, William
Martin, Byron
Matthews, John
Maxwell, Robert
McAubrory, William
McCann, Robert
McDune, William
McEwen, Alexander
McGuire, Hugh
Meintere, Tedeck
Melvin, William
Mitchell, Charles
Moore, Jonas
Morris, Morris
Morris, Peter
Napernery, John
Newland, Thomas S.
Newman, Henry
Newton, John
Nybro, Godfred
O'Neil, Con.
Orstunoser, Jones
Pace, Jonathan
Parsons, Samuel
Patton, David

Battle of Stoney Point

Plants, Edward T.
Price, George
Price, Job
Price, Robert
Prince, John
Quick, Jacob
Rathboun, Jeremiah
Read, James
Rehuhard, Thomas
Reynolds, John C.
Richie, Allen
Robinson, Nathan
Rollins, Thomas
Ross, David
Roupough, Corneilus
Rowe, Michael
Rowley, Nathan
Saunderson, John
Scott, James
Scott, Soloman
Scudder, Stephen
See, Daniel
Sheeps, David
Smith, Elijah
Smith, Jacob
Smith, John
Snow, Assa
Spencer, Nathan
Spink, Anthony
Stanbury, Samuel
Stanhope, C. L.
Stanhope, Curtis L.
Steele, George G.
Storey, Pliney
Stuard, Thomas
Summers, William
Tabott, Benjamin
Taylor, William
Tuffs, William
Valients, William
Van De Venter, Christopher
Van Suraringen, H. J.
Van Veghten, Derck
Vanderherle, Samuel
Von, Samuel
Walker, Simeon
Wavern, Elisha

American Prisoners of War held in Quebec during the War of 1812

Soldiers listed by battles

Battle of Stoney Point	Wayne, Michael	Battle of Stoney Point	Dearborn, Soloman
	Welch, Rupel	(Henderson Harbor)	Dearing, John
	Wells, Caleb		Drew, Ira
	West, Abraham		Easter, Stephen
	West, Hugh S.		Ella, John
	Whagerman, Jeremiah		Evans, Thomas
	Wheeler, Willison		Field, Eli
	Wheller, Anthony		Finney, Elihu
	Whellock, James		Finney, Samuel
	Whitley, David R.		Fitzgerald, Aaron
	Whitman, Stephen		Fobes, Quen
	Wilkins, John		Foster, John
	Wilkinson, Oliver		Goodnow, Elisha
	Williby, George		Graves, Abraham
	Willis, Alfred		Green, Eli
	Wimiss, Daniel		Hagar, Henry
	Winder, William H.		Hall, Lot
	Winton, James		Hamwood, George
	Wolffrom, William		Harrodon, Elisha
	Woodland, Lebai		Harvey, Luther
	Yarrington, Avah		Havwood, Abijah
	Young, William		Hayway, Archibald
			Heath, John
Battle of Stoney Point	Alfen, John		Hooper, John
(Henderson Harbor)	Ames, Oliver		Hooper, Simon
	Ayers, John		Horn, Andrew
	Bacon, Jabbec		Horn, Wentworth
	Bangs, Seth		How, John
	Batehelor, Orsen		Howard, Joseph
	Belcher, Joseph		Howard, Josiah
	Blancet, Levy		Howard, Lewis
	Bonney, William		Howe, Calvin
	Booth, Richard		Howe, William
	Bosson, Thaddius		Hubbard, Thomas
	Boyce, John		Hunt, Soloman
	Carver, William		Hutchins, Eraoh
	Churchill, Oliver		Ingalls, Jonathan
	Clark, Benjamin		Ireland, Jonas
	Cook, Joseph		Jackson, Enoch
	Cook, Robert		Johnson, David
	Cory, Asa		Johnson, John
	Cottes, Edward		Jones, Nathan
	Cranson, John H.		Keith, Lephlmiah
	Daggett, Josiah		Kimball, Abel
	Daggett, Lewis		Kimball, Benjamin W.
	Davis, Moses		Kimball, Hannibal
	Davis, Stephen		Kimball, Nathaniel

American Prisoners of War held in Quebec during the War of 1812

Soldiers listed by battles

Battle of Stoney Point (Henderson Harbor)		Battle of Stoney Point (Henderson Harbor)	
	Kingman, Ebin.		Virgin, Levet
	Knight, Andrew		Walker, William
	Knight, Hudson		Webber, Nathan
	Lamb, Josiah P.		Weiman, Lawrence
	Lamson, John		Wheeler, Stephen
	Lander, Charles		Whitney, Jeremiah
	Lanton, Peory		Whitney, Joseph
	Lawrence, Abel		Wilder, Elihu
	Lewis, John		Wilkins, Aaron
	Linel, Samuel		Wilkinson, Andrew
	Lucas, Ephraim		Williams, Samuel
	Mack, Abner		Wood, Isarrel
	Marks, Ira		Wyon, John M.
	Martin, Silvanus		
	McMillen, Archibald	Williamsburg	Campbell, Frederick
	Merrill, Eli		Whitten, George
	Merrill, Jacob		Woolworth, Elijah
	Mitchell, William		
	Munrow, John		
	Nicholson, Soloman		
	Nute, Jonathan		
	Pearl, John		
	Pennell, Samuel		
	Peterson, Peter		
	Phillips, John Capen		
	Pratt, Nathaniel		
	Price, William		
	Reed, Isaac		
	Round, Amos		
	Rowe, Benjamin		
	Rowe, Jonathan		
	Scott, Abraham		
	Shaddock, John		
	Shaver, George		
	Shute, John		
	Smith, Corneilus		
	Smith, Joseph		
	Smith, Richard		
	Smith, Stephen		
	Smith, Thomas		
	Spencer, Andrew		
	Stevens, Benjamin W.		
	Stevens, William		
	Tabvery, Ephraim		
	Thead, Isaac		
	Tiemell, William		
	Titus, George		

United States Marines

Lyles, William
Joseph, John
Pactaolt, Henry
Sasse, John

U.S. Civilians

Allen, Ira
Beals, William
Bennett, John
Cole, Benjamin
Doti, Ambrose
Gibbs, Eusebais
Gilbert, John C.
Grant, A. T.
Greaves, Philander
Hodge, Benjamin
Johnson, Ross
Knags, Witmore
Kolley, J. W.
La Bonte, Francis
Lovland, Charles
Melage, P.
Ramsey, N.
Rigden, James
Scott, William
Shaver, Frederick
Sloan, Ebenezer
Smith, John C.
Sparks, William
Steele, G. D.
Van Kuven, Abraham
Waite, Brunsey
Warren, Thomas L.
Wheeler, Nathaniel
White, Richard

Woman and Sailor

Romley, Eliza